THE FIFTY-SECOND (LOWLAND) DIVISION
1914-1918

THE FIFTY-SECOND (LOWLAND) DIVISION
1914–1918

BY

LIEUT.-COL. R. R. THOMPSON, M.C.
MCGILL CT., C.O.T.C., CANADIAN MILITIA
LATE CAPTAIN 1/5 ARGYLL AND SUTHERLAND HIGHLANDERS

MAPS AND PLANS
COMPILED FROM OFFICIAL SOURCES AND DRAWN
BY
CAPTAIN J. B. RAMSEY
7TH CAMERONIANS, LATE OF 7TH FIELD SURVEY CO., R.E.

TO ALL THOSE WHO GAVE UP THEIR LIVES
WHEN SERVING IN THE UNITS OF THE
FIFTY-SECOND (LOWLAND) DIVISION, AND TO
THE WOMENFOLK OF ALL THOSE WHO
SERVED IN ITS RANKS THIS WORK IS MOST
RESPECTFULLY DEDICATED BY THE AUTHOR

PREFACE

IN the following pages an endeavour has been made to tell the main story of the 52nd (Lowland) Division during the Great War, and to include a selection of incidents which will indicate to the reader what its men achieved and endured. Limitations of space have prevented the inclusion of much that is well worthy of record, and omission to mention an item does not mean that it has been overlooked.

Since I commenced the work in February, 1921, I have made every effort in all possible directions to secure the essential facts. Briefly, may I say that through the courtesy of the Director, Historical Section (Military Branch), Committee of Imperial Defence, I have had full access to the Records at Hamilton and Perth, have carried on a correspondence which has spread to many parts of the world, and that all the evidence obtainable has been examined. I have received most willing assistance from everyone, and thank them most heartily for it, for without their help this history could not have been written. All possible steps have been taken to ensure accuracy and I have received unstinted support from all ranks. I mention especially my wife, for most loyal help at all times.

The History is fortunate in having had Captain J. B. Ramsey, 7th Cameronians, to prepare its maps. This officer with two others reconnoitred the desert south and south-

PREFACE

east of El Arish, including the Gebel Maghara, in the spring of 1917. He afterwards served in the map section of the Intelligence Department of the General Headquarters of General Sir Edmund Allenby.

The maps have been compiled from official sources, and, in many cases, contain information which was not available during the operations.

In conclusion, I must say that I feel this effort of mine has fallen far short of what is due to so great a subject.

R. R. THOMPSON,
Lieut.-Col.
Canadian Militia.

M'GILL UNIVERSITY,
   MONTREAL,
7th September, 1923.

Grand Quartier Général
des
Armées Françaises de l'Est
État-Major
─────
Bureau du Personnel
(Décorations)

ORDRE No. 15633 " D " (Extrait)

Le Maréchal de France, Commandant en chef les Armées Françaises de l'Est, cite à l'Ordre d'Armée :

Major-Général F. J. Marshall, commandant la 52nd Division d'Infanterie :
" A commandé une Division d'élite qui a porté à l'ennemi des coups incessants d'Août à Octobre 1918, de la région d'Arras à celle de Cambrai, faisant preuve en toute occasion d'un mordant irrésistible, malgré la fatigue et les pertes subies, notamment lors du passage du Canal du Nord, près de Demicourt."

Pour Extrait conforme
Le Lieutenant-Colonel
Chef du Bureau du Personnel
Callemaïs

Au Grand Quartier Général
le 10me Avril, 1919
Le Maréchal
Commandant en chef les Armées Françaises de l'Est
PETAIN.

───────

(*Translation of above extract*)

Extract from the Army Orders of

The Marshal of France, Commander-in-chief of the French Army of the East.

Major-General F. J. Marshall, commanding the 52nd Division of Infantry : "Commanded a 'Division d'élite' which delivered incessant blows against the enemy from August to October, 1918, from the Arras area to Cambrai, giving on every occasion proof of an irresistible dash in spite of hardships and great losses, notably during the forcing of the Canal du Nord, near Demicourt."

PETAIN
Le Maréchal, Commandant en chef les Armées
Françaises de l'Est.

Au Grand Quartier Général, *10th April, 1919.*

CONTENTS

CHAPTER		PAGE
I.	THE MOBILIZATION OF THE 52ND DIVISION AND ITS SAILING FOR GALLIPOLI	3
II.	GALLIPOLI : CAPE HELLES	19
III.	THE BATTLE OF THE 28TH JUNE, 1915	42
IV.	THE BATTLE OF THE 28TH JUNE, 1915 (contd.)	59
V.	THE BATTLE OF THE 12TH-13TH JULY, 1915	76
VI.	THE BATTLE OF THE 12TH-13TH JULY, 1915 (contd.)	102
VII.	AUGUST AND SEPTEMBER AT CAPE HELLES	129
VIII.	OCTOBER AND THE COOLER WEATHER	152
IX.	THE GLASGOW HOWITZERS AT ANZAC AND SUVLA AND SIR CHARLES MONRO'S REPORT	163
X.	THE NOVEMBER FIGHTING IN KRITHIA NULLAH AND THE COMING OF WINTER	173
XI.	THE ATTACKS ON G.11a AND G.12	191
XII.	THE LAST ATTACK IN KRITHIA NULLAH	204
XIII.	THE EVACUATION OF CAPE HELLES	212
XIV.	DUEIDAR	245
XV.	ROMANI	264
XVI.	EL ARISH	295
XVII.	THE ADVANCE INTO PALESTINE	307
XVIII.	THE SECOND BATTLE OF GAZA	312
XIX.	THE RAID ON SEA POST AND OTHER OPERATIONS BEFORE GAZA	335
XX.	THE THIRD BATTLE OF GAZA	355
XXI.	WADI HESI	372
XXII.	ESDUD OR BEIT DURAS	391
XXIII.	BURKAH AND BROWN HILL	400
XXIV.	MUGHAR AND KATRAH	412

CONTENTS

CHAPTER		PAGE
XXV.	NEBI SAMWIL AND EL JIB	429
XXVI.	THE TURKISH COUNTER-ATTACKS AT BEIT UR EL TAHTA AND EL BURJ	458
XXVII.	THE BATTLE OF JAFFA—THE PASSAGE OF THE AUJA	475
XXVIII.	FRANCE	511
XXIX.	THE SECOND BATTLE OF THE SOMME: THE BREAKING OF THE HINDENBURG (SIEGFRIED) LINE ABOUT HÉNIN HILL	515
XXX.	THE SECOND BATTLE OF ARRAS, OR OF THE SCARPE: THE STORMING OF THE DROCOURT-QUÉANT SWITCH OF THE HINDENBURG LINE	534
XXXI.	MOEUVRES	548
XXXII.	THE CANAL DU NORD—HERCHIES—MONS	557

APPENDIX

I.	THE TRANSPORT COMPANIES OF THE LOWLAND DIVISIONAL TRAIN AND THE 10TH (IRISH) DIVISION	575
II.	THE 7TH H.L.I. AND 8TH CAMERONIAN TRENCH MORTAR TEAMS IN MESOPOTAMIA	577
III.	THE LOWLAND ROYAL FIELD ARTILLERY AND THE 7TH (INDIAN) DIVISION	578
IV.	A BRIEF ACCOUNT OF THE 103RD INFANTRY BRIGADE, JUNE TO NOVEMBER, 1918	581

INDEX - - - - - - - - - - 586

ILLUSTRATIONS

	PAGE
Divisional and Brigade Signs - - - - -	*Frontispiece*
Eastward Bound - - - - - - - -	16
Looking North from " X " Beach, Cape Helles - - -	24
River Clyde : " V " Beach, Cape Helles - - - - -	32
" W " Beach, Cape Helles - - - - - - -	40
In the Rest Camp, Cape Helles - - - - - -	48
Vineyard Support Line, Cape Helles - - - - -	144
Vineyard Firing Line, Cape Helles - - - - - -	160
At Kantara : Trench in course of construction - -	248
At Kantara : Trench nearing completion - - - -	256
At Romani - - - - - - - - -	272
In No. 4 Post, Romani, showing common type of Trench in Redoubt - - - - - - - - - -	280
Infantry of the Division on the March through Typical Country in Sinai - - - - - - - - - -	288
Turks surrendering after the Battle of Romani - - -	290
Laying the Wire Road in Sinai - - - - - -	292
Camouflaged Guns, Sinai - - - - - - - -	294
Typical Bivouac Area, Sinai - - - - - - -	296
In the Sea View Defence Area, El Arish - - - -	298
Infantry of the Division marching on the Wire Road between El Arish and El Burj - - - - - - -	300
A Company Cookhouse, Sea View Defence Area, El Arish -	302
Divisional Headquarters, El Arish - - - - - -	304
Divisional Engineers sinking a Large Well at Rafa - -	306
A 60-pounder and 12-horse Team - - - - - -	308
At Khan Yunus : Camel Loads Laid Out - - - -	310
In Khan Yunus - - - - - - - - -	312
Working Party in Wadi Ghuzze before the Second Battle of Gaza - - - - - - - - - -	314
Making a Ramp into the Wadi Ghuzze - - - - -	316

ILLUSTRATIONS

	PAGE
Sheikh Abbas Ridge, Gaza Area	318
Horses and Camels watering in Wadi Ghuzze	320
A Platoon Mess in Gaza Area	336
Bathing at Regent's Park, Gaza Area	340
Wadi Simeon, Gaza Area	348
Wadi Nukhabir, near Dorset House, Gaza Area	352
Samson's Ridge from Hereford Ridge	368
Turkish Trench near Sausage Ridge	384
Ascalon	400
Beit Likia	432
El Kubeibeh	440
Nebi Samwil from the Jerusalem Road	448
Pillar erected to Commemorate the crossing of the Auja	496
Convoy with the Division sailing for France in April 1918	504

MAPS

Trench Plan: Gallipoli, Advance of 28th June, 1915	64
Trench Plan: Gallipoli, Advance of 12th and 13th July, 1915	112
Trench Plan: Gallipoli, Advance of 15th November, 1915	192
Trench Plan: Gallipoli, Actions of 18th and 29th December, 1915	208
Gallipoli: Cape Helles	1 *at end of volume*
Gallipoli: Anzac and Suvla	2 ,, ,,
Northern Sinai and Part of Palestine	3 ,, ,,
Sinai: Romani	4 ,, ,,
Palestine	5 ,, ,,
Palestine: Gaza and Wadi Hesi	6 ,, ,,
Palestine: Esdud, Yebnah, etc.	7 ,, ,,
Palestine: Latron—Jerusalem	8 ,, ,,
Palestine: Nahr El Auja	9 ,, ,,
France and Belgium: British Zone	10 ,, ,,
France: Hindenburg Line	11 ,, ,,

WORKS CONSULTED

The following are among the works which have been consulted :

1/7th Battalion, The Royal Scots, 1914-1918.
Lt.-Col. W. CARMICHAEL PEEBLES, D.S.O., T.D. ; Captain J. N. SHAW, M.C.

Brief Record of the Advance of the Egyptian Expeditionary Force, July 1917 to October 1918.
Compiled from Official Sources.

Desert Mounted Corps.
Lt.-Col. the Hon. R. M. P. PRESTON, D.S.O.

Fifth Battalion, Highland Light Infantry, 1914-1918.

From Gallipoli to Baghdad.
WILLIAM EWING, M.C., D.D., Chaplain to the Forces.

The Book of a Glasgow Battalion.
Lt.-Col. W. M. ANDERSON, D.S.O., M.C. ; Major C. S. BLACK, M.C. ; Rev. A. FYFE FINDLAY, C.F. ; and Others.

History of the Great War.
JOHN BUCHAN.

5th King's Own Scottish Borderers.
Lt.-Col. R. N. COULSON, D.S.O. ; Captain T. D. CRAIG, M.C. ; and Others.

New Zealanders in Sinai and Palestine (New Zealand Official History).
Lt.-Col. C. GUY POWLES, C.M.G., D.S.O.

Record of the 6th H.L.I., 1914-1919.
Lt.-Col. JAMES ANDERSON, C.M.G., D.S.O., T.D.

WORKS CONSULTED

4th Royal Scots.
  Col. A. YOUNG, V.D.; Lt.-Col. A. M. MITCHELL, D.S.O.; and Others.

Sir Archibald Murray's Despatches.

Sir Douglas Haig's Despatches.
  Edited by Lt.-Col. J. H. BORASTON, C.B., O.B.E.

War Record of the 4th Battalion, King's Own Scottish Borderers.
  Lieut. W. SORLEY BROWN.

With the 52nd (Lowland) Division in Three Continents.
  Lt.-Col. JAS. YOUNG, D.S.O., R.A.M.C.(T), O.C. 1/3rd Lowland Field Ambulance.

With the 1/1st Lowland Field Ambulance in Gallipoli.
  Col. G. H. EDINGTON, R.A.M.C.(T).

With the R.A.M.C. in Egypt.
  Sergeant-Major, R.A.M.C.

A Yarn of War.
  Captain E. R. BOYD, 8th Cameronians.

GALLIPOLI

CHAPTER I

(4TH AUGUST, 1914, TO 3RD JULY, 1915)

THE MOBILIZATION OF THE 52ND DIVISION AND ITS SAILING FOR GALLIPOLI

> Then farewell to Kelvin Grove, bonnie lassie, O,
> And adieu to all I love, bonnie lassie, O,
> To the river winding clear,
> To the fragrant scented brier,
> Even to thee, of all most dear, bonnie lassie, O.
> *Kelvin Grove:* THOMAS LYLE.

IN 1908 Lord Haldane re-formed the Volunteers and Yeomanry into the new Territorial Force of all arms and branches, completely organized with divisions of its own similar to those of the regular army. Then it was that the 2nd Lowland Division, as such, came into existence as part of this force, the existence of which made it possible for the Expeditionary Force to leave the British Isles and save the situation in France in 1914.

On Tuesday, 4th August, 1914, Headquarters of the Lowland Division received a wire at 5.25 p.m. containing the single portentous word, " mobilize," and it was known that war between the Germanic Powers on the one hand, and Britain, France, Russia and Serbia on the other, had actually broken out. On its return from camp at Troon, Gailes, and Ayr, it had undertaken some guards and patrols defending vulnerable points, chiefly about Glasgow and the Clyde. By the 10th August the mobilization of the Division was complete, these guards and patrols were handed over to units on coast defence, and it proceeded to its war station.

The scheme for the strategical deployment of the Territorial Army in Scotland against possible invasion provided, in addition to the troops for coast defence, one division as a mobile force. This rôle had been assigned to the 2nd Lowland Division. In general, its disposition was as follows :

BRIDGE OF ALLAN—
    Divisional Headquarters : Major-General G. G. A. Egerton, C.B.
    Glasgow Yeomanry, one squadron.
    R.E., 1st and 2nd Lowland Field Coys. and Signalling Co.
    H.Q. and No. 1 Company, Divisional Train and Supply Column, R.A.S.C.

STIRLING—
    South Scottish (later 155th) Infantry Brigade : Brig.-Gen. F. Erskine.
    4th and 5th Royal Scots Fusiliers.
    4th and 5th King's Own Scottish Borderers.
    3rd Lowland Field Ambulance.
    No. 2 Company, D.T. and S.C.

FALKIRK—
    Scottish Rifle (later 156th) Infantry Brigade : Brig.-Gen. Stuart Hare.
    5th, 6th, 7th, and 8th Scottish Rifles (Cameronians).[1]
    1st Lowland Field Ambulance.
    No. 3 Company, D.T. and S.C.

DUNFERMLINE—
    Highland Light Infantry (later 157th) Infantry Brigade : Brig.-Gen. P. Hendry.
    5th, 6th, 7th and 9th Highland Light Infantry.
    2nd Lowland Field Ambulance.
    No. 4 Company, D.T. and S.C.

[1] The Scottish Rifles are generally referred to in this book as the Cameronians, although the regiment did not take that name officially until after the war.

MOBILIZATION AND EMBARKATION

The artillery brigades of the Division were stationed as follows:

Redford Barracks, Edinburgh, 1st Lowland (Edinburgh and Midlothian).
Larbert, Stirling, 2nd Lowland (Ayr and Kirkcudbright).
Dunfermline, 3rd Lowland (Glasgow).
Stirling and afterwards Tillicoultry, 4th Lowland Howitzer (Glasgow).

The 2nd (Ayr, etc.) Brigade had a battery at Invergordon assisting in the defence of the naval station. The first three R.F.A. brigades had each three four-gun batteries, and were armed with the 15-pounder converted gun. The fourth had two four-gun batteries armed with the old 5-inch howitzer. Each infantry battalion had two machine-guns, and was armed with the long charger-loading Lee-Enfield rifle. The transport of the Division consisted of commandeered civilian carts, lorries, and other waggons.

The Division was billeted in all manner of buildings, including disused factories, schools, private houses, a gaol, and a workhouse. During the end of 1914 and the early months of 1915 defensive positions were entrenched and wired, in view of a possible invasion; guards and patrols were provided, and rigorous training was in progress. Small arms ammunition was short, as a rule, but there was as much musketry training as possible. Of bombs, trench mortars, or rifle-grenades very little was known, and next to nothing was seen.

Under the existing law the Territorial Force could only be called upon for home defence, so that on 10th August, 1914, the Secretary of State for War called for complete units to volunteer for service overseas. Before many days had elapsed the majority of men in every unit of the Division had volunteered. The next step was for each Territorial unit to form a "Second Line," which was to provide drafts for the "First Line," while the latter served overseas, and the Division became the 1/2nd Lowland Division.[1] Recruiting was good and some units formed " Third Lines," despite the competition of the " New Army," and the fear that the Territorials might in the end be cold-shouldered, and left at home. Throughout the winter and spring the wish for active service was father to many thoughts, and numerous rumours arose from time to time that the Division was about to proceed overseas. Hopes often ran very high, and the disappointment that always followed was proportionately keen.

In November, 1914, the 1/9th H.L.I. (Glasgow Highlanders) and the 1/5th Scottish Rifles were taken out of the Division and sent to France. Many envious eyes watched them as they went, and some pessimists forecasted the break-up of the Division. The 1/9th H.L.I. was replaced for a while by the 2/9th H.L.I., its second line, but in its turn this unit was replaced because it was desired that the Division should be composed of first-line units. In April, 1915, when everyone was sure that the Division would go overseas as a Division, a threat of sending a man to the second line for home defence was the most effective of all deterrents from evil-doing.

Christmas and New Year passed amidst many alarms, but not without such festivities as billets would allow, helped out by the kindness of the local inhabitants, who everywhere showed all ranks the warmest hospitality. With the New Year came another change, when the infantry battalions were reorganized from the old basis of eight companies into four double-companies, each with four platoons, each of the latter, in its turn, having four sections. This remained the organization of an infantry battalion throughout the war, and it proved both useful and elastic.

In March, 1915, the 1/6th Scottish Rifles, all Lanarkshire colliers, left the Division for France; but on April

---

[1] A first line unit was designated as follows:—1/4th Royal Scots. Its second line was called the 2/4th Royal Scots. As all the infantry units which went overseas with the Division were first-line units, the writer has usually referred to them as the 4th Royal Scots, and so on.

MOBILIZATION AND EMBARKATION

24th the following first-line units joined the Division from coast defence duties :

    1/4th Royal Scots to Scottish Rifles Brigade.
    1/7th   do.   do.
    1/5th Argyll and Sutherland Highlanders to H.L.I. Brigade.

It had been known on the 5th April that the Division was to proceed overseas, and long Lee-Enfield rifles, with breeches reinforced so that they would take the Mark VII. ammunition of the more modern short rifle, were received and issued to the troops. Everyone's mind was made up for France or Flanders, when on the 7th May, the situation at Ypres being better in hand, the destination of the Division was changed to the Dardanelles where Sir Ian Hamilton was in urgent need of reinforcements. The reinforced rifles were withdrawn from the Division, and the old ones re-issued, eventually to do their duty on the battlefields of Gallipoli.

General service and limber waggons, proper light ambulances, sun-helmets, water-carts, new harness, horses, mules, and all manner of stores poured in on the Division by rail and road from Stirling Ordnance Depôt and elsewhere. The only civilian vehicles retained were the officers' mess-carts. These, being chosen from the lightest and strongest, proved of great value afterwards in the desert, where it was quite usual to meet a homely milk-cart or butcher's trap being pulled round a sandhill by a wicked-looking mule, urged on by a verbal accompaniment in the unmistakable accents of some part of the Lowlands.

On the 11th May the 1/2nd Lowland Division was re-numbered as the 52nd (Lowland) Division, the Infantry Brigades being re-designated as follows :

        South Scottish became the 155th.
        Scottish Rifle became the 156th.
        H.L.I. became the 157th.

The 156th Brigade was now commanded by Brig.-Gen. W. Scott-Moncrieff.

Owing to the difficulties of landing and operating artillery on the Gallipoli Peninsula, and also to the out-of-date pattern of the guns, it was decided that at first only the 2nd Lowland (Ayr), and 4th Lowland Howitzer (Glasgow) Brigades should go to the East. The 1st Lowland (Edinburgh) and 3rd Lowland (Glasgow) Brigades were to remain in the meantime at home for the defence of the Forth.

On 18th May the 8th Scottish Rifles embarked at Devonport on H.M.T. *Ballarat*, and the greater portion of the 155th Brigade at Liverpool on H.M.T. *Mauretania*, the sinking of whose sister-ship, the *Lusitania*, had been reported a few days previously. The remainder of the Division followed rapidly, troop-trains pouring into Liverpool and Devonport.

On the 22nd occurred probably the most terrible disaster in the history of British railways.

Train No. 18 left Larbert at 3.45 a.m. on the 22nd May, carrying Lt.-Col. W. C. Peebles, T.D., the commanding officer of the 1/7th Royal Scots, his Headquarters Staff, and A and D Companies under the command of Major J. D. L. Hamilton and Captain J. M. Mitchell, respectively, a total of 15 officers and 483 other ranks. The remainder of the battalion followed in a second train two hours later. It was a bright and clear May morning, and the men were in the highest spirits, for at last they were really going overseas. A local train had been drawn into a siding at Quentin's Hill Junction, a quiet country place, near Gretna, but its rear carriages had been left projecting on to the main line, some railway officials having forgotten for the moment that Train No. 18 was expected. At 6.45 a.m. the driver of this troop-train, on rounding the curve, saw the obstruction, and at once applied his brakes. But it was too late. The fast-moving troop-train crashed into the local. In a moment, carriages filled with officers and men were telescoped, others were knocked off the rails, and ran bumping over the sleepers, to overturn on the main down line, completely blocking it with their heaped-up wreck. The conscious survivors had hardly realized the horror of

MOBILIZATION AND EMBARKATION

the situation, when, a few seconds after this collision, the London express, travelling north at full speed, dashed into the middle of the over-turned troop-train, and itself piled up and telescoped into a mass of indescribable wreckage. Then a few wisps of smoke were seen to start in different parts of the mass, and soon the wreckage was blazing furiously—and there were no available means of coping with the fire.

The survivors and the people of the neighbourhood, for the whole countryside was quickly roused, risked and suffered anything to save or help the imprisoned victims.

When the fire had burned down it was found that the uninjured survivors amounted to only seven officers and fifty-seven other ranks. The killed and missing included three officers, Major J. D. L. Hamilton, senior company commander, Captain J. M. Mitchell, and Lieut. C. R. Salvesen, all good officers with the highest ideals of responsibility and duty. Numbered with them as dead were 207 other ranks. Of all of these, the bodies of only 53 N.C.O.'s and men were recovered and identified. Five officers and 219 other ranks were injured. The officers had ridden at the front and rear of the train, as it was their duty to do, and almost all the survivors were from the rear compartments. Among the killed in the London express were some officers and men returning from the front on short leave.

The remnant went on to Liverpool, but, although the officers who had escaped injury were allowed to embark, Major-General G. G. A. Egerton, G.O.C., 52nd Division, after conferring with the War Office, sent all the other ranks under a junior officer back to their homes for a rest.

At Liverpool General Egerton received the following telegram from H.M. The King:

" Buckingham Palace. Message from the King to the General Officer Commanding the Lowland Division.

" I remember being impressed with some of the units of your Division which I saw on the occasion of my visit to Scotland last July, and I much regret not to have had an opportunity of inspecting the Division before its departure.

I am confident that the glorious deeds of their regimental comrades at the front will inspire all ranks with the same spirit of devotion to duty. I offer you and the troops under your Command my best wishes for the success of the Lowland Division."

Before the middle of June the Division was at sea, distributed among transports as shown in the accompanying table. The ships left Liverpool and Plymouth Sound after nightfall, and the most stringent precautions were taken to ensure that no lights were showing to guide enemy submarines to their quarry.

Of all the divisions of the British Army, not one was more closely identified with its own recruiting area throughout the Great War of 1914-1918 than the Lowland Division. When it sailed, practically every walk of life from every part of the Lowlands was represented in the Division. Professional and city men, clerks, mechanics, shop-assistants, teachers, students and gentlemen of leisure filled the ranks of the 1/4th Royal Scots from Edinburgh and the H.L.I. and Scottish Rifles from Glasgow. The 7th Royal Scots was recruited from the colliers of the Lothians, from Leith, Musselburgh, and Dalkeith. It had been brought up to its full strength by volunteers for active service, a company strong, from the 8th H.L.I. The latter were from the mines of Lanarkshire, so that it was a wonderful battalion with the pick and shovel. From the Borders and Galloway, Cunningham, Kyle and Carrick came colliers and factory hands, farmers and tradesmen, in the K.O.S.B. and R.S.F. In the 5th Argyll and Sutherland Highlanders came riveters and other shipyard hands from the shores of Renfrewshire, with a leavening of Highlanders from the Western Isles. The Artillerymen, Engineers, Yeomanry, Army Service Corps, and R.A. Medical Corps, coming from the same districts, were recruited from the same types.

The escorting destroyers were left at Ushant, and then, in gorgeous but windy weather, following a course which touched about long. 11.32 W., the ships reached Gibraltar without incident. Zigzagging through the Mediterranean, they called in at Malta, where those who landed were met

MOBILIZATION AND EMBARKATION

DISTRIBUTION OF THE 52ND DIVISION IN TROOPSHIPS ON LEAVING THE BRITISH ISLES IN 1915, DATE AND PORT OF ARRIVAL, ETC.

Date of Sailing.	Port of Embarkation.	Troopship.	Principal Units Transported.	Date and Port of Arrival.
May 18	Devonport	Ballarat	8th Cameronians.	29th May, Mudros.
,, 21	Liverpool	Mauretania	H.Q. 155th Bde.; 4th R.S.F.; 5th R.S.F.; 5th K.O.S.B.	29th May, Mudros.
,, 22	Devonport	Shropshire	Transport Sections of the Division.	31st May, Mudros. (Lay there for 12 days; sailed for Alexandria and arrived 15th June.)
,, 24	Liverpool	Empress of Britain	H.Q. 52nd Division; Divisional Signalling Co., R.E.; H.Q. 156th Bde.; 4th Royal Scots; 7th Royal Scots; 7th Cameronians; 4th K.O.S.B.	4th June, Alexandria.
,, 26	Devonport	Transylvania	H.Q. 157th Bde.; 5th H.L.I.; 6th H.L.I.; 7th H.L.I.	5th June, Alexandria.
June 1	Devonport	Andania	5th A. and S. H.	12th June, Alexandria.
,, 2	Devonport	Mercian	4th (Glasgow) Howitzer Bde.; One Section of 1st Ayrshire Battery, 2nd Lowland Bde., R.F.A.	15th June, Port Said.
,, 5	Devonport	Karoa	Remainder 1st Ayrshire Battery and Bde. Amm. Col. of 2nd Lowland (Ayr and Kirkcudbright) Bde., R.F.A.; 52nd Divisional Cyclists; 1st Lowland Field Ambulance; 3rd Lowland Field Ambulance.	17th June, Port Said.
,, 7	Devonport	Marquette	2nd Ayrshire & Kirkcudbright Batteries, S.A.A.; Sections of 1st & 3rd Field Artillery Brigades.	20th June, Port Said.
,, 8	Plymouth	Maniou	2nd Lowland Field Ambulance.	23rd June, Port Said.

Note.—Almost every ship carried details. The *Mauretania* had on board officer details from almost every unit in the Division.

with long faces, some of which possibly belonged to German agents, and with stories of the sinking of H.M. battleships, *Triumph* and *Majestic* off Gallipoli.

Courtesies were always exchanged with British and French warships, whenever possible, and on several occasions the bandsmen of the Division played the " Marseillaise " to passing French vessels, to which they responded, usually with " God Save The King " and " Tipperary," whilst the men of both nations sent back answering cheers.

As the troopships neared their destinations in the Eastern Mediterranean, the increasing heat began to be felt, and sun-helmets were issued.

In the Aegean Sea, off the Gallipoli Peninsula, lie the islands of Lemnos, Imbros and Tenedos, claimed equally by Turkey and Greece after the Balkan War of 1912-13. They were now occupied by the Allies, Lemnos being used as an advanced base for their armies and navies operating against the Peninsula. For the most part these islands are barren and hilly, and can barely sustain the few Levantines who live in their white-walled, red-roofed hamlets and villages. Samothrace, beyond Imbros, at the mouth of the Gulf of Saros, is mountainous, being crowned with those mighty, red peaks which look over Imbros and Gallipoli and the intervening sea to the plains of Troy. Running in northward from the bleak and rugged south shore of Lemnos is a vast but narrow-mouthed harbour, large enough to hold immense fleets with ease, and named after the grey and dusty little town of Mudros which stands on its inner eastern shore. The barren hills of Lemnos are so grouped as to leave the harbour much exposed to northerly and southerly gales, which spring up very rapidly, making it dangerous for small craft to lie alongside larger vessels. This they were forced to do nevertheless, for there was no other means available for the transhipment of stores and men to the trawlers and small steamers, which took them to Gallipoli. The nearest dry-dock for the repair of ships was in Malta. Lemnos could not even supply the fleet and armies with water. This had to be brought from Egypt with other supplies

MOBILIZATION AND EMBARKATION 13

and stored there, pending transhipment to the Peninsula. An average of eighty tons of water had to be landed daily on Gallipoli to supply the most urgent needs of the army.

On 29th May the *Mauretania* and *Ballarat* entered Mudros Harbour, finding it thronged with a perfect medley of some hundred and twenty vessels in all, including battleships, cruisers, destroyers, trawlers, submarines, transports, and store-ships of every size. Two days later the *Shropshire* arrived. Evidently, it was hoped that the Allied assault of 4th June would result in great gains, and a lengthening of communications with consequent need for land transport. When hope of this was gone, the *Shropshire* was ordered to Alexandria where the *Empress of Britain* and *Transylvania* arrived on the 4th and 5th June respectively, and disembarked their troops, who entrained for Abukir.

Situated on a point of desert, flanked on one side by the Mediterranean and on the other by the historic Abukir Bay,[1] the camping ground was one of the most pleasant that could have been found in such a hot, sandy country as Egypt. It abounded in scorpions, small snakes, flies, beetles, and mosquitoes, but it was possessed of great attractions in first-rate sea-bathing and a fairly constant cool sea-breeze.

On the 8th June the 156th Brigade re-embarked at Alexandria, and, sailing past Crete and through the Greek Archipelago, " a succession of rocky islands shining in the sea like jewels in an azure setting," found themselves on the 11th anchored within the wide bay of Mudros.

On 12th June the 5th Argylls arrived at Alexandria on the *Andania* and had hardly got ashore, when they and the remainder of the Division at Abukir were ordered back to the transports, which sailed on the 13th for Mudros harbour. The next evening they were recalled by wireless, the reasons given being congestion in Mudros harbour, and change of plans on Gallipoli.

[1] In addition to Nelson's victory in 1798, Abukir was the scene of a French victory on land over the Turks in 1799. Sir Ralph Abercrombie reduced Fort Abukir in 1801. British ships made a feint attack here in 1882. The partially excavated remains of Canopus touched the southern edge of the camp. These are a few of the associations of this locality.

They disembarked at Alexandria on the 16th, with the ambulances and other troops which had arrived the previous day in the *Karoa*. Sweating under the sun-helmets in heavy serge, laden with equipment, pack, etc., they got themselves and all the multitudinous vehicles and stores ashore, and entrained for Abukir, in one of the hottest sand-storms recorded in Egypt for several years. The wind " was literally burning, and was comparable with what one experiences when passing in front of the open door of a furnace in an ironwork; and being laden with sand it very quickly hid from view the other vessels in the harbour " (Col. Edington). All the troops of the Division who landed at Alexandria were encamped at Abukir, where training was carried on in the deep, soft sands, between day-break and breakfast. Meanwhile news from Gallipoli was eagerly awaited.

The 156th Brigade, in the *Empress of Britain*, was the first to leave, the principal incident of the voyage being the attempt by an enemy aeroplane to bomb the ship soon after her arrival in Mudros harbour. The movements of various units of the Division, prior to their landing in Gallipoli or elsewhere, are shown in the following statement:

Formation or Unit.	Final Sailing from Alexandria or Port Said.	Arrival at Mudros.	Landed on Gallipoli, Cape Helles, unless stated otherwise.
155th Brigade (less 4th K.O.S.B.)	—	29th May	6-7th June
4th K.O.S.B.	8th June	11th June	14th June
156th Brigade:			12-13th and 14th June
4th and 7th R.S.	8th June	11th June	
7th Cameronians			13-14th June
8th Cameronians	—	29th May	13-14th June
157th Brigade	28th June	1st July	3rd July
1/1st Ld. Fd. Amblce.	22nd June	25th June	27-28th June
1/3rd Ld. Fd. Amblce.	28th June	1st July	3rd July
4th (Glasgow) Howitzers:			
4th Battery	17th June	20th June	21st June
5th Battery	(Port Said)		24th ,, (Anzac)

MOBILIZATION AND EMBARKATION 15

The supply sections of the Divisional Train, R.A.S.C., were with Divisional Headquarters or their infantry brigades, either on Gallipoli or at Mudros. The transport sections of the Divisional Train remained at Port Said until 13/14th October, when they embarked for Salonica on the *Japanese Prince*, arriving there on the 19th. They were attached to the 10th Irish Division, and remained so to the end of the war. The 1/2nd Lowland Field Ambulance was kept at Port Said for about two months. No transport or horses were taken to Gallipoli by the Division.

Owing to the lack of progress on Gallipoli, it was not guns with the range and low trajectory of the 15-pounder that were wanted, so much as howitzers which would throw shells high into the air and drop them into deep, narrow trenches. In addition, not only was Sir Ian Hamilton short of guns, but he was short also of ammunition even for those which he had. The result was that the 2nd Lowland (Ayr, etc.) Brigade, R.F.A., never saw Gallipoli, with the exception of the Small Arms Section of its Ammunition Column, which with those of the 1st (Edinburgh) and 3rd (Glasgow) all went to the Peninsula.

The troops from the *Mauretania* were transferred to destroyers, trawlers, and small cross-channel steamers in Mudros harbour on the afternoon of 6th June. The same afternoon and evening these vessels glided with crowded decks down the still waters of the harbour, receiving a cheer as they passed other ships still at anchor.

On the open sea, outside the two booms of the harbour, everything seemed strangely quiet and lonely after the songs, bugle-calls, shouting, and noise of the bay. Rising and falling to the waves, the small vessels turned towards the Peninsula of Gallipoli over fifty miles away to the eastward.

By day or night the approach to Gallipoli was a most impressive affair. Some of the troops found themselves moving under the grey cliffs of Cape Helles about the time of sunset, when the surrounding isles and mountains were bathed in the glorious tints of evening. Others came in the middle of the night, when those forward in the ships could see a dim mass slowly looming up, intermittently illumined by the flames of red and yellow explosions, and constantly echoing and reverberating with the thunder and roll of the guns.

The transportation of the Division to the Peninsula was not without incident. On the evening of the 12th June, H.M.S. *Reindeer* with 500 of the 4th Royal Scots on board, including the O.C., Lt.-Col. S. R. Dunn, T.D., and his Headquarters, was about thirty-four miles on her journey. She was making about seventeen knots an hour through a fairly calm sea, and, of course, steaming with all her lights out. Suddenly, in the darkness, there appeared another steamer of her own type and size, also without lights, and evidently returning from Gallipoli. She was making directly for the *Reindeer*, as if to strike her on the port bow. In a moment the *Reindeer's* helm had been put hard down. Her nose came round, but the two ships came together, the *Reindeer's* bow cutting deep into the other ship's side almost amidships. The *Immingham*, for such she turned out to be, began to settle down at once. The *Reindeer* tried without success to back away from the sinking ship whose crumpled ironwork was entangled with her own, and it really seemed as if the *Immingham* would pull her down also.

The behaviour and discipline of the hundreds of Royal Scots who crowded on the decks of the damaged *Reindeer* was of the steadiest. Very quietly, they stayed where they were, and took off their equipment, boots, and puttees. These small steamers did not carry life-belts for the crowded human freight they ferried over to Gallipoli; but many of the Royal Scots emptied their water-bottles, in order to have a little extra buoyancy when they were trying to keep afloat.

Those examining the bow reported that the *Reindeer* was cut down, herself, to within a few inches of the water. She was still tugging away to get clear, while the *Immingham* sank lower and lower, dragging more heavily all the time. If the water had once started pouring into the *Reindeer's* torn bows, the two ships would inevitably have

EASTWARD BOUND
On board H.M.T. *Empress of Britain*

MOBILIZATION AND EMBARKATION

gone down together. The crew of the *Immingham*, which had no troops on board, had scrambled over the bows of the *Reindeer*, their only loss having been one stoker killed by the impact.

The two vessels had been locked together about fifteen minutes, when at last the *Reindeer* pulled herself clear, and the *Immingham* went down like a stone.

Steaming slowly, stern first because of her crumpled bows, through a sea providentially only slightly choppy, the *Reindeer* was making back to Mudros when a large steamer bore down on her through the darkness. She hailed the *Reindeer*, and all were much relieved to hear that she was the French transport *Moulourja*, returning almost empty from Gallipoli. The Frenchman stood by until they reached Mudros again, where the Royal Scots were transferred to her.

The following G.R.O. was published to the Army shortly afterwards :

" General Routine Orders
by
General Sir Ian Hamilton, G.C.B., D.S.O., A.D.C.,
Commanding Mediterranean Expeditionary Force.

G.H.Q.
M.E.F.

Adjutant General's Branch.

300. *Acts of Gallantry*

" The general commanding desires to place on record the courage and presence of mind shown by the Officers and Men of the 4th Batt. Royal Scots in the undermentioned circumstances which occurred on the night of the 12th June, 1915.

" This Battalion was on board H.M.S. *Reindeer* when she collided with s.s. *Immingham*, which was sunk. The situation immediately after the accident was critical but at no time was there any sign of panic, and it was largely owing to the gallant behaviour of the troops on board, who upheld the highest traditions of the service, that no loss of life was incurred on this occasion."

Brig.-Gen. Scott-Moncrieff with his staff and this half of the 4th Royal Scots crossed to Cape Helles on two destroyers, arriving and disembarking without loss on the afternoon of the 14th of June.

With the exception of its artillery, none of which it ever saw during the whole of the time that it was on the Peninsula, and the 157th Brigade, which landed on the 3rd July, the Division had gathered all its principal fighting units at Cape Helles by the end of June.

CHAPTER II

(6TH TO 24TH JUNE, 1915)

GALLIPOLI: CAPE HELLES

> Why look the distant mountains
>   So gloomy and so drear?
> Are rain-clouds passing o'er them,
>   Or is the tempest near?
> No shadow of the tempest
>   Is there, nor wind nor rain—
> 'Tis Charon that is passing by,
>   With all his gloomy train.
>   *The Refusal of Charon:*
>   WILLIAM EDMONDSTOUNE AYTOUN.

IN order to realize the circumstances, under which the Division commenced its active service, it is necessary to give a brief résumé of the general situation at the time. The British, French and Belgian armies were just holding their own on a thin line of entrenchments, which ran from the Belgian coast to the Swiss frontier, and some had recognized that a decisive break-through against the Germanic hordes on that front could not be made without such a preponderance of strength as would only be possible after several years of preparation. Russia was already gasping under her efforts to hold back the German invasion, when, on the 31st October, 1914, Turkey entered the struggle on the Teutonic side. The Ottoman Government at once closed the narrow but vital gateway of the Dardanelles to Russia, with the result that but for a small ice-free port on the Arctic, the Trans-Siberian Railway, and Bulgaria—a very doubtful neutral—Russia, during the winter, was practically beleaguered by her enemies, or by barriers of mountains, snow or sand. In summer-time she was no better off, except that the port of Archangel was open. Turkey had struck at Russia in the Caucasus early in January, 1915, and, although the latter had managed to parry the blow, she was having so much difficulty in securing her supplies of munitions that such another thrust from either a German-Austrian or a Turkish army might have been fatal. On 2nd January, 1915, Russia appealed to the British Government for aid, and it was promised, despite Britain's own difficulties. A month later the Turks struck at the Suez Canal from Palestine, endeavouring to sever one of the main arteries of the British Empire. The venture ended in disaster for the Turks, but it showed their ability to cross the Sinai Desert with heavy guns. These events, and their inevitable influence on the minds of the peoples of Asia, Egypt and the Balkans, made it imperative that some immediate blow should be struck at the Turkish Empire.

The British War Council decided to attack Constantinople with a fleet, through the Dardanelles, hoping thereby to achieve the following results:

(1) to sever irretrievably the bulk of the Turkish Empire from the German-Austrian Powers;
(2) to open the Dardanelles so that munitions of war could be poured into Russia, and so that the latter could send out her grain in return;
(3) to distract the Turks from any further attempts against Russia or the Suez Canal, and perhaps to cause a revolution in Constantinople which would put a government in power that would conclude a separate peace;
(4) to bring such doubtful neutrals as Bulgaria and Greece to the side of Britain and her Allies; and
(5) to complete another section of the iron wall which was slowly enclosing the Central Powers.

The long, narrow strait of the Dardanelles, or Hellespont, is the only way by which ships can pass from the outer seas and the Aegean to the Sea of Marmora and Constantinople. That city, the ancient Byzantium, has always commanded the Bosphorus, the final corridor into the Black Sea, whence mighty rivers give access to the very heart of Central Europe and Russia. Great memories brood over this strip of silver water, which cuts asunder the continents of Europe and Asia, from the heroes of Troy to Xerxes, Alexander the Great, Constantine, the Fourth Crusade, and Suleyman. In 1807 and in 1878 British fleets passed through the Dardanelles, encountering little or no resistance, but no hostile fleet has forced the passage of this strait in the face of serious opposition.

At the Aegean mouth of the Dardanelles, between the villages of Sedd el Bahr in Europe and Kum Kale in Asia, the strait is about two miles wide. Running in a north-easterly direction for about fourteen miles, the channel, because of the curve taken by the Asiatic shore, broadens out into that sheet of water about five miles wide, which was to be the theatre of the gallant but disastrous attempt of the Allied Fleet to force the Narrows. Between the minarets of Chanak on the Asiatic side, and the village of Kilid Bahr on the European, the channel turns to the north for about four miles. In the neighbourhood of these two places its shores are less than a mile apart, and, from the heights above to the edge of the water, bristled with the heaviest artillery. This stretch is called the Narrows. Afterwards, the channel runs north-east again for about twenty-five miles with an average width of about three miles, until it passes the large town of Gallipoli, from which the peninsula forming the northern shore takes its name. Here it narrows down again to a width of less than two miles, but widens again to four miles at Bulair on the isthmus of the peninsula, where it opens out into the Sea of Marmora. The land on both sides is broken and hilly, the peninsula heights as a rule dominating the Asiatic shores, although several miles away to the east the ground rises up to the distant, blue mountain range of Ida, 3000 feet, the Turkish Kara Dagh.

On the southern side, just within the Aegean entrance,

lie the green and marshy plains, where could be seen the low hill on which stood the ancient city of Troy, with its reminder of earlier wars for the right to use this waterway. Further east the ground rises to the grey cliffs and heights which overlook the Narrows. The northern shore of the southern reaches is formed almost entirely of precipitous cliffs, which are seamed by deep ravines, and finally overshadow the Narrows and the more low-lying Asiatic shore from a height of over 500 feet. The hills directly behind Kilid Bahr, covered with scrub but with very occasional patches of cultivation like the rest of the countryside, rise to nearly 700 feet, and completely command the forts at the Narrows. The principal elevation is called by the Turks the Pasha Dagh, and is often referred to as the Kilid Bahr Plateau.

The channel itself varies in depth from twenty-five to fifty fathoms. Being the only outlet for the Danube and many mighty Russian rivers, it has a current of very cold water flowing perpetually into the Mediterranean and coming through the Narrows at a speed of four miles an hour. The channel was entirely blocked by numerous mine-fields, and the current could be utilized to carry drifting mines down on to attacking warships.

Between 18th February and 7th March the British and French Fleets destroyed the Turkish batteries at Sedd el Bahr and Kum Kale, and bombarded those at Dardanus, Chanak and Kilid Bahr. On 18th March twelve British and four French battleships, with lesser craft, tried to force the Narrows, but, whilst offering perfect targets themselves, they could not locate and silence the mobile batteries of howitzers which rained heavy shells on them from one hiding place after another away behind the crests of the cliffs. Neither could the accompanying destroyers and trawlers effectively counter the shoals of drifting mines. One French and two British battleships were sunk on this day, while others sustained serious damage, and the Allies had to admit failure, being unfortunately ignorant of the fact that, as we now know, the Turks had hardly any ammunition left.

Meanwhile, it had been realized that the ground commanding the Straits must be in the possession of the Allies, or the narrow water-way would only form a death-trap for the ships, even if they did get through the Narrows, and accordingly a military landing had been decided upon. Unfortunately, through no fault of the army commanders in the Aegean, the troops were not ready. Further, when they were ready, they had to wait for good weather before a landing was possible on the confined and exposed beaches of the Peninsula. Over five precious weeks went past, during which the Turks, now fully warned of their danger, made the cliffs around all possible landing-places as impregnable as mines, machine-guns, entrenchments, wire-entanglements, and concealed artillery could make them.

The Gallipoli Peninsula, referred to afterwards as Gallipoli, is roughly shaped like a foot, the toe being at Cape Helles, the sole towards the Dardanelles, the heel at the town of Gallipoli, and the ankle at Bulair, the latter being bent back to join the mainland of Thrace. It is very hilly and is about fifty-four miles long, varying in breadth from three miles, where the Bulair Lines span the more low-lying isthmus, to over thirteen miles between Cape Suvla and the Straits, drawing in further south to from five to six and a half at the Narrows, then to three and a half at Krithia, and finally shrinking to a mile and a half at Cape Helles, four and a half miles from that village.

It was in this restricted area between Krithia and Cape Helles that lay the arena, little over nine square miles in extent, which was the scene of most of the fighting of the Division on Gallipoli.

There were no railways following either shore of the Dardanelles, and what few roads there were on the Peninsula were very poor, for the sea furnished the normal means of communication. When, later on, our submarines made sea transit almost impossible for the Turks, they still had their European and Asiatic overland routes. The European ran by rail from Constantinople to Uzun Keupru and thence by road to Bulair. The Asiatic ran by rail from Scutari on the Bosphorus to Panderma on the Sea of

Marmora, and thence by road to Chanak. As most of the Turkish reinforcements and the bulk of their supplies, apart from munitions of war, came from Asia, this route, despite the circuitous line followed by the railway in Asia Minor, was really not so inconvenient. Smyrna, for example, was only nine hours from Panderma. Neither overland route presented any considerable difficulty.

The immediate object of the military expedition was to capture the heights commanding the Narrows, and with them the forts and mine-fields which barred that passage. Sir Ian Hamilton decided on a series of simultaneous landings at the extreme southern end of Gallipoli; together with one at that cove now known to history as Anzac,[1] which lies on the western shore almost directly across the Peninsula from the Narrows.

The coast of Gallipoli, south-west of Krithia, is a wall of precipitous cliffs, varying from 65 and 100 feet high at Capes Tekke and Helles at the south-eastern extremity, to 300 feet and more on either shore to the north-west and south-east of Krithia.

In three places this mighty rampart of grey stone and crumbling rock admits of ascent :

(1) at the narrow " X Beach " or " Implacable Landing," which lies a mile north-east of Cape Tekke, where the cliffs are lower, and being very soft and crumbling are less steep ;
(2) at " W Beach " or " Lancashire Landing," where a shallow sandy gully runs in between Capes Tekke and Helles ; and
(3) at " V Beach " or " *River Clyde* Landing," between Cape Helles and Sedd el Bahr, where the cliffs become slopes, making the bay like an amphitheatre about five hundred yards across.

In three places it is cut by gorges descending to sea-level :

(1) at " Y 2 " or " Gully Beach," a mile north-east of " X Beach," where, like a deep, long, narrow gash

---

[1] Taking its name from the initial letters of the Australian and New Zealand Army Corps.

LOOKING NORTH FROM "X" BEACH, CAPE HELLES

in the country-side, the Saghir Dere or Gully Ravine, with cliffs of 100 feet high, barely 100 yards apart at the top, runs south-west with many twists and turns, but roughly parallel to the coast, until the latter turns in to meet it ;

(2) at the curve of Morto Bay, and "S Beach" or "Casson's Landing," where the various watercourses drain the concave interior of the peninsula, and there is a complete break for over a mile between the wooded slopes of Sedd el Bahr and the fine, 200 feet high headland, which overlooks De Tott's Battery at Hissarlik Point ; and also

(3) more than a mile further to the north-east, where the great, wide gorge of Kereves Dere curves round to the south into the Hellespont.

These are the six breaks which concern us principally, and opposite each of them is a strip of sandy beach, over which in the wet season the nullahs or watercourses pour raging torrents into the sea. Morto Bay, *River Clyde* Landing, and most of Lancashire Landing are in full view of the Asiatic coast from a distance of less than three miles.

Two miles to the north-east of the mouth of Gully Ravine lies "Y Beach" or "Koe's Landing," a strip of sand, above which towered, 200 feet high, with its precipitous and crumbling sides seamed by numerous scrub-covered gullies, the height afterwards known as Ghurka Bluff.

With its fringe of cliffs, and the soft graceful lines of its hills, Gallipoli is very beautiful from the sea, and in the springtime has lovely colouring from its flowers, although in summer everything becomes parched and assumes a tawny hue.

As the year advanced, the weather became fine and settled, so that landings on the exposed beaches were possible. On 24th April the collier *River Clyde* was run ashore at "V Beach," and there and elsewhere British troops from all over the Empire struggled ashore, with dreadful losses, through entanglements and cross-fire from machine-guns. Footholds were secured at Casson's, the

River Clyde, Lancashire, and the Implacable Landings at Cape Helles, and at Anzac Cove. Then, short of everything, and with a fickle sea in the rear, the Allies commenced that series of fierce battles for " elbow-room " against an enemy who was never less than twice their strength, and whose lines of communication were secure.

At one time Gallipoli must have been part of a tract of hilly country. The sea, the weather, and other forces of nature have worn away the surrounding land until the present peninsula was formed, its south-eastern end being the remains of a valley, still shut in by the lower inner slopes of the hills which had formed it. The remainder of these hills have disappeared, leaving the peninsula fringed with those huge cliffs. At the south end of Gallipoli is the valley or depression which runs south-west from Krithia, and then curves southward to open on to the Dardanelles at Morto Bay. At its bottom runs the watercourse which is called by the Turks the Kirte Dere, and by the British Krithia Nullah, because of its point of origin. Roughly following the same course about 700 yards to the east runs a lesser watercourse called by the Turks the Kanli Dere, and by the British Achi Baba Nullah, also from its place of origin near the summit of the historic hill.

The three most important heights on Gallipoli are as follows :

(1) Sari Bair, 970 feet high, nearly eight miles north of Kilid Bahr at the Narrows, and about two and a half east of Anzac : from this hill the Narrows and its immediate heights could be dominated at long range ;

(2) Pasha Dagh, or Kilid Bahr Plateau, over 700 feet high, a ridge whose eastern end overlooked the forts near Kilid Bahr and Chanak : this hill was the key to the Narrows ; and

(3) Achi Baba, 720 feet high, a ridge running athwart the peninsula on a line little more than a mile to the north-east of Krithia : this hill was the key to the landings in the Cape Helles area, and from it

operations could be carried on against the Pasha Dagh, six miles to the north-east.

Achi Baba is a ridge about four and a half miles long, forming a barrier right across the peninsula at an average height of almost 500 feet, and little more than five miles from Lancashire Landing, the furthest beach in the Cape Helles area. Its hump or highest point is in the centre, and the southern half of the ridge is rather higher than the northern. At either end it descends sharply, first in terraces, and then in precipices, into the sea. Directly below the central hump of Achi Baba on its south-western face it is scored with gorges, which in many parts are filled with trees that give observers all the cover they want, and which unite to form the Krithia and Achi Baba Nullahs or water-courses. About a mile and a half to the west of the central hump stands the stone-built village of Krithia with its gardens and orchards. On its south-eastern side was a line of five wind-mills which were of the usual Levantine shape, a cylinder crowned by a flat cone, until they were ruined by artillery fire. The buildings of Krithia, standing at a height of 350 feet above sea-level, were most useful to the Turks for observation of the ground within the British lines. In addition they obtained from them plenty of timber for dug-outs.

Because of the hollow configuration of the interior, everything on the surface of the ground within the crest-line of the surrounding sea-cliffs, a few places excepted, can be observed from the ridges of Achi Baba.

From Cape Helles, the ground slopes inwards towards the north-east for about a mile and a half, and then rises in one long glacis about four miles in length to the crest-line of Achi Baba. That slope is almost entirely covered with a low scrub, some of it thorny, and some of it akin to heather, but all giving perfect cover to the defending rifleman and machine-gunner. It offered unlimited possibilities for a whole series of defensive lines. About Sedd el Bahr, and for half a mile inland around Morto Bay, the country is well wooded. In a few other places there are cultivated patches and vineyards with a few trees. With the exception of the village of Sedd el Bahr there were in the entire Allied area less than a dozen stone habitations, a few of these having orchards of figs and olives. In and about the nullahs, mostly in the lower reaches, were a few trees. Apart from these and one or two lonely groups of pines on the higher swells of ground, there was no cover if one walked outside the shallow Krithia and Achi Baba Nullahs, or their shallower tributaries.

These nullahs are shallow gullies with sides about twelve feet high, and for the greater part of the year contain a thin trickle of water, which meanders from one side of the floor to the other, linking up a series of slimy-looking puddles, in which mosquitoes and other insects breed, and where frogs and tortoises make their home. After heavy rain they fill up and become swirling torrents. Even the beds of these nullahs were under observation in many places from Achi Baba, but, by following under some tiny cliff or by using some tiny hillock to block the line of view, they could be used as natural communication trenches to central points in the front line as it moved forward. It must not be forgotten that the gorges of Gully Ravine, and Kereves Dere are of vastly greater depth than the nullahs of the central depression with its intervening tongues of moorland.

Behind Achi Baba, to the north-east, lies a series of beautifully wooded valleys, with unlimited possibilities for concealed artillery positions, supply bases, and rest-camps for troops well clear of our shell-fire.

To sum up, the Turks had almost every possible advantage. In addition, they have been good soldiers ever since they appeared in history, especially when fighting in defensive positions.

The British, with the 29th, 42nd (East Lancashire), Australian, Australian and New Zealand, and Royal Naval Divisions, together with the 29th Indian Brigade; and the French, with the two divisions of their Corps Expéditionnaire Française d'Orient, fought their way up the long moorland slopes of Achi Baba, until by the 21st June a line was held, which ran approximately from the mouth of

CAPE HELLES

Kereves Dere to Ghurka Bluff with a bulge towards Achi Baba in the centre. Because of the shortage of men directly resulting from the difficulties of landing water and supplies to keep alive those who were ashore, the Turks never in the campaign outnumbered the Allies by less than two to one, and were always fresh men opposing men who were worn out with fatigue and privation. Ammunition for the little British artillery that could be landed was desperately short, so that although the Navy gave help, without which many an attack must have failed, the Turkish defences were not properly bombarded with high angle fire, and the losses of assaulting troops accordingly were appalling. This still further reduced what man-power there was, with the result that, when a Turkish line of defences was captured, there were never reserves available to push on. Several times the way to the summit of Achi Baba lay open through great gaps torn in the Turkish lines and there only remained a few shattered remnants of the enemy to be driven out of the way, but there were only the weary survivors of the assaulting troops on the field of battle, and the chances had to be lost. By the time the Allies could make a further advance, the Turks had brought up reinforcements of fresh men and had dug a fresh system of defences, one line of trenches behind another, the higher always enfilading or otherwise commanding the lower.

The British losses were terrible. But those of the Turks were worse, and Gallipoli was like an ulcer in their side continually sapping their strength. In addition, the campaign, because of its very boldness, was one of the influences which caused Italy to declare war on Austria on 23rd May.

The battle fought on 4th June had been a terrible disappointment. The Allies had advanced across the full breadth of the peninsula, and it seemed as if the morrow would have seen them over Achi Baba, but the newly-captured " Haricot Redoubt " on the right had been lost by some French coloured troops, and the new line had been enfiladed so that it had to be given up, and an advance of only a few hundred yards was the net result of the battle.

It must not be forgotten that even when Sir Ian Hamilton had men available at Mudros, he could not always put them ashore for lack of small craft to carry them, and to keep them supplied with ammunition, food, and water, when they were ashore. It was therefore essential to conserve as much as was possible those troops who had already been landed by reducing to a minimum the casualties suffered in assaults. This could only be done by silencing the fire of enemy artillery and machine-guns with a greater volume of fire from British guns on shore. The warships were splendid against the extreme Turkish right, and in shelling main features behind the enemy front line, but could do very little against the concealed artillery and machine-gun emplacements of the Turkish centre and left, because they could not see them, and because the trajectory of their guns was too flat. In those days, when observation by aeroplane was in its infancy, it was dangerous for the Navy to bombard enemy trenches lying near the Allied lines, unless they could see from their own ships the exact places where their shells struck. The saucer-like configuration of Cape Helles caused the inward slopes to commence directly at the edges of the cliffs. This prevented direct observation from the sea of most of the enemy trench systems which were contiguous to the Allied lines. More artillery ashore, especially howitzers, and above all more ammunition, especially high explosive (H.E.), were what Sir Ian Hamilton required. Even for the few guns which he had he was lamentably short of ammunition. The fault for this lay somewhere in the British Isles, for his letters and despatches show that he was continually asking for them, with every possible warning as to the inevitable consequences if he were not supplied. He did not get them until too late, and he and his men had to pay the penalty.

Small assaults and counter-attacks followed the battle of 4th June, and on the 21st the French re-captured the "Haricot Redoubt." By this time, however, the Turks had organized new lines of defences, and the ramifications of their trench systems were rapidly growing.

Turkish heavy artillery could not only shell the Allied

CAPE HELLES

lines from concealed positions behind Achi Baba with fire perfectly directed from its ridges, but, using the same observation posts, they could completely enfilade the Cape Helles area from the Asiatic coast, and shoot right into its rear from Kum Kale. British warships could enfilade the Turkish right from the Aegean, and in the earlier stages had enfiladed their left and covered the southern Allied flank from the Dardanelles. However, enemy submarines and torpedo boats had succeeded in sinking the battleships *Goliath*, *Triumph*, and *Majestic*, after which the ships, with the exception of a monitor and a few destroyers, were withdrawn to more open waters. British warships could shell the Turkish areas north of Achi Baba, but, because of their vast extent, broken nature, and the numerous woods, which gave perfect concealment, it was almost impossible to observe the effects of the fire.

Meanwhile, the Turkish trench systems grew into an immense network, and both sides settled down to trench warfare.

Sir Ian Hamilton has written as follows of Cape Helles: " With the wind in certain quarters no sort of landing is possible ; the wastage, by bombardment and wreckage, of lighters and small craft has led to crisis after crisis in our carrying capacity, whilst over every single beach plays fitfully throughout each day a devastating shell-fire at medium ranges."

Munitions of all kinds, food, and even water had to be brought over the sea and landed at the wonderful piers of wood-piles, stone, lighters and half-sunken ships, which the Allies had erected at Lancashire and *River Clyde* Landings, the most famous being the one of which the old collier formed the principal portion. Here, also, the wounded had to be embarked for Alexandria and Malta.

Because of the miles of fire, and leagues of communication, trenches which the Allies had been compelled to dig through the tangle of tough scrub-roots into the marl and clay, there had been neither time nor labour to do more than scrape a thin layer of earth over the dead where they could be reached.

To this disease-ridden place, where myriads of pestiferous flies tormented the living; where the supply of water was lamentably inadequate; where men's throats were parched with heat, dust, and breathing a foul atmosphere; where the Turks by this time had all important points ranged to a yard; which possessed every possible military defect for the Allies, came the Division, full of life and expectation, to do battle for the first time.

When the 155th Brigade arrived on the night of the 6th June, the troops were landed at the *River Clyde*, and had to clamber up an accommodation ladder on to the much-bombarded old collier, follow a devious path through her battered interior, descend a gangway through a hole in her bow on to a lighter, and then pick their way ashore over a number of half-sunken lighters and boats linked up with simple plank bridges. Every man at the time was necessarily laden up with rifle and bayonet, pick or shovel, pack, other accoutrements, blanket, ground-sheet, and 150 rounds of ammunition. Those who landed in daylight, did so almost free from shelling; but at night the beaches and piers were bombarded by the Asiatic guns, sometimes heavily, and sometimes with only an occasional shell. In daylight one could see how honey-combed with dug-outs were the slopes and gullies round the landings; but at night one had to wend one's way up as best one could through this strange world of cave-dwellings and heaps of stores. To add to the difficulties of the latter, the guides were usually very much at fault, largely owing to the darkness and lack of defined routes with landmarks. As soon as troops crested the rise, they could see the flashes of rifle-fire and flares from Verey pistols in the firing line on the slopes of Achi Baba.

Passing between numerous shell-holes, and occasionally falling into them, they were taken to the " Rest Camp." This was an area on the inner or north-eastern slopes of Cape Helles, completely bare but for a few bushes and stunted trees, and accordingly in full view of Turkish observation posts on Achi Baba a little over four miles away. The only shelter that awaited them on their arrival consisted

RIVER CLYDE, "V" BEACH, CAPE HELLES

CAPE HELLES

of a number of " funk-holes " a few feet deep, shaped like graves, in which men could lie down. A certain amount of shelter from the sun was obtained by pegging a waterproof sheet over the top. There were only sufficient of these dug-outs for a fraction, so that all ranks set to work to dig fresh holes and to deepen and lengthen existing ones. This was the invariable experience of all troops landing at Cape Helles. Those who had to reach the " Rest Camp " in daylight always did so in artillery formation, small columns spread out so that one shell could only put comparatively few men out of action.

The morning of 7th June dawned, and the newly-arrived men could see the low ridge of Achi Baba, with its central hump bathed in early sunlight, many, who knew nothing as yet of its long slope, wondering how it could be such a strong position. At 6 a.m. the Turks started to shell the camp, continuing to do so at intervals throughout the day, until evening. By that time a number had been killed or wounded, and Major Taylor, R.A.M.C. (T), attached 4th R.S.F., had been struck by shrapnel about 7.35 p.m., dying from his wounds the following morning. He was the first officer in the Division to lose his life in action. This shelling was a daily practice, and burst out at odd and unexpected moments, always taking its toll. Despite this, however, the daily life and traffic of the place went on. Animals had to be taken to water. Men had to move about on digging fatigues. There were always sick, wounded and dying to be brought from different points in the motor-ambulances. Processions of the light two-wheeled Indian transport carts moved about all day with stores to and from the trenches and elsewhere. The ground was dry, and its surface had been pulverized until it was covered with a fine yellow and brown dust. The continually moving feet and wheels threw this into the air, where it was caught by air-currents, so that it hung like a thin mist all about and over the " Rest Camp " areas, and away back to the beaches. This had two important effects: everyone had to inhale a foul, thirst-compelling dust, but it also made it very difficult for the Turks to observe their own fire. Looking back from the front line to the "Rest Camp" one could only see a couple of miles, and then the distance was gradually lost in a light, yellow fog. The dust took its toll but it also helped to make life in these areas possible.

At times, when the heat was very great, miniature whirlwinds would spring up, catching up the dust and everything that would lift into a column or "dust-devil," several hundred feet high. When the wind was strong the dust was blown everywhere and into everything. In ordinary times food was always covered with a deposit of this grit and filthy dust, which had to be swallowed with it, but when the wind was high it was best not to attempt liquid food, as it became little better than sandy mud.

Normally, before new troops were sent to hold trenches where the safety of part of the line would depend on them alone, they served an apprenticeship of a few days with experienced troops in the firing line, in order to learn the strange craft of living and fighting in trenches. The battle of 4th June was just simmering down, and it was essential that the 29th Division, which was then in the left sector, should be given an opportunity to secure for a short period whatever rest could be obtained in these surroundings. It was therefore decided to put into the line at once the three Lowland battalions which had landed. The 4th and 5th R.S.F. were to hold the front lines, with the 5th K.O.S.B. in reserve, and accordingly, officers of the R.S.F. units were sent up on 8th June to the 88th Brigade (29th Division) to learn the geography of the trenches and to accustom themselves to the methods of trench warfare.

The trench system at Cape Helles can be best described as a vast system of miles and miles of roofless corridors with walls about seven or eight feet in height, which wound about in all directions with the most complicated ramifications. Apparently, their twists and turns were completely meaningless and without order. In fact, they were decided by the necessity of avoiding outcrops of rock, of linking up trenches, of making frequent traverses and bends to limit the effects of enemy shell-fire, of avoiding observation from enemy trenches on a higher swell of ground, of covering certain ground with fire and of sapping forward to vantage-ground for that purpose, and so on. The result was a tangle of trenches wherever the front line had stayed any time, and a fresh system of communication trenches when it had been pushed forward again. The nullahs only touched a few points, and, because of their width and exact identification on Turkish maps, they were shelled regularly. For this reason they were frequently impassable. "Clapham Junction," where Krithia Nullah was joined by a tributary, was one example of a thoroughly unhealthy spot.

The limited number of trench maps that were available for the infantry were drawings reproduced by a gelatine process, and under the circumstances they were most clever productions, without which the trenches would have appeared an inextricable maze. They were, however, not always accurate, and could not possibly show every turn and blind alley. It had been possible to put up sign-boards (often only of card-board or paper) in very few places in the trenches, and, if anyone lost his way, it was risky to look for a landmark over the top; snipers were everywhere, and, naturally, the worst labyrinths were near the front line. If he did peep over the top along the ground level he usually saw a grisly world, strange and unrecognizable. Useful landmarks were few and far between.

There were a few printed maps, but they did not reach the infantry until later.

The relieving of units in the trenches was difficult enough in daytime, but far more so at night. Those leaving had to point out the positions of enemy trenches, and of Allied trenches which, in these tortuous lines, could easily be mistaken for Turkish; they had to indicate enemy snipers' posts, probable machine-guns, and possible lines of approach; they had to show the newcomers the ramifications of their own section of the line. This could only be done properly by day. It usually took about a couple of hours, after which the tired men relieved could make their way down the miles of trenches to the "Rest Camp," and, possibly before darkness set in, see in what manner and in what hole they were going to lie down.

On the afternoon of 9th June the three battalions, each with a couple of guides, went up to the front lines for the first time. When it was necessary to move a body of men on Gallipoli, the movement had to be made as unobtrusively as possible. Companies were detailed off to their places in the fire and support trenches before any move was made. They left the " Rest Camp " and got into the communication trenches in successions of small sections in single file, each man being laden with rifle, ammunition, and everything he possessed, in addition usually to a pick or shovel. All men stayed in their dug-outs until their section was due to move off. A few stunted trees, some bushes, and folds in the ground gave some cover; but the Turks usually could tell when a move was in progress, probably by noticing extra dust rising from the communication trenches, or by noting an occasional series of rifle-muzzles moving up and down above the parapets. Very soon, for this reason, men were forbidden to carry rifles slung over their shoulders. Turkish artillery always searched the communication trenches with shrapnel during a move, and caused some casualties; but the heavily laden and perspiring men trudged steadily and cheerily on, despite the flies which tormented them, and the heat that struck back from the yellow and white sides and floors of the trench.

The unit of the 29th Division relieved by the 5th R.S.F. was the 5th Royal Scots. This Edinburgh unit had been reduced by battle and disease to about 250 men, and only needed a few trenches for its accommodation. When the Ayrshire men arrived, 850 strong, there was not room for them all, and they overflowed into the communication trenches, a condition of affairs which never occurred again in the Division. Seventy men were sent back to the " Rest Camp," where the quartermasters had their " dumps " or battalion bases.

The trenches having been taken over and sentries posted, all ranks speedily settled down to the novel conditions and became used to the fact that the Turks were only a few dozen yards away. From sunset until nightfall, every man " stood to." No man in the fire trenches was allowed to take his equipment off, or be away from his rifle, which had its magazine filled and bayonet fixed. At night, when not acting as one of the numerous sentries that unceasingly watched " No Man's Land " from almost every fire-bay, men slept in their equipment, lying on the fire-step or the floor of the trench, with their rifles immediately at hand. Officers on duty patrolled quietly up and down, treading in and out of the sleeping men. The sentries used their ears almost as much as their eyes, despite the continual dribble of rifle-fire from the Turkish trenches, and hum and crack of the bullets. Now and again our own sentries sent back an answering shot, or fired at some dark object in " No Man's Land " which seemed to have moved. Many a swollen or shrivelled corpse was shot time and again in this way, for the ground everywhere was littered with them. This shooting served to keep Turkish patrols at arm's length, and did not disturb the sound sleep of the tired men between their turns of duty as sentries. Special vigilance was necessary, because of the recent battle and the possibility of Turkish night attacks. There was a little wire in front of some parts of the British line, but in most places there was nothing between the British bayonets and a Turkish onslaught but the heaps of dead.

An hour before dawn all " stood-to " again, and watched the yellow and grey lines of upturned earth, the forward faces of the Turkish parapets, gradually re-appearing, while the morning light caught the hump of Achi Baba almost three miles away. This was a busy time for the snipers of both sides, watching for unwary look-outs and working parties who did not get their heads down quickly enough.

Many fewer sentries were required in the daytime, but when the men were not trying to sleep despite the myriads of flies that never ceased to pester them, they were kept busy cleaning their arms, and improving the trenches, which had only now been in British possession for a few days. Fire-steps had to be made, parapets to be thickened, traverses to be built, and new communication trenches to be dug. It was best to keep the minds of men occupied, until they had got thoroughly used to finding dead buried in the parapets, and accustomed to breathing an atmosphere which told only too plainly that proper sanitation was absolutely impossible. When the sun was about its zenith, the yellow and white sides of the trenches formed them into sun-baths and the heat was terrific. All were wearing ordinary serge uniforms. Cotton drill never reached the Division while it was on Gallipoli.

Now and again the Turks shelled the trenches heavily, or their snipers became especially daring, and at such times casualty lists became longer.

On the morning of the 11th June the trenches of the 4th R.S.F. shook to a high explosive bombardment, resulting in the loss of Captain A. Logan and one other rank killed, and one officer and twenty other ranks wounded. The dead were buried, the wounded were carried away down the long narrow trenches, and the parapets and traverses were repaired. The next day enemy snipers succeeded in crawling unobserved into some scrub, whence they could shoot at men engaged in carrying up water and rations as they passed a gap where a trench had fallen in. A few more casualties were added to the list before this could be repaired. One has only to look at any heather-clad moorland to realize the amount of cover available for an enterprising sniper on the long, swelling slopes of Achi Baba.

On the 13th the 155th Brigade was relieved and proceeded to the " Rest Camp," the 5th R.S.F. handing over again to the 5th Royal Scots, who distinguished themselves five days later in helping to repel a heavy Turkish attack. Troops in the " Rest Camp " were always worked very much harder, and usually were in much greater danger from enemy shell-fire than those in the front line. Turkish gunners at Kum Kale could shell the " Rest Camp " with ease from its rear, whilst they did not dare to shell the British forward trenches for fear of hitting the defenders of their own front line.

It was quite common for a battalion in the " Rest Camp "

CAPE HELLES

to be asked for larger fatigue parties than it could possibly supply. The need for labour was very great, if only for the digging and deepening of those vital communication trenches. Even after dark this was dangerous, for all night long the Turks sprayed the rear lines with a dropping fire from rifles and machine-guns. On the night of the 18-19th the 4th R.S.F. lost one man killed and four wounded from this cause.

At this time the 155th Brigade (less the 5th K.O.S.B., attached Royal Naval Division) was attached to the 42nd Division. The 156th Brigade, after it landed on the 12/14th, came under the 29th Division.

On the morning of the 15th the " Rest Camp " was heavily shelled from Asia, the 8th Cameronians losing some men. The Turks must have had a number of long-range guns for this purpose, but whenever they opened fire the men always referred to them by the generic term of " Asiatic Annie." Later in the day, Sir Ian Hamilton, accompanied by General Hunter-Weston, G.O.C., 8th Corps, met Brigadier-Generals Erskine and Scott-Moncrieff, and walked round the dug-outs with them, chatting with the officers and men, and gathering a favourable impression of their morale. The 4th K.O.S.B. were sent up to the front lines the same day to spend a night with the 88th Brigade (29th Division) for instruction, and parties of officers and N.C.O.'s from the 156th Brigade went up during the day for the same purpose.

The period that followed was one of continual work on communication and fire-trenches behind the front line, carried out under cover of darkness and usually to the accompaniment of dropping fire from Turkish rifles and machine-guns. Everyone got so used to the " ping " and " plop-plop " of the bullets that they took no notice, but worked steadily on, despite an occasional casualty.

It was not so much the Turkish shells arriving occasionally from front, flank and rear, that kept men from sleeping when in the " Rest Camp," as the myriads of flies, which refused to be driven away, and crawled over faces and hands in maddening persistency. The rations consisted mainly of bully-beef, army biscuits, bread, jam, onions, and tea. Everything had to be kept covered until it was actually going to be eaten. Then it was necessary to wave it about in the hand to prevent flies settling on it before it could be piloted into the mouth. With the accompanying dust and lack of water, it is not surprising that dysentery soon made its appearance, for every fly was a carrier of that disease. The fact that the Allied Armies on Gallipoli were not destroyed in a few weeks by the outbreak of some pestilence is only explained by the inoculations and the wonderful efforts of the R.A.M.C.

On the 18th, the 8th Scottish Rifles started to move up to the trenches in the evening, but a heavy Turkish attack coming on, they spent the night in the Eski Lines, which ran across the peninsula about a mile behind the firing lines. The enemy was repulsed and the next day the 156th Brigade moved up to the trenches, the 8th Scottish Rifles being on the left, and the 4th Royal Scots on the right. The 5th R.S.F. were moved to the reserve lines about Clapham Junction. The communication trenches and "Rest Camp" were shelled heavily whilst the move was in progress, and the 156th Brigade lost 9 killed and 17 wounded before it was complete. Those still in the "Rest Camp" were not immune, the 4th R.S.F. losing one officer and one man killed, and fourteen wounded.

The 21st was the day of the French recapture of " Haricot Redoubt." The attack began at dawn, and Lt.-Col. H. M. Hannan, T.D., C.O. of the 8th Scottish Rifles, a tall man, was watching the battle from an artillery observation post when, at 7.30 a.m., he was shot dead by a Turkish sniper. He had devoted most of his leisure time to his battalion and to work in the Glasgow Battalion of the Boys Brigade, and was beloved and respected by all. The command now devolved upon Major J. M. Findlay.

At 1 a.m. on the same morning Major-General Egerton arrived with the divisional staff. There was no one to tell them where to go, so that they had to lie down on the beach until daylight; generals and privates fared much the same at Cape Helles.

"W" BEACH, CAPE HELLES

CAPE HELLES

The 4th Royal Scots had two crack shots in C.Q.M.S. Dewar, King's Prizeman of 1914, and Coy. Sgt.-Maj. D. Lowe. Both accounted for several Turkish snipers. Comparatively, this was a quiet spell in the trenches. High explosive bombardments at night produced the curious effect of filling the atmosphere more than ever with fine white dust, which coated faces and hung on to hair, until when morning dawned everyone bore a most ghastly appearance. No one escaped this dust, and the moustaches and eyebrows of men in these trenches were often white, quite apart from the age of the owner.

The 156th Brigade was relieved on the 24th, and made its way back to the " Rest Camp " with very few casualties, despite the shelling which accompanied the move.

Whenever it was possible, all ranks were taken in parties for a bathe at one of the beaches, usually either " Y " or " X," although even there they were not free from shellfire. This sea-bathing was of great value and a great relief to everyone. Every effort was made to keep down lice and other vermin, hair being usually cropped to the skull, but the filthy verminous condition of captured Turkish trenches made it impossible to do more than keep these pests somewhat at bay.

CHAPTER III

(25TH TO 28TH JUNE, 1915)

THE BATTLE OF THE 28TH JUNE, 1915

> I've seen the smiling
> Of Fortune beguiling,
> I've felt all its favours, and found its decay;
> Sweet was its blessing,
> Kind its caressing,
> But now it is fled—fled far away.
> ALISON RUTHERFORD (MRS. COCKBURN).

THE use of artillery, particularly with high explosive (H.E.), was such a decisive factor in the Great War, and the lack of it had so much to do with the loss of the campaign at Cape Helles, that we must learn something about the great deficiencies of this arm of the service in that area, in order to understand the battles which followed, and the conditions under which the Division had to fight.

Brigadier-General Sir Hugh Simpson Baikie, who commanded the British artillery at Cape Helles during all the big attacks and counter-attacks of June, July, and August, of whom Lord Kitchener had a high opinion, and whom Sir Ian Hamilton describes as a " deep-thinking, studious, and scientific officer," has included the following in a formal statement on the condition of affairs in that area :

" Although there was only one Battery of 4.5 and one Battery of 6 in. howitzers at Helles there was always an extreme deficiency of howitzer H.E. ammunition. . . . Throughout the above months (June, July and August), constant appeals were made to me by Infantry Commanders to bombard the Turkish trenches with H.E. in order to

BATTLE OF THE 28TH JUNE, 1915

retaliate for the loss our men had suffered from the Turkish guns using H.E. Such requests I had invariably to refuse.

"There were fifty-six 18-pdrs. at Helles when I assumed command on the 29th May, and subsequently they were increased to seventy-two at the end of July. Except for 640 rounds of H.E., which was fired off during the 4th June battle, no more H.E. arrived till the end of July. . . .

"The total amount (of ordinary 18-pdr. ammn.) I could therefore allot justifiably for the artillery preparation before an attack of our four British Infantry Divisions never exceeded 12,000 rounds; as from 6000 to 7000 must necessarily be kept in reserve to assist in beating off the determined hostile counter-attacks. . . . Artillery ammunition was a constant anxiety to the higher commanders on the Western Front also, but never, I believe, had infantry to attack with so little artillery support as the above. . . . In one action at St. Eloi (near Ypres) on 14th or 15th February, in which only the 27th Division was concerned, the artillery of this Division (so the C.R.A. informed me) alone fired 10,000 18-pdr. rounds in one night. . . .

"In comparing the ammunition expenditure in France in 1915 and in the Dardanelles, the enormous discrepancy in the number of 18-pdrs. per division must be taken into account. Reckoning on the scale of the number of 18-pdrs. allotted to a British division in France, we had at Helles little more than sufficient 18-pdrs. for one division, yet with this number we had to give artillery support to four divisions. . . .

"The complete absence of H.E. was severely felt, as shrapnel was of little use for destroying trenches, machine gun emplacements, etc. . . .

"During June two batteries,[1] and during July two more batteries of 5-inch howitzers, manned by Territorials, arrived at Helles. During the last week of July the first two batteries were sent to Anzac. Some of these howitzers

[1] These must be the batteries of the 4th Lowland Howitzer Brigade, of which only one was ever on Cape Helles. The 5th Battery was ordered to Cape Helles, but was diverted to Anzac. It never landed at Helles.

were very old and worn by corrosion, and were consequently inaccurate. ...

"As for heavy artillery, practically speaking there was none! Only one 6-inch howitzer battery (4 howitzers) and one 60-pdr. battery (4 guns) were in action at Helles up to July when four more guns of the latter calibre were landed.... The 60-pdrs. were of little use, as the recoil was too great for the carriages, and the latter broke down beyond repair by our limited resources after very few rounds. At the beginning of August only one 60-pdr. gun remained in action. Consequently we had no heavy guns capable of replying to the Turkish heavy guns which enveloped us on three sides, and from whose fire our infantry and artillery suffered severely. ...

"During June and July one 6-inch howitzer and twenty-five 18-pdrs. (out of a total of seventy-two), as well as one or two 60-pdrs., were put out of action by direct hits from the hostile artillery.... Guns were often further damaged while under repair. Damaged guns had sometimes to wait for days in this workshop (on " W " beach) until other guns had been damaged in a different place by the hostile artillery. Then possibly one efficient gun could be made up of the undamaged portions of one, two or more guns. ...

"As for anti-aircraft guns, they did not exist at all, and the hostile aeroplanes used to fly over and drop bombs *ad lib*. ...

"As regards trench mortars ... I believe there were not a dozen at Helles during the whole period I was there, and these were of such an indifferent type as to be practically useless. ...

"The terrible casualties suffered by our infantry at Helles are well known, and my feelings as Artillery Commander, unable to give them anything like the support they would have had in France or Flanders, may be guessed. ...

"In Gallipoli the 8th Army Corps at Helles, which was composed of four British divisions, never had enough Field Artillery or ammunition to support more than one division, and never possessed sufficient heavy artillery to support more than one infantry brigade."

From the above it will be readily gathered that the arrival of the 4th Glasgow Battery was an event of no mean importance at Cape Helles, although its old 5-inch howitzers had been used at Omdurman seventeen years before, as their history sheets showed. This battery brought the total battle strength of howitzers for the four divisions at Cape Helles up to fourteen,[1] provided that none was under repair. Even at the beginning of the war every division that went to France took with it eighteen howitzers of modern design and workmanship, and had the repair shops of England close at hand.

On the night following their landing, the Glasgow men took their guns by the coast road below the cliffs from "W" beach to their position by Gully Ravine. They used the horses of a regular battery, whose major gave all the help he could. The battery position was at the tip of the narrow tongue of land, which separates Gully Ravine from the sea, and is edged by cliffs of almost 150 feet in height. Before daylight everything was camouflaged. By the next evening, 24th June, gun-pits and dug-outs had been dug; the sector for which they were responsible, which was close to the sea, had been thoroughly reconnoitred; observation posts had been selected in the forward trenches, and telephones had been laid to connect them with the battery position about 2000 yards in rear. In many places the British and Turkish lines were not more than fifty yards apart, and from a few hundred yards away it was most difficult to distinguish the opposing trenches. On the same day the battery had its first shoot for the registration of ranges, etc.

The heat of the day was fierce, but shelter could be had from the pitiless sun in the dug-outs, which were built into the sides of the cliffs. They also gave good shelter from the enemy's shell-fire in the daytime, and random dropping rifle-fire at night. Also, they looked right across the Aegean, receiving thankfully its refreshing sea-breezes, and, after the gorgeous sunsets, the air was

[1] One 6-inch of four guns, one 5-inch of four guns, one 4·5-inch of six guns.

beautifully cool, and there was peace from the loathsome flies.

On the 24th June the 5th Battery of the 4th Lowland Howitzer (Glasgow) Brigade landed at Anzac, and was attached to the Australian and New Zealand Army Corps. The 4th Battery had been secured by Major-General de Lisle for his own Division, the 29th, as soon as it got ashore.

In order that the proposed new landing should be a surprise, it was essential that the Turks should be kept in the belief that their principal danger lay at Cape Helles, where the British and French had already overcome three successive armies. A fourth army of 20,000 fresh Turks was then arriving from Syria with more heavy guns, and the promised attack by Russia from the Black Sea was a disappointment. All this rendered greater the necessity for secrecy as to where the next blow was to come. Sir Ian Hamilton had wished to strike at Cape Helles by thrusting back the Turkish right from Gully Ravine at the same time that the French re-attacked Haricot Redoubt above Kereves Dere, but the British shortage of guns and ammunition would not allow of it. Sir Ian Hamilton wrote at the time: " We cannot think of it until we can borrow shell from Gouraud; and, naturally, he wants every round he has for his own push on the 21st."

At this time the left of the British line ran approximately northward for about 600 yards from the main fork of Krithia Nullah, through Worcester Flat, and thence to the sea at Ghurka Bluff almost a mile away. The Turkish northern flank being exposed to enfilade fire from the warships, they regarded it as a point of great danger, and had dug five regular lines of trenches between Gully Ravine and the sea. From Gully Ravine to the south-east, where they would have little or no artillery fire from the warships to contend with, the Turkish trenches continued generally in two main lines, with innumerable minor systems, branches, junctions, and detached pieces, which can only be faintly realized by seeing a map of them. As a rule these trenches were fronted with entanglements. The Turkish wire was mostly of a very heavy make, being about one-sixth of an

BATTLE OF THE 28TH JUNE, 1915

inch in thickness, entirely defying the ordinary wire-cutters. On the other hand, unless well supported on the Turks' rough wooden trestles, its very weight caused it to lie too close to the ground, and its long barbs could be trampled over. The British wire was lighter, and for that reason was more full of spring and formed a more effective obstacle, while it furnished a much longer entanglement for every cwt. of wire carried up to the trenches.

It was the intention of General Hunter-Weston, G.O.C. 8th Corps (Cape Helles), using a point on Worcester Flat as a pivot, to swing the British left forward until the five lines of trenches running from Gully Ravine to the sea had been captured. This would wipe out the central salient, clear another length of the deep Gully Ravine, and place the British on the sea flank of Krithia.

The general plan of General Hunter-Weston was for a two hours' bombardment, commencing at 9 a.m. by the artillery ashore, and by H.M. cruiser *Talbot*, and H.M. destroyers *Scorpion* and *Wolverine*. At 11 a.m. the artillery were to lengthen their ranges, and the first main assault was to be made. On the west or seaward side of Gully Ravine the 87th Brigade (29th Division) was to capture the first three lines of trenches, whilst on the east or landward side the 156th Brigade (attached to 29th Division *pro tem*.) was to capture the two lines facing its front. At 11.30 a.m. the 86th Brigade (29th Division) was to advance through the 87th Brigade and, with Ghurkas of the 29th Indian Brigade, capture the remaining two lines of Turkish trenches on the seaward side of Gully Ravine. Overhanging this ravine on the landward side was a work called the " Boomerang Redoubt " because of its general shape. It was in the most advanced part of the Turkish front line, and accordingly was to receive special attention from the howitzers, in addition to the concentrated fire of two demoiselle trench mortars lent by the kindness of General Gouraud. This redoubt was to have a special assault of its own by the 1st Border Regiment (87th Brigade) at 10.45 a.m.

Even with plenty of room and supplies, a modern trench-to-trench assault entails a tremendous amount of organization and planning with regard to the resources available and their use. At Cape Helles the difficulties were accentuated. With regard to the artillery arrangements for this battle the writer will quote from General Simpson Baikie's statement, where he deals with the Turkish trenches to be attacked by the 156th Brigade :

" Before the action the Corps Commander sent for me to say that he did not consider that enough guns and ammunition had been allotted to this portion of the Turkish trenches. I replied that I agreed, but that there were no more available, and that to reduce the bombardment of the hostile trenches on the left of our front would gravely prejudice the success of the 29th Division in that quarter, and that I understood success there was more vital than on our right flank. After consultation with the G.O.C. 29th Division, the Corps Commander agreed with my allotment of the artillery. We then did our utmost to obtain the loan of more guns from the French without success and with the result that the attack was beaten off."

On Sunday the 27th June orders were received for the 156th Brigade (Brig.-Gen. W. Scott-Moncrieff) to relieve the 88th Brigade of the 29th Division in that part of the front line which ran from Worcester Flat towards Gully Ravine. The 156th Brigade Headquarters were to be established at those of the 88th Brigade, which was to be in reserve. The move commenced about 2.30 p.m. and the Turks opened a heavy shell-fire on the moving troops. Whilst getting from the " Rest Camp " across the stretch of open country into the communication trench, the 4th Royal Scots and 8th Scottish Rifles lost about thirty men. This, coupled with much congestion in the narrow trenches, delayed the move so that it was midnight before the line was actually occupied, and 6 a.m. on the morning of the 28th before trench stores had been checked, reserve small arm ammunition (S.A.A.) and bombs brought up, and the sub-sector had been completely taken over. There was little sleep for anyone during that night.

IN THE REST CAMP, CAPE HELLES

BATTLE OF THE 28TH JUNE, 1915

It should be noted that, apart from a few days of instruction given to a handful of men from each unit the last thing before they left home, no one as yet had had any experience in throwing or dealing with bombs. The bombs themselves consisted of ordinary 1-lb. jam tins filled with spent bullets, odd bits of metal, etc., and a piece of gelignite, in which was stuck a detonator with a piece of fuse. The whole was kept in place by the lid, which was usually fastened down with short pieces of wire. Later on lids were soldered in their place. The fuse was cut to the required length, lit with a match or cigarette, the thrower counted five, and then threw the bomb, which burst a few seconds after leaving the hand—provided that the fuse had not dropped out as it was flying through the air. The 156th Brigade had 123 of these bombs, of which over eighty failed to detonate. They sent a party down to the beach to draw fourteen boxes of bombs from a dump near 29th Division H.Q., and when they were opened nine of them were found to contain real tins of jam. This mistake was probably caused by the continual casualties due to shell-fire among men working on the beach. Frequently new men would have to take over jobs on which there was no one to tell them where anything was stored, all their predecessors having been killed.

The trenches to be attacked by the 156th Brigade were designated on the British maps as the H11, H12, H12a, and H12b. They followed the general line of a ridge dominating the exits from the eastern side of Gully Ravine. The frontage to be taken measured almost half-a-mile, being about the same length as that to be taken by the 87th Brigade, and included all the Turkish trenches from the pivotal point to the eastern side of Gully Ravine about 300 yards beyond Boomerang Redoubt. The 87th Brigade was to take three lines with overwhelming artillery support; the 156th Brigade was to take two lines with none at all.

The 156th Brigade was never told that none of the artillery support would be given to it.

The assault was to be made by three of the battalions, disposed as follows from right to left :—8th Cameronians

(Major J. M. Findlay), 7th Royal Scots (Lt.-Col. W. Carmichael Peebles), and 4th Royal Scots (Lt.-Col. S. R. Dunn). The 7th Cameronians (Lt.-Col. J. B. Wilson) was to form the brigade reserve in trenches behind. The assaulting battalions were each to be disposed in depth in three lines abreast, having approximately half their strength in the first, the assaulting party; one quarter in the second, the supporting party; and one quarter in the third, the reserve party. It must not be forgotten that the 7th Royal Scots were only two companies strong, one of their own men, and one of H.L.I. attached. In a trench-to-trench attack, whenever possible, attacking lines should form up for the assault in three separate trenches. That, however, could not be done in many cases, because the trenches were not there or could not be dug in time. In this case, the first line were to be in the front line trench by 8 a.m., the second were to join them from the support trenches at 10.30 a.m., and the third were to follow the second into the support trenches as they left them. It was unavoidable that the front line would be packed with troops for half-an-hour before the assault. It had been impossible to arrange for the officers to have a previous personal reconnaissance, although very few portions of the assaulting lines could attack straight to their front, and, of course, no maps were allowed in the front line trenches lest they should fall into the hands of the enemy. To get over these difficulties and to ensure correct direction, officers were to take compass bearings. All watches were to be synchronised through Brigade Headquarters. All bayonets were to be fixed before 10.57 a.m. At 11 a.m. the command "Attack" was to be given and repeated by all the officers and N.C.O.'s, when the first line, using steps which they had cut in the parapet, were to spring out of the front line trench. After they had gone 75 yards, the second line were to move forward, and the third line were to get out of the support trench and follow 75 yards in their rear, crossing the front line trenches on plank bridges previously laid.

Every man in the first line was to have a large rectangular

BATTLE OF THE 28TH JUNE, 1915

piece of tin tied between his shoulders, in order to reflect back the sun's rays and so indicate to the artillery how far they had advanced. Each battalion was to carry forward two screens, painted khaki on the one side and red and white on the other, which were to be exhibited when artillery support was wanted. In addition to his fighting-kit and 200 rounds of S.A.A., every man was to carry two sandbags to be used in repairing and reversing the fire-parapets of captured trenches, and barricading communications which led to trenches still held by the enemy. Three R.E. sappers were to go forward with each company to assist in this work. Each battalion was to take one of its machine guns forward to open fire on retreating bodies of the enemy, and to repel counter-attacks. The remaining four were to go to brigade reserve. Everybody had been given twenty-four hours rations before leaving the "Rest Camp," and no one was to drink any of his water until after the assault. Bombing parties, each of an officer and twelve men, were to be detailed by the 8th Cameronians and 4th Royal Scots. They were to advance on the outer flanks of the supporting companies. There was to be no firing: the bayonet was to be the weapon.

The 155th Brigade, who were attached to the 42nd Division for administration, were in the "Rest Camp" and standing by in reserve during the battle.

The part played by the 4th (Glasgow) Howitzer Battery on the 28th June was entirely concerned with the artillery preparation for the assaults of the 29th Division on the seaward side of Gully Ravine.

During the nights prior to the attack, an observation post had been constructed in the front line and communication with the Battery some 2000 yards in rear completed. At 9 a.m. on the 28th the Battery, along with the other artillery supporting the attack of the 29th Division, opened fire. At 10.45 a.m. the 1st Border Regiment (87th Brigade) rushed the Boomerang Redoubt, and at 11.30 a.m. the second assault by the 29th Division was made, two more lines of trenches being taken. In neither attack was serious opposition met with from the few dazed Turks who survived the very effective bombardments. The assistance rendered by the Battery was most valuable and the congratulations of General de Lisle were afterwards received, but " during the bombardment not one shell fell on the objective of the right of the 156th Brigade and not more than six on the left" (Eye-Witness).[1]

To the 156th Brigade, after a night of hard work, dawn broke at 4 a.m. Brig.-Gen. Scott-Moncrieff came round the lines early, himself, to see that all was in readiness. At about 7 a.m. most of the officers and men managed to get a breakfast of tea, bread and jam, and then, in different ways, waited for 9 a.m., when the Brigade expected the British artillery would commence its bombardment of the Turkish entrenchments that they were to attack. Promptly at 9 a.m. the British guns opened fire, and the Turkish quickly replied, bombarding all front, support, reserve, and communication trenches. The 156th began to suffer from this fire, and the look-outs speedily noticed that the British artillery was only shelling the trenches which lay before the 87th Brigade on their left.

Machine-guns of the battalions and from other units were firing hard to make the Turks in the opposing trenches keep their heads down, but, beyond this, such fire was of little value against earthworks.

About ten minutes before 11 a.m., when the 156th had already suffered many casualties, the Turks put down a very heavy barrage of artillery and machine-gun fire on the front and support trenches, now filled with the three waves of men preparatory to the attack. So many fell that a platoon of the 7th Cameronians had to be sent up to the support trench to fill a gap on the right of the 7th Royal Scots. Major J. N. Henderson, 4th Royal Scots, was being attended to, with both his legs smashed, in a dug-out in the parados of the support trench, and by him lay Captain J. D. Pollock of the same battalion, when another shell burst killing all inside. In that splendid comradeship in

---

[1] The writer is not at liberty to publish the name of this officer, but he saw the whole action from the front line trenches, and during the war rose to high rank in the Army.

BATTLE OF THE 28TH JUNE, 1915

death officers and men were afterwards laid in a common grave.

All this while the Turks before the 156th Brigade were almost immune from shell-fire, but of course were on the alert. The usual conditions were reversed, for it was the attacking force which was receiving all the bombardment.

At 11.2 a.m. the word for the attack was given, and, like one man, the long khaki line sprang forward into the open and rushed on, followed a few seconds afterwards by the other waves of men. "There was not the slightest hesitation on the part of any battalion" (Eye-Witness). As they did so, a perfect storm of machine-gun and rifle-fire burst on them, the bullets whipping up the dust and the Turkish shrapnel coming down like hail. The ground to be crossed was "rough going but nearly flat, and the troops were exposed to view and fire from the moment they went over the parapet" (Eye-Witness).

Men started to fall as soon as they left their own trenches. The first Turkish line was splendidly taken on the centre and left. Thinned in numbers, again they went forward to the second line, but, now, officers and men fell in swathes on all sides.

Less than a hundred yards away on the extreme left was a trench, well supplied with machine-guns and totally missed by the British shell-fire. Many officers and men of the 4th Royal Scots fell as they charged forward. Major James Gray, dropped mid-way between the British and Turkish lines. About here also fell, mortally wounded, Lt.-Col. S. R. Dunn, T.D., to die on board a hospital ship the next day. Keen, just, considerate, and dignified, his personal influence alone gave him great power over all his officers and men.

Pipe-Major Andrew Buchan (4th R.S.), rifle in hand, continued to encourage forward a party of young Royal Scots, although he had been twice wounded. Hit for the third time, he fell dead on the parapet of the first Turkish trench. After a stiff bayonet and revolver fight this trench was captured, and the garrison killed or made prisoners.

The two leading lines had now closed up, and the advance was pushed on, a further length of trench being captured.

The third wave, seeing that the others were under enfilade fire from the right, changed direction half-right, and charged the trench whence the fire was coming. They drove out the Turks, who left behind many killed and wounded.

By this time nearly every officer had been killed or wounded, but one party, numbering fifty-eight, under Coy. Sergeant-Major D. M. Lowe, raced forward about another hundred yards further on over very broken ground, until they gained a footing in the second main Turkish trench, driving the enemy out. This trench, afterwards known as the Eastern Birdcage, ran into Gully Ravine, and word came back that they were being subjected to enfilade fire from across that nullah. This was because their attack had carried them on ahead of the 87th Brigade on their left, and it was fully half-an-hour later before the latter had cleared the trenches on the opposite side of that deep gorge. Lowe's party, now reduced to forty-eight, set to work with their entrenching tools to improvise fire-steps in the deep Turkish trench, and to prepare it for defence, Pte. R. Robertson being one who set a splendid example. Some few had gone far ahead, and could see no more Turkish trenches between themselves and the top of the great ridge. It was useless for this handful to go on, and they were gathered back into the trench. Down in the ravines and beyond, Lowe's men saw parties of Turks retreating, and they scourged them with their rifle-fire. Behind the Royal Scots, the Turks, evidently fearing a further advance by reinforcements out of Gully Ravine, had brought heavy concentration of artillery fire into its depths and about its edges near the first trench captured, setting the whins and scrub ablaze. This cut Lowe's party off for a time from those consolidating elsewhere, but Cpl. G. Cowan and Pte. A. Lunn managed to get through with messages as to the position. Pte. W. Lownie rescued a number of wounded from the gorse-fire and stood in the open for a while trying to beat out the flames with a sand-bag. Cpl. John Rankine, although

BATTLE OF THE 28TH JUNE, 1915

bleeding to death, went out with untended wounds and brought in several wounded lying exposed in the open. He died soon afterwards from loss of blood. Many a man here and elsewhere on that field lost his life in endeavouring to succour wounded comrades.

Lieut. F. B. MacKenzie had followed about fifty yards to the right rear of the leading companies of the 4th Royal Scots with one of his machine-guns, ready for eventualities. He got it forward to the second trench, further to the right than Lowe, where the ground was higher. Turks could be seen retreating everywhere, offering numerous targets in all directions. His crew, with the utmost steadiness, rapidly mounted the gun, and poured burst after burst of fire into these Turks, felling them in groups.

The 7th Royal Scots were led by Major A. W. Sanderson and their own company, the second and third lines being formed from the company of attached H.L.I., with the reinforcement from the 7th Cameronians on the right flank. They raced forward amidst the din for the first trench about a hundred and fifty yards away. Men began to fall within a few yards of their own line, but the majority jumped down into the first Turkish trench, officers and men firing and going at the Turks with the bayonet. Some of the Moslem soldiers fought to the death, but others ran, retiring by the flanks. After a breather in the captured trench, during which the waves closed up, they rushed for the second one about two hundred and fifty yards further on. The leaden storm now caught them in all its fury, and they fell in clumps. Major A. W. Sanderson, a Territorial of twenty years service, was killed half-way across the open with several other officers. Captain J. D. Dawson and Lieut. E. J. Thomson fell dead just at the parapet of the second trench. There, the Turks did not like the glint of the British bayonets and ran. The only officers left out of those taking part in the charge were Lieut. Haws and 2nd Lieuts. Lyell and M'Clelland. These, together with about eighty unwounded men, started on the task of putting the newly-captured trench in a state of defence, under shell-fire, with their right flank for a while " in the air."

The 4th Royal Scots machine-gun came up on their left, and, after inflicting as much loss as possible on the disappearing Turks, Lieut. MacKenzie (4th R.S.) got in touch with them, and moved his gun to their right in order to cover this flank, which was quite exposed. By doing so this gun broke up several concentrations of the enemy for counter-attacks. The situation was similar to that in the line behind, the first trench captured. The British held the section of the trench that ran to Gully Ravine and the Turks held the other to the south. Time and again these brave Moslems tried to force their way along these trenches with bayonet and bomb, threatening to retake the captured lines piece-meal; as often, they were driven back by small and ever-decreasing bands of Royal Scots and Cameronians. Some of the Scotsmen were getting their first lessons in bombing at the time. The most effective grenades were usually the Turkish, which the British managed to throw back at the enemy, before they could explode, because of their long fuses. All the while snipers on both sides were active.

Privates A. Hind and J. M'Intyre (both H.L.I. attached 7th R.S.) did magnificent work in carrying ammunition forward across the fire-swept zone, the former being killed. Both were mentioned in despatches, and Hind got a D.C.M.

" When the position had been taken Capt. A. J. Wightman (7th R.S.) endeavoured to run out a telephone wire, and with Sgt. Rosie (7th R.S.) he led four signallers carrying cables and instruments towards the captured trench. In the course of this brave attempt Sergt. Rosie was killed and Capt. Wightman wounded, though the latter carried on till every man was knocked out and he himself was again wounded and fell. He lay out all day, was hit a third time, but recovered sufficiently to crawl into our lines towards dawn next morning. For this gallant action he was awarded the Military Cross." (Col. Peebles.) This was the only M.C. awarded to the 156th Brigade immediately after this action, largely because there were few

BATTLE OF THE 28TH JUNE, 1915

officers left to make any recommendations. When the 7th Royal Scots had lost all their signal section at Gretna, Captain Wightman had stepped into the breach, and trained his men on the voyage out.

All through the charges and afterwards, the machine-gunners gave of their best with cross and covering fire. Lieut. A. S. Elliot (H.L.I. attached 7th R.S.) was killed whilst observing the fire of his guns.

Just below a plantation, where the ground rose about two hundred yards to the east or behind the first Turkish trench, and not three hundred yards from the right flank of the 8th Cameronians, as they crouched in the front line awaiting the order to attack, was a Turkish earthwork known as H.13. Although it had been previously registered by the artillery it was quite untouched by shell-fire. In reality, this trench was a nest of from six to eight machine-guns, so disposed that they would sweep almost the entire front of the 156th Brigade with oblique fire. In front of the 8th Cameronians were their own direct objectives, also untouched by shell-fire like the other trenches, and crowded with resolute Turks, who ten minutes before the attack were lashing the British parapets with a deadly machine-gun and rifle-fire at less than two hundred yards range. On all sides resounded what one man described as "the sickening cough" of the machine-guns.

There are few troops in the world outside the ranks of the British Army who would have attempted to breast such a fire as did the 156th Brigade on that summer morning, and those few include such religious fanatics as the Mahdists or Japanese, swept along by the belief that, by dying so, they will obtain their eternal salvation.

When the command to attack rang out, away dashed the first line of the 8th Cameronians over the perfectly open grass and moorland, right in the full blast of a tempest of fire from front and flank. Even before the second and third waves could get out and follow them, they were simply mown down. Many of the third line had fallen before they reached their own firing line. Major J. M. Findlay fell severely wounded almost at the start, and his adjutant,

Captain C. G. Bramwell, and many other officers were killed soon afterwards. All ranks were slaughtered literally by platoons. Some tried to work their way up the saps, which ran into the Turkish lines, but they were shot down. A few survivors tried to get on over the open, but still the dreadful storm from front and flank swept their line of advance from end to end.

On the extreme left a few of the Cameronians got forward and reached the first trench, which they blocked and held against bomb and sniper's bullet from their right; but for the rest, the battalion caught the full force of the withering hail and the attack ceased, simply because none were left to advance. In a few minutes nothing was left of the battalion but one officer and a few men who dribbled back to their own front line.

Later in the day the dried grass and scrub caught fire, and many men left comparative safety and gave up their lives in trying to save wounded comrades.

CHAPTER IV

(28TH JUNE TO 6TH JULY, 1915)

THE BATTLE OF THE 28TH JUNE, 1915 (*contd.*)

> I've seen the Forest
> Adorned the foremost,
> With flowers of the fairest, most pleasant and gay;
> Sae bonny was their blooming,
> Their scent the air perfuming,
> But now they are withered and a' wede away.
> ALISON RUTHERFORD (MRS. COCKBURN).

AT 11.47 a.m. the following message was received from the 29th Division by the 156th Brigade:—" H.12 is to be taken at all costs. If necessary you will send forward your Reserve Battalion." Brig.-General Scott-Moncrieff at once ordered two companies of the 7th Cameronians to prepare to re-attack the untaken H.12 trenches. They filed up the narrow communication trenches as fast as was possible past the stream of wounded. The Turkish bombardment was continuing with unabated fury, and several officers and men fell as they moved into their places.

Shortly after noon Brig.-General Scott-Moncrieff decided to go forward to the firing line himself, telling Captain E. Girdwood, his Brigade-Major, that he was only going to the observation post to see how things were going, and would be back in half-an-hour. He handed over to Captain Girdwood his maps and orders as he left.

Again there was no artillery preparation of the trenches to be attacked, and those Cameronians certainly knew, from the evidence that lay before them, that, once over the parapets, death or wounds awaited most of them.

The word was given and they rushed forward. The majority went over the open. Some tried to force their way up an old Turkish communication trench on the right, which later became Bomb Sap No. 30. This trench was barely two feet deep, and was enfiladed by Turkish machine-gun fire. It was a repetition of the previous slaughter. The right and centre could make no progress under the enemy's fire. The communication trench was blocked by a hail of bullets. The kindly and sympathetic Lieut.-Colonel J. Boyd Wilson was killed, and with him many of his officers.

Shortly afterwards, a platoon of 7th Cameronians made yet another attempt to work their way up the communication trench, but its commander, Lieut. H. MacLean, and others were shot down. It was a death-trap, and was already filled with dead and dying.

At 1.5 p.m. the following message was received at 156th Brigade by runner because all wires between Brigade and Battalion Headquarters had been cut by enemy fire.

" Captain Girdwood,
B.M. 156th Bde.

2 Coys. 7th Scottish Rifles have attacked and got into small piece of H.12a opposite the kink in old fire trenches. They are enfiladed from their right and I am sending the last two coys. of my Brigade against the right of H.12a.
12.47
(Sgd.)   W. Scott-Moncrieff."

Eight minutes after General Scott-Moncrieff had despatched this message another was sent off from the firing line stating that he had been shot dead.

Brig.-General Scott-Moncrieff saw that this last attack stood even a smaller chance of success than the others, and those who knew him best think that for this reason he intended to place himself in order to lead the men in person. Others think that he went forward only to reconnoitre the ground more clearly. Whatever his intention, it was his duty to order his men into that hurricane of fire, and it is certain that he, noble and sensitive man that he was, wished to take the same risks as his men.

He hurried up the short piece of communication trench towards the open, and had only gone a few yards when he fell, killed instantly by a shot through the head, near where MacLean lay wounded.

So died the Laird of Fossaway, near the Yetts of Muckart in Kinross-shire, a most fearless and true-hearted gentleman, determined at all costs to do his duty. He had formerly served in the Middlesex Regiment, and was slightly lame from a wound received in South Africa. An ideal leader of men to the end, inspiring both admiration and affection, his loss was deeply mourned by all.

This attack failed as the others had done, and the men were driven back into the front line trench.

By this time, as was inevitable from these repeated assaults, the remains of the 7th and 8th Cameronians had got very much mixed, most of the officers and N.C.O.'s had fallen, and the trenches were crowded with wounded whom it was impossible to evacuate. The 88th Brigade of the 29th Division accordingly took over the firing line and support trenches, so that the Cameronians could be withdrawn and re-organized. Lieut.-Colonel Caley, O.C. 88th Brigade was ordered to take over command of the 156th Brigade as well, and Captain Girdwood obtained permission to go forward and re-organize the remnants. By the coolness and efforts of this officer and the use of scaling-ladders, the congestion in the trenches was relieved. Traffic was organized, the wounded were evacuated, and much suffering was saved.

Later on in the afternoon the 88th Brigade made two attempts on these H.12 trenches, but were repulsed, and these earthworks remained in Turkish hands until the close of the campaign.

We must return to the first assault of the 7th Cameronians, that at about 12.30 p.m. The right of the assaulting troops had been destroyed or driven back, but the left, further away from the machine-gun fire, led by Major W. T. Bird had raced forward and dashed into the first Turkish trench, bayoneting nearly every man in it. Very few Turks were taken prisoner on that day, because those who stayed to fight, and there were many of them, were fanatically brave men. Apart from those killed in the assault, very few dead Turks were found in these trenches, and, of course, they had not been damaged by shell-fire at all. Suddenly, these 7th Cameronians were bombed from the right, and knowing thereby that the company to their right (whose story has already been told) had not reached their objective, they set to work with anything and everything to make a fire parapet, and to build across the trench a block, later known as the Southern Barricade. It was a common thing at Cape Helles for the parapets and barricades to be built partially of heaped-up dead. As these 7th Cameronians were defending their block, and so easing the pressure on men nearer the Gully Ravine, one Turkish bomb fell right into the trench. Lance-Cpl. A. Ross, with no thought for his own safety, at once put his foot on it, even as Pte. Young leant down to throw a coat over it. The bomb exploded, wounding Ross terribly in the feet, legs, hands and face; but he undoubtedly saved several lives by his self-sacrifice. He survived, and long afterwards both men received the D.C.M. for their gallantry on this occasion.

Ordinary language cannot tell of the heroism of the wounded everywhere under these circumstances. They were laid as clear of the ordinary traffic of the trench as was possible, and their comrades did what they could to make them comfortable in all the filth, litter of clothing and rubbish, blankets and food, equipment, rifles and bayonets, invariably found with the dead in a captured Turkish trench. As a rule they lay beneath a cloud of maddening flies, suffering and dying without a complaint, beyond an occasional request for water, for the sun was high overhead and the heat and their loss of blood gave them a burning thirst.

The 156th Brigade had now captured the left half of the

BATTLE OF THE 28TH JUNE, 1915

two lines of Turkish trenches assigned to it, that is to say from Gully Ravine to the south-east, where they had built their two barricades.

After Major Bird had sent back word as to his dispositions, he sent forward 2nd Lieut. E. Watson with two platoons to get into the second Turkish trench. They were a welcome reinforcement, extending the right flank of the men already there, and building the trench-block, later known as the Northern Barricade, to prevent Turks from fighting their way along it from the south-east. Some time afterwards 2nd Lieut. E. Watson (7th S.R.) was awarded an M.C. for his work on this day.

Lieut. F. B. MacKenzie (4th R.S.) had just guided forward a platoon of Cameronians to reinforce the right of the second main Turkish trench, where his gun was placed, when a sniper shot him through the neck. He got no decoration at the time, but several months later was awarded an M.C. for his cool conduct on this day. His sergeant, John Gunn, took charge, and from 1.30 p.m. in the afternoon until 1 a.m. the next morning never ceased to work his gun, until at the end he fell off his seat from exhaustion.

On the left front, early in the afternoon, two machine-guns of the 1st Border Regiment reinforced the party of 4th Royal Scots under Coy. Sgt.-Major Lowe. This was a most welcome addition of strength, as they were holding about a hundred and twenty yards of front line trench, which meant about two and a half yards to every man. During the afternoon this little force checked two half-hearted counter-attacks by the Turks. At about 4 p.m. a staff-captain of the 29th Division came along the front trench bearing the message, "Well done Royal Scots," signed by General de Lisle. On the recommendation of the 29th Division, Coy. Sgt.-Major Lowe was awarded a D.C.M. for his leadership on this day.

Soon after darkness fell the Turks made a heavy counter-attack on the left of the 4th and 7th Royal Scots, but it was repulsed with severe loss to the enemy. Later on, somewhere about 11 o'clock, all seemed comparatively quiet. The new front line was being relieved by the Hampshire

Regiment, the 4th Royal Scots, now under Lieut. Stewart, having actually stood down. Suddenly, without any artillery preparation, large crowds of Turks were seen moving out of Gully Ravine on the left front for an attack. The Royal Scots were back to the parapets in a moment, and they, with the Hampshires and the two machine-guns of the Border Regiment, poured a most devastating fire into the dark masses of the enemy. The Turks pushed the attack to within a hundred and fifty yards of the new front trench. Some men of the Border Regiment had dug a small trench in advance of the firing line, where the ground receded before reaching the level in front of the great nullah. These heroic men died to a man, fighting to the last. At last the Turks had had enough and were falling back when the British artillery caught them, punishing them still further. When daylight came the Turkish dead were seen to be piled, literally, in dark khaki heaps. The 4th Royal Scots machine gun, Royal Scots, and Cameronians further to the right, also had taken their toll.

So heavy had been the casualties, and so weary were those left, because it must be remembered that the night before had been entirely sleepless, that the Headquarters Staff of the 156th Brigade held the bombing saps during the night 28-29th June, and until relieved at about 2 a.m. on the night 29-30th June. There was no one else available to do so.

The medical officer of the 4th Royal Scots had fallen sick prior to the action, but Lieut. James Morham, a combatant officer but also a M.D. and practising dental surgeon, took his duty. He worked for forty-eight hours in what passed for a regimental aid post on Gallipoli, dressing those enormous quantities of wounded, which the regimental stretcher-bearers continually brought in, before they were carried down the long, weary communication trenches by the R.A.M.C. bearers. It was the rule for the medical officers never to spare themselves, whatever the call was and whenever it came. We often discussed on Gallipoli the question of which profession should rank

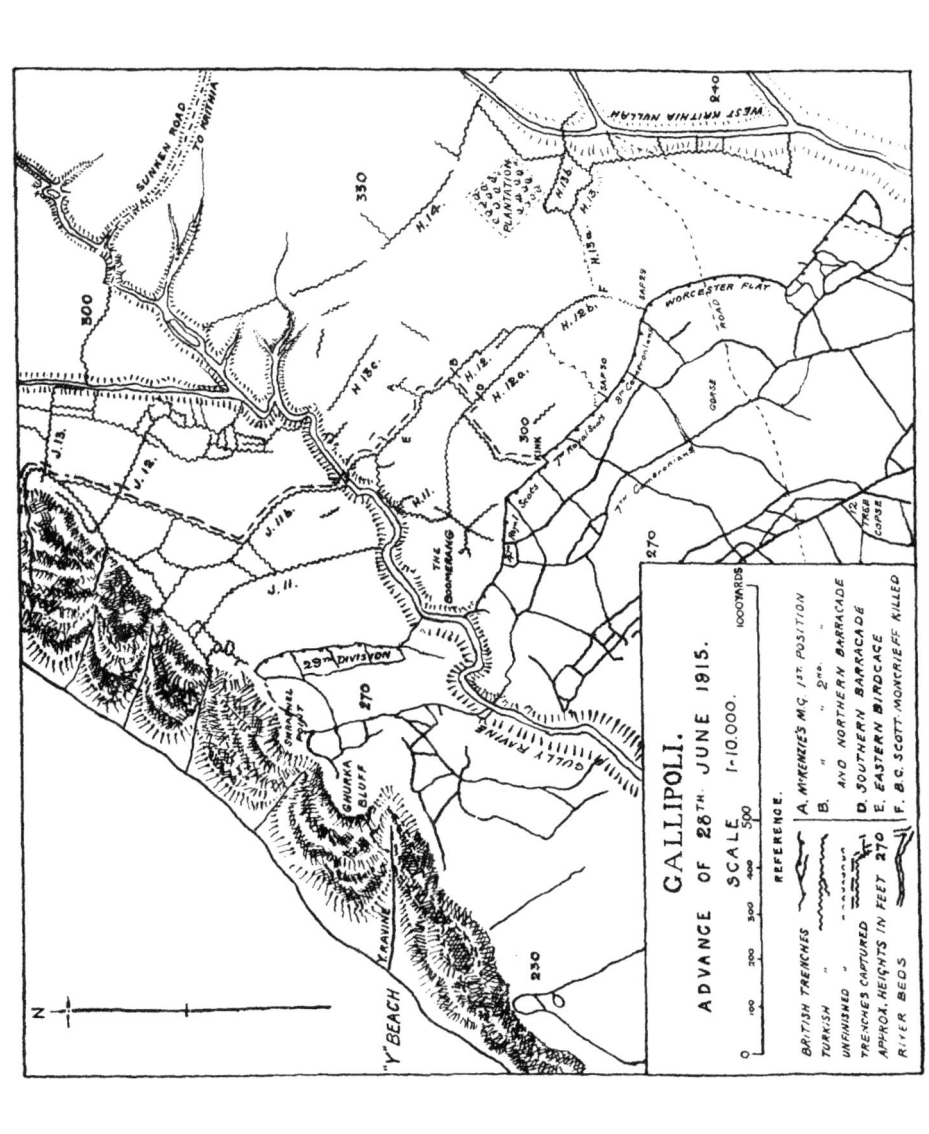

BATTLE OF THE 28TH JUNE, 1915

highest of all, and the conclusion was invariably the same: the healing profession.

The 1st Lowland Field Ambulance, under Col. G. H. Edington, had only landed at 1.30 a.m. on the 29th June at " V " Beach, but, leaving their stores lying on the shore, had sent the bulk of the officers and men away for duty in the forthcoming battle before the sun was high in the heavens.

Major J. W. Leitch's party went to a dressing station in Gully Ravine belonging to the 88th Field Ambulance, attached 29th Division. Captain N. MacInnes' section, on duty with the same unit, were sent to the Pink Farm, a ruined stone steading close to a cart-track, about two miles on the way from " W " Beach to Krithia. Near here, he had to form a dressing station as rapidly as he could, using a disused infantry trench, tarpaulins, and anything that he and his men could get. The 1st Lowland Field Ambulance lost several killed and wounded, but rendered " admirable service throughout the day " (Gen. Egerton).

The R.A.M.C. bearers, writes Col. Edington, " working on a system of relays, plied between the regimental aid posts and our advanced dressing stations. Thence the wounded were carried to dressing stations. These were placed, if possible, within easy reach of a road, and from them the cases were conveyed by motors to the headquarters of the ambulance. Arrived there, they were sorted out in the hospital trench. Cases likely to be fit for duty in a few days were detained for treatment; those requiring a longer period were passed down to the Casualty Clearing Station at Cape Helles. From the C.C.S. they were returned to duty, or sent down the Lines of Communication by hospital ship." Once afloat they might be taken to hospital at Mudros, Alexandria, Malta or home.

During the night of the 28-29th June the 156th Brigade was relieved by units of the 29th Division. It was moved to the reserve trenches in the neighbourhood of Twelve Tree Copse, whence, in addition to other work, it furnished fatigue parties for the clearing of the battlefield and the burying of the dead, so far as that was possible.

The conditions in the captured trenches and in the newly-taken section of the great Gully Ravine were indescribably awful. " To the ordinary litter and filth to be expected where the Turks had been settled for weeks, were added the wreck and ruin wrought by the bombardment, the scattered remains of food, dishes, firewood, articles of clothing and kit, abandoned in the scurry and scramble of flight before our bayonets. The mangled bodies of the dead, unburied, half-buried, or partially dug up by H.E. shells, under the fierce heat, with loathsome clouds of flies, could only be dealt with by fire. The valley with its heaps of rotting refuse, its burning pyres and sickening stench, was a veritable Gehenna." (Dr. Ewing.) Hundreds of Turkish rifles and bayonets, thousands of rounds of their S.A.A., and hundreds of their short-handled entrenching-spades lay everywhere in the trenches and Gully Ravine, and had to be gathered up. Weakened, as the personnel of the burying parties were by their conditions of existence, and working in such a nauseating atmosphere, it was a physical impossibility for them to do more than make a shallow excavation and cover the bodies with earth. It was impossible to burn those in the trenches because of the risk of drawing Turkish artillery fire, and, even if this had been possible, the majority lying out in the open could not be gathered in at all. The result was that " every here and there irregularities in the ground, covered with loose earth and sandbags, and giving off a horrible stench, marked where our men had buried Turkish dead " (Col. Edington). The writer gives these and other terrible details in order that those who read may realise a little of what the officers and men of the Division suffered on behalf of this and succeeding generations, and in order that they may realise how wonderful were the inoculations that warded off pestilences, which otherwise might have swept both armies out of existence in a few weeks.

The exact losses of the 156th Brigade in the battle of the 28th June were not found out until many weeks afterwards, when it was certain that none of the missing were prisoners. Because of this, the writer has put all the

BATTLE OF THE 28TH JUNE, 1915

killed, died of wounds, and missing under one heading. It must, however, be borne in mind that most of the bodies were never recovered, largely because the bitterness of the whole struggle prevented an armistice for their burial, and because the proximity of the opposing lines made it impossible to get them in, even after dark, without further loss of life. In addition, the men had hardly sufficient strength to dig the huge graves that would have been required. The final figures for the four battalions' losses during the battle were as follows :

UNIT.	KILLED, DIED OF WOUNDS, MISSING.		WOUNDED.		TOTAL.	
	Officers.	O.R.	Officers.	O.R.	Officers.	O.R.
H.Q., 156th Bde.	1	—	—	—	1	—
4th Royal Scots	15	198	7	147	22	345
7th Royal Scots	8	116	3	114	11	230
7th Cameronians	10	158	3	100	13	258
8th Cameronians	15	334	10	114	25	448
	49	806	23	475	72	1281

On the 27th June the strength of the 156th Brigade, including all details, was

	OFFICERS.	OTHER RANKS.	TOTAL.
	102	2839	2941
The total loss for the period was	77	1486	1563
Thus by the 30th June it had shrunk to	25	1353	1378

The 7th Royal Scots had left Larbert on the 22nd May at full strength, viz. 31 officers, including attached, and 997 other ranks. The Gretna Disaster, coupled with little more than a fortnight on Gallipoli, had reduced it to 7 officers and 217 other ranks. As a result of this battle and previous losses from sickness and the fire of the enemy, the 8th Cameronians on the 30th could only put one officer and 99 other ranks on parade. On the 28th June the 156th Brigade lost its Brigadier, three commanding officers, including a major, three other majors, three adjutants, and twenty captains, killed or severely wounded. These were the bulk of the most experienced officers of the Brigade. Out of 24 officers of the 4th Royal Scots who went into action on the morning of the 28th, only three came out.

The other officer casualty of this unit was the Quartermaster, wounded the night before. The officers who gave up their lives as a result of this battle were as follows:

156th Brigade Headquarters—
Brig.-Gen. W. Scott-Moncrieff.

4th Royal Scots—
Lt.-Col. S. R. Dunn, T.D.
Major Jas. Gray.
,, J. N. Henderson.
Captain R. W. G. Rutherford.
,, G. A. S. Ross.
,, J. Dunbar Pollock.
,, John Robertson.
,, R. E. Mackie.
Lieut. C. F. Allan.
,, Charles Paterson.
,, P. E. Considine.
,, Arch. Young.
2nd Lieut. T. D. Aitchison.
,, R. J. Gibson.
,, W. J. Johnstone.

7th Royal Scots—
Major A. W. Sanderson.
Captain D. Clark.
,, J. D. Dawson.
,, J. R. Peebles.
Lieut. E. Thomson.
,, A. S. Elliot.
,, R. M. Galloway.
2nd Lieut. F. W. Thomson.

7th Cameronians—
Lt.-Col. J. Boyd Wilson, T.D.
Capt. and Adj. R. Vere Clark.
Captain P. Whitton.
,, J. Howatt.
Lieut. W. Brown.
Lieut. W. Duff.
,, D. M. Taylor.
2nd Lieut. W. Leggat.
,, J. W. M'Lay.
,, A. Duff.

8th Cameronians—
Capt. and Adj. C. G. Bramwell.
Captain W. Campbell Church.
,, C. A. D. Macindoe.
,, C. J. C. Mowat.
,, E. T. Young.
Lieut. J. T. Findlay.
,, R. C. B. Macindoe.
Lieut. H. M'Cowan.
,, G. A. C. Moore.
,, T. Stout.
,, A. D. Templeton.
2nd Lieut. W. S. Maclay.
,, R. M. Pattison.
,, B. H. Robertson.
,, J. W. Scott.

Most of the losses in this action were due to Turkish machine-guns and shrapnel, the latter being especially deadly in the communication trenches, which they had ranged to a yard. The Turkish rifle-fire was usually poorly aimed, but their snipers were very good. With the bayonet the British soldiers were their undoubted superiors.

BATTLE OF THE 28TH JUNE, 1915

The 156th Brigade had contributed very largely to the victory won that day by their capture of the trenches running to the sides of Gully Ravine from the south-east, because these trenches would have enfiladed those on the north-western side where the ground is lower.

Despite the heroic failure to take the trenches at the pivotal point, the battle had resulted in one of the greatest victories ever won on Gallipoli. The gains were much greater than had been expected, for the 29th Division and the Ghurkas had advanced the British left until it was west-north-west of Krithia and almost on the 300 feet contour. At this time, when the British were less than a mile and a half from the crest of the ridge, the Turkish trenches between them and the top of Achi Baba were few and far between. If the advancing army had only had the strength in numbers and artillery to go on, the campaign might have been decided against the Turks within a few days. Sir Ian Hamilton discussed the situation on the afternoon of the 28th with the G.O.C. 8th Corps (Cape Helles), the Commandant of the French Corps, and his own Chief of General Staff, and wrote at the time : " Hunter-Weston, Gouraud and Braithwaite agree that had we only shell to repeat our bombardment of this morning, now, we could go on another 1000 yards before dark,—result, Achi Baba to-morrow or, at the latest, the day after ; Achi Baba and fifty guns perhaps with, say, 10,000 prisoners." A proper supply of H.E. at that time would have meant, almost certainly, decisive success for the whole Gallipoli campaign.

The Turkish morale had suffered severely from the British artillery-fire, and the advance on the left. In addition, the Division had shown them what British bayonets could do, even with no artillery support. The Turkish commanders knew this ; and the C.O. of their right zone published an order immediately after the battle, from which the following are extracts :

" Henceforth, commanders who surrender these trenches, from whatever side the attack may come, before the last man is killed will be punished in the same way as if they had run away. . . .

"I hope that this will not occur again. I give notice that if it does, I shall carry out the punishment. I do not desire to see a blot made on the courage of our men by those who escape from the trenches to avoid the rifle and machine-gun fire of the enemy. Henceforth, I shall hold responsible all officers who do not shoot with their revolvers all the privates who try to escape from the trenches on any pretext. . . .

Commander of the 11th Division, Colonel Rifaat."

The copy of the above, which was captured by the British, had the following note added by the Colonel of the 127th Regiment in sending it to his battalions :

"To Commander of the 1st Battalion. The contents will be communicated to the officers and I promise to carry out the orders till the last drop of our blood has been shed.

Hassan, C.O. 127th Regiment."

Below this were the signatures of the company commanders of the battalion.

During the next few days the Turks tried to get back the trenches by repeated and bloody counter-attacks, but despite the British shortage of artillery-fire, not one of their efforts was successful. They attacked Anzac fiercely at the same time. The result was that their losses on Gallipoli for the period from 28th June to 5th July were estimated to be not less than 5000 killed and 15,000 wounded. These figures were based on the bodies which could be actually seen and counted. The great Gully Ravine and the smaller nullahs were " chock-a-block with corpses " (Sir Ian Hamilton), for the sturdy Anatolian peasants had advanced with the utmost bravery.

However, in a few days time the Turks had dug fresh earthworks, and, but for the attrition of the Ottoman forces, the battle of the 28th June would have been almost a Pyrrhic victory.

On the 29th June the 156th Brigade sent in an estimate of 1343 for its total casualties during the battle, and on the same night Sir Ian Hamilton telegraphed home that he estimated the total casualties at " about 2000, the greater

BATTLE OF THE 28TH JUNE, 1915

proportion of which are slight cases, of which 250 at Anzac, in the useful demonstration made simultaneously there." The comment about the number of slight cases simply serves to confirm the idea that Sir Ian Hamilton was sometimes very much misinformed, and that certain pertinent facts failed to reach him. From the above, the Cape Helles casualties can be taken at about 1750, of which half were Scottish dead and missing. This left a little over 400 casualties for the four Brigades, 86th, 87th, 88th, and 29th Indian, belonging to and serving with the 29th Division. In other words, the 8th Cameronians alone lost more men on this day than the whole of these four brigades added together. In a despatch to Lord Kitchener, dated 3rd July, Sir Ian Hamilton puts the total shrinkage in strength of the three brigades of the 29th Division for the period 28-30th June at 1905. This includes losses sustained in repelling the Turkish counter-attacks. The enormous disparity between the losses of the 156th Brigade on the one hand and the 86th, 87th, and 88th Brigades on the other shows the difference made by the whole of the artillery support being allotted to the Regular brigades in this attack. Sir Ian Hamilton's comment in his diary on the 29th was: "The attack by a part of the Lowland Division seems to have been mishandled. A Brigade made the assault East of the Ravine; the men advanced gallantly but there was lack of effective preparation. Two battalions of the Royal Scots carried a couple of the enemy's trenches in fine style and stuck to them, but the rest of the Brigade lost a number of good men to no useful purpose in their push against H.12. One thing is clear. If the bombardment was ineffective, from whatever cause, then the men should not have been allowed to break cover."

His own note to the above states that "the exact facts (re artillery support) were not known to me until long afterwards" (*Gallipoli Diary*, vol. i., p. 355). This confirms the idea that certain pertinent facts never reached him at all, and others only when they were too late.

At mid-day on the 28th Sir Ian Hamilton signalled, "Well done 29th Division and 156th Brigade," and during the night Lieut.-General Hunter-Weston rang up Major-General Egerton to tell him how thoroughly satisfied he was with the conduct of the 156th Brigade. On the afternoon of the 29th Major-General de Lisle, G.O.C. 29th Division, sent the following telephone message to Major-General Egerton :

" General de Lisle wishes to express how much he valued the help given to the 29th Division in yesterday's attack by the 156th Infantry Brigade. The attack by the 156th Brigade was almost entirely successful. The 4th and 7th Royal Scots succeeded in every detail in the tasks imposed on them. The 8th Scottish Rifles met with enormous resistance owing to the fact that our artillery had not prepared the Turkish position in front of them quite so successfully as in other places. The 8th Scottish Rifles were very gallantly led. This position was attacked twice later by the 88th Brigade (29th Division) with great gallantry but without success. General de Lisle does not blame the 8th Scottish Rifles at all for their failure. He much regrets the death of Brig.-Gen. Scott-Moncrieff."

Regarding the lack of success in the artillery preparation, all eye-witnesses agree that there was no artillery preparation at all on the right of the 156th Brigade's front, and the majority agree that what few shells did fall on the left seemed to be intended for elsewhere.

Shortly after the action General Hunter-Weston conveyed a message of congratulation from Sir Ian Hamilton to the 156th Brigade, and confirmed this on 3rd July with a message referring to " their fine attack which has brought so great distinction on their Brigade and on the 52nd Division."

Despite all this that passed between the 156th Brigade and the Higher Command, the Special Force Order published by Sir Ian Hamilton on the battle, and dated from G.H.Q. on 29th June, praised the gallant 29th Division, but observed complete silence with regard to the 156th Brigade. His despatch dated 29th June contained the following brief statement :—" East of Ravine two battalions Royal Scots made fine attack, capturing the two lines of trenches assigned as their objective, but remainder of 156th Brigade on their right met severe opposition and were unable to get forward." This was briefly restated in his despatch of 26th August, with no mention of the severe opposition. That was all.

One result was that the words, " the remainder of the 156th Brigade were unable to get on " (Despatch, 26th August), were most cruelly misinterpreted by a certain war-correspondent who, incidentally, was so far misinformed as to assign the bulk of the losses to three units in the 86th Brigade (29th Division). Another war-correspondent, referring to the Cameronians, imagined or was wrongly informed that they had " failed to make good their holding." Every trench captured by the Cameronians and every other unit of the Division on Gallipoli was held by them. The H.12 trenches on the right were not captured, simply because corpses cannot walk forward, and no man there got forward more than a few dozen yards without being killed. There was never any question of them failing " to make good their holding." The writer of this work has called attention to these mis-statements, because they were widely read at the time, and neither the public at home nor the army in general knew any more. Naturally, everyone in the Division, and the Cameronians in particular, felt keenly the mis-representation and the official silence. No one grudged the high praise given to the splendid 29th Division, but they should not have had it all, and no one would have said this more strongly than the gallant men who filled its ranks.

Yet the morale of this Brigade did not suffer from the battle, as was shown by their conduct a fortnight later.

That General Simpson-Baikie, the C.R.A. at Cape Helles, had not been informed by those in charge of the operations that the 156th Brigade was under the orders of the G.O.C. 29th Division for the battle, is evident from the following statement of his:

" So successful had been the attack on our left with its capture of five successive lines of Turkish trenches that we had actually some ammunition to spare. In the afternoon it was agreed that there should be another attack on H.12, preceded by a very short but very intense bombardment from every gun and howitzer we possessed. All artillery arrangements for this were completed before 2.30 p.m., from which hour all the guns waited alert and ready for the Infantry to inform us of the hour they wished us to commence fire. I was in direct telephonic communication with the commander of the 52nd Division, having had a private wire laid on to his Headquarters the previous day. Suddenly, to my horror, I received a telephone message from my Artillery Group Commander, Colonel Stockdale, saying the Infantry were making the assault and that he had no time to do more than fire half a dozen shots !"

Brig.-Gen. Scott-Moncrieff and the 7th Cameronians had been dead more than an hour before this attack took place ; and fortunately, realising the futility of piling corpses of their own on to the heaps of the 156th Brigade, the 29th Division did not press their attacks.

We will quote Major-General Egerton at this point :

" It is, therefore, necessary to say that—

" (1) The 156th Brigade were not on this day under the orders of the G.O.C. 52nd Division, having been lent to the 29th Division.

" (2) That no special wire was laid on to 52nd Headquarters.

" (3) That the afternoon assault was made by the 88th Brigade of the 29th Division and that the 156th Brigade took no part in it."

It is futile to speculate as to what might have happened if the 156th Brigade had had the use of the one Lowland Battery at Cape Helles. We all make false steps, and campaigns are won by those who make the fewest, but surely the saddest of the Gallipoli Campaign were those which prevented due honour being done to men who had suffered and given their lives freely.

On 1st July the 7th and 8th Cameronians were formed into one composite battalion, composed of three companies, two of the 7th and one of the 8th, the whole being under the command of Major W. T. Bird of the 7th. The Royal Scots were similarly reorganised on the 6th July, two companies being formed from the 4th R.S., and one from the 7th R.S., the command devolving on Lt.-Col. W. C. Peebles, T.D.

Let us conclude the chapter with a scene which shall be described by the principal actor, a tall chaplain, with white hair and moustache, greatly honoured by all, no matter of what rank or creed. He had promised his own battalion, the 4th Royal Scots, to hold a memorial service for those who had fallen on the 28th June, and on Sunday, 4th July, was making his way to the " Rest Camp " for that purpose. " With some caution," Dr. Ewing writes, " I picked my way in the dark through the various lines until I found my friends. The men were gathered in a little open space and sat round in the form of a half-moon. The stars were very bright, but the night was dark, and we could see each other only as shadows. The enemy seemed to enter into the spirit of the thing, and left us absolutely in peace. So there, in the trenched valley, alive with armed men, in perfect stillness, under the quiet sky, we held our service. We sang familiar words, a few of the lads with good voices standing by and acting as a choir. ' All people that on earth do dwell,' ' The Lord's my Shepherd,' and ' O God of Bethel ' were sung with deep feeling. As the music floated away on the light breeze it seemed to rouse the interest of others, and, attracted by the strains, many dim figures moved silently towards us from the surrounding battalions, considerably swelling our congregation. How our hearts were stirred as we thought of the brave men gone, who had so often worshipped with us in the Grange and in the old Cathedral. One felt in a peculiar way a sense of their presence, as we prayed that we might be worthy to cherish the memory of these heroic friends and comrades."

CHAPTER V

(2ND TO 12TH JULY, 1915)

THE BATTLE OF THE 12-13TH JULY, 1915

> I've seen the morning
> With gold the hills adorning,
> And loud tempest storming before the mid-day.
> I've seen Tweed's silver stream
> Shining in the sunny beam,
> Grow drumly and dark as he row'd on his way.
> ALISON RUTHERFORD (MRS. COCKBURN).

AT the beginning of July the Turks were moving five fresh Nizam (Active Army) divisions into Gallipoli; probably because of the weakness of Russia, and a secret understanding with Bulgaria. Their counter-attacks immediately after the 28th June showed how seriously they regarded their reverse at Cape Helles, and it was essential that their attention should remain fixed on that front.

On the night of the 2-3rd July the 157th Brigade, Brig.-Gen. P. W. Hendry, V.D., was carried over from Mudros to Cape Helles on mine-sweepers and destroyers. During the following day parties of officers of the 157th Brigade were taken to the forward trenches, where the position was explained to them. Some of them spent a night in the Centre Section with the 42nd Division, which was destined to fight by the side of the 52nd in several great battles.

At day-break on 3rd July the first detachment of the 1/3rd Lowland Field Ambulance came ashore at the "*River Clyde*," being accommodated by the 1/1st Lowland Field Ambulance, who were in dug-outs on the cliffs to the south

BATTLE OF THE 12-13TH JULY, 1915

of Lancashire Landing not far from the ruined lighthouse of Cape Helles.

During the night 3-4th July all in the "Rest Camp" worked hard to improve their dug-outs, and, rain coming on, they learnt how tough and tenacious is the Gallipoli clay when wet. Their exertions were very necessary, for the usual shell-fire followed on the 4th, causing a number of casualties.

All night long on the 4-5th the Turks fired heavily and continuously. At 4 a.m., the dawn of a great Moslem festival, they opened fire with every piece of artillery that they could bring to bear on Cape Helles and Anzac. Enver Bey had over-ruled the wiser German decision to let the British and French do the attacking, and had decided to drive the Allies into the sea. "Their Asiatic Batteries alone fired 1900 rounds, of which 700 fell on Lancashire Landing. At least 5000 shell were loosed off on to Helles. A lot of the stuff was 6-inch and over." (Sir Ian Hamilton.) At that time, with the exception of the guns of the 29th Division and the few guns of the Anzacs, our field artillery on Gallipoli consisted of the old 5-inch howitzers and 15-pounders of South African days. In at least one case half of the guns of a brigade were out of repair and useless for the time.

Soon after, the Turks attacked in dense masses. There was no H.E. to spare; but they melted away under the enfilade fire of the British field-guns. The 7/8th Cameronians were in the forward trenches and Captain R. Blair noted in his diary: "We had a great day shooting Turks with machine-gun and rifle, and got some of our own back. The same made me more hopeful than I had felt since I landed here." For the Turks it was a costly failure amounting to a disaster, and seriously damaged the morale of their troops, at any rate for the attack.

The whole Division was standing by soon after 4.30 a.m. An extra fifty rounds was issued to each man, and the quartermasters and cooks hurried breakfast forward. The achievements of the Q.M. departments in the Division were splendid, and the cunning shown in hiding the telltale smoke of the kitchens admirable. Meals were occasionally delayed or consisted of makeshifts, but the writer is sure that not once did the cooks fail the troops in their vital duties, no matter what the hour, the shell-fire, or the weather.

By 9 a.m. the firing had died away, and the Turks had admitted a costly defeat.

Despite the heavy shell-fire directed on the " Rest Camp " and other areas, the losses of the Division were small, because of the digging-in. The 6th H.L.I. lost 1 killed and 9 wounded in the " Rest Camp," and other units even fewer.

After dusk on the 5th July, the 5th H.L.I. were guided up the Eastern Mule Track and through a labyrinth of trenches to Twelve Tree Copse, between Gully Ravine and Krithia Nullah. Here the battalion was split up, the companies being attached to the 1st Dublin Fusiliers, 2nd Royal Fusiliers, and 1st Munsters for instruction in trench warfare.

On the same night the 5th Argylls moved to Ghurka Bluff for the same purpose, having an unfortunate experience with a guide, who as usual lost his way. This was the easiest possible thing to do in the darkness and in such a maze of trenches, but, unfortunately, it was also conducive to much weariness among men who had been up since dawn. The Turks were nervous after their defeat and their lines burst into rifle-fire every now and then, causing a few casualties among the Argylls.

During the 6th the remaining battalions of the 155th and 157th Brigades moved to various places in the forward trenches about Achi Baba Nullah for a few days, the newcomers receiving instruction from more experienced units of the Royal Naval Division. The 5th R.S.F. was an exception, as it had been in trenches near Clapham Junction for some time, and was moved to the " Rest Camp." The 156th Brigade now under the command of Lt.-Col. P. C. Palin of the 29th Indian Brigade, moved on the same day to relieve that brigade at Ghurka Bluff.

On the previous day Brig.-Gen. P. W. Hendry, V.D., had been invalided to hospital with dysentery and fever,

BATTLE OF THE 12-13TH JULY, 1915

and Col. W. H. Millar, 6th H.L.I., had assumed command of the 157th Brigade.

This was the first experience of the trenches for many. "Here we first encountered some of the gruesome spectacles incidental to this style of warfare. Such sights as the withered hand of a Turk sticking out from the parapet of a communication trench, or the boots of a hastily buried soldier projecting from his shallow grave, require getting used to. It was still more trying to look on the unburied dead lying in groups in front of the parapet; and further away, near the Turkish lines, the bodies of so many of the Scottish Rifles who had been swept down by concealed machine-guns only a week before in their gallant attempt to advance without artillery support.

"It is well that this acuteness of feeling soon becomes blunted. One quickly learns to regard such things as an inevitable aspect of one's everyday environment. Thank God for this; life in the trenches would otherwise be unbearable." (*History 5th H.L.I.*)

In these days this moorland, interspersed with occasional olive groves, fig trees, and vineyards, beautiful and speaking of peace although riven and battered by war, had many places where there grew sweet-smelling herbs and flowers, around which bees hummed and butterflies fluttered in the summer heat. Yet one knew that those lovely flowers concealed much that hardly bore thinking of.

Fortunately, the fleshly needs of the practically-minded heroes of the Lowland Division did much to distract their minds from morbid moralizing. Instead, they bore an air of jaunty cheerfulness, making jests of what were really deadly privations and hardships.

The heat became more scorching, and a drink of tea was a god-send. "The drinking water was unpalatable, being heavily chlorinated to sterilise it. Our modest ration of unsweetened lime juice sufficed to remove the unpleasant flavour from one fill to a water-bottle, but would not stand further dilution. In any case water-bottles could not be refilled at will, and it was a long walk to Gully Ravine from which we drew our water. It may be recorded here that this 'trench thirst,' as we dubbed it, remained with us for our first few weeks on the Peninsula. Thereafter it gradually disappeared until our craving for liquid became normal.

"Meanwhile we were rapidly learning to adapt ourselves to circumstances; to sleep soundly on the fire-step of a trench; to extemporise fuel and cooking appliances; to endure the flies which swarmed over our food, pursuing it even into our mouths, bathed (and drowned) themselves in our drink, and clustered on our faces, waiting in queues to sip moisture from our eyes and lips; to live with relish on bully-beef, M'Connochie, tea, hard biscuits and jam; in short, we were becoming able to fend for ourselves." (*History 5th H.L.I.*)

The 5th Argylls lost 2nd Lieut. W. Rodger killed by a sniper on the 7th, and during the same day four of their men were wounded by shrapnel whilst bathing off a beach near by. The next day both the 5th H.L.I. and 5th Argylls moved back to their "rest-trenches" near Pink Farm, and on the 9th they relieved the 7th H.L.I. and 6th H.L.I., respectively, in the trenches. Turkish snipers were very active, using steel loop-hole plates, and rifles from which the woodwork had been cut away so that the barrels could be aimed through a very small aperture. Those before the 6th H.L.I. were especially bold, but that unit took them on in a keen struggle. They lost two killed and several wounded, but it is certain that the Turks lost at least as many. After the relief had taken place and the 6th H.L.I. were moving from the trenches, they were heavily shelled, losing another ten men. By these ways and by sickness the casualty lists steadily mounted up.

The Royal Scots were in the front line at Ghurka Bluff, and about 4 a.m. on the 9th a Turkish officer with a letter for the British Commander-in-Chief met Lt.-Col. Peebles in No Man's Land under cover of a white flag. The letter was from Weber Pasha, Commandant of the Ottoman forces, asking for a five hours truce for the burial of the dead. The British Intelligence made it clear to Sir Ian Hamilton that the Turks requested this because they could

BATTLE OF THE 12-13TH JULY, 1915

not get their men to charge over the corpses of their comrades, and accordingly Sir Ian Hamilton refused it. The answer was conveyed to the Turks in the afternoon by Colonel Palin in person.

The following afternoon, 10th, the 156th Brigade were relieved by the 88th and made their way to the "Rest Camp" by Gully Ravine and the beach. They were only there a day, because at 3 a.m. on the 12th July they received orders to proceed to Backhouse Post, where they were to lie in divisional reserve. The Lowland Division was getting into position for its great attack on the Turkish entrenchments between Kereves Dere and Achi Baba Nullah.

In the meantime, on the 6th July, the remainder of the 1/3rd Lowland Field Ambulance had arrived. After two attempts and one R.A.M.C. casualty, because of the Turkish shell-fire, the trawler got them ashore. They took over the cliff-burrows of the 1/1st Lowland Field Ambulance, who moved to a new site on the inner slope about three-quarters of a mile from "W" Beach. Later, before the 12th July, the 1/3rd Lowland Field Ambulance moved from the cliff-top to a site near the 1/1st Lowland Field Ambulance.

As the 1st and 3rd Lowland Field Ambulance had not had time to learn their way about, and also to avoid a hurried taking over, it was wisely decided that they should send officers and men to assist the ambulances of the Royal Naval Division at their advanced dressing stations. These stations were to serve the frontage of both Divisions.

Let the writer quote here a testimony to the Turks from Lt.-Col. Young (3rd Lowland Field Ambulance) which is borne out by everyone who was on Gallipoli:—"On no occasion did we ever find the Turk disregard the Convention of the Red Cross, and several times we have satisfied ourselves that he exercised special care in steering his shells clear of our camp. We have often had shells in our camp, but we have a strong belief that they were accidental." In such a crowded area as Cape Helles such accidents were unavoidable. Needless to say, the British and French were equally respectful of the Red Crescent of the Turks, which flapped among the trees in a ravine on the face of Achi Baba, and in other places.

In order to maintain the position at Cape Helles it was essential for the Allies to retain the initiative, and, because of the impending landing at Suvla Bay, it was equally essential that the Turks should think that their chief danger lay on the slopes of Achi Baba and not at Anzac.

Little over three hundred yards to the south-east of the main fork in Krithia Nullah lies that patch of vines which was known as "The Vineyard." On its south-eastern side ran the old cart-track of peace time from Krithia to Sedd el Bahr.

At this time the Allied front line ran from just south of this fork in Krithia Nullah to the south-western edge of The Vineyard. Thence, with numerous bends and turns, and with a couple of salients on either side of Achi Baba Nullah, it ran generally in a south-easterly direction, but curving gradually to the south until it reached the western edge of the wide gorge, Kereves Dere, where its cliffs overlooked the Hellespont.

Achi Baba Nullah crossed the Allied lines into the Turkish about 800 yards east of the fork in Krithia Nullah, and about 2000 yards west of the shores of the Hellespont. At this place, to one going up this nullah, its grass and scrub-covered banks, partially sloping and partially scarped, are opening to form one of those shallow watercourses which wind about everywhere on the upper slopes in a hill-country.

It was the intention of the Allies to thrust their line forward and overrun the Turkish trenches between Achi Baba Nullah and Kereves Dere. The Turks did not expect an attack on their left, so much as they did on their right. On the other hand, there could be no naval support from the Hellespont, because of the Turkish forts and drifting mines.

The attack was to be delivered in two phases, so that each could be preceded by a thorough artillery bombardment. The mistake of the 28th June was not to be repeated.

BATTLE OF THE 12-13TH JULY, 1915

The first attack was to be delivered at 7.35 a.m. by the French on the right, and the 155th Brigade in the centre. The second attack was to be delivered in the afternoon at 4.50 p.m. by the 157th Brigade on the left.

Now, apart from the 6th H.L.I. of the 157th Brigade, who were to advance up Achi Baba Nullah, and the French, who were to clear the trenches on the western edge of Kereves Dere, all the assaulting troops were ordered to take three lines of Turkish trenches. It is of extreme importance that the reader should mark well this point, because the official printed map, dated 5th July, 1915, only shows two main Turkish fire-trenches, and all the evidence shows that there were only those two.

From the southern corner of The Vineyard the British front line ran towards the south-east. The Turkish front trench facing it was about 350 yards away, but, when it reached the northern bank of Achi Baba Nullah, it turned in until the opposing lines were separated by less than fifty yards. The Turks had blocked this nullah with seven lengths of heavily-wired trench, laid across or on either side of the water-course. They swept it with cross-fire. On the northern bank it was flanked by a strong earthwork, and the Turks had commenced a redoubt set back a little on the southern bank. This latter was actually a crescent-shaped trench with its ends pointing to the east. Later, it became known as the Horseshoe. All of these trenches were linked up by lesser ones.

From there, two main lines of heavily-wired Turkish fire-trenches ran for about 700 yards across open grass and moorland, to the south-east generally, but curving gradually southward with many twists, and being linked up with numerous lesser trenches. The front line was separated from the British front line by No Man's Land, varying from 100 to 200 yards in width.

The right or southern halves of these two trenches were to be taken by the 155th Brigade, and the left or northern by the 157th Brigade.

For descriptive purposes it is convenient to follow them again from left to right, that is from north to south.

Behind these trenches the aeroplane photographs showed marks which were interpreted to mean a third trench (E.12) running from the unfinished Horseshoe to the southeast for about 350 yards, after which it joined up with the second Turkish fire-trench (E.11). The left and centre of this third Turkish trench came into the objective of the 157th Brigade; the right into the objective of the 155th Brigade. This third Turkish trench (E.12) is marked as a communication trench in the G.H.Q. printed map dated 5th July, 1915, but it is not marked on the multigraph reproductions of the map showing communications, dated 2nd July, 1915, and issued to battalion commanders prior to this battle.

This " third Turkish trench (E.12) " did not exist.

Some marks on the ground as if a trench had been planned, a few short lengths of not more than eighteen inches in depth, even fewer short lengths of over two feet in depth; those were all the signs of digging that were found. Whether the Turks had commenced to dig a trench for their own use, or whether it was intended for a dummy trench will never be known, but it is certain that it deceived the staff of the British Higher Command.

The second matter was as follows. Behind the most southern 350 yards of the first Turkish fire-trench (E.10) was a loop communication trench, sometimes referred to as A-O. Its northern end joined the first Turkish trench approximately in its middle, almost opposite to the point where the third trench (E.12) was supposed to join the second (E.11). This loop-trench was so shallow and narrow to begin with, was so blown about in places by artillery-fire, and was so confused with minor trenches in a like condition, which had not been separately numbered in the orders for the attack, that the assaulting troops passed on without recognising it.

From this it will be seen that, according to the official maps and orders issued, the second Turkish trench (E.11) in front of the 157th Brigade, and the left of the 155th Brigade, became the third Turkish trench for the remainder of the front of the latter Brigade—provided that the loop communication trench (A-O) was counted in, and that the lesser ones were not.

At the risk of tedium the writer has taken pains to make it clear that there were only two main Turkish fire-trenches on these parts of the respective fronts of the two Brigades, because of the succession of cruel blunders which arose out of the idea that there was a third.

The second Turkish trench (E.11) bent back or eastward slightly until it reached a declivity, which ran into Kereves Dere.

The first Turkish trench (E.10) bent forward or southward until it lost itself in a maze of trenches in which no one could imagine three distinct lines of trenches of any kind. In several places there the barricades and trench-blocks of the opposing troops were only a few yards apart.

Thence, the Turkish system, well wired, followed the western side of Kereves Dere until it reached the cliffs overlooking the Dardanelles, about 150 yards to the east of the French front line. Afterwards, the trenches of both sides ran down declivities until they reached the water.

About 1000 yards higher up the slopes of Achi Baba than this system of Turkish trenches there was understood to be, at this time, one long fire-trench, which ran almost right across the peninsula. Apart from this there were probably no more entrenchments of importance.

We are mainly concerned with the 1000 yards of front which ran from Achi Baba Nullah inclusive to a point within the extremely complicated trench system. There, as was general on the middle slopes of Achi Baba, the ground rose gradually from the British lines.

By the 11th July the 155th and 157th Brigades were in the trenches from which they were to make the attack, and the 156th Brigade was being moved forward from the " Rest Camp " to divisional reserve near Backhouse Road.

It was to be a trench to trench attack similar to that of the 28th June. The British front line in this area was then the trench known as Parsons Road. Behind it were three other lines, Trotman Road, Mercer Road, and Backhouse

Road, the last being 400 yards in rear of the front line. All four trenches crossed the entire area of the two Brigades, with the exception of the right which was in the maze of trenches, and the left which was in Achi Baba Nullah.

The attack of the 155th Brigade was to be delivered in four waves of men, with a frontage of about 500 yards. They were to form up in the four lines of trenches and in the confused system on their right. After a preliminary bombardment, the four waves were to rise simultaneously from their trenches. The first two waves were to jump the first two Turkish trenches (E.10 and A-O) and together take the third (E.11). The third wave was to occupy the second, that is the loop communication trench (A-O), and the fourth wave the first Turkish trench (E.10). Their right would advance through the tangle on a corresponding front, and its right flank would be protected by the French advance. To protect their left a special party was told off in the first wave, it being their duty to seize and hold a Turkish communication trench which linked up their two main fire-trenches.

Special bombing parties were to accompany the first three waves to clear the small communication trenches. In the last three waves parties, carrying picks and shovels, and with Royal Engineer personnel attached, were to be detailed for the special purpose of re-building and consolidating the captured trenches. Royal Engineers were to go with the first, third, and fourth waves to search for enemy mines. In order that the artillery might see how far they had advanced, every third man was to have on his back a piece of tin, which would reflect back the sun's rays. For the same purpose the first two waves were to carry biscuit tins, which were to be placed in the rear of the forward captured trenches; and a few men on the left of each wave of the left attack were to carry red flags, which were to be planted in view of the artillery, in order that they would not shell the left of the 155th Brigade when preparing for the attack of the 157th Brigade. Scaling ladders were to be provided, by which the troops were to climb out of the trenches for the

BATTLE OF THE 12-13TH JULY, 1915

assault. Where these were not available, steps were to be cut. The three battalions taking part in the assault were each to detail a platoon to carry up water, ammunition, and bombs when required, but this was found to be quite inadequate during the battle. As many wire-cutters as possible were to be given by the units in rear to the troops in the first two waves. Every man was to have his respirator handy, and it was to be damp but not wet. Respirators at this time consisted of a simple pad to tie over the mouth and nostrils. They were better than nothing, although they dried up with the heat, slipped off, and even when properly on supplied very little protection against gas attacks. Two officers and ten per cent. of the other ranks of each company were to report to divisional reserve. They were to form a nucleus in the event of a company being destroyed.

One great difficulty was that, owing to the slope of the ground, only the front line of the enemy could be seen from the British trenches, so that, as soon as attacking troops had passed the first parapet, they would be beyond the ken of those behind. It was understood that aeroplanes would supply the necessary links, but none were seen. The indescribable complication of the enemy trenches accentuated the problem. A painstaking attempt was made to let each wave and party know exactly where it ought to go. Even with the use of maps and with no enemy fire, it would have been difficult for the waves and parties to have found their way about, because, although Turkish trenches were very clearly designated on our own printed maps, all that the assaulting officers and men could see was a confusion of excavations running in all directions, and, very naturally, not labelled. As it was, in order to prevent information falling into the enemy's hands, no maps, sketches, or copies of orders were to be taken to the front line trenches, and by 6 a.m. on the 12th all such documents had to be no further forward than the Eski Lines. The memory alone could be relied on, and this, amidst the distractions of enemy artillery and machine-gun fire, wounds, and death.

The formation for the attack by the 155th Brigade under Brig.-Gen. J. F. Erskine, M.V.O., was roughly as shown in the following diagram:

1st Wave	{ 4th K.O.S.B. (2½ companies) { R.E., 8 other ranks	4th R.S.F. (3 platoons) R.E., 4 men
2nd Wave	{ 4th K.O.S.B. (1½ companies) { R.E., 16 other ranks	4th R.S.F. (2 platoons) R.E., 8 men
3rd Wave	{ 5th K.O.S.B. (2 companies) { (1 platoon) { R.E., 12 other ranks	4th R.S.F. (2 platoons) R.E., 4 men
4th Wave	{ 5th K.O.S.B. (1 company) { (1 platoon) { R.E., 8 other ranks	4th R.S.F. (2 platoons) R.E., 14 men

The 4th K.O.S.B. (Lt.-Col. J. M'Neile) and 5th K.O.S.B. (Lt.-Col. W. J. Millar) were to deal principally with the southern half of the two main Turkish fire-trenches, together with a portion of the supposed trench E.12. The 4th R.S.F. (Lt.-Col. J. R. Balfour) were to attack through the area where these two trenches joined up with the maze on the right, having to make a big change in direction whilst doing so. This battalion was also to supply a company whose special duty it was to keep touch with the French. The 5th R.S.F. (Lt.-Col. J. B. Pollok-M'Call) were to garrison the old British firing line, to dig communication trenches forward, and to be in brigade reserve with some details. The Royal Engineer personnel was furnished by the 2/1st Lowland Field Coy., R.E.

Diversions to support the attack were to be made at Anzac, and by the 29th Division on the left at Cape Helles.

At 3.45 p.m. on the 11th the French opened fire for two hours on the Turkish trenches in front of the Lowland Division with their field guns, the famous " seventy-fives." This was a preliminary registration for the morrow. Owing to the British artillery being short of ammunition, the French had undertaken the whole of the artillery preparation, and for that purpose generously placed six batteries of seventy-fives, and some howitzers, between thirty and forty guns, under British orders. The British ammunition was to be saved for covering fire during the advance, and for the repelling of counter attacks. The Turkish guns replied vigorously, but the French did considerable damage to their wire and entrenchments before they finished.

The morning of the 12th July broke with bright sunshine and a cloudless sky. The troops were in the highest spirits, " gay and free as usual " (Major Yuille). The ten per cent. nucleus had been sent down the night before, and the order had been obeyed unwillingly, because no one wished to be left behind. Everything was ready, and officers were using what periscopes they had for a last look at the enemy trenches before the attack. The 4th R.S.F. was in touch with the French on its right.

At 4.30 a.m. the French artillery opened fire with shrapnel and H.E. on the Turkish trenches, whilst some warships shelled their back areas and searched for observation stations on Achi Baba. The Turkish artillery replied almost at once, trying to search out the French guns and shelling the front and communication trenches, and soon the roar of cannon was constant. The harsh, ripping crash of the French " seventy-fives " resounded everywhere, as they sent their salvoes of shells with wonderful precision and rapidity on to the Turkish trenches and wire.

The main volume of fire was directed on the trenches before the 155th Brigade. Around this area there was a perfect inferno of din and smoke. The hill-side and the crest of Achi Baba were smothered in clouds of dust and smoke. The 155th and 157th Brigades had many casualties from the Turkish shrapnel as they waited in their trenches ; but the Turkish losses from the deadly fire of the French seventy-fives were also heavy. At 7.30 a.m. the French artillery ceased with startling suddenness. The gunners were lengthening their ranges.

A few moments afterwards there arose a terrific clattering of musketry and machine-guns. The men of the 157th Brigade on the left of the 155th Brigade, were giving covering fire from their rifles and machine-guns, and the Turks were firing their hardest ; for with a burst of cheering the Borderers and Fusiliers were out of their trenches and advancing steadily on the Turkish position, long lines of khaki figures in open order, the sunlight flashing from the plates of tin and their bayonets.

The British and French artillery now opened fire, putting a barrage down in rear of the Turks to prevent them from bringing up reinforcements. As rapidly, the Turks brought every gun which they could spare to bear on the advancing infantry, deluging them with shrapnel and machine-gun fire so that the "bullets fell like rain on calm water" (a 4th K.O.S.B. survivor). The air was filled with dust and smoke, and watchers soon lost sight of the assaulting troops in this convulsed yellow pall that smothered the hill-side, where officers were keeping direction as best they could and looking out for Turkish trenches. The roar of cannon was constant and deafening, and at times the doctors in the dressing stations could hardly hear themselves speaking. Occasionally the uproar died down a little, as if taking breath, and Lt.-Col. J. Young, when at one dressing station, noticed that "just then, during a momentary hush, a yellow-breasted bird flew by, chirping as if nothing were amiss."

"Unless one has seen it there is no imagination that can picture a belt of land some 400 yards wide converted into a seething hell of destruction. Rifle and machine-gun bullets rip up the earth, ping past the ear, or whing off the loose stones; shrapnel bursts overhead and the leaden bullets strike the ground with a vicious thud; the earth is rent into yawning chasms, while planks, sandbags, clods of earth, and great rugged chunks of steel hurtle through the air. The noise is an indescribable, nerve-racking, continuous, deafening roar, while drifting clouds of smoke only allow an intermittent view of the damnable inferno." (Major Yuille.)

Such were the impressions left on the minds of the 4th R.S.F. as they advanced on the left of the French, and tried to wheel and find their way about, over a labyrinth of trenches. For the 4th R.S.F. speed was impossible. The 200 rounds of S.A.A., which were carried by every man in

BATTLE OF THE 12-13TH JULY, 1915

the assault, in addition to a rifle and other necessary equipment weighed them down, and the heavily-laden men had to jump or scramble across one trench after another. They began to lose heavily from the start, Captain Dunn being wounded whilst in the act of altering the direction of his men.

Curving into the centre of the 4th R.S.F. ran the southern end of the first main Turkish fire-trench (E.10), and at the same place this latter was rejoined by its loop communication trench (A-O). Both were joined by numerous lesser trenches forking and running in different directions.

Before the 4th R.S.F. right lay two short Turkish fire-trenches, one behind the other in the tangle of earthworks.

Twelve out of the thirteen 4th R.S.F. officers taking part in the charge had fallen, with the bulk of the men, before these two short fire-trenches were won, together with another trench that ran to the left, towards the loop communication trench.

Somewhere beyond, to the left of their new front, lay the southern end of what was marked on the maps as the second main Turkish fire-trench (E.11). This part (designated S-T), where it ran to a declivity of the great wide gorge of Kereves Dere, they were also to attack; but there were hardly enough left to hold what had been captured until reinforcements could arrive, and the Turkish machine-gun fire increased rather than diminished. To have gone on would have resulted in the destruction of the handful left, and probably the loss of what had been won already. Captain H. R. Young, the surviving officer, got the men together, and they all set to work to consolidate the captured trenches. He was in command of the liaison company, and accordingly ensured that he was in touch with the French on his right. The 4th R.S.F. machine-gun officer was amongst the fallen, but Sgt. T. Murphy brought his guns over the open under a heavy fire, and took up a position whence he materially assisted in covering the consolidation, and in repelling counter attacks.

Meanwhile, the long lines of Borderers had advanced steadily and rapidly. At the start some had been in dead ground, but as soon as they crested a low ridge they were met by a very heavy artillery fire, and men began to drop. 2nd Lieut. A. H. M. Henderson fell here, shot through the head. Before them they could see a line of thrown-up earth, the Turkish front line.

The first trench was captured with bayonet and revolver, and some prisoners that were taken were sent back. The orders were for the 4th K.O.S.B. to carry the first two trenches but not to occupy them, the objective being the third, where both waves were to unite. It was difficult to tell whether some places, where the ground had been riven asunder by H.E., were the remains of trenches and accordingly to be noted, or whether they had been hollows worn by time and the weather and accordingly to be ignored. However, all ranks were on the *qui vive* to count the Turkish trenches as they crossed them, and they went forward for the next one.

Leading the second wave on this day was Lt.-Col. J. C. M'Neile with his adjutant, Captain J. C. Lang, both of them cool, intrepid men. " The survivors of the charge never tire of telling what a magnificent example the Colonel, who had endeared himself to all ranks, was to his comrades that day " (Lt. Sorley Brown). " Come away, Borderers ! don't be beaten ! " was the stirring cry of Captain A. Wallace as he continued to advance, although badly wounded and with blood streaming down his face, until he was hit again, this time to fall a dying man. Lieut. J. B. Innes had one of his arms shattered by a bursting shell. He got his cousin, Lieut. W. K. Innes, to cut it off, asked for a cigarette, and continued to cheer the Borderers on until he died from loss of blood.

They reached a second trench, where the Turks put up a good fight, firing their rifles through loop-holes. Some of the Borderers jumped into the trench, whilst others shot the enemy down from the parapet. By the time it was captured, it was littered with dead and wounded Turks. More prisoners were taken here, and were sent back. Up to this time the casualties of the 4th K.O.S.B. had not been very heavy, considering the nature of the fighting.

BATTLE OF THE 12-13TH JULY, 1915

The adjutant now came down the line pointing out some thrown-up earth which seemed to be the parapet of a third trench about 150 yards away, and the advance went on again. Some men doubled forward to it but only found an untenanted, shallow length of trench, not more than two feet deep. On the left it ran up towards a wood, but stopped about 100 yards short of it. On the right it ran towards another wood, whence seemed to come a great deal of rifle and machine-gun fire. Within both these woods men could be seen running about, those in the left probably being British. In front of them they could see no signs of the enemy at all.

Some think that these men were in what were the preliminary excavations of a new Turkish fire-trench, others think that it was a dummy trench, and others, again, that they had reached a few machine-gun emplacements marked on the map as being about 350 yards to the north-east of Parsons Road, and about 200 yards to the north-west of Kereves Dere.

The remainder of the battalion must have advanced clear of these emplacements, until they had gone about a quarter of a mile, being actually within the zone of our own artillery fire, and under shell-fire from both front and rear. Lt.-Col. J. M'Neile saw that there was a mistake somewhere, and said to Major W. E. A. Cochrane: " We are too far forward, we must get back." There was a brief consultation in which the adjutant joined. Major Cochrane said: " I'll stop the men and get them back," and this they all endeavoured to do.

Every man possible was recalled, but unknown to the others some brave spirits had pressed forward and were well up the slopes of Achi Baba.

The retiral now commenced, and, automatically, any men who had on their backs the plates which were to flash their position back to the artillery, now turned their breasts to the Allied lines, so that, even if the Allied gunners could have seen anything of them, it would only have been a scatter of khaki figures well behind the enemy lines, which could be easily mistaken for a Turkish counter-attack moving on newly-captured trenches. In their advance the Borderers had diverged a little to the right, and now they diverged to the left, which brought them into the French barrage, which was about the Kereves Dere. The shrapnel and H.E. now rained on them from front, flanks, and rear. " The front which had been broken was narrow, and the Turkish machine-guns on the right and left were by this time in position to enfilade the returning men " (Major W. T. Forrest).

" Nothing could live under so cruel a cross-fire from friend and foe " (Sir Ian Hamilton), and the returning troops were almost wiped out.

Nothing more was ever seen or heard of the gallant Lt.-Col. J. M'Neile, his adjutant, five of his officers, and 262 of his men. Some distant heaps of British dead lying well behind the Turkish lines: some reports of helmeted and khaki clad figures seen well up the slopes of Achi Baba: that is all that we know, beyond the picture that the few survivors give us of officers and men retiring steadily down those sunlit slopes, and helping wounded comrades until shot down themselves beneath a deluge of fire from front, flanks, and rear, machine-gun, rifle, shrapnel, and high explosive. It is probable that over 700 of the 4th K.O.S.B.'s crossed the parapets on that day; of these almost half were killed or died of wounds, and considerably more than a quarter were wounded. All but two of the officers taking part in the charge fell. The Royal Engineers with them paid their toll at the same time.

It is because there were so few left to record it that we can give so few accounts of the gallantry of individuals of the 4th K.O.S.B. on this day.

The men who were crowded in the length of shallow trench had filled their sandbags to build up something of a parapet. They had tried to deepen the trench, but " the ground was like flint, and we could make little headway with our entrenching tools " (Cpl. T. Richardson, 4th K.O.S.B.). Machine-gun and rifle fire in enfilade from the wood on the right and a hail of shrapnel made it untenable. An attempt was made to extend the men to the

BATTLE OF THE 12-13TH JULY, 1915

left and some got into shell-holes. Shortly afterwards they saw some of the others doubling back through the bursting shells for the trench behind, and those who were left went back with them, men dropping all the time.

There were not many of the 4th K.O.S.B. left by this time, and as best they could and as quickly as possible, for it was death to move slowly over the open, they hurried back through the stunning din to the next line.

They jumped down into a trench manned by R.S.F. and 5th K.O.S.B., who were busy putting it into a defensible condition, and cleaning it by getting the dead, most of whom were Turks, over the parapet. This trench had been almost obliterated in parts by the French H.E. The parapet had been practically blown away, and in places the trench had been filled up by debris and earth, until its floor was level with the ground outside. They were in the ruin of the loop communication trench (known as A-O) which ran behind the right of the old Turkish front line.

The 5th K.O.S.B. had advanced for the first 150 yards at a run, and then at a walk because of the heat, the rough ground, and the difficulties in getting across the numerous lines of British fire trenches. Never once did the men waver. It was difficult to keep direction, because of the numerous oblique communication trenches, which were inclined to edge men to the left. The Turkish front line trench (E.10) and the loop communication trench (A-O) behind, were occupied, but, as was found out, the latter not at all points on the right.

The first main Turkish fire-trench (E.10) had been as badly knocked about by shell-fire as the loop trench (A-O), which ran on its Turkish side. In places it was filled to the brim with debris of earth, and with dead, dying, and wounded Turks. So much was this the case that in at least one place, having removed the wounded, it was easier to leave the dead blocking the trench and to sap round it.

In the first trench, as in the loop trench, men were hard at work getting the dead over the parapet, and rebuilding with sandbag, pick, and shovel. There was no time for any niceties about burial, for there might be a counter-attack at any time. Others, of the 5th R.S.F., were sapping backwards from the old Turkish front line and forwards from the British in order to link them. Others were getting the wounded to one side, and the regimental stretcher-bearers of all units, as usual, were working steadily, and with no regard for themselves. Machine-guns and ammunition had to be brought forward over the open, there being no other way. The Turkish shell-fire went on all the time, dropping men here and there, and adding to the inevitable congestion and confusion.

About 9 a.m. some men of the 4th K.O.S.B. were driven out of the right end of the loop trench, and fell back to the old British front line, but their three remaining officers rallied them and led them back to the captured trenches.

The special party of 4th K.O.S.B. that had been detailed to occupy a communication trench covering the left of the line had disappeared in the general slaughter. From this direction the enemy were sniping and bombing the garrison of Borderers from the north portion of the Turkish front fire-trench (E.10). On the Borderers' immediate right the Turks were lodged in the tangle of trenches, and Brig.-Gen. Erskine found that the enemy were between the right of the Borderers and the left of the 4th R.S.F. The situation was a very dangerous one, as from this area also came a series of very determined counter-attacks with bombs. The cast-iron spherical bombs used by the Turks at this period were much superior to the converted jam tins of the British. Under cover of rifle and artillery-fire the Turks crept forward, and with their bombs gradually drove the Borderers to the left of the loop-trench (A-O), until there were only about forty men left in it under Lieut. R. Douglas, 5th K.O.S.B. He, however, held on, encouraging his men, fighting the Turks with what came handiest. He was mortally wounded, but they could not dislodge him. Lt.-Col. Millar, 5th K.O.S.B., who was in the forward line, returned over the bullet-swept zone and guided forward two companies of the 5th R.S.F. under Lt.-Col. Pollok-M'Call, practically the whole of the 155th Brigade's reserve. With these reinforcements the Turks

BATTLE OF THE 12-13TH JULY, 1915

were finally held and driven back, portions of the loop-trench being regained.

But the Turks were still as dangerous as ever in the tangle of trenches and portions of the loop-trench (A-O) between the right of the 5th R.S.F. and the Borderers and the left of the 4th R.S.F. All the time they were threatening to break into the British line.

At about this time, 10.30 a.m., a message came from the French saying that they were not in touch with the British right. His own reserves were used up, and accordingly Brig.-Gen. Erskine had to ask for reinforcements from the divisional reserves, the remains of the 156th Brigade. The two 4th Royal Scots' companies were sent up, and ordered to ensure connection with the French on the right. Fortunately, they were not needed, as the 4th R.S.F. " had been in touch with the French on their right from the beginning of the advance" (155th Brigade Operation Report). Lt.-Col. Peebles managed to squeeze in a platoon of his men, but the remainder had to be accommodated in the trenches behind.

The French, advancing with the British, had forced their way along the western edge of Kereves Dere, and their mistake was probably due to one of their company commanders pushing ahead, so that he had formed a small narrow salient of his own. This is borne out by a message sent by Captain H. R. Young, 4th R.S.F. at 4 p.m. The French had not experienced the same opposition here, as their losses showed. The original, erroneous message reached Sir Ian Hamilton, but, unfortunately, the correcting report seems never to have done so.

About mid-day Brig.-Gen. Erskine received information from the R.S.F. in the first Turkish trench that the loop-trench (A-O) was partly unoccupied, and was being enfiladed from the right by machine-gun fire. It was vital that the Turks should be driven out of the tangle of trenches in his right centre, and that the British should fully occupy and hold the loop-trench. The remaining company of the Royal Scots (7th) was sent up, suffering several casualties on the way from shell-fire. After working its way along the communication trenches it made a desperate charge, completely routed the Turks, and recaptured about 180 yards of the left of the loop-trench (A-O). The Turks got over the parapets and doubled towards a cross-trench on the left, where many were shot down. Lieut. D. Lyell (7th R.S.), the coy. commander, was killed whilst preparing to defend his newly-taken position.

On the right of the Royal Scots came a company of the Cameronians (7th). They rushed forward over the open with the bayonet, cleared two trenches of the enemy, barricaded saps leading to the Turkish lines, and got in touch with the Royal Scots in the loop-trench (A-O). This charge allowed the rest of the Cameronians to get into the front line by the communication trenches, and to extend the Cameronian left until it reached the right of the Royal Scots.

The 156th Brigade had now re-established the position in the loop-trench (A-O), so that the whole of it was held, and from then, until the evacuation on the 8-9th January, 1916, it became part of the British front line. They had also cleared the Turks out of the tangle of trenches, from which the latter were threatening the newly-captured trenches right and left. Everywhere men were at work building bombing-saps, barricading trenches, rebuilding parapets. The newly-captured trenches were filthy, and the smell of the dead was dreadful.

Soon after the capture of these trenches Major W. T. Bird (7th S.R.), O.C. the Cameronian Battalion, a most capable and reliable officer, was shot, being killed instantly. After arriving suddenly in a newly-captured trench it was impossible for an officer to look about in it and direct his men without exposing himself many times. Particularly was this so if the newly-captured trench had had many gaps blown in its sides by H.E., and was in such undulating ground as forms these slopes of Achi Baba. Chances had to be taken, and at any moment a Turkish sniper might have his rifle sighted down a communication trench or through a breach in a parapet, and send instant death to some officer thinking out the consolidation, arranging for ammunition, rations and water.

The Cameronians lost heavily again in officers, and the command devolved on Captain R. Blair. This officer was the only one left with the combined battalion for a while, until he got the use of one of the few surviving officers of the 4th K.O.S.B. It is impossible to avoid the mixing up of units once they are launched on to a battlefield, and particularly is this the case when the fighting takes place in a system of trenches. Confusion is inevitable, and officers have to take command of the men available no matter what their unit may be.

The remaining two companies of the Royal Scots (4th) came up and reinforced their portion of the firing-line. The Turks made successive counter-attacks down their old communication trenches, and kept up a galling fire from the next trench in front, but they were held off.

By this time, the whole of the reserves of the Division had been thrown into the line. The 157th Brigade had not been used, but was lying ready for its attack on the left or northern portion of this trench system. The 155th and 156th Brigades were now occupying the right or southern half of the first Turkish trench, and the loop-trench to the eastern or Turkish side of it, together with the bulk of the tangle of trenches, where they linked up with the French. The 5th R.S.F. were digging new communication trenches to link up the old British and Turkish front lines. The two R.S.F. companies that were working on this lost more than half their strength in killed and wounded, before they had finished their tasks.

Sir Ian Hamilton described the situation at this time as follows in his despatch dated 11th December, 1915: " During this fighting telephone wires from forward positions were cut by enemy's shell fire, and here and there in the elaborate network of trenches numbers of Turks were desperately resisting to the last. Thus, though the second line of captured trenches continued to be held as a whole, much confused fighting ensued ; there were retirements in parts of the line, reserves were rapidly being used up, and generally the situation was anxious and uncertain. But the best way of clearing it up seemed to be to deliver the second phase of the attack by the 157th Brigade just as it had originally been arranged."

The continual breaking of telephone wires called for deeds of heroism on the part of signallers and runners, far too numerous to be mentioned here. It also had much to do with some of the mistaken information on which the official despatches were based.

One of the chief difficulties throughout the battle was the evacuation of the wounded down the crowded and narrow communication trenches, and much suffering was unavoidably caused thereby. The stretcher-bearers laboured as long as they had strength. Surgeon-Major D. R. Taylor, 4th K.O.S.B., " worked unceasingly among the wounded during the attack, with shells bursting all around him, and he met death instantaneously while bandaging a wounded man at one of the dressing stations " (Lieut. Sorley Brown).

With regard to the scenes behind the lines, the writer will quote from Col. Edington, who went over at this time to see how the dressing stations were working. He found his " way much impeded by the long streams of wounded coming down the communication trench. Many of them were 'walkers'; but there was a considerable number of stretcher cases, and, although everyone was more or less plagued by flies, these simply swarmed on the faces of the poor fellows on the stretchers, and settled down voraciously on every blood-stained patch of clothing or bandages. And, as if the sights in themselves were not bad enough, the groans of the wounded combined to make the scene pretty much of a Hell. On reaching Brown House I found that our bearer parties had no cause to grumble for lack of work; everyone was at full pitch."

Lt.-Col. J. Young, 1st Lowland Field Ambulance, writes as follows about a scene at an advanced dressing station during the midst of this battle: " These men have more than the mere animal will to live. Through it all their hearts remain smiling and they make others smile too. They are carried on their rude bed of pain and exhaustion into a place that has kept company for many weary hours with the tortured body and with death itself, and the walls of earth and the roof of wood and sand become radiant with a new spirit. The heavy-hearted catch up the cheerful strain. Suffering would almost seem to be a joy. And no one knows exactly how it has all happened, least of all the heroic and simple spirit that itself lies prostrate and yet laughs in the face of death. Their greatness is all unconscious and is only great because it is so. The doctor's smile and word of cheer and encouragement seem puny and irrelevant before such a thing as this. The smile and encouragement have found a thing immeasurably greater than themselves, and they remain the better for the discovery."

CHAPTER VI

(12TH TO 18TH JULY, 1915)

THE BATTLE OF THE 12-13TH JULY, 1915 (*contd.*)

> O fickle Fortune!
> Why this cruel sporting?
> O why still perplex us, poor sons of a day?
> Nae mair your smiles can cheer me,
> Nae mair your frowns can fear me,
> For the Flowers of the Forest are a' wede away.
> ALISON RUTHERFORD (MRS. COCKBURN).

THE 157th Brigade (Col. W. H. Millar) was waiting in the lines of trenches for the launching of its attack. The formation and strength of the actual assaulting troops were roughly as shown in the diagram below:

1st Wave -	6th H.L.I., 100 R.E., 4	5th A. & S.H., 220 R.E., 8	7th H.L.I., 320 R.E., 8
2nd Wave -	6th H.L.I., 50 R.E., 10	5th A. & S.H., 200 R.E., 10	7th H.L.I., 160 R.E., 10
3rd Wave -	6th H.L.I., 50 R.E., 10	5th A. & S.H., 120 R.E., 10	7th H.L.I., 160 R.E., 10
4th Wave -	6th H.L.I., 150	5th A. & S.H., 150	7th H.L.I., 160
5th Wave -	6th H.L.I., 150		
Separate converging attack -	6th H.L.I., 150		

The R.E. personnel, who were to search for mines in the captured trenches and assist in the consolidation, were supplied by the 2/2nd Lowland Field Coy., R.E.

The 6th H.L.I. (Major Jas. Anderson) were to clear

BATTLE OF THE 12-13TH JULY, 1915

Achi Baba Nullah. The 5th A. & S.H. (Lt.-Col. D. Darroch), and the 7th H.L.I. (Lt.-Col. J. H. Galbraith) were to capture the northern half of the lines of trenches attacked by the 155th Brigade in the morning. They also were informed that they had to take three lines of trenches, whilst actually before them to the right or southeast of Achi Baba Nullah there only ran two. General Hunter-Weston had doubted on the previous day whether the "third Turkish trench" (E.12) was not too far advanced to be held, and had written through his chief-of-staff to Major-General Egerton to that effect. He considered that they might get advanced posts in the fifth line across Achi Baba Nullah (E.13a), and in the third Turkish trench (E.12), and that if so, these posts "should be held as long as possible while the other line is being consolidated. It may later be found possible even to connect them together and back, if the Turk gives way badly, as he may. In any case the General wishes a second line across this part, as shown in blue, to be made particularly secure and strongly held as well as the red line." (Extract from Letter from Gen. H. E. Street, 8th Corps, to Gen. Egerton, dated 11th July, 1915, timed 7.30 p.m.) The red line was on an accompanying sketch map and included the Horse Shoe Redoubt and curved back to the second main Turkish fire-trench (E.11). The blue line ran behind on the British side of this redoubt, following F.12 and the second main Turkish fire-trench (E.11). In accordance with this letter orders were issued that, if the third Turkish trench (E.12) was found to be difficult to hold, it was to be vacated.

The general arrangements and orders were similar to those issued to the 155th Brigade. Bombing parties were to be told off. There was a limited issue of Hailes' hand-grenades, missiles like a policeman's truncheon, but the converted jam tins were the bombs on which the grenadiers had principally to rely. Covering fire on the left was to be given by the 42nd Division. The 6th H.L.I. had a very awkward set of trenches from which to start their attack up Achi Baba Nullah, several lines running diagonally to the direction of assault. This also affected the left of the 5th A. & S.H. The 5th H.L.I. (Col. F. L. Morrison, V.D.) were in reserve, and were to garrison the old British firing line with one and a half companies immediately after the start of the attack.

The cannonade was really continuous all through the day, but at 3.50 p.m. commenced the intense bombardment of the Turkish trenches before the 157th Brigade, which was to be the preliminary to its attack.

" The destruction was enormous. Parapets and trenches were scattered in clouds of dust which soon became so dense as to blot out the entire landscape from our sight. The impression was that of a huge black cloud resting on the ground, a cloud incessantly rent and illumined by the red flashes of the bursting shells. Nothing, it seemed, could live under such a smashing fire. In actual fact, as we saw for ourselves after the position had been taken, the enemy's casualties from it were appalling. The morale of the survivors must have been terribly shaken. The marvel is that, after such an experience, they were able to put up so stout a resistance as they did at many points." (*History 5th H.L.I.*)

The Turkish artillery replied on the British trenches and many an Argyll and Light Infantryman fell before he crossed the parapet. Some were wounded, but charged with their comrades despite their wounds.

At 4.50 p.m. the Allied guns lengthened their ranges, putting a barrage behind the Turkish trenches, while a warship pounded the summit of Achi Baba with giant shells so that it smoked as if on fire.

Then, with a burst of cheering and to the skirling of the pipes, the 157th Brigade scrambled over the parapet, and went forward. Again the Turks turned on the assaulting troops every machine-gun and piece of artillery that they could bring to bear, and the din was terrific. Line after line pushed steadily forward through the bursting shrapnel, their triangles of tin twinkling in the sunlight, until each wave of men in turn disappeared into the inferno of dust and smoke that smothered the Turkish trenches.

It will be convenient to deal first with the assault of the right and centre.

The 7th H.L.I. tell of the gallant leading of their first wave by Captain W. H. Gandy, until he was killed. Piper K. M'Lellan (7th H.L.I.) played his pipes until they were blown out of his hands by a shell, after which he tended the wounded in the open. Lieut. J. Rowan of the 5th Argylls fell mortally wounded by a bursting shell, but, holding up his shattered frame as best he could, never ceased to cheer on his Highlanders until he died.

The first main Turkish fire-trench (E.10) was well garrisoned with brave men who had lost heavily already from the French bombardment. The attacking troops trampled over the remains of the wire-entanglement and bayoneted most of the garrison before the trench was captured. The assaulting troops now swept on through the drifting smoke to the next line. Between the two lines before the 7th H.L.I. lay a small detached fire-trench, and before the 5th Argylls lay an extra fire-trench caused by a fork: these were taken in their stride. As they approached the second main Turkish fire-trench (E.11), some Turks were seen to be filing out in an endeavour to get away, but the French seventy-fives caught them and it seemed as if none escaped. A French artillery forward observation officer (F.O.O.) had arrived in the first trench within five minutes of its capture. Again the entanglement was penetrated. Again most of the Turks who had stayed to fight were bayoneted, but a number were taken prisoners.

Sgt. A. MacLachlan, 5th Argylls, cleared one piece of trench by himself, meeting four Turks and killing them one after the other with the bayonet.

The leading waves of the 7th H.L.I. and 5th Argylls, now joined into one surge of men, rushed forward for the third Turkish trench, but found nothing except a few detached pieces of empty trench less than two feet in depth. Some went on to look further, and most of these never returned. Others got into the shallow holes and tried to deepen them and build up parapets. Sgt. A. MacLachlan, mentioned above, held an isolated piece of trench in front with his section until relieved thirty hours afterwards, beating off at least one heavy Turkish counter-attack during the time. It was difficult for the men to make any headway with their entrenching tools in the white gravelly clay. Shrapnel hailed everywhere, and heavy machine-gun and rifle-fire was coming in enfilade from the right. Many were shot down, especially on the right. In no place was there an excavation which was much more than two feet deep, and in most places the ground had been little more than scraped. The assaulting troops hung on for an hour, but the position was untenable, and, in accordance with the letter from the Corps Commander's chief-of-staff, the survivors on the right were withdrawn with little further loss.

During this operation 2nd Lieut. H. G. Russell, 7th H.L.I., returned under heavy fire on two occasions, bringing in two wounded men. Just as he reached the parapet of his own trench with the second, he fell mortally wounded, shot through the thigh with a rifle bullet.

The Argylls and 7th H.L.I. now set about the task of clearing the trenches of their heaped up dead, and of consolidation. Prisoners had to be collected and taken back out of the crowded trenches. Wounded had to be got to one side, until they could be moved. Both first (E.10) and second (E.11) trenches were in a crumbling and ruinous condition from the shell-fire, especially on the right, and it must be remembered that only the northern half of the second (E.11), which was now the firing line, was in British hands. Practically obliterated in places by shell-fire, this trench, which curved back gently into the Kereves Dere, where it was in Turkish hands, was a constant source of danger from Turkish snipers and counter-attacks.

Right along the whole front of the Division there were now going on fierce struggles between snipers and bombers, and these continued almost without intermission. The losses during the charge had been heavy, but those during the consolidation and holding of the trenches against the repeated counter-attacks were equally bad. Officers and senior N.C.O.'s had to be moving about directing their men, and their losses were very heavy. The history of trench warfare had shown, in both France and Gallipoli, that very often trenches could be captured which it was impossible to hold.

Hidden behind a bush in the path of the left of the 5th Argylls and the right of the 6th H.L.I., where they advanced together, was a Turkish machine-gun, which was causing casualties. 2nd Lieut. A. Nicol, 5th Argylls, saw it and ran towards it, firing his revolver at the crew as he ran, but was shot through the head and killed instantly. Immediately afterwards a number of kilted men, Argylls and 6th H.L.I., rushed on the gun's crew, bayoneted them, and captured the gun.

Lieut. W. Millar, 5th Argylls, strode forward leading the left of their first line, armed with a revolver and a spade, waving and cheering on the men. He found himself in the crescent-shaped trench on the south side of Achi Baba Nullah, afterwards known as the Horseshoe. With him were about sixteen men, and later, others joined him, until he had with him 2nd Lieut. J. Wilson, 5th Argylls, and about forty of the 6th H.L.I. and of his own unit. The trench was only partially dug, but they started at once to clear and deepen it, and to build up a parapet with what tools they had. The Turks attacked them with rifle-fire and bombing, but they replied with their rifles and learnt the trick of throwing back at the Turks their own bombs before the long fuses had burned down. Practically all of them had had nothing to do with these missiles before, and, even for experts, this was a dangerous game, because no one knew how far a fuse had burned, when he picked up the bomb. Wilson, a boy of eighteen, was standing on the parapet directing the rifle-fire at one end of the crescent, when he fell shot through the thigh. As he lay wounded, he continued to encourage the men until he was too weak to do any more. At one time the men had been driven back by the enemy bombs to where this lad was lying, but Pte. Coyle, an Argyll, jumped on to the parapet and shot the Turkish bombers down. Coyle was one who set an example in throwing back at the Turks their own bombs. Lieut. Millar held this trench with his party, against the Turks until relieved by men of the Royal Naval Division thirty hours afterwards. During that period this resolute officer repulsed one large organized counter-attack, besides lesser ones, losing a number of his men killed and wounded.

With great dash and determination the 6th H.L.I. charged up Achi Baba Nullah. Blocked by line after line of heavily wired trenches, swept by cross-fire from machine-guns, and flanked by two stronger works, it would have been a perfect death-trap and impregnable to infantry had it not been for the terrible efficiency of the French seventy-fives. Some portions of the enemy trenches had been obliterated by the H.E. One trench (E.12), the second on the left of the nullah, had become " merely an irregular series of shell craters " (*History 5th H.L.I.*). But, even so, there were many fanatical and stout-hearted Turks left, ready to defend their trenches to the last. Despite severe losses from the enemy shrapnel and machine-gun fire, one trench after another was taken, until Lieut. C. S. P. Black with his men took the last Turkish trench on the left or northern side of the watercourse, and Lieut. M. Wyllie with some more men took the last on the right. Wyllie was isolated for a while from the other trenches captured, but held on. Lieut. Black was wounded in the head, but he, with Pte. E. M'Queen, bombed the Turks back with their own bombs, and held them at bay until a barricade had been built behind them across the captured trench, making it secure.

" In the left centre Capt. J. F. Daly was severely wounded early in the advance, but though in danger of bleeding to death, contrived to struggle forward, directing his party until he lost consciousness, when his place was taken by Lieut. Davidson, R.E., who accompanied the wave in charge of a party of sappers." (Col. J. Anderson.)

Owing to losses in officers, and the confusing lines of earthworks, a portion of trench was not taken in the main assault. The 6th H.L.I. threw their own reserve in under Captain C. G. Daly, and made the trench secure.

BATTLE OF THE 12-13TH JULY, 1915

For some hours fighting went on round the furthest objectives, the Turks resisting strongly and counter-attacking frequently.

In different places behind the front of the 157th Brigade working parties were now busy with pick and shovel linking up the old British line and the newly captured systems. They were shelled the whole time, and most of these working parties lost nearly half their strength, but that did not stay them. The work was vital. Ammunition, rations, and especially the rare and precious water had to be carried to the front line. There were countless deeds of heroism on that day by men carrying messages and these necessities across a bullet-swept open, where it seemed that nothing could live. The communication trenches had to be dug forward, and officers and N.C.O.'s had to look about to ensure that the new trenches were so planned that they would take advantage of the lie of the land and not be enfiladed by the Turks. 2nd Lieut. Cowan, 6th H.L.I., was one who fell whilst carrying out this, one of the least exciting and therefore most trying duties of that day.

The troops that stormed a position on Gallipoli had to clear and consolidate the trenches, and hold the ground themselves. There were no reserves available to follow them up for this purpose. The officers and N.C.O.'s who were left, speedily organized this work, and everyone laboured in the heat, " with the body half-drained by perspiration, the throat clogged up with dry powdery dust, and the parched tongue clinging to the roof of the mouth " (Major C. S. Black). What water they had left in their bottles was tepid with the heat, but a draught of it was without price. The water supply was one of the worst problems, and men who tried to carry it forward in biscuit-tins and water-bottles frequently lost their way in the strange and complicated trenches, so that some parties in different units received none at all.

The clearing of the captured lines was a terrible task. " The trenches themselves were littered with the Turkish victims of our shell fire, in places piled on top of one another to the depth of several feet. In one communication trench that had to be used for days until another could be cut, it was necessary to crawl on hands and knees for many yards over the reeking bodies in order to keep within the shelter of the parapet." (Major C. S. Black.) In order to pass one another to get on with their work many had to expose themselves, and in this manner Turkish snipers got many targets.

At about 5.30 p.m. on that evening the 5th Argylls suffered a great loss. Lt.-Col. Duncan Darroch was watching the consolidation, when a sniper shot him, wounding him very severely near the shoulder.[1] A strong, fearless, outspoken leader of men, he thought the world of his battalion and his battalion thought the world of him and would have followed him anywhere. The command devolved upon Major R. A. Clapperton-Stewart.

The searching for the wounded in the thick scrub started immediately after the assault, and went on throughout the night. The company of Sgt. G. Harper (6th H.L.I.) had lost all its officers and its C.S.M., but he led them on to their objective. He had seen two officers lying severely wounded in Achi Baba Nullah, and, having handed over his men to an officer, asked and received permission to return to their help. "Although severely bruised by earth thrown up by a shell and suffering great pain, he went down Achi Baba Nullah, through a very inferno of artillery and machine-gun fire, and helped Lieut. Mavor to the shelter of a trench, killing or scattering a party of Turks who were firing at this officer at close range. Lieut. Laird had meantime been assisted into cover. Sgt. Harper then collected a number of leaderless men and led them up to the company's objective, where he continued to supervise consolidation, remaining on duty for a number of days and declining to receive any personal attention." (Col. J. Anderson.)

All the units that had taken part in the assault had every available man in the line or at work somewhere, and casualties never ceased to thin their ranks. Numerous calls

---

[1] Lt.-Col. D. Darroch never recovered from this wound, although he lingered on for nearly eight years until he died from its effects.

were now made on the 5th H.L.I. in brigade reserve for reinforcements.

The capture and holding of the trenches on the left or northern side of Achi Baba Nullah had been essential in order to protect from counter-attacks the trench system on the right or southern side. Branching off from the last trench captured on the northern side (F.12a) was another (F.13), which ran back into the enemy's lines in a long wide curve to the north-east and north. Just after it left the captured trench it ran generally parallel to the latter for about eighty yards. It was essential that this part should be cleared of the enemy. Both trenches at this place were roughly at right angles to the British front line as it ran south-east from the Vineyard. A company of the 5th H.L.I. were in close support to the 6th H.L.I. in a small work, which was in this line at the end nearest Achi Baba Nullah.

About 6 p.m. Major J. Anderson ordered this company to take the lower portion of this other trench (F.13). They charged in two lines, Major A. M. Downie, 5th H.L.I., leading the first. As they were traversing the area, where the two trenches joined, and where the captured one was a shapeless ruin, he fell mortally wounded in the head. The rest carried on, and drove the Turks about seventy or eighty yards up the trench beyond the junction. "Here the Turks, possibly reinforced, made a determined stand behind a traverse or interior work of some kind and a comparative deadlock ensued, both sides maintaining a heavy fire at a distance of less than thirty yards, but neither being able to gain any ground" (*History 5th H.L.I.*).

Meanwhile, through some mistake, a verbal message had been passed back asking for machine-guns. The day was drawing to its close at the time. Two machine-guns of the 6th H.L.I. were being pushed forward to assist in covering the consolidation. Now, it is extremely difficult for a party moving forward in newly-captured and, to them, unknown trenches to recognise that they are getting into a place of danger, and often a few yards one way or the other will make all the difference. So it was in this case.

The two machine-guns duly arrived in the trench, at the traverse behind which were bombing Turks. They had only been there a very short while when the Turks made a determined counter-attack under cover of a perfect hail of bombs. 2nd Lieut. J. W. Malcolm (5th H.L.I.), who was with the most advanced men, handling and steadying them with great coolness and courage, was killed. As he fell, a bomb burst on one of the machine-guns, disabling it. Men fell killed and wounded, and the rest, deprived of their leader and without bombs, were driven back about twenty yards before they could carry back the guns and the guns were lost.

For a time the situation was critical, their bombs giving the Turks a great advantage, but Pte. T. Melrose (5th H.L.I.) and Corpl. A. R. Kelly (5th H.L.I.) learnt on the spot the dangerous game of throwing back the Turkish bombs. Several H.L.I. were killed and wounded in this way, but the survivors persisted, and the Turkish advance was stopped.

In the meantime Captain G. Morton, who was now in command of this company of the 5th H.L.I., heard of the loss of the guns and decided to make an effort to recover them. He collected six or eight volunteers, " climbed out of the trench and worked his way along the open beside it, making a slight detour, apparently with the intention of rushing the guns from the flank. Dusk was now turning into darkness, and those who were in the trench were unable to see what actually happened. The little party evidently came under heavy fire before they were in a position to make the rush. One or two got back unhurt; one (Private Cleugh) mortally wounded, staggered into the trench just in front of the barricade which was being erected, and was brought in only to die; of Captain Morton and the others nothing more was seen." (*History 5th H.L.I.*)

The whole ground was subsequently regained and thoroughly searched that night, and later by day, but neither gun was found. The Turks had made sure of their booty.

At the same time as the attack of the 157th Brigade, the

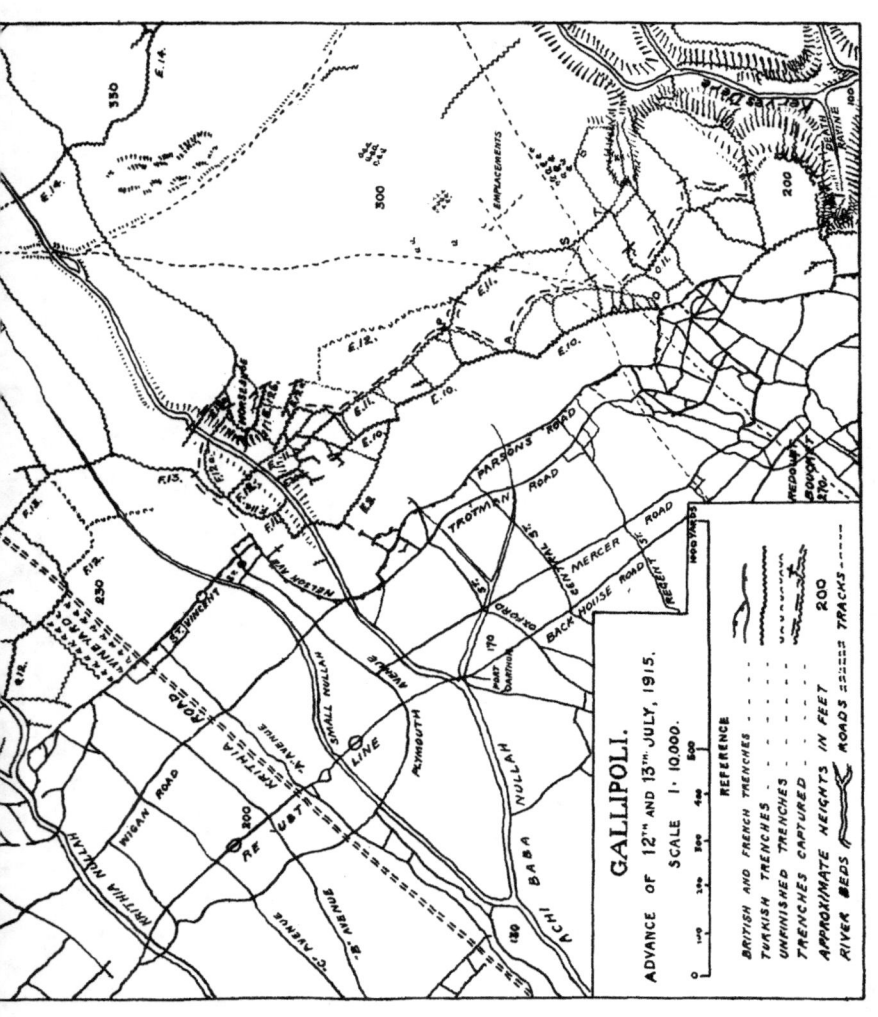

BATTLE OF THE 12-13TH JULY, 1915

4th R.S.F., on the extreme right, had made an attack and captured a further trench immediately to their front.

The general position now was that the 157th Brigade had made a gap (about 650 yards in width) in the principal system of Turkish trenches, whilst the 155th Brigade and the French further to the right had driven the Turks back on to their last important fire-trench in this section to the west of Kereves Dere. Between this trench and the summit of Achi Baba there lay at the time only some disconnected earthworks and the single long trench already spoken of as spanning the peninsula. The Turks had suffered heavy losses, and by nightfall they had been so "thoroughly beaten that officers present were convinced that if troops had been available, in support, to 'leapfrog' through our Brigade (157th), a large further advance could have been made" (Col. J. Anderson). The troops were not available, the artillery ammunition was not available, and accordingly, the only course left was to make sure of holding the ground which had been captured.

"The policy of attack on a limited front and to a limited depth was probably dictated to the Commander-in-Chief by the number of troops and guns available, and these again depended on the conditions at home and on the Western Front, as well as on considerations of space on the Peninsula and of transport, but there can be little doubt that attacks on a limited front tended to be much more costly to the attackers, in that they allowed the concentration of the fire of a large proportion of enemy guns on the area attacked. Further, attacks on a limited frontage simplified, for the Turkish commander, the problem of the handling of his reserves (always the most difficult problem for the defenders), and facilitated the delivery of counter-attacks, not merely by reason of the early movement of reserves towards the threatened point, but also of the short distance from each other of flanks that were not being attacked and were therefore ready points for support to counter-attacks." (Col. J. Anderson.)

So extreme was the shortage of ammunition that night for the British artillery that "all but a limited number of rounds were withdrawn from most batteries and were placed in horsed ammunition wagons, which perambulated from one side of the British position to the other according to where it seemed most likely the next Turkish attack would take place " (Gen. Simpson-Baikie).

The right of the 7th H.L.I. in the captured portion of the second main trench (E.11) got into touch down a Turkish communication trench with the left of the 155th Brigade holding the loop-trench (A-O), and thus linked up there the new British front line.

Every man available was put on the urgent work of linking up the old British front line with the captured trenches before dawn, after which time communication over the open would probably be impossible. Men who had formed the ten per cent. nucleus were brought up for this work, and for the carrying up of rations and water. A 4th K.O.S.B. officer tells how his men had to carry on the tasks of two working parties that had been annihilated by enemy shrapnel. Neither of the saps that they were to work on had proceeded more than thirty or forty yards, and at no place was either deeper than a couple of feet. The correct lines were marked out and the digging was " carried on with feverish haste."

" Flares of all kinds were lighting the whole place every few minutes, and work had to proceed with the greatest caution, as a machine gun was at once turned on our party. As each flare went up every man ' clapped ' and, owing to the fact that the ground was absolutely strewn with corpses, we were not spotted."

As the night went by " every man was becoming absolutely exhausted with the incessant digging, and whenever a man's spell of picking or shovelling was over he was practically asleep before he sat down. This necessitated a constant awakening. On being awakened each man sprang up and bravely buckled to. Every credit is due to these men for the work done that night, as no man had tasted food since the previous day at dinner." They completed their tasks before dawn.

Captain W. Forrest tells how a party of 4th K.O.S.B.

started out before 7 p.m. to carry tin biscuit-boxes full of water, bully-beef and jam from a dump to the newly-captured trenches two miles forward. "Every few minutes there was a halt to allow wounded, walking or on stretchers, to pass" along the unavoidably narrow communication trenches. Carrying parties of other units were frequently met. By one in the morning they had reached the old front line, whence they had literally to force their way up "a zigzag sap not more than two feet wide, varying in depth from two to five feet. In this narrow sap a fatigue party of about forty men were working, and the difficulty experienced in getting a party loaded up with food and water along such a trench can be readily imagined. Practically the whole time machine-gun and rifle-fire was being kept up by the Turks, making it quite an exciting job. The sap itself was about 200 yards long, at the end of which it was found there were still some forty yards of open ground to cross. This was covered at a smart jog-trot, and all dropped safely into what had been a Turkish trench the night before. The hour was 3 a.m. . . . The officer of the party was at once ordered to take charge of a part of the firing line which was very short of officers, while the remainder of the party was split up, and each tried to find the Battalion. Alas ! . . . only here and there could an occasional 4th K.O.S.B. man be found, and at no place were there more than two together. All units of the 155th Brigade were fearfully mixed up. The only thing that could be done was to issue the food and water for the benefit of all and sundry, and sorely were the food and water, especially the latter, needed. One thing will never be forgotten by the writer. If word came along for 'water for the wounded,' a water-bottle would pass through a hundred hands, and be the man ever so thirsty not a sign of hesitation could be seen in passing the water along."

The 6th H.L.I. had obtained the assistance of two companies of the Plymouth Battalion, R.N.D., before midnight, and had returned the company lent to them by the 5th H.L.I. By means of these two R.N.D. companies they managed gradually to withdraw their own men from the newly captured trenches, and to re-organize them in the old British front line during the night, and on the following morning.

Throughout the night the sudden crackle of heavy rifle-fire, punctuated by the detonations of bombs, broke out as the Turks tried in vain to recover some of the lost ground. These counter-attacks were levelled principally against the right of the Division's front, where the Turks could attack from the southern half of their second main fire-trench (E.11) up their old communication trenches, and also against the Horseshoe which was assailed for three hours continuously. Working parties that were near had to down tools, pick up their rifles, and help to man the parapets. 2nd Lieut. R. E. May, 5th H.L.I., fell gallantly in one of these fights on the front of the 155th Brigade. Men had to fight wherever they found themselves in the darkness. The artillery expended some of their precious store of shells, and every attack was beaten off; but it all meant that there was no rest for troops who had been fighting and working hard since dawn, on little or no food. Many were in a fainting condition through exhaustion and hunger, some actually did fall unconscious and slept where they fell. The general conditions, the sights, the smells, and the sounds in the captured trenches can be imagined from what has been written already about this and the battle of the 28th June.

Dawn broke slowly on the 13th, for it was a hazy morning. Every man was standing-to in his place.

Suddenly, in front of the 155th Brigade about 100 Turks appeared from behind a small ridge charging down on the British front, with loud cries of " Allah ! Allah ! " Rifles and machine-guns opened fire on them, and they simply disappeared. Not a man of them got back.

There was a brief lull, and then bayonets could be seen moving along the Turkish trench in front. They were refilling it for another assault. Once again they advanced, but this time in a most halting and hesitating fashion. They moved forward about ten yards and stopped, each man

BATTLE OF THE 12-13TH JULY, 1915

holding one of his hands in front of his eyes, apparently to shut out from his sight what he knew lay before him. The Borderers and Fusiliers thought that they were going to give themselves up as prisoners, and the message was passed along :—" Don't fire ; they are going to surrender." They moved forward a few more halting, hesitating steps. "Apparently this exasperated one of their officers, as he was seen to take his rifle and club a man behind, which one can only imagine roused another man to make some remark, as the officer in question immediately turned round and shot him " (Captain W. T. Forrest).

The Turks at once broke and stampeded, and the watching troops turned on them every machine-gun and rifle which would bear. Only very few can have escaped.

The writer would like to record one out of the many feats of individual gallantry. Sergeant A. Y. Paton, 6th H.L.I., had early in the assault on the 12th " received a shrapnel ball in his shoulder but continued the advance with his company and did not report his wound. In the evening this was discovered accidentally by an officer, but Sgt. Paton expressed himself as being able to carry on and anxious to do so. At daybreak on 13th moans were heard and cries for help from a wounded man in the open forty or fifty yards away from the trench occupied by a party of 'A' Company. Volunteers to bring him in were called for, and Sgt. Paton and a number of privates immediately offered themselves. Sgt. Paton and four privates were chosen and brought in the wounded man (who was found to be an officer of the 5th A. & S.H.), being fired on by Turkish snipers all the time they were out. Sgt. Paton reported that he had seen the body of Lieut. W. A. Broadfoot lying out and the whole party offered to go out again and bring it in, which they did under a brisk fire, for the Turk was now thoroughly alert." (Col. J. Anderson.)

Lt.-Col. J. Young, 1/3rd Lowland Field Ambulance, writes of how he "saw an A. and S. officer with a shattered thigh whose chief concern, as he lay stretched on the table, was that his men would be well supplied with water, as the day was hot." This must have been Lieut.

M. Fleming, 5th Argylls, who had been brought in by Sgt. Paton, 6th H.L.I.

At dawn the 157th Brigade had been assailed by severe sniping, and the Turkish marksmen were particularly active where the uncaptured portion of the second main trench (E.11) ran back into their lines. This gave rise to an incident chiefly remarkable because of the rapid manner in which a very dangerous situation was got in hand, and for the extremely erroneous account of it which appeared in the official despatches, giving rise in its turn to innumerable further mistakes.

The right of the captured portion of this trench was in a very bad condition, in places being partially filled in. It was this right portion, manned by 7th H.L.I., which was so exposed to the Turkish riflemen, working from further south in the same trench.

About 4.30 a.m. this enfilade sniping of the 7th H.L.I. was severe, and ten minutes later Turks crept up the trench and commenced bombing the faint and weary men. It must be remembered that the Turks had plenty of reserves of fresh men hidden safely in Kereves Dere. The 7th H.L.I. tried to draw in their exposed right flank in order to get to a more sheltered position, and a verbal order was passed along the crowded trench for that purpose. In peace time, and when men are fresh and thoroughly awake, the simplest messages passed in this manner will become so changed as to be unrecognizable. It only requires one man to make a mistake, or to condense or to emphasize the message wrongly, and he will totally change its aspect. That is evidently what happened in this case, and the message became an order to retire. In a few minutes, before the surviving officers and N.C.O.'s could stop them and see what it was all about, the men from the front and support lines of the 7th H.L.I. were falling back, some along the communication trenches and some across the open. Drawn in with them, came men from the support and reserve lines of the 5th Argylls in the centre, which unit was holding three lines. The front line of the Argylls, however, never moved, and Captain Jas. Agnew

BATTLE OF THE 12-13TH JULY, 1915

with about thirty-five men stood firm in the reserve line. The left of the 157th Brigade's front, held by the 6th H.L.I., also did not move. Captain A. H. M'Neil, 5th K.O.S.B., by his presence of mind averted the danger from the left of the 155th Brigade, and from the rest of the Division.

Lt.-Col. J. B. Pollok-M'Call, 5th R.S.F., saw what happened from the left of the 155th Brigade, and has stated that "There was no sign of panic among the men I saw. They came back at a jog-trot as if they were carrying out a retiral on a field-day."

Lt.-Col. J. H. Galbraith, 7th H.L.I., was at his headquarters in Trotman Road talking with his adjutant, Captain G. P. Linton, and Major Clark, R.M.L.I., when he saw the men coming back. Major R. A. Clapperton-Stewart, 5th Argylls, saw it at the same moment from his headquarters. All of them, together with officers, N.C.O.'s, and men who were about, set to work at once to rally the others. This they did with little difficulty. As there always are in such cases, there were a few nerve-shattered men who were stopped with difficulty, but the majority halted the moment they were told to do so. Lt.-Col. Galbraith and Major Clapperton-Stewart were worthily seconded by Major E. Armstrong of the 157th Brigade Staff, their adjutants, Captains Linton, 7th H.L.I., and Hewison, 5th Argylls, Major T. L. Jowitt, 5th H.L.I., and Major Clark, R.M.L.I.[1] (Captain Hewison had been wounded on the previous day, but had stayed on duty.) The first parties were led back immediately, reaching the evacuated trenches within five minutes of the retirement. The commanding officers led the men back over the top under a brisk machine-gun fire from the enemy, who apparently had not realized at first that the men moving back were British troops, Major Clapperton-Stewart being wounded but carrying on, and within less than thirty minutes practically all of the men had returned to the evacuated trenches.

[1] Major Clark received a D.S.O. for his services on the strength of a recommendation by Lt.-Col. J. H. Galbraith. He was killed later in the war.

In the meantime Captain John MacDonald, 5th H.L.I., whose company was garrisoning the old British front line, saw that there had been some mistake. He tried to get instructions over the telephone, but there was delay, so he took his men forward, re-occupying the right section of these trenches, apparently about the time that the first parties of rallied men re-occupied the remainder. At the same time six privates of the 7th Royal Scots, the crew of a machine-gun, heard the firing, and without waiting for orders went off with their weapon to the front line to support the 7th H.L.I. It is sad to relate that the gallant Captain MacDonald was killed later in the day.

Touch was obtained on both sides, the defence was set in order, and the trenches were cleared of the wounded. The re-organization of personnel within the cramped spaces of a trench system always takes a considerable time, but by 7 a.m. everything was being carried on as it had been on the previous evening, and the situation was the same.

Information about the re-occupation of these trenches never seems to have reached the Corps Commander, and certainly never reached Sir Ian Hamilton for he ignored it entirely in his despatch of 11th December, 1915.

The day passed without further serious counter-attacks by the Turks, and the Lowland Division were left in possession of all the trenches they had captured. The sniping never ceased, and amongst those who fell was Major T. L. Jowitt, 5th H.L.I., mortally wounded whilst in a piece of detached trench in Achi Baba Nullah, a short distance in front of the Horseshoe.

As the sun mounted higher, the men in those parts of the line that had missed receiving supplies of food and water suffered very much, and the Cameronians, who were among the unfortunate, had men fainting " right and left " with thirst and the heat. A large biscuit-tin full of water, which arrived in the evening, and which was " dished out at a tablespoonful per man " (Capt. Blair) did something to relieve the situation.

The consolidation was pushed on during the day, and

BATTLE OF THE 12–13TH JULY, 1915

two companies of the Nelson Batt., R.N.D., were sent up to join the two companies of the Plymouth Batt., R.N.D., in helping the 6th H.L.I. with the defence and consolidation of Achi Baba Nullah.

At 3 p.m. instructions were received by Gen. Erskine that the Royal Naval Division would attack the right or uncaptured portion of the second main fire-trench (E.11), that is the portion running into Kereves Dere (P-S-T.). The attack was to be made at 4.15 p.m. from Trotman Road, a trench forty to fifty yards behind the old British front line (Parsons Road), and special orders were given for the 155th and 156th Brigades to facilitate the passage of the R.N.D. men over their lines as much as possible. It was to be an attack to secure the remaining Turkish trenches in this section to the west of Kereves Dere. The French were to co-operate by pushing further along the edge of that wide gorge. Whether an attack from the 157th Brigade's front was also intended, because of ignorance of the re-occupation of the trenches temporarily vacated in the morning, is not known; but this last attack was the only one which took place.

One, at least, of the battalion commanders of the R.N.D. did not get his orders until about an hour before the attack, and in that period he had to collect his men who were on various jobs, pass his instructions to his officers, and get his unit into the jumping-off place. The blame for the disastrous blunder which followed does not lie with these officers of the R.N.D. They formed up in the trench Trotman Road, behind the 157th Brigade, and not behind the 155th Brigade. " No attack was made over the trenches of the 155th Brigade towards P-S-T " (155th Brigade's Operation Report). They climbed the parapets of this trench over four hundred yards in rear of the 157th Brigade's front, and advanced over the open, losing heavily from the enemy fire as they did so. They jumped down into trenches filled with surprised men of the Lowland Division, who wondered why they had not walked up the communication trenches. Some reached the Horseshoe where Lieut. Millar, astonished at their method of approach, asked them " What the —— do you want ? " Many of them ran on further looking for trenches held by Turks to attack. A few found the holes which had given rise to the mythical " third Turkish trench " (E.12), and reinforced the Scottish troops who were still holding those on the left. Others went on and never returned. The net result of this assault was to reinforce the existing front line, and so make it possible to hold a slightly improved one. This was done at great cost of killed and wounded to the R.N.D., and could have been done as well and probably with hardly any loss at all if they had advanced up the communication trenches.

Apparently Sir Ian Hamilton did not know the truth about these matters when he wrote his despatch of 11th December, 1915. Referring to the afternoon attack of the 12th, and the later events, he stated that " the 157th Brigade rushed forward under heavy machine-gun and rifle-fire, and splendidly carried the whole of the enemy trenches allotted to their objective. Here, then, our line had advanced some 400 yards, while the 155th Brigade and the 2nd French Division had advanced between 200 and 300 yards. At 6 p.m. the 52nd Division was ordered to make the line good ; it seemed to be fairly in our grasp.

" All night long, determined counter-attacks, one after another, were repulsed by the French and the 155th Brigade, but about 7.30 a.m. the right of the 157th Brigade gave way before a party of bombers, and our grip upon the enemy began to weaken.

" I therefore decided that three battalions of the Royal Naval Division should reinforce a fresh attack to be made that afternoon, 13th July, on such portions of our original objectives as remained in the enemy's hands. This second attack was a success. The 1st French Division pushed their right down to the mouth of the Kereves Dere ; the 2nd French Division attacked the trenches they had failed to take on the preceding day ; the Nelson Battalion, on the left of the Royal Naval Division attack, valiantly advanced and made good, well supported by the artillery of the French. The Portsmouth Battalion, pressing on too far, fell into precisely the same error at precisely the same spot

BATTLE OF THE 12-13TH JULY, 1915

as did the 4th King's Own Scottish Borderers on the 12th, an over-impetuosity which cost them heavy losses.

"The 1/5th Royal Scots Fusiliers, commanded by Lieut.-Colonel J. B. Pollok-McCall; the 1/7th Royal Scots, commanded by Lieut.-Colonel W. C. Peebles; the 1/5th King's Own Scottish Borderers, commanded by Lieut.-Colonel W. J. Millar, and the 1/6th Highland Light Infantry, commanded by Major J. Anderson, are mentioned as having specially distinguished themselves in this engagement.

"Generally, the upshot of the attack was this. On our right and on the French left two lines had been captured, but in neither case was the third, or last, line of the system in their hands. Elsewhere a fine feat of arms had been accomplished, and a solid and enduring advance had been achieved, giving us far the best sited line for defence with much the best field for machine-gun and rifle-fire we had hitherto obtained upon the peninsula.

"A machine-gun and 200 prisoners were captured by the French; the British took a machine-gun and 329 prisoners. The casualties in the French Corps were not heavy, though it is with sorrow that I have to report the mortal wound of General Masnou, commanding the 1st Division. Our own casualties were a little over 3000; those of the enemy about 5000."

With regard to the passages quoted above it will be noted that:

(1) There is no mention that the "third Turkish trench" before the 157th Brigade was not found to be in existence, a few short and shallow pieces excepted; nor that, even if it had been a trench, Gen. Hunter-Weston had doubted on the 11th July whether it was possible to hold it.

(2) The time given for the temporary retiral is wrong by nearly three hours.

(3) There is no mention of the immediate action of the rallied parties of 5th A. & S.H. and 7th H.L.I., and of the detachments of 5th H.L.I. and 7th R.S., despite such definite statements in operation reports as the following in that of Lt.-Col. J. H. Galbraith, 7th H.L.I.: "By 0700

the situation was the same as on the previous evening "; and the following in that of Major R. A. Clapperton-Stewart, 5th A. & S.H. : " Early in morning of 13th inst. the right of the Brigade withdrew and our Support and Reserve retired with them. These were reassembled and reoccupied the position. Our advanced line did not move with Supports and Reserves."

(4) The afternoon attack of the R.N.D. on the 13th is referred to as " a success " whilst it was a disaster ; several writers have understood that it was for the purpose of recapturing trenches lost by the 52nd Division in the morning, there being nothing to show that they were reoccupied at once : this false statement has been the one most often republished in various works.

(5) A battalion of the R.N.D. is described as impetuously pressing too far, and making " the same error at precisely the same spot as did the 4th King's Own Scottish Borderers " ; whilst they made no attack from the front of the 155th Brigade on the 13th—that two different bodies of men under cool and efficient officers were thought to have made " the same error at precisely the same spot " does not seem to have aroused any question.

(6) The question of the " third Turkish trench," in the search for which the 4th K.O.S.B. sacrificed themselves, has been dealt with in the previous chapter : the mistake lay in describing two long fire-trenches and a complicated system of greater and lesser communication trenches, as if they were three distinctly marked lines.

Whether the good work done on the left by the Royal Naval Division, in helping the 6th H.L.I. to man and consolidate the trenches in Achi Baba Nullah, was confused by some ambiguity of description with the supposed results of this attack is a matter for conjecture ; but the assumption that they recaptured trenches " lost " by the 52nd Division is wrong. Incidents similar to that on the morning of the 13th July have occurred numberless times during the Great War, but this one has become unduly prominent because of the incorrect account of it in the official despatches.

It is better that a work such as this should avoid the discussion and correction of the errors of others, and be a simple record of fact. However, the above mis-statements in the official despatches cannot be passed over, because hitherto they have been taken as authoritative and their mistakes have been multiplied by other writers in attempts to interpret them. One historian attributes the non-capture of the "third Turkish trench" by the 155th Brigade to their having lost touch with the French on their right, whilst in fact the 4th R.S.F. were in touch with them throughout the action. This is one example of many.

The night of the 13-14th was quiet, beyond the usual firing.

After their disastrous attack on the 13th the men of the Royal Naval Division were very much mixed up with the men of the 52nd Division, and the sorting of the units had to be effected. About midnight on the 13-14th the Royal Naval Division relieved the 5th Argylls in the front line around the Horseshoe, which they had held continuously for over thirty hours. On the morning of the 14th, before 6 a.m., the Royal Naval Division relieved the 155th and 156th Brigades, and after a day of fatigues burying dead in the front line, these two Brigades were moved on the 15th to the "Rest Camp." In the afternoon of the 15th the 5th H.L.I. relieved the 6th H.L.I. on the west side of Achi Baba Nullah, and the 6th H.L.I. and 5th A. & S.H. occupied the old front line in Parsons Road and Trotman Road. The 7th H.L.I. returned to the "Rest Camp" at 7 p.m. on the 15th. Two days afterwards they relieved the 6th H.L.I., who went back to the Torres Lines in the "Rest Camp." On the 18th the 5th and 7th H.L.I. and the 5th A. & S.H. collected in the same area. It will be noted that the 52nd Division were responsible for and held the whole of the front line until about midnight on the 13-14th, and that they held parts of it until the 18th.

The victory was a great blow to the Turkish morale, because it again proved to the Turks themselves that, man for man, the British troops on Gallipoli were better than they, despite their superior position and bombs.

Let us now count the cost. Again there were large numbers of missing, and the proximity of the opposing lines prevented a proper search of the scrub-covered battlefield. Lives were lost by men trying to recover bodies, so that these attempts had to be stopped. Most of the wounded of the 4th K.O.S.B. were those hit early in the charge, and accordingly close to the captured trenches. Most of their dead lay well behind the new lines which the Turks speedily dug to cover up the gap in their front. A number of the men originally reported as missing turned up as wounded that had been evacuated by the French ambulances. These have been allowed for in the figures, which are not known to be exact in the case of a few units, but have no error of importance. The cost to the Lowlands of Scotland was as follows

155TH BRIGADE.

Unit.	Killed, Missing and Dead, Died of Wounds.		Wounded.		Missing and Prisoners.		Total.	
	Offrs.	O.R.	Offrs.	O.R.	Offrs.	O.R.	Offrs.	O.R.
4th R.S.F.	6	118	6	148	—	—	12	266
5th do.	6	69	1	139	—	—	7	208
4th K.O.S.B.	12	319	6	203	—	13[1]	18	535
5th do.	6	76	5	183	—	—	11	259
Totals	30	582	18	673	—	13	48	1268

156TH BRIGADE.

Unit.	Killed, Missing and Dead, Died of Wounds.		Wounded.		Missing and Prisoners.		Total.	
	Offrs.	O.R.	Offrs.	O.R.	Offrs.	O.R.	Offrs.	O.R.
4th Royal Scots	—	27	—	47	—	—	—	74
7th do.	1	22	1	29	—	—	2	51
7th Cameronians	} 1	43	2	53	—	—	3	96
8th do.								
Totals	2	92	3	129	—	—	5	221

[1] Of these, 12 were wounded when captured, 3 died in captivity, and 1 immediately after his release.

BATTLE OF THE 12-13TH JULY, 1915

157TH BRIGADE.

Unit.				Killed, Missing and Dead, Died of Wounds.		Wounded.		Missing and Prisoners.		Total.	
				Offrs.	O.R.	Offrs.	O.R.	Offrs.	O.R.	Offrs.	O.R.
5th H.L.I.	-	-	-	6	32	1	70	—	—	7	102
6th do.	-	-	-	8	81	3	199	—	—	11	280
7th do.	-	-	-	6	94	2	148	—	—	8	242
5th A. & S.H.	-	-	-	9	123	4	191	—	—	13	314
Totals			-	29	330	10	608	—	—	39	938

The strength of the 7th Royal Scots after this action was 6 officers, 169 other ranks. Several units had not half of their original numbers.

The officers of the 52nd Division who gave up their lives as a result of this two days' fighting were as follows:

4th Royal Scots Fusiliers—

Major W. Stewart.
Captain A. Kenneth.
Lieut. I. Barnett.
Lieut. H. Kyle.
„ G. R. Sturrock.
2nd Lieut. M. B. M'Coll.

5th Royal Scots Fusiliers—

Captain S. A. Cunningham.
2nd Lieut. F. Ferguson.
„ J. G. Hamilton-Grierson.
2nd Lieut. T. Jackson.
„ J. Maxwell.
„ W. H. Mill.

4th King's Own Scottish Borderers—

Lt.-Col. J. M'Neile.
Major J. Herbertson.
Surgeon-Major D. R. Taylor.
Capt. and Adjt. J. C. Lang.
Captain H. Sanderson.
„ A. Wallace.
Lieut. T. M. Alexander.
„ A. Bulman.
„ J. B. Innes.
2nd Lieut. A. H. M. Henderson.
„ J. B. Patrick.
„ P. Woodhead.

5th King's Own Scottish Borderers—

Captain J. J. Dykes.
„ T. Welsh.
Lieut. E. Smith.
Lieut. R. Douglas.
2nd Lieut. R. Carlyle.
„ W. B. MacFarlane.

7th Royal Scots—

2nd Lieut. D. Lyell.

7th Scottish Rifles (Cameronians)—

Major W. T. Bird.

5th Highland Light Infantry—

Major A. M. Downie.
Major T. L. Jowitt.
Captain J. MacDonald.
Captain G. Morton.
2nd Lieut. J. W. Malcolm.
  ,,   R. E. May.

6th Highland Light Infantry—

Captain D. E. C. Easson.
  ,, S. A. Gemmell.
  ,, E. G. Tidd.
Lieut. R. M. S. Boyd.
Lieut. G. L. M'Ewan.
2nd Lieut. W. A. Broadfoot.
  ,,   R. Cowan.
  ,,   J. A. Martin.

7th Highland Light Infantry—

Captain W. H. Gandy.
Lieut. G. Dickson.
  ,, W. B. Galbraith.
Lieut. A. J. M'Kersie.
  ,, G. H. Weller.
2nd Lieut. H. G. Russell.

5th Argyll & Sutherland Highlanders—

Captain W. B. Lang.
  ,, R. F. M'Kirdy.
  ,, J. Nesmith.
Lieut. R. H. Carmichael.
  ,, M. J. H. Fleming.
Lieut. J. E. M'Glashan.
  ,, J. L. Rowan.
2nd Lieut. A. Nicol.
  ,,   J. S. Stewart.

Up to the 13th July, inclusive, the Division had lost about 4800 in killed and wounded out of a total landing strength up to the 3rd July of about 10,900 all ranks. Battalions had been reduced to companies, and companies to platoons.

Great as were the losses of the Division, the losses of the Turks were probably much greater. Many will remember one awful trench on the east side of Achi Baba Nullah, which after this action was almost choked to the brim for about twenty yards with Turkish dead, and how another, on the opposite side, was so densely packed with corpses that it had to be filled in. Truly the Turkish peasantry had good reason for calling Gallipoli, " The Graveyard."

CHAPTER VII

(15TH JULY TO 30TH SEPTEMBER, 1915)

AUGUST AND SEPTEMBER AT CAPE HELLES

"Hope, for a season, bade the world farewell."
Pleasures of Hope: THOMAS CAMPBELL.

THE period that followed the battle of 12-13th July was one in which there suddenly arose a great hope of decisive victory; but it faded away. It arose again for a moment, and then disappeared for ever.

The Division had fought and laboured almost unceasingly ever since it had moved up to the forward trenches for the battle, until latterly everyone was utterly exhausted. They were weary men who dragged themselves into the "Rest Camp." It took the 5th H.L.I. fully four hours to do a journey of less than three miles through the narrow communication trenches, where the scorching heat came down from the sun above, and was reflected from the white and yellow sides and floor. Laden with anything between eighty and ninety pounds of arms, equipment, stores, etc., because everything had to be man-handled, they staggered along, breathing an atmosphere foul with dead and filled with dust. Whenever the men were really suffering there was very little complaint. Some units passed down a trench called Sauchiehall Street near Romano's Well—the one place at Cape Helles where passers-by could get a draught of the coldest and purest water. The Turks knew of it and every now and then would burst shrapnel over it. That, however, did not detract appreciably from its popularity, because one might meet death anywhere or at any time on the Peninsula.

Later, on account of its sinister reputation, orders were issued to prevent there being too large a number waiting at one time for a drink; but the greatest deterrent to crowding was the chlorination of its waters, at a later date.

The writer has only heard of two other natural springs of pure drinking water in the Cape Helles area, one in Gully Ravine, and one in the cliffs near Ghurka Bluff, both of which were little more than trickles of water.

Drill of any kind in the "Rest Camp" was impossible, because, although two or three men might move about without attracting the Turkish artillery, any larger group standing or even sitting in an open space was usually shelled. The troops, however, got plenty of exercise in the day and night fatigues, digging communication trenches, or unloading and stacking stores at different beaches, but principally at "W." Through it all, the shelling and the fatigues, the Division was full of irrepressible Mark Tapleys. The men were encouraged to bathe. "W" Beach was too crowded for this, quite apart from the wreckage, barbed wire, and other grisly reminders of the landings, which lay in the water. "X" Beach was used mostly by the men because of its convenient situation, but the beach was rough and dirty, and the water was coloured by clay and covered with a scum of straw, grain, and other light debris from the unloading of the barges. Many of the officers considered it worth the forty minutes walk to bathe in Morto Bay. There the beach was clean and sandy; the water was clear but for an occasional dead mule; it was shallow for a long way out and usually very cold; and it was really a beautiful spot, with trees fringing the bay in places, and a very fine view of the towering grey cliffs of Hissarlik Point to the left, the blue waters of the Hellespont before us, and on the further side the Asiatic coast, with more grey cliffs, the green plains of Troy, and, beyond, the blue heights of Ida—the Turkish Kara Dagh. It only had one real disadvantage. It was in full view of the Asiatic coast, and was shelled and bombed as the enemy thought fit by their Asiatic batteries and their aircraft. Despite this, the casualties were surprisingly few, and it retained its popularity until the very cold weather stopped the bathing.

The nights on Gallipoli were gorgeous in their beauty, infinite depths of the deepest blue sparkling with millions of points of light. Dr. Ewing describes what he saw on one evening, 15th July, as follows: " Work being over for the day, I went up the hill in the dark to watch, for a little, the flashing shell bursts, the white light of the star shells, the trail of light from the rockets, and the wavering fan of the great search-lights, all picked out in strange distinctness against the gloom. When I turned to come away, a thin, bright silver strip of moon hung in the transparent blue just over the hospital ship, which lay about a mile from the shore. Out of the darkness her lights shone with piercing radiance. You could not see the ship: only a high white light at the bow and stern, a row of green lights along her side, like a string of emeralds, with a great cross of red flaming in the centre, all reflected in gleaming streaks wavering in the water. It gave one the impression of a great fairy lantern, hung on the moon, shining with almost unearthly beauty."

The rest-trenches of the " Rest Camp " ran in irregular lines from north-west to south-east, or generally parallel to the Achi Baba front. It was impossible to plan them without their being enfiladed either from guns on the Peninsula or in Asia. Of overhead cover there was none, such commodities as planks of wood and sheets of corrugated iron being most rare on the Peninsula. One C.O., who had managed to borrow a few beams from the Royal Engineers, was a much envied individual. As a rule the only shelter from the sun, and later the rain and snow, consisted of waterproof sheets or blankets spread over the tops of the grave-like holes and pegged down with pieces of stick. At night, the time when most people were moving about, it was the simplest thing, even when there was the most brilliant moonlight, to step on to one of these delicate structures and to fall in with it on top of some surprised and indignant occupant. At this time sandbags were so scarce that there were hardly enough for the repairing of the front trenches, and certainly none could be spared for troops in the back areas. Any that were available were used for such semi-permanent works as Divisional and Brigade Headquarters, and the trenches occupied by Royal Engineers and other divisional troops. Fortunately, the undersoil was fairly rigid, so that perpendicular sides could be dug without fear of them caving in, so long as the fine weather lasted. Some tried to obtain shelter by undercutting, but this was rather a dangerous practice, because even in fine weather the ground crumbled and it usually resulted in a subsidence. It had been attempted in the front line, but finally was forbidden. Of course, any kind of revetting was out of the question. Every air that blew kept the dust moving over the surface of the ground, and, automatically, the trenches caught what passed their way, distributing it on the body, food, clothing, and all the occupants' possessions. Even the flies were grey with dust. Strange insects, winged beasts, and reptiles used to fall into these holes, but the latter very soon ceased to appear, because there were too many of their mortal enemies, the human animals, on the ground.

From the middle of July to the end dysentery, pyrexia, and jaundice, in the order named, steadily wasted the ranks. It was the older and the very young officers and other ranks who suffered most severely. Practically everyone suffered from dysentery in some form, and only the worst cases were sent to hospital. " Those who could possibly remain on their feet had to carry on, to work and fight in spite of their disease" (Major Black). Brig.-Gen. Hendry had returned to the 157th brigade although still sick, but the fever only gained a firmer grip on him, and on 26th July the doctors ordered him off the Peninsula, and very reluctantly, and to the 157th Brigade's regret, he had to relinquish his command. He was succeeded on 31st July by Brig.-Gen. H. G. Casson, who had commanded the 2nd South Wales Borderers ever since their original landing on 25th April, and the 156th Brigade for a while until it was taken over by Brig.-Gen. L. C. Koe. The total strength of the 157th Brigade when he assumed command was 69 officers, 2476 other ranks.

CAPE HELLES: AUGUST & SEPTEMBER 133

At the beginning of August the men of the Divisional Cyclist Company were sent back to their units as a small reinforcement, those of the 9th H.L.I. being sent to the 6th H.L.I.

The Turks must have known about the arrival at Mudros of the army destined for Suvla Bay, and they probably regarded the last two battles as the preliminaries to larger assaults on the Achi Baba position. The Turks were expecting the landing of fresh divisions at Cape Helles, and, accordingly, they shelled the beaches, the roads, and the "Rest Camps" regularly, particularly the two former. The fire from the Asiatic guns was deadly, and casualties among men of the administrative and non-combatant services became numerous. Usually the whole of a road or track could be seen by the Turks, but they seemed to watch definite lengths, and when a gharry, with its pair of mules and Indian driver, reached one of these areas they would put a large H.E. shell into it. In a moment the gharry and mules would disappear in the huge black cloud of smoke and dust which burst up from the explosion. Very often, when the cloud had drifted on, the driver with his mules and gharry would reappear, still jogging along, quite uninjured. But sometimes they did not, and many of these brave Indians paid the utmost price for the faithfulness with which they stuck to their duty.

On the 6th August the whole Peninsula quaked under a terrific bombardment from sea and land, and Achi Baba was covered with a dense filmy cloud, caused by the bursting shells. In the afternoon the artillery fire died down, the smoke drifted away, and the 29th and 42nd Divisions were flung against the Turkish centre at Cape Helles. There was not sufficient artillery support available to warrant an attack on a larger front. The Turks had recently been reinforced, the fast of Ramazan had just ended, and they were in high spirits from the German successes in Galicia and Poland. For three days the battle for possession of the Vineyard swayed backwards and forwards, and before the campaign was over that little field, which had been fought over already, probably had more blood poured over it than any other area on Gallipoli.

This attack was really a feint, for in those three days the British had attacked at Anzac, made a fresh landing at Suvla Bay, and attacked there also. Hope rose very high, but the crest-line of Sari Bair and decisive victory were missed by a few hundred yards, because of difficulties and reasons which do not concern us here. The fighting continued throughout the month, but once the advantage of surprise had been lost, the Turks had plenty of men, and Sir Ian Hamilton's forces had all the old difficulties of supply and artillery observation.

After Lt.-Gen. Hunter-Weston had been invalided home on 22nd July the 8th Corps had been commanded successively by Lt.-Gen. Sir F. Stopford, prior to his taking command of the 9th Corps for the Suvla Bay landing, and by Major-Gen. Sir W. Douglas of the 42nd Division. On 8th August Lt.-Gen. Sir F. J. Davies took over the command, holding it to the end of the campaign. He visited the 52nd Division on 12th August.

The 4th and 7th Royal Scots became separate units again on 12th August, the command of the former being taken over by Col. A. Young, V.D., who had landed two days previously. The Cameronians carried on as one battalion.

The Vineyard was a rectangle covered with low vine-bushes, not two hundred yards in length, and about a hundred yards in breadth, the two shorter sides each being part of the British and Turkish (G.12) trench systems. The British was known as St. Vincent Street. After the fiercest fighting, this section of Turkish trench (G.12) was captured on the 9th by the 42nd Division. Three days afterwards the Turkish masses retook G.12, and were threatening to bomb their way down a communication trench which ran along a ditch on the north-western side. The 52nd Division had been ordered to take over from the 42nd Division, and, so that they could learn about the ground, some bombers of the 4th R.S.F. and 5th K.O.S.B. were in this trench, which at the time was being barricaded to form a bombing station. A furious struggle ensued. Lieut. W. F. J. Maxwell, of Cardoness, bombing officer of the 5th K.O.S.B., and others were killed, fighting most gallantly, and the Turks were driven back up the trench, our men being led by Capt. J. Howard Johnston, 4th R.S.F. Some of the enemy were driven into a cul-de-sac and then bombed out, being picked off by machine-gun fire as they tried to escape across the open. The trench was hurriedly barricaded, and half of the Vineyard was secured from the Turks.

The permanent barricade in this sap was just about complete late in the afternoon on the 13th, and bombs were being thrown to keep the Turks back, when Pte. D. Ross Lauder, 4th R.S.F., who, like everyone else, had had little practice in bombing, threw one which struck the top of the trench and rolled back inside. Lauder at once put his foot on it and shouted to the rest to clear, which they did. The bomb burst a moment afterwards, blowing off the fore part of his foot completely, and shattering the whole of his lower leg so that he lost it. He undoubtedly saved half-a-dozen comrades from death or wounds, and survived to receive the first Victoria Cross awarded to the Division.

These bombers were subsequently thanked specially by Major-Gen. Douglas, G.O.C. 42nd Division, for their services. The 42nd Division commenced a new trench across the middle of the Vineyard.

13th August found the 157th Brigade in the line here, the 5th H.L.I. having taken over the right, and the 6th H.L.I. the left portion, including the British half of the Vineyard.

The 6th H.L.I. (Col. W. H. Millar) were to join up the trenches which ran on the flanks of the Vineyard by completing the one across it, commenced by the 42nd Division, and continuing it to the south-eastward. They were to have this hundred yards of trench completed before 2.30 a.m. on the 16th, and then were to attack the Turkish lines on the further side of the Vineyard, all of which were heavily wired. In the following seventy-two hours, three companies did sixty hours work, and one did forty-eight hours in order to finish to time. The men were almost dropping from fatigue and lack of sleep at the end, but they completed their task by 10.50 p.m. on the 15th. Whilst they were doing this, the Turks had to be kept at bay by sniping and bombing, so that there was little or no rest at all for anyone in the 6th H.L.I. during this period. Many of the dead of the 42nd Division were brought in and buried.

The attack was intended to be a surprise, but its plan was undoubtedly full of defects.

From 8 p.m. to 10 p.m. on the 15th, while the men were digging the last section, a heavy French " Demoiselle " trench mortar bombarded the enemy trenches, and from then onward until the attack the Turks were left in peace, but they were naturally on the *qui vive*.

The method of advance was an experiment. Under cover of a bombardment the assaulting company was to crawl forward in three lines at three yards interval between the men. As it turned out, this made it difficult for the force to retain cohesion and momentum. On the flanks bombing parties were to attack the enemy sap-heads, which ran out from G.12 on either side of the Vineyard.

At 2.30 a.m. the advance was commenced from the new trench across the Vineyard, which afterwards became part of a long one called Argyle Street. Two minutes later a heavy artillery bombardment was opened on the enemy trenches, coupled with supporting rifle-fire from the 5th H.L.I. on the right. The Turkish artillery was ready and quickly replied, rapid fire burst out from their trenches, and the element of surprise disappeared. The bombing party on the left flank got as far as the Turkish barricade, but the British converted jam tins failed to explode, whilst the Turks bombed them heavily, and they had to fall back. In the centre the attack got within ten yards of G.12, but only a few gaps could be found in the enemy's wire, the already worn-out men were dazed by the explosions, and they could advance no further against the volume of the Turkish machine-gun and rifle-fire. The bombing party on the right advanced up a shallow trench and got as far as F.12, but they also found the Turks too strong and quite ready, and had to fall back with the rest. The 6th H.L.I. lost nine killed and twenty-nine wounded in this small affair.

The previous night the 5th H.L.I. had sent out a patrol

CAPE HELLES: AUGUST & SEPTEMBER 137

to investigate, with a view to their seizure, the Turkish trenches on the northern bank of Achi Baba Nullah. At 2.31 a.m. on the 16th, as the first line of 6th H.L.I. were crawling forward, the 5th H.L.I. opened supporting fire on their whole front. The intensity and volume of the Turkish rifle and machine-gun fire in reply was startling, ripping up the British sandbags, and indicating the number of machine-guns that the Turks had available. Several of these disclosed themselves and were located. Like many other trenches these might have been captured, but could only have been held with heavy loss.

The feint attack at Cape Helles had already served its original purpose. Turkish divisions had been retained there. G.12 was a trench on which, if it had been captured by the British, the Turks could have poured a heavy converging fire rendering it practically untenable. Behind it lay other trenches, so that its capture did not mean a break in the Turkish lines. Accordingly, no further attacks were made on it, and the eastern half of the Vineyard became No Man's Land.

The efficient "Demoiselle"[1] trench mortars of the French, employed on this occasion, and during the battle of the 28th June, threw an interesting sidelight on the unpreparedness of the British for this war. The bomb-thrower most in use, because it could be manufactured on the spot in Royal Naval Division workshops, was a wooden catapult with rubber bands, which threw a bomb between forty and fifty yards. Cast-iron spherical grenades were thrown with this contrivance, as there was great danger of converted jam tins catching in the sling and falling back into the British trench. For three days from the 6th July, during their first tour in the trenches, the Nelson Batt., Royal Naval Division, had kindly lent the 6th H.L.I. a mortar which threw a bomb rather larger than a cricket ball about fifty yards. At the end of August a trench howitzer appeared, which looked like a piece of iron drain pipe of 3·7 inches in diameter, its muzzle resting on two long legs. The propellent explosion was furnished by a blank rifle cartridge

[1] This is also spelt Dumesil and Demizel by various writers.

fired into its breech by a fixed pistol arrangement. This ignited the fuse of a large jam tin bomb, and threw it high into the air, to drop a hundred yards away or more. The elevation was arranged by digging or filling in holes for the breech or legs. At first these were handled by reckless amateurs, but later were manned by special trench mortar companies. But for the rubber and the cartridges, these weapons reminded one of the artillery of Julius Caesar, and Edward III. of England. Despite their primitive nature, they did wonderfully good work in keeping down the Turkish bombing, and bore great testimony to the ingenuity of the men who fashioned them, as well as to the bravery of the men who used them.

That the Germans intended the Turks to keep pace with themselves was proved by a discovery made on the 16th July. Acting on information supplied by a captured Turkish officer who did not like German methods, the 5th H.L.I. found in a shelter in one of the trenches in Achi Baba Nullah two cases marked " Rakaten." They contained fifteen long, slender, asphyxiating bombs, evidently intended to be thrown by a trench mortar.

At the end of the summer the troops were issued with a gas mask, which consisted of a flannel hood soaked in a chemical preparation, entirely covering up the head, being tucked under the tunic, and having celluloid eye-pieces. They were carried in bags hung " at the ready " on the breast. The celluloid very often got cracked, and because of this two were issued to each man. When worn, they gave everyone the appearance of a mediaeval inquisitor. Fortunately, however, the prevailing winds at Cape Helles, in which a gas attack was possible, blew towards the Turkish lines.

In August, Sir Ian Hamilton ordered the 29th Division to Suvla Bay, where he was collecting every available man for another attempt to break through the Turkish lines and win heights which would give him domination of the Narrows. This left three British divisions at Cape Helles, and the 17th saw the whole of the much reduced 52nd in the line. On the 21st August the second great attempt was made at Suvla. Hope ran high for a little on the 21st, but again faded away, this time for ever.

On the 24th August news came that Italy had declared war against Turkey. This was celebrated at night by three cheers from the troops. The Turks thought that it meant an attack, and opened fire with every weapon they possessed, disclosing the positions of some machine-guns hitherto unknown. If these guns were not afterwards destroyed by our artillery, they were at least compelled to move to other parts of the trenches.

Various changes took place in commands within the Division. Brig.-Gen. J. B. Pollok-M'Call had taken over command of the 155th Brigade from Brig.-Gen. J. F. Erskine on 14th August. The latter was invalided home, having remained at his post so long as he could move about. He was a most experienced officer, whose loss was deeply felt. Major Russell, a most capable and universally respected officer, took command of the 5th R.S.F., only to be killed twelve days later.

Everywhere disease was making its ravages felt. Lt.-Col. J. R. Balfour, 4th R.S.F., was invalided on the 16th of August, and Col. W. H. Millar, 6th H.L.I., on the 28th. These are two of the numerous changes which took place in commanding officers during the last five months on Gallipoli. Unfortunately, space forbids the record of them all.

The monotony of the food did a great deal to aggravate the sickness that prevailed. Bully-beef and biscuits do not form a good basis for the diet of human systems already enfeebled by diarrhoea. The M'Connochie tinned meat and vegetable stew was appetising, but it was far too rich for the average digestion on Gallipoli under its tropical sun. The medical authorities recognised this, and about the end of August bully-beef was almost entirely replaced by frozen meat; good bread, baked under shell-fire on the cliffs of Cape Tekke, was issued five or six days per week; the ration of dessicated vegetables was increased; an issue of rice was instituted; cheese was reduced, and fresh milk increased. Jam was always plentiful, but there was a surfeit of apricot. This the men christened " parapet " jam, because, as they said, they were so "fed-up" with it that they simply threw it over the parapet. Bugler Stokes, 6th H.L.I., composed a parody at Cape Helles about this time on *The Mountains of Mourne*, which must be mentioned here, not only because of its popularity throughout the different units, but because of its evidence of the Jock's unfailing sense of dry humour, no matter what he was enduring. One verse runs as follows :

> "We don't grow potatoes, or barley or wheat,
> So we're aye on the look-out for something to eat ;
> We're fed up with biscuits and bully and ham,
> And we're sick of the sight of yon parapet jam.
> Send out steak and onions, and nice ham and eggs,
> Or a fine big fat chicken with five or six legs,
> And a drink of the stuff that begins with a B—
> Where the old Gallipoli sweeps down to the sea."

Friends and committees at home had already sent out the best possible of everything they could, and these parcels began to arrive during August. This helped considerably in solving the food problem, and all ranks will never cease to be grateful to them for this service.

The Divisional Train, R.A.S.C., carried out its supply and transport work without a hitch of any kind during the whole period that the Division was at Cape Helles, despite the shell-fire.

The relations between all ranks of the British and French armies were of the happiest, and complete ignorance of each other's language apparently did not deter the men of both armies from understanding each other completely. The French baked very good bread and got plenty of wine, whilst the British got plenty of jam. As a result, a surreptitious trade flourished between the French lines, which stretched from the village of Sedd el Bahr to Morto Bay, and the British. The demand for French bread waned after the advent of the British field bakeries, but the principal traffic was, of course, for the wine, for which the rate of exchange was one bottle to one tin of jam. Unfortunately, somebody drank too much, and this commercial intercourse was brought to an end by a G.R.O., which rigorously put the French lines out of bounds.

CAPE HELLES: AUGUST & SEPTEMBER

So weak were the forces on Gallipoli that the Division was kept in the forward trenches at Cape Helles in the Central Sector, that is about Krithia and Achi Baba Nullah, for almost five weeks continuously, units taking their turn periodically in the fire, support, and reserve lines. The fighting strength of Sir Ian Hamilton's total force, British and French, on Gallipoli on 23rd August was 68,000; whilst the Turkish was probably about 100,000, of whom at least a quarter were in reserve. In addition, the enemy had every advantage of position. Of reserves at Cape Helles there were extremely few, and it was a very anxious period. Fortunately the Turks were getting short of shells, and their infantry had little stomach for attacking British trenches after the manner in which they had been mown down in every previous attack. If they had once broken through the thinly held forward lines at this time, it is difficult to see what there was to prevent them from walking down to Cape Helles, beyond a few artillerymen and details in the " Rest Camp " at the beaches. For four days during this period the 4th R.S. held about 120 yards of line with sixty-two as the actual rifle strength. The men in the support line had to carry up the water and rations, and do the pioneer work. Men in the front trench had to do an hour's sentry duty alternated with an hour of sleep right through the night, in addition to daily digging fatigues. This was the rule everywhere from now onwards, and yet, whenever wakened, it was also the rule for men to spring up willingly without a grumble; but they fell asleep as they lay down again on the fire-step when relieved. The enemy were less than 100 yards away, and had numerous well-rested reserves. The total strength of the 4th K.O.S.B. on 13th September was 230, which meant that there were only about 150 rifles available for duty in the trenches, as it must be remembered that, whilst the mule carts could bring the rations to a " dump " well up Krithia Nullah, from that point everything had to be carried by men weakened with disease. Water was carried up in camel tanks, old rum jars, or petrol tins. A small section of the trenches was supplied from Romano's Well, a mile and a quarter behind the firing line.

In this case the water had to be carried up entirely by hand, and, despite its coolness when leaving the well, was usually tepid, like all the other water on Gallipoli, by the time that it had reached the front trenches. At this time some officers, discussing the possibilities of a Turkish attack, came to the conclusion that, whilst they knew that their men would try their utmost to do so, they doubted if many of them had the physical strength to push their bayonets home. When the 155th Brigade relieved the 157th Brigade on 3rd October, the latter had been fifty-two days in the trenches, having been continually on working parties in addition to the usual trench duties. The only exception was that the 6th H.L.I. were once in the "Rest Camp" for four days.

Occasionally some of the units were as far back as the Eski Lines, less than 1300 yards from the Turkish trenches. The Turks sprayed these trenches every night with a random dropping fire from machine-guns and rifles, so that the ground was littered with spent bullets, and their high angle of descent often landed them on the bottom of the trench. Casualties were remarkably few considering the steadiness of this fire, but nevertheless it took its toll.

The work of repairing and improving the trenches, letting in iron loop-hole plates for snipers, and putting out wire went on apace. The former especially was unsavoury work, because of the number of dead buried in the parapets, floors of trenches and elsewhere. A curious find was made by a party of the 6th H.L.I. when working on an old Turkish trench. It was a store of twenty-four British rifles with a quantity of ammunition, evidently the dump of some industrious Turks, who had collected them after the June fighting for the purpose of getting the reward offered by their Government for every British rifle brought in. Much salvage work was done by our own patrols and working parties, and many rifles, besides ammunition and equipment, were recovered. Towards the end of September, despite the heat and unfitness of everybody, the labour which some units had to do demanded almost fourteen hours of duty in the twenty-four; whilst at the same time the officers left

CAPE HELLES: AUGUST & SEPTEMBER 143

were so few that in one case, at least, the adjutant had to carry on his ordinary duties in the day-time, and then take a relief in the fire trenches at night. Urgent as this work was, it had to be cut down or units would have disappeared out of sheer physical exhaustion.

All this while the Turks added to their defences until they had a tremendous net-work of trenches on the face of Achi Baba. They also put out wire, and when our wiring parties were at work, at times they could hear the Turks busily driving their stakes, as if they knew that we could not fire on them because of our own men being out.

On the nights of 9th and 11th September the 6th (Lt.-Col. J. Anderson) and 5th (Col. F. Morrison) H.L.I., respectively, dug two new bombing saps nearer the Turkish lines, to keep pressure on the enemy. 2nd Lieut. F. B. Davidson, 6th H.L.I., was mortally wounded in the first case; he had only been on the Peninsula nineteen days.

Patrols were sent out regularly to listen, explore, and sometimes throw bombs into Turkish trenches, but they never met any Turkish patrols. Two men of the 7th Cameronians went out on patrol one night, when there was a good deal of rifle and machine-gun fire and shelling, and a moan coming from No Man's Land was afterwards heard in the trenches. C.S.M. Donald Hunter (8th Cameronians) dashed out and with one of the men, Pte. J. Stewart, managed with great gallantry to carry in the other who was mortally wounded.

Occasionally Turks would creep over to the Division's lines and surrender. Very often they complained bitterly of the treatment which they and even their officers received at the hands of their German taskmasters. They were well set up men and well clad. Those that gave themselves up in the winter time were almost better clad than our own men, but for their footwear, which was often poor. Many a British corpse was relieved of its boots by a footsore Turkish soldier.

The offensive on both sides consisted of sniping, bombing, and the shelling of different parts of the line. It was a general rule throughout the Division that enemy snipers must be kept down at all costs. There was a continual dribble of casualties for this reason, but the Division's snipers invariably got the upper hand. During their tour in the newly captured trenches just after the 12th July, the 5th H.L.I. noticed a well about four hundred yards off, round which, until the Turks realised their danger, occasional parties of them could be easily spotted. One sniper had seven observed hits to his credit, and another five in the same day. Periscope rifles were issued in the first few days of September, and reduced considerably the risks taken by our snipers.

About the middle of September the Turks commenced to fire a trench mortar bomb, which consisted of a long cylinder, sometimes of brass and sometimes of iron, serrated so that it would break up, and usually filled with half-inch diameter shrapnel bullets, nails, and pieces of old iron. It had a stick about four feet long attached, apparently to correct its flight, and because of this was called a "Broom-Stick Bomb." It made a tremendous noise but did little damage, and the broom-sticks were thankfully received by the machine-gunners and snipers for the construction of overhead cover. One dropped on a bomb store of the 5th K.O.S.B. on 24th September, but, whilst it damaged some of them, eighty-seven of the bombs were uninjured. Some of these broom-stick bombs were filled with an incendiary composition, apparently a mixture of bees-wax, sulphur, and saltpetre. They burnt with a great smoke and occasionally destroyed some equipment and stores, but as a form of "frightfulness" were almost a complete failure; although, of course, the possibility of having one lobbed on to one while asleep was not conducive to rest.

Enemy aeroplanes came over fairly often, and dropped their bombs on the back areas and what they thought were battery positions. The nearest base for our own aeroplanes was on Imbros, so that an enemy aviator was usually sure of being able to drop his bombs without interruption. Of anti-aircraft guns we had none, and the wisest course for our artillery was to lie low and not disclose their positions,

VINEYARD SUPPORT LINE, CAPE HELLES

CAPE HELLES: AUGUST & SEPTEMBER

particularly as they were rationed and only allowed to fire a few shells daily without special permission.

Duels with hand-grenades between our own bombers and the Turkish were of daily occurrence. Some very grim situations arose, and, although men would not allow their minds to dwell on them at the time, they must have left their mark. On one occasion a heap of the bodies which had been lying out in No Man's Land near East Krithia Nullah, probably since the beginning of June, and so were completely dried up, caught fire from a bomb explosion. Lest the blaze should attract the Turkish shell-fire, some Argylls who were in the line crept out and threw earth on the fire until it was out. There were many acts of bravery and presence of mind in the daily trench fighting, for instance, on 7th October in a bomb station held at the time by the 5th R.S.F. A thrower had lit the fuse of a bomb and was about to throw it, when he was hit by a splinter from a bullet, and fell back stunned, but still retained the lighted bomb in his hand. At once, Pte. T. Buchanan jumped forward, seized the bomb out of the wounded man's hand, and hurled it into the Turkish trench opposite, where it immediately exploded. His presence of mind saved the other men in the trench, and he was awarded the D.C.M.

One would almost have expected that this detached life in scattered burrows in the earth would have withered the regimental *esprit de corps*, but the spirit of all ranks rose superior to separation and depression, and this spirit was passed on to the few reinforcements of new men that arrived.

During September some drafts arrived, all small with one exception. On the 3rd the 7th R.S. received a draft of thirteen officers, and 440 other ranks, an accession of strength which made a distinct difference in the appearance of the whole 156th Brigade at that time. They, with a previous small draft of officers, included all the fit survivors of the Gretna disaster.

One of the thirteen officers, 2nd Lieut. D. Brown (8th H.L.I. attached 7th R.S.) only lasted a week in the line before he was invalided, to die on board a hospital ship. All services suffered. Capt. G. C. Bell, R.A.M.C., was evacuated sick after very short service with the 7th R.S., dying afterwards in a hospital at Alexandria. These are only two examples to show how rapidly the conditions on Gallipoli told on some men.

The totals of sick and wounded of the Lowland Division in hospital, and remaining on its strength as part of the Mediterranean Expeditionary Force, were as follows for various dates in September and October, 1915:

Week Ended.	Officers.	Other Ranks.	Total.
September 6	66	1493	1559
,, 13	75	1574	1649
,, 20	83	1799	1882
,, 26	82	2037	2119
October 2	93	2293	2386
,, 9	86	2459	2545
,, 17	103	2762	2865
,, 24	112	3020	3132
,, 31	105	3108	3213

All who were sent home to the British Isles were struck off the strength of the Division, and accordingly were excluded from the above figures. It must be remembered that there were many in the trenches who ought to have been in hospital, had there been reinforcements to replace them. At this time, while the ranks of the New Army were kept filled with recruits, the Territorial Force was starved, and it was only with difficulty that small drafts were raised and sent out. The figures quoted above would have increased enormously, in fact the army would have disappeared from pestilence, had it not been for the wonderful results of inoculation against various diseases. By 30th September 93 per cent. of the strength of the Division had been inoculated against cholera, and 97 per cent. against typhoid.

Fortunately the number of fatal cases of disease were few. The most dangerous feature was the manner in which it sapped the vitality of every man. Trench sanitation under the easiest of conditions is a great problem, but on Gallipoli, where there was foul ground everywhere and the pioneers were semi-invalids like almost everyone else, the difficulties were well nigh insuperable. The chief of them was the

CAPE HELLES: AUGUST & SEPTEMBER 147

disposal of the matter. It was not practicable to dig deep pits, sufficient in number, amidst the front trenches. As a result the weary pioneers had to carry the receptacles long distances, under a blazing sun through narrow trenches, where there was other traffic. What this meant for the men, together with the stench and the flies, I leave to the reader's imagination. Lt.-Col. J. Young, 1/3rd Lowland Field Ambulance, writes as follows of the cause of the scourge of dysentery: " The ultimate explanation was, of course, easy—imperfect sanitation." The writer has heard a doctor on Gallipoli describe Cape Helles as a " gigantic morgue and open latrine." The Medical Services fought against this wonderfully from the start, but the doctors, themselves, were semi-invalids and short handed. By splendid exertions they regulated, supervised, and educated the men. They spent themselves freely, physically and mentally, but, beyond a certain point, no man's will-power can fight against sheer physical exhaustion in himself and in others. From the beginning the Division prided itself on the cleanliness and general tidiness of its trenches. Gradually the medical officers got proper sanitation installed everywhere. What they achieved was marvellous and they can never be repaid.

A month's armistice, and a new army to clean up the entire area, and especially No Man's Land, might have made Cape Helles sanitary, but nothing could have got rid of the flies.

Another insuperable difficulty of the medical services was the insanitary condition of the Turkish trenches, which were only a few yards away. The troops could tell at once by the foul smell, when the wind blew from the Turkish trenches. Bad as was the atmosphere in one of our own, it was nothing to that in a recently captured Turkish trench.

The writer thinks that he is correct in stating that in the whole Division only one man died from typhus contracted at Cape Helles. Certainly there were extremely few cases of this awful disease. To the lay mind knowing the circumstances this seems to be almost a miracle.

Dysentery was the dreadful word on Gallipoli. Like most Orientals, the Turks live under such insanitary conditions in their normal mode of life that they are immune from many diseases. Our men were different. Nearly all of them had been brought up in the average Scottish home, where cleanliness is the law. Yet all ranks suffered without complaint; more than this, many heroic souls, officers and other ranks, although they had barely sufficient strength to move about and keep out of hospital, kept brave cheerful faces, laughing off hardships which were really severe.

"I doubt if any, except those who saw with their own eyes, can ever picture the tragedy of hundreds and thousands of brave, strong men battling in vain against a loathsome thing, whilst the flesh left their bodies and their strength ebbed away, till at last they were stretched out helpless as babes. . . .

"Few of us escaped. At times dysentery and fever played a sorry havoc in the ranks of the ambulance. At one time we were working the whole ambulance, including dressing stations, with only two medical officers instead of nine, and one of these was just able to drag himself from bed when a patient was announced": so wrote Lt.-Col. J. Young, 1/3rd Lowland Field Ambulance, of this time.

The 1/2nd Lowland Field Ambulance, under Lt.-Col. Moffat, arrived at 6 a.m. on the 30th August being a very welcome and much needed reinforcement. They camped beside the other two Lowland Ambulances.

On 17th September Major-Gen. G. G. A. Egerton, C.B., who had been appointed to the command of the M.E.F. Base at Alexandria, handed over the command of the Lowland Division to Major-Gen. the Hon. H. A. Lawrence, a son of the great Lord Lawrence of Indian fame. General Egerton had trained his division in peace time, mobilised it for war, and seen it spent in battle and wasted by disease until, despite reinforcements, it had shrunk in three and a half months to less than half of its landing strength of 10,900.

CAPE HELLES: AUGUST & SEPTEMBER

The total effective strength of the 157th Brigade on the 30th September was as follows:

	Officers.	Other Ranks.
Headquarters and Signallers	6	45
5th H.L.I.	14	485
6th H.L.I.	11	426
7th H.L.I.	13	491
5th A. & S.H.	16	425
	60	1872

The above figures include men detached on duties away from their battalion, so that the rifle strength was much less; and this was the strongest brigade in the Division at the time.

In the middle of September there were a few wet, cool days, the flies got clammy, and everyone saw the shadow of approaching winter. However, the sun, the "death-star" of the East, shone again, and kept our minds on present evils.

In spite of all their hardships and the ever busy scythe of Death, the men had a very practical philosophy, and were not of the mould that gives way to depression. Writing of a visit to the 4th R.S. in the trenches, Dr. Ewing tells of how he "found the lads in all sorts of attitudes—reading, writing, chatting, smoking the ubiquitous cigarette, or joining in the strains of a rollicking song. Their uniforms are the worse for wear. They are tanned brown with the sun." The dress of the Division consisted, during the hot weather, of helmet, shirt usually with sleeves cut short, trousers cut short above the knee, or kilt, puttees, socks, and boots. Because of the sun, the khaki cloth, and the Gallipoli clay, everything was brown, with the exception of the grey shirts often issued. In another place, Dr. Ewing describes a visit during October: " I found the lads occupying their respective parts of the line, some keeping a sharp look-out from the points of observation—using the periscope with discretion ; some attending to the periscope rifle, with which a man can take good aim and fire, while keeping well under cover; some were ready at steel-plated loopholes, to exact penalty of unwary foes; some stood by the machine-guns, prepared on a moment's notice to let loose a storm of lead upon any point of danger. Others were absorbed in the homely, but not less necessary, duty of making tea. The fellows bore evident traces of weather and work—brown faces, hands, arms, and knees ; attire not just suitable for Princes Street, in either quantity or quality. The close life of the trenches, and the long strain of constant vigilance, especially after the fierce experiences of action many have come through, have to some extent affected the physique of the men. But you may walk from one end of the lines to the other and never see a gloomy face or hear a grumbling word. They will tell you that they did not come here for a picnic and that they are no worse off than their neighbours. I found a spirit of genial goodfellowship prevailing among them ; and came away with the deepened conviction that our lads are splendid."

During September and October, when the Turkish shell-fire was less, many dead were brought in and buried. This did something to mitigate the conditions, but the majority, lying about the front lines, and hidden everywhere in the scrub, had to be left where they were.

The application of home names to the trenches was widespread, and left no doubt as to the origin of the units responsible for them. "Princes Street," "Sauchiehall Street," "Leith Walk" and "Ayr Road" were communication trenches. "St. Vincent Street," "Renfield Street," "Argyll Street," "Hope Street," "Main Street," "Queen Street," "Great Western Road," "Cathedral Street," "Clunes Vennel," "Govan Street," "Yorkhill Street," "Rosebery Street," and "Dalmeny Street" were firetrenches : "Eglinton Tunnel" ran down from the "Horseshoe" to Achi Baba Nullah near "Symington Bridge." Near the Headquarters of the 155th Brigade in Krithia Nullah was a plank bridge crossing the stream and styled the "Auld Brig o' Doon." Not far off was one of the numerous dug-outs, which honeycombed the banks of the main nullahs, named "Burns' Cottage."

The nicknames given to various Turkish guns, in addition to "Asiatic Annie," were numerous. "Quick Dick", was a high velocity gun, probably the same which the French nicknamed " Marie pressée," because the report of the gun, the shriek of the shell in flight, and its explosion, all followed one another in the space of a couple of seconds. " Creeping Caroline " was the reverse, the shell flying with a soft whistle and arriving after a slow flight, which often deceived men as to the length of time they had in which to get under cover. " Fat Bertha " was named because of the shape of the shell fired. In every case it is probable that there was not one gun but many firing these shells.

CHAPTER VIII

(27TH SEPTEMBER TO 31ST OCTOBER, 1915)

OCTOBER AND THE COOLER WEATHER

> Ay! now the soldiers hear it,
> An' answer with a cheer,
> As "The Campbells are a-comin',"
> Falls on each anxious ear.
> The cannons roar'd their thunder,
> And the sappers work in vain,
> For high aboon the din o' war
> Resounds the welcome strain.
> *Jessie's Dream:* GRACE CAMPBELL.

SEPTEMBER 27th brought news of a great victory in France, and at 7 p.m. all the British troops were ordered to give three cheers for the French Army, whilst, commencing at the same time, one battery in each artillery group was to fire a salute of twenty-one guns on selected Turkish objectives. This was done. The Turks thought that it was the precursor of an attack, put up a brilliant display of Verey lights, and opened fire with artillery, machine-guns, and rifles. There were a few British casualties, the enemy fire died away, and the normal sniping and bombing was resumed. These apparently useless "stunts" left the Turks uncertain as to our real intentions, and proved their utility early in January, 1916.

One Sunday evening, later on in October, a huge bonfire was lit well behind the lines to beguile the Turks into believing that a magazine had caught fire. It was hoped that the Moslems, out of curiosity and joy, would be looking over their parapets to see the blaze, when, on the sending

OCTOBER AND COOLER WEATHER

up of a rocket, a storm of shell and rifle-fire was poured on their trenches, followed by three cheers from the men. How far the ruse succeeded cannot be said, but the Turks replied all along the line with very furious fire.

During these nights, as on others, the high angle of descent of their rifle-fire seemed to indicate that the Turkish infantrymen kept well down, with their rifles pointed high in the air over the parapet, and simply fired at random. Their machine-guns were different. They swept No Man's Land and the opposing parapets with well directed fire. Several of these guns were located, and the artillery put them out of action, at least for a while.

The weakness of the British artillery has been dwelt upon already, and it was always comforting for us to watch the new British monitors, which mounted 14-inch guns, and other warships, shelling the Turkish lines. The long boom of these gigantic guns with their slow burning powder seemed to hit the cliffs of Cape Helles and produce reverberations which one Glasgow Jock described as being "like tummlin' a lot o' dishes aff the shelf." Despite Sir Ian Hamilton's efforts to secure more ammunition, the British artillery ashore had to husband what they had for possible Turkish attacks. However, late in the afternoons, when the air was clearest and the sunlight was nearly behind them, they would let go their daily ration of three or four shells per gun on the Turkish trenches. Very often the troops had had to sit during the day and endure a Turkish bombardment with very little reply from the Allied guns. These evening bombardments of the Turks consoled them somewhat.

There were times, just before darkness fell, when the Peninsula was almost peaceful. Those in the front line could hear Turks chanting in high-pitched voices, as if in prayer. Looking westward from the front trenches down the slopes of Achi Baba, and trying to forget the foreground with its grisly heaps silhouetted darkly against the soft light, we could see across the intervening waters to islands, which were transformed into huge blocks of sapphire, set in a sea of polished silver that reflected the flaming glories of a crimson sunset. In the distance, showing clear and dark against the dying embers of the sun, we could distinguish strange peaks, and wondered whether they were the cone of Mount Athos and other heights of classic lore, or only clouds. Then the pall of darkness would swiftly fall, a crackle of rifle-fire would develop rapidly, and overhead would pass that hum as of numberless bees and those strange resounding cracks, as the harassing bullets sped on their way to the Eski Lines and the back areas. Back we came from the legends of ancient Greece to the stern realities of Gallipoli of 1915.

From August to the end, the different brigades of the Division took their turn in the forward trenches, the reserve lines, and the " Rest Camp." Every time they came down from the trenches some were left to sleep in the little graveyards in Krithia Nullah and elsewhere.

The arrival of a mail with letters, parcels, and newspapers from home always had a great effect in raising the spirits of everyone, and much was done in this direction by means of concerts in the " Rest Camp," when the strains of many an old Scottish ballad and many a modern music-hall song were heard. Undoubtedly, one of the greatest factors in keeping everyone cheerful was the 52nd Divisional Band. Dr. Ewing tells how, on hearing the music whilst riding home one evening, " even my horse pricked up his ears and went forward at a merrier pace." The bandsmen were searched out and recruited from all over the Division. They started practice on 19th October and the first performance was given four days later, the programme being as follows :

      (1) " The Soldiers of the Queen ";
      (2) " May Blossom ";
      (3) " Jock O' Hazeldean ";
      (4) " Row, Row, Row ";
      (5) " It's a long way to Tipperary."

Lieut. Watson, as Bandmaster, started with about a dozen men, but, at the time of the evacuation of Cape Helles, these had been increased to forty-three other ranks, of whom nineteen were pipers. Every battalion in the 52nd Division was represented in its ranks.

The band was in universal demand by units outside the Division, and for church services. The selection for one of the last services, on 13th December, was as follows, and is typical:

Psalm—" God is our refuge and our strength ";
Hymn—" All hail the power of Jesus' Name ";
Hymn—" Fight the Good Fight ";
Hymn—" Stand up, stand up, for Jesus."

The men liked hymns in which they could use their lusty voices to the full. Such well-known metrical psalms and paraphrases as " The Lord's my Shepherd," " O God of Bethel," " I to the hills will lift mine eyes," " O thou my soul, bless God the Lord," " God is our refuge and our strength," and " All people that on earth do dwell " were especial favourites, because they could be sung from memory as it was too dangerous or impossible to have any illumination, all services being held under cover of darkness.

The last service was held on 29th December, and the last secular programme was on Christmas Day at the quarters of the Royal Naval Division. Apart from the " Marseillaise " and " God Save the King," which finished up every programme, one of the last pieces played was " Are we downhearted ? "

At the beginning of October the weather was still very warm during the day-time, and the flies just as active as ever, but the nights became extremely cold. With blood thinned by the hot weather, everyone suffered greatly from these extremes. In the second week the first of the autumnal rains fell, and it was with an apprehensive feeling that many watched the first drops fall on the little canopies of waterproof sheets which were their only shelters. A battered sheet of corrugated iron was a priceless possession, because, even at that date, there was no material available to provide shelter for the British troops in the trenches. Officers and men had to huddle under what shelter they could get, while the rain poured down and the dust of Gallipoli became deep, tenacious mud. Many of the grave-like dug-outs of the "Rest Camp" were flooded, and their occupants had to walk about in the open under the cold, drenching rain until the morning. They could be heard laughing and chaffing one another about their "hames," treating it all as a huge joke.

Everything has compensations : from this time onwards the flies grew less and less in number.

The rain passed, the trenches gradually dried up, and the heat became tempered with cool breezes, now from the south and now from the east.

There was no lack of signs that winter was rapidly approaching. Immense clouds of migratory birds began to pass over us, flying southward. Our own men were forbidden to waste ammunition on these birds, which flew at a great height. One day a heavy and foolish fusillade started, and it was rapidly followed by a telephonic message from someone in the Higher Command saying that the men doing this were to be stopped at once. It was pointed out in reply that to do this would necessitate a small battle, as the men in question were Turks.

Early in the autumn a training camp was instituted at Imbros with the idea of giving the men a relief from the shell-fire and a chance to recuperate, without having to wait until they became so ill that they had to go to hospital. Only very few men could be spared, and naturally only the very weakest were sent, and at first the camp rather missed its object by emphasizing too much the smartening up and outdoor exercise processes. This was soon put right, and for the few who could get to it, this camp at Imbros, and later at Lemnos, was a great boon.

Towards Morto Bay there were several fields surrounded by trees and bushes, which prevented their being easily observed from Achi Baba. Here were all the requisites for football, and accordingly Sir Francis Davies offered a trophy, to be called the "Dardanelles Cup," to be won in a knock-out competition. The writer remembers watching a match between the 5th A. & S.H. and the 6th H.L.I. The game was being played not a hundred

OCTOBER AND COOLER WEATHER 157

yards from a French battery, which at the time was shelling and being shelled by the Turks. A shell burst rather near one of the goals, so the spectators moved to the other end of the field, but the game went on. After a few more shells in different places, one struck a gun epaulement and the gunners deemed it wise to leave. The Frenchmen walked past the end of the field, glanced at the game still going on, and then at each other with expressions that said very clearly, " All that we have heard is quite true. The British are completely mad." The game went on and in due course was finished. These matches supplied the men with subjects for interminable discussions and arguments, and for that reason were a great boon. The 5th H.L.I. had won through to the final round with the Anson Battalion, Royal Naval Division, when the Evacuation took place.

As October went on, very warm days alternated with others when bitterly cold winds blew from the north and north-east. The month went out with a violent thunderstorm from the south-west, accompanied by heavy rain, a dust-storm, and then more rain.

The difficulties of transportation between Mudros and Gallipoli, with which Sir Ian Hamilton and his staff had to contend, can hardly be exaggerated. The work of the British Navy and Mercantile Marine cannot be praised too highly. " On the Dardanelles Peninsula it may be said that the whole of the machinery by which the text-books contemplate the maintenance and supply of an army was non-existent. The zone commanded by the enemy's guns extended not only to the landing places on the Peninsula, but even over the sea in the vicinity." (Sir C. Monro.) Ships were sunk by collision and torpedo, lighters and even steamers were driven ashore and wrecked. Storms swept the piers of wooden piles, stone embankments, and sunken vessels, breaking them down, but they were rebuilt. The bombardment of the beaches and stores of the Army Service Corps and Ordnance never ceased, but as men fell others replaced them, " learnt the ropes," and carried on until they fell.

"The sea, the ships, lighters, and tugs took, in fact, the place of railways and roads, with their railway trains, mechanical transport, etc., but with this difference, that the use of the latter is subject only to the intervention of the enemy, while that of the former was dependent on the weather . . . For all personnel and material there was at least one trans-shipment, and for the greater portion of both two trans-shipments," (Sir C. Monro) before they could be landed on the shell-swept beaches. At times the sea was so rough that stores could not be landed, but, although the Cape Helles army was occasionally cut off for a few days and had to live on bully-beef and biscuits, never once was it without food and water. The Naval and Military Staffs achieved this by working together with most perfect harmony and skill.

It was the lot of some to lose their lives without setting foot on the Peninsula. During the night of 28-29th October, H.M.S. *Hythe*, bringing across the 1/3rd Kent Field Company, R.E., as a reinforcement to the 52nd Division, was sunk in collision, and about 155 officers and men perished in the waters of the Aegean.

Mining companies were formed under the Royal Engineers from the colliers of the Division, and these, working from various sap-heads, began to run out tunnels under the Turkish trenches.

Trench mortar companies were also formed early in the autumn, and, using French " demoiselles " principally, frequently took up positions in the trenches and bombarded the enemy's lines and bomb saps. Their winged bombs had a distinct effect on the morale of the Turkish infantry, who could often be heard calling out " Allah ! Allah ! " in terror stricken tones, as the missile could be seen swiftly descending. For this reason the Turkish artillery were always very quick in retaliating, and searching the trenches with shrapnel and H.E. for these trench mortars. The British infantry had to endure this, often long after the trench mortar battery had completed its " shoot," packed up, and left; and, accordingly, the infantry officer gave the coldest reception possible to any trench mortar personnel

OCTOBER AND COOLER WEATHER

whenever they appeared in his trenches. Nevertheless, these mortars did good work in wearing down the Turks. Lieut. J. Wilson, 5th A. & S.H., a lad of eighteen, who had returned to the Peninsula from hospital after being wounded in the " Horseshoe " fighting on the 12th July, died of dysentery on 16th October. He was serving with the trench mortars at the time, and the O.C. of the 8th Corps Mortar Group, Capt. A. Burrows, R.G.A., on hearing of his death, wrote to the O.C. 5th A. & S.H., as follows : " As one example of many, I should like to mention that during our operations against the ' Gridiron ' the Dumesil Heavy Mortar Battery was heavily shelled. In spite of his being twice covered with debris and more or less buried by shells striking the parapet in front of him, and one of his guns being put out of action, the pit being filled in by a shell, Mr. Wilson continued to keep the other gun in action until the end of the operations in a most satisfactory manner. On his way back to camp he was again half buried by a shell, but arrived smiling, and told me that he was afraid the operations had been somewhat delayed as so much of the men's time was occupied in ' digging him out.' It is needless to state the effect an example such as his had on the men. I am afraid his illness was somewhat exaggerated by his insistence in remaining on duty as long as he could."

Lieut. R. Orkney, 5th A. & S.H., who had served with the trench mortars for a while, was killed on 20th October during one of these retaliatory bombardments, by a shell which also wounded Lt.-Col. K. H. M. Connal, T.D., Glasgow Yeomanry, and his adjutant.

During the middle of October, besides some returned sick and wounded, the Division received a welcome reinforcement from the Lowland Mounted Brigade, when the Ayrshire, Lt.-Col. J. Boswell; Lanarkshire, Lt.-Col. Lord Dunglass; and City of Glasgow Yeomanry, Lt.-Col. K. H. M. Connal, were landed on the Peninsula, and distributed through the three infantry brigades. These yeomen, thorough going sportsmen as they were, set to work at once to learn their jobs as infantrymen carrying on trench warfare. They were big, lusty men, and it was good to see them digging and filling sandbags, before the diseases of the place began to affect them. This reinforcement amounted to 55 officers and 1070 other ranks, so that, in addition to the health and strength of its men, it was of great value for its numbers alone. The total strength of the 157th Brigade, the strongest of the three, at this time was 68 officers and 1511 other ranks. These figures included 150 recovering health in the training camp at Mudros, besides all detached men. The sick and wounded in hospital, but still on its strength, amounted to 1155. The average effective rifle strength for a brigade of the Division in the trenches at this time was less than that of a normal battalion.

The work of pushing forward various bombing saps at night was carried out several times in October and with complete success. From this time we may date the commencement of the systematic operations which finally drove the Turks out of the trench marked on the British maps as G.11a, and accordingly out of the main fork of Krithia Nullah. After this watercourse divided, the two branches were called respectively West and East Krithia Nullahs.

On the 9th the 5th K.O.S.B., Lt.-Col. W. J. Millar, advanced a bomb-sap on the east side of East Krithia Nullah to within about twenty-five yards of a Turkish trench. During the night of the 12th the 4th K.O.S.B., Lt.-Col. G. Wilson, pushed the North-East Bombing Station forward about fifteen yards. This brought it within fifteen yards of the Turks, and the first intimation of the change to the latter was a salvo of bombs at daybreak. Five nights later the 5th H.L.I., Col. F. L. Morrison, advanced the North-West Bombing Station from the Vineyard to very close quarters with the Turkish trenches guarding East Krithia Nullah.

The 7th Royal Scots, Lt.-Col. W. C. Peebles, had drawn up a scheme to capture a trench which ran along the west side of West Krithia Nullah, but, before they had time to put it into effect, they were relieved by the 7th H.L.I.,

VINEYARD FIRING LINE, CAPE HELLES

OCTOBER AND COOLER WEATHER

Lt.-Col. J. H. Galbraith, who put the projected plan into execution. On the 20th, under bright moonlight, a party of 7th H.L.I., under Capt. E. Watson, stole across No Man's Land to this trench (part of H.11a), and found it unoccupied for the time being. Before the Turks realised what had happened, the 7th H.L.I. had erected a barricade, and dug a communication trench of their own across to it without the loss of a man. The portion captured ran along the top of the cliffs of West Krithia Nullah, directly overlooking and almost enfilading the Turkish trench G.11a, which ran across the more low-lying tongue dividing the two watercourses. The Turks showed their appreciation of this very clever theft from them of a valuable trench, by making a heavy bomb attack on the new barricade at 9.45 p.m. on the next night. Lieut. Arber, 7th H.L.I., and one other rank were killed, and seven other ranks were wounded, but the attack was beaten off. In the afternoon of the 22nd the enemy tried to creep up and throw bombs over the barricade, whilst their artillery shelled it and their machine-gunners swept it with fire. Meanwhile, a party of Turks left G.11a as if to attack, but they were driven back, and the attempts to retake the trench failed. The Turks put bridge-traverses across G.11a, and, because of the hollow in which that trench ran, it was very difficult for British guns to destroy them without imperilling their own lines.

All of this made the Turks very nervous, and they became extremely active in making overhead cover, putting out wire, and otherwise strengthening their lines. They also tried to destroy our bombing stations by bombing and shelling, but without success. Frameworks, covered with wire-netting and fixed at the end of bomb-saps, made it much more difficult for the Turks to throw grenades into the British T heads, and they copied this means of defence.

On 30th October the 5th R.S.F., Lt.-Col. A. H. Leggett, D.S.O., pushed forward for a few yards a barricade in the trench H.11a, on the cliffs of West Krithia Nullah, making it possible for the British bombers to throw bombs over two of the bridge-traverses in G.11a by hand. By the end of October there was no question that our men could throw bombs by hand much further than the Turks, and this prowess can be traced to the good training of the bombing schools in the " Rest Camp."

At the same time the Lowland Division ran out T-headed saps in other places, digging new fire trenches, so that it steadily ate into No Man's Land about East Krithia Nullah.

The stage was now almost set for the battles to capture the junction of East and West Krithia Nullahs. This was in the Turkish centre, and, because of the utility of these nullahs as communication trenches, its capture would constitute a direct threat against Krithia and Achi Baba.

CHAPTER IX

(29TH JUNE TO 20TH DECEMBER, 1915)

THE GLASGOW HOWITZERS AT ANZAC AND SUVLA AND SIR CHARLES MONRO'S REPORT

> Few and short were the prayers we said,
> And we spoke not a word of sorrow;
> But we steadfastly gazed on the face of the dead,
> And we bitterly thought of the morrow.
>
> We thought as we hollowed his narrow bed
> And smoothed down his lonely pillow,
> That the foe and the stranger would tread o'er his head,
> And we far away on the billow.
>
> *Burial of Sir John Moore*: CHARLES WOLFE.

FOR the 4th (Glasgow) Battery at Cape Helles, the period following the 28th June was one of retaliatory bombardments and of repelling counter-attacks. The Lowland artillerymen were ordered to stand by for the 12th July, but to their great disappointment were not called upon. Orders arrived a fortnight later for the 4th Battery to proceed to Anzac to strengthen the Australian and New Zealand Army Corps, with which the 5th Battery, under Major R. R. Stewart, had already done good service. It landed on the nights of 27-28th and 28-29th July.

Anzac was the most confined area on Gallipoli. It was a maze, less than three hundred acres in extent, of ridges and gullies, the coastward fringe of the range of Sari Bair. No part of its front line was more than 1000 yards from the sea, and all night long Turkish bullets spluttered in the waves. It took a hundred men on the drag-ropes of each gun to pull it up the tracks which passed for roads on the faces of the cliffs, but by daylight each one was in position with a supply of ammunition. The batteries had to shoot through an arc of over 180°, that is to say in every direction excepting out to sea. The British front line was only a few hundred yards in front of their positions, which were close together, and they were constantly annoyed by snipers and machine-guns from front and flanks.

Because of the Russian collapse in Poland, Sir Ian Hamilton decided that his wisest plan was to strike without further delay from Anzac at Sari Bair, the capture of which would give him the Kilid Bahr Plateau, the Narrows, and finally cut the Turkish Army in two. Of his five new divisions two had not actually arrived, but the autumn was at hand, reinforcements for the enemy were approaching and further delay might spoil all chance of success. Briefly, his plan was to distract the Turks by attacks at Helles and from the right of Anzac on Lone Pine Ridge, and by feints at Mitylene and Bulair, coupled with the dissemination of false reports. The real attack was to be made from the left of Anzac on Sari Bair, and was to be covered by a surprise landing at Suvla Bay further to the north. This latter was to protect the left flank of the main assault by capturing the heights north of Sari Bair, and to assist in the capture of that dominating ridge.

At 5 a.m. on the 6th August the Glasgow Howitzers opened fire in support of the Australian attack on Lone Pine Ridge, an immensely strong field fortification, which was captured by 6.30 p.m.

On the following day both Glasgow batteries were turned on the German Officers' Trench, a position which had resisted all previous attacks. During the preceding night New Zealanders and Australians had burst out from the left of Anzac, until by 9 a.m. on the 7th they were on Rhododendron Ridge, close up to the summit of Chunuk Bair, one of the most prominent peaks of Sari Bair, the key position. Early in the afternoon the Glasgow Howitzers assisted in dispersing Turks, who were massing in Legge Valley for a counter-attack on Lone Pine Ridge. Throughout the day the Lowland gunners toiled and sweated in the

THE GLASGOW HOWITZERS 165

great heat, throwing shells from their ancient howitzers, wherever they were needed.

Meanwhile, the 9th Army Corps had commenced landing at Suvla Bay in the early morning of the 7th. Very little water could be got ashore for the troops and animals, and the advance inland to the north of Sari Bair did not take place to support the attack of Imperial and Colonial troops on Chunuk Bair, which was made at dawn on the 8th. The Glasgow Howitzers had joined the other artillery in bombarding the height through the night from 10 p.m. to 4.15 a.m. A footing was secured on Chunuk Bair, but enemy reinforcements from the north hopelessly outnumbered and drove back the troops assaulting Koja Chemen Tepe. The Lowland gunners hardly ceased firing throughout the 8th.

On the following night there was no rest for the Glasgow men, who were engaged in replenishing their ammunition from the beach. From midnight until 5.15 a.m. on the 9th, all of the British artillery, afloat and ashore, was in action, shelling the Turkish positions for another assault on Chunuk Bair. Imperial troops assaulted, and for a few minutes a little band of English and Gurkhas captured the saddle east of Chunuk Bair, thus cutting it off. Below them, in the distance, they could see the silvery waters of the Narrows. The fate of the campaign trembled in the balances, but a salvo of heavy shells and a counter-attack by swarms of Turks drove the heroic handful off the ridge, and the balance swung definitely against us. The 9th Corps had landed more troops at Suvla, and tried to advance on this day, but they were almost without artillery ashore and were held back.

The following night passed quietly, but on the 10th a Turkish bombardment was poured on the 900 British troops clinging to the edge of Chunuk Bair, and then 12,000 of the enemy overwhelmed them. Afterwards, the Turks tried to retake Rhododendron Ridge, but the British artillery, afloat and ashore, could get at them, and they were driven back. The 9th Corps again tried to advance on the 10th, but the Turks were ready, and this day saw the final extinction of all real hopes of a British victory in the Gallipoli campaign.

On the 11th, and again on the 15th, the 9th Corps tried to advance in order to outflank Sari Bair from the north, but it was too late, and these attempts failed.

General Birdwood, in a letter circulated among the troops of the Australian and New Zealand Corps, referred to the " enormous and self-sacrificing assistance " of the artillery, mentioning the 4th Lowland Brigade.

As a result of these operations from 6-15th August, the British were holding a strip of land about nine miles long, and averaging less than two miles wide. Lone Pine was only about 1000 yards from the sea, whilst inland from the shores of Suvla Bay the line was in places about 4000 yards from the coast. The area generally consisted of open country, covered with plenty of scrub, and seamed by watercourses. The ground rose gradually to ranges of hills, which completely shut it in. The highest of these in the south was Koja Chemen Tepe (1000 feet) on Sari Bair; and in the north Kavak Tepe (970 feet) and Tekke Tepe (950 feet). Only on the extreme flanks did the British lines include the crests of ridges, at Kiretch Tepe Sirt (650 feet) on the northern shore and at Lone Pine (410 feet) in the south. Everywhere else they were completely dominated by the surrounding heights, which were fast being entrenched by the Turks, and turned into a series of mountain fortresses. In the south the British trenches crept up to Rhododendron Ridge (700 feet) on Sari Bair, but as a rule they ran across low ground, which could be easily observed from the heights above.

Sir Ian Hamilton made another attempt on the afternoon of the 21st of August to improve his position by the capture of a ridge, which ran towards the sea from the centre of the Turkish position, and which terminated in two heights, Scimitar Hill, and Ismail Oglu Tepe. The 4th Battery was moved to Suvla Bay to assist in the attack. The British attacking force, nominally of five divisions of infantry and one of cavalry, had ashore less than one-sixth of their complement of artillery, and this attack also failed. Usually

THE GLASGOW HOWITZERS 167

the hills, when viewed from Suvla Bay in the afternoon, stood out clear and distinct, but this afternoon the whole arena was wrapped in a mantle of pearly mist, which prevented the British artillery from observing their fire.

On leaving the Australian and New Zealand Army Corps, Lt.-Col. Sheppard received a letter from Gen. Birdwood thanking the Brigade for its first-class work, and expressing the general regret of the Colonials at their departure.

Apart from a small gain on Kaiajak Aghala and some localised trench warfare, there followed a period of enforced and wearisome inactivity for the British, whilst the Turkish position gradually developed into a series of impregnable hill-fortresses. Meanwhile, sickness, and especially dysentery, ravaged the ranks still further. By the 3rd of September the personnel of the 5th Battery of the Lowland Howitzers had been reduced to one officer and twenty other ranks, and the night firing in response to S.O.S. calls had to be carried out by men who ran from gun to gun. The 5th Battery remained at this strength for about four weeks. The 4th Battery was more fortunate, but for a while its personnel were reduced to two officers and thirty-five other ranks. Normally, each of these batteries should have had with them in the field five officers and 194 other ranks. Both batteries had to maintain observation posts several thousand yards from the gun positions, but they never once failed to fire when called upon, whether by day or by night. Except in response to an urgent call, the artillery dared fire little, because their daily ration for general purposes was only about two shells per gun.

Before the end of August the antiquated 5-inch howitzers began to show signs of wear and tear. " No hope of new ones and no chance of repairs, so we must continue. Error in some cases, through ammunition and gun, sometimes 500 yards—a serious matter when the Turkish trenches are only 20 yards from our own," wrote Capt. W. Watson in his diary at the time.

On the 20th September it was known by the Entente Powers that Bulgaria was siding in an unnatural alliance with Turkey against Russia, her co-religionist, Slavonic like herself, to whose armies she owed her very existence. This meant the release of Turkish forces on the Bulgarian frontier, the seizure of the Serbian railway between Belgrade and Pirot by the Central Powers, and a stream of munitions pouring down it into Turkey. On 5th October the Entente withdrew their representatives from Sofia, and Bulgaria entered the war on the side of the Germanic Powers. Greece was under an obligation to help Serbia, if she were attacked by Bulgaria, and, under the influence of Venizelos, she got so far as to order the mobilisation of her armies. But, the policy of King Constantine gaining the day, she decided that she was not bound to help Serbia, if Bulgaria attacked in company with other powers.

For the time being Greece was a doubtful neutral and Venizelos resigned. The British Government, fighting on half-a-dozen fronts already, had to consider whence it could get together an army to help the Serbians, who were attacked in front and flank, and with the shifty King Constantine in their rear. In this extremity, Sir Ian Hamilton was asked what troops he could spare—this being at a time when the average division on Gallipoli was little stronger than a brigade. He sent from Suvla the 10th (Irish) Division, one of his strongest, and the French sent a composite division from Cape Helles, leaving behind one division half-composed of Senegalese, black troops who could not be relied on under a bombardment of H.E. or grenades. This movement left only three British divisions at Cape Helles, the 42nd, 52nd, and Royal Naval Division, totalling 13,300 worn-out men; but most serious of all it took away forty-four French guns, which had always been amply supplied with ammunition.

At the end of August it was reckoned that Cape Helles was being held by the minimum garrison, but now, with greatly reduced forces, the tired British troops had to take over a large portion of the French line. The most that Sir Ian Hamilton could do to ease the situation at Cape Helles was to send the 87th Brigade of the 29th Division, at this time equal in strength to an ordinary battalion. The fact that, even under these circumstances, the Turks could not induce their troops to make a proper attack on the British is eloquent testimony as to their opinion of the British soldier. Sir Ian Hamilton had to rely on the hardiness, cheerfulness and fighting spirit of the remaining British troops.

The British Government decided that their only line of action now was to end the Gallipoli expedition altogether. Sir Ian Hamilton, thinking of the difficulties of the landing, of all that had since been achieved, and of the effect on Egypt and the Mahomedan world, remembering also how the blunders of the Crimea had been followed by the Indian Mutiny, advised strongly against evacuation. He estimated the probable loss at 50 per cent. of his entire force. At an earlier date, when circumstances were not so difficult, Gen. Gouraud, who commanded the French Army Corps until wounded, had estimated a loss of two divisions out of six in case of the evacuation of Cape Helles.

On 17th October Sir Ian Hamilton received a telegram recalling him, and directing him to hand over the Gallipoli command to Lt.-Gen. Sir W. R. Birdwood, until the arrival of his successor, Gen. Sir Charles Monro. The War Council " desired a fresh, unbiased opinion from a responsible Commander upon the question of early evacuation." With a sore heart Sir Ian Hamilton penned his farewell order to the M.E.F. on the day that he received this cable. Writing to his troops in this order, he expressed his admiration at the " noble response which they have invariably given to the calls he has made upon them. No risk has been too desperate; no sacrifice too great. Sir Ian Hamilton thanks all ranks, from Generals to private soldiers, for the wonderful way they have seconded his efforts."

Lord Kitchener made a hurried visit to Gallipoli to see for himself how matters stood. He conferred with Sir Charles Monro, Sir H. McMahon, the High Commissioner, and Sir John Maxwell, Commanding the Forces in Egypt. On 12th November he was ashore for a few hours at Cape Helles, seeing all that he thought necessary from the Headquarters of 8th Corps and Sedd el Bahr. The next day he visited Anzac and Suvla, and climbed up to the most advanced positions. He went home to recommend evacuation to the War Council.

With the possibility of having the Peninsula cut off for a fortnight at a time owing to storms, the certain loss of prestige in the East consequent on the evacuation seemed to hold less risk than the chance of greater disaster through attempting to fight on.

The Mediterranean Expeditionary Force was now divided into two distinct bodies, the "Dardanelles Army," under Lt.-Gen. Sir W. Birdwood, and the "Salonika Army," under Lt.-Gen. Sir B. Mahon.

In the course of time History will pass final judgment on Sir Ian Hamilton, and the Gallipoli campaign that might have been. Some writers, with all the audacity bred of great ignorance, have criticised and condemned, but without possession of the full facts opinions are valueless. Three things, however, we know already :

(1) The Mediterranean Expeditionary Force was starved for troops, artillery and ammunition from the commencement, despite Sir Ian Hamilton's appeals.

(2) Several times during the campaign decisive victory was nearly won, but was lost through lack of reinforcements and of shells.

(3) The first ruinous break-through in that great front of the Central Powers, which stretched from the North Sea to the Aegean, took place in the Balkan Peninsula. After that, Austria-Hungary collapsed, and it became a question of how long it would take to move troops through Central Europe into the German rear.

Sir Charles Monro assumed command of the M.E.F. on the 28th October, and reported on the British positions. "The Force," he wrote, "held a line possessing every possible military defect. The position was without depth, the communications were insecure and dependent on the weather."

The Turks enjoyed full powers of observation, and had abundant artillery positions. So strong were the Turkish defences now that they could hold the British and French, who were on the Peninsula, with a small force, whilst prosecuting their designs on Egypt, Mesopotamia and Russia. At the same time there was no sufficiently large area in which either to mount the number of guns or to deploy the number of troops necessary to take these positions even if these guns and troops had been available.

He then dealt with the sufferings and condition of the troops. Nowhere could they obtain rest from shell-fire. They were enervated by the diseases of the place. There was less actual sickness now that the weather was cooler, but on the other hand a Balkan winter was approaching. Those that were there would soon have to be replaced, or they would disappear into hospitals or graves. The only course left seemed to be to " divert the troops locked up on the Peninsula to a more useful theatre " (Sir C. Monro).

The value of the operations of the 52nd Lowland Division against the junction of East and West Krithia Nullahs, the last serious offensive on Gallipoli, can be readily understood. Such operations had to be assigned to troops who would press them with the utmost vigour, or the enemy might realise that they were only feints, and see through everything.

On the 27th September Lt.-Col. H. C. Sheppard went to hospital, and the command of the 4th Lowland Howitzer Brigade devolved upon Capt. W. Watson, all his seniors being in hospital.

On the 17th of November there broke out a terrible gale which thundered on the beaches at Anzac and Suvla, and left them littered with piled-up shipping and wreckage of all sorts. Ten days later the wind rose again for another storm, bringing with it torrents of cold rain, and finally that dreadful blizzard of snow which covered bleak hillside and open plain and morass with a white cloak of misery. To crown everything the blizzard was accompanied by biting frost. The storm lasted for four days and nights. Sentries were found frozen dead at their posts. Some men were bereft of their reason. The blizzard cost the Gallipoli armies as many men as a first-class battle. The 9th Army Corps alone lost 200 dead, and over 10,000 frost-bitten and prostrated men were removed from Suvla, Anzac, and Cape

Helles, more than two-thirds of whom were from the northern front. Many of the Australians had not seen snow before in their lives, but their fortitude was worthy of the highest traditions of the British race. This great disaster hastened the decision to evacuate, and on 8th December Sir Charles Monro received the necessary orders from the War Office, and ordered Gen. Birdwood to proceed at once with arrangements for leaving Suvla and Anzac.

During the first week of December, the 4th Battery was withdrawn from Chocolate Hill, where it had been stationed, to Lala Baba, for both of the Lowland Batteries had been detailed for the rearguard, the 4th at Suvla and the 5th at Anzac. Every artifice possible was employed to delude the Turks, while troops and guns were embarked each night. The enemy suspected nothing. Between the occasional bursts of rifle-fire from their trenches the last parties to leave could hear dull rumbling explosions as the Turks blasted new entrenchments in their rocky fastnesses. They were known to be constructing cement platforms behind Kavak Tepe and elsewhere for large howitzers. The Turks respected the fighting qualities of those armies of invalids to the last.

The last night, 19th December, was calm, with bright moonlight, and the Turkish Higher Command was having its attention drawn to Cape Helles by the attacks of the 157th Brigade in Krithia Nullah. The 5th Battery had to leave behind one old howitzer at Anzac, but it was blown up after dark. The remainder got away quite safely before midnight, and the whole evacuation was completed at 3.30 a.m. on the 20th. In all, ten disabled guns, some tents, and destroyed stores were left behind. It was not until H.M.S. *Cornwallis* began to shell the piers soon after 7 a.m. that the Turks realised what had happened.

CHAPTER X

(1ST TO 30TH NOVEMBER, 1915)

THE NOVEMBER FIGHTING IN KRITHIA NULLAH AND THE COMING OF WINTER

> Few, few shall part, where many meet.
> The snow shall be their winding-sheet,
> And every turf beneath their feet
> Shall be a soldier's sepulchre.
> *Hohenlinden* : T. CAMPBELL.

WINTER was approaching, and winter quarters of some kind had to be provided, with as much appearance of permanence as possible. Life was scarcely tolerable with blankets and greatcoats soaked by chilly rain, when mud grew deeper and encased feet and legs as though in plaster of Paris casts. Anything in the nature of a fire was impossible. The only overhead cover available for troops in the trenches consisted of canopies made by their blankets or waterproof sheets. Even these flimsy coverings could not be allowed in the front line. The enemy were only a few dozen yards away, and it was essential that men awakened from sleep should jump into position on the fire-step, rifle in hand, and with no entangling canopy to get clear of. Accordingly, men slept in their equipment on the fire-step, their loaded rifles with bayonets fixed leant against the parapet, and with nothing between them and the rain, sleet, and snow but so much of their blankets and waterproof sheet as did not slide off in their uneasy rest. The vermin were bad, and, as officers and men lay sleeping, one could see them stir and move frequently, as if the lice would never let them rest. The Medical Services made unending efforts to keep down this pest with Serbian boilers and extemporised equipment, but the odds were all against them. " Many times each night one would waken shivering and chilled to the bone. Hard rubbing and a brisk walk brought the circulation back. Then a little more sleep—and frozen again." (Major C. S. Black.)

On 5th November Col. A. Young was invalided to hospital, and after that date the 4th and 7th R.S. were again administered as one battalion under Lt.-Col. Peebles.

The strength of the Division had been so far reduced, in spite of reinforcements of yeomanry, and returned sick and wounded, that on 15th November, after the deduction of men serving with the trench mortars, mining companies, and on other special work, the average strength of a brigade in effective rifles was only about 675. At this period in the front fire-trench there were frequently not sufficient men in a unit to man every fire bay, and some had to be left empty. Officers and senior N.C.O.'s in the front line were usually on duty the better part of the night. Other ranks continued to do sentry duty on the fire-step, the periods being an hour on and an hour off.

Many, who should have been in hospital, saw the shortage of officers and men, and how few and small were the reinforcements that came, and they volunteered to stay on in the trenches. If a man felt that he could " stick it out " for only a few days longer, it was a help. Some of these men were killed in the trenches, when they could have been in comfortable and clean hospital beds. And this was a time when the Turkish shell-fire was steadily increasing and their trench mortars were bombarding trenches well behind the front line with incendiary and other bombs, for on 5th November Nish fell and the Central Powers obtained direct railway communication with Constantinople and an ample supply of ammunition was made easy.

The religion of the trenches was a very practical one, and was not limited by creeds. In the main, it was one of brotherly love, and self sacrifice, and it was fitting that it should have been practised under a flag which is a Union of Crosses.

Turkish soldiers crawled across occasionally in ones and twos to surrender, and without exception they were treated with kindness by the men, who always gave "Johnny" some of their own small store of cigarettes or food.

Quantities of corrugated iron sheeting were landed at Cape Helles during November, and rows of roofed dug-outs were constructed on the high ground above "X" Beach, an area where a drainage system was possible. A few of these were ready for occupation at the end of November. For those who could use them they were an unspeakable luxury. Later there were so few troops that there was accommodation near them for everyone.

Col. Edington gives the following description of a hospital camp at Cape Helles: "The camp was laid out in the form of parallel lines of trenches, running north-west and south-east. These trenches were three feet wide, and were cut to a depth of four feet. Opening off one side of the trench was a series of bays or recesses with intervening butts of earth. One trench was designed for hospital purposes, and each of its bays was sufficiently large to accommodate three to eight stretchers. The bays in the living trenches were smaller, accommodating two men in each. The height of the bays was increased by a parapet of the excavated earth, improved later by the addition of sand-bags. Roof shelter was obtained by stretching out tarpaulins and ground sheets. In the hospital trench these were supported by wooden frames; later, in this trench, tarpaulins and sheets were replaced by corrugated iron." Our hospitals feared only stray shells as the Turks were consistently scrupulous in their conduct to the Red Cross.

With the advent of the cooler weather and rains in October dysentery had waned, but instead there commenced an epidemic of jaundice. Few died from this disease, but many sickened. The totals of sick and wounded in hospital, but still on the strength of the 52nd Division, at various dates in the last two months of 1915, were as follows :

	Officers.	Other Ranks.
November 7th	92	2964
,, 14th	104	3219
,, 21st	105	3227
,, 28th	126	3261
December 5th	127	3359
,, 12th	122	3552
,, 19th	126	3248
,, 26th	107	3056

All officers and other ranks sent to the British Isles were struck off the Division's strength, and consequently not included in the above figures.

It must not be supposed that either officers or men of the Division allowed life to become one long procession of gloom and misery. The ordinary amenities of social intercourse were carried on. After every arrival of a parcel mail little dinner parties were arranged, in which the company was invariably excellent, and the menu ranged from Devonshire cream and peaches to bully-beef and biscuits. Even in the trenches the men sang their choruses and were cheery. An especially heavy shelling by the Turks was dismissed with the comment that "Johnny" must have received another "paircel."

At the commencement of November the weather was usually fine, but very cold and frosty, and there were several heavy rainfalls. The loyal service of the cooks was one of the factors that made life possible. The sides of Krithia Nullah were honeycombed with the dug-outs of Advanced Dressing Stations, Royal Engineers and others ; and in one part above Clapham Junction was "Dixie-Land," named after the "dixies" or camp kettles. Here were the field-kitchens of the Division, which served the men in the trenches. Because of the gradual upward slope, and the brushwood which concealed the smoke until it diffused a little, it was a long time before the Turks located these field-kitchens exactly, and they were strangely immune from shell-fire. The enemy shrapnelled Krithia Nullah from end to end daily, and occasionally dropped a few H.E. into it,

FIGHTING IN KRITHIA NULLAH

but the cooks never failed their comrades in the fire-trenches. The banks were about twelve feet above the level of the stream, and, taking cover under the steep upper portion, they tended their fires, and always produced some kind of a meal, which the W., A. and R. C. (water, ammunition and ration carriers) took to the trenches. Before dawn, on many a cold and wet early morning stand-to, one could see the glow of their fires in the darkness, as they prepared porridge, mostly from oatmeal sent out by friends at home, soup, or cocoa. The rum ration was usually issued at this hour, as it brought out a temporary glow, which made the men feel warmer until the sun rose and improved things a little.

About the 14th November winter clothing was drawn from ordnance and issued to the troops. "References have been made to deficiencies in the fighting equipment of the troops on Gallipoli, which were doubtless due to the initial unpreparedness of the nation for a European War, to the enormous demands on our resources made by the fighting on the Western Front, as well as to the rapid and unlooked for increase in the equipment required by the Gallipoli force itself. The clothing and feeding of the troops, however, were more than creditable to the departments concerned, and the issue made at this time was an admirable example of forethought and organization as the following list will show:

1 waterproof cloak	per W.O., N.C.O. and man.	
1 leather jerkin	,,	,,
1 pair woollen-lined leather gloves	,,	,,
1 woollen muffler	,,	,,

Rubber boots, first issue 80 per battalion, afterwards increased for battalions in the trenches." (Col. J. Anderson.)

By this time the bombers had been issued with the Mills hand-grenade, and there is no need to point out what a vast improvement this was on the converted jam tin or the spherical bomb with a fuse, some of which latter had been manufactured in Egypt and were mostly too defective for use. Spherical bombs had to be used for the catapults.

Grenades of all kinds were strictly rationed, and if a bombing officer expended more than his allowance he had to give good reason why.

Lance-Cpl. J. Temple, 4th R.S., was throwing a Mills bomb on the 13th of November, when it struck the top sandbags, for the barricades had to be very high, and rolled back into the trench. He promptly threw a sandbag damper on it, put his foot on top, and shouted to the rest to clear out. They did just in time to avoid the explosion. When he was picked up, it was found that his foot was blown off. He was awarded a D.C.M.

The amount of ground which could be captured and held by the Allies on Cape Helles was limited by the means of communication between the new front line and the old one. If water, ammunition, and rations could not be brought up, the ground could not be held. This need could usually be supplied only by digging trenches forward, a laborious and costly process; but, where a nullah of any depth was available, forming a ready-made communication trench, the possibilities of being able to hold a larger area of captured ground were much increased. For these reasons the Turks probably regarded the forthcoming operations against the junction of East and West Krithia Nullahs as the prelude to further attacks on Krithia, and finally on Achi Baba.

The western banks of West Krithia Nullah rise in a series of steep cliffs of marl and clay, probably forty feet in height. The ground on the eastern side of East Krithia Nullah descends more gradually to the watercourse. The tongue of land between the two nullahs before they join is more low-lying, and after steep banks of about ten feet high on the watercourses, it rises in a small swell. A strong Turkish trench system followed the cliffs on the west side of West Krithia Nullah, being designated as the H trenches on British maps. It crossed the tongue of land with the G.11a and other trenches. Then it ran up the slope on the east side of East Krithia Nullah to the Vineyard with the G.10, G.11, and other trenches. All fire-trenches were heavily wired.

FIGHTING IN KRITHIA NULLAH

The first move was on the 15th November, when the 156th Brigade, under Brig.-Gen. L. C. Koe, captured a portion of the trenches on the eastern slope (G.11), and others on the western cliffs (H.11a). Those in the centre (G.11a) between the nullahs were left in Turkish hands for the present.

The general plan was as follows. The attack on the right (G.11) was to be made by the Cameronians Battalion, Lt.-Col. B. G. Bridge, reinforced by Lanarkshire Yeomanry; the attack on the left (H.11a) by the Royal Scots, Lt.-Col. W. C. Peebles, reinforced by Ayrshire Yeomanry. Both attacks would be made from parts of the line where three or four bombing-saps ran down old trenches towards Turkish bombing-saps, which in some cases were only twenty yards away. The attack was to have no artillery preparation, but was to be a surprise, the signal being the explosion of three mines, which the mining detachments, working under the Royal Engineers, had run under the enemy trenches.

Supporting fire was to be given by the 4th R.S. and machine-guns from all the brigades of the Division, whilst the 155th Brigade (Brig.-Gen. J. B. Pollok-M'Call) were to demonstrate with their bayonets as if going to attack, and so confuse the Turks.

Every man possible was gathered to swell the very thin ranks of the 156th Brigade. Fourteen of its men in the Divisional Band returned to their units on the day previous to the attack.

It had been very wet on the night before and was showery during the afternoon of the 15th.

At 3 p.m. everything was ready, the three mines went off with mighty explosions that shook the whole ground in the vicinity, and immense brown and black columns of dust, earth, and smoke were flung into the air, in form like a row of gigantic elm trees. As this happened, two monitors, each mounting 14-inch guns, and the cruiser *Edgar*, all "blister ships" to protect them from submarine attack, began to pound the enemy's support and reserve trenches. The British artillery also joined in, and between the explosions could be heard the continuous chatter and rattle of machine-guns.

One mine had destroyed a Turkish bombing station in the trench (H.11a) to be taken by the 7th R.S. The other two had almost ruined G.11, the objective of the Cameronians, and had blown most of its garrison into the air.

While the dust and debris were still in the air, Cameronians on the right and Royal Scots on the left had dashed forward. The Turks appeared to be demoralized by the explosion, and could be seen running backwards and forwards in a communication trench on the tongue of land, discharging their rifles in the air. British machine-guns were turned on them, and added to their confusion.

The surprise was complete. The Cameronians met with little opposition. Led by Lieuts. Meiklejohn and Watson, they were soon in full occupation of the mine craters and ruined trench, which had been the Turkish G.11, and ready to defend them against counter-attacks. The task of consolidation amounted almost to rebuilding the trench, but this had been provided for, filled and empty sandbags were ready, and despite enemy snipers the work was pressed on. Lieut. Meiklejohn was shot dead whilst directing this work. At 3.37 p.m. some Turks tried to get over the parapet opposite this captured trench, but our machine-guns drove them back.

In the British trenches on the top of the cliffs the bombers of the 7th R.S., led by Lieut. J. Scott (8th H.L.I. attached), tore through a gap that had been prepared under the advanced barricades, and rushed up to the top of H.11a. Numbers of the enemy left their dug-outs to see what was happening, and were either killed or made prisoners. In the melee a huge Turk, emerging from a dug-out behind Lieut. Scott, took aim at him with his rifle from only a few yards distance. The Turk could not get the breech to close. Cpl. Kelly saw him and, with a shout of, " Look out, Mr. Scott," shot the Turk dead. The latter had forgotten that he had one cartridge in the chamber, had put another in the breech, and was too excited to notice why the bolt was jammed.

FIGHTING IN KRITHIA NULLAH

The Royal Scots had now obtained their objective, but, working further down a cross-trench, found the Turks sitting in niches with their bayonets just appearing. They threw a few bombs at the Turks, and then retired a few yards and erected sandbag barricades to defend what they had taken. Here, also, the mine explosion had filled in part of the captured trench, and much digging was necessary to clear a passage. Enemy snipers and machine-gunners were busy, and Lieut. J. E. Flett, 7th R.S., was killed whilst directing a digging party from the top crater. The Turkish artillery commenced to shrapnel the captured trenches, getting H.11a completely in enfilade. Capt. A. M. Mitchell and Lieut. D. B. Allan carried on the work of repairing and rebuilding from the time of the assault, 3 p.m. on the 15th, until 6 p.m. on the next day. 2000 sandbags had been filled and laid in readiness before the attack. These were passed forward by men at yard intervals. Altogether, over 10,000 sandbags were used by the 7th R.S. in this work of reconstruction. The Cameronians had similar and equally well organised arrangements.

The captured trenches were strongly made, with well-built dug-outs. Good timber had been used, and in some places walls were bricked. It was fortunate that the attack had not been postponed, because the Royal Scots found an enemy mine-shaft leading below one of their own bomb-stations. It was within two hours of completion, well built and lined with wood, and the charge was ready to place in position. In addition to this, running from the enemy bomb-station which had been blown up, was another mine which led below the very bombing-sap from which the Royal Scots had rushed up H.11a. The entrances to both were blocked and destroyed by the Royal Scots. The first one was just in front of a barricade, which they had erected and which covered it.

The monitors continued to throw their three-quarter ton projectiles into the Turkish rear until 6 p.m. on the 15th, by which time the troops on both sides of the nullah junction had obtained a good hold on the captured positions. About 160 yards of trench had been taken on the eastern side, and about 120 on the western. So far the casualties had been wonderfully light, and this was largely due to the skilful organization and execution of the attack.

On that night, 15-16th, there burst a heavy storm of thunder, lightning and rain. It turned the trenches into canals, and flooded the " Rest Camp " area, until most of the dug-outs there became treacherous pits, in which clothing and kit floated or lay submerged, until they could be fished out in the morning. In the captured trenches everyone worked all night under cover of the darkness. The occasional flashes of lightning made everything look unusually weird and awesome.

During the night small parties of the Turks crept or rushed forward in frequent attempts on the barricade, which covered the entrance to the mine-shaft which had been first discovered. As a rule they were bombed, shot down, or driven back, but continued their attempts throughout the day. The Turks had evidently set great value on that mine-shaft and had intended to do much with it.

The 16th was bright and fair, and an enemy aeroplane flew over the lines at 7.30 a.m., evidently trying to find out what was going to follow the attack of the previous day. Consolidation proceeded, the Cameronians running out bombing-saps towards East Krithia Nullah, and 4th and 7th R.S. digging a new fire-trench, Forrest Road, which ran west of H.11a, now called Rosebery Street. Lieut. A. Muir, 7/8th Cameronians, was killed by snipers on this day, whilst on the work of consolidation.

At 8 o'clock on the evening of the 16th, the Turks made a determined effort to recapture Rosebery Street. A party crept up from the low ground at the edge of the cliff, and rushed the barricade. They held it for a few moments and had managed to pull part of it down, when bombers of the Royal Scots and Yeomanry, led by Lieut. J. B. Greenshields, 7th R.S., and Lieut. J. A. Neilson, 1/1st Ayrshire Yeomanry, drove them out with bayonet and grenade. The Turks had left behind a small but very heavy, white, wooden box in the bombing station. Remembering the mine-shaft, the Scotsmen pushed this over the parapet out of the way.

FIGHTING IN KRITHIA NULLAH 183

The barricade was rebuilt a dozen feet further back, clear of the debris of the old one. The Turks made further attempts on it during the night, and two after daylight, but were unsuccessful.

During the night (16-17th) four attempts were made on the Cameronians, but they, also, were ready for the Turks. Most of the attacks were half-hearted, but one, more serious than the others, was gallantly repelled by Lieut. J. Fyfe, Sgt. J. Clark, Pte. Braidwood and other bombers.

During the 17th the Royal Scots heard a voice in Turkish come from the ground in their mine crater, and rescued a very hungry Turk, who had been imprisoned for two days in the Turkish mine-shaft leading from it. Calls were heard on the 19th from the other mine-shaft, which was in front of the barricade, and the Royal Scots put up a white flag, intending to save these imprisoned Turks. No response was made from the Turkish lines, and these men had to be left to their fate.

For a couple of days the Turks lay low. But they had been caught napping and were uneasy. They started digging very hard in G.11a, and the other trenches on the tongue of land.

The cost of the operations to the 156th Brigade was small, but nevertheless was a severe strain because of the much reduced strength of the units. Very few were lost in the assault, the principal casualties being in the consolidation and holding of the trenches. The figures given for the period 15-20th November in the War Diary of the 156th Brigade is as follows:

	Officers.	Other Ranks.
Killed	3	22
Wounded	2	85
	5	107

More than half of these belonged to the Cameronians.

The Turkish losses were much greater. Between seventy and a hundred dead Turks were seen, all killed by rifles and bombs; and a wounded prisoner reported that over thirty were buried in the explosion of one mine. To these must be added the Turkish dead we did not see, and their wounded. The 8th Corps Headquarters estimated that twenty were killed by the fire of the 155th Brigade's machine-guns.

The weather became rapidly worse, and bitterly cold, with spells of frost. During the afternoon of Wednesday, 17th November, a southerly gale blew, raising a most vile dust storm. At night the heavens opened, and the water from the slopes poured into the trenches, converting them into flowing rivers, in places two feet deep. The low-lying " Rest Camp " was flooded, and the most confirmed optimists felt within themselves that although the enemy might kill them, they could not make them more cold and miserable.

At the landing places great foaming billows plunged in white cataracts over the sunken hulks and piers, breaking up the wooden and stone structures of the latter, and tearing lighters, picket-boats, and other small craft from their moorings, to pile them up in a chaos of wreckage on the sand.

With spells of bright frost this coarse weather was now to be expected, for winter was upon us.

The 157th Brigade (Brig.-Gen. H. G. Casson) had just taken over the line on either side of Krithia Nullah, during the afternoon of the 21st, when the Turks commenced an attack, which was an attempt to capture the new grenade stations about Krithia Nullah, and to follow this up by breaking through the British line.

From mid-day onwards there was some shelling of these grenade stations, and other parts of the line east of Krithia Nullah. No special attention was paid to this; but at 4 p.m. the Turkish artillery opened a heavy bombardment of shrapnel and H.E. on the same places, and also on the communication and support trenches, cutting most of the 157th Brigade's telephone wires. Their machine-guns also opened fire on the front line trenches. The 7th H.L.I., Lt.-Col. J. Galbraith, were on the high ground on the western side of the nullah, whence they could bring flanking fire to bear on any attack launched on the 5th H.L.I., Col. F. L. Morrison, who were on the eastern side. Despite

FIGHTING IN KRITHIA NULLAH

the shelling and machine-gun fire, these two units kept up a steady play with rifles and machine-guns on the enemy trenches, where considerable activity was observed. The British artillery fire was slow in opening, but, when it did, was effective. Grenadiers of the 6th H.L.I., and 5th A. & S.H. were helping to hold the bombing-saps, and reinforcements from these units were also moved up in anticipation of attack. At 5 p.m. the Turkish bombardment slackened, and forty minutes later ceased, having completely failed to quell the fire from the 157th Brigade's rifles and machine-guns. The British shelling became heavier.

Turkish officers on both sides of the Nullah now tried to get their men to assault, supported by heavy machine-gun and rifle-fire. A red flag was waved from the enemy's trenches, and all along their line bayonets appeared above the parapets. Here and there small parties of Turks left their trenches, led by officers, but the machine-gun and rifle-fire dropped many, and the survivors bolted back to their trenches.

One or two attempts were made to induce the Turkish infantry to advance, but each one was abortive. Whenever a few Turks showed their heads they were met by a burst of fire, which showed that the 157th Brigade were completely masters of the situation. Apparently, the Turkish infantry remembered the repulse of their counter-attacks a few months earlier.

The units of the 157th Brigade had maintained circuitous communication with their Brigade Headquarters through the 5th K.O.S.B. and by runners, but by 5.30 p.m. all the wires were repaired again. Many quiet acts of bravery were done by battalion signallers, and direct communication was re-established.

After nightfall the slopes were lit by some further bursts of shell-fire, but the Turkish attack had completely failed. There was a bitterly cold wind blowing, but all ranks were in the highest spirits and felt increased confidence in themselves.

This abortive effort had been intended to restore the Turkish soldiers' morale and spirit for attack; but it had precisely the reverse effect. The total losses of the 157th Brigade were eight other ranks killed and thirty-seven wounded, which said much for the British trench construction. Of these twenty-five were grenadiers. The Turkish losses are unknown, but cannot have been light.

For a week the Turks did their utmost to harass the numerous bombing-saps which had been pushed towards their trenches about the junction of East and West Krithia Nullah. They swept them with machine-gun fire at night, and, under cover of this, their men tried to creep up and bomb them; but the grenadiers of the 157th Brigade were too watchful for them, and could throw better. Incendiary bombs were used by the Turks, but to no purpose. This was a very trying time for the grenadiers, because, excluding the Vineyard bombing-saps, there were five main ones to be held on the eastern side of the fork, and four on the western. After a battalion of that period had supplied all the bombing teams necessary for these bomb stations, there were very few riflemen left for the trenches. For the bombing teams themselves, it meant spending most of the time in the bombing-saps, whether their unit was in the front line or in support. Some grenadier officers were on duty in the bombing-saps for several days together. When it is remembered that they were only a few yards from a thoroughly alert enemy, the need for ceaseless vigilance will be understood. To add to this, grenades had to be severely rationed, and only a limited number were allowed for general purposes.

The 26th November was cold and bright, but as evening drew on the wind became gusty, and a heavy storm of thunder and lightning broke out, with intermittent rain squalls. The thunder rolled away before midnight, but the rain fell steadily in torrents. The trenches became channels of water, so that in many parts of the line, everyone had to move about on the fire-step. Even under these circumstances, some irrepressibles could be heard chaffing about "Venice in Gallipoli." Where the trench floors were drained, the mud was ankle deep. Duck-boards

FIGHTING IN KRITHIA NULLAH

were an unheard-of luxury in Gallipoli. The nullahs became raging torrents, which could hardly get rid of the water that poured into them, and swelled until they filled many of the dug-outs with which their sides were honeycombed. In places, such as the Small Nullah between Krithia Road and Achi Baba Nullah, trenches had been replaced by breastworks, and these had been constructed with gaps, that when the rain came, they might not act as dams, until burst by the water confined behind them. Down these torrents swirled all kinds of grim and horrible things. Every dug-out in the " Rest Camp " was flooded, most of them to the brim, and the more level areas became lakes, across which horses and mules were taken at the risk of breaking their legs.

On the next day, the 27th, the wind again rose suddenly and blew a full gale from the south-east with cold, drenching rain, which soaked everything that was not already thoroughly wet.

Great seas thundered on the light piers, breaking them down again, smashing the landing-stages, and hurling a litter of wreckage on the beaches. At noon the wind veered round to the north-west, and later to the north. There was to be no escape, no shelter. The rain became colder and more pitiless, and then turned to sleet. Despite all of this, the Divisional Band, Lieut. W. J. Watson, managed a performance on the afternoon of this day.

All through the night the bitter hurricane blew a cutting blast of icy rain and sleet right into the aching faces of the sentries at Cape Helles. It was a mercy to the Allies there that their men could keep well up to the parapets. But doubtless the Turkish look-outs cowered in their trenches and left No Man's Land to take care of itself.

Then the snow came, and there burst over Gallipoli that blizzard which seemed as if it would overwhelm both armies in a common, gigantic and appalling misery. The biting wind froze the sodden clothing as it hung on the benumbed bodies. Joints would hardly work, and fingers would not move. The physical pain alone of the cold was hard to bear. The blood of everyone had been thinned and their constitutions enervated by the hot weather and the dysentery. On Sunday, the 28th, the heavens were black, and whirling, blinding snow fell heavily, collecting in drifts in the trenches and dug-outs, and overspreading the ground. The pools in the trenches and the streams in the nullahs were frozen over. Some of the motors of the ambulances were frozen and useless. The taps of the water-carts were also frozen. Finally, it was found that many of the machine-guns were in a like state and would not work, and that when the triggers of rifles were pulled, the cocking-pieces had frozen and would hardly move the strikers. This left the troops little more than their bayonets to fight with.

The snow and the bitter frost seemed as if they would end everything; but it is wonderful what can be endured. The Lowland Field Ambulances were on the northern slope of Cape Helles and, accordingly, they had been able to make drains some weeks previously to prevent the water flooding the hospital trenches. Col. Edington relates how he " overheard one of the men telling his pal, apropos our deep drains, which showed black in the snow-covered ground, ' There's one thing about this snow, it lets you see where you're going.' "

A few oil stoves were available, but braziers and perforated buckets were the best for heat when dry fuel could be procured. An extra ration of rum was given on the 28th, and helped to save the health and lives of many. This was one of the few occasions, when the cooks of some units were defeated by wet fuel, and had to give the men a cold breakfast.

If the Turks had attacked on this day, it would have been impossible to have offered any serious resistance, for everyone was too cold to move. The enemy, however, were in a worse case than ourselves, being very short of blankets.

The 156th Brigade relieved the 155th in the trenches on this terrible 28th November, and as many as possible of the latter were accommodated for the first time in the new roofed dug-outs erected on the high ground above " X " Beach. These winter quarters " were in all respects a credit to our divisional R.E., both in the planning of the

FIGHTING IN KRITHIA NULLAH 189

structure and in drainage. The latter was of the highest importance, on account of the torrential rains which fell frequently. Dug to the average depth of between three feet six inches and five feet, with roofs of corrugated iron carried on stout timber and upper walls of sandbags, they were palaces indeed to tired men. Sandbags on the roofs rendered them proof against shrapnel bullets and splinters." (Col. J. Anderson.)

The wind was much less violent on the 29th, but it blew from the north and was very keen, keeping up the hard frost. The water in the wells, whence the animals' drinking water was obtained, was frozen, as also were the pumps and water-carts. On this day the Turkish artillery opened on the "Rest Camp" again, shelling it very heavily. Tuesday, 30th, St. Andrew's Day, dawned in great beauty, "the sun kindling his fires on the snowy peaks of Imbros and Samothrace" (Dr. Ewing). The frost remained, but the weather became calm, bright, and invigorating. Everywhere, the earth below was as hard as rock, and the sky above unclouded. This weather lasted for a few days, but with it came heavier and heavier shell-fire from the Turks. The projectiles were larger, there was more H.E., and there were fewer "duds."

We could now look round and see what had happened. Owing to the previous good work of the medical officers in instructing everyone in the "rubbing with snow" and other treatment necessary, and the promptitude and persistence with which officers and men dealt with bad circulation and other symptoms, there were very few cases of frostbite or trench feet. The 157th Brigade, although in the front trenches during the blizzard, had only one case. The Gallipoli forces had received circulars from home instructing as to how frostbite and collapse through exposure were dealt with in France. One recommendation was that suffering troops should be lodged in buildings well clear of shell-fire behind the front line !

The hurricane had blown from opposite directions, and every anchorage and beach had felt its full force. Nowhere had it been possible to land stores. At Imbros craft had been sunk and driven ashore. A destroyer had been wrecked at Suvla. There, as at Cape Helles, piers had been destroyed, and the shores strewn with wreckage. A slight protection had been given by the hills at Anzac and Cape Helles from the blizzard from the north; but on the Suvla front there had been no protection, and the sufferings of the troops there had been worst of all.

CHAPTER XI

(1ST TO 20TH DECEMBER, 1915)

THE ATTACKS ON G.11a AND G.12

> Then all him answered with a cry,
> And with unanimous voice and high,
> That none for fear of death should fail
> While yet the fighting did prevail.
> *The Bruce* : BARBOUR
> (rendering by D. A. MACKENZIE).

OF course, if the proposed evacuation had been hinted at to the troops, the garrulous gentlemen, who congregated about the various " dumps " and beaches, would have spread the news over the whole of Cape Helles in less than half-an-hour. Nevertheless, the 8th Corps could not fail to draw an inference from the very weakness of its own numbers. The combined 7/8th Cameronians were in the trenches at the time with a rifle strength of 120. This was one of the weakest battalions, but the others were little better. Of those who went to hospital sick or wounded, less than half returned.

As the numbers of men available decreased, the need for larger working parties increased. After every spell of rain the sides of the trenches disintegrated for a couple of inches and fell in. It was impossible with the men available to clear out more than a fraction of this debris. Accordingly, it was mostly trampled into the floors of the trenches. The result was that the miles of communication trenches were gradually getting wider and shallower, quite apart from the effects of Turkish shell-fire. Some estimated that, if nothing else had happened, the trenches by February would have filled themselves in sufficiently to render the whole Cape Helles position untenable.

The 157th Brigade came out of the line on 5th December, and half of it was accommodated for the first time in the new quarters. During the previous 115 days this Brigade had spent:

In the Firing and Support Lines	48 days.
In Sub-section Reserve	38 ,,
In Divisional Reserve	11 ,,
In the " Rest Camp "	18 ,,
	115 ,,

This may be taken as typical of the other brigades also.

By 14th December the Turks were throwing trench-mortar bombs as far back as the Redoubt Line, one of the defensive lines which ran across Cape Helles, and over 700 yards distant from the enemy firing line.

The last troops at Suvla and Anzac were to leave on the night of 19-20th December. It was essential meanwhile that Turkish attention should be riveted on Cape Helles, and it was therefore decided that the 157th Brigade should attack the Turkish trenches, G.11a and G.12, because their capture would give the British the junction of East and West Krithia Nullahs, besides cutting out what was now an enemy salient. This attack was to be made by the 5th H.L.I., under Col. F. L. Morrison, assisted by the other units, the total force engaged being as follows:

	Officers.	Other Ranks.
5th H.L.I., whole battalion	18	271
6th H.L.I., two grenade teams	1	18
7th H.L.I., three ,, ,,	2	26
5th A. & S.H., two ,, ,,	2	18
	23	333

In addition, the 7th H.L.I. were to hold two companies in reserve. This was a tiny force with which to try to distract the attention of the Turkish General Staff from Suvla and Anzac to Cape Helles, but a larger was not available, and the determination of the attack had to make up for its weakness in numbers.

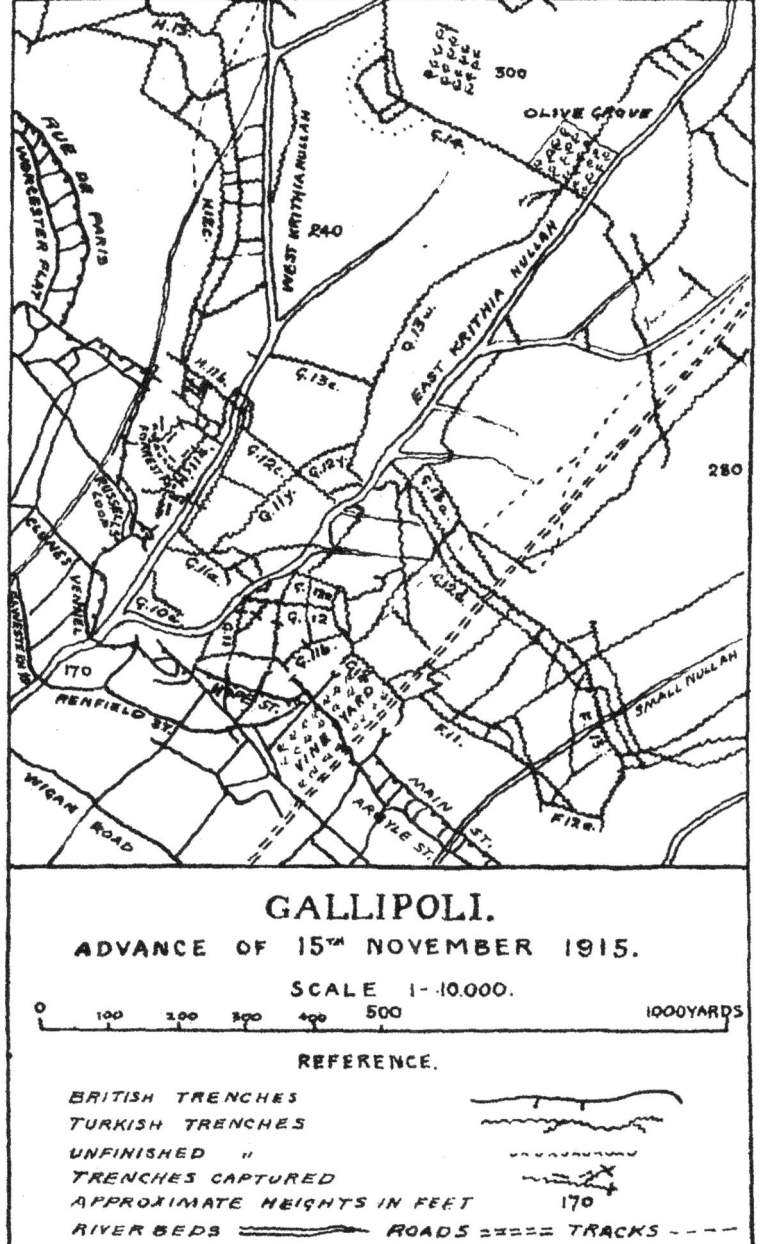

GALLIPOLI.
ADVANCE OF 15TH NOVEMBER 1915.
SCALE 1:10,000.

REFERENCE.

BRITISH TRENCHES
TURKISH TRENCHES
UNFINISHED "
TRENCHES CAPTURED
APPROXIMATE HEIGHTS IN FEET   170
RIVER BEDS   ROADS ===== TRACKS - - - -

THE ATTACKS ON G.11A AND G.12

The tongue of land between East and West Krithia Nullahs had a trench at the tip, known as G.10a. Eighty yards behind or to the east of this, the Turks had the trench G.11a, which ran right across the tongue, being about 120 yards long. Neither of these trenches was occupied by the enemy in the day-time, because they were commanded from the British trenches on the cliffs which formed the north-western side of West Krithia Nullah. They were thought to be occupied at night.

From G.11a there ran back to the Turkish lines two main trenches, one along the south-eastern side of West Krithia Nullah, and the other along the centre or crest-line of the tongue. This second trench was held day and night and was known as G.11y.

There were some other trenches about the south-eastern end of G.11a, but they do not concern us here.

The attack was to be a surprise, and was divided into two, named the East and the West Attacks, respectively. The West Attack was to seize G.11a as far as and including the junction with the crest-line trench, bombing barricades being erected in the crest-line and other trenches. If possible, the remaining or south-eastern portion of G.11a was to be taken and held. The intention was to seize the trenches of G.10a and G.11a during the afternoon of the 18th, before the Turks garrisoned them for the night. Several frontal attacks had been made on these trenches earlier in the year without success. They were now to be taken in flank.[1]

The great difficulty lay before the West Attack. The assaulting troops had to get from Rosebery Street on the top of the cliffs above West Krithia Nullah into the north-western end of G.11a below. To make this possible the Divisional Royal Engineers had tunnelled a narrow passage down through the cliffs to a point directly opposite the end of G.11a. The last foot of the earth opening the tunnel on to the bed of the nullah was to be broken through

---

[1] Major J. B. Neilson and Lieut. Leith (5th H.L.I.) had previously made a reconnaissance of the position by crawling into the nullah one night and examining G.11a.

immediately before the attack. The assaulting and consolidating parties would have to issue from the tunnel one man at a time, and assemble in turn in the open bed of the nullah, probably under heavy machine-gun fire, before they could be led into G.11a. The Turks in the crest-line trench would probably rush down to occupy G.11a, as soon as they saw that an attack was commencing, and a race with these Turks was almost certain to ensue. To have allowed the men to rush across the nullah one at a time would have saved casualties at that point, but would have led subsequently to inevitable confusion and disaster. It was the necessity for this concentration in the nullah, which rendered the capture of the north-western end of G.11a such a difficult feat of arms.

For such an attack the highest organization was necessary. In addition to the assault and grenadier parties, special parties were told off for the removal of enemy barricades, and the building of fresh ones to block the captured trenches and the bed of West Krithia Nullah. These parties would have to get through the tunnel, collect, and move to their objectives with as little delay as possible. It must be remembered that the Turkish machine-gunners and riflemen would be firing at ranges, which would be measured as a rule, not by hundreds, but by tens of yards.

The East Attack was to be made from the long bombing-saps which ran down to East Krithia Nullah. It was to seize the portion of the Turkish fire-trench facing them (G.12), which ran down to East Krithia Nullah—about sixty yards of trench. This, also, was to be protected by the erection of bombing barricades in the trenches which linked it up with the rest of the Turkish system.

Concurrently with these attacks the 5th R.S.F., Lt.-Col. A. H. Leggett, D.S.O., working on the right of the East Attack, was to push forward No. 1 bombing station, bringing it into line with the North Vineyard bombing station and the portion of G.12 which was to be captured.

The 155th Brigade, Brig.-Gen. J. B. Pollok-M'Call, was in the line and was to give covering fire for the whole

THE ATTACKS ON G.11A AND G.12

attack, besides looking after all arrangements for supplies of sandbags and other stores to the attacking troops.

By 2 p.m. on 18th December every party was ready and in position. At 2.15 p.m. four mines were exploded below the Turkish lines. All were at important enemy trench junctions. One was in the Turkish continuation of Rosebery Street, and brought down portions of the cliffs of West Krithia Nullah disposing, it is believed, of several machine-guns, which might have played down the nullah. The other three were before the East Attack, two at a junction dividing off the portion of the trench (G.12) which was to be captured; and one, further to the right, at the junction of four trenches before No. 1 and the North Vineyard bombing stations. The effect of these mine explosions was to disorganise the enemy communications on the outer sides of the East and West Krithia Nullah. To add to the confusion, the British artillery opened up a heavy shell-fire on the trenches behind those to be attacked. Monitors and other warships joined in the bombardment. Krithia Nullah was avoided during the fight as a route for the carrying down of the wounded, because of the manner in which it was swept by enemy shrapnel.

Before the earth and other debris of the explosions had fallen to the ground, those engaged in the East Attack, led by Major J. A. Findlay, 5th H.L.I., were racing over the open through clouds of dust and smoke, while the West Attack, under Major J. B. Neilson, 5th H.L.I., was smashing down the thin curtain of earth which blocked the entrance to the tunnel.

The Turks were not surprised. Probably they had heard the tunnelling. They opened at once a heavy bombardment with, in addition, considerable machine-gun and rifle-fire. The men of the 155th Brigade who were in the line gave covering fire which quickly established their ascendancy and beat down the rifle-fire in the trenches before them; but in the captured trenches and West Krithia Nullah fierce fighting was proceeding, and the shell-fire of both sides was incessant.

Lieuts. Oliphant and M'Intosh, 5th R.S.F., advanced

down the sap from No. 1 bombing station and put up two barricades where it forked. These were held and made secure. The 5th R.S.F. losses were two other ranks killed and thirteen wounded, mostly by falling debris from the mine explosions.

The assaulting parties and grenade teams of the East Attack, two of the latter being from the 7th H.L.I., doubled forward and reached their objectives, several men on the right being injured by falling debris. Some Turks, among whom was an officer, were shot down on the edge of the crater. Following at a brief interval went the consolidating parties. It was necessary to barricade three trenches and saps. This work, with the repairing and rebuilding of the trenches, was commenced at once. These trenches had been bombarded continually for months, so that they were in ruins, and large quantities of broken earth and loose soil had to be cleared away before hard and workable undersoil was reached. The trenches wound about and limited the field of fire of the barricades to anything from eight to fifteen yards. Turks crept along and threw bombs into every barricade. Fierce duels ensued. By 3 p.m., that is in less than an hour, there were very few unwounded grenadiers left at two of the barricades (marked F. and G. on the map) and Lieuts. Davie and Strachan (7th H.L.I.) had to draw on the reserves. At the barricade (E.) in the main fire-trench (G.12) Lieut. W. M'Culloch (5th H.L.I.) had been wounded almost on arrival, but one N.C.O. after another stepped into his place and, despite many casualties, the work proceeded satisfactorily. By 6 p.m. the Turks were throwing heavy bombs into this sap with a catapult, and our grenadiers were driven back up the trench. Lieut. Scott (5th H.L.I.) went forward with another team and regained the barricade. Intermittent bombing never ceased, Turks being able to creep close up before being shot down or bombed. At 9 p.m. the enemy launched a counter-attack against two of the bombing barricades (G. and F.), running forward from the captured trench (G.12), but it was repulsed. A few minutes before midnight another counter-attack was made, but the Turks

THE ATTACKS ON G.11A AND G.12

were seen under the bright moonlight and driven back by rifle and machine-gun fire. Two other attempts later on in the night were stopped before they fully developed.

By morning the consolidation here, under Capt. N. R. Campbell, 5th H.L.I., was well in hand. Very high and, in two cases, overhead traverses had to be erected because of the steep slope into the nullah. At 7 p.m. on the evening of the attack the 5th R.S.F. had offered to take over and complete one of the saps which had to be run forward. The 5th H.L.I. gladly accepted the proffered assistance, for out of their small force engaged in the East Attack they had lost between fifty and sixty officers and other ranks.

We must now retrace our steps and follow the fortunes of the West Attack. G.10a was quite unoccupied. The question was whether the 5th H.L.I. grenadiers could seize any portion of G.11a before the Turks in the central communication trench (G.11y) on the crest-line could run down the hill and secure it.

The Turks opened heavy rifle and machine-gun fire on the mouth of the tunnel about a minute after the explosion of the mines. Soon afterwards a considerable volume of machine-gun fire came down West Krithia Nullah from cliffs a hundred and fifty yards up on its southern side, making the slope from the watercourse to the northern end of G.11a almost a death-trap. In addition their grenadiers were waiting at the G.11a end of their central communication trench (G.11y).

As soon as the tunnel was opened at 2.15 p.m., Lieut. Aitken, 5th H.L.I., collected his grenadiers under the cliffs, dashed across the nullah-bed and within two minutes was moving up the slopes outside the western parapet of G.11a. Within five minutes two other grenade parties were following him. Lieut. Aitken's objective was the central communication trench, but his party came under heavy rifle-fire, so they dropped into the trench (G.11a) and started to work their way along it. The bridge-traverses of the Turks had been bombed frequently and were in such a ruinous condition that they formed a series of obstructions in the trench, consisting of baulks of splintered timber and sandbags, one to every few yards, with very low and narrow passages below them. It was only with an effort that men managed to wriggle through, and all of this caused delay. The aperture under the fourth traverse was very small. Lieut. Aitken and a bayonet man [1] crawled through first, and had advanced to the bend by the fifth traverse when the man was shot dead, and Aitken was shot in the arm and leg, from a loop-hole a few yards away. Aitken managed to crawl back through the hole in the fourth traverse, where he found Lieut. E. M. Leith. The Turks were now hurling bombs from the crest-line (central communication) trench, and as they were throwing downhill they were able to reach G.11a behind the fourth traverse. Two officers and a number of men were wounded. Different parties, totalling about forty of all ranks, were crowded in about twelve yards of trench. Another party was entering the trench at the north end, and the tunnel was still full of people coming down. The low and ruinous bridge-traverses prevented any quick advance up G.11a. It was impossible to organise an attack over the top in that trench, congested with wounded and dead, and in any case the Turks were obviously ready for them with bomb and machine-gun. Lieut. Leith, the only unwounded officer in the trench, decided to erect a barricade at the fourth traverse, and secure the footing gained, in all about thirty yards of G.11a. He got men to work on this, while the 5th H.L.I. grenadiers, throwing uphill, did their best to cope with the Turks. The barricade was completed by 3.30 p.m.

Another party under Lieut. D. M. Pitchford, 5th H.L.I., had orders to block the communication trench which ran along the south-eastern edge of the nullah. He turned up this communication trench, but most of his men became entangled with others moving along G.11a. Some Turks were behind a barricade of logs about twenty yards up the trench. A single grenadier, who had followed Lieut. Pitchford, bombed them and they fell back. Pitchford saw that his men were not behind him, and so went back for

[1] A team of grenadiers included men specially told off as throwers, carriers, bayonet men, etc.

THE ATTACKS ON G.11A AND G.12

them, the Turks re-occupying the barricade and opening a brisk rifle-fire. Gathering some men, he erected and loop-holed a barricade at a point where he had clear observation for twenty to twenty-five yards.

Enemy machine-gun fire was sweeping right down the nullah, and dead and wounded were lying about its bed and on the further slope. Capt. Frost, 5th H.L.I., leading an assault party into G.11a, was mortally wounded as he reached the northern parapet to climb into the trench. Despite his wounds he crawled back and continued to direct his men who, seeing all around them the slaughter which had already taken place from the hail of bullets pouring down the nullah, were inclined to hang back. Coy. Sgt.-Major M. M'Kean, who was in rear, pushed forward, aud led them into the trench.

Lieut. Dow, 5th H.L.I., in charge of a party with instructions to remove the Turkish barricade at the nullah end of G.11a, was killed as he entered the trench. Lieut. Kirbe, 5th H.L.I., was in charge of another party instructed to erect a barricade across the nullah which was to give protection from the devastating machine-gun fire. He was killed a few minutes after emerging from the tunnel. Sgt. J. Waddle, 5th H.L.I., carried on his work. This barricade with a fire-step was completed by 4 p.m.

Another party under Lieut. Turner, 5th H.L.I., set to work to establish a dump of stores and ammunition in the captured trench. Lieut. Turner was mortally wounded and Coy. Quartermaster-Sgt. Stewart was killed before this was done.

All these officers fell within a few minutes of leaving the tunnel.

The consolidating party had the utmost difficulty in getting through the narrow tunnel, as each man was carrying a rifle, pick, and shovel. Rifles could not be slung, and so the shovels were fastened on the men's backs. When they were half-way down they were stopped to allow bombs to pass. However, by 3.30 p.m. every party was clear of the tunnel.

Bombing had gone on continuously. By 3.30 p.m.

most of the grenadiers of the 5th H.L.I. had been killed or wounded, and the survivors were exhausted with throwing. The two grenade teams of the 6th H.L.I. under Lieut. Hardie were now ordered into the trench to hold the two barricades.

By 4 p.m. of the ten officers detailed for the attack seven were killed or wounded, including all from one company, and accordingly Capt. R. Morrison was sent to take command in G.11a.

The light was beginning to fail. It could be seen that further progress up the trench or over the open across the tongue of land was barred. In addition to the strongly-held central communication trench, there was a machine-gun nest, concealed just west of the middle of G.11a. About forty officers and men, almost a third of those actually engaged in this attack, had been killed or wounded, and many of them were still lying about between the tunnel exit and the barricade in G.11a, a distance of forty yards. The difficulties of evacuating wounded up the tunnel while stores and men were coming down can hardly be exaggerated.

At 6.50 p.m. Col. Morrison decided that further progress was impossible. About twenty men were removed from the crowded trench, the remainder of the wounded were evacuated, and it became possible to get on with the work of consolidation under Lieut. Leith.

One of the bombers of the 6th H.L.I. " was in the act of throwing a Mills bomb, when, owing to the crowding in the trench, it was knocked out of his hand, in the dark. Pte. J. Greig (6th H.L.I.), who was then throwing from the parapet, seeing the occurrence, jumped down, searched for and found the bomb and had just time to throw it when it burst, but outside the parapet of the trench. He undoubtedly saved several lives by his promptitude." (Col. J. Anderson.) For this he was awarded a D.C.M.

All went well until 8 p.m., when the Turks made a determined counter-attack. There was a burst of grenade throwing, several exploded inside the barricades, Lieut. Hardie was wounded, more of his men fell, and out of the eighteen bombers of the 6th H.L.I., only five were left.

For a short while the southern or innermost bombing station was empty.

Lieut. M'Lardie, 5th Argylls, hurried up the trench with a team of grenadiers from his battalion. As they reached the untenanted southern barricade, two Turkish bombs exploded in the trench, hurling them back in a heap, killing or wounding every man, and stunning the officer. Of all the bombing teams prepared for the West Attack, there was now only one of the 5th Argyll teams left.

Lieut. A. O. Deas, 5th Argylls, took this team down the tunnel into G.11a, which was once more littered with dead and wounded men. Rushing up the trench towards the southern barricade, Cpl. R. MacIntosh leapt up on to the parapet on the side nearest the central communication trench, and within less then twenty yards from it. Standing up, so that he could see whence the Turks were throwing their bombs, he threw grenades back himself, and was able to direct the aim of a tall Argyll, another MacIntosh, throwing from the trench. Others threw grenades from near the barricade. A Turkish bomb fell into the bombing station, but it was damped with a wad of blankets, and did no harm. A hail of bombs was now poured on the Turks and they were driven back up their trench. Meanwhile, Lieut. Deas with a grenadier had got a catapult, which was lying there, into working order. With this bombs were sent further up the central communication trench, and the Turkish bombing was quelled. Cpl. R. MacIntosh received a D.C.M.

For the rest of the night the 7th H.L.I. supplied a new garrison, but the bombing teams of the 5th H.L.I. and 5th Argylls were left as they were. The situation was one in which the giving of explanations to new men had to be avoided.

It was decided to erect a second barricade a few yards within the southern one, that is the one near the central communication trench, and a chain of men was arranged, who passed sandbags forward. Throughout, the supply arrangements of the 155th Brigade worked well. Hot meals were provided for the attackers, sandbags were filled and stacked, and stores were carried forward in plenty.

By 1 a.m. matters were much quieter, and it was possible to reduce the garrison of G.11a.

The inner barricade was completed by 5.30 a.m. on the 20th, and the catapult moved back to it, a sniper being left at the old barricade.

The West Attack resulted in the capture of about thirty yards of G.11a, giving the British a footing on the tongue between the two nullahs. The attacking forces there lost sixty-eight officers and other ranks, or a little more than two per yard of trench captured. The final cost to the 157th Brigade for both attacks was as follows :

	Killed and Died of Wounds.		Wounded.		Total.	
	Officers.	Other Ranks.	Officers.	Other Ranks.	Officers.	Other Ranks.
5th H.L.I.	4	17	5	67	9	84
6th H.L.I.	—	—	1	13	1	13
7th H.L.I.	—	—	—	7	—	7
5th A. & S.H.	—	2	—	8	—	10
	4	19	6	95	10	114

Some of the wounded afterwards died. This represented almost half of the officers and over one-third of the men of the little force engaged. The losses at the British entrance of G.11a were caused by rifle and machine-gun fire, and at the inner end by bombing. The bulk of them fell on the 5th H.L.I., reducing it to less than the strength of an ordinary company.

The 155th Brigade lost two other ranks killed and twenty-six wounded.

The Turkish losses can only be guessed at, but twenty dead were seen and counted before the trenches captured on the right, and they must have suffered severe losses from the bombing about G.11a and the mine explosions.

The determined efforts of the Turks to retain their hold on this fork in Krithia Nullah showed the value that they placed on it. To them it was a danger point, and the attack had kept the attention of their Headquarters Staff fixed on it, and away from the north.

On the 20th December Lt.-Gen. Sir Francis Davies

published a special order to the 8th Corps, on the evacuation of Suvla and Anzac. After writing of the successful withdrawal of the previous night from those places, he added the following paragraphs :

"The position at Cape Helles will not be abandoned, and the Commander-in-Chief has entrusted to the 8th Corps the duty of maintaining the honour of the British Empire against the Turks in the Peninsula, and of continuing such action as shall prevent them, as far as possible, from massing their forces to meet our main operations elsewhere.

"This duty is one for which we are fully prepared, and is only the continuation of the operations which have gained the strong position we now hold. In front of this position Division after Division of the Turkish Army has been worn down, and so many Turks have been killed that this part of the Peninsula is known amongst them as 'the Slaughter-House.'

"We can only hope that the Germans will force the Turks, already heartily sick of the war, to attack us again and again, being confident that the same fate will befall all fresh troops that are brought against us as befell their predecessors.

"Reinforcements of artillery and increased supplies of ammunition have already arrived, and further troops will be available shortly. In the meantime, Sir Francis Davies wishes every Officer, Non-commissioned officer, and Man to know how confident he is that, one and all, they will put their whole hearts in the work before them, and that they will show, both to the Turks and to those at home, who are so anxiously watching our deeds, that the 8th Corps will continue to do more than pull its weight.

"We must, by strenuous labour, make our positions impregnable, and while driving back enemy attacks, we must ever seek to make steady progress forward and maintain both in spirit and action, that offensive which, as every soldier knows, alone leads to success in war."

CHAPTER XII

(20TH TO 31ST DECEMBER, 1915)

THE LAST ATTACK IN KRITHIA NULLAH

> " I, with my Carrick spearmen, charge ;
>   Now, forward to the shock ! "
> At once the spears were forward thrown,
> Against the sun the broadswords shone ;
> The pibroch lent its maddening tone,
> And loud King Robert's voice was known—
> " Carrick, press on—they fail, they fail !
> Press on, brave sons of Innisgail,
>   The foe is fainting fast !
> Each strike for parent, child, and wife,
> For Scotland, liberty, and life—
>   The battle cannot last ! "
>   *The Lord of the Isles :* Sir Walter Scott.

After they had recovered from their surprise, the Turks commenced to withdraw their artillery from Suvla and Anzac, and to concentrate it on Cape Helles. The shell-fire from this time onwards became more severe than at any time since the landing. " Strafes " and " Hates," as the heaviest bombardments were termed, followed one another in rapid succession, and, throughout the daylight, sniping by the enemy artillery at any moving object never ceased. Casualties became increasingly numerous, and the R.E., whose duty it was to provide wooden crosses for graves, had more work than they could cope with. Enemy aeroplanes bombed the back areas daily.

On the 20th December the 157th Brigade, Brigadier-General H. G. Casson, took over the line about Krithia Nullah, and until relieved again by the 155th Brigade on

LAST ATTACK IN KRITHIA NULLAH 205

the 26th, was constantly repelling Turkish counter-attacks on G.11a. These were usually made under cover of machine-gun fire and at night, but they were all beaten off with loss to the enemy.

Heavy rains came on again, and where the trenches were not flooded, they were covered with tenacious mud, caused by the gradual collapse of the trench walls. Fortunately there were spells of fine weather, usually in the day-time.

The 87th Brigade, of the 29th Division, was temporarily attached to the 52nd Division at this time, and was in the front line to the left of the 157th Brigade. Its section included a number of bombing-saps which ran towards the Turkish lines, one (No. 8) being the continuation of the trench, Rosebery Street (late H.11a), which ran along the western cliffs of West Krithia Nullah. The 5th Argylls, Major P. M'L. Thomson, were holding the line to the right of No. 8, including the next bombing-sap, which overlooked the nullah. Early in the morning the Argyll on the look-out in this sap saw some parties of Turks make an ugly rush on No. 8 station to their left. The Highlanders repelled this attack with rifle-fire, and warned the 87th Brigade men in No. 8 of their danger. A few minutes later it transpired that the Turks had made a surprise attack on the other bombing-saps to the left, and had captured them all from the 87th Brigade with their ammunition stores. This was undoubtedly the first step in an attempt to drive the British back from their trenches on the cliffs, to cut off G.11a, and to push them back from the fork of Krithia Nullah. Fortunately, the saving of No. 8 bombing station, at the corner of the line, made the next step not so easy. Before it could be attacked again, the 87th Brigade had been replenished with grenades from the 157th Brigade stores, and had retaken the saps. The danger was over for the time, but the Turks could be heard working hard to improve their covered work near G.11a, and the other trenches on the tongue of land, in order to prevent the junction of the nullahs falling entirely into British hands.

The British trenches on the cliffs could be easily enfiladed, and they were repeatedly shelled with shrapnel and

H.E., the bridge-traverses being frequently destroyed and as often rebuilt.

On the morning of Christmas Eve the 5th Argylls lost their commanding officer, Major P. M'L. Thomson (5th H.L.I. attached), by a shrapnel bullet through the heart. His cool bravery, knowledge of his duties, and quiet consideration for others had endeared him to all ranks of the Argylls. Up to this time the 5th Argyll and Sutherland Highlanders had lost the following officers, who had held command at different times on the Peninsula :

Lt.-Col. D. Darroch, wounded 12th July.
Major R. A. Clapperton-Stewart, wounded 13th July, to hospital 2nd August.
Lt.-Col. B. H. H. Mathew-Lannowe, 2nd Dragoon Guards, invalided 23rd November.
Major J. Agnew, wounded 8th December.
Lt.-Col. F. Lyle, wounded 8th December.
Major P. M'L. Thomson, 5th H.L.I., killed 24th December.

The command fell for a while on the shoulders of a young officer, Major R. Brown.

The bombardment of the right and centre of the British line on the 24th December was the most violent ever experienced at Cape Helles. During the day grenade stations in G.11a and at the Vineyard were fiercely assailed with bombs, but the enemy were driven off. It seemed as if they were suspicious and were anxious to know whether we were going to attempt evacuation, or make yet another attempt on Achi Baba. That we must do one or other was evident.

Major Thomson was buried in the evening at the cemetery of the Division on the bluff above " X " Beach. As the mourners stood around the grave-side a German aeroplane bombed them, and the blanket-shrouded bundle had to be taken off the stretcher, so that wounded and dying could be taken to hospital. Altogether, three aeroplanes dropped bombs. Some were apparently intended for the hospitals, but luckily they all fell on the boundaries of the

LAST ATTACK IN KRITHIA NULLAH

camps. This was taken as a sure sign that they were German and not Turkish aeroplanes. The Turks were always careful not to fire on the Red Cross; for instance, about this time they apparently wished to reach with high-angle fire the magazine cave which had been cut into the cliffs of Cape Helles above "W" Beach. The hospital, No. 11 Casualty Clearing Station, was in their way, and so they gave three days' notice for it to move before opening fire.

On Christmas Day there was an exceptionally heavy bombardment by the Turks of the trenches behind and about Krithia Nullah. A great number of 9-inch or heavier howitzer H.E. shells were thrown over, interspersed with storms of shrapnel. In the morning and afternoon the 5th A. & S.H. lost 2nd Lieut P. M'Lardie and a number of men killed and wounded by shell-fire. 2nd Lieut M'Lardie and his servant, Pte. H. Kennedy, were among those who could well have gone to hospital before this, but preferring the harder path they remained at duty and later were laid together in a common grave.

The enemy began to "get" the cook-houses; a number of Christmas dinners were destroyed, and there was a crop of casualties. The 30th was a bad day for the quartermasters' departments. Two company cook-houses of the 7th Royal Scots were blown to pieces, with a loss of six killed and seven wounded. A H.E. shell landed in the dump of the 5th R.S.F., killing R.Q.M.S. M'Kie, a fine old soldier, and wounding several others. The 5th A. & S.H. had two of their brave and faithful Indian muleteers killed.

Including reserves, there were probably 120,000 Turkish troops on the Peninsula at this time, and the Allies at Cape Helles must have been outnumbered by at least three to one. Early in December information had been received that a battery of 12-inch howitzers and two or three batteries of 9-inch guns were on their way from Germany. Very often the best defence is in attack, and the boldest course the safest; and now the Division was ordered to carry out another offensive, maintaining that moral superiority over the enemy, which it had done so much to establish. After the Vineyard fighting in August every important offensive at Cape Helles was carried out by the Lowland Division.

Two mines, the work of the 2/1st Lowland Field Coy., R.E., had been run out from the British portion of G.11a, one below the covered machine-gun nest which the Turks held just west of the centre of the trench, and the other below their central communication trench (G.11y). This nest was afterwards found to be a work which was proof against ordinary shell-fire, and had very deep dug-outs. The mines were to be exploded at 1 p.m. on the 29th, and the 155th Brigade, Brigadier-General J. B. Pollok-M'Call, was to seize and barricade the remainder of G.11a and other trenches, linking up with the British line to the east of Krithia Nullah.

The attack was to be a surprise, without previous artillery bombardment, and to allow time for the heavier debris to fall, it was to be made ten clear seconds after the explosion of the mines. The assaulting troops were to be provided by the 5th R.S.F., Lt.-Col. A. H. Leggett, supported by four grenade teams from the 4th R.S.F., and 4th and 5th K.O.S.B. To guide the Allied artillery observation officers as to how far they had advanced, the leading parties were to wave large blue flags occasionally. Covering fire through loop-holes and with periscopic rifles was to be given by the remainder of the 155th Brigade, with all its machine-guns and six from the 156th Brigade. Simultaneously with the advance, British artillery, trench mortars, and bomb catapults, with French howitzers were to open fire on East Krithia Nullah and the trenches leading into it above the objective, in order that the latter might be isolated.

All was ready for the attack, and the assaulting troops were taking shelter in the tunnel and below bridge-traverses in G.11a in anticipation of the mine explosions, when at 12.45 p.m. the Turks started to shell heavily with H.E. the trenches about the nullah fork. One machine-gun section was completely destroyed and all telephone communication cut. Despite this action the Turks apparently did not expect this attack.

At 1 p.m. the mines went up. As their reverberations

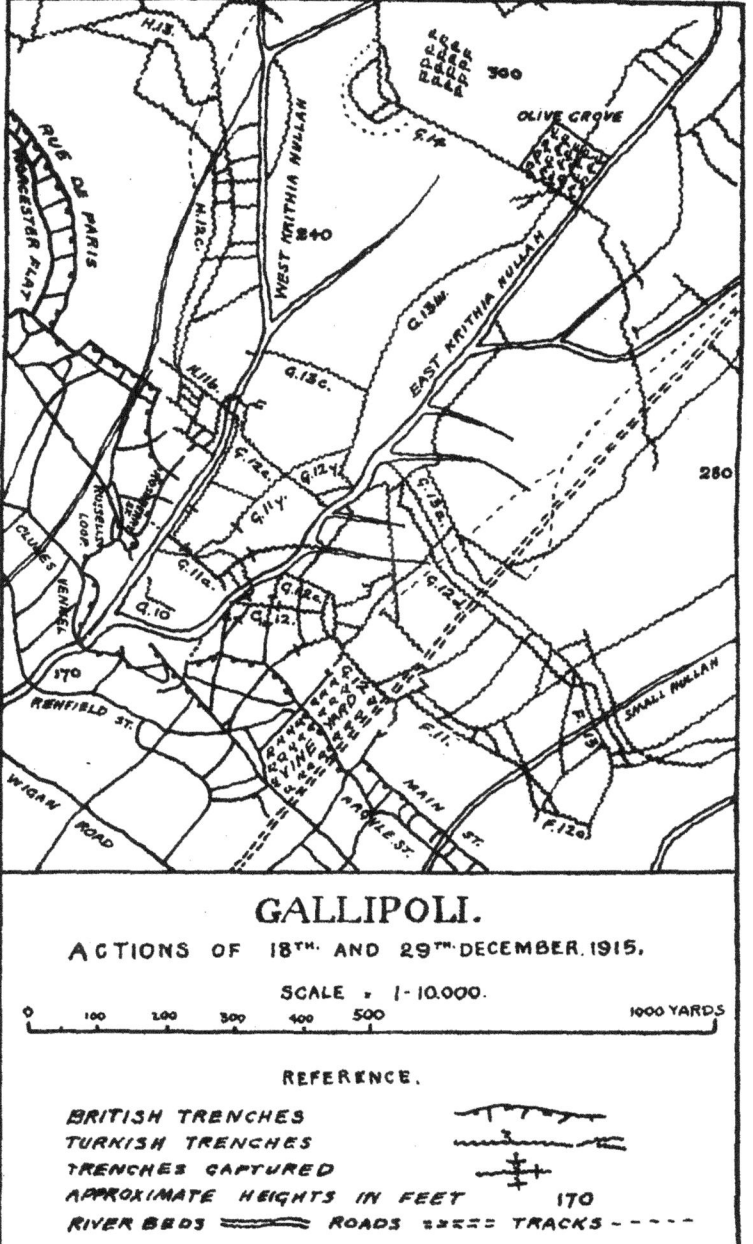

LAST ATTACK IN KRITHIA NULLAH

died away on the slopes of Achi Baba, the men in the adjoining trenches broke into prolonged cheering, and the assault parties, accompanied by mine-searchers from the 2/1st Lowland Field Coy., R.E., ran for the craters, led by Captains Rodgers and Wilkie, and Lieuts. M'Intosh and M'Naughton. Although surprised, the Turks offered a stubborn resistance, but in a short while all the trenches had been captured. One party of fifteen Fusiliers took a wrong turning down a trench and ran into a party of twenty-six Turks who were trying to escape. The latter were big men, but surrendered at once to the Fusiliers. Afterwards, it was found that they were members of the Constantinople Fire Brigade.

At least twenty Turks were killed in this attack, but the losses of the Fusiliers up to this time were very small. As was the rule, casualties mounted up in the repelling of counter-attacks, and from sniping during consolidation, before our men had found out what points were exposed to enemy marksmen.

Immediately after the attack, the Turkish artillery poured shell of all kinds into this hollow at the junction of the nullahs, which had now become the cockpit of Cape Helles. After an interval of a couple of hours, the enemy shelled it again for an hour and a half, and then counter-attacked at 5.10 p.m., but the Fusiliers were ready and drove them off with ease.

By 4 p.m. the signallers of the 4th and 5th R.S.F. had linked up telephones across East Krithia Nullah to G.11a. By 9 p.m. consolidation was complete, and all barricades erected. Parties from the other units of the Brigade and 2/1st Lowland Field Coy., R.E., helped in the work.

Three times during the night did the Turks counter-attack, and as often were they repelled. Six officers and nearly forty other ranks of the 5th R.S.F. had fallen by the time the last attack had been repelled. Among the killed was 2nd Lieut. Austin.

The next day the Turks turned this nullah junction, together with the cliffs about it, into an inferno of bursting shrapnel and H.E., blowing down parapets and causing many casualties. The hollow that was receiving this deluge of fire was only about 150 yards across, and the bulk of it was directed on G.11a and Dalmeny Street. At 7.40 p.m. the enemy crept up and blew up one of the newly erected bombing stations with dynamite, killing or wounding everyone in it. Another team of the 5th R.S.F. grenadiers re-occupied it immediately, drove the Turks off, and rebuilt the barricade. The battalion stood to arms all night, but no further attack was made and all remained quiet.

On the 31st December, after another bombardment, the 155th Brigade was relieved by the 88th Brigade, 29th Division, which had been brought to Cape Helles to reinforce the 8th Corps.

The fighting on the 30th cost the lives of Lieuts. Mitchell and M'Naughton, and 2nd Lieut. Anderson, 5th R.S.F. The losses of the 155th Brigade during this fighting were as follows:

	Killed and Died of Wounds.		Wounded.		Total.	
	Officers.	Other Ranks.	Officers.	Other Ranks.	Officers.	Other Ranks.
4th R.S.F.	—	10	3	20	3	30
5th R.S.F.	4	24	5	62	9	86
4th K.O.S.B.	1	—	—	7	1	7
5th K.O.S.B.	—	7	—	13	—	20
	5	41	8	102	13	143

Lieut. Cairns, 4th K.O.S.B., was shot through the heart while laying wire in front of the firing line on the evening of the 29th, when all was apparently quiet. The figures for the casualties look small, but, when compared with the number of troops available and engaged, they were important. They would have been much larger but for the mining work of the Lowland Field Coys., R.E. The same applies to the casualties of the 156th and 157th Brigades in their attacks.

During the two days, 29th and 30th, the 156th Brigade, who were in the line on the right, lost eleven killed and twenty-four wounded by shell-fire.

The Turkish losses must have been heavier. Of the twenty-nine prisoners taken, seven were wounded, twenty dead were found about G 11a. At least thirty were

LAST ATTACK IN KRITHIA NULLAH

killed when the counter-attacks were repulsed, and the snipers of the 5th K.O.S.B. alone claimed to have shot eighteen Turks, whilst they were trying to get away.

The attack had resulted in the wiping out of a Turkish salient, but its worth was not to be assessed by yards of captured trench, or by casualties. Its principal value lay in the depth of the impression created on the Turkish mind that this attack was merely the prelude to further operations against Krithia.

On December 29th the following message was received from 8th Corps Headquarters and passed to all ranks :—
" 8th Army Corps will shortly be relieved by the 9th A.C."

CHAPTER XIII

(24TH DECEMBER, 1915, TO 9TH JANUARY, 1916)

THE EVACUATION OF CAPE HELLES

> What hallows ground where heroes sleep ?
> 'Tis not the sculptured piles you heap :
> In dews that heavens far distant weep
>   Their turf may bloom,
> Or genii twine beneath the deep
>   Their coral tomb.
>
> But strew his ashes to the wind,
> Whose sword or voice has served mankind ;
> And is he dead, whose glorious mind
>   Lifts thine on high ?—
> To live in hearts we leave behind
>   Is not to die.
>   *Hallowed Ground :* THOMAS CAMPBELL.

ON the 24th December Sir Charles Monro directed Gen. Birdwood to " make all preliminary preparations for immediate evacuation in the event of orders to this effect being received." Four days later the necessary orders came.

Gen. Birdwood's problem was to bring away, unnoticed, over 35,000 troops, about 110 guns, some 4000 animals, and over 100 tons of stores. Sir Charles Monro reminded him that, conditionally on not exposing the personnel to undue risk, every effort should be made to save all 60-pounder and 18-pounder guns, 6-inch and 4.5-inch howitzers, with their ammunition, mules, army transport carts, limbered wagons, and other equipment.

Now, one of the most difficult of all military operations is to bring away an army from open beaches fully exposed

EVACUATION OF CAPE HELLES

to the fire of an enemy in possession of ample artillery. Prior to the evacuation of Suvla and Anzac, it had been regarded as impossible to do this with even a modicum of success, without previously inflicting a heavy defeat on the enemy and driving him back. Even under these circumstances heavy losses were regarded as certain. In the problem that lay before Gen. Birdwood a general defeat of the Turks was impossible. Not only this, but many of the last troops would have to steal away from points only a few dozen yards distant from the Turkish trenches. All the difficulties of the first evacuation were repeated, and accentuated by the enemy having had the warnings of Suvla and Anzac to put him thoroughly on the alert.

The orders were kept secret as long as possible. The value of everything, which might help to give the Turks the impression that we intended to retain our hold on Cape Helles, was manifest. It is certain that Sir Francis Davies' message on the 29th December was duly passed on by some spy. "Authoritative" rumours were spread around. Sedd el Bahr was to be heavily fortified, deep concrete dug-outs were to be built, and the Dardanelles were to be barred by "another Gibraltar," and submarine base. Those who looked at Achi Baba and wondered how this Torres Vedras plan could be possible were met with another rumour. There was to be an overwhelming attack on Achi Baba through Krithia. The attacks of the 52nd Division were opening up the way for this. Fresh troops and guns were being landed for the purpose. This was borne out by the concentration of the 29th and 13th Divisions at Cape Helles during the end of December. The worn-out troops of the 42nd Division and French Corps were withdrawn, in order, so it was said, to give room in the cramped area for the troops who were to carry out this great attack.

Artillery was landed, some being planted on Hunter-Weston Hill above Cape Helles. Reinforcements of troops could be seen in the morning cresting the sky-line as they climbed from the beach, where they had landed overnight. The Turks saw them, as they were intended to,

and shelled them. Fresh emplacements were dug for heavy
artillery, and here and there, when morning dawned,
mysterious guns appeared, completely enshrouded in canvas
coverings, ostensibly to conceal from enemy aeroplanes their
size and power, but really to hide their decrepit condition.
Rumours of great howitzers were current everywhere.

Early in December a Christmas card was issued to various
units, and, in due course, was sent to many homes in the
British Isles. It showed a bulldog with " 8th Army Corps "
on his collar, tugging, as if he would never let go, at the toes
of a foot representing the Peninsula. In due course,
doubtless, the inference thus suggested was passed to the
German Intelligence, as the Turkish spies on Cape Helles
had passed on the other " authoritative information."

For a long while even the British troops on Cape Helles
were deceived by all this, but observers at the beaches
noticed that, although troops were landed during the day-
time much larger numbers were leaving at night. Field
Ambulances were ordered to retain no cases unless they were
likely to be fit again for duty in a day or two. No letters
arrived, and there was no Christmas parcel mail. All the
Greek Labour Corps disappeared, and with them, doubtless,
many spies. Finally, men asked why heavy shells should
be taken off to the transports when a new Army Corps
was arriving and would need them ?

" Eventually," writes Lt.-Col. J. Young, 1/3rd Lowland
Field Ambulance, " we received definite orders to prepare
to evacuate. The Peninsula was to be emptied gradually,
but every effort was to be made to maintain the ordinary
routine appearance of things. Our camps were to be undisturbed and the evacuation of wounded and sick two or three
times a day from advanced dressing to main dressing station
was to continue whether there were patients or not. The
patients naturally grew less as the troops dwindled in
numbers, but dummies were to be used and the performance
of loading and unloading the waggons was to go on as before.

" A good deal of natural amusement was to be extracted
from this theatrical show. The spirits of the men rose
higher and higher each day as the hour of their deliverance

EVACUATION OF CAPE HELLES

drew nigh. They threw themselves with zest into the construction of dummy water-carts and motor cars to replace those which were sent to the beach to be shipped. At that time we had one motor ambulance car. The chassis was sent off, whilst the hood was mounted on four wheels in the usual place by the hospital entrance.

" It almost seemed as if the Turks had grown suspicious, for the roads round our camp were shelled more heavily than usual and the camp itself did not escape.

" A few days before the end of the year we received orders to send off any officers or men who were in any way unfit. It was with great difficulty that any men could be induced to admit they had not felt better in all their lives. But a party was mustered and sent off under our old quartermaster."

This, as a rule, was the spirit throughout the Division. All wished to go, but they did not like the idea of others staying behind to cover their retreat. The youngest private knew what the increasingly heavy bombardment meant. Everyone must have seen the possibility—nay the probability of the Turks finding out everything, when the trenches were empty, and the last troops were crowded in ordered lines about the beaches and on the open slopes of Cape Helles, which, it will be remembered, were tilted towards the Turkish lines. A deluge of H.E. and shrapnel over the whole area from front, flank, and rear would have followed, and, beyond a few dug-outs, of cover there was none.

Everything depended on puzzling the Turks as to the real intentions of the Allies.

About Christmas time a scheme was propounded, the ostensible purpose of which was to induce the Turks to attack, and accordingly to suffer very heavy losses. The general idea was for the British to pretend that they were going to evacuate Cape Helles by acting as the troops at Suvla and Anzac had done before the evacuation of those places.

For several days before the evacuation of Suvla and Anzac, there had been a gradual slackening off in the British trenches of rifle-fire, bombing, the discharge of flare pistols, and other noise from midnight onwards, until finally there was complete silence which lasted till dawn. As the light grew, the British trenches awoke into life, and the men sniped any unwary Turkish working parties with the usual glee. This conveyed the impression that the British soldiers were tired out, and only too glad of a night's rest. The Turks got used to this, and their fire slackened off also. Finally, the evacuation of Suvla and Anzac took place, and the trenches became silent, as usual, but for a different reason—they were empty. As the morning advanced the British lines remained silent, and the Turks found that they had been hoodwinked.

Commencing on the night of 29-30th December, the troops at Cape Helles were to do the same. Close watch was to be kept on the Turkish lines, and, on a signal from Corps Headquarters, when it was thought that No Man's Land was full of enemy patrols anxious to peer into our trenches, or possibly of Turkish infantry advancing to the attack, the whole line was to open fire. Everyone at Cape Helles knew of the ostensible purpose of this scheme, and it is probable that the Turkish Intelligence Department was also informed of it.

On the first night the counter-attacks about G.11a prevented proper silence along the entire front, but on the next, 30-31st, from 7 p.m. onwards, the British fire rapidly died down until there was complete and uncanny stillness in the British lines. " The Turkish sentries kept on firing occasional shots as usual," writes Lieut. Sorley Brown, of the 4th K.O.S.B., which was in the line, " but as the night wore on their rifles spoke at longer intervals, and towards midnight scarcely a sound disturbed the still air.

" One of our guns, stationed not far behind ' Wigan Road,' kept firing for short periods at long intervals. It was always the same gun that spoke, but the Turkish artillery made scarcely any effort to reply to it, and the monotonous sound it made only served to render the silence more acute. Only too ready to fall asleep on other nights when the noise of rifles and shell-fire always prevailed, I found it impossible on this particular night to let sleep steal over my eyelids, and there were many other tired soldiers near me who were in the same state. And so we lay more or less awake the whole night through.

"The night seemed as if it would never end. In the almost intense stillness the senses became exceptionally acute, and one had the feeling that something was going to happen. As it was, nothing happened. Unable to sleep, I lay and smoked, and several times I went out of the dug-out into the trenches and looked around. The darkness shrouded everything, and the silence of the great night had clearly cast a curious spell upon the imagination. I was looking up at the stars above me when suddenly a man lying on the fire-step of the parapet said in a low voice, which almost startled me—' Do you think Johnny Turk will come over ? ' "

Johnny Turk did not. Grey dawn appeared, and the silence continued, punctuated only by occasional shots from the Turks, who were wondering what it all meant.

At 12.25 p.m. on the 31st the silence was broken by every man in the British front line, including the 155th and 156th Brigades, firing " five rounds rapid," and the artillery shelling the enemy for fifteen minutes. The Turks were evidently taken by surprise, and thought that a general assault on their lines was about to follow. Their infantry poured a nervous fusillade over the parapets, and their artillery, after a preliminary burst of fire, kept up a heavier shelling than was usual during all the afternoon. Nothing more happened, however, from the British lines.

Apparently, the ruse had failed. The Turks had not been deceived into thinking that the British were going to evacuate. They had neither attacked nor sent over a large number of patrols. The scheme had been too widely published and was too obvious, thought some, and accordingly, the Turks had not been drawn into the trap.

In point of fact, the scheme was a success. The Turks had seen through it, as they were intended to—but only so far. On the night of the 1st January the British started doing exactly the same thing over again, all firing ceasing after 1 a.m. Herein lay the puzzle for the Turks. Was this a real preliminary to evacuation, or was it another of the "foolish stunts" of the British, as the last had been?

On the 30th December Sir Charles Monro handed over his command in the Eastern Mediterranean to Lt.-Gen. Sir Archibald Murray, K.C.B., C.V.O., D.S.O., and left Mudros on his way to France. Before leaving, he had selected Major-Gen. the Hon. H. A. Lawrence to take charge of all embarkation operations. This he did on the 31st December, Brig.-Gen. H. G. Casson taking command of the 52nd Division, and Col. F. L. Morrison of the 157th Brigade and "Rest Camp." General Lawrence, a banker in civil life, was described by Sir Ian Hamilton as "a man of tried business capacity and great character."

Before the close of December spare kits and other stores were sent down to the beaches to pave the way for "the relief by the 9th Corps." The New Year was ushered in with desultory bombing, artillery, rifle-fire, and by the rumble of waggons going down to the beaches heavily laden, but returning empty. By this time even the troops in the fire trenches knew that the evacuation of Cape Helles was afoot.

Preliminary operation orders for the evacuation on the final or "Z" day were issued on New Year's Eve. The 156th Brigade, Brig.-Gen. L. C. Koe, was to have the honour of forming the final garrison for that section of the line which the Division was to hold to the last. This Brigade now consisted of the two composite battalions, the 4/7th R.S., Lt.-Col. W. C. Peebles, and the 7/8th Cameronians, Major R. N. Coulson. It was to be reinforced by the 6th H.L.I., Lt.-Col. J. Anderson, and the 7th H.L.I., Lt.-Col. J. H. Galbraith, in addition to a section of the 1/3rd Field Company, Kent Royal Engineers.

The areas held by the four divisions during the last days at Cape Helles fronted as follows: from the Aegean to the west side of Gully Ravine, the 13th; from the east side of Gully Ravine to the east of Krithia Nullah, the 29th; from there, to the right of Achi Baba Nullah, the 52nd; and from the right of the 52nd to the Hellespont, the Royal Naval Division. It seemed improbable that many

EVACUATION OF CAPE HELLES

of those left on the Peninsula for the last night could escape, and it was certain that, in the event of a heavy Turkish attack before the time came for the last garrison in the front lines to get away, the latter would have to die where they stood.

Hospital accommodation had been prepared at Mudros for over 10,000 casualties, and as far as was possible the hospitals in Egypt had been cleared.

On New Year's Day the reinforced 156th Brigade was in position. The Lowland Mounted Brigade, Lt.-Col. J. D. Boswell, T.D., had been in the trenches as a unit, and had been relieved on the 29th December. It had suffered very heavy losses by men being blown to pieces or buried by enemy shell-fire, especially on the 28th December whilst extending and improving the new trench " Main Street," in front of " Argyle Street."

The 1/1st Lowland Field Ambulance had been attached to the 29th Division on the 25th December, and was to remain with it until after the evacuation. This unit and the 1/3rd Lowland Field Ambulance were on the Peninsula until the very last.

On the 31st December divisions sent 10 per cent. of their strength down to the beaches for evacuation, starting with the weakest and sickliest men. The first party from the 52nd Division went off on the same night, numbering 7 officers and 325 other ranks, from the 157th Brigade. The total strength of the 155th Brigade at this time, including all detached men, details, and yeomanry attached, was little more than 1200 of all ranks. This Brigade arrived down from the line on New Year's morning, and with the exception of the bulk of the 4th R.S.F., and a machine-gun section of the 5th R.S.F., was sent off the Peninsula entirely during the following week. With it were evacuated officers and men of the Headquarters Staff of the Division, Ayrshire, Lanarkshire, and Glasgow Yeomanry, Royal Engineers, Divisional Ammunition Column, R.A.S.C., R.A.M.C., together with small advance parties from the 156th Brigade. Some of these were included in the 1200 strength given above for the 155th Brigade. The numbers for the various parties of the 52nd Division which embarked were as follows :

	Officers.	Other Ranks.
Night of 31st Dec.-1st January	7	325
1-2nd ,,	20	433
2-3rd ,,	10	241
4-5th ,,	2	20
6-7th ,,	21	233
7-8th ,,	13	183
	73	1435

The other three British divisions similarly were sending away their men. The French division had been reduced during December until only about 4000 of their men were left at Cape Helles. These, with the exception of some artillery, were embarked on French warships during the night of 1-2nd January. The French artillery left behind included one or two old heavy guns and a number of "seventy-fives." They were to keep up the sound of guns to which the Turks were accustomed, and were attached to the 8th Corps. At the end of the first week in January the British Army garrisoning Cape Helles had been reduced by more than one half. This was the minimum which could keep up the appearance of force, so that the whole of those left would have to be taken off in one night.

Before the chaplains left, the Presbyterians of the Division held a celebration of the Lord's Supper in a dugout of the winter quarters, which presented a scene worthy of some modern Rembrandt. At this time the Turks were continually throwing shells into these winter quarters. The celebration took place at night. On a rough table of packing-case wood stood a few candles in bottles, and a small communion service. The dim light revealed some of the stern, resigned faces of the men crowded around under the low corrugated-iron roof. Others could barely be seen in the dark shadows, as they leant against the walls of sandbags and clay. Two or three officers acted as elders. For those remaining on the Peninsula, it was likely to be their last act of assembled worship. Everyone felt this, and the beautiful and comforting words, which told of the World's

EVACUATION OF CAPE HELLES

Greatest Sacrifice, quietly spoken and punctuated by shellbursts near and far, were peculiarly appropriate. All of the men present were prepared to die in order to save the Army, and although they had not to do so on this occasion, many of them did give up their lives before the end of the war.

Various precautions were taken, and devices used to cover up signs which might indicate the shrinkage in strength to the watchful aeroplanes and look-outs of the enemy. Some had been used at Suvla and Anzac, but they were to be used again.

The bright moonlight which prevailed, and the watchful "stand-off" patrols which were put out by the British, rendered it unlikely that any venturesome enemy would be able to creep up to listen or peer into the British trenches, but, nevertheless, the use of the word "evacuation" was forbidden lest it should be overheard through someone's carelessness.

Everything, as viewed from above or from Achi Baba, was to appear unchanged. All hospital and other tents were left standing. Strict orders were given that no waterproof sheets or blankets, which had been used to roof dug-outs or to form canopies in the trenches, were to be taken down. Dummy sentries were propped against the water-carts. In the place of soldiers lying motionless and face downwards in the dug-outs in order to escape observation, enemy aeroplanes saw dummies, which looked from above exactly like living men. Long sections of trench were entirely without any garrison other than the dummies placed to represent sentries and men sleeping on the fire-step. The men obtained a good deal of quiet amusement out of all this, but, nevertheless it became increasingly trying for the nerves of those left on the Peninsula to know that their supports were only lifeless effigies of men. These motionless figures in their silent trenches seemed strangely akin to the dead, who lay so close at hand all around. All lamps and fires, which had been habitually kept burning in the "Rest Camp" or elsewhere, were kept alight. There was something eerie about those lonely candles burning on unused tables in the empty dug-outs of abandoned camps.

During the first few days of January the traffic and dust-clouds of the "Rest Camp" became obviously less, and the area began to have a deserted look. After this the appearance of traffic was kept up by strings of mules and horses and small processions of mule-carts being led backwards and forwards across the "Rest Camp" from cover on one side to cover on the other, and re-appearing in different sub-divisions and in different places. Single large general-service waggons were seen moving about, sometimes with only one corrugated-iron sheet for a load. This was most dangerous work, as the shell-fire never ceased. The clouds of dust which had been usual, and which had curtained much in the past, were not now so easy to raise, but it was hoped that the previous wet weather would explain their absence.

From the 28th December to the end the weather was usually fine, but always raw and cold, and especially so at night. The 28th, 29th, and 30th were fair and bright. From the 31st December to 5th January it was cloudy, and on the 4th there was a north-east gale with rain. On the next day it looked as if another blizzard were pending, but, after a very cold night, the 6th broke fine with hoar frost. After that the weather was clear and frosty, with bright sunshine. This was more comfortable than the rain, but it helped the Turkish observers considerably. The enemy aeroplanes, having convenient bases behind Achi Baba, could slip over whenever the coast was clear of Allied aircraft, and get back before the latter could cross from the neighbouring islands. At least twice a day German or Turkish aeroplanes flew over the British lines, so low, as a rule, that the guns detailed for anti-aircraft work dared not fire. On the 5th January the Allies had five aeroplanes up watching for them, but there was no landing-place for them at Helles. The enemy simply waited until they had gone, and then flew over and back again.

The evacuation of Anzac and Suvla had put the Turks on the *qui vive*, and they were certainly suspicious.

EVACUATION OF CAPE HELLES

Their observers on Achi Baba must have noticed the reduction in the traffic during the first few days of January, and their aeroplane photographs must have shown that the beaches were crowded with stores. The German and Turkish Intelligence Department may have decided that this meant an attempt at evacuation, and not the arrival of troops and stores for another attack, but doubt must have remained in their minds as subsequent events clearly proved. Two enemy patrols were dispersed by the 156th Brigade on the night of the 3-4th. On the same night there was very little Turkish shell-fire, possibly to avoid retaliatory shell-fire on their own working parties, but their suspicions of something must have been thoroughly aroused on the next day, for during the following four nights their artillery steadily and heavily bombarded the communication trenches, with the tracks leading between them and the beaches, as if to catch troops on the move. In many places the shell craters actually intersected one another. On the night of the 4-5th enemy working parties were seen by the 156th Brigade to be digging hard, improving their defences: this was during the silent period, so that they were not fired upon.

Even if the Turks did think that the British were going to evacuate Cape Helles, it is certain that neither they, nor even our own troops, had any idea when the last or "Z" night was to be. The Turks were quite deceived as to the weakness of the British forces. They must have thought that there were so many Allied troops on Cape Helles that it would be impossible to evacuate them for several weeks to come, before which time they would have sufficient large howitzers and shells to overwhelm them and force a surrender, if, indeed, by that time some Balkan winter storm had not intervened and done the work for them.

While the 156th Brigade, with the 6th and 7th H.L.I., were garrisoning and working about the front trenches, the other units of the Division, until they were taken off, were supplying parties to help to deal with the immense quantities of stores which had to be disposed of. Artillery, ammunition, bombs, vehicles, animals, and other valuable stores were loaded into lighters and saved.

"W" Beach was shelled very badly on the 2nd January. Major Wardle, Glasgow Yeomanry, attached to 4th K.O.S.B., was killed on that day by a H.E. shell.

"At 'W' Beach there was a look-out man at the top of the cliff, and whenever he saw the flash of the Turkish guns a warning bell was rung, which gave our men a few seconds in which to run for any shelter they could obtain. A faint boom in the distance, the shout of 'look-out' and then the crash of a shell on the beach—this pretty accurately describes the happenings at 'W' Beach. The duties of the the Military Landing Officer and his assistants were most nerve-trying in the circumstances. Great difficulty was experienced in getting the stubborn and nervous mules off. Sometimes, after being collected for embarkation, a shell would come over, burst in among them, killing some and causing a general stampede among the others. And then the work would recommence, and the same thing would happen time and again." (Lt. W. Sorley Brown.)

The casualties from shell-fire were numerous, but not as numerous as one would have expected from the quantities of ammunition expended by the enemy. This was because everyone quickly became an expert in taking cover, and because the troops were so few and scattered that at times the Turks wasted their H.E. and shrapnel on trenches and areas empty but for the dummies.

The bulk of the stores had to be destroyed. Waggons were left standing in their usual place, but with every shaft, pole, and wheel-spoke sawn through, until the whole would collapse as soon as some Turk attempted to move them. Paraffin was poured over biscuits and flour. Bags of currants were emptied into cess-pools. Harness was cut to pieces and thrown after them. Tins of preserved meat and other food were punctured so that they would putrefy. Rum and other spirits were poured over the ground. Sandbags and rubber boots were ripped open. Spare tents, waterproof sheets, blankets, shirts and other clothing were torn into shreds. Spare rifles, stoves, bicycles, and lamps were smashed. Boxes of S.A.A. were buried. The heavy coast-defence guns captured in the batteries on Cape

EVACUATION OF CAPE HELLES

Helles were burst. Men went round winter quarters, as soon as they were permanently vacated, driving holes in the corrugated iron roofing with crow-bars, and ripping open the sandbags in the walls with hedging tools or sickles, the latter being afterwards broken, buried, or thrown into pits of water. Many horses and mules were shot. These and many other things were quietly done, principally towards the end of the first week in January, 1916.

Fire could not be used in this destructive work, because of the warning it would have conveyed to the enemy. The incinerators for the destruction of refuse had to be kept smouldering as usual, but there had to be no extraordinary smoke. Mounted yeomen acted as police and they watched this very carefully. Once or twice dense volumes of smoke arose by mistake, and watchers trembled lest, before it could be damped, it should be the signal for that hurricane of shells which might burst at any moment on the devoted and dwindling garrison of Cape Helles. It was a case of "touch and go" during these anxious days.

Stores that could be neither saved nor destroyed were gathered round the beaches, or otherwise placed, so that the warships could shell them after the evacuation.

In the meantime everything that human ingenuity could devise was being done in the front trenches and elsewhere to hold up or at least delay any Turkish advance. The entanglements before the three front lines were repaired and added to. A fourth line, consisting of a series of posts, was made, and fronted by a belt of wire stretching from De Tott's Battery on Morto Bay to a position which had been prepared at the mouth of Gully Ravine to cover Gully (Y.2) Beach. A "last stand" position was entrenched and wired to protect "V" and "W" Beaches. It ran across the north-east slopes of Cape Tekke, and of Hunter-Weston Hill, the height which forms Cape Helles. This last had to be done very carefully, because it was in full view of the Turks, and the reason of its construction was self-evident. Transverse lines of wire were made in different places, so that a break-through of the enemy would leave them in a pocket surrounded by wire.

Mines and traps were prepared with demoiselle and other bombs, ready to be connected on the last night with trip wires. They were laid mainly at the junctions of fire and communication trenches, along which the enemy would pour if they tried to break through to the beaches. The belts of wire would prevent any rapid advance over the open. These traps were a military necessity. The knowledge that we had done the same at Anzac and Suvla would make the Turkish infantry cautious and therefore slow in any advance. A few explosions taking place at Cape Helles would make them realise that the same had been done there, and would probably check any headlong rush.

The general scheme for the last night was for the troops to leave Cape Helles in three trips, embarking in lighters at all the beaches available. From the lighters they would be transferred to waiting transports and warships, which would come to Cape Helles from various hiding places under cover of darkness. The left of the line would evacuate at Gully Beach, and the centre and right at Lancashire Landing ("W") and the River Clyde Landing ("V").

The first trip was to be the largest, so that in the event of some lighters being destroyed there would be spare craft available for the last two. The troops in the "Rest Camp" were to be taken off first. They would leave their dug-outs, and would form up on the open north-eastern slopes, after night had fallen. The troops in the front trenches would be thinned down, leaving only skeleton garrisons. "The second trip was timed so that at least a greater portion of the troops for this trip would, if all went well, be embarked before the final parties had left the front trenches.

"The time fixed for the last parties to leave the front trenches was 11.45 p.m., in order to permit the majority of the troops being already embarked before the front line was vacated. It was calculated that it would take between two and three hours for them to reach the beaches, at the conclusion of which time the craft to embark them would be ready." (Sir C. Monro.)

By ingenious arrangements that had been used at Anzac

EVACUATION OF CAPE HELLES

and Suvla, desultory rifle-fire and the shooting off of flare pistols was to be maintained until 1 a.m., the usual hour for the commencement of the silent period. The Royal Engineers fastened rifles and Verey pistols in frameworks, which would point them in the necessary directions. Attached to them were two biscuit tins. The upper ones, filled with water, would drip into the lower, until the latter were heavy enough to pull the triggers to which they were attached. The corks in the upper tins would be pulled out by the last officers in the trenches.

The routes to be followed to the beach on the last night were carefully limited and defined, and all trenches which led off those to be used were blocked with wire and made "fool-proof." In the maze of trenches now spread over the Cape Helles area, this in itself was a huge undertaking. Where the routes crossed the open slopes to the north-east of Capes Tekke and Helles on their way to the beaches, they were marked with white posts. Every officer and many W.O.'s and N.C.O.'s who would be in the front lines on the last night were sent in daylight over the route that they were to use, in order to be thoroughly familiar with it.

At various junctions on the routes there were to be "control stations," consisting of one officer and four grenadiers. They were to stay there until every man higher up on their route had passed the station, or had otherwise been accounted for. After that they were to block their trench with trestles of wire, which were to be lying ready. The officer would then report by telephone that this had been done, and he and his men would retire in their turn. If attacked before this, their orders were simple. With grenade, rifle, bayonet, and revolver they were to hold out to the last.

The numbers and positions of all officers and men, the parties they were to join, and the routes they were to follow had to be checked and re-checked, time and again. One mistake might cause much confusion and the loss of many lives. That these were avoided is great testimony to the efficiency of the staff and regimental officers left on Cape

Helles. Col. Edington, 1/1st Lowland Field Ambulance, writes: "On the 4th January, the O.C. 88th F.A. and myself had just finished the revision of the numbers for the day, when a message was received that in one party no fewer than eight of our men had been knocked out by a shell. Their places had to be filled, and this meant revising the list of parties of the unit which were being made up for early embarkation before 'Z' day."

At 4.30 a.m. on the 7th January all the troops surplus to the final "battle strength" of the reinforced 156th Brigade were sent down to the "Rest Camp." This left the following troops to hold the 52nd Division's firing line:

	All Ranks.
Cameronians	160
6th H.L.I.	141
7th H.L.I.	185
	486

With the above were fourteen machine-guns and their teams from the various units of the Division. Of the Royal Scots battalion 300 officers and other ranks were in the support and reserve trenches. Another 100 Royal Scots were in a fourth line near the Eski Lines. For the last two nights the strength of the garrison of the firing line averaged one man per four yards of trench.

A most remarkable piece of good fortune occurred on this day. From noon onwards the enemy artillery gave the whole of the line a bombardment which was reported to be the heaviest since April, the Asiatic guns being turned on the Royal Naval Division on the right. Their fire was principally directed against the 13th Division on the left, and many trenches were blown in and telephonic communications destroyed. The British guns quickly replied, the watchful British Navy joined in, and a general attack seemed to be developing. There was great danger of the Turks noticing a shortage in British artillery, but the fire of the warships did much to conceal this. From 3 p.m. the enemy bombardment became intensive until 3.30 p.m., when the Turks sprang two mines below the British lines near Fusilier Bluff, which cost us many men. The Turkish

EVACUATION OF CAPE HELLES

trenches were seen to be full of men, and their officers appeared urging them on to the assault. A few parties who rushed out were swept away in disorder by the British fire, but the bulk of the Turkish infantry refused to advance. By 5 p.m. the enemy artillery fire had died away, and the attack had failed. The Turkish soldier still regarded the British remnant on Gallipoli as too formidable for his own army, which by this date probably outnumbered it by seven to one. The British losses were two officers and fifty-six other ranks killed, and four officers and a hundred and two other ranks wounded, principally by the mine explosions. The 156th Brigade lost two other ranks killed and five wounded by enemy fire.

The Turks had happened to time their attack for the precise period when some units of the 13th Division were changing over in the trenches. The incoming troops had not completed the taking-over from those outgoing, so that the lines were doubly manned and held plenty of machine-guns. If the Turks had suspected that the British trenches were thinly held, they must have been astonished by the volume of fire poured on them, and at the number of British troops that appeared. This coincidence must have caused further confusion in the calculations of the enemy staff. If they could believe that we were really going, they had still to decide when we would be weak enough to be overwhelmed in a victory which should resound throughout the Mohammedan and Christian worlds. If Kut had been preceded by a great disaster at Cape Helles one trembles to think of what would have happened in the East.

The British were not accustomed to such good fortune on Gallipoli, and many looked anxiously that sunny afternoon at the "mackerel" sky overhead with its long and bent "mare's tails," which promised an early change in the wind and then plenty of it. Those who went off that night were considered very fortunate.

During the same night the 156th Brigade saw a party of Turks putting out wire in front of their trenches before the silent period, and dispersed them. So far were the enemy from anticipating the evacuation of the entire British remnant on the following night, that they were actually taking precautions against an attack.

When the morning of the 8th broke with bright sunshine, and the ground white with frost, the Division had been reduced until it was made up as follows :

Headquarters and Divisional Signallers	75
Royal Engineers	153
Infantry	2359
Royal Army Medical Corps	212
	2799

Every unit that had served with the Division at Cape Helles was represented in the above. An unusually large proportion were officers, because of the number required in the line as Control Officers, Military Landing Officers, and otherwise. The infantry were mainly made up of the bulk of the following units : 4th R.S.F., Major J. Alexander ; 4/7th R.S., Lt.-Col. W. C. Peebles ; 7/8th Cameronians, Major R. N. Coulson ; 5th H.L.I., Major J. B. Neilson ; 6th H.L.I., Lt.-Col. James Anderson ; 7th H.L.I., Lt.-Col. J. H. Galbraith ; and half of the 5th A. & S.H., Major H. Thompson.

The 8th was a calm, summery day, the sun being very warm but tempered by a pleasant, south-westerly breeze. The Turkish artillery were unusually inactive, probably because of the attack on the previous day. The British and French guns replied as usual. The last preparations were made in the trenches. " During the afternoon and early evening of the 8th surplus material was buried, blankets were torn and the floors of the front trenches carpeted with them, and sandbags were issued to be put over the boots, to muffle the sound of marching men, lest a sharp-eared patrol should overhear it." (Col. J. Anderson.) The last figures and lists were checked again. The destructive work was completed. The last animals were shot—or surreptitiously released.

The coolness and matter-of-fact attitude of everyone on that day was remarkable. Nevertheless, as night drew on bringing with it deliverance or possible disaster, the

EVACUATION OF CAPE HELLES

nervous strain and suppressed excitement, necessitating the greatest self-control, must have been extreme for everyone.

The " Rest Camp " troops were to go with the first trip. Darkness having fallen and all the usual lights and fires having been tended, promptly, at 6 p.m., 1211 officers and men of the Division silently formed up in parties in column of route at a rendezvous in the " Rest Camp " area. Each party was 100 strong, had officers at the head and tail, and was accompanied by four R.A.M.C. and plenty of stretchers. All wore overcoats and were heavily laden. Many officers carried rifles and bayonets. No smoking was allowed and absolute silence was maintained. Despite the gathering clouds, the heavens that evening were glorious, being powdered with myriads of stars that shed a soft glow, just revealing the dark bodies of troops, which were drawn up on the open slopes. Now and again a distant rifle cracked, or a red, green, or white Turkish flare went up. Occasionally a British flare was noticed. Anxious eyes looked towards Asia, or watched the searchlight beams of the Narrows flickering behind Achi Baba. At any moment they might see the ridges and hills blaze from end to end with the red and yellow light, which would show that the retreat was discovered, and would herald a bombardment that would end everything. Strangely enough, the Turkish guns were quieter than usual, and only an occasional shell came singing over. Old British 15-pounders and other guns sent occasional shots back again.

Gradually, the columns began to move. With perfect order and quietude they reached, about 7 p.m., the main rendezvous for troops and guns evacuating at " V " Beach about 1000 yards north-east of its shores. This rendezvous was in telephonic communication with the control-posts along its line, with " V " Beach, and through Embarkation H.Q. with the other beaches. There was some unavoidable delay here whilst parties of 400 were made up. Meanwhile, the slopes were crowded with shadowy masses of men. " All round the camp fires burned as if there was nothing to disturb the ordinary routine of the night . . . As we gazed into the dark, waiting for the first trip, we watched four large French guns pass towards the Beach, each drawn by twelve pairs of fine horses. There was no fuss. They moved past us in a silence that was impressive." (Lieut.-Colonel J. Young.) [1]

The breeze had freshened considerably, and was blowing from the worst quarter, the south-west, right into the bays and against their flimsy piers. The old *River Clyde* was grounded in " V " Beach below Sedd el Bahr, and was to be used for the embarkation of guns and animals. Running out from the north-western or opposite side of this bay was a stone embankment connected by ordinary steamer gangways with a half-sunken French steamer, similarly connected in its turn with an old dismantled French battleship, which also rested on the bottom. This was the pier to be used by the 52nd and Royal Naval Divisions.

Stage by stage, occasionally only by a few steps at a time, the long procession wound over the ridge, down a steep slope, and along the beach, under the shadow of the cliffs, to the pier. Once or twice were seen the distant flashes of Asiatic guns. There could be no question of taking cover, although everyone was fully exposed, because the slightest disorder would have brought hopeless confusion. Despite the nervous strain the discipline was perfect, and the masses of men never moved. Fortunately, the shells burst harmlessly over the dark waters of the bay, and their reports went echoing round its amphitheatre. Probably they were intended for the *River Clyde*, where waiting men could hear the rumble of the wheels of French " seventy-fives," British 60-pounders, and other guns.

By the time that the leading troops of the Division, now two deep, were being hurried across the two gangways to the first of the hulks, the sea had risen under the freshening wind, and large waves were thundering against the iron sides of the old hulk. Not for a moment was the human stream allowed to cease rushing across these narrow plank bridges, which were the only avenues of escape for thousands

---

[1] In his preface Lt.-Col. Young thanks Major W. W. Greer, M.C., for the materials for his chapter on the evacuation of Cape Helles.

EVACUATION OF CAPE HELLES

of men. Those who passed were counted by naval and military officers. From the gloomy interior of the hulks men were passed on to the motor lighters that swayed and plunged alongside. Each lighter would take about 400 men. The one carrying the Headquarters of the 157th Brigade had 439 persons crowded and clinging to various erections on its decks. No attempt was made to keep parties together. As soon as they were filled, these lighters, handled with the most consummate seamanship, were steered clear, and started for one of the transports or warships that loomed up on all sides.

The feeling when once aboard the transports was one of great relief and safety, but in point of fact there was still great danger. Quite apart from the possibilities of an artillery bombardment, reports had been received early in the evening from the right flank that a hostile submarine was moving down the Straits.

Troopships and warships waited around until their full quota was made up, and then steamed for Mudros.

Meanwhile, at 8.30 p.m. more than half of the garrison of the front trenches had been withdrawn, and, with perfect organization, the men of the 156th Brigade and 6th and 7th H.L.I. were formed into parties and started on their march of three and a half miles to "V" Beach.

This left about one officer and twenty men to defend each 400 yards of line, and to keep up appearances by the discharge of odd rifles and Verey pistols. The 7th-8th Cameronians, 6th H.L.I., 7th H.L.I., machine-gunners, signallers of 156th and 157th Brigades were all represented in that last garrison of the firing line.

As each party passed down the communication trenches, it was checked as to numbers and composition by control-officers at the firing line, the support line, the exit from the communication trenches laid down for each section of the front line, and the final rendezvous where the parties of 400 were formed.

All distances had been carefully measured and timed to prevent overcrowding at the beaches, and, if a party was ahead of its time at any control station, it had to wait. At the last checking, parties came under the control of the Navy.

The weather was freezing and no packs were carried, but they were hot, dusty, and tired men, who at last passed the Divisional rendezvous. By 10.30 p.m. when the last machine-gun in the firing line set out for the beach, these men were still awaiting embarkation.

The wind had increased in violence so much that by 11 p.m. the connecting pier between the hulks and the shore at " W " Beach had been washed away, and further embarkation into destroyers from these hulks became impossible. This necessitated re-organization and the diversion of troops to " V " Beach. Despite this, the embarkation of the second trip commenced at 11.30 p.m. When the last troops left the firing line at 11.45 p.m., and were on their way down the miles of trenches, the embarkation for the second trip was still proceeding under grave difficulties, with seas running so high that the decks of waiting destroyers were frequently swept by waves. As soon as each control officer was able to telephone to the main rendezvous that his list was complete, he took away or smashed his instrument. He and his grenadiers then blocked the communication trench, and set off for the beach. The Division's fourth line was held by 100 Royal Scots under Major A. M'L. Mitchell. The last garrison of the firing line having passed and being well on its way, these quietly filed out of their posts about midnight into the communication trench. Now, nothing lay between the Turks and the remaining troops, who were massing about the beaches, except empty trenches, entanglements, mines, and a firing line manned by dummies and biscuit tins. Surely these last formed the strangest garrison that ever bore arms and fired them against a brave and numerous foe.

At midnight a large number of the 156th Brigade and 6th and 7th H.L.I. embarked, and after fifteen minutes tossing in a lighter, reached H.M. Battleship *Prince George*, which with the other ships had been lying off Sedd el Bahr. Several times it seemed that she had been lit up by the enemy searchlights. She had embarked about

EVACUATION OF CAPE HELLES

2000 troops, and had started for Mudros, when she was struck by a torpedo which fortunately failed to explode.

Anxiety had been acute whilst the troops for the second trip were being embarked, but now everyone was at the utmost tension. Yet, looking back to the dark slopes of Achi Baba everything appeared normal. " Still the rifles cracked on the hillside and still our flares climbed into the skies at the far-off trenches as if everything were as usual " (Col. J. Young). The devices of the R.E. were working splendidly. White, red, and green Turkish flares went up regularly, and one wonders if they did any more digging and wiring on that night.

Lt.-Col. J. Young, 1/3rd Lowland Field Ambulance, has written of this time as follows :—"At last No. 1 Control Post at the front line rang up to say he was cleared and was removing his instrument. A few minutes later No. 2 Post did the same, then No. 3. The excitement was now extreme. The stage of final crisis was on us. The next few minutes would decide our fate. In succession the remaining posts rang up to announce the passage of the last trip. No. 4, then No. 5, then No. 6, then No. 7, and finally No. 8 reported that all was well and that they were lifting their instruments . . ."

" At last, just as the moon began to peer over the distant hills of Asia away beyond the Hellespont, our straining eyes picked out the first few men of the last batch. Their dour Scotch faces were set in a look of mingled determination and suspense as they approached. They had come miles through trench and over the open without a moment's pause, for this was not a night for dallying by the way. The sweat poured down their faces although the night was cold. As they gathered in front of us to be marshalled for the final count the excitement that animated them spread to us.

" In a short time the ' all correct ' was announced, the Staff closed their office at the rendezvous, and the procession turned its back on Achi Baba and made off for the Beach, the ambulance, or what was left of it, taking its usual position in the rear. . . .

"The way to the Beach, which we had often marched and thought nothing of, seemed a very long trek that night. But we pushed on as quickly as the length of our procession and the darkness of the night would allow. The rifle bursts still broke the silence of the far-off slopes of Achi Baba, and the lights of the flares still rose into the heavens. The Turk was still unsuspecting, though every now and then a gun from the Asiatic side of the Hellespont would hurl a shell over to the Beach near us.

"Gradually our pace became slower as the head of the procession reached the narrow track that runs between the sea and the cliffs. In places it is only a yard or two wide and the column was by now a long one. At one time 'Asiatic Annie' served us the last thrills which she was fated to do. We could by this time see the far coast of the Dardanelles showing distinctly in the moonlight. Every now and then we caught the flash of the large gun and then, eleven seconds afterwards, the shell burst with a shriek and a crash. It fell near us in the sea, but it was still thirty yards away. Our luck was still holding.

"We marched past the *River Clyde*. With one last look at the famous old tattered liner we passed on. We continued our course past "V" Beach to the rocking, ramshackle wooden pier and thence along the breakwater to where we could just make out in the darkness a torpedo boat destroyer tossing on the sea.

"Here the delay seemed to be interminable, and 'Asiatic Annie' was rousing herself into renewed activity. But we steeled our hearts to patience although it at one time looked as if daylight would still find us on the shores of Gallipoli. One by one the men scrambled on to the slippery rocking deck of the T.B.D. across the gangway steadied by stalwart bluejackets. Our gallant boys still clung heroically to their salved stretchers, but this was more than the sailors could stand. A stentorian voice rang out, 'Chuck these —— things away!' and it rained stretchers in the vicinity of that gangway till all the R.A.M.C. men were safely on board.

"We slipped our moorings and were off. The moon was

hidden behind storm clouds and we could see little of the shore as we bade good-bye to the land which had held us captive for these many months past. We were cold and sodden, for the seas broke over us as we huddled together on the deck. But we were happy as we breathed the breath of liberty once more after months of bondage. As we watched the searchlights in the Narrows grow more and more distant behind us, even the greatest discomforts of body and the buffeting of the elements could not rob us of the relief we felt at the ending of our long chapter of trial. The sailors, with the proverbial cheery kindness of the sea, did their utmost to lighten the troubles of the passage. Within a few minutes every man who had not fallen into a sleep of exhaustion where he lay was served with a pannikin of steaming cocoa."

It is remarkable that no one was drowned, the only losses into the sea being a few rifles. Col. Edington, 1/1st Lowland Field Ambulance, who came off at 11.3 p.m. at "W" Beach, describes how, when their lighters cleared the protecting headland they "got the full force of the south-west gale. We made slow progress. The night was dark and the skipper had some difficulty in finding our transport. He kept hailing through his megaphone the various shadowy vessels we approached, but drew a succession of blanks. At length the answering hail came back, and we were speedily laid alongside the S.S. *Partridge* (in peace time one of Messrs. Burns' Belfast boats). A gang-plank was passed through a doorway in her side on to our deck. With the motion of the vessels it swung up and down like a see-saw; but transhipment was accomplished by seizing the chance as the plank approached the level and rushing along through the doorway. . . . Most of us . . . dropped off to sleep on chairs, or on the saloon floor, or anywhere."

Gully Beach was only two miles from the firing line on the left, and the embarkation there was complete at 1.50 a.m. A lighter carrying 162 men, including some of the Division, was being towed, when it broke clear and drifted up to Gully Beach, grounding in the surf there at

2.10 a.m. After vain attempts to get it off, the men were hurried off along the road under the cliffs to " W " Beach for re-embarkation. At 2.40 a.m. the breakers were so bad that the Naval Transport Officer had the greatest anxiety as to the possibility of embarking the remaining troops, if their arrival was much deferred. However by 3.30 a.m., just in time, the evacuation was complete; the miracle had happened.

Time fuses to the magazines, dumps, etc., were lit, and in a few moments abandoned tents and heaps of stores and supplies burst into flames, which lit the heights of Capes Helles and Tekke and flickered over the surrounding waters. At last the Turks realised that something unusual was happening. Red flares soared into the air from the enemy trenches, and the ridge of Achi Baba and the whole Asiatic coast burst into fire, as every gun that could bear threw a hurricane of high explosive and shrapnel on to the abandoned trenches and beaches. At 4 a.m. the two magazines under Cape Helles were blown up with a thunder that was heard above the diapason of the bursting shells. For three hours the enemy artillery poured this deluge on the abandoned positions, and then, as daylight grew, it died away.

So, amidst a final blaze of mighty pyres and bursting shells that lit up the black clouds hurrying overhead, amidst detonations that reverberated among and seemed to shake the surrounding isles and mountains, and amidst the storm and fury of the wind and sea, the Gallipoli campaign came to an end.

When day broke on Sunday morning, the 9th January, destroyers, motor barges, and other craft could be seen making their way over the storm-swept waters to the shelter of Imbros, still within view of the Peninsula. Among them was the T.B.D. *Bulldog* with the last of the Division's rearguard, control and other staffs on board.

As the Turkish bombardment continued " one explosion was observed, like the eruption of a small volcano, which showed that one at least of the giant howitzers, tardy Teutonic gifts, was in position at length, and ready for action, but just too late to cause us anxiety " (Dr. Ewing).

EVACUATION OF CAPE HELLES

In all, fourteen well-worn 15-pounders, a 6-inch gun, and six old French fortress heavy guns were destroyed and left behind. 508 horses and mules were killed or released. Vast stores were burned, or later on shelled to pieces by warships.

But not a man was lost.

The R.A.M.C., who had volunteered to stay behind in the dressing stations with any wounded that could not be brought away, came off with the last parties. There were no wounded. There were one or two slightly injured who were easily evacuated, but nothing more. For this reason the evacuation of Cape Helles, coming as it did after the warnings of Suvla and Anzac, deserves to be ranked as one of the most wonderful of all military achievements. It surpassed every precedent of its kind in history.

The credit for this triumph of organisation, discipline, and cooperation between the Army and Navy belongs to Gen. Sir W. Birdwood, Lt.-Gen. Sir F. J. Davies, Major-Gen. the Hon. H. A. Lawrence, Vice-Admirals Sir J. de Robeck and Wemyss, and Capt. C. M. Stavely, R.N., with their staffs, and also to the coolness, steadiness, and intelligence of the officers and men of the evacuating force. The fact that not a life was lost does not detract one iota from the extreme bravery of the officers and men, who competed for the posts of honour in garrisoning the trenches, manning the control stations, and acting as embarkation officers on the beaches. But for the calibre of the whole personnel of the 52nd and of the other divisions, disaster would have been inevitable.

During the Gallipoli campaign the Division lost by battle casualties at least 70 per cent. of its officers, and over 50 per cent. of its other ranks.

The total losses in battle of the British Imperial and Colonial Armies in the Gallipoli campaign were as follows:

	KILLED.	WOUNDED.	MISSING.	TOTAL.
Officers	1,745	3,143	353	5,241
Other Ranks	26,455	74,952	10,901	112,308
Total	28,200	78,095	11,254	117,549

At least three-quarters of the missing were killed. The sick admitted to hospital between 25th April and 11th December, 1915, numbered 96,683, and at least 5 per cent. died. 36,000 is a fair estimate for the total loss of lives of British soldiers during this campaign. The Turks have admitted to a loss of well over 100,000 in dead alone, and it is known that this does not include all. It is probable that half of this total of over 140,000 dead lay in the Cape Helles area. Truly was the long, nullah-seamed depression, running from Morto Bay to Achi Baba, a Valley of the Shadow of Death.

Gallipoli had proved a terrible ulcer in the side of Turkey, sapping her strength. With bitter but brave fighting, and invariably acting with chivalry, her soldiers had held her coasts against some of the bravest onslaughts that the world has ever seen, and at last she felt relief and was free to prosecute her designs elsewhere.

None will deny that we were glad to leave Cape Helles. " Oh, how glad ! Here was an end to all the weariness and suffering. But when we thought more deeply of it, the joy was far from unalloyed. Cape Helles had no happy memories for us; no one wanted to see the place again. But what of the men we were to leave behind us there? The good comrades, who had come so gaily with us to the wars, who had fought so gallantly by our side, and who now would lie for ever among the barren rocks where they had died. Never a kindly Scot would there be to tend their graves; their memory was left to the mercy of foes and strangers, though, thank heaven, gallant foes. No man was sorry to leave Gallipoli; but few were really glad." (Major C. S. Black.)

During the hours of waiting, as the long silent columns moved slowly over the bluff to the beach, despite the very present anxiety, we could not help looking up the dim moorland slopes and thinking of all that had been achieved by blood and the agony of weariness, and of all the tens of thousands of brave men who slept, scattered over its ridges and nullahs. To the imaginative it seemed that they knew that we were going and that we had done our best, and now they were watching us go.

So, we left them, these men of British birth and lineage from the Homeland, the Antipodes, Newfoundland, and the ends of the Earth, sleeping with their comrades from Hindustan and France.

" Beside the ruins of Troy they lie buried, those men so beautiful ; there they have their burial-place, hidden in an enemy's land." *The Agamemnon*, 453-455.

SINAI AND PALESTINE

CHAPTER XIV

(9TH JANUARY TO 26TH APRIL, 1916)

DUEIDAR

> We that held the Lone Post, north of Dueidar,
> Know the morning sunshine and the evening star,
> Wakeful when the day breaks, watchful through the night,
> Hearts that beat for Britain, and whose faith is bright.
>
> Behind us creeps the railway the brown-skinned toilers lay,
> To serve the needs of Britain and keep her foes at bay;
> Cleaving the pathless desert, they bind it to her will,
> What time the lonely outpost keeps guard upon the hill.
> *The Lone Post:*
> the late CAPT. W. F. TEMPLETON, 4th R.S.F.

ONE transport after another arrived in Mudros harbour during the morning of 9th January. The last parties of the 52nd Division disembarked at Sarpi and other piers, and moved into tents on the bleak slopes, where they found those who had left the Peninsula on previous nights. Gradually, the wonderful news spread around that not a man had been lost, and that the acres of hospital tents were not needed.

At Lemnos training was commenced, but little could be done because of the storms of cold wind and rain, which swept over the exposed clay slopes, often blowing down many of the tents. The men speedily picked up their drill again, but few were really fit, and a smart appearance was difficult with the ragged clothes and varied headgear. The latter ranged from glengarries and balmorals to field service caps, sun helmets, and woollen mufflers. The sick lists increased, largely because many, who should have been in hospital before, could go now without thinning a firing line.

The Royal Scots once more became two battalions at Sarpi, on the 26th January, Lt.-Col. A. Young, who had returned from hospital, taking command of the 4th and the 7th remaining under its original C.O., Lt.-Col. W. C. Peebles. The 5th H.L.I. played off the final tie for the Gallipoli Cup early in January, losing to the Anson Battalion of the Royal Naval Division.

As troopships became available during January and the beginning of February, the Division commenced to move to Egypt. As they arrived, the units were first concentrated at the Abbassiah suburb of Cairo, where training was continued. The Division was fated to visit places whose history was reckoned not by centuries but by thousands of years. Heliopolis, the few remains of which lay near the camp, was the city of On in the days of the patriarch Joseph, and had been a place of note 3000 years B.C.

Whilst at Abbassiah some drafts of men and officers arrived, but at the same period some time-expired men had to go home, for voluntary enlistment was still the law in the British Isles. Nevertheless, new clothing, including an issue of cotton "drill," made a big difference to the appearance of the different units. Cool weather prevailed, with occasional showers of rain.

In the middle of February the Division was moved to the Suez Canal defences, the 155th Brigade to Port Said, and the 156th and 157th to Ballah. Many an adjutant and quartermaster made his first acquaintance on this occasion with the supercilious but indispensable camel as part of his unit's transport.

A glance at the map will show that the northern portion of the peninsula of Sinai forms the only connecting link of land between the continents of Asia and Africa. Prior to the cutting of the Suez Canal, which is about 100 miles in length, it was the only barrier to the short sea passage from Europe to the further East. For these reasons this area of scrub-covered sand, lying where the highways between three continents cross each other, has been one of the chief strategic features of the world ever since the ancient Egyptians crossed it to settle on the banks of the Nile, more than 7000 years ago.

The central and southern portions of Sinai, the scene of the migratory wanderings of the ancient Hebrews, are covered by a barren and almost waterless tract of mountains. Between this hill country and the Suez Canal to the west lies a belt of sandy, scrub-littered desert, in width from twelve miles in the south to fifty further north. To the north of this mountainous area lies a similar belt, about ninety miles in length, and about twenty miles in breadth. From Palestine into Egypt there are two main routes, by which armies can move. One runs through the northern portion of the hill country. It is not so well supplied with water as the other, and depends a great deal on the cisterns of Moya Harab. The Turks had a railway running to the eastern end of this route, and had used it for their main attack on the Suez Canal defences in January and February of 1915. Difficulties of transportation and supply, or, in other words, sand and lack of water, had prohibited the use of a large force by the enemy, and the attack had ended disastrously for them. The other route runs through the northern belt of desert from El Arish, on the ancient River of Egypt, to Kantara [1] on the Suez Canal. This route has a succession of oases with fairly plentiful supplies of water, and within about thirty miles of Kantara lies the great Katia [2] group of oases, where water is abundant and there is ample shade under acres of palm trees from the rays of the desert sun. The Katia oases could be used as a temporary base for an army of 20,000 men. This fact had a direct bearing on the course of the campaign.

From time immemorial this latter route has been the main caravan track between Africa and Asia, and many great conquerors have passed along it with their armies. Thothmes III. and Rameses the Great of Egypt; Sennacherib, Esarhaddon, and Ashurbanipal of Assyria; Cambyses and Darius of Persia; Alexander the Great; Ptolemy Philadelphus of Egypt; the great Roman Caesars, Julius and

---

[1] Kantara means " a crossing."   [2] Katia means " plenty."

Augustus; Amru, the soldier of the Caliph Omar; Saladin, the prince of Saracenic chivalry; and the Great Napoleon with his dreams of world conquest; all these and many others have passed along this ancient highway.

The patriarchs Abraham and Jacob, and the captive Joseph, used this track, but One infinitely greater than all these twice passed this way. It is certain that this was the route used by the Holy Family in their flight into Egypt—where they rested for a while near Heliopolis—and in their return to Nazareth.

Along this route the Division was to fight and to make a road into the Holy Land, with their comrades from England, Australia, and New Zealand.

For nearly two-thirds of its length this northern caravan route is separated from the Mediterranean by a vast, dried-up salt lake, the Sabket el Bardawil.[1] It is bounded on the north by a narrow strip of sand, a vast natural embankment. During 1916 the surface crust of this sabket, which is very like ice in appearance, was passable anywhere for horses and camels. Heavy transport, however, could not be risked on its surface. It is said to have collapsed and swallowed up an entire army belonging to the Persian Emperor, Darius Ochus, over 2000 years before. Its western end is to the north-west of Katia, and near it lies Mahemdia[2] or Chabrias.[3] Eight miles to the east lie the ruins of Pelusium, at one time on a mouth of the Nile which has long since dried up. In the days of its greatness it was regarded as the key of Egypt, because of its situation at what was, at the time, the end of this northern caravan route.

The triangular Plain of Tina, which lies between Port Said, Kantara, and Pelusium, had been the delta of this branch, and is absolutely flat but for a few mounds and

---

[1] The name Bardawil is said to be an Arabic corruption of Baldwin, King of Jerusalem. It is the Serbonian bog of the classics; see also Milton, *Paradise Lost*, ii. 592.

[2] Mahemdia is variously spelt Mahemdiya, Mehamdia, etc.

[3] Chabrias was probably named after an Athenian general, who served (*circa* 370 B.C.) under an Egyptian king against the Persians.

AT KANTARA
Trench in course of construction by Divisional R.E.

DUEIDAR

hardly distinguishable elevations. When the Division came there much of it was flooded, and after heavy rains most of it became an impassable swamp covering Port Said.

The Turco-Egyptian frontier ran from Rafa, which lies eastward of El Arish, to the Gulf of Akaba. After the outbreak of war with Turkey the whole of Sinai had been abandoned to the enemy, and a line for the defence of Egypt was taken up on the west bank of the Suez Canal. By this means that greatest of all military barriers, a desert, had been placed between the defenders and the Turks, and the Canal had been made to fulfil the part of a gigantic wet ditch. The great disadvantage of this defence line was that it allowed the enemy to bring up artillery close enough to shell vessels in the Suez Canal. In the attack during January and February, 1915, they had done so. It was evident that a similar attack along the great northern caravan route, with its better water supplies and the possibility it gave of using greater forces, might be very much more dangerous. If the Suez Canal was to remain an artery for steamer traffic, the Turks would have to be kept at arm's length.

General Sir John Maxwell, the G.O.C. in Egypt, decided on pushing his front line of defence seven or eight miles out into the desert east of the Canal. To the Dardanelles army, after its arrival, was assigned the task of protecting Egypt against attack from the east, and the Division was stationed in the northern, or No. 3,[1] of the three sections into which the Canal defences were divided. Sir Archibald Murray, after taking over from Sir John Maxwell, decided that the Katia area ought to be held by him, and for that purpose commenced the construction of a railway from Kantara to that place. He also began to collect camels for the transport service of the force, which consisted of one division and one mounted brigade, with which he intended to clear and hold the Katia district.

On the 21st February, whilst at Ballah, the Cameronians were reformed into their original units, the command of the

[1] No. 3 Section was commanded by Lt.-Gen. H. S. Horne, C.B., at this time.

7th being taken over by Lt.-Col. J. G. P. Romanes, and of the 8th by Lt.-Col. R. N. Coulson. The Queen's Own Glasgow Yeomanry, who had been attached to the 4th K.O.S.B., were detached on the 26th February, and left for Kantara, where they were mounted once more. Similarly, yeomanry and others attached to various units returned to their own formations, and the Division gradually assumed its normal aspect. On the 27th February the 155th Brigade entrained for Kantara, and by the 2nd March the 156th Brigade had also concentrated at that place. On 28th February the 157th Brigade moved out to Ballybunion, a group of self-supporting entrenchments in the desert six miles east of Ballah. There it was busy on fieldworks until 11-13th March, when by road and by canal barge it moved to Kantara. In the meantime, since 29th February, the 155th Brigade had been pushed out into a series of posts in the desert from five to seven miles east from Kantara, barring the main caravan route. All of these posts were on gentle elevations on the flat Plain of Tina. Beyond them, fourteen miles out, was another at the oasis of Bir el Dueidar, where the sandhills begin to rise from the levels towards the great dune, Katib Abu Asab, 383 feet in height.

Kantara was a fortified bridge-head, and the 156th and 157th Brigades were kept busy on its defences, in addition to carrying on with their training. From the swing bridge of boats, which crossed the canal at Kantara, there ran out into the desert, following a gentle elevation, the main caravan route, and close beside it the metalled road which eventually reached Bir el Gilban. Alongside, also, lay the beginning of the new broad-gauge railway, already sometimes called the " Jerusalem Railway." By means of lines of redoubts and strong points across this elevation, and flooded areas to the north and south, Kantara had been transformed into an immensely strong field fortress, finally barring the main caravan-route. It was constructed almost entirely by the Division under the direction of its own Royal Engineers.

Sir Archibald Murray closed the caravan route through

DUEIDAR

the mountainous area by draining the cisterns at Moya Harab and elsewhere.

The chief difficulty with trench construction in the desert lay in the looseness of the sand. As soon as holes were a few inches deep the sides began to collapse. Revetting by sandbags was tried at first, but proved a failure. The sand in the sandbags, after the latter had been filled and placed in position, became completely dry and loose under the hot sun, and trickled out between the interstices of the fabric, until the bags were so empty that the walls collapsed. This was obviated by placing an old bag inside a new one, and filling the inner one with sand. This was a success, but entailed heavy consumption of bags, of which the supply was limited. The difficulty was overcome by revetting " by means of wooden hurdles, to which matting was attached on the inside. The trenches were dug the correct width at the bottom, the front and rear sloping at about 45°. The hurdles were then placed at their correct slope, and anchorages, consisting of sandbags or wooden pickets, placed about five or six feet from the top of the hurdles and one or two feet below ground level. The hurdles were then wired to these anchorages and sand filled in behind them to form the parapet and parados. The tops of the parapet and parados were finished off with two or three layers of sandbags." (Capt. G. Streeten.)

Whilst at Kantara, the 2/1st and 2/2nd Lowland Field Companies, R.E., joined the Division. As the standard-gauge railway was pushed out towards Katia, the Divisional R.E. were sent to railhead to arrange the water supply. The water was brought by rail, and run into tanks constructed of canvas with supporting walls of sandbags. It was syphoned through a hose into the fanatis, fantasses, or camel tanks, as they are variously called, which held from ten to fifteen gallons, and these were carried by long strings of camels to the covering troops and working parties.

The artillery of the Division began to concentrate at Kantara in March. The 2nd Lowland Brigade, Lt.-Col. H. Wilson, had been at El Kubri, north of Suez, on the

Canal defences since 7th January, but on the 6th March it rejoined the Division at Kantara, being followed by the 4th Lowland Howitzer Brigade, Lt.-Col. G. S. Simpson. When at Kantara two sections of the 2nd Lowland Brigade were detailed for duty on the Egyptian Western Front to act in defence against the Senussi. After leaving the railway they had a two days march over the desert towards Sollum, the old 15-pounder converted guns, which they took with them, being drawn by camels with harness converted for the purpose. Sir Archibald Murray inspected the Division on the 24th March, with the Prince of Wales as a Captain on his staff. On this occasion the Kirkcudbrightshire Battery paraded with a full section of their guns and wagons drawn by camels.

On the 27th of March the Mediterranean Expeditionary Force in Egypt became the Egyptian Expeditionary Force (E.E.F.).

About this period the employment of machine-guns (Maxims) in separate tactical units was decided upon, and personnel and guns (of which there had been four with each infantry unit) were all withdrawn, and formed into brigade machine-gun companies. Each company took the number of its own brigade. In place of the Maxims, battalions were issued with the light Lewis guns. At the same time the Stokes trench mortar made its appearance, and the training of officers and men in these new weapons proceeded, together with that of grenadiers and other specialists.

Digging under the scorching rays of the desert sun was hard work. The hottest part of the day was the hour before the sea breeze commenced to blow, about 9 a.m. When the sun was high men in ordinary single tents had to wear their helmets. Largely because of the strictness with which the wearing of the sun-helmet was insisted upon, there were wonderfully few cases of sunstroke.

"Almost a greater enemy than the sun is the hot south or south-east wind, or Khamsin,[1] which usually occurs from time to time during the months from March to July. It

---

[1] Taken from the Arabic word for fifty. These winds are supposed to occur within a period of fifty days.

may blow strongly or moderately, but is excessively hot. The air is filled with sand, sometimes so thickly as to obscure the sun and to appear like a fog, and this sand fills eyes, nose, ears and mouth. The body streams with perspiration, to which sand sticks, and life for the time being is barely endurable. Food, water, cooking-vessels, dishes, everything in short is covered with a fine powdering of grit, and there is nothing to be done but summon all one's patience, and hope for a speedy change. This may take place in forty-eight hours, but may not for several days. If troops must march by day during weather of this description, men may fall unconscious or delirious in large numbers, and only the most urgent necessity can justify such movement." (Col. J. Anderson.)

The sand of the Sinai Desert is deep and soft, so that at every step the foot of the heavily laden soldier sinks deeply into it. The foot has then to be dragged out of the hole, in which it has partially buried itself. This produces an effect as if every foot is smouldering, and a marching column sends up a white smoke which lifts slowly and drifts to leeward in any wind there may be. Through this hot dust the desert sun throws its rays, these are reflected by the dazzling sand, and men march slowly and painfully forward in a sun bath of intense and enervating heat. Loose marching formations to permit the free passage of air are essential.

Early in 1916 Sir Archibald Murray had information that the enemy had 250,000 troops in Syria. On the 16th of February the Russian Grand Duke Nicholas's army inflicted a heavy defeat on the Turks at Erzerum, the effect of which was to draw Turkish troops from Syria to that quarter, but, nevertheless, a large army was left available for the defence of Palestine, and for operations against Egypt. The conditions of desert warfare in general, and the condition of the Turkish railways in particular, prevented the use of more than a fraction of this army as a striking force in the desert. However, that fraction, if it could have established itself in the well-watered district of Katia, would have been large enough to threaten very gravely the Canal defences, and possibly to have caused a rising among the pro-Turkish party in Egypt.

On the 9th of April Yeomanry had reconnoitred the main caravan route as far east as Bir el Abd, before they met any of the enemy. Meanwhile, the standard-gauge railway had been pushed out steadily, and on the 21st had reached Bir el Arais, near the ruins of Pelusium, about seven miles north-east of the entrenched post of Bir el Dueidar, and about seven north-west of Katia. Gen. Murray saw that "the railway towards Katia had reached a point upon which a serious advance to hold the whole district could be based." The Turks realised his intention, and determined to drive the British troops back on to the Canal before he could execute it. They planned to overwhelm these posts by surprise attacks and to cut the railway before help could arrive. This was undoubtedly intended as a preliminary to their larger advance during the summer.

About Katia, and Oghratina, further east, was the 5th Mounted Brigade, two squadrons [1] being at the latter place, where a party of the 2/2nd Lowland Field Company were digging wells.

Proceeding eastward from Kantara, the main caravan route parts into two tracks just before it reaches Bir el Dueidar,[2] through which the southern one passes. After about fifteen miles the two tracks rejoin just before reaching Katia. Again proceeding eastward from Kantara, six miles west of Dueidar the railway makes a wide sweep to the north, which avoids some difficult sand-hills and brings it well clear of both routes.

The small post of Dueidar covered this bend in the railway and the junction of the two caravan tracks, besides defending the last important wells on the southern route as it left the high sand-hills. On the 22nd April its

---

[1]

CAVALRY UNIT.	WAR ESTABLISHMENT OF PERSONNEL.
Squadron - - - -	6 officers, 149 other ranks.
Regiment (Headquarters and three squadrons) - -	26 officers, 514 other ranks.

At this time these units were probably up to about two-thirds of their full strength.

[2] A "bir" is a well; a "hod" is a hollow with date palms.

DUEIDAR

defences were held by the following garrison: One company, 5th R.S.F., 180 rifles and 2 Lewis guns; 1 officer and 12 men of the Bikanir Camel Corps; details of Yeomanry, R.E., R.A.S.C., and R.A.M.C.; in all there were about 256 rifles under the command of Capt. F. Roberts, 5th R.S.F. The remainder of the 155th Brigade were distributed at the time in the line of posts, Turk Top and others, which lay from five to seven miles to the east of Kantara. Lt.-Col. A. H. Leggett, 5th R.S.F., took over command of the 155th Brigade, temporarily, on the 22nd April, the information available and passed on to him being that no large body of the enemy existed within seventy miles of any of his posts. The 156th and 157th Brigades were about Kantara.

The Royal Flying Corps had already made many bombing raids and reconnaissances throughout the Sinai Desert, and on the 22nd April reported new bodies of the enemy encamped in the oases of Mageibra and Bayud, ten and seventeen miles respectively to the south-east of Katia. By marching in the cool nights under the brilliant stars and moonlight, and encamping in the hot day-time beneath the shade of the palms which fill many of the deep hollows lying between the sand-hills and ridges, the Turks were able to move large bodies of troops considerable distances without their being observed. As a rule, the existence of these hollows is not noticed, even from the height of a camel's back, until the observer is a few dozen yards from their edges. The interlacing, broad, green leaves of the palms provide excellent cover from aeroplane observation. In this case a force of over 3500 Turks with five small guns had moved within striking distance before its approach was observed.

Three squadrons of yeomanry moved out from Katia during the night of 22nd April to attack the Turkish camps, but found them empty, the enemy in the meantime having marched to attack Oghratina, Katia, and Dueidar. About 2500 of them with four guns had advanced on the first two places, and 1000 with one gun on Dueidar, the latter following the southern track of the main caravan route. Prior to this, the Bedouin had been allowed by the British to come in to a weekly market near Kantara, and, without doubt, the enemy were guided to Dueidar either by some of these Bedouin or by spies who had travelled through our lines with them.

The little force of yeomen and engineers at Oghratina was surprised in an early morning mist and destroyed. The 2/2nd Lowland Field Company lost 4 officers and 60 other ranks missing, one of the four officers being killed. Katia was attacked next, and two entire squadrons were lost, including part of the force which had returned from its intended attack on the Turkish camp. The remainder, little more than 400 men, fell back unhindered, one portion towards railhead and the other towards Dueidar. Three days later an Australian Light Horse patrol counted over 200 Turkish dead about Katia alone, which seemed to indicate that the enemy had not followed up the retreating yeomanry because of their heavy casualties.

Meanwhile, the other Turkish force had made a thrust at Dueidar and the railway.

The date palms, which form the oasis immediately to the west of the wells of Dueidar, stretch for about 440 yards from east to west, and for about 150 yards from north to south. The camp of the garrison was within this oasis. The caravan route runs in from the east, following the northern edge. On the north-east, east, and south sides were five small entrenchments. All around rise high, rolling sand-hills. On one sandy knoll about 150 yards south-east of the eastern end of the oasis was a small redoubt with a semi-circle of wire and garrisoned by 50 men with a Lewis gun. This redoubt and the five smaller works were held day and night. On another dune, 500 yards to the east-north-east, was another redoubt, which was held only by day.

This is an opportune place to describe another feature of the desert which must be borne in mind when considering cover and fields of fire in any desert fighting. As the scrub and camel-weed, the latter a diminutive cactus, grow in the dew-moistened desert, they collect the wind-driven sand about them, and with them there rise up hummocks of

AT KANTARA
Trench constructed by Divisional R.E. nearing completion

sand, usually about three feet in height but sometimes as much as six and over. These hummocks occur every dozen yards or so in all parts of the desert where the sand is firm enough for the roots of the scrub to fasten. They form ready-made breastworks for the sniper, and usually have a fringe formed by the leaves and branches of their bushes. To clear only a small area of these heaps of sand involves immense labour.

On the night of the 22nd Capt. F. Roberts' information was that there was no hostile body within seventy miles. Nevertheless, the fullest precautions were taken. At 4 a.m. it was reported that the telephone wire to the Yeomanry at Katia was cut. This was nothing unusual and might have been done by some horse or camel, but he took no risks, despatched a linesman to find the break, and visited all the posts to ensure extra vigilance. At 4.30 a.m., just before dawn as was customary, the whole garrison stood to arms and the different posts were reinforced. At the same time the usual yeomanry patrol was sent out to the south-east, but there was a dense mist everywhere, and they returned twenty minutes later having seen and heard nothing. Daylight floods the desert in a few minutes, but this morning it shone through a fog which would take some time to melt, and everyone remained standing-to. The garrison for the outer redoubt could not be sent out until the fog had cleared, and for that reason it was unoccupied at the commencement of the action.

At 5.17 a.m. some cans, hung on the wire of the inner redoubt, were heard to rattle, a dog kept in the redoubt ran out to the wire and commenced barking furiously, and the next moment a look-out, peering into the mist, suddenly saw a large number of men appear not thirty yards away, approaching from the south-east. He fired at them, and they at once made a determined rush over the sand, but 2nd Lieut. M'Diarmid, who commanded in the redoubt, was ready, and met them with a burst of fire from his Lewis gun and rifles. About twenty fell killed and wounded, and the remainder recoiled a short distance and got under cover.

Whistles blew, heavy rifle fire was opened on the redoubt and oasis from the east and south-east sides, an enemy machine-gun also joined in, the Fusiliers replied at once, and the action became general. Only occasionally could the Fusiliers get glimpses of the enemy through the mist, but they shot at everything that moved. Casualties occurred in the different works, and Lieut. Miller, R.A.M.C., with his men and the R.S.F. stretcher-bearers were soon moving about through the fire attending to them. Such a heavy cross-fire had developed, sweeping the ground between the redoubt and the oasis, that no casualties could be carried back out of the earthwork. Men in the oasis tell how the enemy bullets, which flew high, cut off and sent down small showers of fronds from the palm leaves. Capt. Roberts' first estimate of the strength of his attackers was only 150, but he was soon undeceived.

The Turks also brought into action their mountain-gun about 400 yards from the oasis, but its aim was erratic and it only fired a few rounds.

After about two hours of this fighting the enemy fire became more intense, and it was evident that they were trying to work round the southern flank. In a small circular trench on a ridge on this side was Cpl. J. Hill, 5th R.S.F., with six men. So steady and accurate was their fire that this small party held the out-flanking movement in check. About the same time (7 a.m.), with loud cries of " Allah ! Allah ! " the Moslem soldiery made a second determined rush on the redoubt. Again they were mown down with Lewis gun and rifle fire by the garrison, and they did not get within twenty yards.

About 7.30 a.m. Capt. Roberts gave instructions to the R.A.M.C. detachment that a man, who had been struck down about fifty yards from the trees when carrying a message to the redoubt, should be brought in. The men of the 1/3rd Lowland Field Ambulance who were in the garrison, acted without hesitation. " M'Donald rushed out and bandaged him up, and Ritchie followed with a stretcher. Just before Ritchie reached him, M'Donald was struck in the face, but, merely wiping the blood away, he gave Ritchie a hand with the stretcher. Ritchie was immediately afterwards struck on the shoulder. In spite of their wounds, they carried the stretcher about twenty yards. By this time blood was gushing freely from M'Donald's wound. Wright and Wood rushed out and brought the stretcher under cover of the trees. Corporal Raffin, seeing both Ritchie and M'Donald struck, rushed out to give them a hand, and was wounded by bullets through both thighs, just when he got beyond the trees."[1] Raffin had managed to crawl twenty yards when Private J. M'Aslan dropped some water bottles which he was carrying, rushed across, and dragged him in. Private M'Donald dressed his own wounds and stayed on duty until 8 p.m. that night, by which time all the wounded had been dressed and sent away. Private Wood was shot dead beside him in the dressing station.

From 7 a.m. onwards there ensued a fierce fire-fight at ranges of two hundred yards and less. The enemy attacked with great resolution, and under cover of the mist, which still hung about, crept up close on the eastern and southern sides. Their firing line extended from the caravan route on the east to the camel camp south-west of the redoubt. Camels were always kept well clear of the general camp because of their stench. Horses were afraid of them and were usually kept within the general camp.

The enemy were evidently a picked force of Germans, Turks, and Arabs. They were firing behind good cover at close range, and outnumbered the Ayrshire men by at least eight to one, but the latter were quicker and better shots, and their fire was very deadly. Yeomanry, Bikanirs, R.E., and A.S.C. all took a hand in the defence.

About seven miles of soft sand does much to isolate a post, but the vigilance of the R.S.F. had spoilt the Turks' surprise, they were being held at bay, and relief was approaching. About 6 a.m. Capt. Roberts telephoned Lt.-Col. A. H. Leggett, telling him what had happened. In little more than an hour (at 7.5 a.m.) all the necessary arrangements had been made, and the relief force had set

[1] Quoted from a narrative in Lt.-Col. A. Young's book.

out from Hill 70 along the caravan track for Dueidar seven miles away. It consisted of two companies of the 4th R.S.F. and two Lewis guns, with eleven Glasgow Yeomen as a cavalry screen in front, about 250 in all, under Major Harold Thompson, 4th R.S.F.

Now, two miles an hour is good marching over the sand of the desert, but on the track the sand was firmer, the Fusiliers were on their mettle, and they did the seven miles in less than two hours. Heavy white mist prevailed when they set out, but at 8.15 a.m. it lifted and the chances of their running into an ambush laid for any relief force became less. Above them was the blue sky, around the dazzling white and yellow desert smirched with lines of scrub, to the south-east lay the shining yellow mass of Katib Abu Asab, and before them were the palm groves of Dueidar, resounding with the rattle of musketry. Overhead a British aeroplane could be seen dropping a smoke-ball on the enemy's main position.

They came under rifle-fire three hundred yards west of the palm trees, the advance guard extended, and then the main body. To Major Thompson's right front were Cpl. J. Hill and his men, now reinforced by a few dark-skinned Bikanirs, firing hard and preventing the enemy's left from creeping further round to the west. Some 4th R.S.F. were diverted to reinforce them, and the remainder of the lines of sweating but eager men took cover in the palm grove. The cheering effect on the defenders can be understood.

After a brief consultation with Capt. Roberts, Major Thompson reinforced the line at the knoll east of the grove with the two Lewis guns and about half a company, and sent another half-company to increase the volume of fire from the defenders' right flank. Lieut. C. S. Brindlay, 4th R.S.F., and five men were shot dead as the first party got into position. While the enemy's attention was thus being drawn to the inner redoubt and the oasis, Major Thompson detailed a party to work its way along folds between rising ground, and, as best they could, to get into the hitherto unoccupied outer redoubt five hundred yards to the east-

DUEIDAR

north-east, from which they could enfilade the enemy's right flank.

Soon after the arrival of the relief force, an aeroplane dropped a message that the enemy main body was in retreat through the dunes towards the south-east, that is towards Katib Abu Asab.

About this time Lieut. and Adjutant Crawford, 4th R.S.F., was sent forward to see how matters stood in the inner redoubt, but was shot down before he had gone thirty yards. Capt. A. C. A. Bruce, A.S.C., ran out and was helping Crawford back when he fell mortally wounded, Crawford being hit again at the same time. Others managed to drag them into cover, where the gallant Bruce died half-an-hour afterwards.

Lieut. Miller, R.A.M.C., had been hard at work attending to casualties in the inner redoubt, when he saw men dropping amongst the palm trees. Determined to get to them, he took his chances and dashed across the bullet-swept open, but fell soon after leaving the redoubt, shot through both thighs and in the hand. He did not know that two medical officers and some R.A.M.C. had arrived with the relieving troops. During his absence in the redoubt, Cpl. Raffin, R.A.M.C., had supervised the collection and dressing of the wounded after he was wounded himself.

A 4th R.S.F. telephone was available, and a wire was now run across the fire-swept zone from the oasis to the redoubt by Signalling Cpl. Clifford, 4th R.S.F.

The party detailed to occupy the outer redoubt apparently got into position without the Turks realising it, until they found themselves subjected to a galling flanking fire. As soon as this fire was opened, Major Thompson, knowing that Lt.-Col. A. H. Leggett was following him with the remaining half of the 4th R.S.F., besides Australian Cavalry, put his reserve of about half a company into the firing line. The Turkish fire now slackened off considerably under the enfilade fire from the outer redoubt, and it became a question as to when a British counter-attack should be made on the enemy rearguard left behind.

At noon a squadron of Australian Light Horse arrived

at Dueidar and moved off towards Katib Abu Asab to pursue the enemy's main body. Their horses were, however, fatigued with the march from Kantara. About the same time some survivors of the Yeomanry, who had been cut up at Katia, passed by the post with news of that disaster.

At 1 p.m. Major Thompson counter-attacked with the whole of his line from the inner redoubt and oasis. Lieut. Sutherland, 4th R.S.F., dashed on ahead of his men for a body of thirteen Turks. He bayoneted one and the rest immediately surrendered. This was the end. The Turks fled, and the Fusiliers chased them for about a mile and a half, taking nineteen more prisoners.

Half an hour after the launching of this attack Lt.-Col. Leggett arrived with the remainder of the 4th R.S.F. and some Australian Light Horse. The cavalry went in pursuit of the Turks, but their horses also were weary and thirsty, and the enemy had made too good a start for them to be found and rounded up in the maze of sand-hills about Katib Abu Asab. The colonials took eight prisoners.

The British losses in this affair were as follows:

	Killed and Died of Wounds.		Wounded.		Total.
	Officers.	O.R.	Officers.	O.R.	
4th R.S.F.	1	5	2	5	13
5th R.S.F.	—	13	2	9	24
R.A.M.C., A.S.C., Bikanir Camel Corps, etc.	1	5[1]	1	10[1]	17
	2	23	5	24	54

The camel camp had come under heavy Turkish fire, and fifty-two camels had been killed. In addition, eight horses had been shot.

Seventy-five Turkish dead were counted and buried on the battlefield. When we consider those who limped away to die of their wounds in the retreat through the sand-hills, and those who were wounded, we cannot estimate the Turkish losses before Dueidar at less than two hundred men. In addition to quantities of rifles, small arms ammuni-

[1] The total of 15 other ranks is correct, but the proportion of killed and wounded is not certain.

DUEIDAR

tion, and equipment, they left behind cases of shells for their mountain gun.

Major Thompson received a D.S.O., and Capt. F. Roberts an M.C. for this affair. Two of the Bikanir Camel Corps received the Indian Order of Merit.

The 5th K.O.S.B., 4th R.S., and 8th Cameronians were hurried off by rail on that Easter Sunday to railhead at Pelusium. The remainder of the 156th Brigade, with the 157th Brigade, marched out to reinforce Hill 70 and the fringe of posts which barred the caravan route east of Kantara.

The Turks in the Katia oasis were not allowed to rest. At dawn on the 24th eight British aeroplanes bombed and machine-gunned them from low altitudes, killing many, scattering the remainder in disorder, and destroying their camp. Raid succeeded raid about Bir el Abd and Bir Bayud during the 24th and 25th, driving them eastward, and by the 26th Australian cavalry were patrolling all the country about Katia.

As an attempt to stop the advance of the British railway towards Katia, this raid of the Turks was a failure. By their cleverly concealed advance and rapid blows they had destroyed the posts at Oghratina and Katia, but they had been checkmated by the garrison and relief force of Dueidar.

CHAPTER XV

(24TH APRIL TO 12TH AUGUST, 1916)

ROMANI

> Shoulders galled by the braces,
>   Knees that tremble and creak,
> Sores in a hundred places,
>   Scarcely the breath to speak;
> Hark to the oaths we utter,
>   Husky and hoarse and low,
> Dragging our weary footsteps
>   After a fleeting foe.
>
> We are the Mobile Column,
>   Dirty and dour and dry,
> Slogging it over the sand-hills
>   Under a blazing sky;
> Bending our backs to our burdens,
>   Staggering four by four,
> We are the Mobile Column,
>   God, but we're tired and sore.
>
> *The Mobile Column:*
> the late CAPT. W. F. TEMPLETON, 4th R.S.F.

CAMBYSES, Alexander, and Antiochus IV. have all fought battles outside Pelusium, the key-city of ancient Egypt. British and Turkish armies were now gathering here for a struggle in which the latter were to be hurled back finally from the defences of the Suez Canal, and were to be deprived of the initiative for all subsequent operations in this theatre of war. The two great empires were fighting at the ends of very long lines of communication, so that only comparatively small forces could be kept in the field. That, however, does not alter the magnitude of the decisions arrived at in the operations about to be described.

ROMANI

The 2nd (Ayr and Kirkcudbright) and 4th (Glasgow Howitzers) Artillery Brigades had been joined by the 3rd (Glasgow) and by a new brigade, the 5th, formed of the Essex, Hants, and West Riding Territorial Force Batteries of Royal Horse Artillery. All were now armed with the new 18-pounders, with the exception of the 4th, which received new 4.5-inch howitzers. These brigades were renumbered as follows:

The 2nd (Ayr and Kirkcudbright) became the 260th.
The 3rd (Glasgow) became the 261st.
The 4th (Glasgow Howitzers) became the 262nd.
The 5th became the 263rd.

Each battery contained four guns.

The artillery prepared themselves for an advance across the desert. At Kantara they adopted pedrails in preference to sand tyres, and ascertained that the best method of drawing the guns was by harnessing ten horses, four and four abreast, with two leaders. By these means the guns could go anywhere over the sand and keep pace with the infantry. About this time the draught horses were sent to France, and were replaced by mules, which proved more capable of hard work over soft sand, when rations were short and water was poor.

Mention must also be made of experiments in the use of nets for camouflaging guns from the air. These were carried out chiefly by the 1st Ayrshire Battery under Major Walker, and had been commenced in September, 1914. They were actively encouraged by the C.R.A., Lord Denbigh, who brought the results to the notice of the War Office. Soon after, the whole artillery of the desert column were equipped with nets, the use of which became general throughout the E.E.F.

About this time the Transport Section, R.A.S.C., of the 31st Divisional Train, Lt.-Col. P. C. de la Prynne, joined the 52nd Division and took its number. The original Supply Sections were still with the Division.

On 29th April the British garrison in Kut el Amara, Mesopotamia, had to surrender to the Turks. The pro-

Turkish section of the Egyptians knew of this before the British Headquarters. It was essential that the Turks should be kept well clear of the Canal. Horse and camel patrols watched the whole Sinai front, pushing as far east as Hod Salmana. To the west of the Nile Valley various operations were carried out, suppressing the activities of Turkish agents and allies. Enemy aeroplanes bombed Port Said and the camps. The Royal Flying Corps retaliated, and warships destroyed the old castle at El Arish, leaving unharmed the mosque and houses near by.

After consultation with Major-Gen. Lawrence, who now had command of No. 3 Section in addition to the 52nd Division, Sir Archibald Murray decided to prepare a position for about 2000 men to the west of the Katia group of oases, which would cover Mahemdia and Romani three miles inland to the south. The railway was to be pushed through the northern oases to a point (Um Ugba) about two miles to the east of Katia, where a larger position to hold about 4000 troops was to be constructed. East and south of this latter position the oases were to be controlled by mobile troops. The defences of Dueidar, well behind both of these positions, were to be considerably increased.

These were really preliminary dispositions for an advance on El Arish planned for the autumn. The troops to be used consisted mainly of the Australian and New Zealand Mounted and the 52nd (Lowland) Divisions. About Kantara and Dueidar the 5th Mounted Brigade of English Yeomanry and 42nd (East Lancs.) Division were to be stationed.

On the 11th May the 156th Brigade, still temporarily commanded by Lt.-Col. A. H. Leggett, marched from railhead over ten miles of soft sand to Mahemdia, where it was set to work building defensive posts as a nucleus for the first position mentioned above. This march, like many which had preceded it and more which were to follow, called for the utmost powers of endurance. The heat ran from 108° F. to 110° F. in the shade, and the water was limited to half a bottle per man per day. Even the natives felt the heat during the summer. At times, when a khamsin blew, the thermometer reached 125° F. in the shade. On 3rd and 4th June the 155th Brigade, with the exception of one company of the 4th R.S.F., moved by train to railhead, at that time at Romani. They also commenced digging redoubts, as did the 157th Brigade, which moved out by rail between 6th and 9th July. A small garrison of 5th A. & S.H., with some details, about 120 all ranks, were left at Canterbury Hill, a redoubt covering the railway south of Pelusium. These rail-journeys were done in open goods trucks, nothing else being available.

The company of the 4th R.S.F. referred to was that of Capt. J. Hamilton, which marched firstly from Kantara to Dueidar, then from Dueidar to Canterbury Hill, and from there to Romani. From the Romani position the whole Division marched across the desert into Palestine, so that this company did the whole distance to Jaffa on foot, over soft sand or the rough tracks of Palestine. The wire road, which others used, naturally did not exist when the 52nd Division crossed the Sinai Desert.

During July the following units of the Divisional artillery moved out to Romani:

260th Brigade—the two Ayrshire batteries.
262nd (Howitzer) Brigade—both batteries.
263rd Brigade—two batteries.

Many times during May and onwards did the Australian and New Zealand Mounted Division harry detached posts of the enemy in the desert at Bir Salmana and elsewhere. The Royal Flying Corps also bombed and machine-gunned enemy aeroplanes and camps at El Arish and at other places. Enemy aeroplanes retaliated, and the Division came in for its share of the bombs, losing men killed and wounded.

The 11th July saw the second change in the command of the Division since its first sailing overseas, when Major-Gen. Lawrence handed over to Major-Gen. W. E. B. Smith, C.M.G. General Lawrence was a man in whom everyone, above and below him, had complete confidence. Another important change took place on the 3rd of July, when Brig.-Gen. L. C. Koe handed over the command of the 156th Brigade to Brig.-Gen. E. S. Girdwood, who had originally been its brigade-major. General Koe had commanded the 156th Brigade for about a year, and was respected throughout the formation.

Work on the Mahemdia and Romani defences was pressed forward by the men of the Division, and by the Egyptian Labour Corps. The heat was terrific, and there were cases of sunstroke. Water was issued only twice a day, and the full ration was only half a bottle. The only water for washing was that of the sea and of a few brackish wells, available to those who happened to be within reach of them. The pure, blue waters of the Mediterranean were a blessing, indeed, for those who could get into them. Little washing could be done by the units inland, and the sand blew everywhere. As on Gallipoli, the slightest scratches became septic sores from which nearly everyone suffered. Sand got into every kind of food, and as usual in the desert and in Palestine, except for a short period in the winter, flies were everywhere. The health of few was good, and the Division was up to little more than half its proper strength. Nevertheless, the sea breeze, parcels from home, scratch entertainments, a few footballs, occasional grants of leave, and the general quiet buoyancy of officers and men kept the Division in good spirits. A rest camp at Sidi Bishr, near Alexandria, to which many Lowland units went, wholly or in detachments, was a great success.

The great problem in maintaining the Anzac Mounted and 52nd Divisions out in the desert was, of course, that of water supply. The water from the wells is brackish, and it produced sickness among the men. But for the work of the R.E. in ensuring a considerable supply of good water, we could have maintained very few troops in the desert, and the battle of Romani might have ended in a Turkish victory through overwhelming superiority in numbers. Concrete reservoirs for water were constructed at Romani and Mahemdia. Old wells were cleaned and improved, and new wells were found and dug.

The Romani position, on which the Division was at work, ran from the coast inland due south for nearly six miles.

A branch railway ran from the main railroad northward to Mahemdia about four miles away. The defence line was over a mile to the east of this. Transportation of stores and water from the railway to the earthworks and camps was almost entirely done by regimental camel transport. The men took charge of the camels as if they had been born and bred in Sinai instead of in Scotland.

In accordance with Sir A. Murray's plan to advance on El Arish in October, great preparations were on foot. Immense numbers of camels and horses were being collected. Mountains of stores were being accumulated at Kantara. The laying of a pipe-line to convey water from Kantara into the desert was carried on. The railway was pushed on through Romani towards Er Rabah, one of the northern oases of the great Katia group. The infantry units of the Division were practised in route-marches through the soft sand. These were a few of the preparations in progress.

More than half of July passed quietly, and Anzacs penetrated on the 9th July as far as Salmana, half-way along the main caravan route, without finding any of the enemy. The nearest enemy camp known of was one, with between 1500 and 2000 men, at Mazar, about fifty miles from Romani. It seemed that the great heat would stop even the Turks from moving troops on a large scale, and that, apart from aeroplane bombs, the Anzac Mounted Division and 52nd were to have a quiet summer. Some authorities regarded a desert campaign by either side in the months of July and August as virtually impossible.

The situation was changed with dramatic suddenness. On the 7th July enemy aircraft appeared over Romani and Dueidar, and on the next day Australians exchanged shots with an enemy camel patrol. On the 19th July an evening reconnaissance of British aeroplanes detected a large force of the enemy, estimated at about 9000 men, in the oasis between Bir el Abd and Bir Bayud, less than twenty miles away as the crow flies. The whole British desert army was on the *qui vive*. The Turks had made another swift and unseen advance across the desert.

Reconnaissances on the next day disclosed that the Turkish army had moved further west, to Oghratina, where they were entrenching only about eight miles from Romani, and also south-west, to Bir el Mageibra. They had made another rapid advance in the night, and had spread out on a wide front. From this time forward the Colonial cavalry never ceased to harass them, capturing a number of prisoners, from whom valuable information was obtained as to their strength and formations.

Other enemy troops were coming up behind, and, in fact, although this was not known until after the operations had developed, the Turkish force was at least 18,000 strong, mainly consisting of infantry and artillery, but including a body of Arab camelry. They were bringing with them 8-inch, 5.9-inch, and 4-inch howitzers, in addition to anti-aircraft and mountain guns, the artillery being manned by Turks, Germans, and Austrians. The guns were brought along roads constructed by filling shallow trenches with brushwood, which was kept in place by a thin layer of sand. Very loose sand was crossed by running the wheels over broad planks, which were picked up after the gun had passed over them, and laid down in front again. The whole of the force was in fine physical condition, and was admirably equipped. It was amply supplied with machine-guns, which could be carried on specially designed camel saddles. Its great weakness, however, was lack of cavalry. The whole army was under the command of the German General, Kress von Kressenstein.

The 7th R.S. and 7th Cameronians were in Sidi Bishr Rest Camp at the time, and were recalled on the 20th, arriving at Romani in the early hours of the following morning. The 158th Brigade of the 53rd Division commenced to move up to Romani to reinforce the 52nd, and the 42nd, an old Gallipoli neighbour, was moved to Gilban and the posts from five to seven miles out from Kantara. Work on the Romani position was pressed forward. A Mobile Column was organised by the 52nd Division from its fittest men, so that the infantry could strike at the Turks across the desert, when the time came.

For this purpose, also, 10,500 transport camels had been concentrated under Gen. Lawrence by the 1st August. A general attack on the Turkish position by the whole of Gen. Lawrence's army was, however, impossible, until a much larger number of transport camels had been collected, so that, until that could be done, his troops had to await the enemy.

Gen. Lawrence's instructions for the first stage of the impending operations were for the two divisions at Romani (the Australian and New Zealand Mounted and the 52nd) " to allow the enemy to involve himself in an attack on our defences, if he would, and not to hinder any such intention by a premature counter-attack" (Sir A. Murray). The plan of Generals Murray and Lawrence was to leave the British right flank at Romani apparently exposed, so that the enemy, in an endeavour to get round it, would become entangled in the dunes, and render themselves open to counter-attack in their flank. If the enemy would not attack, it was their intention to attack them about 13th August, the date of full moon, when troops could be manoeuvred in the coolness of the night, and by which date sufficient camels would have been collected. The Intelligence Department of Gen. von Kressenstein, however, had much under-estimated the strength of Gen. Lawrence's troops and of their position, and the Turkish army took the initiative.

Running approximately south from Mahemdia is the main line of Romani heights, marking the eastern edge of a vast sea of sand-hills. The greatest of these is Katib Gannit, a dazzling yellow cone of shifting sand, towering 100 feet above the surrounding dunes, which reach 140 feet above sea level. This giant sand-hill is about 9000 yards from the coast as the crow flies, and can be seen for miles across the desert in almost every direction. To the east of this main line of heights runs a line of lesser ones, after which the ground sinks down in the north to the dry bed of the Sabket el Bardawil, and further south to a tract of low-lying dunes, interspersed with the dried salt-lakes, marshes, and oases of Romani and Abu Hamra. Eastward, the ground does not rise again to dunes of an altitude equal to the

Romani heights until eight or nine miles have been passed. The main British position consisted of a series of thirteen redoubts following the line of lesser heights immediately east of the main Romani range. Thus, they were not on the sky-line, but still had fields of fire of between 1000 and 2000 yards.

A man standing on these heights and looking eastwards, sees directly below him the grey-green foliage and dark shadows of the oases of Romani and Abu Hamra, and further east, running from Abu Hamra, masses and clumps of palms as far as the eye can see.

Looking south-eastward, over more open ground and higher swells, the eye rests on the immense Katia group of oases, the tomb and ruins of Katia being about 9000 yards east-south-east of Katib Gannit.

South of Katib Gannit the line of redoubts bent back and was continued to the north-west for a couple of miles by four more earthworks. Thus, the main line was formed like a hook, with the point to the north-west.

South of Katib Gannit are other large sand-hills, two outstanding ones being Mount Meredith, 1200 yards directly south of that dominating height, and Wellington Ridge, less than 800 yards to the west and outside of the British redoubt line.

To the south-west of Katib Gannit, ten or twelve miles away, lay the fortified post of Dueidar. It was echeloned to the right rear of the main Romani position. Between the two positions lay the sea of dunes, already referred to, in which was but one post, the single redoubt of Canterbury Hill, about a mile south of the railway near Pelusium. About 3000 yards to the south-east of Canterbury Hill the great group of dunes, known as Mount Royston, lay directly in the path of the forthcoming attempt of the Turks to cut the railway near Pelusium.

This gap had been deliberately left by Gens. Murray and Lawrence between the two positions for the purpose of enticing the Turks into this expanse of drifting sand-hills. As soon as the Turks were involved in this area, they were to be attacked from the north by infantry brought to

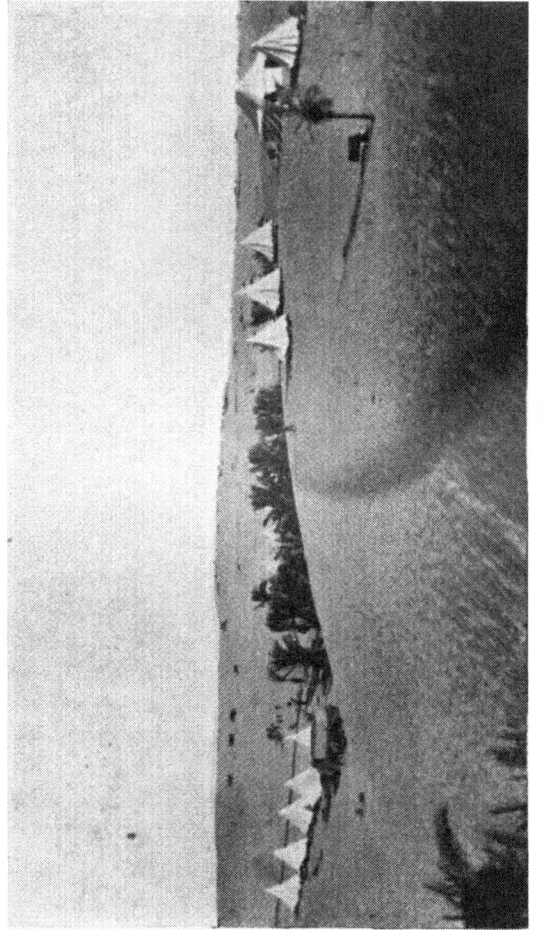

AT ROMANI

Pelusium, and from the west by mounted troops from Dueidar. At the same time the Imperial Camel Corps and more cavalry, operating from the direction of Ismalia, were to threaten their rear. As early as the 22nd July the two divisions holding the Romani position took steps to conceal their real strength from enemy observation, and, apparently, with great success.

There are six facts to be borne in mind in connection with the main Romani position.

(1) If the Turks had established themselves across the railway at Pelusium Station, nothing would have lain between them and the coast but the perfectly flat and open sandy Plain of Tina. A few guns mounted on the northern edge of the sand-hill country could have swept this area with shrapnel.

(2) The redoubts had wire all round them, but not until about the 2nd of August was permission given to link the redoubts up with wire fences. This was probably for the purpose of husbanding the wire and of concealing the strength of the position. Now, the distances between the outer edges of the wire encircling the redoubts averaged about 900 yards. This space usually had gullies, hollows, and other means of approach. When the necessary orders came, the wiring was pressed forward, and by the evening of the 3rd August, Redoubts No. 5 to No. 22a, those on the right flank and round the bend of the hook, had been linked up with wire fences.

(3) It was forbidden to level sand-mounds in the vicinity of works. Their clearance would have made open spaces, and their retention was probably intended to conceal the exact strength and location of the redoubts. On the other hand it allowed enemy riflemen to establish themselves in good cover within 150 to 200 yards of some works, and from there to snipe the redoubts and to cut the wire fences.

(4) The main ridge behind the right was about 140 feet above sea level, and had a few small works, such as Anzac Point and Strong Point. It could form a second line of defence.

(5) The redoubts north of the railway were in an advanced state of construction. Those south, that is in the centre and

on the right, were, as a rule, but half-completed and some not even that. Lack of time and the necessary material had prevented the construction of deep, covered dug-outs, suitable for shelter from a H.E. bombardment. The railway had only a single track, and it had to carry everything for the whole army about Romani.

(6) As originally planned, Nos. 21, 22, and 23 were the only redoubts covering the right rear for a distance of about two miles. Thus, if No. 22 had been put out of action, there would have been a 3000 yards long gap in the right rear, which the redoubts at the extremities (Nos. 21 and 23) could not have covered even in day-time, because of the proximity of Wellington Ridge, and of the innumerable scrub-covered valleys and hollows. Infiltration by the enemy would have been easy. "Work 22 ... had been constructed in low ground and possessed nearly every possible military defect" (Lt.-Col. Leggett). Enemy riflemen could have crept up with ease to commanding ground within short range and picked off the garrison, which would have been helpless. Two other works were constructed just prior to the engagement in front of No. 22. These denied the high ground to the enemy, and formed effective outworks to meet attacks from the long, scrub-covered Wellington Ridge, less than 800 yards to the west. These two works were numbered 21a (southern) and 22a (northern), and were built by the 5th R.S.F., Lt.-Col. A. H. Leggett.

During the last few days of July the Division, with its attached brigade, 158th, were working their hardest on the Romani position, while British cavalry and aeroplanes kept the enemy under ceaseless observation.

Meanwhile, von Kressenstein built a ten-mile line of entrenched positions and posts from the neighbourhood of Oghratina to Bir el Mageibra, where a cluster of redoubts was dug. This gave him a series of prepared works behind which he could retire, and saved his army from complete disaster later on. His advanced base was at Bir el Abd. He also closed up his troops for the attack, which was intended to end in the cutting of the Suez Canal, and to secure the Turkish communications with Arabia, where the Hedjaz rebellion was developing.

On the night of the 27/28th von Kressenstein's left was swung forward until the line rested on Abu Darem. His right was held back by the stubborn skirmishing of some New Zealanders. On the 29th the Royal Flying Corps began to harass the enemy vigorously with bombs. The following day two monitors lying off Mahemdia commenced shelling the Turkish works and the palm groves about Oghratina and Negiliat, continuing this harassing fire daily until the close of the battle. On the morning of the 31st enemy aeroplanes bombed the British lines about Romani and Mahemdia, the 157th Brigade losing a few men killed and wounded. Each battery of the Glasgow Howitzers (262nd Brigade) had a gun ready on a special platform with the trail dug in, so that it could shoot into the air right overhead. These howitzers were the only British anti-aircraft guns at Romani, but they forced many enemy aeroplanes to higher altitudes, from which their bomb dropping was less accurate.

Up to the beginning of August it had been uncertain whether the Turks were going to attack, or to seize a position which would bar a British advance and force Gen. Murray to attack them. Von Kressenstein's next forward move was on 2nd August, but this time only his right could push the Colonial cavalry back. The next day left no doubt that he intended to attack. He moved his whole line forward on the 3rd, until it reached the eastern edge of the Katia oases, and ran from Er Rabah to Bir el Hamisah. All the British mobile troops possible were freed for action.

Briefly, it was von Kressenstein's intention to overwhelm some of the redoubts on the right with H.E. and to penetrate and crush that flank with an infantry attack. At the same time other Turkish infantry were to work round into the rear of the British right, completing its ruin, whilst another force advanced behind them to the northwest and cut the railway and the British line of retreat at Pelusium Station. Success depended on his outflanking troops being able to obtain or carry with them sufficient water, and to establish themselves across the railway before the British could interfere from the west and north-west. It would not be easy for the British to move their reserves great distances over the soft sand. If von Kressenstein could cut off the Romani army from its water supply, it must have come to disaster through thirst, however well it fought. Unfortunately for him, he had miscalculated the strength of the Divisions opposed to him. Before the action he informed his troops that they only had mounted troops to deal with, and he certainly acted as if he estimated the infantry holding the Romani position at about a brigade.

The British army defending the Romani position numbered about 14,000 men, of whom 3000 were mounted, namely the 1st and 2nd Australian Light Horse Brigades of the Anzac Mounted Division and a detachment of the Bikanir Camel Corps. The infantry and artillery, almost entirely from the 52nd (Lowland) Division, were disposed as follows:

STATEMENT SHOWING GARRISONS OF FRONT LINE ROMANI REDOUBTS ON THE 4TH AUGUST, 1916.

Number of Redoubt, in order from Mahemdia to Katib Gannit, and thence to the North-west.	Garrison.
No. 11	157th Bde., 5th H.L.I., Col. F. Morrison.
,, 10	,, ,, ,, ,, ,,
,, 10A	,, ,, ,, ,, ,,
,, 9 (Blair's Post)	,, ,, ,, ,, ,,
,, 8	158th Bde., 1st Herefords, Major Drage.
,, 7	155th Bde., 4th R.S.F., Lt.-Col. H. Thompson.
,, 7A	,, ,, ,, ,, ,,
,, 6 (Katia View)	,, ,, ,, ,, ,,
,, 5	,, 5th R.S.F., Lt.-Col. A. H. Leggett.
,, 4	,, 52nd Div. Cyclists, Capt. H. F. Hodge.
,, 3	,, 52nd Div. Cyclists and 5th R.S.F.
,, 2	,, 5th R.S.F., Lt.-Col. A. H. Leggett.
,, 1	,, ,, ,, ,, ,,
,, 21	,, ,, ,, ,, ,,
,, 21A	,,
,, 22A	,, 4th K.O.S.B., Lt.-Col. G. T. B. Wilson.
,, 23	156th Bde., 7th Royal Scots, Lt.-Col. W. C. Peebles.

The garrisons of these redoubts varied in number from 40 to 171 all ranks, but they averaged about 100. Each redoubt had from one to three machine-guns, the average being two per redoubt, mostly drawn from the 155th Brigade M.G. Coy. The 161st Brigade, 54th Division, M.G. Coy. had guns in Nos. 3, 4, and 5. Each redoubt had Lewis guns in addition. Nos. 1, 21, 21a, and 22a, that is those guarding the right rear where innumerable gullies ran from Mount Meredith and Wellington Ridge towards them, each had a Stokes trench mortar.

The bulk of the 157th Brigade was in reserve on the left about the inner position at Mahemdia. The remainder of 158th Brigade (53rd Division), less one battalion, was in reserve just north of Romani railhead. The 156th Brigade, with the 5th Royal Welch Fusiliers attached, was in reserve on the right centre about Redoubt No. 23. The remainder of the 155th Brigade was in reserve on the extreme right, immediately north of Katib Gannit. Of necessity, the reserves were distributed over the front, because of its length and the impossibility of moving with speed over the drift-sand that prevailed. Each brigade was up to about two-thirds of its strength.

The artillery of the Division was disposed as follows :

One 18-pdr. battery (Ayr) of the 260th Brigade was dug in as a battery of position on the extreme left near the shore at Mahemdia. Another 18-pdr. battery (Ayr) of the 260th Brigade was attached to the two batteries of Glasgow Howitzers, and formed No. 1 Group, being stationed on the right in the bend of the hook. Two 18-pdr. batteries of the 263rd Brigade were more in the centre, south of the railway. The remainder of the Divisional artillery took no part in the action.

It had been intended that the Kirkcudbright battery of the 260th Brigade should be moved up to Romani, but the battle intervened before the railway could transport the guns. The 261st Brigade (Glasgow), also, could not be moved to the front, and remained at Kantara. It will be seen that the 260th Brigade, as a unit, was split up. In connection with this, mention must be made of the extremely gallant conduct of Lt.-Col. A. Brown, its commander, who, as things were, found himself bereft of nearly all his guns. He managed to get up the railway prior to the opening of the battle, and was looking over the battery attached to the Glasgow Howitzers when the fighting commenced. He served right through the action as a section commander in this battery under one of his own majors, being frequently under rifle-fire.

A battery of 60-pdrs. near the railway, and the Ayr and Somerset Batteries, R.H.A., operating with the Anzac Mounted Division, completed the artillery of the Romani army, making in all thirty-six guns.

The main strength of the artillery in the position was on the right, the exposed flank.

The advanced dressing stations of the 3rd, 1st, and 2nd Lowland Field Ambulances were grouped in the order named behind the right, centre, and left. In addition to the usual flags flown, each had a large flag fastened to the ground with a red cross painted on it. The British had taken the trouble to notify the Turks that one of their ambulances was in an exposed situation. The Turks had replied on the 27th July with a message dropped from an aeroplane, thanking " l'Officer Commandant de Romani," and stating that they could not pick out the British ambulances from the air.

The collection and transportation of wounded over such a vast area of sand, as the impending battle would cover, was a serious problem. The principal means used were the light, two-wheeled, desert ambulances or sand-carts, camels with litters or cacolets, and the regimental stretcher-bearers, working on foot.

The sand-carts had broad-flanged tyres, so that their wheels would ride over, instead of ploughing through the sand. The sand about Romani is unusually loose and even these wheels sank deeply into it, and the broad flanges were covered with sand, but at least they prevented the wheels sinking too deeply to move. At a later date the Divisional R.E. boxed these wheels in entirely, and this worked very well. These carts were drawn by teams either of two mules or of two camels.

The camel cacolets were improvised. Some, for lying-down cases, consisted of stretchers slung one on each side of the camel. The swaying motion of the camels caused terrible suffering to the wounded, but very often this was the only means of transportation possible, and the poor fellows simply had to endure it. Each ration camel was provided with nets on either side for its load. By an ingenious arrangement of bars these were converted into hammock-seats for sitting cases, and the wounded, being below the centre of gravity of the animal, were subjected only to a gentle swinging, as opposed to the violent pitching and rocking of the high-perched stretchers. From railhead the wounded had to go to Kantara, where the main stations of the Lowland Field Ambulance were situated, by ordinary springless goods trains, there having been no time to complete a hospital train.

To return to the dispositions of the fighting forces. On that night, 3-4th August, the Colonial cavalry put out a strong outpost line, stretching from the gullies that ran into the right flank south of Katib Gannit, over Mount Meredith, to Hod el Enna, three miles to the south. This was to prevent the enemy executing one of their silent night-moves into the waterless area of sand-dunes southwest of Romani in the British rear.

Behind the redoubt of Canterbury Hill at Pelusium Station was a battalion of the 127th Brigade, 42nd Division. The remainder of this brigade was to proceed there as soon as the over-burdened single-track railway could carry them, but, as events turned out, it could not do this until the middle of the ensuing battle.

At Dueidar were the New Zealand Mounted Rifle Brigade, the 5th Mounted Brigade of English Yeomanry, totalling about 2500, with some guns and other units.

The 42nd Division and some other units were between Gilban and Kantara, and an Australian Light Horse Brigade, was ten miles to the south, at Ballybunion.

About 11.30 p.m. the sentries in the redoubts near Katib Gannit heard heavy rifle-fire to the south. The Turks had collided with the Australian outpost line, and

were fighting to break through. Several assaults were
beaten off, but the Australians were greatly outnumbered
and had to fall back or be surrounded. At 3 a.m. the
garrisons of the redoubts, all of whom were standing to,
could see the flashes of the rifles of both friend and foe
gradually moving westward. The skirmishing of the
Australians through the darkness was superb, but the
night covered the advancing Turks until they were close up,
giving them the full advantage of their numbers, and the
brilliant star-lit heavens made it easy for the enemy officers
to keep correct direction.

By daylight the line had bent back until it faced south,
running over Wellington Ridge, and it was evident that the
Turks meant to get into the British rear. The Australian
and New Zealand Mounted Division threw every available
man into action to thicken and extend the long drawn-
out line of riflemen, but the Turks kept working round its
right flank, and it still had to retire slowly northwards
towards the railway. The Light Horsemen's outpost line
and their delaying action had spoilt the intended surprise
night march of the enemy into the British rear, but the
Turks were making better progress than had been expected.
Wellington Ridge was lost, the Turkish infantry were
pressing closely on the retiring Australians, and large
bodies of the enemy were moving towards Mount Royston,
Canterbury Hill, and Pelusium railway station.

At 4 a.m. stray bullets began to drop in and about the
redoubts on the southern, and south-western fronts about
Katib Gannit. Day dawns with great swiftness in these
Eastern deserts, and it was a beautifully clear morning at
4.45 a.m. on this 4th August, when an Australian patrol
passed one of the redoubts and reported that large bodies of
Turks were gathering in the oasis of Bir Abu Hamra.

A few minutes after daylight, a fleet of enemy aeroplanes
flew over the position and the camps behind it, bombing
them from end to end. This was the signal for practically
the whole Turkish artillery, from 8-inch howitzers downwards, to open fire on the posts, Strong Point, Anzac Post
and others on the high ridge of dunes, and also on Redoubts

IN NO. 4 POST, ROMANI, SHOWING COMMON TYPE OF
TRENCH IN REDOUBT

Nos. 1 to 6 below them. Their aim was good, and the first two rounds dropped within the wire of No. 6 (Katia View). At the outset, the bulk of the bombardment was directed behind the main line on to the high range and areas behind it, and these were covered with the white puffs of Turkish shrapnel interspersed with the huge black and yellow columns of smoke and sand thrown up by the bursts of their H.E. Later the shell-fire was directed on the main line of redoubts before Abu Hamra.

This was the commencement of von Kressenstein's attack on the east front of the right, and it will be convenient to deal with it first, up to mid-day, by which time the great crisis of the battle had been passed.

Up to this day the Lowland gunners had had no opportunity of firing their new guns. They were now to do this for the first time in action against the Turks. The artillery of the Division, under Brig.-Gen. Parker, replied about 5.40 a.m., as soon as they knew that the screen of cavalry among the low dunes towards Abu Hamra had withdrawn, and as soon as their forward observation officers could give them targets. No ammunition could be wasted, because of the limitations of supply. The forward observation officers were observing from the main ridge behind, and one, Lieut. R. Guest, Glasgow Howitzers, was on Katib Gannit. This towering cone of shifting sand was deluged with enemy shell-fire from the beginning to the close of the day, but this officer and Lieut. G. F. Scott-Elliott, 5th K.O.S.B., 155th Brigade, rendered most valuable service throughout. They sent a steady stream of clear and prompt messages to their respective brigade headquarters, notifying concentrations far afield, besides dangerous movements of bodies of the enemy, who were creeping up hollows and elsewhere, unseen from the lower heights and main redoubt line. There was also a party of seven 5th K.O.S.B. in this vantage point, who did some excellent long-range sniping as the attacks developed.

No. 1 Artillery Group, Lt.-Col. G. S. Simpson, because of its position in the extreme right with guns covering that flank to east, south, and west, had the principal part in dealing with the attacks of the Turkish infantry, besides replying to the enemy artillery.

Under cover of the Turkish bombardment, bodies of enemy infantry were seen trying to debouch from the palm groves of Abu Hamra, less than half a mile away, but the British artillery caught them, and scattered them or drove them back. The Turks, however, commenced to work their way forward in small parties up hollows and behind low dunes, making for Redoubts Nos. 3, 4, and 5. Word had come at 6.25 a.m. that the enemy infantry had crept close up to Nos. 3 and 4, and were digging themselves in. 'A' Battery of the Glasgow Howitzers, under Major W. Watson, had just been turned on them with effect, when the Turkish attack into the British right rear, or south-western front, developed seriously, and these guns had to be swung round to fire to the south-west. Shortly afterwards the Ayrshire 18-pounders, 'B' Battery, under Major J. Milligan, also had to turn its guns to shoot south-west instead of east. To do so, it had to change position under a fire of enemy shells, bullets, and aeroplane bombs. In addition to being shelled, the artillerymen of No. 1 Group worked their guns throughout the day under long range rifle and machine-gun fire. At this time the guns of this group were shooting through an angle of almost 180°, but this was no new experience for the veterans of Anzac.

Shortly before 7 a.m. the enemy gunners shortened their range and concentrated most of their bombardment on Redoubts No. 3, 4, 5, and 6. An idea of the concentration of this fire may be gained from the number of shell-holes caused by H.E. and percussion shrapnel alone in three of these works during the action. They were as follows:

for No. 3, Capt. Glendinning, 52nd Divisional Cyclists,
    23 in the work, 27 inside the perimeter of the wire;
for No. 4, Capt. H. F. Hodge, 52nd Divisional Cyclists,
    108 in the work, 61 inside the perimeter of the wire;
for No. 5, Capt. R. W. Paton, 5th R.S.F.,
    89 in the work, 43 inside the perimeter of the wire.

It was evidently von Kressenstein's intention to overwhelm

Nos. 4 and 5, and so make a breach of about 2000 yards in the British front. Whilst this bombardment was blowing in parts of the trenches, and inflicting casualties on the garrisons, the enemy had crept forward and dug a firing line from No. 2 to No. 5. Before No. 2 (Capt. Brotherstone, 5th R.S.F.) they were 1100 yards away, but opposite No. 4, the redoubt nearest Abu Hamra, they were in places only 150 yards away. Despite the showers of Turkish shrapnel, Fusiliers, Cyclists, and Machine-Gunners could not be driven from their parapets. The dropping fire and shrapnel of the British guns was quick and accurate, the garrisons of the redoubts exacted a heavy toll, and the Turks could get no closer.

Meanwhile, the British monitors were shelling the oases in enfilade, their fire being observed by the Ayrshire Battery at Mahemdia; British 60-pounders were searching for the Turkish guns; British aeroplanes were systematically bombing the enemy camps and communications; and German aeroplanes, working by relays in groups of four, were bombing the British positions and railhead. In the right rear the Turks were pressing, and forcing their way over the desert towards Pelusium.

At 7.30 a.m. the Turks made another determined attack from the palm groves of Abu Hamra, moving thither under cover of the oases, which stretched eastward. This time they made for No. 5. They struggled forward to within 400 yards of the British wire, when, under the concentrated artillery, machine-gun, and rifle-fire, the attack completely broke down.

About the time that this attack was developing, the observers on Katib Gannit detected a party of four Turks, who had crept up a hollow between Nos. 2 and 3 and were cutting a gap in the wire fence. These redoubts were about 1000 yards apart, and neither could see what was going on. Cpl. W. Curran, 5th K.O.S.B., who had already distinguished himself carrying messages from Katib Gannit and elsewhere, crawled out and stalked them. He shot one dead and wounded two, the fourth managing to escape.

At 8.30 a.m. the Turks made their third assault on this front, this time towards Nos. 4 and 5. Some 3000 of them were seen moving forward, but 'B' Battery of the Glasgow Howitzers, Capt. G. C. F. Speirs, was turned on them, and immediately began to drop shells on their line. The attacking force was broken up, and only a few small parties succeeded in getting forward, where the garrisons of the redoubts killed them or held them at bay. The rapidity and accuracy with which the guns of No. 1 Group were handled did much to wreck von Kressenstein's plans.

Redoubts Nos. 4 and 5 were now badly knocked about, and the former had lost a number of its garrison. Forty picked shots of the K.O.S.B. lined the main ridge overlooking these two posts, and from there sniped the Turkish snipers. The enemy artillery searched for these Border riflemen with shrapnel, but did not find them.

The sun was now approaching the zenith and the midday summer heat was terrific. On this front the British had won in the fire-fight, and the Turkish infantry were thirsty, exhausted, and disheartened. They had only succeeded in pushing their firing line into a perilous position before the redoubts which they had intended to capture, and for the time being could do no more.

We must retrace our steps to follow the Turkish attempt to penetrate the British right rear, the southern and south-western front of the 155th Brigade.

From daylight onwards, bodies of Turks were seen south of the position moving westward following the retiring cavalry. Whenever they got targets, the 155th Brigade machine-guns opened fire, and many times broke up these parties, punishing the enemy severely. The enemy infantry never got within 1200 yards of the works on the extreme right, and none of the garrisons suffered much from enemy artillery fire.

Whenever a gun could be spared from one of the howitzer batteries, it was turned on the enemy aeroplanes. The enemy artillery continually tried to find the British guns and observation posts.

Before 7 a.m. Brig.-Gen. Pollok-M'Call had come to the conclusion that the chief danger on the right lay in an attack from Wellington Ridge, which by that time had been occupied by enemy infantry, who from the higher ground were carrying on a long range fire-fight with Redoubts No. 21a (Lieut. J. Lees, 5th R.S.F.), and No. 22a (Capt. P. L. P. Laing, 4th K.O.S.B.). An attack was expected, and the Ayrshire 18-pounders shrapnelled the reverse slope of Wellington Ridge, where Turks were known to be collecting. Shortly after 7 a.m. large numbers of enemy infantry tried to charge down Wellington Ridge towards Nos. 21a and 22a; but they were met with the fire of a battery of the Glasgow Howitzers, one of Ayrshire 18-pounders, and an 18-pounder battery of the 263rd Lowland Brigade, Lt.-Col. C. C. Robertson, stationed further north, besides the machine-gun and rifle-fire of the redoubts, and of two companies of 5th Royal Welch Fusiliers, which had been brought from reserve and were now lining the ridge on either side of 22a. The enemy infantry suffered heavy losses and the attack completely collapsed.

From this time onwards the Turks tried to dribble men forward, and managed to get snipers within 300 yards of No. 22a, but the defence was too well prepared for them. Some of the hollows and gullies proved veritable death-traps. The sand in them was so loose that men in them could neither run nor dig a trench. Once Turks were located in such hollows there was no escape from the dropping fire of the Lowland howitzers, which, because of their curved trajectories, could get right into the bottoms of such places. After the action, 205 enemy dead, mostly killed by shrapnel, were counted in the immediate front of No. 1 alone. By 9 a.m. the British had complete superiority of fire, and this attack, which, with that on Nos. 4 and 5, was intended to cut off and destroy the British right round Katib Gannit, was completely held. The artillery repeatedly shelled the reverse slope of Wellington Ridge, and, although a reinforcement of about 250 Turks was seen to arrive after noon, the enemy could only hold on and trust to their thrust at Pelusium station. Soon after mid-day the British artillery had the situation completely in hand, and commenced to husband their ammunition.

By 8 a.m. the 4th and 7th Royal Scots of the 156th
Brigade, Brig.-Gen. E. S. Girdwood, were holding and
supporting a series of small entrenchments, which ran from
No. 22, south of No. 23, to the north-eastward towards the
railway. So far had the British line been bent back that
these units were covering the centre of the British rear, and
were under rifle-fire from Wellington Ridge. The remainder of the 156th Brigade was moved to the neighbourhood of No. 23, to stop any further Turkish advance
in this direction.

The general situation to the west of the 156th Brigade
at about 8 a.m. was as follows. The two brigades of
the Anzac Mounted Division, originally about 3000 in
number, had suffered heavy casualties and were spread out
in a line of skirmishers to the west. This line had stretched
until it was about 5000 yards long, and was so thin that it
could extend no further. Most of these men had been
fighting and retiring continuously since midnight. A
squadron of the Gloucester Yeomanry had reinforced their
right, but that flank was completely " in the air." The
Turks had occupied Mount Royston, and were lining the
ridges facing Canterbury Hill before 9 a.m. If they could
only advance in force the necessary two miles or less past the
flank of the mounted troops, nothing lay between them and
the precious railway but this single redoubt on Canterbury
Hill, and a battalion of the 42nd Division with some details.
There had been " unfortunately, more delay than had been
anticipated, in moving the infantry of the 42nd Division
up to Pelusium station " (Sir A. Murray), and the remainder of the 127th Brigade, 42nd Division, did not
arrive until about 3 p.m. This was the gravest time in the
battle. The British Romani army was gradually assuming
a triangular formation, with the Turks on two sides, and the
sea and the almost impassable flats of Tina on the third.
To watchers at Romani, who " could see the Turkish
shrapnel bursting on the hills far behind us, it looked
almost as if the Turk had succeeded in his object and that
we were being caught in a trap. It looked as if our only
escape would be northwards by the sea. The enemy

circled so far round our position and was so far abreast of our rear that his shells were falling on the railway between us and Pelusium, the railway station immediately behind Romani, and all traffic was held up." (Lt.-Col. J. Young.)

However, factors, on which Generals Murray and Lawrence had calculated, had been in operation. The soft sand had tired out the Turkish infantry, the blazing heat had caused them to drink their water, and they were entangled in an almost waterless area. This great outflanking movement of von Kressenstein's, which had been planned to finish before the heat of the day, was still two miles from its goal, and the Turks were almost completely played out. Nevertheless, it had moved with greater speed than some had thought possible.

" The result of the somewhat rapid advance of the Turks from the south was that General Lawrence was obliged to divert the cavalry, originally destined to operate against the enemy's rear, to strengthen the line of resistance on the north" (Sir A. Murray). The 5th Mounted Brigade were moved from Dueidar to Pelusium, and at 9.45 a.m. came into action, reinforcing and extending the thin line of the Anzac Mounted Division. The New Zealand Mounted Rifles Brigade moved from Dueidar to attack the Turkish left flank, and more Australian cavalry was ordered up from the south.

The Turkish advance reached its limit at 12.30 p.m., when their line ran from the north of Mount Royston, through Bir Abu Diyak, to Wellington Ridge, and thence round the Romani position to Bir Abu Hamra.

Shortly after 1 p.m. the cavalry began to attack towards Mount Royston from the west and north, gradually pressing the Turks back in spite of a desperate resistance. The Turkish infantry had been supplied with sandbags made of white cotton. When they filled and placed these bags in front of them, they showed as lines of pure white specks against the blazing yellow sand, indicating exactly to British observers the Turkish positions. This cost the Turks many of their men, especially when the artillery of the mounted brigades started to burst their shells over

Mount Royston. The Turkish shrapnel was good and well-timed, but the steady advance of the cavalry continued, until they were within from 400 to 500 yards of Mount Royston.

The hour fixed for the commencement of the counter-attack was 3 p.m., and at that time Canterbury Hill passed on a message that the Turks were fought to a stand-still, and that the whole line closing on Mount Royston and the Turkish left flank was to press forward. At 4 p.m. Mount Royston was taken by the cavalry, and three battalions of the 127th Brigade, which had marched south from Pelusium, cleared up the position. Over 500 prisoners were taken, with machine-guns, and a battery of mountain artillery. Among the captured was a Turkish engineer officer specially detailed to look after the destruction of the Suez Canal.

The Turkish left flank had now crumbled away, and fugitives, with rifles and equipment thrown away, were making for the south-east. After them went the weary Australians, New Zealanders, and English Yeomen.

News that his left flank was held up by the arrival of the 5th Mounted Brigade, and therefore in extreme danger and cut off from supplies, must have reached von Kressenstein not later than mid-day. His attack had failed and his concern now was to save his army and guns. A machine-gun in No. 4 had been destroyed by a shell soon after mid-day, and the redoubt had just been reinforced by the 4th R.S.F., when at 1.30 p.m. the Turkish artillery opened a heavy shell-fire on this post and No. 5 opposite Abu Hamra, and on No. 1 on the extreme right. The enemy battery bombarding the latter was located behind a dune nearly four miles away to the south-east, and was silenced by the artillery. The bombardment of Nos. 4 and 5 continued for two and a half hours, and enemy aircraft bombed the lines again. In order to prevent their guns being located by the dust raised by each discharge, the enemy gunners had been ordered to spread large mats on the sand below the muzzles. This had been effective and they were not easy to find.

INFANTRY OF THE DIVISION ON THE MARCH THROUGH TYPICAL COUNTRY IN SINAI

At 4 p.m. the Turkish infantry sallied from Abu Hamra wood for their fourth attack on No. 5 Redoubt. Von Kressenstein was sacrificing his infantry to cover the withdrawal, which he saw was very urgent. Again the Turks came under rifle, machine-gun and artillery fire, and again they simply melted away. After the battle a captured Turkish officer stated that the British " mitrailleuse fire was terrible, and cut down the men like reaping corn." The dead, found after the action lying immediately in front of Nos. 2 to 5, and killed mostly by rifle-fire, numbered as follows :

No. 2	26
,, 3	126
,, 4	97
,, 5	52

Men killed by shrapnel lay scattered further out, and the wounded who crawled away must have been numerous.

This was the last effort of the Turkish infantry, and, even as it was being made, Mount Royston was being captured, and orders were being issued for the 156th Brigade to retake Wellington Ridge.

Two battalions of the 156th Brigade, Brig.-Gen. E. S. Girdwood, moved southward in artillery formation from behind Redoubt No. 23 shortly before 7 p.m. The 7th Cameronians, Lt.-Col. J. G. P. Romanes, was on the left, and the 8th Cameronians, Lt.-Col. J. M. Findlay, on the right. Each unit had four guns from the 156th Brigade M.G. Coy. In desert warfare it is almost useless to choose a natural feature as a point by which to march, and accordingly the left, the directing flank, was to pivot on Redoubt No. 22a. Their right was to be covered by the Anzac Mounted Division.

As darkness gathered, the Borderers in 22a could see the mounted troops and East Lancs. infantry cresting the sky-line of the ridges to the east. Both battalions of Cameronians deployed under desultory sniping, and advanced, the 8th keeping touch and direction despite inevitable difficulties, and making for the crest of the ridge. The unevenness of the ground, the darkness, and the firing in front and on the flanks made the movement increasingly difficult. As soon as the 8th neared the crest, the Turks, who were entrenched on top less than 100 yards away, opened a heavy fire on them, and there followed a night of rifle and machine-gun firing, bombing, and digging in a prone position, during which the German and Turkish officers decamped. One company of the 7th Cameronians was in close touch, and the remainder were linking up with No. 22a. Orders were given to hold fast till dawn, and then to charge the enemy positions.

As the morning light rapidly drove away the darkness and disclosed the desert once more to the Turks on Wellington Ridge, this was the spectacle that presented itself. Immediately before them, across the ridge, lay lines of the 8th Cameronians with bayonets fixed preparing to assault. Behind the 8th Cameronians was a company of Royal Welch Fusiliers being brought up in support, to the right of the firing line. To the right flank of the Turks was a company of the 7th Cameronians already working round either to enfilade or to attack them in flank. Below, on the desert, to the west and south, were innumerable parties of mounted troops commencing to move eastward, some being close in to their left flank.

At the same time, the rifle, machine-gun, and Lewis gun fire from the Cameronians swelled quickly in volume, and the redoubts also joined in. The Cameronians commenced to advance with the bayonet, and this decided the matter. The Turks put up a white flag, the firing ceased, and, throwing down their arms, the whole body stood up, and left their trenches with their hands up. 864 Turks surrendered to the 8th Cameronians with machine-guns and quantities of ammunition and equipment. Just at this time men of the Anzac Mounted Division moved out on the right of the 8th Cameronians, and assisted in rounding up more Turks to their front and flank. In all about 1500 prisoners were taken on Wellington Ridge, nearly all of whom were brought into the camp of the 156th Brigade. This was the end of von Kressenstein's sweeping movement into the British rear.

During the night of the 4-5th parties of Turks made

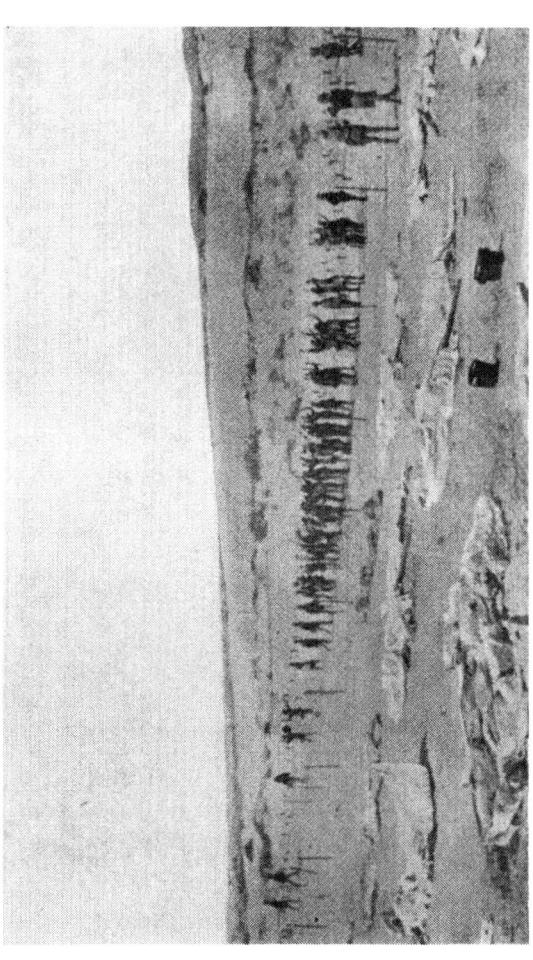

TURKS SURRENDERING AFTER BATTLE OF ROMANI

Taken on 4th August, 1916, at 7.30 a.m., one minute after the Turks hoisted the white flag. In the foreground are tents which were lowered directly the attack appeared imminent.

several attempts to penetrate the wire between Redoubts Nos. 2 and 5, but they were driven off by patrols, artillery fire, and machine-gun fire played along the fences. The enemy had made several gaps in the fences, and twice had blown openings with gun-cotton, but when day dawned not a Turk was to be seen to the west of the British wire. Lieut. S. Findlay of the Divisional Cyclists on patrol work was shot dead by some Turks between Nos. 2 and 3. The persistence of the Turks in trying to penetrate the British wire, despite their severe ordeal of the day before, showed their excellent calibre.

As the morning advanced the enemy could be seen in full retreat everywhere. Some, however, could not get back, and at 6 a.m. a white flag was hoisted about 200 yards east of No. 3, and two officers and 117 other ranks, twelve of whom were wounded, surrendered in a body. This was the end of the attempt to pierce the Division's front.

Beyond a few shells fired by the Ayrshire 18-pounders stationed at Mahemdia, the troops north of Romani had been able to take no part in the engagement, although they had been occasionally shelled by the enemy artillery and bombed by their aeroplanes.

The British cavalry with tired horses were following up the enemy to their front south and east of Katib Gannit. An attempt was now made to round-up the exhausted Turks, who still lingered in the oases about Abu Hamra. Shortly before mid-day the 157th Brigade, Brig.-Gen. H. G. Casson, was ordered to form a mobile column and move south to attack Abu Hamra in flank, while a similar column formed from the reserves of the 155th Brigade, Brig.-Gen. J. B. Pollok-M'Call, was to attack it in front. By the time the 157th Brigade had collected its men over the soft sands of Mahemdia it was past mid-day and the same factors which had ruined von Kressenstein's flanking movement, heat and sand, made this one a failure. Under a little shell-fire the 157th Brigade completed the eight miles it had to cover, and reached Abu Hamra as darkness fell, only to find that the Turks had fled. The cavalry were fighting the enemy's rearguards, and this brigade was again on the move soon after dawn on the 6th. The 155th Brigade, whose previous orders had been cancelled, moved off at the same time, with the 7th R.S. attached. Both brigades reached El Rabah on that day, but the cavalry had pressed the pursuit much further to the eastward. The heat on these marches was intense; some of the men fell unconscious, and some became delirious. The pursuit by the infantry finished at El Rabah, and both the 155th and 157th Brigades remained in the Katia oases for over a week, during which period they were frequently bombed by enemy aircraft.

British (Imperial and Colonial) aviators and cavalry did their utmost to turn the retreat into a rout, but von Kressenstein's forethought in preparing rearguard positions did much to save his army from complete destruction, and his machine-gunners fought well. One rearguard action succeeded another in different places, and more prisoners were captured. At Bir el Abd he brought up fresh troops, and counter-attacked four times with a force of over 6000 men, in an attempt to save his heaps of stores, but he had to set fire to them and retreat. The pursuit finished at Salmana on the 12th. Bir el Abd was held by the cavalry from this time onwards, the main body of the infantry was withdrawn to Romani, and work on the railway and pipeline was resumed with all speed.

The Turkish losses in personnel during the battle and in the pursuit can only be estimated. The British actually buried 1251 of their dead, and, when we consider the wounded who died during their retreat and those who survived, we cannot put their losses in killed and wounded at less than 5000. In addition, 3930 prisoners were taken, so that von Kressenstein must have lost one-half of the force he had before Romani. The prisoners included forty-nine officers, of whom twenty-five were Germans and Austrians, an entire German machine-gun company being also among the prizes. Among other things, we captured one mountain battery, nine machine-guns, great quantities of rifles, shells and other ammunition, 600 camels, horses and mules, and a large amount of equipment and miscellaneous stores, besides two complete field hospitals.

LAYING THE WIRE ROAD IN SINAI

The British losses, the greater portion of which fell on the Anzac Mounted Division, who fought the opening rearguard action, were as follows up to 6th August :[1]

	Killed.	Wounded.	Missing.	Total.
Officers	12	36	—	48
Other ranks	94	338	52	484
	106	374	52	532

To these must be added the casualties sustained in the pursuit.

The casualties of the 155th Brigade were as follows :

	Killed or Died of Wounds.	Wounded.	Total.
Officers	3	1	4
Other ranks	32	44	76
	35	45	80

The 52nd Divisional Cyclists lost Lieut A. Henderson and fifteen other ranks killed in Redoubt No. 4. These with Lieut S. Findlay were all their dead. Lieut. A. H. Pollard, 5th K.O.S.B., was the third officer killed. The remaining casualties were spread almost evenly over the garrisons and reserves. These small losses are great testimony to the hurdles which made properly shaped trenches possible.

The casualties of the 156th Brigade were as follows :

	Killed or Died of Wounds.	Wounded.	Total.
Officers	1	4	5
Other ranks	19	26	45
	20	30	50

The 8th Cameronians lost Lieut. G. Lawson killed, and two officers wounded, besides sixteen other ranks killed and fifteen wounded.

The casualties of the 157th Brigade were as follows :

	Killed or Died of Wounds.	Wounded.	Total.
Other ranks	3	13	16

The losses of the artillery were very small : the artillery of the 52nd Division only lost six other ranks killed and four wounded, eight of these being in the Glasgow Howitzers.

[1] These figures are taken from the Official Communiqué published in the *Egyptian Mail* of 10th August, 1916.

In all, the casualties of the 52nd Division were considerably less than 200.

The disparity in numbers between the casualties suffered by the two brigades, 155th and 156th, and the Lowland artillery, and those inflicted on the enemy by these formations, is tremendous. It may be said quite truly that the battle of Romani was won as soon as Gen. von Kressenstein decided to walk into the trap laid for him by Gens. Murray and Lawrence, with the Anzac Mounted and 52nd (Lowland) Divisions. The Colonial horsemen spoilt his night surprise, led him into the trap, and fought right through the action: the Lowlanders formed the wall against which he broke himself, and they destroyed every attack on it: the English yeomanry and infantry helped to checkmate and finally overwhelm his thrust at Pelusium railway station. Sir Archibald Murray and Gen. Lawrence had been ready for every move.

Judged from the standpoint of numbers, this action seems relatively unimportant; yet it effected far more than many of the gigantic battles fought in Europe, and was one of the decisive battles of the war. It drove the Turks back from the Suez Canal and Egypt finally, and from that time onwards they were on the defensive on this front. It resulted in the British recovering possession of one of the greatest and most ancient strategic highways of the world, and helped to seal the fate of Turkish rule in Arabia.

CAMOUFLAGED GUNS, SINAI

CHAPTER XVI

(7TH AUGUST, 1916, TO 5TH MARCH, 1917)

EL ARISH

> We have seen the dried-up salt lake spread below,
> One vast opal 'neath the dawn and afterglow,
>   And its mid-day pearly hue
>   Blending into turquoise blue;
> But we saw the sapphire sea at El Madan.
>
> In a night we heard a whirr of wings, so we
> Asked if home-birds southwards passed, and merrily
>   Sang one morn a north-land bird;
>   But the sweetest sound we heard
> Was the murmur of the sea at El Madan.
>
> *The Sea at El Madan*, 16th Decr., 1916.

CAPT. R. S. TAYLOR of the 1/1st Lowland Field Ambulance was searching the country between Katib Gannit and Katia with a mobile section on the 7th August for any wounded still lying out. He found none, but on his way back picked up some sick. One was seriously ill, and he suspected cholera. He examined the man closely, and was confirmed in his belief, the man having contracted it from drinking water from some butts left behind by the Turks. On his return he immediately had the patient isolated and wired the news to Divisional Headquarters. All diarrhoea cases were segregated, and an isolation camp was laid out. " In view of the risk to nursing orderlies in this camp and the irksomeness of the strict isolation entailed, volunteers were called for. The men rose to the occasion as always, and there was no lack of willing offers." (Lt.-Col. J. W. Leitch, 1/1st Lowland Field Ambulance.) Capt. Taylor took charge with six orderlies and a cook.

Every possible step was taken. The troops already had rigorous instructions to avoid drinking water from native wells. A mobile laboratory under Col. Martin, Australian Army Medical Corps, was sent forward, and reported on all cases of diarrhoea. All who had been in contact with cases were isolated. No one was allowed to journey westward across the canal until he had spent eight clear days in a quarantine camp on the east bank and been certified clear of infection. The whole army, together with the native camel drivers and labourers, were inoculated. The sanitation of native camps was more strictly supervised than ever. The Turkish prisoners had to be taken out of the war area, but they were put in quarantine. In Egypt, isolation hospitals and compounds were made everywhere. Other preparations were made too numerous to mention here, as a result of which the disease was quelled by the end of October, and there were only thirty cases in all. The first man died within a few days, and there were six other fatal cases. Not a single case occurred among the Egyptian labourers in Sinai, and the disease was kept out of Egypt.

In 1883 the loss of life in Egypt from the cholera epidemic had been 60,000. In 1896, among 21,693 cases of cholera reported in Egypt, there had been 18,105 deaths. From these figures the magnitude of the disaster which was averted can be understood, and it is no exaggeration to say that the army might have been well nigh destroyed but for the prompt measures taken by the R.A.M.C. under Surgeon-General Maher, C.B. The British forces kept more than a petrifying tyranny out of Egypt when they drove back the Turkish army, for cholera was raging in Syria at the time. For the prevention of this disaster "most of the credit is due to Captain R. S. Taylor for his early recognition of the serious disease we had met with" (Lt.-Col. J. W. Leitch).

Cholera was only one of the diseases against which the R.A.M.C. fought silently, unremittingly. Enteric fever, "plague," dysentery, and many others were only kept at bay by the constant alertness of the doctors and their men.

The Assyrian monarch Sennacherib on one occasion lost

TYPICAL BIVOUAC AREA, SINAI

EL ARISH

an entire army in these very parts, outside Pelusium, either by disease or thirst. That it was possible for the British column to cross this desert without similar disasters is due to the R.A.M.C., and to the R.E., who developed the water supply, bridged the desert with the railway, and laid the pipe-line which brought a continuous supply of water, eventually right across the desert. Nor must we forget the supply services, and the Camel Transport Corps, with their single-file caravans of camels, which were literally miles in length.

Water suitable for animals is found in a narrow belt immediately to the south of a line from three to five miles from the coast, and usually at the foot on the north side of a steep dune, or at the edge of a sabket. South of this belt palatable water as a rule is unobtainable. The usual method adopted by the Lowland Field Companies was to erect a four-sided box of galvanised iron vertically in an excavation. The hole was dug deeper until the box sank into place, holding up the sandy sides. The water which filtered into the hole was drawn out by means of a hand-pump, or an adaptation of the native "shaduf."[1] Fresh water was also found by boring on the sea-shore west of El Arish. Apparently it was retained by a lip of clay which underlay the sand and gravel.

The whole of the Transport Section of the Divisional Train was left behind at Kantara, camels taking the place of the wheeled vehicles for the advance over the desert. Some seventy camels were attached to each battalion, the native camel-drivers being under their own "reis." The drivers had no knowledge of English, but all ranks of the Division and especially those of the quartermaster's department gradually acquired a vocabulary of Arabic. This latter was most fearful and wonderful, but, when it was helped out by signs, etc., the natives managed to understand it, through the mutual good humour of themselves and of our own men.

[1] A "shaduf" consists of a long pole fixed as a lever to an upright. One end is weighted, and the other, the further from the upright or fulcrum, has attached to it the receptacle which is lowered into the well for the water.

A camel's load is always about 350 lbs., and must be well balanced, or the saddle will cause a bad gall and the load may fall off. The loading of tools and miscellaneous stores was a complicated problem, and the loading officer had to be a man of infinite tact and patience. After the transport of water, supplies, ammunition, blankets, equipment, etc., had been provided for, there was very little carrying capacity left, so that only the barest necessities could be taken, when on the march, or on " mobile," as it came to be termed.

" The eye might be charmed by the stately motion of the creature but the nose was offended by its exceedingly unpleasant smell. Camels are very delicate. They have vile tempers, and in late autumn become frankly impossible. The native word ' macnoon,' by the way, in spite of its suggestion of respectable Highland clans, was regarded as the only one adequate to describe a camel at this time of year, and was therefore added to our vacabulary. They are noisy, vicious, un-accommodating and aggravating to a degree." (*History 5th H.L.I.*)

Generally, the camel acts and looks like an overbearing aristocrat continually suffering injustice. He has a most supercilious lower lip, and seems to regard the human animal with contempt and the barest tolerance, and on occasion bites him viciously. Nevertheless, he carried our burdens, and whether through stupidity or bravery we know not, would do so through a shell-fire that horses and mules would not face.

During September the Divisional artillery was renumbered as follows :

260th Brigade (Ayr and Kirkcudbright) became 261st Brigade.
261st   (Glasgow) became 262nd ,,
262nd ,, (Glasgow Howitzers) became 263rd ,,
263rd ,, (Horse Artillery) became 264th ,,

For the advance these brigades were reorganized into two groups, No. 1 and No. 2, each with two batteries of 18-pdrs. and a battery of howitzers. The 264th Brigade and 'C' Batteries of the 261st and 262nd Brigades were detailed for lines of communications.

IN THE SEA VIEW DEFENCE AREA, EL ARISH

EL ARISH

The Division kept brigades out at El Rabah until 12th September, various reliefs taking place. During this period it was bombed daily by enemy aeroplanes; but the casualties were few, excepting on the 3rd September, when a bomb burst among the officers' bivouacs of the 6th H.L.I., killing Lieut. J. S. Osborne and wounding five other officers and a private. Camel lines were favourite targets of enemy aviators, and a few days previously the 1/1st Lowland Field Ambulance lost two native camel drivers killed and three wounded.

On 12th September the 42nd Division took over the Katia oases, whilst the 52nd (the 155th and 156th Brigades at Mahemdia and 157th at Katib Gannit) went into training for the forthcoming advance. Early in October four extra Lewis guns were received by each battalion, making the complement two per company. All ranks had become acclimatised to conditions of life in the desert, the sun had lost some of its heat, and mornings and evenings were cooler. The standard of training reached was never higher than at this time. Unfits were weeded out, and although the Division was up to only about two-thirds of its strength, it was never more efficient.

On 2nd October Brigadier-General H. G. Casson, C.M.G., left the 157th Brigade to take over command of the Delta District, handing over his command to Brigadier-General C. D. Hamilton-Moore. General Casson was well known for his careful and thorough methods. His men remembered how he had come twice a day round the front lines in Gallipoli, no matter what the conditions were, and the dunes rang with their farewell cheers as his train steamed out.

A reconnaissance in force of mounted troops and artillery against Mazar on 16th and 17th September so much impressed the Turks with the increased radius of British action that they withdrew all their men from there to El Arish.

On 12th October the move on El Arish commenced. The 155th and 156th Brigades marched to El Afein, and the 157th to El Rabah. The desert column, which was to carry out this advance, consisted of the Anzac Mounted Division, the 52nd (Lowland), and the 42nd (East Lancs.). Throughout this advance, with the exception of one period, the 52nd Division led the way with a screen of horsemen, sometimes a brigade and sometimes a division. "Consequently much the largest proportion of the pioneer work of selecting and preparing fortified positions, developing water supplies, forming dumps, etc., fell on our division. We were of course assisted by Egyptian labour companies and Indian pioneer battalions, in the later stages of the development of each locality, but the planning and most of the pioneer work may be said to have been done by the Lowland Division." (Lt.-Col. J. Anderson.)

Between the 13th and 17th October a small force of mounted men carried out a reconnaissance into the Gebel Maghara, which lay right along the flank of the route and was held by the enemy. It was ascertained that the Turks were not maintaining a large force there. Because of the broad belt of waterless country which lay between the Gebel Maghara and the railway, any force intended to attack the latter would have to carry most of their water with them, and so could not be of considerable strength. Nevertheless, a raid on the railway and pipe-line by 500 or 1000 men on camels had to be provided against, and this threat immobilised some troops of the desert column, but was finally met by the construction of block-houses.

The advance was conducted by a series of bounds. As the railway, the pipe-line, and the wire road were pushed forward, the 52nd Division, with its screen of horsemen, kept moving from one position to another, each position in turn being entrenched. At times these positions had two exposed flanks, because of the flats of Bardawil intervening between the left and the sea, but never once did the Turks dare to attack them. Romani had taught them a lesson, and they could only watch our deliberate advance.

Enemy aeroplanes periodically bombed the camps of the Division, but the R.F.C. retaliated and the cavalry "kept the initiative." The aeroplane bombs caused a thin dribble of casualties from the Division, but did no more.

INFANTRY OF THE DIVISION MARCHING ON THE WIRE ROAD BETWEEN EL ARISH AND EL BURJ

EL ARISH

The principal forward moves of the various brigades were as shown below:

Date.		Brigade.	Journey.
1916.			
October	12	155	to El Afein
		156	to El Afein
		157	to El Rabah
,,	13	155	to El Abd
		156	to El Abd
		157	to El Afein
,,	14	157	to El Abd
,,	27	155	to Salmana
		156	to Ganadil
		157	to Salmana
December	1	155	to Tilul
		156	to Tilul
,,	2	155	to Mazar
		156	to Mazar
,,	7	157	to Tilul
,,	8	157	to Mazar
,,	16	157	to El Maadan (kilo. 128)
,,	20	156	to El Maadan
,,	21	155	to El Maadan
		156	to El Meshalfat
,,	22	155	to El Bittia
		156	to El Arish
,,	23	155	to El Arish
,,	29	157	to Bardawil Station (kilo. 139)
1917.			
January	5	157	to Masaid (kilo. 152)
,,	8	157	to El Arish

A few miles were covered over the edge of the surface crust of the Sabket Bardawil.

Colonel J. Anderson gives the following picture of a battalion on the march as part of a brigade column:—
" Bivouac has probably been left soon after sunrise, shelters having been struck in darkness, blankets rolled and loaded and breakfast taken before the sun is well above the horizon; battalion stores have been loaded, the battalion bivouac area cleaned and the refuse burnt. The battalion marches with fours well spread out in width, but not in length, to minimise dust and allow free passage of air; all ranks are in shirt sleeves, the lower arms bare and the neck open; the drill jacket is strapped to the haversack or inside the pack, if the

latter is being carried, but pack and haversack were never worn together while we were on trek, one or other being left behind to be brought up later. The company commander is probably walking at the head or by the side of his company. At the rear of each company are its pack animals, carrying its Lewis guns and a proportion of ammunition. In rear of the battalion, though sometimes marching parallel with it, are the 1st line transport limbers and camels carrying ammunition, tools, water and cooking pots. The 2nd line transport, with blankets, stores, etc., is in rear of the brigade."

Bivouacs were usually made out of blankets, although many were equipped with the excellent German-made light waterproof sheets and collapsible poles captured from the Turkish army. A few of the officers had managed to purchase Egyptian Ordnance bivouacs, and after El Arish was reached most of them obtained them.

> " Who can the desert's strength subdue ?
> Pipe, Rail and Road.
> Pipe to carry your drink to you ;
> Rail to speed your rations through ;
> Road to march on firm and true
> Past bir and hod."

So wrote the gunner-poet, Crawsley Williams, but unfortunately there was no road for the 52nd Division. They were the pioneers. They trudged through the sand and took a large share in laying the wire road along which those who followed them marched. This road was a purely British invention, the result of a simple but brilliant idea. It consisted of a belt of wire-netting, three or four rolls broad, laid on the sand, which prevented the foot sinking more than an inch into it and was constantly pulled to the surface by the general beating of the feet. Animals and vehicles tore the wire, and so were ordered not to use this road, frequent gaps for crossings being provided for them. These wire roads were much used over the sand and deep dust before Gaza. They doubled the speed with which troops could march, and the saving in human energy was incalculable.

A COMPANY COOKHOUSE, SEA VIEW
DEFENCE AREA, EL ARISH

On the 28th of November the 42nd Division passed through the 52nd and took up a position covering railhead, which at the time was five miles east of Mazar. The 52nd caught up on the 16th December, and on 22nd the 42nd was sent back to Mazar because of a shortage of water. For the remainder of this long trek the 52nd led the way with the cavalry.

Lt.-Gen. Sir P. W. Chetwode took over the desert column on the 7th December.

East of Bir el Abd, water is found in comparatively few and widely separated localities. As the railway advanced the water difficulty increased, and long waits had to be made while the supply was developed. The Turks had placed their troops to cover all the available water about El Arish and Masaid, and had taken up a very strong position with the lines of defence disposed in a depth of four miles. The long parallel ridges and sand-hills south-west of El Arish are extremely steep and bare, forming a most difficult terrain for attacking troops. It was known that the Turks at El Arish expected reinforcements and their aircraft became increasingly active, but the water supply prevented the British from hurrying their attack.

When the 157th Brigade arrived at El Maadan, and from the crest of a ridge saw the sea for the first time since leaving Mahemdia, it was with the expectation that they would have to fight their way to the spire of the mosque in El Arish, and the dome of Nebi Yesir's Tomb perched on its knoll, which they could see about twenty miles away, along the surf-fringed coast. However, the Turks concluded that their reinforcements could not arrive in time, and on the 20th December hurriedly withdrew. During the following night, a moonless one, the British cavalry surrounded the enemy position, and at sunrise entered El Arish. The 156th Brigade was following close behind, and, after a hard night-march over very soft sand, reached the town at 11.15 a.m. on the 22nd.

El Arish is the usual oriental town, flat-roofed and filthy, and containing nothing of any value, but, because of its position at the Asiatic side of the Sinai Desert, its capture was of the highest importance. To the east of it the ground grows harder for marching and becomes increasingly fertile. The desert had been bridged, and the British could take the offensive into enemy territory.

While the 155th and 156th Brigades were occupying positions around El Arish on the 23rd, British mounted troops were moving swiftly on the Turkish garrison, which had retired up the Wadi el Arish and dug itself in very strongly at Magdhaba. After a stiff battle the entire enemy force was destroyed, 1282 prisoners and four guns being captured. This was followed on the 9th January by the mounted troops swooping down on the Turkish force holding Rafa.[1] Over 1600 unwounded prisoners with four guns were taken, and the Turks realised that no detached force within a few days march of the British was safe. The Gebel Maghara and other places were evacuated, with the result that Sinai and the district south of El Arish was clear of the enemy. Von Kressenstein began rapidly to prepare a position near Weli Sheikh Nuran to cover the communications of Beersheba with the north.

It was a welcome relief to eyes, tired of the monotony and endless sands of the desert, to see the group of palms at the mouth of Wadi el Arish, the strips of green along its banks where the crops were sprouting, and the plain covered with fig trees. As the year advanced the weather had become cooler and the flies less numerous. By the middle of December it was very cold when the sun was not up. A heavy shower of rain fell on Christmas night, and at El Arish there were several storms of bitterly cold wind and rain during January. Heavy rains in the mountains to the south turned the Wadi el Arish into a flowing river, and entirely justified the bridge which the Royal Engineers had thrown across it on sandbag piers. During this period the heat of the sun was so great at mid-day that sun-helmets had to be worn, and these extremes were very trying to all ranks. The men dug themselves deep dug-

---

[1] This battle was fought over the same ground as that of Raphia (217 B.C.) between Kings Ptolemy IV. and Antiochus, in which both sides employed fighting elephants.

DIVISIONAL HEADQUARTERS, EL ARISH

outs to escape the cutting winds, as well as the bombs and machine-gun fire of enemy aeroplanes, which came over night after night. This nightly bombing and machine-gunning by low-flying enemy aeroplanes was checked by the retaliation of the Royal Flying Corps. On the 3rd January the 7th Cameronians had a bad accident. The sides of a dug-out collapsed, suffocating one man and imperilling the life of another, and the depth of these holes had to be limited.

Trawlers had commenced sweeping the roadstead of mines on the 22nd December, and, while the railway was being advanced to El Arish, invaluable work was done by the Navy in landing stores. A trawler was driven ashore on 29th December during one violent tempest of wind and rain. Several strong swimmers from the 52nd tried to get out to her with ropes, and various attempts were made with flare pistols and the like to shoot lines over her, but these efforts failed because of the furious surf and wind. The whole crew were finally saved on the next day by jumping into the waves, and, before the backwash could draw them out to sea, being caught by two lines formed by some officers and men of the Division joining hands.

Early in January the Divisional artillery were again reorganized. The 18-pounders were changed from four to six gun batteries by allotting a section from each 'C' Battery to 'A' and 'B.' The two howitzer batteries remained part of the two groups, which now became the 261st and 262nd Brigades. Each of these brigades now had four howitzers and twelve 18-pounders.

The 42nd Division followed the 52nd into El Arish, where both toiled with the native labour corps in transforming the place into a field fortress with a long perimeter of redoubts, because it was to be the advanced base for operations into Palestine. At the end of January the 42nd (East Lancs.) received orders for France, and we said goodbye to these old Gallipoli friends. They were replaced by the 53rd (Welsh), and about the same time the 54th (East Anglian) commenced to move to El Arish.

Gen. Murray's force on this front now consisted of three infantry divisions, two mounted divisions, and another infantry division, the 74th, in process of formation out of dismounted yeomanry. The railway was creeping along the coast to Rafa, the Egyptian border town. By the end of February the Turks had discreetly retired from Khan Yunus in Palestine before the Colonial cavalry. Preparations were on foot for an attack on the position at Weli Sheikh Nuran, on which the Turks had been labouring hard for many weeks. However, on the 5th March it was found that they had become nervous for the safety of their force there, and had retired on Gaza and Beersheba.

Gen. Murray was getting further from his base in Egypt, but the Turkish army seemed to be falling back with their main forces still intact. He wished to destroy the garrison at Gaza, as he had done that at Rafa, before it could withdraw any further, and so decided to strike, as soon as the railway had reached Rafa, and his army could be supplied from that place.

DIVISIONAL ENGINEERS SINKING A LARGE WELL AT RAFA

CHAPTER XVII

(27TH FEBRUARY TO 27TH MARCH, 1917)

THE ADVANCE INTO PALESTINE

> March, march, Ettrick and Teviotdale,
> Why the deil dinna ye march forward in order?
> March, march, Eskdale and Liddesdale,
> All the Blue Bonnets are bound for the Border.
> Many a banner spread,
> Flutters above your head,
> Many a crest that is famous in story.
> Mount and make ready then,
> Sons of the mountain glen,
> Fight for the Queen and our old Scottish glory.
> SIR WALTER SCOTT.

GAZA, a city of probably 40,000 inhabitants at this time, has an unlimited water supply. To the south, about fifteen miles away and well inland, there is an abundant water supply at the wells of Shellal on the Wadi Ghuzze, to protect which the Turks had dug their abandoned Weli Sheikh Nuran position. These wells, however, are ten miles from the main caravan route, which here follows the coast. Apart from these and some isolated pools and wells, there is no water supply between Gaza and El Arish, which is fifty miles distant, and, after all, is little better than a desert oasis. The wells of Beersheba and Esani are too far inland to be of any use to caravans travelling on the main route between Africa and Asia. For these reasons, Gaza was a " strong city " at least 3500 years ago, at a time when ancient Nineveh, even if it existed, had not grown to be more than a small provincial town. The country immediately around Gaza has few wells of importance, and, because of this and of its natural features, Gaza has often withstood a siege. It took Alexander the Great two months to capture the city. The battles for Gaza [1] were like almost all other battles in Eastern campaigns : they were battles for water.

The forthcoming attempt to seize Gaza by a *coup de main* was to be made with the 53rd and 54th Divisions and all the available strength of mounted men.

The 52nd Division was to be in reserve. On the 27th February the 155th Brigade was moved to El Burj, which marks the end of the desert, and beyond which lie stretches of sparse grass-land with patches cultivated by the Bedouin. On 7th March the 155th Brigade reached Sheikh Zowaid, where it was joined next day by the 156th and 157th Brigades. During March the Transport Section of the Divisional Train rejoined the Division.

Prior to leaving El Arish, on the 6th, Brig.-Gen. A. H. Leggett, late 5th R.S.F., took over the command of the 156th Brigade from Brig.-Gen. E. S. Girdwood, who had been appointed to command the 74th Division with the rank of Major-General. Gen. Girdwood had obtained great popularity with all ranks, his dash, efficiency, and geniality having endeared him to all.

Whilst the 52nd was at Sheikh Zowaid, the desert column held the " First Spring Meeting " of the " Sinai Hunt Club " on the battlefield of Rafa. The races took place on the 21st March, and, although the Lowlanders were well represented, very naturally the prizes mostly went to the mounted troops.

The 53rd and 54th Divisions moved ahead of the 52nd during March, although from 23rd March to the 26th the 4th R.S.F. was attached to the 53rd, and lay alone as a detached post during that time at Khan Yunus, covering the advance. On the 26th, the 53rd and 54th Divisions moved across the Wadi Ghuzze with the mounted troops for the first ill-fated attack on Gaza. On the previous day,

---

[1] It is impossible in a work of this size and nature even to indicate all of the historical associations of the places near which the 52nd Division fought and marched. One could easily fill a book with the history of Gaza alone.

A 60-POUNDER AND 12-HORSE TEAM

THE ADVANCE INTO PALESTINE 309

the 155th, 156th, and 157th Brigades, the 155th leading, crossed the frontier at Rafa, whilst the Divisional Pipe Band, stationed beside the boundary pillar, played them into Palestine to the tune of " Blue Bonnets over the Border." After nightfall they reached the narrow lanes and low hills of Khan Yunus, a village " with a ruined castle, dating probably from the time of the Crusaders, embosomed in groves of palm and orange trees, while the neatly laid out orchards were hedged by great rows of cacti with their fleshy prickly leaves and brilliant yellow flowers " (*History 7th R.S.*). This was the scene that refreshed the eyes of the Lowlanders as the morning of the 26th advanced. The 155th Brigade moved to In Seirat on the same morning, arriving there before the battle started. Before midday the sound of guns was heard, but, as the sun sank, word came that all was not well before Gaza, and the 157th Brigade was ordered to In Seirat, which it reached about midnight.

Gaza lies in a shallow fertile valley, which is about two miles wide, and runs parallel with the sea between a belt of coastal sand-hills and an extensive table-land. The belt of dunes is almost two miles wide. The table-land rises gradually, and in the distance can be seen the blue Judean hills. On its coastal and southern sides, this table-land is fringed by ridges and hills. The southern are referred to as the ridges of Mansura and Sheikh Abbas. On the side overlooking Gaza there rises up the great rock of Ali el Muntar, 272 feet in height, just south-east of the city, the gates of which are said to have been carried up this hill by Samson. It is a commanding height overtopping everything within several miles to the south. This is the key-position. From Muntar there runs southward, for nearly five miles, the ridge of El Sire, terminating at the Wadi Ghuzze. Parallel to it, from the southern edge of the table-land, two other ridges run down to this great wadi, the centre one of the three being called El Burjaliye after a small garden. These ridges are separated by a labyrinthine tangle of nullahs, from ten to twenty feet deep, which twist and turn in every direction.

The Wadi Ghuzze is a deep, wide nullah, running generally from east to west, and joined by innumerable other nullahs. South of this great wadi rises more high ground, fringed immediately to the south-east by the ridge of In Seirat.

Gaza is the usual white-walled Eastern town, with red roofs and minarets showing here and there. It is embosomed in palm trees, and all around it is a belt, to the southward almost three miles deep, of small fields and gardens, each surrounded by high cactus hedges. These cactus hedges grow out of mud banks, are from six to twelve feet high, and about a yard or more deep. They form natural barbed entanglements, and give perfect cover from view. Shrapnel does little more than pierce their leaves. Direct hits from H.E. shells will blow holes in them, and, after much labour, gaps can be cut in them with hedging tools and sickles, but such expedients could have little effect, since they ran for miles. The Turks made use of these hedges by digging their machine-gun emplacements, fire-trenches, and snipers' posts below them. Tanks alone can cope with them effectively.

The story of the first battle of Gaza is soon told. By nightfall our mounted troops, principally Australian and New Zealand, had thrown a cordon right round the town to the sea. The 53rd Division had gallantly captured Ali el Muntar. The 54th Division and more mounted troops were disposed to the east of Gaza about Sheikh Abbas and elsewhere, trying to hold back Turkish relief forces, which were attacking from the east and north-east. So near was Gen. Murray to a brilliant repetition of Rafa, that Colonial cavalry had captured the Turkish commander with his staff trying to escape, together with two Austrian howitzers. But communication with the headquarters of the Army was difficult; there was a gap of two and a half miles between the 53rd and 54th Divisions, and the latter was threatened by Turkish forces moving from Beersheba, that is from the south-east. A dense fog which had lasted from dawn until 8 a.m. had delayed everything, so that the Turkish relief forces arrived just at the crisis of the battle,

AT KHAN YUNUS. CAMEL LOADS LAID OUT

and not several hours afterwards. Horses were about to collapse through lack of water, and the cavalry had to withdraw. There was danger of the Turkish forces from Beersheba cutting in south of the forces scattered round Gaza, and bringing about a great disaster. It was this last which brought the 157th Brigade hotfoot to In Seirat, the 156th Brigade being left to guard Khan Yunus.

All through the 27th, the 155th Brigade lined the ridges of In Seirat. The force advancing from Beersheba was bombed and disorganized by British aeroplanes. However, the elements fought against the British arms. A khamsin came on and the troops scattered round Gaza were terribly short of water. Gradually they were withdrawn, the Turks attacking them fiercely all the time. Those holding Muntar and the hills about could not believe that they were really to retire. The enemy in front of them were known to have been demoralized. Positions were evacuated and re-taken. The Gaza garrison was reinforced, and Muntar became the apex of a dangerous salient. It would have become a waterless, detached post, and had to be given up. As night fell, the 157th Brigade took up a position on the ridges south of the Wadi Ghuzze, and through the lines of the Division came the worn-out troops who had made the attack. The British casualties were heavy, and many machine and Lewis guns, besides other equipment, were left behind. Some of this equipment was afterwards recovered by the 52nd Division, which lost no men in this battle. Of the Turkish casualties we know nothing, but they were probably less than the British. Gaza had had a narrow escape, but the enemy had saved it, for a time.

It is foolish to criticize Gen. Dobell, who directed the attack, for not chancing all by throwing in the 52nd Division as a forlorn hope to take Gaza and its precious wells. Firstly, it would have taken time to concentrate the Division, and, secondly, there was no water available for such a move. Sir Archibald Murray was campaigning in a country where whole armies have perished from thirst.

CHAPTER XVIII

(28TH MARCH TO 21ST APRIL, 1917)

THE SECOND BATTLE OF GAZA

> Some night, long ages hence, sounds of a fray,
> The Celtic slogan fierce, the Saxon roar,
> Shall haunt that belt of dunes along the shore
> By Sheikh Ajlin, and those grim ridges, bare,
> Carved deep with labyrinthine nullahs, where
>   The wounded crawled to die.
>
> El Sire, Mansourah, shadowed 'neath the sway
> Of Muntar, lion of rocks with ruin and scar,
> Shall echo with a shouting, near and far,
> Like thunder rolling deep amidst the hills,
> Or when some fierce opposing tempest fills
>   A flowing sea with wrath.
>   *A Legend of an Old Beersheba Road.*[1]

SIR ARCHIBALD MURRAY's despatch reporting the battle gave the War Cabinet the impression that he had won a victory, but that adverse circumstances had prevented his troops from gathering in all of its fruits, and on the 30th March he received orders to advance on Jerusalem. At that time the tide of war in Mesopotamia was changing in the British favour.

There now followed a period of feverish preparation on both sides. The Turks knew that the attack was coming and dug a series of immensely strong entrenchments, which ran from the sea, east of Gaza, through the cactus gardens, to the hills about Muntar. Thence it ran north-east along the ridges for a couple of miles, so that Gaza was

---

[1] These verses are reproduced by permission of *Chambers' Journal*.

IN KHAN YUNUS

THE SECOND BATTLE OF GAZA

covered on two sides. South-east of Muntar, where the table-land was lower, there was an apparent gap of two or three miles, a death-trap for an attacking force if the high ground on either side were held by the defenders. Beyond this to the south-eastward, where the ground rose, were more trench systems as far as the Atawineh ridge seven miles from the town. A chain of posts continued the line to Tel el Sharia, another nine miles, prohibiting any wide outflanking movement. Practically every earthwork had a perfect field of fire. On the Mansura and Sheikh Abbas ridges there were a few trenches and observation posts. South-west of this there were no trenches of importance. The Turkish forces defending this natural fortress, and the position on its left flank running to Beersheba, eventually amounted to one cavalry and five infantry divisions, with plenty of heavy artillery, probably about 25,000 men,[1] or about three-quarters of the strength of Gen. Murray's force.

For nearly three weeks the 52nd Division laboured. The position was entrenched in case of a Turkish attack. Parties worked under the Divisional Royal Engineers digging wells in the bed of the Wadi Ghuzze, deep down below which fresh water was percolating in an erratic course to the sea. Others, with skirmishers to protect them, were digging numerous ramps, so that all kinds of transport and vehicles could cross the wadi at several places with ease. Occasionally Turkish shells " got " these working parties. Other parties escorted camel caravans of water and quietly filled the old cisterns scattered on the north side of the Wadi Ghuzze towards Mansura. One important result of the earlier operations had been that the British held both sides of the Wadi Ghuzze, otherwise much of this work would have been impossible. The Turks came no further south

---

[1] This estimate is taken from the New Zealand official history, and is made up as follows :
        8500 at Gaza
        4500 immediately east of Gaza
        2000 Atawineh Redoubt
        6000 Abu Hareira and Tel el Sharia
        4000 elsewhere
        25,000

than the El Burjaliye garden, unless they were reconnoitring. The railway and the pipe-line were hurried forward to Deir el Belah, where stores of all kinds were accumulating. At the end of March the Division was issued with new anti-gas box respirators.

The British line ran from the mouth of the Wadi Ghuzze to In Seirat, and thence to Shellal, the last place being held by mounted troops. On the 30th March the 156th Brigade rejoined the Division at In Seirat.

This was a period of much aircraft activity, of many artillery duels, and of reconnaissances by both Turks and British. On the 9th April the 7th H.L.I. commenced the almost daily game of sending a company to turn a small Turkish post out of the orchard-garden of El Burjaliye, after which they retired at dusk. This apparently meaningless procedure was continued by other units of the 157th Brigade, always at a different time and in a different manner. It was really a cunning move to accustom the Turks to the British moving troops to this point. It produced much rifle-fire, but very few casualties.

On the 16th April all was ready. El Burjaliye had been cleared as usual, but the company of the 5th H.L.I., which was concerned, only retired to a convenient hollow, and after nightfall re-occupied the garden.

The operations were to cover three days. On the 17th, the 52nd Division was to seize the El Sire[1] Ridge as far as Kurd Hill, and the Mansura Ridge, whilst the 54th Division was to seize the Sheikh Abbas Ridge. This would bring the British arms on to the edge of the table-land, and within striking distance of the main Turkish position.

The 18th was to be occupied in bringing up stores of water, heavy artillery, and tanks, ready for the morrow.

On the 19th, after a bombardment, the assault was to be made. The 52nd Division was to take Muntar and its group of hills, the key to the whole position. When this had been effected, the 54th Division was to swing round the right of the 52nd Division and capture the hills in rear of Gaza. The attack of these two divisions was to be under

[1] Sometimes spelt El Sier.

WORKING PARTY IN WADI GHUZZE BEFORE
THE SECOND BATTLE OF GAZA

THE SECOND BATTLE OF GAZA

the command of Major-Gen. W. E. B. Smith, C.B., C.M.G., G.O.C. 52nd Division. The right and rear of this attack was to be covered by mounted troops, who also were to be disposed round Shellal watching the enemy forces at Hereira. The 53rd Division was to attack towards Gaza along the coast, seizing Sheikh Ajlin and a knife-edged dune named Samson's Ridge. The 74th Division, which was only partially formed, was to be in reserve.

Everything depended on the storming of the great rock-fortress, Ali el Muntar by the 52nd Division, and the Turks knew that the attack was coming.

As soon as darkness fell on the 16th, the whole army commenced to move. By 1 a.m., on the 17th, the 157th Brigade, Brig.-Gen. C. D. Hamilton-Moore, was in position at the El Burjaliye garden, and in touch with the 54th Division on its right. This move, effected without a hitch, in total darkness, over a country seamed with nullahs, reflected the greatest credit on the guiding of the Brigade-Major, Capt. A. E. Williams. The 155th, Brig.-Gen. J. B. Pollok-M'Call, following the crest of the El Sire Ridge, had occupied Kurd Hill, and entrenched their position, with movements equally well regulated. This also was a difficult move, because of the narrowness of the path, and the doubt whether the Turks had posts established on it at night. The 156th Brigade, Brig.-Gen. A. H. Leggett, was in reserve at the Wadi Ghuzze.

Punctually at 4.45 a.m., before dawn, the 157th Brigade advanced up the El Burjaliye Ridge to the attack of the Mansura Ridge, which presents a face of cliffs scarred with ravines. The line from right to left was formed of the 6th H.L.I., Lt.-Col. Jas. Anderson, 7th H.L.I., Lt.-Col. J. H. Galbraith, and the 5th H.L.I., Col. F. Morrison. The 5th A. & S.H., Lt.-Col. B. Mathew-Lannowe, were in reserve. As the light grew, the Turkish posts on Mansura saw the scouts followed by lines of men already approaching, and opened a brisk fire. At the same time, guns of the 262nd Brigade,[1] Lt.-Col. Farquhar, commenced to shell

---

[1] Because of the firmer ground, pedrails were removed from the wheels and the extra teams were dispensed with after the first week in April.

Mansura. When their bombardment ceased, patrols scaled the cliffs under the fire of the enemy snipers, and in a few minutes were looking over the top, shooting at small parties of enemy cavalry and infantry retiring across the plain towards Muntar. The enemy artillery now opened fire, together with their machine-guns, on the heights on El Sire nearest Mansura, but the H.L.I. pushed steadily on. The 6th H.L.I. were on the southern end at 6.40 a.m., and by 7 a.m. the 157th Brigade was in full possession of its objective. The Turks had been taken completely by surprise.

The patrols pushed out well beyond the crest into the plain, and consolidation was begun. The enemy artillery had now wakened up and "plastered" the ridge and nullahs south of it with 5.9s and shrapnel. Their machine-guns also swept it with enfilade fire. However, the work proceeded steadily. During the afternoon this fire slackened off, and by nightfall trenches had been dug and partially wired, 800 yards north-east of the edge. All preparations were made for a counter-attack, but none came. The casualties of the 157th for this operation were five officers and ninety-five other ranks. The former included 2nd Lieut. W. G. Grant, 7th H.L.I., killed. A battery of the 261st Brigade, Lt.-Col. G. S. Simpson, had been in action near the El Sire Ridge, and both artillery brigades had several casualties. A direct hit on an observation post of the 261st killed a man, and severely wounded the forward observation officer and another man. The position taken was one of great strength, in which a few men could have held a large number at bay for many hours and caused them many losses, if the capture had not been carried out by means of a surprise.

The 54th Division, meanwhile, had seized Sheikh Abbas, and the first day's operations had resulted in complete success. The value of these positions to the British became more and more manifest later on in the year, as the operations against Gaza developed. The area captured is threaded by the countless tributary nullahs of the Wadi el Nukhabir, which form a vast system of communication trenches to the

MAKING A RAMP INTO THE WADI GHUZZE
Many of these were made before the second battle of Gaza.

south-east of El Burjaliye Ridge. Happy Valley, lying between the latter and El Sire, is more open, there being a depression separating the ridges of Mansura and El Sire.

During the 18th thousands of fantasses of water, besides stores, were dumped behind Mansura and elsewhere, tanks crept forward, and artillery got into position in the captured area. The Turks, now thoroughly on the *qui vive*, completed every preparation possible to meet the attack, which they saw to be close at hand. There was intermittent shell-fire from them all day. In the afternoon a hostile aeroplane dropped smoke-balls over the battery positions, and the area south of Mansura was well searched with shrapnel, which caused some further casualties, chiefly to the 157th Brigade. The aircraft of both sides were busy. After nightfall the 156th Brigade moved up behind Mansura Ridge.

The story of the Second Battle of Gaza is chiefly one of the desperate attacks of the 155th Brigade on Outpost Hill. From Kurd Hill to the north-east, the El Sire Ridge for two and a half miles rises at regular intervals into a series of elevations, known as Queen's, Lees, Outpost, Middlesex, and Green Hills, gradually increasing in height, the last being overtopped by the precipitous sides of Muntar with its mosque and single tree. Innumerable nullahs have bitten deeply into the ridge on both sides, almost to the crest-line. The ground is generally crumbling grey rock and sandy clay, so that secure footholds are hard to find in their sides, and the nullahs act as countless scarped dry ditches. Unless men climb in and out of these nullahs every few yards, it is only possible to advance along the ridge by following the narrow crest-line.

Outpost Hill had been strongly wired and entrenched by the Turks, and, from there north-eastwards, each height was crowned with earthworks and entanglements, each group commanded by those further north, and the last commanded by Muntar. From Middlesex Hill to the north of Muntar, the area is a confusion of narrow dongas, holes and fissures in between minor crags and heights, and interspersed with cactus hedges, and bushes. This area is more than 2000 yards across, and contained trench systems, well named the Labyrinth and the Warren. It gave perfect cover from shell-fire and view, and was sown with machine-guns.

The table-land below the ridge to the east is devoid of all cover. The countless gardens on the slopes and in the valley to the west were defended by at least two lines of trenches and redoubts, strongly held, well placed, and concealed behind endless and impenetrable cactus hedges.

The 52nd Division was ordered to storm this vast fortress, and could only do so by frontal attack. The 155th Brigade was to advance up the El Sire Ridge, capturing it as far as Green Hill. The 156th Brigade was to advance over Mansura on the right of the 155th, and, when the attacks of the latter had succeeded, and it was threatening Muntar from the south-east, the Royal Scots and Cameronians were to storm the rock-fortress from the plain. The 157th Brigade was to swing over the open to their right and to storm the ridge further north, linking up with the 54th Division.

Day dawned on the 19th with a gentle breeze blowing to the northward. The total land artillery available to deal with the entire Turkish position was about eight 8-inch howitzers, eight 60-pounders, twenty-four 4.5-inch howitzers, and eighty-four 18-pounders.[1] The 261st and 262nd Brigades were massed behind Mansura, and to the east of El Sire. This artillery was supplemented by the guns of the French battleship, *Requin*, and of two British monitors, but, considering that the enemy had had three weeks within which to wire and entrench, it was quite insufficient to do any real harm to such a strong and extensive position. The only hope for a successful attack lay in the use of gas shells. Unfortunately, the efficacy of these latter was much overestimated.

At 5.30 a.m. the two brigades detailed for the first phase of the attack were in artillery formation ready to advance, the 155th on Kurd Hill, the 156th behind

[1] Compare this total of 124 with the 230, including 78 heavy guns and howitzers, which, with the guns of nine warships, bombarded the Gaza defences for six days prior to the third and successful assault.

SHEIKH ABBAS RIDGE, GAZA AREA

THE SECOND BATTLE OF GAZA 319

Mansura, and at that moment the whole of the artillery opened fire, throwing gas shells and H.E. on to the Turkish positions. The guns of the Division, the few heavies that were available, and the warships shelled the Muntar area. Those of the 53rd and 54th shelled their objectives, near the sea, and on the high ground about Khirbet el Bir and Khirbet Sihan east of Muntar. The gas shelling on the front of the 155th Brigade was entirely confined to the woods west of El Sire. In point of fact the quantity of gas shells used was quite insufficient, and the gas was so diffused and limited in area that the Turks were able to withdraw nearly all their men from the threatened localities. They knew that they would be able to see the British troops advancing long before the latter could get near their trenches, which could be re-manned in plenty of time. Meanwhile, the Turkish artillery replied, and searched the El Sire Ridge and the area behind Mansura with a heavy fire of shrapnel and H.E. Many casualties were caused, and it was obvious that the Turks had plenty of artillery and were quite ready. They obtained direct hits on some guns and waggons.

At 7.30 a.m. the gas shelling ceased, the 155th Brigade commenced to advance along El Sire, and the Divisional artillery put down a creeping barrage before the leading line. So little effect had the bombardment had on the Turkish trenches, that ten minutes after it ceased the enemy machine-gunners and snipers were hard at work from their posts, interfering with the little reconnaissance that time permitted.

The right of the 155th was formed by the 4th R.S.F., Lt.-Col. H. Thompson, and the left by the 5th K.O.S.B., Lt.-Col. Simson, each battalion advancing in successive waves of men. The 5th R.S.F., Major J. B. Cook, was advancing behind the leading battalions, in order, as the brigade advanced, to take up a series of positions on the west of the ridge to protect it against counter-attacks from troops hidden among the gardens and trees to the westward. Ahead of the leading battalions advanced two tanks. Close behind came guns of the 155th Machine-Gun Company.

Following, 800 yards behind the 5th K.O.S.B., was the 4th K.O.S.B., Lt.-Col. J. M. B. Sanders, in reserve. It was evident from the start that, because of the nullahs, the 155th Brigade could only advance on a very narrow frontage. A large portion of this advance and of the subsequent fighting on this bare and prominent ridge was done in full view of sections of both armies.

At 7.50 a.m. the right of the 155th was in line with the 156th, and the latter commenced to move forward towards Green Hill and Muntar, hundreds of dots in eight ordered lines, scattered over a green plain. The right of the 156th was formed by the 7th R.S., Lt.-Col. W. C. Peebles, the centre by the 4th R.S., Lt.-Col. F. H. Goldthorpe, and the left by the 8th Cameronians, Lt.-Col. J. M. Findlay. The 7th Cameronians, Lt.-Col. J. G. Romanes, was in reserve behind Mansura, where also the battalions of the 157th Brigade were waiting.

A few minutes before the 155th got into line with the 156th, the tank ahead of the 4th R.S.F. nose-dived into one of the treacherous nullahs, and was not extricated until the close of the battle. The infantry had orders to keep behind the tanks, and waited a few moments until Lt.-Col. Thompson could send word to continue the advance.

Enemy shrapnel and H.E. was poured over the ridge, officers and men began to fall, but the advance continued steadily until the 5th K.O.S.B. reached the gullies between Lees and Outpost Hills. Like the rest of the ridge, the ground there is almost completely devoid of cover, rock and stony clay being only clothed in places by sparse grass and stunted scrub. As the leading platoons cleared these gullies, there burst on them a tempest of machine-gun fire and shrapnel from the front and left, ranged to a yard. Officers and men dropped on all sides, and, automatically, everyone faced towards the fire, and the advance bore to the left. An order to right incline only resulted in two platoons getting on a ridge to the east of Outpost Hill, which they held through the day, galling the Turks with their fire, and repulsing at least one counter-attack. Lieut. Turner struggled forward and eventually reached his

HORSES AND CAMELS WATERING IN WADI GHUZZE

Taken during the first morning of the Second Battle of Gaza. The storage tanks shown were filled with water during the night previous, some 4000 camels being employed for this purpose. Shortly after the photo was taken the wadi was heavily bombed at this place.

THE SECOND BATTLE OF GAZA

objective, Middlesex Hill, but only with three or four of the thirty men that he had started out with, the rest having been shot down. He got in touch with the 4th R.S.F., and held on until nightfall, when he fell back with the rest.

Meanwhile, storming parties of the 5th K.O.S.B. were being mown down in gallant attempts to take the Turkish earthwork on Outpost Hill.

The 5th R.S.F., who were carrying picks and shovels for consolidation, had occupied Queens, Lees, and Blazed Hills in succession, and from the latter were giving all the covering fire that they could to the attack. The Divisional Cyclist Company, attached 5th R.S.F., under Capt. T. H. Glendinning, had taken up a position west of Outpost Hill, but he found himself ahead of the attackers and had to withdraw to where the 5th K.O.S.B. were spending themselves in attempts to get at the Turkish lunette, which crowned the height. These Cyclists and another company of the 5th R.S.F., who had been following, now threw down their picks and shovels and joined the Borderers in their assaults. Capt. Glendinning was killed later near the lunette. Most of the camels carrying the reserve ammunition had become casualties soon after the advance started, so that boxes of small arms ammunition had to be man-handled forward along the bullet-swept ridge. On this, as on many another occasion, the Egyptian camel men behaved with striking bravery and coolness, and earned the respect of the British fighting men.

Meanwhile, the 4th R.S.F. had pushed on under the shell-fire, along the eastern side of the ridge, until they were within two hundred yards of Outpost Hill, when there burst on them a terrible storm of machine-gun fire and shrapnel. The bullets caught the lines in enfilade and men fell in groups. For a while the advance was delayed, and men were drawn into the fight for Outpost Hill. However, the firing line was pushed on again and by 11 a.m. had worked its way on to Middlesex Hill, and had driven the Turks from some of their trenches.

A gap had now developed between the troops on either side of the ridge. Many officers had fallen, and Lt.-Col.

H. Thompson set to work to fill it up with any men he could get. Whilst doing so, he fell mortally wounded, shot through the throat. His second in command, Major Hugh R. Young was helping him, and about the same time and place he also fell mortally wounded in the head. The battalion was now scattered over a fire-swept area; for a time no one knew who was left to take command, and the advance was stayed.

It was a few minutes before 10 a.m. that the 155th Brigade was first held up for a while, and the 156th had to stop in conformation. As the 4th R.S.F. got on to Middlesex Hill, the left of the 156th also reached its slopes, but after 11 a.m. the 155th could get forward no further. The 156th's front line now faced towards Muntar, its right, almost a mile away out in the plain, being about 700 yards south-east of Green Hill. Its situation was a most trying one. The Royal Scots and Cameronians were lying in extended order completely in the open, with their right flank quite exposed, the left of the 54th Division being hung up about a mile to the east. Before and above rose a range of hills, from which was poured on them throughout that long weary day, a continual shell, machine-gun, and rifle fire. The 156th Brigade Machine-Gun Company did good work in enfilading some Turkish trenches on Outpost Hill, but the rest of the Brigade could make little or no effective reply. They had to lie and be shelled and shot at. The ambulance-waggons of the Divisional R.A.M.C. came right into the firing line, and several had their hoods riddled with bullets. Capt. W. W. Greer, 1/3rd Lowland Field Ambulance, was decorated for his gallant work in succouring the wounded in the open.

We must now return to the men trying to advance from the gullies west of Outpost Hill to take the lunette on its summit, called by many "the redoubt." This work had been constructed with its ends drawn back, so that it could be swept by fire from three directions, and it was completely commanded by the entrenchments to the north-east. There is no record of all the heroic assaults in that fierce and stubborn struggle, but we know that the lunette was taken

THE SECOND BATTLE OF GAZA

and lost three times during that forenoon. Time and again did the Fusiliers, Borderers, and Cyclists sweep up the slopes and capture this work, only to be driven out by a hail of shrapnel, H.E., minnenwerfer bombs, machine-gun and rifle bullets. Those who tried to work up the slopes from the west, were swept away by enfilade fire. Major J. C. Kennedy, 5th K.O.S.B., led one successful assault, and was severely wounded. 2nd Lieut. Campbell and Coy. Sgt.-Major Townsend, both 5th K.O.S.B., together rallied the men and led two more, Campbell being killed. Lieut. Nicholson, 5th K.O.S.B., was going to help Capt. Dun, 5th K.O.S.B., who was lying wounded, when both were shot dead.

The 261st Brigade, R.F.A., Lt.-Col. G. S. Simpson, was supporting the Borderers and Fusiliers. Over and over again the gunners swept the Labyrinth, the Warren, and Muntar, and incessantly bombarded a long trench running to Outpost Hill from the cactus hedges to the west, which was the main artery to the lunette for Turkish reinforcements. The gas shelling of these woods to the west of El Sire had apparently been quite abortive. At 8.30 a.m. the gunners were shelling the lunette prior to a successful assault. Shortly afterwards, as early as 9 a.m., the 261st Brigade received word that ammunition must be economised ;[1] but every available gun had nevertheless to be turned on the hills and ravines behind Outpost Hill to help the guns of the 155th Machine-Gun Company to keep down the galling machine-gun and rifle-fire. Little could be done, however, with the enemy artillery, and neither their trenches nor their wire were seriously damaged by the British bombardment. The British guns were quite insufficient in numbers, and the battleship *Requin* was driven off by a submarine attack.

About 11 a.m. the tank *War-Baby* advanced under cover of the fire of the 261st Brigade, crushed down the Turkish wire on Outpost Hill, and got across the lunette ; but it

---

[1] The shortage of 18-pounders, the wire-cutting guns, was much accentuated by the shortage of ammunition. Compare this with the abundance of ammunition at the Third Battle.

was completely exposed, was struck several times with direct hits from the enemy guns, and its tractor was broken. The Lowland infantry had followed and once more Outpost Hill was captured. Shortly afterwards, a strong force of Turks counter-attacked, drove back the garrison of the redoubt, and the tank was left burning on the hill. The guns of the Division put down a barrage to protect the retiring Lowlanders, and then, as the Turkish infantry appeared, scourged them with shrapnel, scattering them and driving them back to the trenches.

Shortly before mid-day the 4th K.O.S.B. was ordered to recapture this earthwork, and Major W. T. Forrest, the Scottish International Rugby player, went forward with two companies, another following in support. He made his way to the nullah, whither the remnants of Borderers and Fusiliers had been driven. Units were mixed up, and he found the gallant Capt. W. D. Kennedy, 5th R.S.F., busy reorganizing them. This work Major Forrest carried on, coolly walking about on the edge of the nullah. Despite what they had been through, these Borderers and Fusiliers were ready for another assault. When all was ready, Major Forrest, the Wattie Forrest of the football field, led his men forward for the last time. This charge of men from almost every unit in the 155th Brigade was a most inspiring sight. Under a murderous fire, which struck down many, they rushed up the hill. About fifty Turks saw them coming, leaped from a ravine, and bolted away into the cactus hedges on the western slopes. Major Forrest was mortally wounded as he entered the work, and there fell one of the best of soldiers, best of friends, and best of sportsmen in the Division.

Lieut. J. M. Pollok, 5th K.O.S.B., describes what happened: "The fire from the enemy's machine-guns was terrific, spelling certain death to nearly all who were in the open. About twenty yards from the redoubt I obtained shelter in a shell hole for a few minutes, and while lying there I saw Capt. Cochrane rush forward and bend over the body of Lumgair, who was lying wounded between the barbed wire and the redoubt trench. He appeared to be

THE SECOND BATTLE OF GAZA

just on the point of lifting Capt. Lumgair up, when a man near me said—' Look at Capt. Cochrane; he'll be killed as sure as fate,' and these words had scarcely been spoken before I saw Capt. Cochrane stagger and fall to the ground. I eventually rushed forward with the Lewis gun team and got into the redoubt. The Turks were holding one-half of the circle of the redoubt. Some were within bombing distance, while others were not a hundred yards away, and they were causing great havoc with machine-gun and rifle-fire, especially from the slope of the hill overlooking the redoubt. Our losses were very heavy, and, as we were badly in need of reinforcements, urgent messages asking for them were repeatedly sent back by runners and by slightly wounded men," but not one of them ever got through to 155th Brigade Headquarters.

Capt. Lumgair was a general favourite and Lieut. W. R. Ovens and Sgt. Waugh made a desperate attempt to get him in. Waugh had lifted him up, when he was shot again, this time fatally.

There was not room for all of the assaulting party in the lunette, whose shallow trenches were choked in places with bodies, and some of the men had to line the trenches on the ridge on either side. The Turks were quick to counter-attack, but were driven back. Some Borderers chased the retreating Turks, and tried to penetrate further, but they were outnumbered and had to return. There were about 350 of all ranks holding the work on Outpost Hill, and now there ensued a bitter struggle with bayonet, bomb, and Lewis gun, whilst the Turkish artillery and trench mortars never ceased to deluge it with shrapnel and H.E.

Capt. Pirie, Lieut. Stewart and two men of the 155th Machine-Gun Company managed to get a machine-gun into the lunette, but it was destroyed by a shell; Pirie and a man were killed, and Stewart was wounded. Pirie was standing up and encouraging his men with great gallantry when he was killed. In addition to this machine-gun, five Lewis guns were smashed by shell-fire, and two were blown to pieces with most of their crews.

Lieut. Gibb, 5th K.O.S.B., on his own initiative, collected a few men and tried to get at the enemy machine-guns, which were steadily reducing the garrison. He got as far as some cactus hedges, but had to retire, and was killed later on. Officers fell rapidly. Every captain was killed. On one occasion Major Crombie, 5th K.O.S.B., in an endeavour to ease the situation by pressing the Turks back, gave the order to fix bayonets and charge the front, but every man who mounted the parapet fell back at once, killed or wounded. The 155th Brigade could advance no further. The position before them was impregnable.

The command of the lunette finally devolved upon Lieut. R. B. Anderson, 4th K.O.S.B. Through most of the afternoon its garrison was cut off from communication. Out of a dozen runners sent back by Lieut. Anderson only one won through at sometime after 3 p.m. His message asked for artillery support, as the garrison was losing heavily and was sorely pressed. Half an hour after this, Lieut. Logan, 4th R.S.F., made an attempt to get a telephone to the lunette, but the wire was much too short. Logan set out to get more wire forward but was never heard of again. During the afternoon messages came over this telephone to 155th Brigade Headquarters from an officer, who thought that he was on Outpost Hill and in command there. He repeatedly reported that all was well, and that no help was needed. In point of fact the instrument was several hundreds of yards from the lunette, and in the absence of other information this created a false impression until well on in the afternoon. There is no space to tell of the heroism of the runners, and of those who carried forward ammunition and water.

Several times the Turks tried to work up from the cactus hedges, but they were driven back with heavy losses by the 5th R.S.F., machine-gunners, and a party of Borderers and Fusiliers with Lewis guns on a crest west of the redoubt. This party was commanded by Lt.-Col. D. Simson, 5th K.O.S.B., until he was mortally wounded late in the afternoon. When he fell, the Division lost one of its most

THE SECOND BATTLE OF GAZA 327

efficient battalion commanders, and one of its coolest, shrewdest, and sternest fighting men.

Those on the eastward side of the ridge could see a tank on the rising ground 2000 yards north-east of Sheikh Abbas, disabled and pouring out dense volumes of smoke. Behind it lay the perfectly open plain, across which it had advanced, and in the midst of which lay the 54th Division, completely held up by enemy machine-guns with perfect fields of fire. The containing attacks of the mounted troops and the Royal Air Force were effectively covering the right and rear. The 53rd Division on the sea flank had taken Sheikh Ajlin and Samson's Ridge, but advanced no further, with the result that the Gaza garrison could devote most of its attention to the 52nd Division.

When the 4th K.O.S.B. went forward, the 155th Brigade had practically no reserves left, and the 6th H.L.I. was sent across to Lees Hill at 11.40 a.m. to come under Gen. Pollok-M'Call's orders, being followed by the 5th Argylls later on. By the time they had reached the El Sire Ridge Gen. Pollok-M'Call saw that nothing could be effected by an advance in any direction by these two battalions, and that it would simply mean useless waste of life. After midday it was evident that the 157th Brigade would not be called on to storm the ridge north of Muntar, because, of that great fortress, the southern outworks alone had been captured and they were barely held. British aviators had reported that a large counter-attack was impending from the gardens and orchards north of Outpost Hill. The situation was very dangerous, and accordingly, at 1.44 p.m. the remainder of the 157th Brigade was ordered across the Happy Valley to Lees Hill. The Turkish concentration in the gardens near the Dueidar Trench was dispersed by the Divisional artillery. When Gen. Hamilton-Moore arrived on the El Sire Ridge he confirmed Gen. Pollok-M'Call's opinion, as to the situation.

The 156th Brigade, facing north, had now lain in the open, shelled from front and right flank, for five or six hours, and had lost several hundred officers and men. The left of the 8th Cameronians had been adjusted several times, as the battle had swayed backwards and forwards on Outpost Hill. At 2.45 p.m. Turkish artillery opened on the rear of the 7th R.S. from the south-east. The position of this battalion was extremely precarious, and Col. Peebles set about drawing back his line, to refuse his right to the enemy, a most difficult manoeuvre under fire. At the same time another flood of Turks overspread Outpost Hill, and their skirmishers worked along the eastern slopes of Middlesex Hill behind the 4th R.S.F., until they were shooting into the left of the 8th Cameronians, which was driven in. The 156th Brigade was now being fired into from every direction excepting the south-west and south, and its situation was intolerable. The 7th R.S. could be seen retiring, and, because of flanks being exposed, the rest of the line did the same, platoons constantly turning round, lying down, and firing to cover the withdrawal. The Turks saw the brigade falling back, and suddenly the sides of Delilah's Neck, just north of Muntar, were black with thousands of advancing figures, as their men left their trenches for a counter-attack.

The Divisional forward observation officers were alert, and the liaison between them and their batteries was excellent. In less than two minutes the whole of the guns of the Division were pouring a storm of shrapnel on to the masses of the enemy. The Turkish infantry were smothered by the shell-bursts, broke, scattered, and doubled back to the shelter of their trenches. A very little delay in the sending of word to the guns and in their acting on it might have resulted in a very serious situation. The whole crisis was over in a few minutes.

Gen. Leggett reinforced his firing line with two companies of the 7th Cameronians, and the 156th Brigade gradually fell back, until at nightfall its left was about 500 yards south-east of Outpost Hill, and its right faced north-east in touch, near Camel Hill, with the 54th Division. It had been extricated from a most dangerous position. After darkness the various units linked up, and the line was entrenched.

As the sun set, the situation in the lunette on Outpost

THE SECOND BATTLE OF GAZA

Hill was bad. The Turkish fire had never ceased. Less than seventy of the garrison were left. Only by lying down could they get cover in the shallow trenches. Turks could be seen working round its flanks, and the next attack meant annihilation. Lieut. R. B. Anderson, a most gallant young officer, decided that they must retire after nightfall, and passed word for men to dig gaps in the Turkish parapets for that purpose. Every two unwounded men were to help one of the wounded back, and to leave in turn. Shortly afterwards, Anderson was shot through the heart, being killed instantly. Night fell about 6 p.m., and those who were left, saw the Turks closing in. Word was given, and the garrison slipped away.

As the survivors made towards Lees Hill, they ran into the 7th H.L.I. and the last company of the 4th K.O.S.B. moving up under cover of the moonless night to re-occupy the lunette. Following the latter were two companies of the 5th A. & S.H. By that time the voices of Turks could be heard in different places on Outpost Hill, and the only landmark was the tank a few dozen yards down the western slope, still burning and red hot. Gen. Hamilton-Moore, whose brigade was taking over from Gen. Pollok-M'Call, arrived shortly afterwards and directed Col. Galbraith to send two officers' patrols to locate the lunette in the darkness and to find out the strength of the Turks holding it. At the time they were standing within 120 yards of the enemy. The patrols had only gone a short distance when a heavy machine-gun and rifle-fire was opened on them. 2nd Lieut. A. W. Philip got up to the lunette with one patrol, and returned wounded with word that it was strongly held. 2nd Lieut. Lamb advancing from another direction, got inside the wire, but, with most of his patrol, never returned. It was evident that any further attempts to storm this work would only result in useless bloodshed.

A line was now drawn across the ridge. The 7th H.L.I. on the eastern slope linked up with the 8th Cameronians. The two companies of the 5th A. & S.H. on the western slope faced up the ridge, and also towards the cactus gardens. Meanwhile, covering parties had been put out, because

Turkish voices could be heard, and a fire had been lit near the lunette, by the light of which Turks could be seen clearing that work. Suddenly, a collection of dark figures were seen moving near the tank and voices were heard, but the Argylls were ready and poured a heavy and low-aimed fire at about forty yards range into these Turks, who replied vigorously for a few minutes and then retreated. This was probably a strong patrol moving down the ridge, to see how far the British had fallen back. It was not far, as the Turks found out. Lees Hill was held, and this had an important bearing on the remainder of the operations, as from it Mansura could have been attacked in enfilade.

After nightfall the R.S.F. who were still holding points on Middlesex Hill fell back. 2nd Lieut. J. R. Foster, 4th R.S.F., left with the last party at 10.15 p.m.

A Turkish counter-attack was anticipated, but the night passed with only spasmodic bursts of fire. The enemy had evidently suffered severely and were exhausted. Both 7th H.L.I. and 5th A. & S.H. dug unceasingly throughout the night, but the ground was very hard, and the trenches of the former were only two or two and a half feet deep by dawn. The Argylls facing the tank had improved some trenches made by the 155th Brigade, and so had a little more shelter. When day broke the Turks opened on the trenches of both sides of the ridge with machine-guns, rifles, and later with trench mortars. 2nd Lieut. A. Cumming, 5th Argylls, was killed trying to extricate his men from an exposed place. There is no space even to mention all the gallant deeds of this battle, how two of Cumming's men brought him in, how some 7th H.L.I. were killed trying to get water forward to the exposed trenches, all of which were completely cut off by the enemy fire during daylight, and so on. The 7th H.L.I. lost thirty-four men by this sniping on the 20th.

At dawn on the same day the 7th Cameronians shot down several Turks and Bedouin, who were looting the dead that lay out between Mansura and Muntar.

Meanwhile, the remainder of the 157th Brigade were behind, digging and wiring a more defensible line across

THE SECOND BATTLE OF GAZA

the fronts of Lees and Blazed Hills, under the supervision of the Divisional Royal Engineers. This was principally done at night, when water, etc., was taken forward to the advanced trenches. Everywhere, both sides were digging in. On the 21st, the 7th H.L.I. lost Capt. J. R. Brown, Lieut. F. Davie, and 2nd Lieut. A. Grant, all killed directing and encouraging the men.

At midnight the new line was ready, and the garrisons of the advanced trenches were withdrawn. British riflemen in these trenches were at a continual disadvantage because of their low position, and to have held them would have entailed the cutting of very long communication trenches through hard clay and rock, a tedious, if not an impossible task. On the same night the 156th Brigade at Mansura withdrew to a better line.

Midnight on the 21st April may be said to have been the close of the second battle of Gaza. Sir Archibald Murray gave the casualties for this battle as " some 7000." Of these the 52nd Division had suffered the largest share. The losses of the 155th Brigade were as follows:

	Killed and Died of Wounds.		Missing.		Wounded.		Total.
	Officers.	O.R.	Officers.	O.R.	Officers.	O.R.	
4th R.S.F.	5	25	1	31	11	200	283
5th R.S.F.	4	22	0	14	6	140	186
4th K.O.S.B.	6	16	0	28	9	152	213
5th K.O.S.B.	10	47	1	52	8	226	344
Totals	25	110	2	125	34	718	1026

The total strength of the 155th Brigade before the action was about 2500. Most of the casualties were about the lunette on Outpost Hill.

The losses of the 156th Brigade were as follows:

	Killed and Died of Wounds.		Missing.		Wounded.		Total.
	Officers.	O.R.	Officers.	O.R.	Officers.	O.R.	
4th Royal Scots	1	13	—	4	6	110	134
7th Royal Scots	1	20	—	—	7	120	148
7th Cameronians	1	2	—	—	—	24	27
8th Cameronians	2	30	—	17	9	144	202
	5	65	—	21	22	398	511

The losses of the 157th Brigade were as follows:

	Killed and Died of Wounds.		Missing.		Wounded.		Total.
	Officers.	O.R.	Officers.	O.R.	Officers.	O.R.	
5th H.L.I.	—	10	—	—	3	59	72
6th H.L.I.	—	3	—	—	3	75	81
7th H.L.I.	4	14	1	7	3	116	145
5th A. & S.H.	1	7	—	—	—	31	40
	5	34	1	7	9	281	338

The losses of the Divisional Artillery were as follows:

	Killed and Died of Wounds.	Wounded.	Total.
Officers	—	2	2
Other ranks	2	8	10
	2	10	12

The total casualties of the 52nd Division were about 2000. Of the missing, less than half a dozen other ranks turned up as prisoners-of-war. Of those included above as wounded, many afterwards died of their wounds.

As usual, the mortality among the officers was very heavy, the names being as follows:

155TH BRIGADE.

4th R.S.F.—

Lt.-Col. H. Thompson.   Major H. R. Young.

5th R.S.F.—

Capt. T. H. Glendinning   Capt. J. Lees.
   (Divisional Cyclists).   Lieut. R. P. M'Kenzie.
„ W. D. Kennedy.

4th K.O.S.B.—

Major W. T. Forrest.   Lieut. R. B. Anderson.
Capt. W. F. Cochrane.   2nd Lieut. A. Ainslie.
„ R. R. M. Lumgair.   „ J. C. Moore.

5th K.O.S.B.—

Lt.-Col. D. Simson.   Lieut. Nicholson.
Capt. A. R. Clark-Kennedy.   2nd Lieut. J. Campbell.
„ T. Dun.   „ Gibb.
„ W. G. D. Watson.   „ Henery.
Lieut. S. P. Crombie.   „ A. Tweedie.
„ Law.

155th Bde. M.G. Coy.—Capt. Pirie.

THE SECOND BATTLE OF GAZA 333

156TH BRIGADE.

4th Royal Scots—2nd Lieut. G. B. Care.

7th Royal Scots—Lieut. G. Pender.

7th Cameronians—2nd Lieut. John Russell.

8th Cameronians—

Lieut. L. W. Thom.   2nd Lieut. N. R. Edwards.

157TH BRIGADE.

7th H.L.I.—

Capt. J. R. Brown.   2nd Lieut. W. G. Grant.
Lieut. F. Davie.   „   A. W. Philip.
2nd Lieut. A. Grant.

5th A. & S.H.—Lieut. A. Cumming.

The following verses by the late Capt. W. F. Templeton, 4th R.S.F., are inserted because they are descriptive of two splendid men of different types which were very often found in the 52nd Division :

LT.-COL. H. THOMPSON, D.S.O.

He was ever a fighter, and joyed in the press of the fray,
  Where even the bravest would falter he cheerfully sped,
Like a schoolboy out for a holiday, smiling and gay,
  To fill with the breath of his valour those that he led ;
And often we thought, as he towered at the head of his men,
'Twere a wonder of wonders if ever we saw him again.

MAJOR H. R. YOUNG.

In after years we'll tell of him,
  His great-souled friendliness,
And all the charm and spell of him
  Which loving hearts confess ;
And memory will bring clear to us,
  Long after grief has passed,
How good he was, how dear to us,
  How faithful to the last.

This was an indecisive battle. The British had suffered a bad repulse, but they retained almost all the ground they had captured. The Turks were unable to follow up their victory, although at the close of the action their reserves were practically intact. During the night of 19-20th April Gen. Murray with Gen. Dobell, who had commanded the attack, considered resuming the offensive next day, but the latter, supported by the generals commanding the desert column and the divisions, dissuaded him. The prospect of success was small, and of very heavy casualties very great.

The Turks had had three weeks in which to wire and entrench their fortress. The British artillery available for the attack was utterly insufficient, and the gas bombardment was a failure, and did not make up for the great shortage of guns, as everyone had been led to expect. The tanks, manoeuvring in perfectly open country, received the inevitable direct hits. The enemy were never seriously distracted by a determined attack along the coast, which would have threatened the city of Gaza and helped to cover the exposed left flank of the 52nd Division. The attack failed because, without any effective bombardment, an assault had been attempted of a great fortress in broad daylight, with the defenders fully apprised of the attack. It is useless to discuss what would have happened if the Muntar fortress alone could have been thoroughly gassed, and the tanks used for an attack in the enclosed country near the coast. It is believed, however, that before the battle the weight of opinion of the 52nd Division was thrown against a frontal attack on Muntar, and for a determined attack against the extreme Turkish right, where success was eventually achieved in the third battle of Gaza.

CHAPTER XIX

(22ND APRIL TO 28TH OCTOBER, 1917)

THE RAID ON SEA POST AND OTHER OPERATIONS BEFORE GAZA

> They plainlie throw the countrie rides;
> I trow the meikle devil them guides;
>   Where they onset
>   Ay in their gate
>   There is na yett
>   Nor door them bidis.
> *Aganis the Thievis of Liddisdale*:
>   Sir Richard Maitland.

THERE now followed a period of inaction, which lasted until the end of October. This was a time of entrenching and wiring, digging for wells under the Royal Engineers, training, and so on, interspersed with raids and minor actions.

The British front line before Gaza ran south-east from Sheikh Ajlin on the coast, over Samson's Ridge, across Kurd Valley about 600 yards south of the cactus gardens, over Lees Hill, and across the fronts of Mansura and Sheikh Abbas Ridges to the Abbas Apex. At the latter point it formed a salient, and, doubling back, followed the ridge, running south-west to Dumbell Hill. During the months succeeding the second battle of Gaza, a very elaborate system of earthworks and entanglements was constructed along this line, and at Mendur, an important wadi-junction south of Dumbell Hill, a ring of nine mutually-supporting redoubts was dug. From there to Shellal, and further south, the line was watched by cavalry, but, because of the vast extent of the front and the innumerable wadis, it seemed easy for an English-speaking German wearing a British uniform to get into the British lines. Nevertheless, when it came to the crucial time at the end of the summer, and the enemy were badly in need of knowledge as to where the British were concentrating, their information was wrong.

The Division had a large share in the construction of the main system from Sheikh Ajlin to Mendur, and occupied all parts of it at different times. Everyone agreed that the unhealthiest spot was the Abbas Apex, because it was shelled from both flanks and front; and that the quietest was Mendur, about the only fortified locality of any size which could not be observed in some way from Muntar. Tel el Ahmar, south of Mansura, was another favourite depositing ground for surplus Turkish 5.9's and other shells. Samson's Ridge also received a good share of these. This shell-fire caused a constant dribble of casualties. Lieut. M'Leod, 8th Cameronians, was killed and six other ranks were wounded on the 19th July, during an enemy bombardment of Sheikh Abbas. The losses from sniping, however, were very few because of the width of No Man's Land, which, at its narrowest, on the El Sire Ridge, and before Umbrella Hill in the sand-hills, was about 500 yards wide. On 22nd April Lt.-Col. G. S. Simpson, D.S.O., 261st Brigade, was studying the enemy lines, together with a forward observation officer, on Lees Hill, when he was shot through the right lung. During one tour in June, in the trenches before Umbrella Hill, the 5th R.S.F., Lt.-Col. J. B. Cook, had twenty-two authenticated cases of Turks being killed or wounded by Scottish snipers. The loss of these Fusiliers from the same cause was much less.

The Divisional artillery had a number of casualties in their repeated duels with the enemy, and on several occasions had guns damaged, for the enemy aeroplanes were much superior to the British on this front and their observation was very good. The British machines were much slower, and not until the end of the summer, when a store ship laden with new aeroplanes managed to avoid being sunk by submarines, was this disheartening superiority of the enemy

A PLATOON MESS IN GAZA AREA

This method of messing was adopted throughout the Division for cleanliness

OPERATIONS BEFORE GAZA

reversed. The British airmen, many of them recruited from the Division, were the bravest of the brave, and did wonderfully with their old machines, but they could not do the impossible, although they freely spent their lives in trying. The British anti-aircraft guns did good work, and once or twice had busy times defending, from enemy aeroplanes, the sausage balloons, which were moored about the Wadi Ghuzze, and which gave us a much greater altitude for observation than the battered rock of Muntar. Lieut. and Quartermaster H. Bowen, an 8th Cameronian Gallipoli veteran, was lying in his dug-out on the 21st May, when a Turkish anti-aircraft shell, which had failed to explode, fell near him, bursting on contact and killing him instantly.

The losses inflicted by the British bombardments were certainly heavier than those inflicted by the Turkish. A Turkish sergeant, who surrendered to the 157th Brigade, said that his unit alone on 29-30th May had lost thirteen killed and fourteen wounded by British shell-fire. As more projectiles became available later on in the summer, the British bombardments increased in intensity, and on occasion an earthwork was almost obliterated. Tank Redoubt, before Sheikh Abbas, was a favourite target of the Divisional guns, and, so continually was Muntar shelled with heavy H.E., that its steep sides gradually became heaps of scree. Since the Germans used the minaret of the Great Mosque of Gaza as an observation post it was knocked down by the guns of a French warship. Turkish deserters took delight in pointing out the quarters of German officers in Gaza, and the areas indicated were thoroughly shelled by the Divisional guns. Kurd Hill was a good observation post for this work. During May alone the surrenders to the 157th Brigade were four officers, two sergeants, forty-four other ranks, and two bicycles. On the 31st August a major, a lieutenant, and two privates came over in a party to the 7th R.S. The reasons usually given were overbearing conduct on the part of German officers, over-work, and shortage of food.

This shortage shows the utter inefficiency of the Turkish

administration in Palestine and elsewhere. The British brought stores and water right across the desert. Deir el Belah had only an open roadstead, but supplies were landed from steamers in surf boats, the latter being manned by expert surf navigators from all over the British Empire, from the West Coast of Africa to the islands of the Pacific. The very firewood had to be transported overseas by the British, being thrown overboard opposite Deir el Belah to drift ashore through the breakers before an onshore breeze. Behind the Turks lay Gaza, which they pulled down for its timber, and stripped of every kind of cloth for the making of sandbags. Gaza suffered infinitely more from this than from British shell-fire, as the bulk of the latter was directed on the Turkish works. The city, now deserted by its inhabitants, was only shelled when the British artillery were searching for some enemy headquarters or store-house.

The natives, whose huts were in the battle area, were not the only ones inconvenienced by the war. The miles of communication trenches proved traps, into which fell hundreds of inoffensive yard-long grass snakes. Naturally, they seriously engaged the attention of many a Jock who wanted to get past them and was unused as yet to having close dealings with such " beasties." All the snakes killed were amply avenged by the fleas of Sheikh Abbas. Whenever the Bedouin vacated a mud-hut, the myriads of fleas which infested it made for the nearest trenches. Flies, tarantulas, scorpions, and centipedes were as bad before Gaza as anywhere else.

The sand-storms of the desert had their parallel in the dust-storms of Palestine, whose effects were equally unpleasant. One of the worst was on the 19-20th May. The weather was uniformly hot and dry, and consequently the lower atmosphere was filled with dust, and the plague of septic sores did not abate. The best remedy available was sea bathing, but this was only possible for units when stationed near the coast. The vast system of defences constructed, the wells dug, and so on, had entailed heavy calls on the energy of all, and many were much run down. Everything possible was done by the authorities, and there was a 52nd Divisional Rest Camp at the beach near Deir el Belah, besides the Corps Rest Camp at Rafa, and another at El Arish.

Two bad incidents occurred at Deir el Belah. Several times hospitals had suffered from stray shells, aeroplane bombs, and machine-gun bullets, and such affairs had been put down as accidents. Nevertheless, the Lowland Field Ambulances had made a practice of preparing shelter trenches, which could be entered by patients within the hospital tent, and which opened out of it. On the night 7-8th May the 1/1st L.F.A. and 1/3rd L.F.A. had considerable tentage erected near the south bank of the Wadi Ghuzze, and the camp was clearly marked with the Red Cross. There was bright moonlight, and enemy aeroplanes returning from a raid on railhead deliberately machine-gunned the camp. On the following night the patients were carried out before moonrise to some disused infantry trenches, about 100 yards away. Lt.-Col. J. W. Leitch, O.C. 1/1st L.F.A., remained in his camp with four other ranks. Before long, two hostile aeroplanes commenced bombing and machine-gunning the hospitals, and Col. Leitch and two of his men were wounded. A battalion of another division was passing the camp, and one bomb dropped into its midst. The single explosion cost forty lives besides the thirty-six wounded who lived and who were carried into the Lowland Ambulances. It is unlikely that the airman saw the battalion and what terrible havoc he had wrought, or he would have turned, and, at least, machine-gunned them. There is no doubt that he was aiming for the white tents, which he could see. This showed that the ruthless German spirit was permeating the whole enemy resistance.

Two days after the close of the second battle of Gaza, the 7th Cameronians captured two Turks prowling outside the wire at Mansura. Such audacity called for action by the Division's patrols, and there commenced a struggle for the possession of No Man's Land, which on the Mansura side of El Sire, varied from one to two miles in width, and in the belt of dunes from 500 to 1000 yards. By day it was an area of apparently peaceful stretches of green plain or dune. By night it was often black pandemonium, in which officers and men occasionally disappeared and were never heard of again.

As a result of the two battles, British telephone wires were running in many directions into the disputed area, as well as behind the British lines. It was impossible to remove these wires at once, and there was danger on such an extended front, with its innumerable nullahs, of enterprising Turks tapping lines which were in use, and taking down British messages. To provide against this, each brigade was given a code name for use over the wires, the battalions and batteries being designated by numbers. Those of the Lowland Division were as follows :

155th Brigade	-	-	-	Hearts.
156th „	-	-	-	Bairns.
157th „	-	-	-	Rangers.
261st „	R.F.A.	-	-	Celts.
262nd „	R.F.A.	-	-	Hibs.

The first recorded offensive exploit by a patrol took place on the night of 18-19th May, when some 5th R.S.F. crept up and threw bombs into the Turkish trenches on Umbrella Hill. This was a high sand-hill running out from the Turkish lines like a bastion on the edge of the sand-hills. Its crest was covered with green bushes and trees, and it took its name from one of the latter, which from a distance looked like a " Sairey Gamp " umbrella. This hill became famous later on.

From this time the Division's patrols set to work to waylay enemy patrols, bomb their sentries, and so on. When two patrols clashed in the darkness, success usually went to the one which had seen the other first, so that there was a large element of chance in these affairs. The Turks as usual proved brave enemies, and would creep up to throw bombs into the British trenches.

On the 5th June the Turks tried new tactics. The 5th R.S.F. were holding the line before Umbrella Hill, where the sand-hills are gradually merging into the wooded country. This part of No Man's Land is accordingly covered with

BATHING AT REGENT'S PARK, GAZA AREA

OPERATIONS BEFORE GAZA

stray thickets, patches of bush, and clumps of trees. To watch this difficult area, a day post of eight other ranks was kept on an elevation about a hundred and eighty yards in front of the British firing line.

The morning " stand-to " had taken place without incident, sentries had been posted, and the reliefs had settled down to get what rest they could under the hot rays of the rising sun. Suddenly, about 6.15 a.m., from a thicket about a hundred yards away, both sentries were shot dead, and some twenty Turks rushed for the post.

Those in the fire trenches could see none of this. Their first intimation of something being wrong was the sudden appearance of a Fusilier in the trench fighting with a Turk, whom he bayoneted. The next moment a bomb burst in the post, and the N.C.O. in charge of it appeared, wounded, and shouting for help. He then returned to the post. That is nearly all that we know about these men.

In a very few seconds 2nd Lieut. J. M. Craig, 5th R.S.F., was doubling over the expanse of soft sand with a rescue party. They found the N.C.O., disembowelled and dying, together with another man mortally wounded. Around lay three other men dead, but of the remaining three they could find nothing. Sgt. Graham, with some men, followed up the tracks of the Turks into the bushes to a point where an enemy covering party of about twenty had waited, but found nothing but bloodstains and marks on the sand, which showed that the Turks had dragged them away into the greenery, as soon as all had been felled. Evidently their bodies were to form proof that the post had been " scuppered."

The dead and wounded were being brought in when the Turks in Umbrella Hill Redoubt, little more than 400 yards away, opened fire on the rescue party with rifles, machineguns, and later on with light field guns sending over H.E. and shrapnel. The Fusiliers went coolly on with their work, there being no lack of willing helpers. A man fell wounded, and a moment afterwards a sergeant was shot down in an exposed place. Capt. E. D. Gairdner, R.A.M.C., arrived at that moment, and immediately went to the sergeant's assistance, but himself fell shot, with a broken thigh.[1] At this, 2nd Lieut. Craig went out and carried the sergeant to some cover. The Turks had concentrated a considerable fire on the spot. 2nd Lieut. Craig next went out with Lance-Cpl. Colville to bring in Capt. Gairdner. The gallant Craig was now wounded, but persevered in his efforts until he had got the doctor under cover of a fig tree, where he scooped with his hands a shelter for him and the wounded sergeant.

All of this had only taken a few minutes, but the artillery had received word, and the battery, 'B' of the 267th Brigade, covering this point, with great promptitude brought a sustained and accurate fire on Umbrella Hill Redoubt, completely quelling its fire. This greatly assisted the safe evacuation of the wounded, which took place a few minutes afterwards.

For his great personal bravery on this day 2nd Lieut. J. M. Craig, 5th R.S.F., was awarded the second Victoria Cross which came to the Lowland Division.

Within a week the 5th K.O.S.B., Lt.-Col. A. Kearsey, had taken revenge for this in their night raid on Sea Post, a Turkish work on the cliffs overlooking the beach, and lying about 600 yards from the Turkish redoubt, Beach Post, and about 1200 yards from the British lines at Sheikh Ajlin.

For over a week prior to the raid, the troops concerned were practised in their work by day and by night, over an exact replica of Sea Post prepared from aeroplane photographs. The distance to the position of readiness, the point close to the redoubt from which the final rush was to be made, was carefully paced by patrols. Helmets whitened by sun were re-dyed. Major-Gen. Smith personally extracted information about the redoubt from two Turkish deserters, when no one else had managed to do so. He, Gen. Pollok-M'Call, Lt.-Col. Kearsey, and everyone concerned carefully considered every contingency, and the following operation was the result.

---

[1] This was the fourth time that Dr. Gairdner was hit whilst succouring wounded.

Two parties, each consisting of forty of all ranks and bombing teams, were to raid the redoubt, advancing across the scrub-covered depression which sank gradually from the British lines, but rose more steeply up to the Turkish. Midway in No Man's Land a force of about a hundred, with four bombing teams, was to lie ready to reinforce the raiders, or to cover their retreat.

On the beach a party of forty with two teams of bombers was to guard that flank from a counter-attack, and behind it was to lie another small force in close support.

For several days the artillery had been blowing gaps in the wire of Sea Post. These gaps were watched by day and sniped by machine-guns at night. At 5 p.m. on the 11th of June another seventy-seven rounds were fired at them, and afterwards the guns kept sniping them.

A patrol reported the front clear and at 8.20 p.m., under a moonless sky, the raiding party, armed with rifle, bayonet, bomb, and revolver, and some carrying sharpened axes to cut down barriers, silently set out for the position of readiness, reaching it in twenty minutes. After them the other parties moved out. At six minutes to 9 p.m. the artillery opened an intensive bombardment of the post, deluging it with shrapnel and H.E. This lasted for about four minutes.

When this stopped the 5th R.S.F., Lt.-Col. J. B. Cook, about two miles to the right, sent up three red flares, the Turkish S.O.S., from such a point that, to look-outs on Muntar, they appeared to come from Umbrella Hill Redoubt. With commendable promptitude the Turkish artillery put down a heavy barrage in No Man's Land before that redoubt, and on the front and support lines of the 5th R.S.F., keeping it up for a full hour. A nervous rifle-fire broke out from Umbrella Hill, and whenever it showed signs of abating the R.S.F. started it again with short bursts of their own. This cost the R.S.F. three killed and one wounded, but it completely bewildered the Turks, for guns were now firing in all directions.

At the same time, in No Man's Land, before Outpost Hill, men of the 5th H.L.I., Col. F. Morrison, were raising and lowering dummies with strings about 300 yards from the Turkish trenches, and from behind the dummies were firing flares and rifles as if an attack were being made. The Turks responded to this with fire of different kinds until 3 a.m., and the next night they were found to have occupied the ridge where the dummies lay.

Meanwhile, the real attack was taking place on Sea Post. For two minutes before 9 p.m. the artillery were silent, as were the two raiding parties now lying ready within about 100 yards of the redoubt. At 9 p.m. the guns opened again, putting down a barrage about 200 yards behind and to the landward flank of Sea Post, whilst howitzers shelled Beach Post and other Turkish trenches near by. At the same moment, led by Capt. Penman, 5th K.O.S.B., and his officers, the two raiding parties dashed forward, one on the right and one on the left, stumbling in and out of shell-holes, but keeping their organization.

They could dimly discern heads above a trench, cries were heard, an ineffective rifle-fire was opened by the enemy, and a Turk was seen wildly trying to undo something, afterwards found to be a puttee wrapped round a Lewis gun. In a few seconds, and without difficulty, the Borderers were through the gaps in the wire with a fierce rush, and the machine-gunner was bayoneted, together with every other Turk on duty. One enemy rifleman bolted along the front of a trench, but Pte. Ferguson ran after him and with one terrible blow of his axe shore the Turk's head clean from his body. A few moments afterwards Ferguson met another Turk and decapitated him also.

At the same time the bombers, under Lieut. H. Burt, 5th A. & S.H. attached 5th K.O.S.B., had dashed for the four communication trenches, and by the light of the bursting shells were busy building trench-blocks to face both ways, barring off reinforcements, and cutting off those avenues of escape for the garrison. Some Turks, trying to get away, ran into these barriers, and were all killed but one, who was captured. At the blocks in the trench leading to Beach Post Lieut. Burt was attacked from both directions, but the relief party was driven off by the

OPERATIONS BEFORE GAZA

superior bombing of the Borderers, and left behind a number of dead.

Within Sea Post the various parties proceeded rapidly on their missions, stumbling over the Turks killed by the bombardment. One party was making for the dug-out of the post commandant, when a Borderer threw a bomb into it, blowing the whole place and all it contained to pieces. At almost the same moment the signal office was blown up by another bomb. The trenches appeared to be empty, but Capt. Penman, with Lieuts. Turner, M'Kinnon and M'George, using electric torches, found the remainder of the garrison cowering in their dug-outs. They seemed too paralysed to move, but as many as could be caught hold of were dragged out to take the life offered to them. The remainder were disposed of with bombs, and not a man can have survived beneath the heavy timbers of those shattered dug-outs.

Other parties had been smashing the wire around the work, and carrying out further devastation. Every place was examined. Beyond the twelve prisoners, one of them badly wounded and on a stretcher, not a Turk was alive within the trench-blocks. The booty was collected, a Lewis gun, relic of the first battle of Gaza, a few rifles, bayonets, and other things; the parties were checked off; and fifteen minutes after the first storming of the redoubt the raiding parties, followed by the bombers when the former were clear, set out for the return journey. The Borderers had not lost a man. A private had cut his foot badly with a hatchet, but not a single Turk had got his blow home first against these descendants of the old Border raiders.

The beach party, on reaching the enemy wire, had been fired on by a picquet of six or eight men, whom they drove off with their own rifles. They remained at their vantage post until their allotted time without incident, and then returned safely, as did all the other parties.

The Turkish dead in this affair cannot be estimated at less than sixty and probably were over a hundred. We do not know what happened with the mines, left by the Borderers in the trench-blocks and elsewhere, when the

Turks came in the morning to re-occupy the battered shambles, but the wiping out of the garrison must have had a serious effect on the Turkish morale.

Camped behind Sea Post was a working party of 150, who, if they had not all bolted at the first bombardment, might have done something to avert the total disaster to the Turkish garrison.

This was the first trench raid on this front. Others were made by the 52nd and other divisions,[1] but none were so completely successful. It is remarkable that, although several times parties of Turks were driven back from the British lines as if they had contemplated a raid, never once did they get in and destroy a British garrison.

During the close of June the old long rifles were withdrawn from the Division, and the new short rifles were issued. Hitherto it had been necessary to carry two classes of small arms ammunition, because the Lewis guns took the more powerful ammunition which was used with the short rifle. Henceforward, the one class was carried and much worry was saved.

On the 28th June Gen. E. H. H. Allenby, G.C.B., G.C.M.G., took over the command of the Egyptian Expeditionary Force from Gen. Sir A. J. Murray.

At the end of July there commenced a series of patrol-fights and raids on the Mansura-Sheikh Abbas front which continued into September. Most of this fighting was done by the Lowland Division. Battle patrols of between thirty and seventy men were sent out, armed with rifle, bayonet, bomb, and Lewis gun. The Turks sent out patrols varying from eighty to three hundred men, similarly armed. Confused and deadly struggles in the darkness were the result, and, although these actions were often apparently indecisive, their net result was to drive the Turkish patrols well to their own side of No Man's Land, leaving the greater portion for the British to wander over at will. This was eloquent testimony that their patrols must have suffered heavy losses, but, of course, at the time of a fight, only the

---

[1] Notably those on Umbrella Hill and other places by the 54th Division.

dead actually seen or felt and the prisoners taken could be counted.

Between Sheikh Abbas and the Turkish trenches known as the Tank System, which took their name from the tank wrecked there on 19th April, are a series of features whose names sufficiently indicate their character. From east to west they are, Suffolk Ridge, Old British Trenches, Northampton Mound, and Wadi Endless. On the night of 25-26th July a patrol of 8th Cameronians, Lt.-Col. J. M. Findlay, consisting of four officers and sixty-six other ranks with two Lewis guns, under Capt. D. Hannan, ran into an enemy force near Suffolk Ridge. In a moment the place was lit up with the flash of small arms and bombs, showing that the Turks were about two hundred and fifty strong and had two machine-guns. Under a fierce fusillade at close quarters, Capt. Hannan withdrew his patrol, bringing all the wounded that could be found. On his return his losses were found to be four other ranks missing and ten wounded. On the following two nights patrols searched the same place for these missing, but could find no trace of them or of the enemy.

The difficulties of the Division's patrols in finding their way about cannot be exaggerated. The country was undulating enough to be deceptive in the darkness, but at the same time almost devoid of landmarks of any kind, apart from a few tracks which could only be seen when one stood upon them, and a few wadis which often could only be located when the edge was felt with a stick. Many Clyde yachtsmen were in the officers' ranks, and " in these days compasses were our constant companions and Cassiopeia and the Great Bear valued friends " (Capt. E. R. Boyd). The smallest errors in action or direction might bring disaster, and one could never see the enemy until they were within about thirty or forty yards. The mental attitude of some of the men was wonderful in its calmness. If a patrol had halted and lain down for a while, very often an N.C.O. would have to get up to awaken some man who had quietly dropped off to sleep and was snoring. For most, however, every nerve was tense and alert. The

Turkish patrols were usually too noisy on the move, and on occasion they had to pay for this dearly.

On the night of 31st July a patrol of forty-one officers and men, thirty-two from the 4th R.S. and nine from the 5th H.L.I., were fired on and bombed by eighty to a hundred and twenty Turks near Suffolk Ridge. The Lowlanders replied, but their Lewis gun jammed, and they had to withdraw with the loss of 2nd Lieuts. J. Wallace and J. M. Brunton, 4th R.S., and three other ranks, wounded and missing, and of one man wounded who was brought back.

Now, about half a mile behind the Turkish lines ran the Gaza-Beersheba Road, and opposite the gap between the Muntar and Tank trench systems could be seen a telegraph wire on poles. Lieut. Coltart, signalling officer of the 7th Cameronians, was sent out by his C.O., Lt.-Col. Romanes, to ascertain the practicability of laying a wire from the British lines to tap the Turkish wire. He reported favourably, and on the following night, with his signallers, and protected by a patrol of 7th Cameronians under Capt. H. MacLean, he laid the wire over the intervening two miles. No results were obtained, so Lieut. Coltart set out again on the third night for another long tramp over the dark plains to ensure that satisfactory contact had been obtained. He had reached the Gaza-Beersheba Road and was perched at the top of the telegraph pole examining the wires, when he observed a party of Turks approaching. He hurriedly slid down and concealed himself in some scrub near by. Along the road came a Turkish working party of about fifty, with rifles slung over their shoulders and all unconscious of the Cameronian who lay watching them not twenty yards away. After they had passed, he returned safely and made his report. The next night, that of 1st August, Lieut. Coltart sallied out for the fourth time to penetrate the Turkish lines. This time there accompanied him a fighting patrol of sixty picked Cameronians under Capt. H. MacLean, whose object was to waylay this Turkish working party within their own lines. Unfortunately, the Turks did not turn up. Capt. MacLean had

WADI SIMEON, GAZA AREA

OPERATIONS BEFORE GAZA

commenced to return, when his patrol detected some movement on their flank. He quickly disposed his men for an ambush, and, when the Turks had walked into it, attacked them, getting his blow in first. A regular melee took place some two hundred yards from an enemy post. The fighting was hand-to-hand, and two Cameronians had respectively a sword-bayonet and a muzzle of a rifle blown off by enemy rifle discharges. The Turks, completely surprised, made off, leaving behind eight killed that the Cameronians could count, besides three prisoners. Delays under these circumstances are undesirable. Capt. MacLean ascertained that he had not lost a man, and then quietly and rapidly withdrew. The Turkish losses were probably much heavier than those actually ascertained. Unfortunately, Lieut. Coltart's exploit did not have the success it deserved in the tapping of enemy messages.

There was almost nightly patrol fighting in the early days of August by the units of the 157th Brigade, until finally the Turks ceased to approach Wadi Endless. A trick played on the Turks several times by the 4th R.S., Lt.-Col. A. M. Mitchell, was to send out a patrol, with a telephone. This patrol would locate a Turkish standing patrol, possibly waiting to ambush a British patrol. It would then quietly telephone the location of the Turks to the artillery, who would suddenly deluge the place with shell-fire.

The most important action took place on the intensely dark night of 8-9th August. According to plan, two platoons of 6th H.L.I., Lt.-Col. Anderson, searched the Wadi Endless, but met no one. A platoon of 5th H.L.I., Col. F. Morrison, then proceeded along a track towards Tank Redoubt. This platoon was to decoy the Turks into an ambush already lying in wait, and formed of two companies of 5th Argylls, Col. B. H. Mathew-Lannowe. The latter were under the command of Capt. R. Brown, and were disposed, one to cover the right and rear, and the other ready to charge. The first intimation of the proximity of Turks to the platoon of 5th H.L.I. " was the sight of a line of sparks from bombs being lit (the Turk then used brassards for lighting the fuses); then began quite a battle. Rifles and our Lewis guns opened out rapid fire, ceased fire, and opened again, and then began to withdraw. It was time, as the Turks were enveloping us. Several men had been hit and half the butt of the Lewis gun blown off by a bomb. It was difficult to estimate the number of the enemy, but an officer found himself in the third extended line of advancing Turks and reckoned we were up against a big roving patrol which had a good reputation for this sort of work. This officer, with a balmoral as a headdress and armed with a rifle and bayonet escaped in the dark by his resemblance to a Turk and by his bayoneting one of the enemy. The patrol extricated itself with ability, much helped by Cpl. M'Lean in charge of the Lewis gun section, who took the gun after all of his team had been wounded and kept off the enemy by firing it from his shoulder." (*History 5th H.L.I.*)

Suddenly the 5th H.L.I. came past the waiting Argylls, and after them came a crowd of pursuing Turks. The Argylls went for them with the bayonet, and found themselves fighting with Turks on all sides. The enemy were evidently led by Germans, and one party advanced up to the Argylls, shouting, " 5th H.L.I. !——5th H.L.I. ! " Another party of enemy came up shouting, " Don't shoot ! We are escort to prisoners." The result was an indescribable melee, after which the opposing forces separated and returned to their own lines.

Lieut. J. S. Milne, 5th H.L.I., died of his wounds in a Turkish hospital. Lieut. R. Munro, 5th A. & S.H., was shot dead. The losses in other ranks for this affray were twenty, of whom one killed, four missing believed killed, and seven wounded were Argylls. The Turkish casualties were estimated at from thirty to forty.

The British Intelligence Department had information that the Turks anticipated a raid on Tank Redoubt, and were employing specially trained " storm troops " to oppose the British here. These Turks were clever and formidable antagonists, and had a habit of going about in overwhelming masses. During the first fortnight in August the 6th H.L.I. lost in patrol fights in this area, one officer

OPERATIONS BEFORE GAZA

wounded and missing, four other ranks killed, and twenty wounded.

During the night of 11-12th August, the 156th Brigade moved out to cover a raid by the Imperial Camel Corps on Sana Redoubt, a work to the eastward. The garrison bolted in time, so that only a dozen Turkish casualties resulted from it. For the 156th Brigade the affair was without incident. During the summer the Colonial cavalry repeatedly raided the Turkish railway south of Beersheba, blowing up bridges and generally making a complete wreck of it.

On the night of the 20-21st August, the last night affray of any size before Sheikh Abbas occurred. The Old British Trenches, 500 yards south-west of Tank Redoubt, were occupied by the Turks as a night post. It was decided to place a box barrage around them, formed on its three sides severally, from west to south, by the fire of howitzers, 18-pounders, and machine-guns. This barrage was to move towards Sheikh Abbas, shepherding the Turks within it into the Old British Trenches. The fourth side of the rectangle was to be a line formed of one company of the 5th H.L.I. on the right, and one company of the 6th H.L.I. on the left, the whole being under the command of Lt.-Col. J. Anderson. This line was to rush the trenches with the bayonet. The objective of the 6th was the work, Old British Trenches, and of the 5th that part of Suffolk Ridge in a line immediately to the east. Touch was to be maintained between the two companies by a special officer's party, and behind this line were flank guards and reserves.

The Turks were thoroughly on the *qui vive* for an attack on that night. At 9.45 p.m. a patrol pushed close up to the Old British Trenches and found the Turks in position. The patrol fired on them, but the Turks lay silent until the H.L.I. men got so close that the enemy were forced to reply.

The barrage came down at 10 p.m., and all went well until about half an hour later, when the line was within a few dozen yards of the Old British Trenches. There was some rifle-fire from Turks to one side of that work, and the party keeping connection in the centre were all wounded, and with them the officer on the inner flank of the 6th H.L.I. The sudden destruction of the link connecting the two wings caused them to diverge rapidly, and in the darkness and shell-fire both parties approached their objectives separately, the 5th H.L.I. getting on theirs, and the 6th H.L.I. being met with a burst of rifle-fire from about thirty rifles and two machine-guns. The officers on both inner flanks tried to get into touch, but failed. The Turks before the 6th H.L.I. were receiving reinforcements from their rear in spite of the barrage. They heavily outnumbered the H.L.I. and were waiting for them. There was little more than half a company of 6th H.L.I. in front of the Old British Trenches, and the enemy began to move out to surround it. These were driven back, and Lt.-Col. Anderson withdrew his men. The Turks did not attempt any pursuit, probably because of the previous ambush. The 5th H.L.I. waited for a while on Suffolk Ridge, and then they also retired, probably about the same time. Not until the parties were well on their way back did the Turkish artillery open fire.

Our losses in this affair totalled thirty-four.

	Killed.	Missing, believed Killed.	Missing and Wounded.	Missing.	Wounded
Officers, 6th H.L.I.	–	1	–	–	2
Other ranks, 5th H.L.I.	2	–	2	2	9
,, ,, 6th H.L.I.	1	–	1	–	14
	3	1	3	2	25

2nd Lieut. J. Edmond, 6th H.L.I., was mortally wounded and must have died soon afterwards, as he never returned. The 5th H.L.I. missing were two stretcher bearers, who lost their way carrying one of the wounded.

About twenty freshly killed Turks were found by the 6th H.L.I. immediately before the Old British Trenches, and the enemy must have had casualties from the barrage. A Turk, who deserted a week later, stated that he knew of thirty, and that, whilst on that night they had out three machine-guns, afterwards they took out five. When the

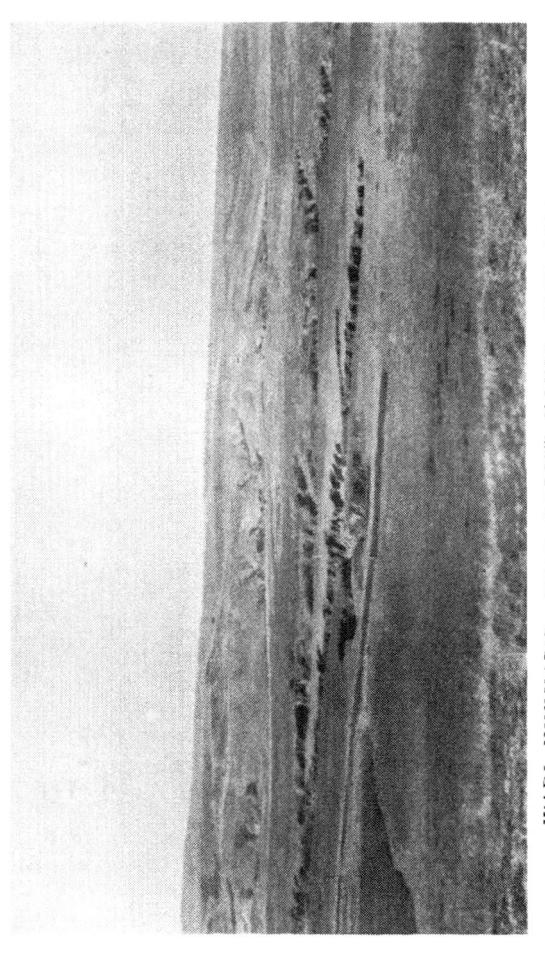

WADI NUKHABIR, NEAR DORSET HOUSE, GAZA AREA

OPERATIONS BEFORE GAZA

157th Brigade left Sheikh Abbas on the 1st September Turkish patrols seldom dared to come on the British side of Suffolk Ridge. This was the general result of these night affrays.

The last officer to lose his life in this night patrol fighting was Captain J. G. Hart, 7th H.L.I., missing believed killed, on the 28th August.

During October the 155th Brigade turned their attention to the Turkish patrols in the sand-hills area, fighting several small actions, which cost us a few men, but which succeeded in keeping the enemy to their own side of No-Man's-Land.

The Division got its first taste of a rain-storm in Palestine on the night of 27-28th October. The 157th Brigade was in reserve about the Wadi Nukhabir, and its units were lying asleep in those natural shelter trenches, the sandy and sun-baked nullahs. Elsewhere, several other units of the Division were in similar places. Suddenly a tempest of extraordinary violence burst. " The rain came down in torrents, and in a few minutes every wadi was full of roaring waters, which swept the companies out of house and home and sent clothes, blankets, equipment and the slender comforts of our nomad life ' doon the burn.' It was not exactly pleasant, but even so, the indomitable humour of the British soldier hailed this ' end of a perfect day ' with the cry : ' Fall in for washing water.' " (Rev. A. Fyfe Findlay.) It took two days to put to rights the mess that resulted.

The 12th of September saw another change in the command of the Division, when Major-General W. E. B. Smith, C.M.G., handed over to Major-General John Hill, C.B. It is unnecessary in a work like this to call attention to General Smith's skill as a tactician and an organizer, but we cannot pass by without mentioning his constant care and forethought for the welfare of those under him.

Hard training and drafts had by this time made the Division one of great fighting efficiency, and, towards the end of October, everyone knew by the preparations behind the lines, the bridging of the Wadi Ghuzze, and the steadily increasing bombardment of Muntar, that the third attempt on Gaza was not far away.

There had been a saying current in Palestine that the Turks would not leave that country until the waters of the Nile flowed into its borders. This had been understood to mean that the Turks would hold the country for all time. Yet at this time the pipe-lines were bringing the waters of the Nile from the Sweet-Water Canal of Egypt, across the desert, and pouring them across the frontier at Rafa.

CHAPTER XX

(29TH OCTOBER TO 7TH NOVEMBER, 1917)

THE THIRD BATTLE OF GAZA

"The 1st Royals ... moved steadily on with the noble mien and gallant bearing of men bent upon upholding, at any sacrifice, the honour and glory of their country."
History of the War in 1815 : CAPT. W. SIBORNE.

BAGHDAD, with all its tremendous prestige for the Oriental mind, had passed under the British flag in March, 1917. The collapse of Russia had released the Turkish army in the Caucasus for service elsewhere, and, during the end of the summer, General von Falkenhayn and Jemal Pasha, the Governor of Syria, were arguing with Enver Pasha as to how they could make best use of it. The East, from India to Egypt, was permeated by German propaganda, and was simmering with revolt. Another British reverse in that part of the world might have brought irretrievable disaster to the cause of the Entente, so that the wisdom of the War Council in strengthening General Allenby's force, in the face of strong opposition, cannot be emphasized too strongly. Von Falkenhayn had much under-estimated the rate at which the British home authorities were reinforcing General Allenby's strength, and favoured an attack by his army during the latter half of October in order to clear the way for an attempt to recapture Baghdad; after which India and Egypt were to be brought under the Turco-Germanic sway. However, the only results of the enemy deliberations were indecision and delay, and the collection, under von Falkenhayn in northern Syria, of a much advertised force of picked units, called the " Yilderim," or Lightning Army Group, out of compliment to its prospective exploits. As usually happens when such names are given in advance, it never struck at all. At last, in the middle of October, a decision was arrived at. General Allenby was to be attacked first; but it was too late. Troops were still on their way back from the Mesopotamian front, and enemy aeroplanes were still being unpacked, when von Falkenhayn, at the time on the railway proceeding south, learnt that Beersheba had fallen to the British on 31st October.

While the enemy councils were vacillating, General Allenby and his army, with a foresight and organization that was as perfect as men could make it, were quietly training and preparing for the attack that was to wreck the Turkish army before Gaza, and to carry the small Union Jack of the Commander-in-Chief into Jerusalem, a city whose significance to the Moslem world must be measured with that of Mecca, of Cairo, of Baghdad, of Adrianople, and of Stamboul.

When considering the terrain over which this campaign was to be fought, certain physical features of Palestine stand out before all others. Running north and south, about twenty miles from the coast, is a mass of hill country, rising at the central plateau to over 3000 feet. On the north it is bounded by the Plain of Esdraelon and tapers off into Mount Carmel above the port of Haifa, and as far south as Beersheba it sinks down to a narrow ridge at an elevation of 1500 feet. Further south the hills rise again and run into Sinai. This compact mass of hills consists largely of moorland covered with boulders and outcrops of rock, between which grow rough scrub and thorns, although, after the winter rains, there is considerable herbage. In some places there are hollows with olives, figs and vines, but there is little permanently running water. The hills are rounded, and between them lie deep valleys with sides which are often terraced. These valleys run off into innumerable ravines and nullahs, which usually end in blind alleys. The transportation difficulties of armies in this

THE THIRD BATTLE OF GAZA 357

hill country have always been immense. At this time these hills were traversed by only two good roads ; one from Jaffa through Jerusalem to Jericho and El Salt ; and the other from Shechem (Nablus) and the north through Jerusalem to Beersheba and the south. The villages are perched on hills and are surrounded by enclosures with cactus hedges. The whole area is full of places where a few machine-guns might with ease hold up a brigade, and this mass of hills, with its narrow passes, has proved a vast natural fortress ever since history began. In the midst of this mountainous area lies Jerusalem.

To the east the country sinks down to the deep valley of the Jordan and the Dead Sea, 1300 feet below the level of the Mediterranean. Further to the east ran the railway from Damascus to the south, the jugular vein of the Turkish resistance to the Hedjaz rising.

To the west these Judean hills sink down through the elevated rolling country of the Shephelah, which produces barley and wheat, figs, olives, and vines, to the belt of fertile plain, called Sharon at its northern parts. This is a region of firm soil, with a number of wells, and some extensive areas of cultivation. Orange groves are numerous, and in the spring it has a fair show of verdure and numerous wild flowers. It could, however, provide little to supply the needs of an advancing army, the Turks having already almost completely denuded it. Small towns and villages, surrounded by gardens, are scattered about, and here and there rise low hills and ridges, all of which could be rapidly turned into very strong positions for defence with almost perfect fields of fire. . This plain was traversed from north to south by the railway, which ran from Damascus, skirted the northern edge of the Judean Hills, sent a branch line from Junction Station to Jerusalem, another to Gaza, and reached Beersheba on the edge of the hill country. South of that point the Colonials had turned it into a useless wreck. Junction Station was to be General Allenby's first great strategical objective. Its capture would sever the railway communications of Jerusalem.

Between this fertile plain and the sea stretches a belt

of dunes about a mile wide. The distance between the sand-hills of the coast and the 1000 feet contour is usually about twenty miles, and within that belt, part of it the "Land of the Philistines," was to be fought the greater portion of one of the great decisive campaigns of the war.

The Turkish line of defence ran from Gaza to Beersheba, about thirty miles away. East and south of Beersheba the country is extremely broken, and the water supply is very poor, so that the enemy regarded an outflanking movement by cavalry as virtually impossible. From Gaza, now a modern fortress with line after line of redoubts and trenches fronted by leagues of wire entanglements, so that the Turks thought it to be impregnable, ran a series of fortified localities and trench systems, as follows:—the Sihan group of works, which included the Tank system; the Atawineh group; the Baha group; the Abu el Hareira—Abu el Teeaha trench system (near Sharia); and, finally, the works covering Beersheba. "These groups of works were generally from 1500 to 2000 yards apart, except that the distance from the Hareira group to Beersheba was about four and a half miles. The enemy's ... lateral communications were good and any threatened point of the line could be very quickly reinforced." (General Allenby.) By the end of October these strong localities had been joined up so as to form a practically continuous line from the sea to a point south of Sharia, well embedded in the hills. The defences of Beersheba were practically a detached system in front of the Turkish left, guarding, in addition to its own seven precious wells, the road over the hill country through Hebron into Jerusalem. So secure against frontal and flank attacks did the German Staff consider the whole position, that they had almost neglected any second-line system of defence on the line of the Wadi Hesi.

To hold this position the enemy had nine Turkish divisions and one cavalry division, organized into two armies. The 8th Army under Fevzi Pasha had its right on the coast, and the 7th under General Kress von Kressenstein had its left in Beersheba. At the time of the

THE THIRD BATTLE OF GAZA 359

attack General von Falkenhayn was on his way from Aleppo to Jerusalem. " The general staff of all the enemy formations was in the hands of the Germans. All ranks of the flying corps, heavy artillery and motor transport corps, and the officers of the engineer and supply services and of the railway administration were also Germans. There were a few German and Austrian infantry battalions." (Col. Preston.) This force totalled 49,000 fighting men, of whom 3000 were mounted, with 360 guns.

To drive them from their position General Allenby had ten brigades of mounted troops, from Australia, New Zealand, the British Isles, and India, and seven divisions of infantry. The whole of the ten brigades formed the Desert Mounted Corps under Lt.-Gen. Sir H. G. Chauvel. The 10th, 53rd, 60th, and 74th Infantry Divisions formed the 20th Corps under Lt.-Gen. Sir Philip Chetwode, destined to attack Beersheba and to break through the enemy's left, and the 52nd, 54th and 75th formed the 21st Corps under Lt.-Gen. Sir Edward Bulfin, destined to attack Gaza. This force consisted of some 76,000 fighting-men, of whom about 20,000 were mounted, with 350 guns.

The British had a great preponderance in cavalry, but the full effect of that could only be felt after the enemy had been driven from his tremendously strong line of fortifications. This would have to be done principally by the artillery and infantry, in which arms our superiority was not so great. The arid state of the country, the absence of local sources of supply, and the great distances to be covered should have easily outweighed General Allenby's superiority in numbers. That they did not was due to the superiority of the average British soldier over the Turkish as an all-round fighting man, and to British staff work and organization, which were so much better than the enemy's that full advantage could be taken of the element of surprise, and exploits carried out successfully which the enemy thought impracticable.

The first stage of General Allenby's plan was to capture Beersheba by the very manoeuvre which the enemy thought impossible, a wide flanking attack from the east and south-east, as well as an attack from the west. After this, a containing attack was to be made on Gaza, so as to pin the enemy's reserves down to that area. This was to be followed by the main infantry attack being launched against the Turkish left at Hareira, after which it was hoped to roll up his line from east to west, driving the Turks towards the coast, and leaving a gap through which cavalry could move to seize the wells near Huj and elsewhere, and continue the pursuit to Junction Station. Beyond that, nothing could be planned at this stage.

There is no space here to do more than indicate a few of the preparations made. A railway line was pushed forward in the direction of Beersheba to Karm, in the front line. The difficulties of water supply were immense. To carry water alone to the infantry for the attack on the Turkish left, 6000 camels would be required.

On 27th October the bombardment of the Gaza defences commenced amidst a terrible thunderstorm with rain that flooded the dug-outs. Three days later nine warships commenced to co-operate, working in relays. The artillery ashore included seventy-eight 8-inch and 6-inch howitzers, 6-inch and 60-pounder guns, besides the guns of the divisions: a hundred and eight 18-pounders, thirty-six 4.5-inch howitzers, and eight mountain pieces, a total of two hundred and thirty. Hundreds of tons of shells were available, and, as the days went on, this bombardment gradually increased in volume. The British aviators had command of the air, so that the advantage of superior observation was now lost to the Turks.

The artillery of the 52nd Division, under the command of Brig.-Gen. E. C. Massy, C.B., C.M.G., D.S.O., was in position among the sand-dunes, and included the following brigades : 261st, Lt.-Col. J. Farquhar, 262nd, Lt.-Col. J. C. Gaskell, and 264th, Lt.-Col. H. H. Elliot. The trench artillery consisted of the 133rd and 134th (Medium) Trench Mortar Batteries.

Having left behind standing camps to deceive the enemy, marching by night and lying hidden by day, successive forces always using the same camping ground to avoid too

THE THIRD BATTLE OF GAZA

many signs that enemy aeroplanes might detect, the Desert Mounted and 20th Corps moved stealthily on Beersheba. Owing to the difficulties of the country, the countless nullahs and the areas of sand, practically the whole of the transport available in the army, including 30,000 pack camels, had to be allotted to this force in order to keep it supplied at a distance of from fifteen to twenty-one miles in advance of railhead. Nevertheless, so completely were the enemy deceived, that an appreciation of their's for 29th October contains the following passage : " An outflanking attack on Beersheba, with about one infantry and one cavalry division, is indicated, but the main attack, as before, must be expected on the Gaza front." The empty camps about Deir el Belah led the enemy to believe that there were "six infantry divisions in the Gaza sector, deeply echeloned."

On the evening of 31st October, Beersheba fell after a surprise attack, which owing to water difficulties had to be fought exactly to time-table. As it was, the wells of Beersheba were not equal to the demands on them, and some cavalry had to be withdrawn. The news of this victory was flashed at once to the troops of the 21st Corps.

The containing attack on Gaza was now due. The assault was to be delivered by the 54th Division, Major-Gen. S. W. Hare, on the defences from Umbrella Hill, inclusive, to the sea. The 156th Brigade, Brig.-Gen. A. H. Leggett, was attached to the 54th for the purpose, and to them had been assigned the capture of the two greatest earthworks in this part of the Turkish line, Umbrella Hill and the El Arish Redoubt. Major-Gen. Hare had once commanded the 156th Brigade, and on the 1st November called personally to renew acquaintance with the battalions and tell them that the attack was to commence that night.

Umbrella Hill, an advanced post on a dune connected by trenches with the main line, could bring flanking fire to bear on any troops assaulting the El Arish Redoubt which lay nearer the sea, so that the former would have to be taken first. This was the task of the 7th Cameronians, Lt.-Col. J. G. P. Romanes, reinforced by a company of the

8th Cameronians, Lt.-Col. J. M. Findlay. A company of the 7th R.S., Lt.-Col. W. C. Peebles, was to cover the right flank of this assault, which was timed for 11 p.m. Four hours afterwards, the 4th R.S., Lt.-Col. A. M. Mitchell, with a company of the 8th Cameronians in reserve, was to storm the central and eastern portions of the El Arish Redoubt. At the same time the 54th Division was to assault the remainder of the Turkish line as far as the sea, the 1/5th Suffolks being detailed for the western portion of the El Arish Redoubt. The whole assault was to include a front of 5000 yards and was intended to penetrate to a depth of 3000 yards. To two companies of the 8th Cameronians fell the dangerous and laborious task of carrying ammunition, water, wire, stakes, and other Royal Engineers' material to the troops that were holding and consolidating the captured positions across No Man's Land, which in front of Umbrella Hill was 500 yards wide, and before the El Arish Redoubt was about 900. The 412th Field Company R.E., and one section of the 410th Field Company had been detailed to construct communication shelters and trenches across to the newly captured positions, and to help in the consolidation. The 155th Brigade, Brig.-Gen. J. B. Pollok-M'Call, was holding the British front line facing these two earthworks.

For many days previously, the 156th Brigade had practised this attack over models of the trenches they were to assault. Loads for men and mules of the carrying parties had been carefully measured and stacked ready. The Royal Engineers had constructed a system of Decauville light railways to bring stores of all kinds close to the front line. No small proportion of this work, together with the building of bomb-proofs, etc., had been done by the Royal Engineers of the Division, the 410th, 412th, and 413th (Lowland) Field Companies, under Lt.-Col. L. Fortescue Wells.

For several days and nights the bombardment of the Turkish trench systems around Gaza had been increasing in volume, and every night a creeping barrage had moved across No Man's Land and the enemy lines, so that, when it moved to cover the actual assault, the Turks would notice

THE THIRD BATTLE OF GAZA

nothing unusual until they actually saw the advancing troops. The area being shelled was very extensive, and accordingly the British fire was concentrated on definite points and areas. In addition to the artillery, a hundred machine-guns, twenty-eight of them from the Division, opened on the Turkish lines. Besides its own machine-guns, the 156th Brigade was supported by six from the 230th Company and six from the 155th. The Turkish and German artillery replied, and had at least a hundred guns available to pour shells over the British lines. On this night the mighty diapason of the British artillery was sounding to the full, and had increased to the intensity of drum fire. " Looking back toward our own gun line, the darkness was gashed and torn by constant flashes, while the continuous bark of the field guns and the roar of the heavier pieces made conversation impossible. The air was alive with the whine of the shells overhead." (Capt. E. R. Boyd.) One eye-witness describes the culminating bombardment as follows : " It was as if the furies had at last burst loose. For hours a tornado of high explosive and shrapnel poured on the Turkish positions, and, standing on the sandy knoll on which our camp was placed, we could watch the storm of fire breaking beyond the summit of Samson Ridge. Though several miles away we could see the sand crests in front of Gaza lit into distinctness, as the brilliant flashes rent the darkness of the night." It was a new experience for the Division to have plenty of artillery support. Each battery fired about 1000 rounds every day.

In connection with this bombardment a piece of good work by the Divisional Intelligence Staff should be noted. Long and definite, though barely visible, lines had been noted on aeroplane photographs of the enemy's areas in the sand-hills. After much thought and examination they were identified as the long but tiny mounds of sand which were raised when telegraph wires were buried. By following these up, all the various headquarters of the enemy were located exactly. The artillery did not fire a shot at them until the night of this attack, when, suddenly, all of these dug-outs were overwhelmed together by H.E.

The 155th Brigade had cut gaps in the wire during the day, and through these the Cameronians filed for the assault on Umbrella Hill, deploying a few minutes before 11 p.m. on tracing tapes laid out in readiness among some trees known as Fisher's Orchard. They were observed, and the Turks in the redoubt, 150 yards away, opened a machine-gun and rifle-fire on them. Beyond causing some casualties, it had not the slightest effect on the organization. To the right of the Cameronians the company of the 7th R.S. moved to its position to cover the assault.

As the Turks opened fire on the deploying Cameronians, the British bombardment attained its greatest intensity, and the Turkish small-arm fire died away. The Cameronians moved forward, and in a few minutes had taken the front line trenches with little opposition. Further on, the enemy resistance increased, and there was fierce fighting with bomb and bayonet on the final objective, many Turks being killed. This was taken by 11.28 p.m., and consisted of the trenches in rear of Umbrella Hill, which ran across the communications between it and the main system. So impetuous was the rush of the Cameronians, that it was hard to restrain them from following the Turks into our own barrage, which now fell across the communication trenches north of Umbrella Hill. It was a night in which all did well, but special mention must be made of the gallant deed of Lance-Cpl. D. Pollock, 7th Cameronians, who, having discovered a Turkish machine-gun causing mischief on his left, rushed forward, bayoneted two of the gunners, drove away five others, and stood by the gun until his section came up. The captured earthworks covered an area over 600 yards square, and it took some time to clear the numerous dug-outs of the parties of enemy secreted in them, some of whom fought to the last.

The enemy artillery had put down a barrage at 11 p.m. across No Man's Land, and this increased until 5.9 and 4.2-inch shells rained on this area, across which the carrying parties of the 8th Cameronians were bringing bombs, small arms ammunition, wire, pickets, etc., and across which the Royal Engineers were trying to construct a

THE THIRD BATTLE OF GAZA

series of shelters and trenches for communications. Many casualties were caused and the carrying parties were much hindered, but fortunately a good supply of everything had gone forward behind the assault. The labours of the Royal Engineers had to be suspended for a while, as men could not work in the open under this deluge of shells.

By about 1.20 a.m. the enemy had apparently realized that this was not merely a raid on Umbrella Hill, such as had been made by the 74th Division on the previous night on Outpost Hill, but that the Cameronians had come to stay. The Turks opened a heavy fire from rifles, machine-guns, and light artillery on the new front trenches of Umbrella Hill, and launched a small bombing attack. Ten bombers forming one party were all killed, and the counter-attack failed, but the hail of shells and machine-gun bullets on the captured redoubt continued unabated for over an hour.

The hour was now approaching for the second, and main phase of the assault. This had been fixed to give the extra artillery activity of the enemy, caused by the capture of Umbrella Hill, time to die down a little. The troops had moved forward to the front line under considerable shell-fire, and about 2 a.m. the 4th R.S., with the two companies of the 8th Cameronians, moved out and deployed in four waves on tapes already laid out 500 yards from the El Arish Redoubt. They were observed by the enemy and a heavy machine-gun fire was opened on them, causing some casualties, but in no way dislocating the movement of formations. Two tanks had moved out with them, and two minutes before 3 a.m. went forward. One broke down before it reached the enemy wire, but the other pushed across the first two lines of trenches before it was hit and set on fire.

At 3 a.m. the British artillery once more poured all its fury on the Turkish front lines; the Turkish guns turned from Umbrella Hill to the newly-threatened areas; and, with magnificent steadiness, the 4th R.S., followed by two companies of the 8th Cameronians, advanced in four lines, each with a front of 300 yards, on the El Arish Redoubt.

On their left they were in touch with the 1/5th Suffolk Regiment, 163rd Brigade, whose objective was the western portion. Ten minutes afterwards, the British barrage had moved behind the threatened works, and the leading ranks of 4th R.S. swept over the Turkish front trenches to the third and fourth lines of the enemy, the succeeding waves following to clear up the first and second. As the leading wave of men swept over, at least two contact mines exploded, blowing many of the men to pieces, and filling the air with clouds of dust and sand. Only for a moment was there a slight disorganization. Led and encouraged by their officers, the remaining men swept forward steadily to their objectives. One company, wheeling in the darkness and the uproar with perfect discipline, swung to the right with the object of rolling up the enemy resistance in the Little Devil Trenches, which connected up with the Mazar work.

Severe fighting now occurred in all parts of the redoubt and in the Little Devil Trenches. The Turks resisted stubbornly in dug-outs and saps, but our men with bomb and bayonet killed the enemy in large numbers, and forced the remainder back. More contact mines (at least four in all) were exploded in different parts of the El Arish Redoubt and these trenches. Although there is nothing more demoralizing to troops than to feel that they cannot rely on the ground under them, and that any moment they may be blown into the air, the Royal Scots with their attached Cameronians went steadily about their deadly work amid the pandemonium.

By 3.35 a.m. all objectives had been gained, but, on the left, the 54th Division had not been able to get so far forward, and the left of the Royal Scots had to be swung round to conform to their line. The Turkish machine-gun and rifle-fire sweeping the captured trenches was very heavy, especially from a building known as Bedouin Hut in rear of the El Arish Redoubt. A young officer, 2nd Lieut. W. Dalgleish, 4th R.S., hastily gathered a small party, rushed through the British barrage in rear, stormed the hut, killed all of its defenders, and smashed up a machine-gun which he found in position on the roof. He then returned, and the work of consolidation proceeded.

The Turks had no intention of losing this redoubt, as it was part of their main line, and they had in it some of their best troops defending Gaza, with orders to hold it at all costs. Twice they counter-attacked with great determination, but each time were repulsed with heavy loss. The assaulting troops had suffered very heavy casualties, and at 6 a.m. a company of 7th R.S. arrived in the Redoubt as a welcome reinforcement.

The fighting in the Little Devil Trenches was hard and bitter. They had no depth and were exposed to enfilade fire from the earthworks behind In one desperate counter-attack about 6.30 a.m. the Turks drove back the Royal Scots a little. Here fell Captain R. D. M'Rorie, 4th R.S., and near by all his officers and N.C.O.'s were killed or wounded. Lieut. H. W. Winchester, 4th R.S., came up with a platoon, rallied the men, and drove the enemy off the higher ground commanding these trenches, consolidating it as far as possible, despite the shallowness of the trenches and the severe fire. Shortly afterwards, reserves from the 8th Cameronians were pushed into these trenches. Heavy bombing attacks followed, but the Royal Scots and Cameronians held their own until daylight, when it became evident that these trenches were untenable, and Brig.-Gen. Leggett ordered a withdrawal to the western portion, which was on higher ground, and denied the eastern part to the enemy.

From daylight until 3 p.m. on the 2nd the whole of the captured area was subjected to such a heavy shell, rifle, and machine-gun fire that work on the defences was out of the question. The bombardment of Umbrella Hill was not so severe, and there consolidation could be carried on steadily.

All through that night the carrying parties of the 8th Cameronians went to and from the El Arish Redoubt across the 900-1000 yards of No Man's Land. This work called for the greatest possible determination and endurance. It was not carried out in the heat and excitement of an assault, but entailed many weary trips backwards and forwards across a stretch of soft sand. All the time the area was alive with shell-bursts, and swept by enemy machine-guns, but the work was steadily and unflinchingly done. With the carrying parties went the quartermasters and their men carrying dixies of hot tea for the men in the front trenches.

The signallers had a busy time keeping up telephonic communication with the two captured redoubts. At one time on the morning of the 2nd the wire to the El Arish Redoubt was found to be cut in seven different places. It was cut on seventeen different occasions during the first twenty-four hours. Eventually, a line was laid by a different route, and buried by night to a depth of eight inches.

At 3 p.m. on the 2nd the hostile fire died down considerably, and the work of consolidation in the El Arish Redoubt could be carried on methodically. After darkness, quicker progress was made, chiefly in wiring and the improvement of communications. Matters were much helped by ample supplies of wire, pickets, and other material having been already brought across to the redoubt by the carrying parties. In this constructional work the R.E. assisted with their customary coolness and bravery.

At 11 p.m. the Turks again attempted to counter-attack the El Arish Redoubt from the cactus-hedged garden to the north-east. At the same time the enemy artillery fire became intense. A few Turks could be made out close at hand amongst the cactus, but their main body was still in mass further behind, when the British barrage descended on it, breaking it up at once. Half-an-hour afterwards the enemy artillery fire died away, but continued intermittently throughout the night.

By this time the 4th Royal Scots had lost over 200 of all ranks, and it was decided to relieve them with the remaining three companies of the 7th Royal Scots. Again, however, the enemy artillery and machine-guns deluged the El Arish Redoubt, so that the relief could not take place until the fire had died away at 4.30 a.m. on the morning of the 3rd. By this time Umbrella Hill was well consolidated and the great El Arish Redoubt definitely in British hands, thanks

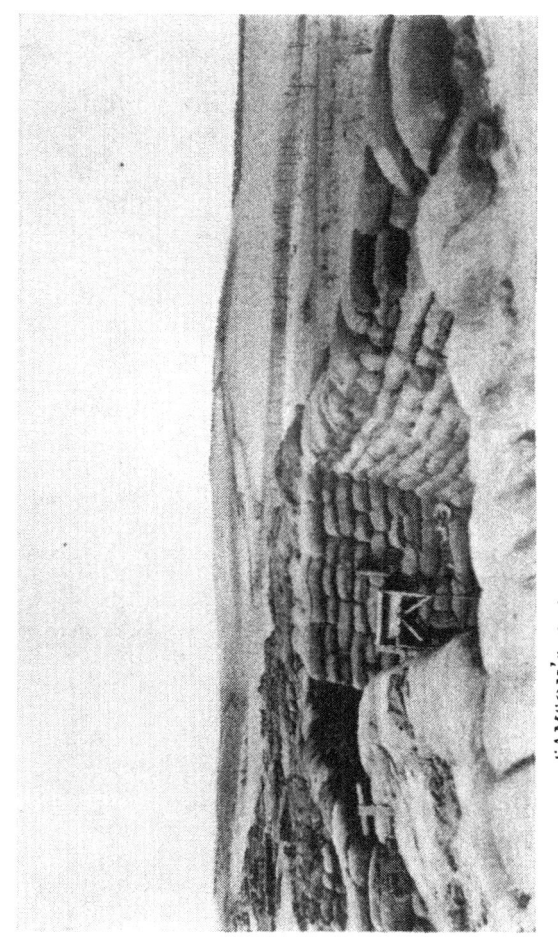

SAMSON'S RIDGE FROM HEREFORD RIDGE

THE THIRD BATTLE OF GAZA 369

largely to the dash and determination displayed by the Royal Scots and Cameronians.

Many of the 156th Brigade were at work for thirty-six consecutive hours before they got any rest. The attack of the 54th Division was not completely successful, the Turkish support lines having stubbornly resisted in most places. Sheikh Hassan was reached at 6.30 a.m., and in the afternoon two heavy Turkish counterattacks on it were broken up with great slaughter by naval and military guns. Another from the Magdhaba trenches was also repulsed. The following systems west of Gaza were, however, still in the enemy's hands on the 4th :—Magdhaba, parts of Rafa, Yunus, and Belah. Beyond Sheikh Hassan lay a string of posts from the sea to the outskirts of Gaza. The Turks hung on to their trenches with tenacity, and the city still held out.

Meanwhile, the Turks had taken the whole of their reserves to the extreme east of their line, and on the 4th and 5th made bold counter-attacks, but these were repulsed without General Allenby essentially altering his plans. The water supplies found about Beersheba were, however, very disappointing, and cavalry had to be withdrawn or their horses would have died from thirst, all of which naturally hindered the preparations for the main attacks of the Desert Mounted and 20th Corps on Sharia and its accompanying trench systems, which had been timed for 6th November.

November 3rd was fairly quiet before Gaza, but from that date onwards enemy shell-fire continued to play over the captured trenches, and especially the El Arish Redoubt. At times it was intense. At 11.30 a.m. on the 6th, they began to rain shells on this redoubt, and it is now thought that they were trying to get rid of ammunition that they could not carry away. One shell hit the regimental aid post of the 7th R.S., blowing a man to pieces and wounding the medical officer and four others. Pte. J. MacKay, the only survivor, continued to dress the wounded. This bombardment lasted until 5.30 p.m., when it died away.

Another attack on the Gaza defences had been ordered for 11 p.m. on that night, by the 75th Division against

Outpost and Middlesex Hills, and at dawn on the 7th by the 54th against Belah Trench, east of Sheikh Hassan. It was not, however, to be, for at 10 p.m. on the 6th patrols of the 4th and 7th Royal Scots found the trenches between the El Arish Redoubt and Gaza empty. Other patrols were pushed out in different directions, and all brought back the same story; the Turks had gone. At 11 p.m. the 74th Division occupied the fateful Outpost and Middlesex Hills, and the patrols that they pushed forward reported that they, too, had found nothing but silent trenches. The troops occupied Ali el Muntar, now pounded into a heap of rubble, without a man being hurt.

As dawn broke that morning, there was a wonderful stillness and calm. Captain E. R. Boyd tells how he " ran to the top of the sand-dune in front of Headquarters, and looked away toward Gaza and the north. As far as the eye could reach every dune and hillock held small parties of our men looking in wonder toward the now silent city." Well they might, for Gaza the Impregnable had fallen.

The Turks had been worn down by the bombardment, and in places their trenches had been reduced to pulverized depressions. The loss of the two great El Arish and Umbrella Hill Redoubts to the 156th Brigade, and their western front line with Sheikh Hassan to the 54th Division, had convinced them that they could only expect a similar fate for the remainder of their defences. To save the Gaza garrison from annihilation, they had evacuated in the night, and left the ancient city, a heap of smouldering ruins.

The losses of the 156th Brigade during the period from the 1–7th November were as follows :

Unit.	Killed and Died of Wounds.		Wounded.		Total.	
	Officers.	O.R.	Officers.	O.R.	Officers.	O.R.
4th Royal Scots	2	56	12	174	14	230
7th Royal Scots	—	8	4	79	4	87
7th Cameronians	1	36	4	122	5	158
8th Cameronians	3	32	4	100	7	132
156th Bde. M.G. Coy.	—	4	—	7	—	11
156th (Light) Trench Mortar Battery	—	—	—	2	—	2
	6	136	24	484	30	620

THE THIRD BATTLE OF GAZA

The officers killed were as follows :

4th Royal Scots—
Captain R. D. M'Rorie. Lieut. E. Dawes.
7th Cameronians—Lieut. J. O. Smith.
8th Cameronians—
2nd Lieut. P. E. Frankau. 2nd Lieut. J. T. Neilson.
2nd Lieut. S. J. Rowland.

The 410th and 412th Field Companies, R.E., lost twenty-seven killed and wounded, including Lieut. W. S. Young, 412th, at the El Arish Redoubt, and 2nd Lieut. D. F. Roberts, 410th, at Umbrella Hill.

Over 400 of these 650 losses were about the El Arish Redoubt. The total British casualties for this third and last battle for Gaza were about 2700.

The 155th Brigade lost an officer and twenty-one other ranks from enemy shell-fire.

Under Col. Tweedie, A.D.M.S., the arrangements of the 1/1st, Lt.-Col. J. Leitch ; 1/2nd, Lt.-Col. M. Dunning ; and 1/3rd, Lt.-Col. J. Young, Lowland Field Ambulances for the evacuation of the wounded worked rapidly and with absolute smoothness.

The casualties of the 156th Brigade were heavy, but they were light compared with those known to have been inflicted on the enemy. Their ascertained losses in and about the two redoubts were as follows :

Redoubt.	Turkish Dead Buried.	Prisoners. Officers.	O.R.	Machine and Lewis Guns Captured.
Umbrella Hill	201	3	58	5
El Arish	169	2	41	1
	370	5	99	6

Machine-gun mountings and great magazines full of small arms ammunition, bombs, and other stores were found in the two works. The Turkish losses in this area were about three times those of the 156th Brigade. Elsewhere, the 54th Division buried 739 enemy dead.

Strangely enough, none of the 52nd Division actually entered Gaza until long afterwards. The Division had to hurry past on the wonderful fighting march under Major-General John Hill, which had a decisive influence on the whole course of this campaign.

CHAPTER XXI

(8TH TO 9TH NOVEMBER, 1917)

WADI HESI

"Suppose, ah ! suppose, that some cruel, cruel wound
Should pierce your Highland laddie and all your hopes confound ? "
"The pipes would play a cheering march, the banners round him fly ;
The spirit of a Highland chief would lighten in his eye."
        O Where, Tell Me Where ? : MRS. GRANT OF LAGGAN.

ON the 6th of November, whilst the Turks were pouring into the British lines the shells that they could not remove, the 20th Corps was assaulting the series of trench systems about Sharia. After an obstinate resistance the Turkish line was completely broken through at 4.30 p.m., and the railway station occupied. "On the 7th November the intention had been for the Desert Mounted Corps to pass immediately through the gap in the Turkish line made by the three infantry divisions at Kauwukah, but the Turks were not yet too disorganized to offer sturdy resistance in places, and the 60th Division had some difficulty in dislodging them from Tel el Sharia at 0600[1] as a necessary preliminary to an advance of two miles beyond the Wadi Sharia." The way was finally cleared, and the Anzac Mounted Division passed through, but found itself "engaged with enemy rearguards and was only able to advance . . . a distance of two and a half miles by nightfall. . . . The lack of water was severely felt."[2] This last, coupled with the desperate resistance of the enemy, was delaying

[1] 0600 means 6 a.m.
[2] These quotations are from General Allenby's *Brief Record of the Advance of the Egyptian Expeditionary Force.*

WADI HESI

the advance on the right, and Gen. Allenby was faced with the possibility of the Turks gaining time and being able to hold him up on the line of the Wadi Hesi. If they could do that long enough to be able to fortify another line, further north, from the coast into the hills, then they would have saved Junction Station and Jerusalem, and he would have to fight another battle similar to the present one before he could reach his intended objective. There were numberless lines of depressions, elevations and hills, suitable for this purpose. If the Turks had not been pursued hot-foot, and had been allowed to make such a stand, the situation might have been dangerous in the extreme, when we consider with it the general position in France early in 1918. How the Division, under Major-Gen. J. Hill, was largely responsible for turning them out of these defensive lines one after another, it is our business to relate.

Gen. Allenby rapidly re-adjusted his plans. The main thrust was now to be made up the coast. On the 7th the 75th Division lay in front of the Sihan and Atawineh systems, which still held out. The 54th Division was in the trenches. Of the 52nd Division, the 155th Brigade was in the trenches, and the 156th Brigade was reorganizing, but the 157th was in reserve, ready to move at half-an-hour's notice.

The Division was ordered to carry out the pursuit, and almost all of the tens of thousands of camels and of the other transport which had been allotted to the 20th Corps for the attack on Beersheba and its intended advance after the break-through at Sharia, trekked back, and were turned over to the 21st Corps.

It must be remembered that if a 1000 gallons of water be used for infantry, it will maintain a force of higher rifle strength than if it is used for cavalry, as the latter have their horses to supply in addition to the men.

The 157th Brigade, Brig.-Gen. C. D. Hamilton-Moore, received orders at 9.45 a.m. to make for the mouth of the Wadi Hesi, and moved at once for Sheikh Hassan. From there, with the 6th H.L.I., Lt.-Col. Jas. Anderson, and a battery of artillery as advance guard, it marched along the beach, the outer files being at times on the edge of the water. With it went the 264th Brigade, R.F.A., its wheels once more fitted with pedrails, and the 410th Field Company, R.E. The heat was very great, for the sea breeze had failed and the sand was soft and deep. The men were carrying double rations and an increased supply of ammunition, and everyone was wearing a steel helmet. It was inspiriting to see the flashes from the guns of British monitors and other warships, as they harried the enemy in their retreat. Just before reaching the Wadi Hesi, the 157th Brigade was joined by a squadron of cavalry. On its right more cavalry were covering the flank. The Royal Flying Corps had complete command in the air, and on one occasion eighteen of our aeroplanes were seen flying north on some bombing expedition.

At mid-day the 155th Brigade set out to follow the 157th up the coast.

By 5 p.m. shots between the 6th H.L.I. and Turks, on opposite banks of the Wadi Hesi, could be heard. The 6th was threatening the Turks about Herbieh. Darkness fell a few minutes afterwards, and the 5th H.L.I., Col. F. Morrison, was ordered to move into the coastal belt of dunes and to seize the sand-hill, Ras Abu Ameirah, from which the Turks could closely observe and shell the mouth of the wadi. The 6th H.L.I. cleared the wadi and the sand-hills on its left bank, taking some prisoners, and then put out an outpost line, facing north and east, on the high ground inland.

Before we proceed further it should be noted that the only map in use, which showed the line of connected hills covering the railway and known later as Sausage Ridge, and also Ras Abu Ameirah, was a section of the general map made by Lieuts. H. H. Kitchener, R.E. (afterwards Earl Kitchener), and C. R. Conder, R.E., in May, 1878. They had no time to survey the country as exactly as is done for an ordinary British ordnance map. The work that they did was wonderful, and recorded all the main features correctly, but, very naturally, the innumerable minor features of a

WADI HESI

countryside had to be inserted on what seamen would term "dead reckoning." The result was that errors crept in in matters which were of critical importance to troops in action, where an extra 500 or 1000 yards of frontage or distance might make all the difference between victory and defeat.

The distance between Ras Abu Ameirah and the sea is about 1500 yards according to this map. Actually, according to the latest survey, it is nearer 2000 yards. This is a small error when we consider the relative unimportance of this sand-hill as compared with the physical features of the whole of Palestine, but such errors were to have a large bearing on the course of this battle.

The 5th H.L.I. moved up the wadi bed just in time to make out Ras Abu Ameirah before it disappeared in the gloom. Turkish riflemen and machine-gunners were hard at work on all sides. The 5th H.L.I. found their hill in the darkness, attacked, and captured it, with a few casualties to both sides.

Sniping went on all night long, and, as one man expressed it, "hameless wee bullets were dinging the air" in all directions. Just as the first suggestions of morning light appeared, the 5th H.L.I. made out a Turkish trench close at hand. Before the Turks had time to see anything, they were rushed by a party of the 5th from the rear, a very hot machine-gun and nine prisoners being taken.

Because of the heavy firing, the 7th H.L.I., Lt.-Col. E. S. Gibbons, had been sent forward to clear up the ground to the westward of the 5th H.L.I., and to continue the outpost line to the sea. They also were met by rifle and machine-gun fire from all directions, but pressed forward. The frontage was longer than was expected, and they were reinforced by a company of 5th A. & S.H., Lt.-Col. C. L. Barlow, then in reserve, in order to complete the line. Men, tired from a twelve mile march over soft sand, and working in the darkness, had secured an outpost line on both sides of the Wadi Hesi, including the most important height, which would have commanded the passage of its mouth.

As soon as they had arrived, the Royal Engineers had set to work to develop the water supply, driving their spear-points into the sand.

In front of the 5th H.L.I. to the eastward, when day broke, there "stretched a wonderful view of a plain studded with orange and lemon groves with fresh green foliage, odd plantations, cactus hedges and a village or two" (*History 5th H.L.I.*). Beyond, running north and south, lay the long yellow elevation, known as Sausage Ridge. With daylight came the bullets of the sniper, and some casualties, an officer of the 157th Brigade Machine-Gun Company being killed in this way, in addition to a few N.C.O.'s and men.

A sand-ridge to the westward of Ras Abu Ameirah was still occupied by the enemy, and gave direct observation on the mouth of the wadi, where the Division was collecting. The Turkish artillery soon turned a sprinkling of shrapnel on the crowds of men and animals on the shore, causing many casualties, but a company of 7th H.L.I. advanced under a heavy shell, machine-gun, and rifle fire over the bare sand-hills as if it was carrying out a parade movement, and carried the ridge. After this, the enemy's shell-fire on the thin flat strips of beach at the mouth of the wadi had to be directed from Sausage Ridge, but, although it became less effective, it continued throughout the morning and caused many casualties among the men, horses, mules, and camels crowded there. These, with guns and limbers, huddled close under the shelter of the low sandy cliffs and banks. In the midst, with white-hooded sand-carts tipped up to form shelters for the wounded, were the 1/2nd and 1/3rd Lowland Field Ambulances already at work under their Red Cross flag.

The general position on the morning of 8th November was as follows: the two Turkish divisions that had garrisoned the Sihan and Atawineh Systems had escaped in the night, and were making for the Wadi Hesi; the infantry of the 20th Corps could advance no further, because of their transport having been taken away for the 21st Corps; the Desert Mounted Corps was spread out mainly east of Gaza, in a bad country, with great difficulties as to water supply, fighting Turkish rearguards which disputed the advance. The retreating columns of the enemy had been heavily bombed by the Royal Flying Corps, and were much disorganized, but the Turks have wonderful powers of recuperation, and it would have imperilled the success of the campaign if they had been allowed to make a proper stand.

Sausage Ridge runs approximately parallel to the coast, its crest-line being about 6500 yards away from the sea, and its southern point overlooking the village of Deir Sineid on the right bank of the Wadi Hesi. To the eastward of it run the road and railway, up which Turkish troops were retreating. It offered a refused right flank to an attack from the sea, and, so long as the Turks held it, together with the sand-hills south of Ascalon, a further British advance up the coast was impossible. A delay of a few days on the line of the Wadi Hesi would have been of incalculable value to the enemy, and they had every intention of holding Sausage Ridge as long as possible.

This ridge had therefore to be taken as soon as possible, and at all costs, and the result was one of the fiercest struggles of the campaign.

Between Sausage Ridge and the belt of coastal dunes lies a stretch of rolling country about one and a half miles wide. In its southern portion it is low-lying, and is littered with orange groves and cactus-hedged gardens, in the midst of which lies the village of Herbieh. A mile north of the wadi the ground becomes more open, with an elevated tongue of land (about 150 feet) running southward, not quite in the centre but nearer to the Sausage Ridge side than the other. This tongue increased in height as one moved northward.

The 155th Brigade, less 4th and 5th R.S.F. on outpost duty two or three miles south of the wadi, had arrived at the mouth of the Hesi on the previous night, and the 156th Brigade, Brig.-Gen. A. H. Leggett, had set out at 5.30 a.m. on the 8th from Sheikh Ajlin. Orders came from Corps Headquarters that the Division was to attack Sausage Ridge from the north-west, avoiding the low ground round Herbieh, with the object of capturing the troops defending the position, and cutting the railway. The 155th Brigade, Brig.-Gen. J. B. Pollok-M'Call, was detailed to carry this through.

Now, according to the map in use, the northern end of Sausage Ridge lies 4500 yards to the east-north-east of Ras Abu Ameirah, whilst according to the latest survey it is shown to be 5500 yards in approximately the same direction. Again, the information available for the Headquarters Staffs made Sausage Ridge consist of dunes of not more than sixty or seventy feet in height. Actually, it was a ridge of rock and sandy clay of more than 230 feet in height over nearly all of its length, rising gently from a level plain, and with numerous spurs and gullies. It was therefore further away, and a much stronger position than was shown by the information on which the orders were based, and, in order to carry out the orders of Corps Headquarters, a much wider sweeping movement would have to be carried out than was contemplated.

"No members of the Corps or Divisional Staffs had had time to see the ground, and orders consequently were based upon such information as could be deduced from existing maps, which, as has already been stated, were inaccurate.

"General Pollok-M'Call who had carefully reconnoitred the ground was not slow to realise that the orders he had been given were based on a faulty appreciation of the conditions of space and country generally, and that all unwittingly he had been directed to carry out a movement fraught with inordinate risk, and one which was not likely to result in what was hoped for and expected by Corps and Divisional Headquarters. General Pollok M'Call did, therefore, what any responsible commander would have done and should do in similar circumstances. He reported the situation to his Divisional Commander, emphasizing the immense difficulties and risks which the enterprize entailed.

"He fully appreciated that the strategic situation called for quick and decisive action, and that this was one of the occasions in war where, if big results are to be obtained, time has to be estimated in minutes and not in hours, but he rightly estimated that his chances of success if he were to carry out to the letter the orders he had received not only were nil, but that he ran the almost inevitable risk of sustaining a reverse which might have most serious effects on subsequent operations. He was, however, directed to carry out his original orders, this decision no doubt being adhered to mainly by reason of the continuous pressure exercised by Corps Headquarters on General Hill to push on at all costs, and because the all important question of ' Time ' forbad any change of plan involving loss of precious hours, not to say minutes." (General Leggett.)

The 7th H.L.I. was still fighting for the sand-ridge when the 4th K.O.S.B., Lt.-Col. R. Dashwood-Tandy, and 5th K.O.S.B., Lt.-Col. A. H. C. Kearsey, of the 155th Brigade commenced to arrive within the line held by the 157th. The latter was now very scattered. The 5th and 7th H.L.I. with part of the 5th Argylls were holding an area north of the wadi, and the 6th H.L.I. were in the dunes which ran along the south bank as far as Sausage Ridge. The latter could not be moved without endangering the guns of the 261st Brigade, R.F.A., which had arrived and taken up a position there, largely because of the Turkish shell-fire sweeping the crossings of the Wadi Hesi as far as its mouth.

The 7th H.L.I. captured the sand-ridge soon after the 155th Brigade commenced to arrive, but the dunes north of Ras Abu Ameirah increase in height as one advances and they were still in possession of the enemy, who were so close that individuals could be seen by Brig.-Gen. Pollok-M'Call sniping at him and his staff, as they tried to reconnoitre the ground. This area would have to be cleared before the 155th Brigade could get into position to make its attack ; the 157th Brigade had no men available ; and accordingly the 5th K.O.S.B. moved out to clear the ground. This they did with nineteen casualties, and by 10.30 a.m. all the high ground was in our hands, and it was possible to reconnoitre the ground for the attack on Sausage Ridge. To the north lay a vast sea of sand-hills, into which the enemy had been driven, and beyond which, a little over three miles away, lay the ancient town of Ascalon. At 11 a.m. a report was obtained from a detachment of the Duke of Lancaster's Yeomanry, that had been scouting to the north. It showed that the enemy were in considerable strength in the coastal sand-hills, and very aggressive, the Yeomanry detachment having been driven in by them. The Turks were also holding in force the whole of Sausage Ridge, together with the village of Burberah on its northern end. A 5.9 battery was firing from the sand-hills south of Ascalon, there were two field-gun (.77 mm.) batteries at Burberah, and at least another about the southern end of Sausage Ridge. A battery of the 264th Brigade had got forward through the soft sand to Ras Abu Ameirah, but the artillerymen had difficulty in getting proper observation, because of the lie of the land. The Divisional artillery south of the Wadi Hesi were, of course, too far away to have helped this attack, even if they could have observed their fire. The open mouth of the wadi was being heavily shelled by the Turks, and no animals could be taken across it.

    The 4th R.S.F., Lt.-Col. R. G. Maclaine, and 5th R.S.F., Lt.-Col. J. B. Cook, left the position in the sand-hills south of the wadi, where they had been on outpost duty during the night, and, after an exhausting march of more than five miles over soft sand, joined the remainder of the 155th Brigade at 10.30 a.m. It could be clearly seen now that the map was wrong, and that, to carry out its orders, the 155th Brigade would have to form up for its attack with its left about a mile and half north of Ras Abu Ameirah, and then advance in a south-easterly direction over another [1] 3000 yards of bare dunes and open rolling ground on its objective, the centre of Sausage Ridge. This meant that it would be open to counter-attack, not only against its left flank, but into its left rear. The line of the 157th Brigade was already stretched to the utmost, and it was covering the mouth of

---

[1] This distance is taken as the crow flies, and not as men have to march. The marching distance was probably at least two miles.

the wadi, which it would be very dangerous to leave open to counter-attack. The best provision that could be made was to order the left battalion of the attack, the 5th R.S.F., to hold one company in hand to watch for an attack from the north, and to request the detachment of Yeomanry—less than 50 rifles—to assist. A company of 4th R.S.F. had to be left behind as escort to the Divisional Ammunition Column.

The battery of the 264th Brigade, R.F.A., had moved forward to the Headquarters of the 155th Brigade and opened a long range fire on the enemy.

The assaulting battalions moved out in artillery formation, and, after executing a wide wheel to the right, reached the place of deployment in the following order from right to left :—5th K.O.S.B., 4th R.S.F., 5th R.S.F. The 4th K.O.S.B. was in reserve. At 2.30 p.m. the troops advanced to the south-east, and, as soon as they descended from the ridges of dunes to the lower ground, came under an accurate barrage from four enemy batteries, including one of 5.9 howitzers. 200 officers and men fell within 400 yards, one 5.9 shell killing 2nd Lieut. G. M'Kinnon, 5th K.O.S.B., and killing or wounding fourteen of his men. Lt.-Col. R. G. MacLaine, 4th R.S.F., also fell wounded, a serious loss at such a time. Nevertheless, the Fusiliers and Borderers advanced with the utmost steadiness. Enemy cavalry could be seen to the north, and many parties, varying from 100 to 200 in strength, could be seen entrenching in the same direction and on Sausage Ridge. This meant that there were many more unseen. It was afterwards confirmed that this ridge was strongly held, and had many rifle-pits on its western face, with plenty of machine-guns ready to repel with cross-fire any attack from the sea-coast across the perfectly open plain, which lay below its northern and central portions.

After passing through the barrage the assaulting battalions reached the dead ground caused by the high tongue of land, which ran down into the lower ground from the north. Between this point and Sausage Ridge there was a level glacis, 1000 yards broad. These battalions were now completely detached. When they began to go over this tongue of land they came under heavy enfilade fire from about a hundred of the enemy with a machine-gun dug in on a sand-hill higher up to their left. To have left them there would have meant a murderous flanking fusillade for the whole of the assaulting troops, and Lt.-Col. J. B. Cook, 5th R.S.F., did the only thing possible. He deflected his men to the left, drove the Turks out, and secured the hill. After this the 5th R.S.F. pressed on, and actually reached the outskirts of Burberah, forcing the Turks to abandon a battery of field guns. The 5th R.S.F. was advancing to capture these guns, although another enemy battery behind was firing at them furiously, when further heavy shell-fire descended on them, so that they had to fall back. The Turks now re-manned the abandoned guns and poured a hot fire on the Fusiliers at point-blank range, blowing some men to pieces by direct hits. The Fusiliers had to fall back behind the crest-line, and for an hour and a half underwent a fierce shelling.

By this time a gap had developed between the 5th R.S.F. and the 4th R.S.F. The telephone wire out to the assaulting battalions had been cut, but Brig.-Gen. Pollok-M'Call went out and personally kept touch with his Brigade, now a couple of miles from his Brigade Headquarters. He ordered them to close up to the right, sent up the 4th K.O.S.B., less two platoons, as a reinforcement, and directed the assault to proceed.

The Yeomanry to the north had been held up by the Turks, just as the 155th Brigade had completed its wheel for the attack, and afterwards were driven in completely.

The closing-in movement of the 155th Brigade was being effected, and nightfall was not far off, when, about 4.30 p.m., Lt.-Col. Cook detected a force of about two battalions of Turks moving from the north as if to attack the assaulting troops of the 155th in rear, when they were preparing to continue their isolated advance across the open. He watched it carefully, mentally calculated the distance this counter-attack would have to travel, saw the imminent danger, sent a company of his men under Major Paton to ward off the attack, and notified the battalion on his right that he was going to retire. The remainder of the assaulting battalions conformed with his movement. The enemy came on with great boldness in the gathering gloom, shouting out " 156th ! " and whistling. They opened fire but were driven back in disorder. Major Paton and his men contested ridge after ridge. After fire was opened, the enemy sent up flares, and looked for the British flank. They got within 300 yards of the firing line, but at 7 p.m. retired, leaving traces of considerable losses. By that time the remainder of the Brigade had managed to withdraw to the sand-hills with its wounded, and had taken up a position, facing north and east along the ridge just north of Ras Abu Ameirah. Lt.-Col. J. B. Cook's cool and timely action probably saved the brigade just in time. An assault of a strong position in the darkness, with a heavy counter-attack developing in the rear of the attacking troops, could hardly have been a success. As the 155th Brigade retired, a column of about 1000 Turks was seen from Ras Abu Ameirah to fall in on Sausage Ridge and to march away to the northward, indicating that that objective had been strongly enough held.

Meanwhile, Brig.-Gen. Pollok-M'Call had tramped back to his Headquarters in the sand-hills. As soon as he arrived, about 5 p.m., a heavy rifle-fire was opened on it from a point 700 yards to the north. The 264th Brigade guns were only 200 yards behind his Headquarters. As rapidly as they could be moved, the two remaining platoons of the 4th K.O.S.B. in reserve, neither of them strong in numbers, together with the gunners and every man in the 155th Brigade Headquarters, lined a ridge facing north and replied to this fire with their small arms. These were the only men available. The situation was dangerous, and the artillerymen limbered up, ready to withdraw their guns, but fortunately, although the Turks got within 400 yards of 155th Brigade Headquarters, the bold front shown kept them from finding how weak the defenders were, and after the assaulting battalions had returned and taken up their position facing north, the enemy retired.

The losses of the 155th Brigade in this battle were as follows:

Unit	Killed and Died of Wounds		Wounded		Total	
	Officers	O.R.	Officers	O.R.	Officers	O.R.
4th R.S.F.	1	6	5	70	6	76
5th R.S.F.	—	8	7	92	7	100
4th K.O.S.B.	—	—	1	—	1	—
5th K.O.S.B.	1	12	2	80	3	92
	2	26	15	242[1]	17	268

The second officer killed was Capt. L. L. M'Keever, R.A.M.C., attached to the 4th R.S.F. He had done especially good service on the night of 1-2nd November. All of the wounded were brought in.

Of the Turks' losses we know nothing, beyond that they must have lost many before they abandoned their guns at Herbieh, and before they abandoned their counter-attack from the north in the evening. On the following morning 5th R.S.F. patrols found evidence of a four gun 10-cm. howitzer battery having been in the dunes to the north.

Three battalions of the 156th Brigade were pushed across the Wadi Hesi during the afternoon to guard against a Turkish counter-attack from the north. They arrived after nightfall behind the lines of the 155th Brigade, and the 7th R.S. went forward to link up the left of the line with the sea.

During the day the 6th H.L.I. had observed large bodies of troops, estimated at about 500 cavalry and 3000 infantry, retiring north from Deir Sineid, and it was urgent that this avenue of retreat should be blocked. The arrival of the 156th Brigade made it possible for Major-Gen. Hill to use the 157th Brigade for an attack on the southern portion of Sausage Ridge, and at 1.30 p.m. he ordered Brig.-Gen. Hamilton-Moore to attack with his whole brigade as soon as possible. At this time Brig.-Gen. Pollok-M'Call was preparing to launch his attack away to the north, and it could not be delayed. The 157th Brigade was partially in action, and still scattered from the north of Ras Abu Ameirah (7th H.L.I.) to the south of the Wadi

---

[1] Some of these afterwards died.

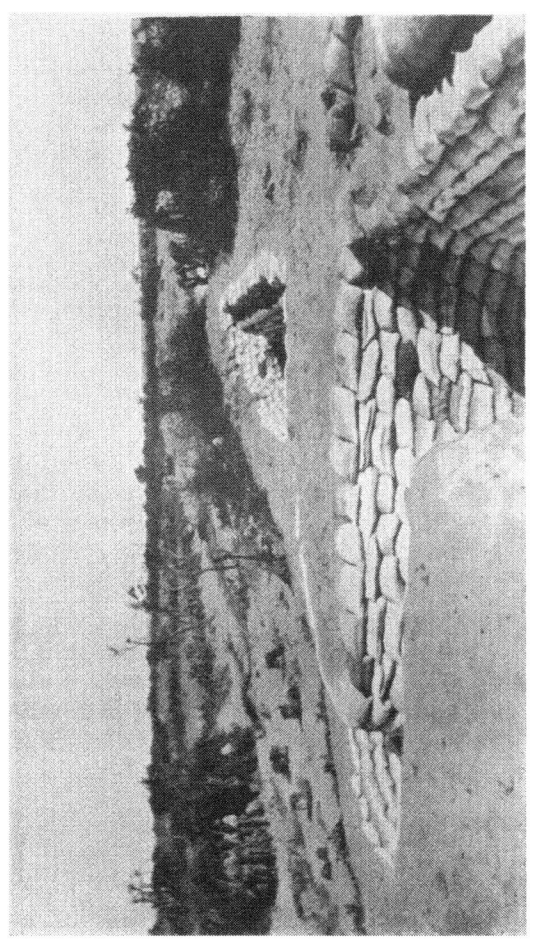

TURKISH TRENCH NEAR SAUSAGE RIDGE

WADI HESI

Hesi opposite Herbieh (6th H.L.I.), so that it would take several hours to collect the battalion commanders, and get everyone into position for the attack. Accordingly, there could be no co-operation between the two brigades, but that could not be helped.

The plan of the 157th Brigade was to attack with two battalions, from the Ras Abu Ameirah Ridge, westward through Herbieh, on the southern portion of Sausage Ridge. This was to be carried out by the 5th H.L.I., Col. F. L. Morrison, on the left, and the 5th Argylls, Lt.-Col. C. L. Barlow, on the right. At the same time the 6th H.L.I., Lt.-Col. James Anderson, were to advance from their position in the sand-hills south of the wadi, across its bed, and to attack the south-western end of the ridge, changing direction on arrival there and sweeping northward along the ridge. The attacking troops were to leave their packs behind, and the ridge was to be taken as soon as possible. The remainder of the brigade was in reserve.

At 4 p.m. the 5th H.L.I. and Argylls descended the Ras Abu Ameirah Ridge in artillery formation, making towards the orange and olive groves of Herbieh. There was an hour's daylight left, and they had a march of almost three miles before them, before they could attack. Away to the north they could hear the shelling and small-arm fire as the 155th Brigade fought before Burberah. Each battalion had a frontage of 400 yards, and, during almost all of the advance over the low ground and through the gardens, they had to march by compass, the bearing being 118°. As the men passed through the gardens they found time to fill their pockets with oranges, even though the enemy guns were bursting shrapnel over them. The British artillery, also, fired a few shells at Sausage Ridge during the first stage of the advance; thereafter there was no artillery support.

As the troops debouched from the gardens, the bullets of machine-guns and rifles commenced spitting in the sand, and the men extended at once, but the Turks seemed to withhold most of their fire until the 5th H.L.I. and Argylls were in the open and getting close to Sausage Ridge, when, in the dusk, they poured in a very heavy fire which caused severe losses. Darkness soon fell, and the enemy fell back fighting stubbornly and throwing up flares.

The western face of this portion of the ridge is steep, and at the base, under shelter of the heights, the troops were given time to recover their breath. Then, about 6 p.m., with bayonets fixed, they climbed up the hill, at times on their hands and knees, and, with a rush at the top, captured it. The 5th H.L.I. found themselves on an isolated mound in the centre of an indentation, and on part of the main ridge behind. The 5th Argylls found themselves on part of the main ridge further to the right. Immediately, they came under a heavy frontal and flanking machine-gun, minenwerfer, and rifle-grenade fire, from higher portions and minor features further back on the main ridge. This fire swept the 5th H.L.I. and Argylls from end to end causing heavy losses. Quick digging-in was impossible in that rock, and hard, dried clay. Fierce hand-to-hand struggles were going on in some parts, and gradually the attacking troops were forced off the main ridge, but hung on to this mound. There, a mixed body of 5th H.L.I. and Argylls made an effort at consolidation.

From this time onwards there ensued a stern and confused battle, in which the troops of both sides struggled with the most desperate determination, driving each other off the hill, returning time and again to the attack, and fighting without quarter. The condition of the British dead found on the ridge after the fight showed how fierce and merciless the enemy had been in their bayonet work.

After they had been driven off for the first time, the 5th H.L.I. with some Argylls rallied in a nullah behind and retook part of the ridge at the point of the bayonet, but only to be driven off again. " Another time and yet another did they return and capture the ridge, only to find it untenable. Then Major Findlay decided that it was useless to make a further attempt, and that it was better to hold on to the mound, which had been to some extent consolidated, and try to establish a line running north-north-west from it. But the enemy pushed his machine-guns forward and concentrated all his fury on our precarious position, which he enfiladed from the left and left rear. Gradually its defenders were driven westwards along the west of the mound into the depression behind, where they rallied and reformed, and from which they retook the position. After a game effort to hold on they were once more compelled to retire. By this time the fog of battle had enveloped everything. Major Findlay and Capt. Townsend were dead on the top of the hill. Major Brand and eight other officers were out of action; 190 men were dead or wounded. The remaining officers decided that it was useless to make any further attack and withdrew to Battalion Headquarters with the remainder of the men." (*History 5th H.L.I.*)

The Turks had had a bombing school behind the ridge, and, accordingly, they had an unlimited supply of bombs and other stores. The hill was so steep that they could roll large tin canisters filled with explosives down on the attackers. One enemy machine-gun at least had been laid so that it swept two successive crests, with the result that when men tried to rush it they only found themselves on another elevation swept by its fire, and the gun apparently as far away as ever. Despite all of this, parties of Argylls and H.L.I. kept returning to the attack. Capt. A. C. King, 5th Argylls, who had led the first company of Highlanders, and R.S.M. Monteith, 5th A. & S.H., won Military Crosses on that night for the manner in which they kept gathering men together, restoring their cohesion, and trying to consolidate what had been gained.

In the meantime the 6th H.L.I., who had had a much longer distance to travel, and a number of steep ridges of very soft sand to cross on the south side of the Wadi Hesi, were making for the southern end of Sausage Ridge in the darkness. The draught and pack animals had had no food and very little water all day, so that several dropped from exhaustion. Enemy bivouac fires were visible, dotted all over the plain to the eastward up to within a few hundred yards of the line of the advance. Half of the battalion's Lewis guns were left on the south side of the Wadi Hesi, and a half-section of the 157th Brigade Machine-Gun

Company were placed on some rising ground on the north side to cover the right flank and rear of this attack. The remaining Lewis guns and half-section of machine-guns were left behind in the wadi to wait for orders.

Guided by the Turkish flares, which soared into the darkness showing the forward ridge in silhouette, and the light and noise of the continual explosions, the 6th H.L.I. advanced on the ridge in extended order. Above rose the black mass of the main ridge, itself covered with confusing minor ridges, and varying from 100-500 yards in width at the top.

Capts. W. D. Macrae and Macquaker, who commanded the two companies that now led the 6th H.L.I., carried out a brief reconnaissance and found that the Turks were still in possession of the ridge. With bayonets fixed, the 6th H.L.I., and some Argylls and 5th H.L.I. who had joined them, now climbed the heights, and formed up on the crest-line facing the flares ahead. The attention of the Turks was naturally directed to the west, and the flank attack was a surprise for them. There was stern work in the darkness with the bayonet, and the Turks fought hard with every weapon and missile, but, numerous as they were, they had already had the 5th H.L.I. and 5th Argylls to contend with, and this last attack settled the matter. The 6th H.L.I. swept along the ridge for several thousand yards, bayoneting the Turks or driving them pell-mell down the gullies and slopes.

The Turks made one more ineffectual counter-attack after this, but it failed, and by 9 p.m. the 157th Brigade was consolidating the position. It was afterwards found that a force of 3000 of the enemy had bivouacked near the ridge for the night, but the capture of it had sent them on their way again and effectually settled any question of the Turks making a stand on the Wadi Hesi. When morning broke, it was discovered that a highly-organized and well-developed trench system, in two or three lines and with good shelters, had been captured, but that it had been planned mainly for an attack from the south, whilst the assaults of the 5th H.L.I. and 5th Argylls had been into the rear, and that of the 6th H.L.I. into the flank of the defences.

WADI HESI

At the time when the 6th H.L.I. was about to make its decisive charge along the ridge, Brig.-Gen. Hamilton-Moore was making arrangements for a fresh attack from the west. He had directed the old assaulting line to remain at the foot of the hills, until he could withdraw the 5th H.L.I., which had suffered very heavily in officers, for a rest, push in the 7th H.L.I., and then continue the attack.

Beyond some snipers, who were all cleared off by 2 a.m., the Turks had abandoned the ridge, and when day dawned the 6th H.L.I. and 5th Argylls were in uninterrupted possession.

On the morning of the 9th patrols of the 6th H.L.I. found Deir Sineid and Burberah clear of the enemy. This day was spent in reorganizing, burying the dead, and taking possession of the spoil. Immense dumps of artillery ammunition and grain were captured near the railway, to save which the Turks had evidently intended to make every effort. Large supplies of arms, small arms ammunition, bombs, stores, equipment, and documents fell into the hands of the victors, but only twelve Turks were taken alive. This last fact, with the numbers of enemy dead that were found, bore evidence of the desperate nature of the struggle.

The price paid by the 157th Brigade for the capture of this important ridge was as follows :

Unit.	Killed.		Missing.		Wounded.		Total.	
	Officers.	O.R.	Officers.	O.R.	Officers.	O.R.	Officers.	O.R.
5th H.L.I.	2	13	—	45	11	134	13	192
6th H.L.I.	—	6	—	1	2	17	2	24
7th H.L.I.	—	6	—	6	1	55	1	67
5th A. & S.H.	—	15	—	33	5	60	5	108
157th M.G. Coy.	1	1	—	—	—	3	1	4
	3	41	—	85	19	269	22	395

Most of the missing were killed, although a few afterwards turned up as wounded. Several of the wounded afterwards died.

Major J. A. Findlay, 5th H.L.I., was one of the type of senior territorial officer in which the Division was singularly rich. He was quiet, kindly, shrewd, and a fine leader.

On the day of the battle of the Wadi Hesi, the cavalry, between Gaza and the hills, were fighting their way to water at Bir Jemameh and elsewhere, capturing prisoners here and there, and attacking Turkish rearguards, who fought stubbornly and offered determined opposition. The Turk "well knew that, if he could keep our cavalry away from water for another forty-eight hours they would have to be withdrawn" (Col. Preston). At 11 a.m. the enemy counter-attacked near Tel Nejile on the right of the British line, and so strongly as to stop the advance for some hours. Further east, the Yeomanry Division had to break off from an attack and withdraw to Sharia for water. The advance in the centre was necessarily slow, because of the continuous, isolated troop actions, but large numbers of enemy guns were stalked and captured by the Colonials. In addition to the battle of the Wadi Hesi, another most remarkable action took place on this day, when 170 English yeomen near Huj charged and captured eleven howitzers and field guns and three machine-guns, in the face of two battalions of Turkish infantry.

The victory of the Division at the Wadi Hesi was decisive. The blow had shaken the whole Turkish right, and, henceforward, the advance of the British left up the coast dominated the whole campaign.

CHAPTER XXII

(9TH TO 10TH NOVEMBER, 1917)

ESDUD OR BEIT DURAS

> ... " You must die where you stand."
> The men answered his appeal, saying :
> " Ay, ay, Sir Colin ; we'll do that."
>
> Sir Colin Campbell and the 93rd (Sutherland) Highlanders at Balaclava.
> *Invasion of the Crimea:* KINGLAKE.

ON the morning after the storming of the heights above the Wadi Hesi, Brig.-Gen. Leggett, to whom the command of the squadron of the Duke of Lancaster's Yeomanry had passed, received orders to send mounted reconnoitring patrols forward to Ascalon and Mejdel. The Yeomanry were, however, incapable at that moment of movement, their horses having been neither fed nor watered for thirty-six hours. However, the 156th Brigade Headquarters formed a small mounted patrol of its own, consisting of nine signallers and grooms, led by Capt. T. M'Clelland, the Assistant Brigade-Major, and mounted on horses and mules. This was the British force that captured the ancient Crusaders' city of Ascalon, together with Mejdel.

Ahead of them lay a country that had been full of Turks on the previous day, and might be full of ambuscades. They were well in front of any British cavalry screen. After a journey of about seven miles, during which they rode down a sniper armed with an automatic rifle, this assorted troop of 'Mounted Infantry' entered Ascalon, with its gardens, ancient ruins, and modern houses, but found it empty of Turks. M'Clelland decided to push on at once to Mejdel, four miles to the north-east. At its outskirts he left a rearguard of two men, and with the remainder pushed boldly up the village street. There seemed to be few people about, but he noticed two armed Turkish soldiers disappearing hurriedly through a gateway. He was not sure whether they had run in with the object of rousing a garrison, but, taking the risk, he immediately followed. Fortunately, there were only two Turks there, both of whom surrendered; but there might have been 200, so far as M'Clelland was concerned. Inside, he found a large store of ammunition and 150 rifles, besides other stores. He was wondering what to do with his capture, when a squadron of Australian cavalry arrived. To them he handed over his captured dump, and duly obtained a proper receipt. He then returned with the valuable information that the Turks had fallen back certainly beyond Mejdel.

On this day, the 9th, the cavalry inland were beginning to feel keenly the want of water. For this reason the Yeomanry Division was delayed at Huj, and the Australian Mounted Division could not move far. Only the Anzac Mounted Division and 7th Mounted Brigade could advance. A rapid advance of the 52nd Division was accordingly of great importance.

By 7 a.m. the 157th Brigade, Brig.-Gen. C. D. Hamilton-Moore, was already on the move for Esdud (the Ashdod of the Philistines), to continue the pursuit. Somewhere ahead was Colonial cavalry with orders to occupy Esdud in advance. The march was about thirteen miles, and very trying for men in marching-order with packs. A large portion of it was over soft sand, and a khamsin came on, tormenting the sweating men with its scorching breath.

"The junction between the sand and the firmer soil is marked abruptly by the grass and vegetation that covers the latter with a uniform surface of green, in contrast with the yellow, barren surface of the desert" (Col. Young). Of good roads there were none in Palestine, but, even so, and despite the foot-soreness which naturally followed for men who had marched for months on yielding sand, it was a

ESDUD OR BEIT DURAS

great relief for everyone to step on to the utterly neglected, uneven, and dusty tracks of the harder ground. The route lay through Mejdel with its orange groves, where some were fortunate enough to obtain ripe Jaffa oranges plucked fresh from the trees. A pathetic feature of the march northwards, but also a great tribute to British rule, was the stream of natives, with their animals and humble possessions, flocking southwards from their hiding-places, back to their homes within the British lines.

As the perspiring men of the 157th trudged forward through the dust, they passed many dead and dying animals, broken waggons, piles of shells, and all the litter left behind by the Turks. The further an army advances the more difficult becomes the question of its supply, and, in order to push on ahead, the 157th Brigade had had to go on half-rations. With the 157th went 'B' Battery of the 261st Brigade, R.F.A., and the 413th Field Company, R.E. The cavalry attached to the Division, and detailed to advance with the 157th Brigade, did not do so because neither horses nor men had had water or food.

When about four and a half miles from Esdud it was noticed that the enemy were shelling it. Riding on ahead, Brig.-Gen. Hamilton-Moore found that the 1st Australian Light Horse Brigade was holding the line of a wadi north and east of the place, but that the Turks were holding some hills above Kummam, about two miles directly east of Esdud, and about 800 yards east of the wadi. From this position they were threatening to turn the right of the 1st Australian Light Horse Brigade, and were also preventing the 2nd Australian Light Horse Brigade from watering their horses at the wells of Kummam. These animals had not been watered for two days, and it was primarily to capture these wells that the 157th Brigade fought the action that followed.

Brig.-Gen. Hamilton-Moore hurried up his 18-pounders ahead of his troops, and they commenced shelling the Turkish positions by the light of the westering sun. As the 7th H.L.I. advance guard marched into Esdud at 4 p.m., fondly anticipating a good night's rest, they were met with word that another two or three miles of marching and an attack still lay before them. There was no time to reconnoitre the position, and the dispositions of the enemy could only be guessed. A speedy attack was essential. Packs were left behind, the necessary orders were given, compass bearings were taken, and within twenty-five minutes the 157th Brigade was advancing to the attack. The Division seemed destined in this campaign constantly to undertake long marches with night-attacks on unreconnoitred positions at the end of them.

The average strength " with the units " of the battalions of the 157th Brigade on the 1st November had been twenty-four officers and 750 other ranks. The wastage of war and battle casualties especially, as a glance at the Wadi Hesi casualty list will show, had already reduced these figures.

The 5th Argylls, Lt.-Col. C. L. Barlow, was on the right, and the 7th H.L.I., Lt.-Col. E. S. Gibbons, on the left, the latter directing. In reserve, echeloned to the left behind the 7th H.L.I., to protect that flank, was the 6th H.L.I., Lt.-Col. J. Anderson. The 5th H.L.I., Col. F. L. Morrison, remained behind at Esdud as rearguard. Away to the eastward, beyond the plain across which they were moving in artillery formation, was the landmark on their objective, a white domed tomb on a hillside that looked very peaceful in the setting sun. Three batteries of Turkish .77-mm. guns had turned their fire on the advancing brigade and on the 18-pounders.

Major-Gen. Hill had pressed forward personally, and reached Esdud with his staff in time to see the 157th Brigade move off.

Before the assaulting troops had got half-way to these hills above Kummam, darkness had fallen, and the artillery had to cease fire, but the advance was continued by compass bearings.

Immediately at the foot of the main ridge to be captured was a smaller one, on which the enemy's front line was entrenched. The infantry were extended, as soon as they were judged to be near their objective, and, a few minutes afterwards, a great volume of machine-gun and rifle-fire was opened on them from the lower ridge, between 400 and 500 yards away. The advance never ceased, and, when about 100 yards from the enemy trenches, with bayonets fixed and with cheers and yells, the leading companies charged. Two enemy machine-guns fired away until their crews were bayoneted. Most of the Turks fled, but no prisoners were taken. Up the long slope of the main ridge rushed the H.L.I. and Argylls, and at last found themselves on what seemed to be its crest-line. So far, the casualties had been very few, thanks to the darkness, and consolidation was commenced at once.

Suddenly, a heavy machine-gun and rifle-fire was opened on them from another ridge higher up, and only 150 yards away from the Argylls on the right. It was sighted so as to skim the top of the captured ridge, and Turks, aided by a strong wind, commenced throwing rockets and flares among and behind the Highlanders, lighting them up and showing them sharply in silhouette, as they worked on the top of the ridge. Casualties now became frequent, but the consolidation went on.

The difficulties of working over strange and deceptive ground, in darkness, and under a heavy and accurate fire at close range, are better imagined than described. The western portion of the occupied ridge was held by the 7th H.L.I., and the eastern, which turned to the south a little, by the 5th Argylls. Overlooking the eastern portion was the higher ridge, which, after running parallel to the line of 5th Argylls, turned eastwards for about a mile and a half towards its highest point. This ridge was entirely held by the enemy, and the wells, for which the 157th Brigade was fighting, were south of and commanded by it. Most of the above was not learned until the following morning, and the map in use (a section of the 1878 survey) simply gave a general indication of two elevations at Kummam, east of Esdud, and north of Beit Duras.

Where the two ridges ran parallel, there lay between the Turks on the higher and the British on the lower, a rocky gully. Patrols of Argylls pushed across, but came back with word that the Turks were in strength. There now ensued one of those confused night actions, in which it is almost impossible for a commander to tell exactly what is happening, and in which he must rely in a large measure on the initiative and resolute bravery of his men. Parties of Turks crept across the gully and threw bombs at the Argylls as they worked to dig shallow trenches in the rocky soil or to build breastworks of stones, galled all the while by the enemy machine-guns. These parties were driven off by the bombs and rifle-fire of the Highlanders with heavy losses, and Sgt. Gemmell distinguished himself by his deadly work with a Lewis gun. Capt. R. Brown, who commanded the two companies of Argylls on the ridge, retaliated by sending out exploiting parties that crept across and bombed the Turks on their own ridge. At one time all of the officers with Brown on the ridge were lying either killed or wounded. Many of the men also fell from this close-range fire, but, wearied though they were from their long march, they hung on stubbornly to the captured ridge.

In order to quell the accurate grazing fire of the enemy, eight of the 157th Company's machine-guns brought cross-fire to bear on the enemy guns as they were located from time to time. This work under Lieut. J. Webster, 157th Machine-Gun Company, caused them to keep changing their positions, and considerably diminished their fire, thus reducing our casualties.

The Turks knew the run of every ridge and gully, whilst to the British the whole situation was obscure. Brig.-Gen. Hamilton-Moore went over the whole of the firing line, personally, immediately after the capture of the ridge. Any further development of the attack in the darkness could only be founded on guess-work, and the only course open was to hold on and make a further attack at daylight. However, the Turks were digging in further north on a line north of the Nahr Sukereir, running through Burka and Tel el Turmus, to Beit Jibrin in the mountains, in order to hold up the British advance, and they were preparing a second line behind this one, still further to the north. In order to gain time the British would have to be driven back by every counter-stroke possible, and especially would the Turks have to stop the advance along the coast, which was bending their right flank back so that if not stopped it seemed that something would have to break. The Turks forming the bulk of the enemy army were tall and sturdy Anatolians, filled with the fiercest religious hatred of the infidels opposed to them, and their commanders could generally depend on their delivering counter-attacks with the most reckless courage. A wounded Turkish officer, afterwards captured, stated that the enemy troops engaged consisted of the remains of the infantry of the 3rd Turkish Division. Of this force, about 600 infantry with six machine-guns were firing from the main ridge, whilst another 400 or 600 with six more machine-guns were in support on the slope behind. There had been several minor counter-attacks with bombs on the 7th H.L.I. and 5th Argylls, all of which had been repelled, but the Turkish commander now decided on a more formidable attempt. His own force had suffered considerably. One company of the battalion to which the captured officer belonged had lost about sixty killed or wounded. On the other hand the Turkish commander knew that his machine-guns had been laid in the daylight.

About midnight a very heavy machine-gun fire was opened on the British position, and the lower ridge was swept by a tempest of bullets which caught it in front and in enfilade. A few moments afterwards a large body of Turks crept up quietly, threw a shower of bombs into the right of the 7th H.L.I., and rushed a portion of the position, Further to the left the 7th H.L.I. hung on, fighting the enemy with every available weapon. Pte. Jack, 7th H.L.I., was on the right of these men, and kept his Lewis gun in action all the time, helping materially to defend the remainder of his battalion's line. Those who had been driven off soon recovered from their surprise. Somebody put up a flare, and, in the glare that followed, Lt.-Col. Gibbons, who had had his revolver shot out of his hand, was seen to grab hold of a rifle, and, shouting to the rest to follow, charged up the hill. After him went the men of the 7th. A platoon also of the 6th H.L.I., led up by Sgt. A. Mackie, joined in the final rush with the bayonet. Not many of the Turks waited, and, only a few minutes after they had gained their footing on the ridge, they were driven off it again.

After this the Turks contented themselves by keeping up a brisk rifle and machine-gun fire, which caused more casualties before 3 a.m., when it died down. When this happened, patrols were at once sent out, and they found that the enemy had retired. The main ridge was then occupied, and to the south lay the great prize, the wells.

The tenacity of the 157th Brigade had been too great for this Turkish force. In spite of the latter's strong defensive position, and the cleverness with which it had fought this rearguard action, the Turks were forced to retire and allow the British advance to proceed.

The marching and fighting powers of the Turks are very great. Time and again, day after day, they would carry out a long march, fight a rearguard action, and then retreat again in the darkness, finding time to destroy all the water-lifting apparatus of the wells that they passed. Unfortunately for them, the powers of the British troops were greater, and the 52nd Division was now fairly in its stride, driving them in a few hours from a series of positions, which they had planned to hold for some days, if not indefinitely.

During the early morning following the action the Turkish artillery shelled the captured ridges for a while at long range, causing a few more casualties. The total losses of the 157th Brigade in this operation were as follows:

Unit.	Killed.		Wounded.		Total.	
	Officers.	O.R.	Officers.	O.R.	Officers.	O.R.
6th H.L.I.	—	—	—	2	—	2
7th H.L.I.	—	5	2	23	2	28
5th A. & S.H.	3	16	4	38	7	54
157th M.G. Coy.	—	1	1	3	1	4
	3	22	7	66	10	88

The three officers of the 5th Argylls who were killed were Lieut. J. Baxter, Lieut. J. S. D. Clarke, and Lieut. R. Harrison.

ESDUD OR BEIT DURAS

When we consider the issues at stake, these losses, apart from the officer casualties, cannot be considered proportionately heavy.

Thirty enemy dead, including a German officer, were found lying between the two ridges. None were found on or behind the main Turkish position, but there were bloodstains in plenty on the ground, and rifles, bayonets, and equipment were lying everywhere. Apart from this and what was told by the Turkish officer who was taken prisoner, we know nothing of the enemy's losses. Three machine-guns were captured by the 157th Brigade in this engagement, besides quantities of arms and stores. The greatest immediate prize was the water supply, but greater than that was the fact that the pursuit was now catching up with the enemy's main body.

All the wells in Esdud had to be condemned, but the Divisional Royal Engineers got to work very rapidly, and a "sump" which had been dug close to the sea provided a supply of comparatively pure water. A campaign is won by every branch of the service doing its part, and the Royal Engineers were not behind the others. The surface of the water in many of the wells which had to be used was over 100 feet below the ground level.

During the night of the 10-11th the weary 2nd Australian Light Horse Brigade and other cavalry had been withdrawn to water and rest at Kummam. To the left of the 157th Brigade was the 1st Australian Light Horse holding a thin outpost line that reached the sea. To the right of the 157th was a scattered screen of cavalry patrols. Behind, were the 156th Brigade at Mejdel, and the 155th at Herbieh, both preparing to move forward. The 75th Division had reached a point south of Mejdel. The remainder of the infantry divisions were being concentrated at Gaza and Karm, where, in order to save transportation, they could be supplied either direct from depots, or from a railhead. The cavalry, with the exception of a force watching the enemy in the mountains north of Beersheba, were preparing to continue the pursuit.

CHAPTER XXIII

(10TH TO 13TH NOVEMBER, 1917)

BURKAH AND BROWN HILL

We must follow with the convoy till the job is fully done,
Over sand-dune, scrub and wadi, 'neath a blazing noonday sun;
Over rock and stone and boulder, up the friendless pathless hill,
When the sweat runs cold and chilly 'neath the rain-drenched khaki drill.
We must follow through the darkness of a night that's black and blind;
We must search for dregs of humour where's there's not a drop to find.
The Song of the Camel Convoy:
CAPTAIN E. R. BOYD, 8th Cameronians.

ON 11th November " the enemy was beginning to show signs of recovery and made efforts to reconstruct his line of resistance, and make a front in hopes of maintaining control of the lateral line of communications along the railway from Ludd to Jerusalem. . . . The importance of a further advance, before the line could harden into a prepared front, is obvious." [1]

The success of a pursuit is dependent not only upon the valour and physical endurance of the troops, but also on the power to keep them furnished with ammunition, water, and food. In this, no division received better service at this crucial time than did the 52nd from all concerned, from Lt.-Col. J. S. Matthew, the Senior Supply Officer, with his staff, to the quartermasters, transport officers and their men. It must be remembered that the camels, and the men who accompanied them, usually had a double journey to make. When they had taken one set of supplies to their units,

[1] From the *Record of the Advance of the Egyptian Expeditionary Force.*

ASCALON

BURKAH AND BROWN HILL

they had to retrace their steps to the refilling point for the next load.

The effect that such services had on the campaign is shown by the following incident.

The Staff-Captain of the 157th Brigade was at the refilling point south of the mouth of the Wadi Hesi, on the morning of the 10th, when he received word that his brigade had set out for Esdud, " fifteen miles up, three miles inland." His supplies had not arrived, but he at once sent off the camels with the water, and they caught up to the 157th Brigade before it left camp.

His rations did not arrive until after dark, and it was 6 p.m. before his convoy was loaded up and moved off. The only maps available were one that ended at Burberah, and a small map of Palestine in a Bible. Somehow, he found his way through the labyrinth of sunken, sandy lanes and cactus hedges about Herbieh. He remarshalled his camels, and, working in the darkness by compass across a trackless country, had reached a point south of Burberah, when he saw an array of lights to the east. They were from a convoy of motor cars sent on by the Divisional Staff, who, concluding that the Staff-Captain could not possibly find his way, had collected these cars and loaded them up with supplies for the 157th Brigade. The D.A.Q.M.G., who was in charge, directed the Staff-Captain to the main track northward, and then pressed on with his own convoy.

The Staff-Captain followed on, but at 2 a.m. was told that the Egyptian drivers were dropping from fatigue. He halted, and, with the exception of the guard, everyone slept. At 4 a.m. he awoke, roused the convoy, and started off again. Only those who have had experience can know all that was entailed before those growling camels had been got on to their feet with readjusted loads. The Staff-Captain made up his mind not to halt again for anything until he reached his brigade.

The narrow lanes and streets of Mejdel were packed with Australians trying to water their horses and mules at a pool at the side of the road. The camels stampeded the mules, but the convoy got through complete. Mile succeeded mile of that sandy track. Day dawned, and the khamsin still blew with its fiery, blighting breath. At last, the Staff-Captain staggered into the camp of the 157th Brigade near Kummam. He reported to Brig.-Gen. Hamilton-Moore, and then collapsed. As a result, there were rations forward for two brigades, and it was possible for the 156th Brigade to advance and fight the battle described in this chapter, before the Turks had put one or two more days' work into their defences.

Two and a half miles over the flat, open, wadi-seamed plain to the north-east of Esdud lies the village of Burkah, a collection of cactus-hedged gardens and mud-huts, with ridges behind it to the north running east and west. About a mile to the east of Burkah, commanding that place and in a measure the approaches for Turkish reinforcements from the north, and at the same time dominating any approach from the south against the eastern side of it, lies a hill, conical in appearance from the south, and from its colour called Brown Hill. The occupation of Burkah would have to be coupled with the occupation of Brown Hill, and the capture of both would bring the British army a stage nearer its strategical objective, Junction Station. The information supplied to the Division was that both places were lightly held. Burkah was reported to be held by four hundred Turks with four guns, and Brown Hill by not more than a company.

The 156th Brigade, Brig.-Gen. A. H. Leggett, marched forward from Mejdel on the 11th, having picked up the 7th Cameronians, who had been occupying a defensive line to hold Ascalon. This brigade reached Esdud and Kummam by 3 p.m., after a trying march through most oppressive heat. Every man carried his pack and a blanket, besides extra small arms ammunition, his arms, etc., yet only seven men fell out on the line of march. The 156th Brigade took over the defences from the 157th Brigade soon after its arrival.

Orders were issued on the same day for the 156th Brigade to be clear of Esdud by 1 p.m., to move to Burkah, and there to develop the water supply.

BURKAH AND BROWN HILL

Throughout the 11th, enemy guns opened fire on any bodies of troops moving between Esdud and Kummam, and a reconnaissance in the afternoon by Brig.-Gen. Leggett of Burkah and Brown Hill disclosed that both places were held and entrenched. Two patrols of the Duke of Lancaster's Yeomanry, who had come up by this time and had been placed under the orders of the 156th Brigade, reconnoitred the positions at daybreak and reported that both places were not only held, but held strongly.

In point of fact, the positions were of great natural strength, and the Turks had entrenched them for a prolonged defence, because their loss meant the thrusting back of their right flank from the sea and a great lengthening of their line. Certainly, they expected to hold them until they had entrenched and reinforced their last line for the defence of Junction Station, which ran from El Kubeibe through Mughar and Katrah to Tel el Turmus and thence to Beit Jibrin in the hill-country. The cactus hedges of Burkah were natural entanglements and provided excellent cover for machine-guns and riflemen. Through the village, and extending along ridges for about a mile to the west, were two lines of trenches, known later as " A " and " B." These curved to the north-west to protect the Turkish right flank. Behind, following another ridge, lay a third line, also curving to the north-west, and with its eastern flank drawn back. Brown Hill, a mile to the east, was also entrenched. Afterwards, these positions were found to have been held by two or three thousand of the enemy, with about fifty machine-guns and several batteries of artillery. Between 500 and 600 Turks were on Brown Hill and the remainder about Burkah. These troops included some fresh units of the Yilderim Group, which had commenced to arrive about this time.

Brig.-Gen. Leggett delayed his advance until 11 a.m. in order that he might have the use of two 60-pounders, which Brig.-Gen. Massy had sent forward by caterpillar tractors, and that his officers might have ample time to examine the enemy defences, and to get into position for the attack. There were no troops available for him for an enveloping movement, so that the attacks on both positions had to be frontal. Brig.-Gen. Leggett divided his force as follows :

For the attack on Burkah :

7th R.S., 7th and 8th (three companies) Cameronians ;

Two 60-pounders, one battery 264th Brigade R.F.A. ; [1]

Three sections (twelve guns) 156th Machine-Gun Company.

This force was to operate from Esdud. The assault was under Lt.-Col. W. C. Peebles, and consisted of the 7th R.S., Major W. T. Ewing, and the three companies of the 8th Cameronians, Lt.-Col. J. M. Findlay, together with two machine-gun sections. It was to advance with its left slightly refused, in order to meet any counter-attack from the north. The 7th Cameronians, Lieut.-Col. J. G. P. Romanes, with four machine-guns were to establish themselves in reserve in the Wadi Mejma, about 2000 yards short of Burkah, as soon as the 7th R.S. and 8th Cameronians had cleared it.

For the attack on Brown Hill :

4th R.S., one company of 8th Cameronians as escort to artillery ;

Two batteries, 264th Brigade R.F.A. ; Hong Kong and Singapore Mountain Battery ; [2]

One section (four machine-guns) 156th Machine-Gun Company ;

One squadron (less one troop) Duke of Lancaster's Own Yeomanry.

This force was to operate from Kummam under Lt.-Col. A. M. Mitchell, 4th R.S. It was to advance with the other

[1] When this Brigade arrived at Esdud its horses had not been watered for forty-eight hours, and the watering parade at that place entailed a march of about five miles.

[2] The Hong Kong and Singapore Mountain Battery was one of the most ubiquitous and hard-working units in the army, and its history should make very interesting reading.

BURKAH AND BROWN HILL

force at 11 a.m., and, leaving the village of Butani on its left, was to attack Brown Hill from the south and southeast. Its outer or eastern flank was to be watched by Yeomanry.

Advancing, and echeloned to the right rear of the 52nd Division, was the 75th Division.

The attacks on Burkah and Brown Hill, although delivered simultaneously and forming one complete and co-ordinated movement, had to be carried out separately by distinct forces, and it is necessary for the sake of clearness to recount them separately.

Promptly at 11 a.m. both forces moved out in artillery formation from the wooded outskirts of Esdud, and from the ridges about Kummam. As they commenced to move over the flat coverless plain, they came under heavy shell-fire from several enemy batteries to the north. Fortunately, at the outset, the Turks burst their shrapnel too high. The British artillery opened fire on machine-gun positions and other targets situated on both enemy positions, but they were very short of ammunition owing to the difficulties of transportation, and had to try to make up for lack of volume by accuracy.

Col. Peebles' force advanced astride of the Burkah road with the 7th R.S. leading, and reached the Wadi Mejma with hardly any loss. After that, the enemy shell-fire became more effective, and with it came an accurate long-range rifle and machine-gun fire from the cactus enclosures of Burkah. The assault pressed on until it reached a shallow wadi about 400 yards south and south-west of the first position, " A." The Turkish defences had suffered very little from our shells, so that the attackers had to quell the enemy's fire themselves, and from this wadi they opened with machine-guns and rifles on the Turkish trenches. There now ensued the rattle of a fire-fight, in which the Royal Scots, Cameronians, and Machine-Gunners gradually gained the ascendancy over the Turkish defenders. The forward machine-guns managed to enfilade the enemy position by working round the flanks. The Turks were killed or driven from this " A " line, and it was taken at 2.45 p.m. The

Turkish snipers in the gardens and the artillery quickly turned their fire on the captured position.

The attacking troops were reorganized in some dead ground behind position " A." Enemy snipers were dislodged from cactus hedges on the right. Another fire-fight followed, and at 4 p.m. the line again went forward, carrying the " B " position.

Night was drawing on, and there remained the third position, " C," 800 yards away and the strongest of all. The Turks were defending it stubbornly. Three companies of the 7th Cameronians were sent forward to the right under Major Blair, and, although they had suffered many casualties, the Royal Scots and Cameronians prepared for their third assault. As darkness set in, they attacked, and after a short fierce bayonet struggle captured the last line. Reorganization of the troops and consolidation of the captured position was at once proceeded with, but the Turks had had enough. There was no counter-attack, and, with the exception of those actually on duty, officers and men, without any covering but their thin drill uniforms, could get what sleep was possible, in the bitter cold of the night that followed.

In the meantime, Lt.-Col. Mitchell's force had attacked Brown Hill. This force, owing to the heavy casualties which the 4th R.S. had already suffered, was given what was believed to be the least difficult objective.

Advancing in artillery formation, with one company echeloned back to protect the right flank, and with the artillery shelling Brown Hill, the 4th R.S. and Machine-Gunners by mid-day with very little loss had reached a wadi north of the village of El Butani.

From this point, which was about a mile from the enemy position, and onwards, fire of all kinds was opened on the advancing troops, and casualties became numerous. Most of the enemy artillery fire came from hills to the east of Brown Hill, so that their shrapnel swept across the numerous small columns of Royal Scots. To the left, they could see the remainder of the 156th Brigade, like themselves, moving steadily over the plain.

Capt. J. Gray, 4th R.S., was in command of the assault,

BURKAH AND BROWN HILL

and, by rushing his men forward in small parties at a time, he gathered them for the final advance in a wadi from eight to ten feet deep and three hundred yards from the foot of the hill.

At 3.30 p.m., under cover of fire from the four machine-guns and the artillery, the Royal Scots commenced to work their way forward, and to climb the hill. Three companies attacked to the front, and one moved to operate against the Turks' left flank. Many fell, but within half an hour they had fought their way to the top, rushed the enemy trenches, and captured two machine-guns, which they at once turned upon the retreating enemy. Unfortunately, both guns jammed after firing only a few rounds.

A few moments after they had taken the crest, the Royal Scots realised that, on the rather gentle reverse slope and within bombing distance of the captured trench, was a second line, untouched by the artillery, from which a hot fire was now being poured on them. Large Turkish reserves were hurried forward, and, at 4.20 p.m., enemy infantry, in overwhelming numbers, sallied out with bayonet and bomb to counter-attack those Royal Scots, who were left on the crest. There was bitter hand-to-hand fighting, but weight of numbers prevailed, and the Royal Scots were driven back, fighting, off the hill.

Meanwhile, 2nd Lieut. D. Noble, 156th Machine-Gun Company, brought his guns into the open, and gave effective covering fire, holding back the Turks from following up their success.

By this time every company officer of the Royal Scots but one junior had fallen. The remnant, however, gathered together in the wadi, from which they had made their first attack, and commenced to reorganize for a second attack under cover of the darkness, which was fast closing down.

In the meantime, the 2/3rd Gurkhas, a unit of the 232nd Brigade, 75th Division, had appeared to the south-east of Lt.-Col. Mitchell's headquarters. On hearing of what had happened, and knowing how few men he had left, he asked the O.C. of the Gurkhas for the help of one or two companies. The answer was prompt. Two companies were sent, and their arrival was greeted with a burst of cheering.

A difficulty now arose: these Gurkhas had lost every English-speaking officer. Fortunately, Capt. Bolton, one of the survivors of the assault, an Indian Civil Servant who had returned home to join up, could make himself understood. There were only sixty or seventy Royal Scots available, but they were mixed among the Gurkhas, and, pointing and directing in the darkness, showed them which way to go. The delight of the Gurkhas at the prospect of an attack in company with the " Jocks " was manifested in many ways, and all thoroughly understood each other, despite the blackness of the night, and the fact that neither could speak a single word of the others' language.

At 5.20 p.m. Royal Scots and Gurkhas, led by Capt. Bolton, made another attack on the hill, covered by the fire of artillery and machine-guns, the latter being brought to within 300 yards of the Turkish machine-guns entrenched on the hill. Within fifteen minutes the assaulting troops had scaled the height, and swept over the crest and beyond it, killing large numbers of the enemy and routing the remainder. The enemy poured in machine-gun fire, but did not counter-attack again. They now knew that more British troops, the 75th Division, were coming up on the right of the Division, and this, coupled with their losses, must have decided them that a further attempt to regain Brown Hill was hopeless. The casualties of the Gurkhas were almost nil in this advance, a great tribute to the effectiveness of the machine-gunners' and artillerymen's fire.

The losses of the 156th Brigade were heavy. Those who crossed the battlefield on the bright, clear day that followed, saw, here and there, many khaki-clad figures showing above the green grass, and the burial parties busily at work. The exact figures were as follows:

Unit.	Killed and Died of Wounds.		Wounded.		Total.	
	Officers.	O.R.	Officers.	O.R.	Officers.	O.R.
4th Royal Scots	3	49	4	157	7	206
7th Royal Scots	—	32	6	86	6	118
7th Cameronians	—	1	—	3	—	4
8th Cameronians	1	12	3	67	4	79
156th M.G. Coy.	—	—	1	5	1	5
	4	94	14	318	18	412

The officers who gave up their lives were as follows:
4th R.S., Capt. G. M. Clark, Lieuts. W. Dalgleish and
W. R. Robertson; 8th Cameronians, Lieut. R. S. Cree. The
4th R.S. had now lost over one half of its fighting strength
in the casualties of two battles. The gallant remnant of
this unit was relieved at about 7 p.m. by two companies
of the 6th H.L.I., who arrived in time to take part in the last
scuffling in the darkness, losing one man killed and another
wounded.

At Burkah, where the day was principally decided by
the efficiency in musketry of the 156th Brigade, 170
Turkish dead were found, although the whole area was not
searched. The enemy killed at both Burkah and Brown
Hill were estimated at over 300. The captures included
one officer and fifty-five other ranks. Of the latter twenty-
one were seriously wounded. There were also captured
three intact and two badly damaged machine-guns, a gun
limber, 200 rifles, 200 boxes of .77-mm. shell, and quantities of small arms ammunition, bombs, wagons, etc. The
Turkish casualties showed the value that they placed on
these positions, and the heaps of shell, which they were
compelled to leave behind, gave some indication of the
artillery that had been available for the defence.

This was much more than a rearguard action. The
156th Brigade, assisted at the last on the eastern flank by
the 75th Division, had broken down the right of the line
of advanced Turkish positions, and caused the enemy to
swing that flank back from the coast until their position ran
almost north and south. Because of this, the cavalry were
enabled to push their patrols forward almost to Beshshit, and
the 155th Brigade could carry the pursuit on the 13th up to
the last enemy line of defence for the railway, before it was
fully entrenched and consolidated. If a couple of regiments
of cavalry had been available to operate in conjunction with
the infantry, this action would probably have been turned
into a complete disaster for the Turkish western wing.

Strangely enough, Gen. Allenby only referred in his
official despatch to the operations of this day in the following
words : " The 12th was spent in preparations for the attack,

which was ordered to be begun early on the morning of the 13th, on the enemy's position covering Junction Station."

On this day the cavalry were hampered everywhere by the exhaustion of their horses on account of lack of water. Two brigades had to be withdrawn because of this, and, although they were replaced by others moving forward the mounted men were prevented from exercising their full strength and mobility. Col. Preston writes of this time as follows: "Had water been available in abundance throughout the advance, there is little doubt that our cavalry would have been able to overwhelm the retreating Turkish armies, and the capture of Jerusalem might have been accomplished by a rapid raid of mounted troops. As it was, each night was spent by a large part of the cavalry in a heart-breaking search for water, that too often proved fruitless, while the enemy, moving in his own country, utilized the hours of darkness to put such a distance between his troops and their pursuers as enabled him generally to entrench lightly before our cavalry came up with him in the morning."

On the day of this battle the cavalry on the right made a hard-fought advance, but eventually had to give up two or three miles of captured territory owing to a heavy counter-attack of fresh Turkish troops, directed, it is believed, personally by Marshal von Falkenhayn. On the extreme left the 1st Australian Light Horse forced the passage of the Nahr Sukerier at its mouth, securing a height, Tel el Murre, on its northern bank, and with it a temporary landing place for ammunition and other stores brought up the coast by trawlers. At this time the ammunition for the artillery had to be landed by surf boat at the mouth of the Hesi, and taken forward by motor traction to dumps where the limbers could be loaded. This difficulty accounted for most of the shortage of artillery support which so often threw the infantry almost entirely on their own resources. How serious this shortage was can be judged from the fact that at the close of this battle one battery of the 264th Brigade had only eight rounds left per gun. The capture of this new landing place for stores saved almost twenty miles of carriage for the over-strained land transport service.

The Turks were to be allowed no rest. The 155th Brigade had left Mejdel on the day of this battle, and at 1 p.m. had reached Esdud after a very hot march. Inland, the men could see the conflict of the 156th Brigade. Packs were discarded, and at 7 p.m. the 155th Brigade was off again northwards in the darkness along a track which led to Yebnah, the Jamnia of the New Testament period and the Ibelin of the Crusades. After proceeding six miles, the 155th Brigade passed through the cavalry screen, which reported having had to retire owing to the strength of the enemy rearguards. The South Scottish Brigade, however, went on. Its objective was a point on the map west of Beshshit, but in a moonless night there was nothing by which to distinguish it. Moving, by sending forward its advance guard 1000 yards at a time and then closing up the main body, the Brigade advanced another eight miles. At 1.35 a.m. it halted, dug in, and lay down blanketless in the intensely cold night. The whole distance had been paced by Capt. A. K. Ramsay, 5th R.S.F., and, when morning dawned, it was found that the Brigade was within 400 yards of its exact destination. Brig.-Gen. Pollok-M'Call's orders were to take Beshshit, Katrah, and Mughar; for the direction of the advance was now to change towards the east where the mountains held Jerusalem in their midst.

CHAPTER XXIV

(13TH TO 16TH NOVEMBER, 1917)

MUGHAR AND KATRAH

> Little know you of the hearts I have hidden here;
> Little know you of our moss-troopers' might—
>   Linhope and Sorbie true,
>   Sundhope and Milburn too,
> Gentle in manner, but lions in fight!
>   *Lock the Door, Lariston :* JAMES HOGG.

THE Turkish position covering the railway ran due south from El Kubeibe, through Zernuka, Mughar, and Katrah to Tel el Turmus, whence it ran south-east through Balin and Berkusie to Beit Jibrin. This position had been dictated to the Turk " by the rapidity of our movement along the coast, and the determination with which his rearguards on this flank had been pressed " (Gen. Allenby).

Mughar and Katrah, at the centre of the northern wing of this position, are within six miles of the railway north of Junction Station. The intervening country is not as difficult for an advance as that which lies between Junction Station and Balin, Berkusie, and Beit Jebrin on the southern wing. The capture of Mughar and Katrah would not only place this railway at the mercy of the British, but would certainly entail the collapse of the whole Turkish line to the south, a line on which the Turks had already resisted the cavalry with success. The enemy knew this and prepared to fight accordingly.

The country, through which ran the northern and central portions of this Turkish position, consists mainly of an undulating, treeless plain, out of which, here and there,

MUGHAR AND KATRAH

rise ridges and isolated hills. It is fairly populous, and the villages are usually perched on low, rocky hills. Each collection of huts and houses, some of the latter quite modern, is surrounded by strong mud walls, palm and other trees, gardens, and extensive cactus hedges, and forms a ready-made fortress for machine-gun defence. The Turkish position ran along a line of these ridges and isolated village-crowned hills. The whole plain around is cultivated, but at this time of the year was absolutely bare, the crops having already been gathered. These excellent fields of fire gave an immense advantage to the Turks, and it seemed as if only a prolonged bombardment by heavy artillery could drive them out.

At hand to defend this line, which was about twenty miles long, the Turks probably had only 20,000 rifles, but many of these were entirely fresh troops; they had the advantage of interior lines of communication with a railway, and were fighting on the defensive.

Immediately available for the work of driving them out, Gen. Allenby had two divisions of infantry, the 52nd and 75th, and three of cavalry, the Yeomanry, Australian, and Australian and New Zealand Divisions. Of these five, the first and last two had already suffered heavy casualties. Moreover, the British had to attack, and at the end of long and difficult communications.

It was decided to attack at once before another Gaza position could be made, and the honour of making the principal assault, that on Mughar and Katrah, fell to the 52nd Division because of its advanced position. On its left the Australian and New Zealand and Yeomanry Divisions were to operate, and to its right the 75th Division was to attack El Mesmiye, the last with its right flank protected by the Australian Mounted Division.

Major-Gen. Hill sent the following message to his Division on the morning of the battle: "The Divisional Commander wishes all ranks to be informed that to-day, 13th inst., will be the decisive day of the war as far as Turkey is concerned, and that, hardly as everyone has been tried, we have got to make a superhuman effort to-day.

The Commander-in-Chief intends to seize the Jaffa-Jerusalem Railway . . ."

After a hurried breakfast on the morning of the 13th, the 155th Brigade, Brig.-Gen. J. B. Pollok-M'Call, moved out from its bivouac to attack Beshshit, with the 5th K.O.S.B. echeloned on the left flank to watch for a counter-attack. On the same flank were thirty sabres of the Duke of Lancaster's Yeomanry, with instructions to get in touch with the Yeomanry Division as soon as they appeared. The latter were to seize Yebnah, a village on the west side of the Wadi Janus, and opposite to the extreme northern flank of the Turks. After occupying Yebnah, the Yeomanry Division was to continue its advance and seize the village of Akir behind and to the north-east of Mughar, the railway north of Junction Station being the final objective. The Yeomanry drove the Turkish snipers out of Yebnah at 8 a.m., but further progress by them to the east was held up by the machine-guns of the Turkish northern flank, and they came to a standstill.

The 156th Brigade, Brig.-Gen. A. H. Leggett, and 157th Brigade, Brig.-Gen. C. D. Hamilton-Moore, were also on the move, the former for Beshshit whence they were to proceed to garrison Mughar and Katrah after their capture, and the latter to occupy Yebnah and to cover the northern flank of the advance.

The village of Beshshit lies on a slight rise about a mile and a half to the westward of Katrah and Mughar, giving an uninterrupted view of both places. After a march of about two miles, it was occupied at 9.30 a.m. by the 5th R.S.F., practically without opposition, eighteen wounded and six unwounded prisoners being taken. Major-Gen. Hill arrived at this point, and, after a brief consultation with Brig.-Gen. Pollok-M'Call, ordered the 155th Brigade to attack Katrah and Mughar simultaneously, in order to prevent the one sending reinforcements to the other.

These two villages, with their red and white roofs peeping through acres of trees and cactus, stand about a mile apart, each on a knoll which rises abruptly from the surrounding plain. Between them runs a low ridge cut by the Wadi Janus, the Scriptural Brook Kedron, which runs to the north-west, in front of Mughar. To the south of Katrah are more ridges and knolls. The height on which Mughar stands is continued for several miles to the north-east by a long range of low ridges and hills, which spread out further north until they reach Zernukah and El Kubeibeh, the extreme Turkish right. The plain which lay between the 155th Brigade and Mughar was a dead level of black cotton soil. Before Katrah the ground was of a rolling character, affording some slight cover against an approaching enemy. Everywhere it was quite open, but intersected by numerous wadis, tributaries of the Janus. This section of the Turkish position had a frontage of 4700 yards, and the Turks could be seen feverishly entrenching in front of the villages and on the ridges. It was afterwards found that the Turkish garrison for this position numbered about 3000, with two batteries of artillery and at least fifty machine-guns.

The 4th K.O.S.B., Lt.-Col. R. Dashwood-Tandy, was ordered to attack Mughar, and the 5th R.S.F., Lt.-Col. J. B. Cook, to attack Katrah. The 5th K.O.S.B., Lt.-Col. A. H. C. Kearsey, was to be prepared to assist either and also to watch the left rear of the Mughar attack, as it was still uncertain whether the Yeomanry Division would get far enough forward from Yebnah to cover that flank. The 4th R.S.F., Major J. Bruce, was moved up to Beshshit in brigade reserve.

It was a beautiful sunny morning, and in the eastern distance " the Judean hills with their steep defiles, rocky spurs and deep re-entrants stood out in all the grandeur of dancing sunlight and deepest shade" (Capt. E. R. Boyd). Nearer at hand "on the surrounding hillsides sheep and goats could be seen grazing and birds were whistling. Everything appeared so calm, and it was difficult to believe we were about to be engaged in battle." (Capt. J. S. Allan.)

A battery of the 261st Brigade, R.F.A., moved up to cover the advance, and the assaulting battalions went forward in artillery formation. There was little enough artillery and machine-gun support available for the attack on even one village, and, throughout the battle, most of it was given to the operations against Katrah, because the Division was hourly expecting the Yeomanry Division to support the attack on Mughar with an outflanking movement to the north against Aku.

Although the attacks on Mughar and Katrah formed part of the one battle it will be convenient to describe them separately.

After a very short interval of time the 5th R.S.F. was advancing towards the southern portion of the Katrah position. Covering fire was given from six guns of the 155th Machine-Gun Company. As the battalion moved forward, three enemy columns were seen to leave the village and make towards the high ridges to the south to oppose this attack. These were fired on by our artillery, but apparently reached their destination without great loss.

As the Fusiliers topped a ridge within 1500 yards of Katrah, the place, which hitherto had been fairly quiet, burst into life, and a heavy rifle and machine-gun fire was turned on them. Their small columns at once deployed into extended order. When the Fusiliers got nearer, it was seen that the ridges south of Katrah were strongly held, and that they were guarded by broken ground, a sunken road, and cactus hedges. From north to south the cactus-hedged enclosures of Katrah extended for almost a mile, and this great area had to be attacked by this single battalion with very little artillery support, because of the shortage of ammunition. Further south, the country had fewer obstacles, but it was very bare and had no dead ground.

The Turkish artillery had now joined in, and the enemy, who were far more numerous than the Fusiliers, moved out from Katrah at 10.30 a.m. to counter-attack. The 5th R.S.F. reinforced their firing line with their reserve company and the Turks were driven back.

Major R. W. Paton, 5th R.S.F., now pushed forward and well out to the right with four Lewis guns. He got these into a position from which they enfiladed the first ridge held by the Turks, felling many of them, and driving the survivors through the cactus and low trees to the slopes of the higher ridge behind, where they came under fire of the 155th Company's machine-guns. This enabled the whole firing line on the right to advance, until at 11.30 a.m. it had reached a wadi 800 yards from the main Turkish position.

An outflanking movement to the right was then attempted with two companies of the 4th R.S.F., whilst another company reinforced the firing line. The two companies made too short a circuit, and only extended the right of the firing line, failing in their main object. About 11 a.m., when there was only one company of the 4th R.S.F. left in reserve, thick columns of Turkish reinforcements could be seen arriving, and the Fusiliers, who were outnumbered and had lost heavily, could make little headway. Nevertheless, the accurate fire of the Ayrshire men prevented the Turks from counter-attacking.

About 1 p.m. Major R. W. Paton crept forward again with his Lewis guns, and an hour later, under cover of their fire, the centre and right of the Fusiliers got within 600 yards of the enemy position, and the left into the cactus gardens within 400 yards of Katrah. However, they were too weak to advance further into the close country without support of some kind.

Lt.-Col. J. Young, whose command, the 1/3rd Lowland Field Ambulance, had its advanced station working at this time at Beshshit, writes as follows: " During the fight at Katrah, as we watched it from the higher ground, there were two incidents which we saw and remembered. Walking up the village street a man could be seen in the distance, in the middle of the fight, with a metal piece of the equipment on his back flashing in the sun. Unhurried and apparently unconcerned, he continued on his way as if nothing was amiss. As we watched, also, we could every now and then see a window on the right of the village thrown up and a machine-gun commence to fire on our advancing troops. It was all deliberate. The window was lifted, the gun was placed and fired. Just as deliberately the gun was removed, the window was closed, and the man disappeared. It was a supreme piece of gallant bravado, with a strong element of humour. Later on we found the window, and were not surprised that the house walls were riddled through and through with our bullets."

The German and Turkish machine-gunners, in an endeavour to command the whole area, had their guns placed, if anything, at too high an altitude, with the result that most of their fire was plunging into, instead of sweeping over the flat surface of the ground.

We must now leave the Fusiliers pressing hard against Katrah, but held off by the superior numbers of the enemy, and follow the fortunes of the Borderers before Mughar.

In eight waves of men, the 4th K.O.S.B. advanced towards the gardens and village on its hill. A short while after 10 a.m. a sudden and dramatic change was wrought upon the calm of the morning. The Turks opened a heavy and accurate machine-gun fire, and poured shrapnel and H.E. over the advancing lines. Everywhere, the bullets threw up clouds of dust, and men began to fall. With short dashes, the 4th K.O.S.B. pushed forward, until they had got within 400 yards of the edge of the gardens, reaching the Wadi Shellal el Ghor near an old well, Khurbet Hebra, a ruin with a garden, and an advanced part of the Wadi Janus. Before them lay a perfectly open level stretch, beyond which were acres of thick cactus hedges hiding hundreds of Turkish riflemen and several dozens of machine-guns. Thirty of the latter were captured later in this position and others must have been got away by the enemy. These guns lashed the whole front of the Borderers with a terrific barrage. The 4th K.O.S.B. had lost heavily and could get no further.

As in the case of the Fusiliers, there ensued long hours of fighting. The ground was hard, and it was almost impossible to dig cover. Shortly after mid-day three companies of the 5th K.O.S.B. reinforced the firing line, and the fourth tried to work along the Wadi Janus to attack Mughar from the south. This watercourse, it will be remembered, ran into the Turkish line between the two villages, and the enemy effectually barred it with their

MUGHAR AND KATRAH 419

fire so that the fourth company was also held up, and could only extend the firing line.

This was the most critical time in the whole battle. Many Borderers had fallen. The Fusiliers could make very little progress against Katrah, and there was still no sign of the Yeomanry Division carrying out its outflanking movement to the north of Mughar.

About 1 p.m. Major-Gen. Hill had a consultation with Brig.-Gen. Pollok-M'Call, and arranged for as heavy an artillery bombardment as was possible on Katrah from 3.30 p.m. to 3.45 p.m., to be followed by a general assault on both villages. He then motored to the Yeomanry Headquarters, where it was arranged that the 6th Mounted Brigade should make a charge against the Turkish right. It was to be an assault of both cavalry and infantry over the entire front on the whole Mughar and Katrah position.

Behind the enemy position lay a flat plain, ideal ground for the operations of cavalry and artillery against a retreating enemy, and this the Turks knew. If this, their last position guarding the railway, fell, wide and irrevocable disaster was certain. This explains the desperation with which many of the enemy fought, and especially their machine-gunners.

Meanwhile, Brig.-Gen. Pollok-M'Call had issued orders for the last company of 4th R.S.F. to make another flanking movement against the south of Katrah, and for the assault on that place to be made. He then made his way to the wadis where the Borderers, who had now pushed every available man, including the headquarters staffs of the two battalions, into the firing line, were doing all that was possible to reply to the Turkish fire. As soon as he arrived he proceeded to reorganize the firing line, ready for the moment of the assault on which so much depended.

Then the Berks Battery, R.H.A., and a Machine-Gun Squadron of the Yeomanry came into action against Mughar, the former from amidst the trees north of Beshshit and the latter from the Wadi el Ghor. About 3 p.m. the Berks, Bucks, and Dorset Yeomanry were seen galloping with almost perfectly ordered lines across the two miles of plain, which lay between them and Mughar and its ridges to the north. This was the signal for the guns of both sides to open up a heavy fire.

For a few moments the charging cavalry drew the fire of the machine-guns about Mughar and its ridges to the north, and their advance was noticed to swerve slightly to the left. Seizing the opportunity, Brig.-Gen. Pollok-M'Call snatched up a rifle and bayonet, shouted to the Borderers to follow him, and dashed out into the open. Here, there and everywhere, the Borderers, shouting and cheering, jumped out, and there ensued a wild but steady advance in lines across the open for the gardens of Mughar.

The Brigade Commander led his men all the way, a bullet piercing his shrapnel helmet. Wounded men were carried forward by the enthusiasm of that charge. Officers and men fell on all sides, but in a few seconds they were through the plunging machine-gun barrage, had crossed a gully, and were racing breathless for the cactus hedges in front. To the left, the lines of Bucks and Berks Yeomanry with swords flashing were galloping up the ridges north of Mughar. Further north still the Dorset Yeomanry had dismounted and were attacking a ridge on foot. The plain resounded with the chattering of machine-guns.

By 3.30 p.m. the Yeomanry had captured the ridges north of Mughar, and the Borderers had hacked or found gaps in the cactus hedges and were fighting their way through the belt of gardens. Fighting in close country is always exciting. Ranges are point blank, and it is the man who sees his opponent first, who gets in the first shot or first bayonet thrust. Capt. J. S. Allan, 4th K.O.S.B., relates how " after crossing the gully a party of us doubled forward to a cactus hedge at the foot of one of the village gardens, and opened fire on the Turks, who were ensconced at the top of the garden, and it was at this time that Lieut. Wood was killed. Capt. Nimmo was again wounded, this time very badly. Lieut. Graham was wounded in the leg, and while lying on the ground was again wounded in the shoulder. Lieut. Ross was also wounded in the leg, and I was wounded in the arm ... all these casualties occurring in quick succession as the result of rifle or machine-gun fire. At this time Private Fox of 'D' Company fell mortally wounded, and whilst endeavouring to bandage his wound he spoke to me with his last breath ... one of the many touching incidents that occurred amidst the roar of battle, and one that I shall never forget."

Lewis guns proved of immense value as weapons of opportunity against enemy machine-guns. The Turkish defence collapsed. In different places, parties of Borderers were driving the Turks through the village, and taking prisoners right and left. Capt. Laing, R.S.M. Murray, Lance-Cpl. Ramsay, and three privates, all of the 4th K.O.S.B., caught about forty Turks, including an officer, hiding in a quarry. They had thrown away their rifles and surrendered in a body.

As the Borderers were fighting their way into the village from the west, two squadrons of the Berks Yeomanry had galloped from the captured ridges, and were fighting their way in from the north on foot. Borderers and Yeomen met within the village, and the battle here was decided. The Borderers had already taken between 300 and 400 prisoners, besides artillery and machine-guns, and these they handed over to the Berks Yeomen, who, as mounted men, could take them back more easily. Some Turks were still putting up a stiff fight in different places, and these the Borderers hunted down. Before 5 p.m. the victory was complete, and before sunset the village was consolidated.

As the Turks tried to retire, they were caught by the machine-guns of the Yeomen on the ridges to the north, and the plain was covered with their dead. Darkness alone saved them from annihilation.

Meanwhile, the Royal Scots Fusiliers had captured Katrah. From 3.30 p.m. until 3.45 p.m. the guns of the 261st and 264th Brigades, together with a mountain battery which had arrived, poured every shell that they could into Katrah, while the 155th machine-guns searched its hedges and thickets. At the same time, Capt. H. E. Sutherland, 4th R.S.F., led the fourth company of his battalion in another attempt to outflank the Turks from the south. He was determined to make a proper detour, and led the way a considerable distance ahead of his men. With him were a Lewis gunner with a single drum of ammunition, and a grenadier with only two bombs. Sutherland moved rapidly over the ridges, and struck the end of a trench filled with Turks which marked the end of their support line. The Lewis gunner emptied his only drum into them, the grenadier threw his two bombs, and nine Turkish officers with sixty-four other ranks surrendered to these three Fusiliers. The company closed up, and, having seen the prisoners under guard, Capt. Sutherland continued his attack on the Turkish left.

At the same time, the main body of the 4th and 5th R.S.F. had been closing in for the final rush. The shell-fire of the artillery was most effective, causing many casualties, and the Turks, who hitherto had been well concealed, were obviously becoming restless.

At 3.45 p.m., as the Borderers were fighting their way through the cactus hedges of Mughar, the Royal Scots Fusiliers, under Lt.-Col. J. B. Cook, rose up and went forward steadily and boldly to storm Katrah. Again, there were many casualties. Lieut. George M'Quaker, 4th R.S.F., fell mortally wounded, but continued to urge on his comrades as he lay dying on the ground. Although the Turks were in superior numbers the sight of the advancing bayonets was too great an ordeal for them. Their spirit broke, and all but their machine-gunners commenced to retire. Some of the latter remained firing their guns until they were shot down at point blank range. Large bodies of the enemy in front of cactus hedges could not get away, and surrendered *en masse*. Others, who had a clear road were pursued by all kinds of fire, and the road was littered with the bodies of their killed and wounded. The Fusiliers burst through the Turkish defences at a salient at the south-east corner of their line, where a track led through the orchards. The Ayrshire men carried all before them, swept through the village, cleared the houses, and by 4.48 p.m. the whole of the Katrah plateau was in their hands, with eight machine-guns and about 400 prisoners. Patrols

MUGHAR AND KATRAH 423

were immediately pushed through the village to the plain on the other side.[1]

The outflanking company of the 4th R.S.F. attempted a pursuit, but the Turks took up a position on high ground further east and held it off. However, two of the machine-guns captured in the village were turned on the retreating masses. Soon afterwards, the sun sank, and darkness enshrouded the plain with its fleeing Turks, pursuing Yeomen, and Lowland stretcher-bearers busily at work.

As soon as Mughar had been captured by the Borderers and Yeomanry, the 22nd Mounted Brigade rode forwards to attack Akir, the original objective of the cavalry, " but was held up till nightfall by unexpectedly strong enemy opposition. The Brigade rounded up seventy prisoners and a few machine-guns retiring from El Mughar " (Col. Preston).

Including reinforcements, the Turkish force holding the Katrah–Mughar position had totalled 5000 men. Their casualties were severe. Their dead were never fully counted, because of the extent of the cactus-hedged orchards and the plains across which they fled, but we know that 400 Turks were buried by the 155th Brigade about Katrah and Mughar, where a large number had been killed by shell-fire. At least 200 were killed by the Yeomen when

[1] Lt.-Col. R. M. P. Preston makes some curious blunders with regard to this battle in his book, *The Desert Mounted Corps*. He states that the 155th Brigade first captured Katrah, and then advanced on Mughar, but were held up by enemy machine-guns and riflemen. In his diagram illustrating the action at the time of the cavalry charge, he places the 155th Brigade almost entirely within what were the Turkish lines at the time, the right of the Brigade being shown as lying behind what was really the right rear of the Katrah section of the Turkish position. He ascribes the actual capture of Mughar entirely to the action of the Yeomanry Division, and makes no mention of the charge of the Borderers. Actually, the two places were attacked and captured almost simultaneously by the joint action of the cavalry and infantry. The writer's account of the 52nd Division's action is based on the official operation report of the brigade chiefly concerned, besides the reports of many responsible eye-witnesses. In works of little standing these mistakes could be ignored, but in a work of such authority and undoubted excellence as Col. Preston's attention must be called to them. The scope of his book is very great, and, where even the most careful of writers have not got all possible evidence before them, such errors are bound to occur. May the writer take this opportunity to bear testimony to the many generous tributes that Col. Preston pays in his book to the work of the infantry in this campaign.

they captured the ridges. How many lay hidden in the orchards, or littered the plain, slain by artillery, machine-guns, rifles, and sabres in the pursuit, we do not know. 1096 prisoners were taken by the Yeomanry and Borderers in Mughar and on the ridges to the north. About 400 were taken by the Royal Scots Fusiliers in the Katrah position. 70 were taken by the Yeomanry in the rout which followed. This made about 1500 in all, divided evenly between the cavalry and infantry.

Altogether, thirty machine-guns and two field guns were taken in and about Mughar, and eight machine-guns at Katrah. General Kress von Kressenstein is believed to have galloped out of Katrah half an hour before the R.S.F. entered, taking most of his artillery with him. Another field gun and two machine-guns were taken at Akir by the Yeomanry on the next morning. The ammunition and supplies captured were very great, and the shells were made use of later on in the campaign when General Allenby turned the captured artillery on positions of the enemy.

The northern wing of the Turkish army had been smashed, and only disorganized fragments remained. After nightfall their extreme right evacuated El Kubeibeh and Zernuka, and retired in considerable confusion. This disaster to the Turks was brought about by the magnificent charge of the English Yeomanry, King's Own Scottish Borderers, and Royal Scots Fusiliers. The dash of the cavalry for the ridges to the north shook the morale of the whole Turkish defence, and the infantry, after bearing the burden and heat of the day, were the principal factor in sweeping the Turks from their main positions of Mughar and Katrah.

General Allenby commented on this battle in his official despatch as follows :—" This Katrah–El Mughar line forms a very strong position, and it was here that the enemy made his most determined resistance against the turning movement directed against his right flank. The capture of this position by the 52nd (Lowland) Division, assisted by a most dashing charge of mounted troops, who galloped across the plain under heavy fire and turned the enemy's position from the north, was a fine feat of arms."

MUGHAR AND KATRAH

The losses of the 155th Brigade in this battle were as follows:

Unit.	Killed and Died of Wounds.		Wounded.		Total.	
	Officers.	O.R.	Officers.	O.R.	Officers.	O.R.
4th R.S.F.	1	19	5	61	6	80
5th R.S.F.	—	15	2	64	2	79
4th K.O.S.B.	4	31	9	138	13	169
5th K.O.S.B.	1	20	2	110	3	130
	6	85	18	373	24	458

These were heavy losses for a brigade already much below strength—the 5th R.S.F. was less than 500 strong when the battle commenced—and the severity of the fighting for Mughar is evident, the Borderers losing half of their officers and one-third of their men. The officers of the 155th Brigade, who gave up their lives on this day, were as follows:—4th R.S.F., 2nd Lieut. G. W. M'Quaker; 4th K.O.S.B., Captain and Adjutant J. M. Watson, Captain A. P. Nimmo, 2nd Lieut. L. D. Robertson, 2nd Lieut. J. Wood; 5th K.O.S.B., 2nd Lieut. J. Kerr.

The two regiments of Yeomanry that were engaged lost a total of 129 all ranks, the heaviest losses falling on the squadron which had dismounted and stormed its objective on foot.

Further south on this day, the 75th Division had captured El Mesmujeh, and pushed on to Kh. el Mugharah on the southern railway line, taking 292 prisoners and seven machine-guns. It was strongly counter-attacked during the night by the Turks covering Junction Station less than two miles to the east.

The Turkish line to the south-east had now collapsed everywhere, and their forces retired during the night in two different directions, eastward for the hills, and northward astride the railway towards the waters of the perennial River Auja.

There still remained the actual cutting of the railway communications of Jerusalem with the north. This was accomplished through the gallantry of Lt.-Col. B. I. Rolling, 412th Field Company, R.E. Early in the morning he rode out with two others far ahead of the mounted troops, reached the railway north of Junction Station, and blew it up, preventing the enemy saving any of their rolling-stock to the south. The troops at Katrah saw the last enemy train steam out of Junction Station, and shortly afterwards saw the clouds of smoke and heard the sound of Lt.-Col. Rolling's explosion. Soon after daybreak Brig.-Gen. C. D. Hamilton-Moore had left the 5th and 6th H.L.I. holding Yebnah, and was on the move with a composite force, aiming for Mansurah about two miles north of Junction Station. This force was composed of the 7th and 8th Cameronians, 7th H.L.I. and 5th Argylls, besides batteries from the 261st, 262nd, and 264th Brigades, R.F.A., heavy guns, Royal Engineers, and Corps cavalry. Motors and horses, however, can move much faster than infantry. British armoured cars dashed into Junction Station early in the morning, killed and wounded half of a crowd of 400 Turks who were setting fire to the buildings, scattered the remainder, and captured the place. Further north, the Yeomanry Division pushed on through Akir to Naane, north of Mansurah, and Australian cavalry seized El Tine Station to the south of Junction Station. The Turks were thoroughly demoralized from their defeat of the previous day, and Brig.-Gen. Hamilton-Moore's force occupied Mansurah without opposition, beyond a little long-range rifle-fire and a heavy shelling from Abu Shusheh in the hills to the east. Apart from about a dozen men wounded, the composite brigade escaped casualties, and this was due to its excellent artillery formation, which was the subject of comment among the cavalry who witnessed its advance over the plain.

The 75th Division entered Junction Station shortly after the armoured cars.

Of the situation on 14th November, Gen. Allenby writes : " The enemy's army had now broken into two separate parts, which retired north and east respectively, and were reported to consist of small scattered groups rather than formed bodies of any size." The cavalry pursued the enemy into the hills and towards the Plain of Sharon, fighting a series of brilliant actions, whilst the Turks, true to their

MUGHAR AND KATRAH

character, turned and counter-attacked whenever they could. By the evening of the 16th, Jaffa, Ludd, and Ramleh were in British hands, and the two sections of the Turkish army were cut off from each other by a tract of mountainous country, whose numerous and deep valleys and gorges, and almost complete absence of practicable tracks made inter-communication and co-operation difficult in the extreme. The Turks about Jerusalem were at the dead end of a narrow-gauge railway, and the only good road connecting them with their army on the coastal plain ran north over the mountains for about forty-five miles, through Nablus (Shechem), before it reached the railway at Messudiyeh and with it dropped down in a detour to the Auja, over twenty-five miles away to the south. The nearest point on the Hedjaz railway east of Jerusalem, Amman, was separated from the Holy City by the deep Jordan Valley and sixty miles of difficult roads.

The Division had played a leading part in this campaign. Advancing at times ahead even of the screen of cavalry scouts, they had driven back the Turkish right, smiting it repeatedly, and finally, with the cavalry, had dealt the last blow which had shattered it altogether. "The 52nd (Lowland) Division had covered sixty-nine miles in this period" (Gen. Allenby). This had been done in great heat and over bad roads in a week, during which it had fought the enemy for four nights and three days. In less than a fortnight the Division had fought five actions, four of them mainly by night, and every brigade had gone twice into the assault, usually at the end of a long march.

Gen. Allenby estimated that, during this great advance from Gaza to Beersheba and Jaffa, his army had inflicted " losses amounting to nearly two-thirds of the enemy's original effectives. Over 9000 prisoners, about eighty guns, more than a hundred machine-guns, and other stores had been captured."

The Turks, however, were hurrying reinforcements southwards to Jerusalem and the coastal plain. Gen. Allenby's army was now on two sides of a vast hill fortress, which could soon be made impregnable, and from the valleys of which, as soon as the defence was organized, the enemy would be able to issue, attacking him where they choose. Before they could complete their defences he must capture this mountain system on his flank, and with it would go the great prize, Jerusalem. Because of the wild mountainous nature of the country, infantry would have to do most of the work, and the only infantry immediately available were the 52nd and 75th Divisions.

During the past fortnight its strength had been reduced by rather more than one-third, and with these thinned ranks and practically no rest, the Division was now to set its face towards the hills and the great goal of the Crusaders.

CHAPTER XXV

(17TH TO 27TH NOVEMBER, 1917)

NEBI SAMWIL AND EL JIB

> For you fought like devils, your only rivals,
> When you were at Dunkeld, boys!
>> From an old Jacobite song, addressed to the Cameronians, and written after the Battle of Dunkeld, 1689.

AFTER the capture of Junction Station there ensued a delay of a few days, whilst Gen. Allenby manœuvred his troops into position for the thrust into the Judaean Highlands. This, it was hoped, would cut the communications of Jerusalem with the north before the enemy could recover from their demoralization, and force them to evacuate the Holy City without any fighting in its immediate vicinity. During this period the Australian and New Zealand cavalry pushed the broken enemy in the coastal sector, back to the line of the Auja, whilst the Yeomanry on the north-east penetrated into the hill-country within two miles of Beit Ur el Tahta (Lower Bethhoron). The 54th Division marched up to Yebnah and Kh. Surafend behind Ramleh, their presence so far north of railhead greatly increasing the strain on the transport organization. The 60th Division, which, owing to transport difficulties, was still in the Gaza area, now made ready to follow. The Turks holding El Dhaheriye on the Beersheba–Jerusalem Road fell back, because of the tactical pressure of the advance along the coast, to Hebron on the 3000 feet contour.

Up to the 18th the Division was disposed as follows: the 155th about Katrah, the 156th between Akir and

Mansurah, and the 157th about Yebnah. Steps were taken to disarm the inhabitants, and, by fixing prices, to prevent them from taking advantage of the mild rule of Britain by profiteering out of her soldiers. The effect of the reading of the proclamation at Akir (Ekron of the Philistines) is thus described by Capt. E. R. Boyd : " During the succeeding hour there was a constant stream of villagers making their way to the verandah at Battalion Headquarters (8th Cameronians) carrying the most weird assortment of weapons and firearms. There were ancient Arab sabres with ivory handles, smaller swords and daggers, long Arab blunderbusses, rough leather belts filled with ancient and villainous blunt-nosed cartridges, spare parts of machine-guns, excellent automatic revolvers, long pistols with carved handles and hammer action, modern shot guns, a gunsmith's appliances for the manufacture of cartridges, thousands of rounds of ammunition, and countless other weapons of all dates from barbaric times to the present day." The *History 5th H.L.I.* contains the following shrewd remark with regard to the surrenders that took place at Yebnah : " Of modern rifles, Turkish or British, there was none. They were probably too deeply buried to be dug up at half an hour's notice."

On the 18th the 156th and 157th Brigades were moved to Ramleh and thence to Ludd, the ancient Lydda, the burial place of St. George. They marched over a road which was simply a track covered with black dust, and which was strewn with the jetsam of the retreating Turks. The 155th Brigade reached Ramleh on the same day. During the march of the first two brigades to Ludd, which was completed in darkness over a road literally packed with troops and transport, the weather turned very cold and rain began to fall, transforming the whole countryside into a black morass. Some battalions had actually to bivouac on the road itself. After their long sojourn in great heat, all felt the cold severely, but, nevertheless, the wearied troops slept.

At Ramleh the Division had crossed the first metalled road it had seen since it left Kantara. This was the main highway from Jaffa to Jerusalem, but the Division was not to

NEBI SAMWIL AND EL JIB

make use of it for its forthcoming advance eastwards. A " Roman Road " from Ludd to Jerusalem was marked on the map three or four miles north of this highway, and this was most misleading, for the road did not exist, and only at isolated points could one find signs that it ever had existed. Yet this was the route to be followed by the 52nd Division, and it consisted almost entirely of the open hillsides, covered with outcrops of rock and strewn with boulders over their entire area. There was no continuous ridge for it to follow, but only a series of terraced limestone heights, gradually increasing in altitude, with deep saddles or cols between them.

Parallel with the 52nd Division and to the south of it, the 75th Division was to advance by the metalled road from Jaffa to Jerusalem. This Division consisted of English Territorials, and of Indian troops skilled in mountain warfare. The cavalry were to form a screen round this double spearhead, but it could only be a very thin and ragged one, because of their casualties and the inaccessible nature of those rugged hills and defiles.[1] A glance at the map will show that the Lowlanders had not only to watch this front, but also their left flank, for this was practically a movement across the enemy's front, actually in places within range of their machine-guns.

About three miles south of the road to be followed by the 75th Division lay the railway from Junction Station to Jerusalem.

The 156th Brigade had arrived at Ludd after midnight in pouring rain. "About 2 a.m.," writes Capt. E. R. Boyd, 8th Cameronians, " John Nicholl returned with the news that the Brigade would march again at 8 a.m., and that, as water and rations were to be drawn, the convoy must move forward at once to the Battalion, which lay about a mile further along the road. So there was nothing for it but to wake up the men, get the camels loaded and start away." At 8 a.m. on the 19th the 156th Brigade set out

---

[1] The three Brigades of the Yeomanry Division and the 5th Mounted Brigade took part in this movement. On the 16th November the 5th Mounted Brigade had only 690 men mounted and fit for duty.

from Ludd, being followed by the 157th. The 155th Brigade set out at 6.45 a.m. from Ramleh, bringing up the rear. Before them lay, piled one on top of another, the barren and forbidding masses of the Judaean Highlands.

"We thought of the Crusaders of old," writes Lt.-Col. James Young, "of Cœur-de-Lion, of Godfrey de Bouillon, and all the rest, who challenged these mountain ramparts to free the Holy City from the bond of the Saracen. We thought, with a sympathy born of kindred struggle, of the despair and disaster that often followed them. . . .

"We felt that every rock was hallowed by sacred memories. Every peak as it looked down on us in its stern, unchanging dignity, had watched the hundred holy battles that swayed to and fro along the valleys round Jerusalem. And we felt that they stood over us in judgment."

At first, until the Lowlanders were into the foot-hills, the route was merely very rough and difficult, but beyond Berfilya it gradually became impossible for ordinary wheeled transport. "Starting from the lower slopes, the hills are covered throughout their entire extent with boulders of all sizes, which have broken from the parent limestone. They are scattered thickly over the surface of the hills from base to summit, and give to them and to the valleys between, an appearance of singular wildness, and in some places a certain element of stern grandeur such as one occasionally sees in the remote recesses of the Scottish Highlands." Most of the wheeled transport had to be left behind before passing Berfilya, and hardly even a half-limber [1] of the remainder got within two miles of Beit Likia, at this first thrust into the mountains. Many carts had been forsaken *en route* with wheels and axles broken and twisted under the strain. Those which got furthest were man-handled over the rocks and boulders on the road. Very little of the artillery got far beyond Berfilya at the first attempt, and the horses, streaming with sweat, had to pull the guns off the road, ways having to be cleared through the boulders for this purpose.

---

[1] A limbered-wagon consists of two parts, hitched together by a pole. Each part has two wheels, and can be detached and taken forward alone, when it is spoken of as a "half-limber."

BEIT LIKIA

NEBI SAMWIL AND EL JIB

The transport camels managed to struggle forward. Adapted through countless generations for sand and blazing heat, the soft pads of their feet fell on sharp fragments of rock at every step, whilst their bodies were chilled by wet and cold weather, which tried even the systems of the lightly-clad but hardy northerners of the 52nd Division. Long before the Division had reached Beit Likia it was wholly dependent on these beasts for the transport of its supplies from the base many miles behind, but by constant attention to torn feet, and continual readjustment of loads, most of the camels were saved, and this momentous advance into the hills was made possible. Many camels, however, fell by the way. The ground was slippery from the rain, especially at some smooth outcrops of rock, greasy with mud, which had to be passed by the 157th Brigade in the darkness before they reached Beit Likia. The camels fell down frequently, and each time they had to be reloaded before they could be raised to their feet again. Some poor beasts slipped down greasy inclines, and tumbled into ravines below, where they floundered with legs split apart until they could be mercifully shot. Wagons also slid into these gullies, and were irretrievably lost.

Daylight failed, and the 157th Brigade did the last six hours in the Stygian gloom of a dark and rainy night, in which the sky was almost as black as the intense blackness that covered the ground and hid the pitfalls and ravines on every side. Only the most experienced troops working under the most careful arrangements could keep touch in such a country on such a night; but it was done. All of this caused much delay, and it was 1 a.m. on the 20th before the last of the 157th Brigade arrived near Beit Likia. The head of the 156th Brigade arrived there at 4 p.m., and the 155th reached Berfilya on the same afternoon. Despite the rain, drinking supplies would have been a problem, but fortunately the bottle-shaped well-cisterns of Beit Likia were full of valuable supplies of good water.

The night was one of bitter cold and pouring rain. The troops had only thin khaki drill jackets and shorts, or, of course, in the case of the 5th Argylls and 6th H.L.I., kilts. Packs had been left behind at Ludd. Haversacks were carried filled with two days' rations to last for three days. No blankets could be carried, with the result that the only extra covering for each man was a cardigan jacket. The 157th Brigade, Brig.-Gen. Hamilton-Moore, had received orders to capture Beit Dukka, about five miles further on, before 8 a.m. on the 20th, so that his battalions had to parade at 4.30 a.m., ready to move in the utter darkness which preceded the cheerless dawn.

Beyond Beit Likia the track climbed rapidly, following the bottom of a cleft that lay between two hills, and was littered and heaped with rocks and boulders that had tumbled into it. The path became nothing more than a goat-track, until after a short distance all trace of it was lost on the stony hillsides. Its gradient was about one in six, and the rate of the transport's advance could not exceed a mile in two hours.

No previous reconnaissance of the objective, Beit Dukka, had been possible, and, when daylight appeared, it was found that the map did not in any way represent the features of the surrounding country. Dukka, which had been described as a village set on a hill and commanding considerable surrounding country, had first of all to be identified among the many dull grey villages, set on the summits of grey speckled, rugged hills, and separated by deep narrow valleys and gorges about 1000 feet deep. It was found to be on one of an isolated clump of hills commanding the junction of two valleys, north of the Roman Road heights, but itself commanded by a ridge 1200 yards behind. To the south-west of Beit Dukka, and on the Roman Road route, was a similar village, Beit Anan, which, with good fields of fire, completely barred the 157th Brigade's line of advance, and would have to be taken. The highly unsatisfactory native guides said that the Turks had fallen right back to Jerusalem, and so far there had been no signs of the enemy. Nevertheless, the 157th Brigade took no unnecessary risks.

Gen. Hamilton-Moore directed the 7th H.L.I., Lt.-Col.

NEBI SAMWIL AND EL JIB

E. S. Gibbons, to drop down into the valley to the north in order to attack Beit Dukka from that direction, whilst the remainder of the Brigade moved towards Beit Anan, the 5th H.L.I., Col. F. Morrison, forming the advance guard.

About two miles short of Beit Anan the 5th H.L.I. was ordered to crown the heights on either side of that village, whilst their scouts pushed on towards it. The heights were occupied, and shortly afterwards, at 7 a.m., the head of the column appeared in sight of Beit Anan. As it did so, a very sudden and heavy rifle and machine-gun fire was opened on it from the village and the ridges behind. Prisoners afterwards stated that there were at least seven hundred enemy infantry with machine-guns holding the place, a considerable force to oppose an attack on such a strong position by a weak infantry brigade completely without artillery. The 5th H.L.I. and the whole of the 157th Brigade Machine-Gun Company were at once brought into action to take Beit Anan, and the 6th H.L.I., Lt.-Col. Jas. Anderson, was ordered to push a company across the intervening gorge on to the heights west of Dukka.

Meanwhile, the 7th H.L.I. was feeling its way forward with the doubtful help of a native guide, along the stony and muddy bed of the Wadi Selman, the Scriptural valley of Ajalon. To have advanced along the ridges would have entailed several extra thousands of feet of climbing and descending, a wider detour and ruinous delay and fatigue. These wadis twist and turn, and are joined by tributaries with gorges as large as their own in all directions, so that without local knowledge or a perfect map, it is most difficult when down in their depths to tell which is the main water course. The guide led the 7th H.L.I. astray by turning south too soon and it attacked Beit Anan from the north in mistake for Beit Dukka just as the 5th H.L.I. was developing its attack.

It was very difficult through the atmosphere thick with mist and rain to locate the Turkish riflemen and machine-gunners hidden among the grey rocks, but by 8.15 a.m. they had been driven out of the village position on to the commanding ridges behind, and Beit Anan had been occupied. The 5th and 7th H.L.I., supported by covering fire from the 157th Brigade Machine-Gun Company, now set out to drive the Turks from the ridges behind by working forward to outflank them from the south. The rain descended in sheets, and the hills smoked with mist, rendering visual signalling impossible. The depth of the valleys and the distances rendered communication by wire out of the question, so that Gen. Hamilton-Moore could only keep in touch with his units by means of runners. He was completely cut off from Divisional Headquarters.

At 1 p.m. every available machine-gun and rifle was brought to bear on the position behind Beit Anan, and the enemy had to evacuate it and fall back. About three hundred of them, however, with some machine-guns, occupied a walled enclosure, about a mile further east on the crest-line of the same ridge, which from its elevation commanded all approaches from the west. This enclosure was a garden belonging to the Italian and Spanish Franciscan Monastery at Kubeibeh, the Emmaus of the New Testament.

From the south, the 157th Brigade could hear the thunder of the guns of the 75th Division, as it advanced up the metalled road towards Jerusalem.

Meanwhile, the 6th H.L.I. had captured Dukka by a frontal and flank attack. To get to it, the 6th, with their pack-ponies and mules, had to descend about seven hundred feet into a gorge. The ascent of the opposite side, about twelve hundred feet in height, was so steep and rocky that the animals had to be left behind until tracks could be cut and cleared for the pack-ponies. And so, without the help of the mules, the Lewis guns and ammunition were man-handled up the crags. To those further to the rear the men looked like ants crawling up the hillside.

At Beit Dukka, also, the Turks fell back to a delaying position behind, from which they sniped the village with two machine-guns. Two platoons of the 6th H.L.I. were sent to clear them out, but nightfall and a dense mist prevented them doing anything until daylight, when they continued their advance, and, with the loss of only three wounded, bombed the Turkish rear party out of their sangars.

Gen. Hamilton-Moore decided not to attack the monastery garden that afternoon, because of the exhaustion and hunger of his troops, feeling confident that in the morning he could quickly force the Turks out by working round their flanks, if they did not, as he expected they would, and as they actually did, evacuate it after dark without awaiting a further attack.

That night, 20-21st, the rain developed into torrential showers of hail, driven by a strong and bitterly cold wind. This further drop in the temperature was extremely trying to all ranks.

Everyone's clothing had become very ragged. The shorts of some were torn to ribbons. Kilts stood the hard wear better. The boots of many were now bundles of rags bound together with string and puttees. Many were very foot-sore, and men had been seen to take their boots off and bind their puttees round their wounded feet, continuing to march over the rocky ground in this way, cheerful and keen as ever. Very few had fallen out. Mark well that these men were not labouring forward to comfort and rest, but to further hardships and fighting, and possibly to wounds and death.

" For twenty hours the 5th H.L.I. company, which held the line nearest the monastery garden, in their tropical kit endured the enemy's sniping and machine-gun firing, and the bitter cold and hunger and misery, hearing in the early morning the wind-borne chimes of the chapel bell in Kubeibeh calling the brothers to matins, until dawn found many of them unable to speak " (*History 5th H.L.I.*).

Detachments of other units had similar experiences, and behind stone walls or rocks they got what shelter they could. It says much for the stamina of the troops that comparatively few were evacuated to hospital on the following morning as a result of exposure, the number from the 6th H.L.I., for example, being only five.

The 155th Brigade and a composite battery of the 264th Brigade R.F.A. reached Beit Likia on the 20th, where the

156th Brigade was in position. Each battery sent only one section, so that double and on some occasions quadruple teams could be harnessed to each gun, and these, with, at times, a hundred men on the drag-ropes, pulled them up the hillsides.

"At three o'clock in the morning of the 21st," writes Capt. E. R. Boyd, of the men, "while the rain was driving up the valley in solid sheets, I saw them standing round in the glow cast by three fires, which they had lit from the branches of some almond trees, singing in chorus the popular songs of two years ago."

"The mind of man is a strange thing and capable of providing strange contrasts," writes Col. Jas. Anderson, 6th H.L.I., of the morning of the 21st. "In the midst of fighting, wet to the skin and chilled from exposure to a night of storm, someone discovered a little bunch of jonquils peeping from a cranny in the rocks, and presently several headquarters' officers were busy in search for more. It was a presage of spring with its message of refreshing and hope."

At dawn on the 21st Lieut. Agnew, accompanied by C.Q.M.S. Kelly and Sgt. Black, all of the 5th H.L.I., set out to find whether the Turks were still in the monastery garden or not. Lieut. J. S. Agnew was the first to climb the wall and found that the enemy had gone. The 5th H.L.I. then moved into the garden, and occupied Kubeibeh, where state calls were exchanged between Col. Morrison and the Father Superior of the Franciscan monastery. Kubeibeh, with its trees and gardens tended by the long-robed monks, was a peaceful and beautiful place, and to it came many of the Division for their last long sleep.

The 157th Brigade had now secured a footing well into the hill country, being on the 2500 feet contour.

The 6th H.L.I. held Dukka, and the remainder of the 157th was about Kubeibeh on the Roman Road heights. During the night of the 20-21st a patrol of the Hyderabad Lancers rode across the hills from the 75th Division to the 157th Brigade, a splendid feat in an enemy country and on such a night. They brought word that the 75th Division had reached a point roughly parallel on the metalled road to the south. This Division had carried the Kuryet el Enab position at 6 p.m. during a thick mist.

The battle casualties of the 157th Brigade for this operation were as follows :

Unit.	Killed and Died of Wounds.		Wounded.		Total.	
	Officers.	O.R.	Officers.	O.R.	Officers.	O.R.
5th H.L.I.	1	2	—	10	1	12
6th H.L.I.	—	1	—	3	—	4
	1	3	—	13	1	16

Capt. W. L. Buchanan was mortally wounded on the 20th, gallantly leading his men on Beit Anan.

That the 157th Brigade, without any artillery support, suffered so few casualties in turning the enemy out of these strong positions, is great testimony to the skill with which its attack was directed and carried out by all ranks. Either an incautious advance into the hills, or undue delay would have entailed, if not disaster, at any rate heavy losses before such natural fortresses could be captured.

Of the Turkish losses we know little, beyond that some prisoners taken reported them to be heavy.

From the 20th and onwards, from Berfilya to Biddu, the brigades of the Division, whenever they were not climbing and fighting their way into the mountains, were road-making under the guidance of the Divisional Royal Engineers. With blasting charge and crowbar, pick and shovel, and by herculean efforts, a way was cleared, until by the 23rd heavy artillery could pass as far as Biddu. The construction of this road within four days, over about fourteen miles of most rocky hill country, by men who were hungry, cold, and at the end of a tremendous advance, is one of the achievements of which the Division can be very proud. As an engineering feat alone, it was wonderful.

Little more than 1000 yards beyond Kubeibeh, and on the same ridge, stands this village of Biddu. The track between the two runs below the crest-line along the northern slope of the ridge, and is in full view of the heights to north-eastward, and therefore, at this time, in full view of numerous Turkish observation posts.

About two miles to the east of Biddu and about a mile south of and parallel to the Roman Road from that place to El Jib, lies the dominating ridge of Nebi Samwil, the traditional burying-place of the prophet Samuel, the Mizpeh or watch-tower of the tribe of Benjamin, and the Mountjoye of the Crusaders. The main ridge is about 2800 feet in height, and runs for about a mile to the northeast. The highest point, with an altitude of 2942 feet, is nearer the western end, and has a conical appearance from the west.[1] On its summit, surrounded by a small village and numerous stone-walled gardens and orchards, is a large mosque, referred to as " The Mosque," which at this time had a long, slender minaret, a landmark for miles around. This hill commands all the heights to the east, and all within six or seven miles to the north of Jerusalem. The Holy City stands on its own hills four and a half miles to the south-east, and can be clearly seen from the summit of this eminence. In January, 1192, A.D., the followers of Richard Cœur de Lion first looked upon the City from its summit, and pointed out its white buildings to him, but he, hiding his face in his helmet, prayed : " Lord, let me not set mine eyes upon Thy Holy City till I have rescued it from the Infidel."

Nebi Samwil was " the key that opened to us the gates of the Holy City " (Col. R. M. P. Preston).

On the 21st the Yeomanry out on the northern flank made a final attempt at Beitunia to reach the road from Jerusalem to the north, but were outnumbered three to one, were overwhelmed by artillery,[2] and had to retire after nightfall to a three mile line running approximately north and south through Beit Ur el Foka, a village about 4000 yards north of Beit Anan. The very badness of the

[1]. The following heights are given to assist the reader to realize these altitudes :

Scotland (Highlands).	Scotland (Lowlands).	England.
Ben Lomond, 3,192 ft.	Goat Fell, 2,866 ft.	Skiddaw, 3,054 ft.
Ben Ledi, 2,875 ,,	Merrick, 2,764 ,,	Cheviots, 2,676 ,,
Ben Venue, 2,393 ,,	Hart Fell, 2,651 ,,	

[2] The Yeomanry had one mountain gun, with which to reply to the fire of a number of field and mountain batteries.

EL KUBEIBEH

country served for a while as a protection from counter-attack from the north. On the same day the line of the 75th Division's advance converged on that of the 52nd's. It left the metalled road and pushed the 234th Brigade[1] through Biddu, across the intervening saddle, on to Nebi Samwil, capturing the Mosque late in the day, before the Turks had properly realised what was happening. To cover the left flank of this movement, the 6th H.L.I., Lt.-Col. Jas. Anderson, cleared about 500 Turks out of the village of Beit Izza, about 1500 yards north of Biddu, losing two men wounded in the operation. The thrust into the Judaean Highlands had now formed a salient narrower than ever ; it was no wider than a single ridge. The enemy, realising the importance of what they had lost, were gathering on all sides for the purpose of retaking Nebi Samwil.

During the 22nd the Turks brought a gradually increasing shell-fire to bear on the summit from the north and east, and the 75th Division was sorely pressed. Meanwhile, the 156th Brigade, Brig.-Gen. A. H. Leggett, had set out from Beit Likia at 5.30 a.m., without reserve ammunition or reserve water, to relieve the 75th Division at Biddu and Nebi Samwil. The weather had now cleared and was fine, and, as the thin column of men wound along the ridge from Kubeibeh, they could see the shells bursting about the Mosque. The 7th and 4th R.S. relieved the 75th Division near Biddu, and at Beit Surik. The 7th and 8th Cameronians, with guns from the 157th Machine-Gun Company, the whole under Lt.-Col. J. M. Findlay, pushed on for Nebi Samwil. Artillery formation saved them from serious losses as they crossed the valley to Nebi Samwil, despite their being in full view of the Turks, who raked the valley with shell-fire.

A more particularised description of Nebi Samwil is now desirable. To the north-east of " the Mosque the ridge is, for some 1200 yards, broad, flat, and devoid of cover, and then falls sharply towards the wadi just south of

[1] The 234th Brigade was commanded at this time by Brig.-Gen. C. A. H. Maclean, D.S.O., late of the 52nd Divisional Staff.

Bir Nebala. The western slopes of the ridge were not so steep, but were all swept by fire from El Jib, which was held by the enemy.

"The immediate vicinity of the Mosque consisted of stone-walled enclosures, courtyards and stone buildings, spreading for a distance of 450 yards to the north and north-east (where there was also a small mosque and native village) but elsewhere extending for no greater distance than 100 yards.

"Once clear of enclosures, the ground to the east fell sharply to the Wadi Hannina, and to the west in a series of natural rock terraces and gentler slopes to the Roman Road." (Gen. A. H. Leggett.)

To the south-east the ground falls away to the valley of the Wadi Abbeideh, which is apparently quite shut in by high, rocky hills, but finds an outlet to the south.

El Jib, the ancient Gibeon, the chief city of the Hivites, was captured by Joshua, and has been a stronghold from time immemorial. The village and its enclosures lie on the summit (2578 feet) of a mighty terraced, tower-like hill, which completely bars the valley north of Nebi Samwil, and is connected with hills to the north by a ridge, slightly lower in altitude.

Lt.-Col. J. G. P. Romanes, whose command, the 7th Cameronians, was leading, went on ahead, and received a request from the Brig.-Gen. Commanding 234th Brigade for both battalions to reinforce his line as quickly as possible, because he was being continually counter-attacked and a relief at the time was impossible. This reinforcement was completed at 2.30 p.m., and the defence line was found to include the Mosque, and the buildings and enclosures which were just north and south of it, the Turks holding the remainder of the ridge to the north-east, and being behind walls not forty yards away. The musketry and machine-gun fire of both sides, and the Turkish shell-fire, never ceased.

After nightfall, about 6 p.m., it seemed possible to proceed with the relief. Commencing from the left, the taking-over was partially complete, when the Turks seized the opportunity to counter-attack. Between 400 and 500 of them rushed for the Mosque, the centre of the line, and still partially held by the 234th Brigade. They broke through, and a wave of Moslem soldiery surged round the Mosque and its buildings, and spread over the gardens round about, but there its forward momentum ceased. A company of 7th Cameronians, reduced by casualties to about thirty men and a Lewis gun, and commanded by Lieut. Watson, had been guided to a courtyard at the southeastern corner of the Mosque. Lieut. Watson had just placed Lance-Cpl. J. Lipsett with four men and the Lewis gun in position to hold a lane which led to the centre of the Mosque, when the confused babel and explosions of the counter-attack burst out. The walls and roofs surrounding the courtyard were hastily manned, and, although completely isolated and attacked on all sides, this party kept the Turks from entering the Mosque by their steady, rapid and deadly fire. To the right of the courtyard a British machine-gun, also apparently isolated, kept up a persistent fire, and, to the left, Lipsett and his men held a large body of Turks at bay. The situation was critical; bombs were being thrown into the right rear of the courtyard; the darkness covered the weakness of the defenders, but vigorous action by the enemy would soon disclose to them the true state of affairs, and an immediate British counter-attack was thus essential.

The headquarters of Lt.-Col. Findlay were under a low cliff, a few hundred yards east of the Mosque, and close by were those of the 234th Brigade. Their first intimation of a counter-attack was the sight of some men of the 234th Brigade being pushed back past this locality. Some twenty men of the 234th Brigade were collected here, and, with some Cameronian headquarter details, were lined up on the top of the cliff. A company of 7th Cameronians was hurried forward. There was no time to inform any but its commander, Capt. James Anderson, of what was happening. His Lewis guns with part of their crews were left behind as useless for bayonet work, so that his company went forward not more than seventy strong. Only by a swift counter-attack could they hope to succeed, and many of the men had to fix bayonets as they groped and scrambled up the low cliff.

To the left, that is on the north side of the Mosque, runs a lane, about six or seven yards wide, and shut in by stone walls and cactus hedges. Forming his seventy Cameronians into four thick waves, Capt. Anderson led his men along this lane. Abreast of the Mosque was a crowd of Turks, estimated at over 200. These he rushed with the bayonet, and, after a desperate hand-to-hand clash, in which 2nd Lieut. J. B. Elliot was killed and thirty of his men fell, he drove them back beyond the Mosque. A continuance of the advance would probably have turned victory into disaster, so he wisely stopped his men, who engaged in a rifle duel with the Turks in the open at a range of fifteen yards.

The remainder of the Turks in the village, deluded as to the strength of these Cameronians by the ferocity of their attack, withdrew under cover of the darkness beyond the Mosque. The Cameronians shortly afterwards completed their relief of the 234th Brigade, the 8th being to the south of the Mosque and the 7th to the north. The position was then cleared and consolidated, three Turkish snipers and two other prisoners being taken behind the line.

The area was littered with the bodies of dead and wounded British, Ghurka, and Turkish soldiers, and of dead animals. The stretcher-bearers were busy throughout the bitterly cold night that followed, and Chaplain J. Spence gave himself no rest, thinking only of the wounded and dying. Camel cacolets were the only transport available for the wounded from the regimental aid posts, over the crags and ravines, to the hospitals at Kubeibeh, and thence to Beit Likia. Even a short journey in these might jostle to death a badly wounded man, and so only the slighter cases were sent beyond Kubeibeh by the Field Ambulances.

Blanketless and with only half rations, the Cameronians snatched whatever sleep or rest was possible.

The Turks, however, had no stomach for any more counter-attacks during that night.

NEBI SAMWIL AND EL JIB 445

There are many occasions in every campaign when tremendous issues hang on the action of a very few men, and there can be little doubt that the tenacity and promptness of these Cameronians saved a situation which might have delayed indefinitely the capture of Jerusalem. If the Turks had retaken Nebi Samwil, they would probably have transformed it into another Ali el Muntar, or even an Achi Baba or Sari Bair. As it was, the narrow passes from the plain to the plateau of the Judaean range, which had been forced, were made secure by the capture and retention of Nebi Samwil. These passes have seldom been forced, and have proved fatal to many invading armies. "Had the attempt not been made at once, or had it been pressed with less determination, the enemy would have had time to reorganize his defences in the passes lower down, and the conquest of the plateau would have been slow, costly and precarious" (Gen. Allenby).

It is sad to relate that the gallant Capt. James Anderson, 7th Cameronians, was mortally wounded on the following day, the 23rd, and died in the monastery at Kubeibeh (Emmaus).

At dawn on the 23rd about fifty Turks were seen making for Lance-Cpl. Lipsett's post, calling upon the men to surrender. He let them approach within thirty yards, and then greeted them with a burst of fire from his Lewis gun and a shower of bombs, annihilating the entire party.

During the 22nd and 23rd the 75th Division made attempts to take El Jib, but the Turks had been driven back towards their own depots, so that fresh men, guns and supplies were becoming increasingly plentiful for them, and no progress could be made. The good main road from Jerusalem northwards ran east of their positions, and they placed many of their guns along it, where they could easily keep them well supplied with ammunition. The enemy knew that they had lost the key position and were determined to retake it. The result was that from a semicircle stretching from Ram Allah in the north, through Er Ram in the east, to Beit Iksa in the south, they poured a converging fire on the crest of Nebi Samwil, deluging it with H.E. that soon commenced to shatter the delicate minaret and solid masonry of the Mosque. Not until the evening of the 23rd, when a gun of the 5th Battery (Major W. Watson), Glasgow Howitzers, got forward and into action near Biddu, firing the first rounds from British artillery in the neighbourhood of Jerusalem, could any attempt be made to reply to this fire. The rifle, machine-gun, and bombing duel in the enclosures outside the Mosque, never ceased, and many Cameronians fell; but they held the Turks at bay.

During the night of the 23-24th the 75th Division was withdrawn from its operations against El Jib, and took over the line about Biddu from the Royal Scots, and that about Dukka from the 6th H.L.I. The 156th Brigade then concentrated behind the Mosque, the 8th Cameronians taking over the whole Nebi Samwil defence line from the 7th, who had lost seven officers and ninety-four men from their already thinned ranks.

The 4th R.S. was not relieved until 6 a.m., so that this unit had to cross the valley to Nebi Samwil in broad daylight. The men were dribbled across and suffered few casualties, but the losses in transport animals were heavy. The 157th Brigade was at Kubeibeh, Beit Dukka, and Beit Anan. The 155th Brigade moved forward from Beit Likia on the 23rd.

The weather was fine, and at one place, after the Fusiliers and Borderers had been climbing abruptly for some considerable time, on turning their eyes, they found "outstretched before us, in a gap between the peaks, the long expanse of the plain of Sharon, with Ludd and Ramleh in the nearer distance, and far back, standing on the shore, the large town of Jaffa. Behind it all, the Mediterranean sparkled in the setting sun, with the warships riding on its surface, and showing in the distance as small black specks. A few more steps, and this panorama was blotted from our sight. As we reached the higher levels, every now and then we got a sight of the prominent peak of Nebi Samwil with its tower shining white as it caught the sun." (Lt.-Col. J. Young.)

NEBI SAMWIL AND EL JIB

The writer of the War Diary of the 5th K.O.S.B. for this date tells how the " men's hearts burned within them as they heard the chimes of the clock on the tower of the modern Franciscan Latin Hospital " at Emmaus. Some had not heard the familiar, home-recalling sounds since they had echoed to them along their own Lowland dales.

The track from Kubeibeh through Biddu, and across the valley to Nebi Samwil, was in full view of the Turks during most of its course, they knew the exact range, and their artillery shelled everything that they could see moving along it. The south-east corner of Kubeibeh was under constant shell-fire. Coming down the track to Biddu, a shell burst among the 4th K.O.S.B., killing two and wounding fourteen men, including ten battalion signallers. The 155th Brigade took up a line north-east of Biddu, and also occupied Beit Izza permanently.

This thrust into the Judaean Highlands was a phase in the campaign which could not be ordered to a set plan. The general intention was to cut the communications of Jerusalem with the north ; the exact details had to be settled as the operations developed. The 52nd Division was now little more than a brigade in strength, and it had achieved much, but it was to make one more effort. On the 24th it was to attempt to throw itself across the Jerusalem–Nablous (Shechem) road at Er Ram. With cavalry demonstrating on its left, the 155th Brigade was to advance from Beit Izza and take El Jib, and thereafter was to move on Jedireh and Kulundia. The 156th Brigade was to attack from about the Mosque, clear the Nebi Samwil ridge, and capture Bir Nebala. The 157th Brigade, advancing through or past these brigades, had, as its objective, Er Ram.

By superhuman efforts, and the use of every horse available, the Divisional Artillery, under Brig.-Gen. E. C. Massy, had pushed forward to Biddu four 4.5-inch howitzers and six 18-pounders, chiefly from the 264th Brigade. At one place, after three hours' work, the Glasgow Howitzers found that they had only got one gun forward about a mile. Major-Gen. Hill asked for twenty-four hours' delay in order to await the arrival of the 60th Division and more artillery, and so to attack on a wider front, but 21st Corps Headquarters told him that he must attack at once.

The 75th Division sent over four 4.5-inch howitzers, and the small guns of the ubiquitous Hong Kong and Singapore Mountain Battery also arrived. The supply of ammunition for all of the guns was limited.

Around the storm-battered 52nd Division there lay in a semi-circle a Turkish army of many thousands of men, some of whom were quite fresh. The enemy had hundreds of machine-guns and a numerous artillery, and were embattled on a series of rugged and precipitous heights, which were fronted by open, rock-strewn valleys. Every brigade of the Division would have to attack under enfilade fire, and if they penetrated far enough, would be fired into from behind also. The communications of the British force in the hills were already very precarious. The reader must remember that the rifle strength of the Division, which was to assault and hold these mile-long positions, averaged about 300 per battalion, and its artillery support consisted of eighteen guns.

In fact, because of its own weakness, its negligible artillery support, and the strength of the enemy in position, numbers and guns, the task which the Division had been called upon to undertake was an impossibility.

The British artillery fire could only be of use if it were concentrated on a small target. El Jib was the point selected. The larger British guns were in position among the heights about Biddu, and the mountain guns, because of their short range, were near Beit Izza in the valley running towards El Jib. The artillerymen fought well, but the contribution of the British guns to the general chorus has been described as " pathetically insufficient," and, moreover, the Turkish gunners had far superior opportunities for observation.

The 155th and 156th Brigades advanced to the attack at noon on the 24th.

The assaults of the 75th Division had been made against the precipitous cliffs on the southern front of El Jib. Brig.-Gen. J. B. Pollok-M'Call decided that the 155th Brigade

NEBI SAMWIL FROM THE JERUSALEM ROAD

NEBI SAMWIL AND EL JIB

should attack further to the north, and, pivoting its right on an orchard or walled garden eight hundred yards west-south-west of El Jib, assault the rock fortress from the north-west. The 5th K.O.S.B., Lt.-Col. A. H. C. Kearsey, was on the left, and the 5th R.S.F., Lt.-Col. J. B. Cook, was on the right. The 4th K.O.S.B., Lt.-Col. R. Dashwood-Tandy, moved forward in support, and the 4th R.S.F., Lt.-Col. A. G. Stewart-Richardson, was in reserve. Guns of the 155th Machine-Gun Company took up positions to support the attack. A squadron of the Mysore Lancers, who were attached to the 155th were sent out to cover the left flank and to get in touch with the Yeomanry Division. The latter were to cooperate with a demonstration, but, as events turned out, were too far west to make their presence felt.

Supported by the mountain battery, but heavily shelled by the Turkish guns, the 155th Brigade moved coolly forward along the stony valley north of the Nebi Samwil ridge, towards El Jib. The troops were advancing over the battleground of the Five Kings of the Book of Joshua. The sections kept their places well in their artillery formation, the rain-washed khaki drill blended with the ground, and there were few casualties at the outset of this advance. The first 1000 yards had been covered rapidly, when enemy machine-guns opened fire from the village, and the ridges right and left, causing the sections to extend.

From that time, as the 155th Brigade pushed forward, the enemy fire from El Jib and from both flanks, but especially so from the left, became more merciless. Casualties increased; more and more care had to be taken in dribbling the men forward, and the advance became slower. Within thirty-five minutes the 5th R.S.F. had worked their firing line forward across slopes and valleys, with no cover beyond loose stones, until their right got through the walled garden as far as the side nearest El Jib, and about 700 yards from that village. Batches of men were pushed up by quick rushes, and at 1.30 p.m. they were joined by about fifty men of the 5th K.O.S.B., which battalion had advanced with extreme difficulty, being most exposed to the heavy fire from the ridges to the north. The Mysore Lancers could do nothing to check this fire, and had been pushed back by the Turks. There was no sign of the Yeomanry Division, and this flanking fire from the left, to which we could not reply, made a successful advance practically impossible. The 156th Brigade had been held up on Nebi Samwil, so that, to carry out its orders, the 155th Brigade would have to advance further into a pocket, in which it would be under fire from three sides. In front of it, beyond an open zone swept by fire, rose up tier upon tier of rock, crowned by the hill fortress of El Jib. The Turkish guns now shelled the orchard garden and the advance was held up.

Distances made communication most difficult, but preparations were made to press the attack. Half of the 4th R.S.F. was sent forward to reinforce the right, and the whole of the 4th K.O.S.B. the left, which was the most exposed flank and was suffering most severely. Here, Lt.-Col. Kearsey, 5th K.O.S.B., his adjutant, and several other officers had already fallen. From 3.45 p.m. to 4 p.m. the artillery bombarded El Jib as heavily as it could, and then another attempt to advance was made. Major R. W. Paton, 5th R.S.F., with about fifty men, reached a ridge within 600 yards of the high part of the village, but the terrible cross-fire, now severe from the right as well as from the left, made further forward movement impossible in the daylight.

About this time Lt.-Col. J. B. Cook, D.S.O., 5th R.S.F., was killed near the orchard. He died as he had lived, quietly and fearlessly doing his duty. He was a born soldier, never spared himself, and considered his own comfort last of all. He was loved and respected by all who knew him.

Brig.-Gen. Pollok-M'Call was preparing to assault El Jib with the bayonet after dark, when Major-Gen. Hill sent word that the Corps had ordered the action to be broken off. The troops were then about 400 yards from the outskirts of El Jib. It is wonderful that they had got so far.

The 156th Brigade, Brig.-Gen. A. H. Leggett, had to

NEBI SAMWIL AND EL JIB

deliver its attack over a maze of stone walls and gardens, where a numerous and brave enemy lay in many places within bombing distance. Of artillery preparation to breach the stone walls there could be none. Each wall was a barricade about five feet in height. Each enclosure was a death trap, swept by hidden trench mortars, machine-guns, and rifles. Each wall had to be climbed, and the difficulties of deployment alone were enormous. There could be no concealment. Turkish artillery fired on Nebi Samwil, until the summit and the Mosque were almost hidden by the dust and smoke of bursting shells, which came from every side but the west.

The 8th Cameronians, Lt.-Col. J. M. Findlay, was in the line. Advancing from either side of the Mosque, the 7th R.S., Lt.-Col. W. C. Peebles, was to clear the enclosures and native village on the ridge, and to dig in after reaching its northern end. On the left of the 7th R.S., the 7th Cameronians, Lt.-Col. J. G. P. Romanes, was to advance up the valley on the low ground, parallel with the 155th Brigade. After El Jib fell, this unit was to capture Nebala. When the 7th R.S. had taken the ridge, the 4th R.S., Lt.-Col. A. M. Mitchell, were to take up a line facing east, and linking up the 7th's right with the Mosque area, which the 8th Cameronians were to garrison. The 155th Machine-Gun Company and two Stokes trench mortars were to assist the attack whenever possible.

Two companies of the 7th R.S. were to deploy and attack from the right of the Mosque and two from the left. They moved forward promptly at noon.

The leading company on the right managed to get forward about 100 yards when it was held up, suffering many casualties from frontal and enfilade machine-gun and shell-fire. An attempt was made to crawl round the eastern slope of the hill to get below the fire-beaten zone, but all who tried were hit. Lt.-Col. Peebles, whilst trying to see if there was any possibility of an advance in this quarter, had his coat shot to ribbons, but escaped unwounded. One platoon was reduced to three men. Many more Royal Scots fell here, and the movement was held up.

The company on the left made better progress. "Advancing past the left of the Mosque a courtyard was reached, in front of which was a big flat-roofed stone shed. Bombs, rifle and machine-gun bullets seemed to come from all quarters, the only exit being through a doorway commanded by enemy machine-guns. Capt. Rogers cleared the shed in front and led some men on to the roof to fire down on the enemy behind the garden walls. Enemy machine-guns at once opened fire, sweeping the roof, killing Capt. Rogers and several of the men. Capt. Malcolm Smith assumed command and attempted to force a passage on the left so as to turn the enemy's right flank. The only exit was through a gap in the wall through which the men rushed, and the enemy guarded the point with his machine-guns. Bombing was tried, but the machine-guns were out of range. A bomb station was now established to guard the left flank while a party of bombers, riflemen, and one Lewis gun section made a determined and successful rush through the gap, though at heavy cost, and cleared the Turks from the first wall which was taken and held. However, the position became untenable owing to concentrated and enfilade fire, the Lewis gun and team being blown up, and it became necessary to withdraw. This was done, the dead and wounded were collected and taken behind the gap in the wall, which was again held." (Lt.-Col. W. C. Peebles.)

Every effort was made to cooperate with the 155th Brigade by pressing back the Turkish right on the ridge, but a total advance of 200 yards was all that was attainable.

Meanwhile the enemy, using a hidden gully on the eastern slope, had thrown an additional 200 to 300 men into the enclosures on his left.

The advance of the 7th Cameronians on the left was held up along with the troops on both of its flanks. The remainder of the 156th Brigade had to lie and endure the raking bombardment.

Preparations were being made by Gen. Leggett for a supreme effort, and two battalions of the 75th Division had been brought up to hold the line, so that the whole weight

NEBI SAMWIL AND EL JIB

of the 156th Brigade could be used in the attack, when orders came about 4 p.m. from Divisional Headquarters not to attempt any further advance.

In the meantime the 157th Brigade had been searching for a route by which to get forward. To avoid entanglement with the attack of the 156th Brigade, Brig.-Gen. C. D. Hamilton-Moore at first decided not to advance along the north-western side of the Nebi Samwil ridge, but along the south-eastern. As his Brigade moved along the ridges from Biddu, it was heavily shelled from Beitunia by the Turks, who had the track ranged to a yard. A little shelter was obtained by diverging further to the south, but when the leading battalion, the 5th A. & S.H., Lt.-Col. C. L. Barlow, got on the top of the ridge south of Nebi Samwil, its ranks were again heavily shelled from Beitunia, in the north, and Lifta in the south. From between these points they faced a crescent of fire from machine-guns and rifles. A company of Argylls doubled forward into this bullet-swept area, and in the next two and a half hours three separate attempts were made to force a passage along the eastern slopes of the Nebi Samwil Ridge; but the enemy were too strong. The slightest movement brought a storm of cross-fire, and Gen. Hamilton-Moore saw that a further advance this way would be too costly.

Seeing that nothing further could be achieved here, he left the 5th Argylls to guard this flank, and decided to try the north-western slope with the 5th, 6th and 7th H.L.I., concluding that the attack of the 156th Brigade would have advanced far enough to allow him room for this. He diverted these three battalions for this purpose, but, on reaching the Headquarters of the 156th Brigade, found that there was no room for this movement, and that further attempts to advance along the Nebi Samwil ridge would only result in heavy casualties. After a consultation with Major-Gen. Hill over the telephone, it was decided that the 157th Brigade should join in the attack on El Jib. The 6th H.L.I., Lt.-Col. James Anderson, the nearest battalion, had moved forward to the right flank of the 155th Brigade, and had actually commenced to advance with the bayonet to storm the hill, when the order to break off the battle reached Gen. Hamilton-Moore.

The 5th Argylls were withdrawn from their exposed position after nightfall, and, about midnight, the 157th Brigade took over the outpost line before Beit Izza from the 155th, which, like the other Brigades, had been withdrawn in good order, with all wounded, guns, and most of the dead. The 155th went into bivouacs at Kubeibeh, the last camel clearing the exposed track before 4 a.m. The night that followed was bitterly cold, and even the most fortunate units lay among the stones with perhaps one blanket to four men.

Mention must be made of the signallers, who invariably did so much to help the 52nd Division to deserve success. They had to work coolly and methodically, often in the most exposed places, and with the closest attention to tiny details. On the 24th, Lieut. A. Hewison's battalion, the 5th Argylls, was in the open swept by fire from front and flanks, but, at great personal risk, and despite repeated failures, he kept the firing line in touch with battalion headquarters.

"The 52nd Division was directed to discontinue the attack,"[1] just as it was about to launch another series of assaults. Even though they were outnumbered and wearied, the Lowlanders were ready to continue their efforts. The task set them was, however, impossible. Nevertheless, the safest defence is often a bold attack, and the great key position for Jerusalem had been held for another two days, whilst fresh divisions with much shorter casualty lists marched forward from the south.

The 75th Division was relieved on the 25th by the 60th Division from Gaza. So reduced were the 52nd and 75th by casualties, that this fresh division could adequately relieve both.

The 156th Brigade held Nebi Samwil, Biddu, and Beit Surik until the night of the 25-26th, when it was relieved by troops of the 60th Division. Nebi Samwil and Biddu

---

[1] See *Record of the Egyptian Expeditionary Force*, compiled from official sources.

were heavily shelled during this time, and the Mosque rapidly crumbled into ruins. Further losses were suffered, but the enemy were too exhausted by the fighting of the previous day to make any serious counter-attacks on the 25th. After relief, the 156th Brigade moved back during the night-time over the exposed valley and ridges to Beit Anan.

The 157th Brigade held the line east of Beit Izza until the evening of the 27th, when it also was relieved by the 60th Division.

Whilst facing El Jib for these three days, the 157th Brigade was shelled continually, the explosions echoing up and down the valley and ravines. On the 25th about 120 shells fell in the Brigade Headquarters area. The heaviest bombardment was on the 27th, when the 5th H.L.I. lost two men killed, and its adjutant and eight men wounded. On the same day the 7th H.L.I. lost seventeen men wounded, besides forty-two camels, three horses, and four pack mules, a serious matter considering transportation requirements. Pte. Clark, of the 7th H.L.I., displayed great coolness and fearlessness in walking down the transport lines, and setting the animals loose. On the 25th and 26th reports were received that the Turks were supposed to be evacuating their present line, and night patrols were sent out towards El Jib, but they found the reports untrue. 2nd Lieuts. D. L. MacIntyre and D. B. Lockhart, 6th H.L.I., did markedly well in this work. Possibly these reports were inspired by the enemy, in the hope that the great counter-attack, recorded in the following chapter, would find the British entangled in a disastrous attack on El Jib.

During the evening of the 27th the Turks made one of that series of desperate counter-attacks on Nebi Samwil, which showed how seriously they regarded the loss of this key position. A party of Turks crawled through the lines and got as far as the battery positions of the Lowland Howitzers, but were wiped out. The 157th Brigade was ready to assist, but the 60th Division repelled the attack, and the Brigade moved back under cover of darkness to bivouacs around Beit Anan. The whole Division was now out of the line.

The losses of the three Brigades for the fighting around Nebi Samwil and El Jib were as follows:

155TH BRIGADE.

Unit.	Killed and Died of Wounds.		Wounded.		Total.	
	Officers.	O.R.	Officers.	O.R.	Officers.	O.R.
4th R.S.F.	—	2	—	9	—	11
5th R.S.F.	1	3	4	50	5	53
4th K.O.S.B.	1	2	—	20	1	22
5th K.O.S.B.	—	16	7	64	7	80
155th M.G. Coy.	—	1	—	9	—	10
155th T.M. Batt.	—	—	1	1	1	1
	2	24	12	153	14	177

With Lt.-Col. J. B. Cook, D.S.O., 5th R.S.F., there was numbered among the dead, 2nd Lieut. A. N. Wilson, 4th K.O.S.B.

156TH BRIGADE.

Unit.	Killed and Died of Wounds.		Wounded.		Total.	
	Officers.	O.R.	Officers.	O.R.	Officers.	O.R.
156th Bde. H.Q.	1	1	—	—	1	1
4th Royal Scots	—	—	—	7	—	7
7th Royal Scots	2	17	3	89	5	106
7th Cameronians	3	31	5	95	8	126
8th Cameronians	—	20	4	82	4	102
156th M.G. Coy.	—	2	—	6	—	8
	6	71	12	279	18	350

The following officers of the 156th Brigade gave up their lives:

156th Bde. H.Q.—Captain and Bde. Major T. A. Franklin.
7th Royal Scots—Captain A. N. Rogers.
  2nd Lieut. J. W. Hutchison.
7th Cameronians—Captain J. K. Anderson.
  2nd Lieut. J. B. Elliot.
  2nd Lieut. G. Porteous.

For such a weak brigade these losses were very heavy, and show the severity of the fighting. The ration strength of one company of the 8th Cameronians had dropped to twenty-three.

157TH BRIGADE.

Unit.	Killed and Died of Wounds.		Wounded.		Total.	
	Officers.	O.R.	Officers.	O.R.	Officers.	O.R.
157th Bde. H.Q.	—	—	—	2	—	2
5th H.L.I.	—	2	1	8	1	10
6th H.L.I.	—	3	1	30	1	33
7th H.L.I.	—	—	—	27	—	27
5th A. & S.H.	—	14	1	49	1	63
157th M.G. Coy.	—	1	—	9	—	10
	—	20	3	125	3	145

Considering the shell-fire directed on this brigade, these losses were very small, and are explained by the effective use of artillery formation and the poor quality of percussion shrapnel used by the Turks.

The total loss of seven hundred was heavy for such a weak division, but, when compared with the magnitude of the achievement, was very small. The British had secured a footing within the keep of the great fortress of the Judaean Highlands, holding its topmost tower, Nebi Samwil, the key of the whole situation. The Turks continued their efforts, by assault and bombardment, to recover this hill, but the British had had time to consolidate the position. Where there had been only rocky hillsides, there was now a road for wheeled traffic. The gallant men who took and occupied Jerusalem in December were able to do so because the 52nd Division had maintained its hold on this dominating height when the situation was at its worst.

CHAPTER XXVI

(26TH NOVEMBER TO 2ND DECEMBER, 1917)

THE TURKISH COUNTER-ATTACKS AT BEIT UR EL TAHTA AND EL BURJ

> King George II. : " Ah, Sir Agnew, the *gens d'armes* got in among you to-day."
> Sir Andrew Agnew : " Yes, please your Majesty, but they did not get out again."
>> King George II. and Sir Andrew Agnew, who commanded the 21st Royal Regiment of N.B. Fusiliers (later the Royal Scots Fusiliers) at the battle of Dettingen, when it opened its ranks, allowed French cuirassiers to charge into the lane so formed, and then annihilated them.

THE 52nd Division had now been fighting and marching without cessation for more than three weeks. It was reduced to a shadow of its former self, and it was time for other and less battle-scarred formations to take up the standard of the advance. How gallantly they did so is told in histories of this campaign. It was a great disappointment to many that the Division was ordered to turn its back on the Holy City before it had fallen, and deprived of the honour of taking part in its capture. Like Moses and many other pioneers, they were only permitted to see from afar off the promised land, to which they had found the way.

Nevertheless, it was obvious that the 52nd Division was badly in need of rest and reinforcements. The 155th Brigade leading, it now started back to the low country, down the road which it had made over the hills.

All were looking forward to sleep, clean clothes, a change in diet from bully-beef and biscuit, some cigarettes, for all

BEIT UR EL TAHTA AND EL BURJ

their tobacco was gone, a good home mail, and perhaps even a comparatively comfortable place in which to lie down; but it was not to be yet. More work lay before the Division, and the roll of those who were to sleep their last long sleep amidst those Judaean Hills was not yet complete.

The Lowland Division was now to take a prominent part in warding off one of the deadliest counter-attacks attempted by the Turks in this campaign.

At this time the northern front of the British in Palestine ran inland from the mouth of the Auja, and was continued into the Judaean Highlands by the northern side of the great Nebi Samwil salient. This continuation was held by the Yeomanry Division. The Yeomen had sent back their horses to Ramleh on the 23rd November, but, even so, they could only muster about 800 rifles. With these they were holding a line which was nearly four miles in length, and ran through this country of hills, ridges, and deep narrow gorges, from the north of Beit Dukka, around Beit Ur el Foka to Beit Ur el Tahta.[1] This " line " consisted of a few posts, and a number of small, roving patrols. North of Ludd, and to the left of the Yeomanry, which was about Beit Ur el Tahta, the line was held by the 54th Division, but the latter's right rested on Shilta, so that between the two divisions there was a gap of about five miles. Parallel to, and less than two miles south of this gap lay the road from Ludd to Nebi Samwil, the principal channel of ammunition, supplies, and reinforcements for that place. If the Turks should awaken to this fact, there was apparently nothing to prevent them from walking through the gap and blocking this road, thereby rendering the retention of Nebi Samwil extremely difficult.

An advance of a few miles to the south would carry them across the metalled road to Jerusalem, would practically cut off the British divisions in the salient, and would inevitably bring about a collapse of the thrust for Jerusalem.

Encouraged by the set-back of the Yeomanry, and the failure to take El Jib and clear the Nebi Samwil ridge,

[1] Beit Ur el Foka and Beit Ur el Tahta were the Upper and Lower Beth-horons, respectively, of Joshua's days.

the Turks did attempt to break through the northern side of the great salient, but, fortunately, their effort was made just at the moment when the 155th, the leading brigade of the 52nd Division, was approaching the gap, the point of greatest danger. At this time the 156th was concentrating at Beit Anan, but the 157th was still holding the line before Beit Izza.

On 26th November the 155th Brigade, Brig.-Gen. J. B. Pollok-M'Call, had crossed the valley of Ajalon and reached Beit Sira. It halted there during the following day, and on that afternoon, with artillery and machine-guns, the Turks attacked a small post, a mile east of Beit Ur el Foka, on the extreme eastern flank of the Yeomanry Division. With the help of a small reinforcement, the post held out until the morning of the 28th, when it had to be given up, and, with it, a section of the line had to be drawn in.

During the evening of 27th November all the wires were broken, so that all messages had to be sent by despatch-riders. One of these men was trying to find his way to 52nd Division Headquarters, in order to deliver a message from Corps Headquarters, when he reached the Head-quarters of the 155th Brigade. From this message Gen. Pollok-M'Call learnt of the existence of the gap, and of the danger. He at once got ready to move his brigade to the threatened area. About midnight came orders from Gen. Hill to send a battalion at 5.45 a.m. to stop the gap between Shilta and Beit Ur el Tahta. At the time named the 4th R.S.F., Lt.-Col. N. G. Stewart-Richardson, set out with a section of the 155th Machine-Gun Company. At 8 a.m., Gen. Pollok-M'Call was ordered to proceed with another battalion at once to Suffa, which lay midway in the gap. On the way he encountered an armoured car, and, so serious was the news that it brought, that he ordered the remainder of his brigade to follow immediately.

Using the tracks which run westwards and southwards from the Jerusalem–Nablous road, throughout the 28th the Turks were moving troops towards the gap, and, when the 155th Brigade arrived before Suffa, the horses of Turkish cavalry could be seen tied to trees west of the village.

BEIT UR EL TAHTA AND EL BURJ

The place was strongly held by the enemy, who opened a heavy machine-gun fire on the Fusiliers and Borderers as they came in sight. So full of hills and ridges is this rugged country, that it is almost impossible to be sure that any particular point may not be under observation from some grey height, whose outline can barely be distinguished in the general tumble of spur and crest. Major D. Yuille, the veteran Quartermaster of the 4th R.S.F., tells how his transport suddenly found themselves caught in the open by machine-guns and snipers. " We made for a spur of a hill across a hundred yards of open with the bullets spurting all around. Heaven only knows how we got across that with only one camel struck. I led them out, leading my horse, or rather pulling it behind me. . . . We got in behind the spur and the camels perched like seagulls among the rocks, and there we had to sit the whole day absolutely marooned by machine-gun fire, with bullets pinging against the rocks. At nightfall I got all the transport disentangled and behind another hill where only dropping bullets were the menace."

Shortly before the arrival of the 155th Brigade, a party of Turks with machine-guns had taken up a position overlooking the road to Berfilya. They had wiped out a section of the Yeomanry Divisional Ammunition Column, and had nearly shot a motor cyclist, whose first warning of danger had been the dead men and horses and wrecked wagons lying about the road. Shortly afterwards the 155th Brigade found these Turks, and drove them away.

The general position of affairs at this time was as follows : The enemy were attacking from Beit Ur el Foka on the right to Shilta on the left, that is to say from the 2000 feet contour to the Shephelah, or foot-hill country, and were using a force which included 3000 storm troops, four batteries of .77s, and some camel guns. There now ensued a series of actions, in which the troops nearest to hand, usually portions of the hard worked 52nd Division, were hurried forward wherever the danger point might lie, to stop a gap or reinforce a line.

Units found themselves broken up, brigades found themselves intermingled and reconstituted, and, by the 29th, the whole of the Division was back again in the line, fighting to save the salient, and so to make it possible to continue the campaign for Jerusalem.

The action of the 155th Brigade was vigorous. The 4th K.O.S.B., Lt.-Col. R. Dashwood-Tandy, with one company of the 5th R.S.F., were ordered to attack Suffa, covered by the fire of ten guns from the 155th Machine-Gun Company. Major R. W. Paton, who commanded the 5th R.S.F., was sent with three companies of his own battalion, two of the 5th K.O.S.B., and a sub-section of machine-guns, to make a wide detour through the defiles and attack Suffa from the south-west. The 4th R.S.F., Lt.-Col. N. G. Stewart-Richardson, which was then north-west of El Burj, was ordered to cooperate with him. The remaining two companies of the 5th K.O.S.B., and a company of the 5th R.S.F., were in reserve.

A long and hard day's fighting ensued, and the enemy could be clearly seen on the opposing heights. Lt.-Col. Dashwood-Tandy's force drove the Turks off a ridge and held it in spite of losses, but, although Major Paton's force formed a junction with the 4th R.S.F., it could not get round the Turkish right flank, because to do so it must cross an open valley, which was swept by machine-gun fire from the direction of Shilta, in the west. There was no artillery available to deal with this fire, the guns in the Nebi Samwil salient having been left with the 60th Division, and the remainder being still on the western edge of the foot-hills.

At 1 p.m. Gen. Pollok-M'Call received an urgent appeal for help from the G.O.C. Yeomanry Division, whose line at Hellabi, north-west of Tahta, was hard pressed and nearly breaking. In response to this call he immediately sent the remaining half of the 5th K.O.S.B. This left the 155th Brigade almost without reserves. It was a time of extreme danger as both right and left flanks of its long thin line were exposed. However, it fought on, and continued to hold up the Turkish advance which, otherwise, would have lapped round the left flank of the Yeomanry.

Meanwhile, on the same day, the 156th Brigade, Brig.-Gen. A. H. Leggett, had marched to Beit Likia. By this

BEIT UR EL TAHTA AND EL BURJ

time the Yeomanry had been compelled to evacuate Beit Ur el Foka, and had fallen back to a wooded ridge half-way to Tahta. As the 156th Brigade filed along the track from Beit Anan in full view of the Turks, they could see the bursts of the enemy shells following the retiring Yeomen along the ridges. The Turks were now close enough to shell the Roman Road, and they brought a very accurate fire to bear on a pass two miles east of Beit Likia. Before the 7th R.S. got through it, they lost an officer and four men wounded, besides four camels killed.

At 1 p.m., the 4th R.S., Lt.-Col. A. M. Mitchell, with a few machine-guns, was detached from the 156th Brigade and moved to the west of El Burj, which was under fire at the time. There, it extended the left of the 155th Brigade, to which it was now attached, and endeavoured to obtain touch with the 54th Division at Shilta.

At 3 p.m. the 156th Brigade was ordered into the line about a mile north of Beit Sira, coming up on the right of the 155th, part of whose line it took over, the 4th K.O.S.B., to the south of Suffa, being attached to the former Brigade. To the right of these Borderers were the 7th R.S., Lt.-Col. W. C. Peebles, and then the 8th Cameronians, Lt.-Col. J. M. Findlay. Half of the 156th Brigade Machine-Gun Company was in the front line. The 7th Cameronians, Lt.-Col. J. G. P. Romanes, was in reserve.

The 155th and 156th Brigades were now strung out almost in a single line, with their lateral communications swept at places by enemy artillery fire, with the Yeomanry on their right barely hanging on, or falling back fighting desperately, and with the Turks pressing everywhere.

The 4th K.O.S.B. fought the Turks all through the 28th, their Lewis guns putting several enemy machine-guns out of action. One attack was only repelled after a loss of twenty-nine officers and men, including Lieut. W. M. Mercer, killed. The attacking Turks, however, lost heavily in this fighting, as an officer prisoner disclosed, this being due to the storm of bullets poured on them by the Borderers, and the heavy fire of some 74th Division guns, that had been brought from Latron to the Roman Road south of Beit Sira.

After darkness the 155th Brigade withdrew from its operation against Suffa, and fell back to a defensive line north-east of El Burj. Next to the 4th R.S. was the 4th R.S.F., then the combined force of three companies of 5th R.S.F. and two of 5th K.O.S.B. One company of the 5th R.S.F. was in reserve at El Burj. Because of the stony nature of the ground, it was impossible to dig trenches, so that, in order to obtain shelter behind rocks and to build sangars, most irregular defence lines had to be taken up. As the units became spread out in small posts over miles of ridges, communications became more and more difficult, and so, when darkness fell, the situation became more obscure and obviously more perilous.

Half an hour after the 155th Brigade had taken up its new position, a burst of firing and bombing was heard to the north-west, followed by silence. Gen. Pollok-M'Call telephoned Lt.-Col. Mitchell, of the 4th R.S., to enquire what was happening. " After some delay Col. Mitchell replied in the most matter-of-fact way that the nearest post of the unit on his left, consisting of half a company, had been rushed and captured, leaving a gap of two miles in the line " (Gen. Pollok-M'Call).

The Turks had annihilated a detachment of 120 men of the 54th Division at Shilta. This laid open the whole of the line of the 155th Brigade to enfilade. However, the situation was taken calmly. El Burj formed a strong *point d'appui* behind its line, and could have been held indefinitely, and its machine-guns could sweep the ground to the north-west, that is towards Shilta. The Brigade therefore did not modify its dispositions, although the Turks held commanding positions and throughout the night poured a good deal of harassing machine-gun fire on the places held by the Lowlanders.

At 6.30 p.m. Brig.-Gen. Leggett had to send the 7th Cameronians to Tahta, where the 7th Mounted Brigade were struggling desperately to hold back the Turks.

This left the 155th and 156th Brigades with no reserves, but for the single company at El Burj. Nothing was known at the time of the strength of the Turkish attacking force,

BEIT UR EL TAHTA AND EL BURJ

and the situation was one of the greatest anxiety. The 157th Brigade was awaiting relief by the 74th Division, and had orders from Gen. Hill to march at once to take up a position to defend the Roman Road between Beit Anan and Beit Likia, the portion south-west of Foka, opposite which the Turks were pressing so hard. Dukka was still defended by the cavalry, but it will be noticed how the lines of defence were moving back until they were beginning to rest actually on the lines of communication. It was a time when no one could be certain where the line was, and whether troops firing from the rear were British or a Turkish raiding party.

The 5th Borderers, who had been sent to help the Yeomanry north-west of Tahta, were very soon in the front line at an exposed place called Two Tree Post. The line was very thin and at 7 p.m. on the 28th a Turkish patrol got through and was firing into the rear of this post, until driven out by the Borderers. At midnight the Turks attacked Two Tree Post but were repelled, and the Borderers were reinforced by some Australians. Three hours later the enemy again attacked with great determination, but their bombers were held off by Lewis guns and rifles, and they were finally driven away.

It will be remembered that the 7th Cameronians, with companies of a rifle strength of about forty each, were also fighting with the Yeomanry to save Tahta. The Turkish fire had worked havoc among the animals and the place reeked with the stench of their corpses. Three Cameronian companies were soon in the widely extended line, and under heavy shell and machine-gun fire from the front and in enfilade.

Capt. A. J. M'Guffie, on taking over part of the line, found that it was near the foot of a precipitous hill held by the enemy. He set out with about forty men to scale and capture the height. With a final, desperate charge the position was taken, but the gallant M'Guffie was killed whilst leading his men forward, and enfilade fire drove the Cameronians out, so that they had to fall back in ones and twos to their original line. The attack failed, but, nevertheless, such counter-movements were useful in damping the Turkish ardour for an advance. All through the 29th the Cameronians fought on under heavy shell-fire and kept the enemy back, killing many Turks and taking seventeen prisoners.

2nd Lieut. A. R. M'Gillivray was shot through the forearm but carried on. He was shot again through the thigh, but stayed on in the firing line to direct and encourage his men. Finally, he was shot through the head and killed.

The 7th Cameronians had nearly fifty casualties here, and so determined were some of the Turkish attacks, that some thought that the battalion would be wiped out. The orders to every unit in the Lowland Division were the same : the Turk must be held back at all costs.

28th November was probably the most critical period, but the gap had been closed and the enemy were held up by the Lowland Division, with the assistance of some Yeomen,[1] Australian cavalry and artillery of the 74th Division who had been hurried forward from the south and west. During the 29th reinforcements of cavalry, infantry, and artillery were collected from various quarters, and thrust forward to defend the line. The sound of the British guns was heartening to the defenders after the gruelling they had endured without effectual artillery support.

The Lowland Howitzer artillerymen had reached Amwas on the 28th, and had taken over the guns of the 60th Division, when they received orders to proceed at once to Beit Likia. By a forced march they came into action before dawn on the 29th, just where they had been a week previously. All day long they shelled the Turks who were attacking Tahta, breaking up the enemy attacks. The task of the observers, who had constantly to change their positions as the battle swayed among the hills and ridges, was a most difficult one. To carry out his duties, a forward observation officer must be as close to the enemy as possible, and in fighting such as this, when the line can only consist of a series of fragments, the risks they had to run were innumerable. On one occasion, Major Campbell, of the Lowland

---

[1] As distinct from the Yeomen already fighting in the line of the Yeomanry Mounted Division.

BEIT UR EL TAHTA AND EL BURJ 467

Howitzers, was quietly looking about for a good observation post, when he found himself confronted by an armed Turk, whilst at the moment he possessed nothing more deadly than his slide-rule. He pulled this out, however, and pointed it at the Turk, who surrendered and was brought in.

The relieving troops for the 157th Brigade did not commence to arrive until 3 a.m. on the 29th, but before dawn it managed to get into its new position, covering the Roman Road south-west of Foka.

The general position on the 29th was better. On the left of the danger area, the 155th Brigade had got machine-guns into good positions at and behind El Burj, from which they opened a harassing fire on the Turks, wherever they were known to be, pouring 12,500 rounds into Shilta alone.

About 8 a.m. the men of the 155th Brigade were busy building sangars, when the Turks were again seen advancing to attack them. They came on in small parties at a time but only half-heartedly, and were swept by machine-gun and now also by artillery fire. Shortly after mid-day, some had crept forward and were lying on stony ground about 250 yards in front of the 155th's line.

A 5th R.S.F. Lewis gun was sent out to enfilade the Turks from the east, and a 4th R.S.F. gun to catch them from the west. When these were ready, Stokes trench mortars opened on the Turks from the front, and the enemy suffered heavily.

Latterly, during that day, said a Border officer, " it was for all the world like a day's ferreting at home," the trench mortars of the 155th routing out the enemy, while the machine-guns and rifles picked them off as they ran.

By nightfall only a few snipers were left, and a patrol, which went forward 350 yards, found all quiet. The Turks before El Burj had been thoroughly discomfited, and the situation restored.

Late on 29th November, the 3rd Australian Light Horse Brigade relieved the 155th Brigade, which then proceeded to Beit Sira, with the exception of the 4th R.S.F., which was left in reserve at El Burj. This brought the 155th close to the 156th, which the 4th R.S. rejoined. The 156th had been sniped and machine-gunned all through the 29th, but in the course of the Turkish attacks the Royal Scots and Cameronians had settled many an old account, and the enemy had made no headway. By nightfall the Turks were tired of sending their assaulting parties to scale those deadly grey speckled ridges, only to be shot down and bombed from above, and they contented themselves with artillery work and sniping.

During the evening of the 29th and the night following, the right of the Yeomanry Division, about Dukka and elsewhere, was relieved by a brigade of the 74th Division, and its left, including the defence of Tahta, had been taken over by the 157th Brigade. This relief, like many others carried out by the Lowlanders, took place in darkness, over unknown ground, with the situation uncertain, and the enemy close at hand and aggressive. The 6th H.L.I., Lt.-Col. Jas. Anderson, was on the right, on the scene of Joshua's famous victory, as also was the 5th H.L.I., Col. F. L. Morrison, in the centre, to the north-east of Tahta. The 7th H.L.I., Lt.-Col. E. S. Gibbons, was on the left, its western flank being less than a mile south of Suffa, and in touch with the 8th Cameronians. The line of the 7th H.L.I. was anything between twenty and fifty yards distant from the Turks, so that they received the help of a larger share of the machine-guns and trench mortars which were distributed about the line. The 5th A. & S.H., Lt.-Col. C. L. Barlow, was in reserve just south of Tahta. Rifle and machine-gun fire went on throughout the night.

The Turkish Higher Command was determined to break through at Tahta. At 1 a.m. on the 30th, the 5th H.L.I. had taken over a rocky ridge, which fell away sheer for about seventy feet. Sangars, outcrops of rock, and depressions, here, as elsewhere, afforded the only protection. At 3 a.m. the Turks made a succession of bombing rushes up the hill and the whole line became engaged.

The severest fighting was on the left at Two Tree Post, which had been held previously by the 5th K.O.S.B. Capt. L. M'Lellan, in charge of the post, had been killed earlier in the night, and the Turks began to press the point

BEIT UR EL TAHTA AND EL BURJ

dangerously with bombs. At a critical time Capt. Campbell, in charge of that part of the line, was hit, and one of the two Lewis guns in the post knocked out of action. On hearing of this 2nd Lieut. T. W. Woodhead, 5th K.O.S.B., dashed over the open into the post with a Lewis gun and a party of his men. He got both guns into action, and saved what might have been a most awkward situation. Later, this post was held by men from the 5th K.O.S.B.

About 6 a.m. a strong and concerted attack developed on the whole battalion front, and, with bomb and bayonet, the Turks broke through the centre of its line. The position was dangerous in the extreme, because this ridge was just above Tahta, but the men fought stubbornly, and Major J. B. Neilson, hurrying forward a reserve company, charged with the bayonet and drove the Turks back. In this last struggle 2nd Lieut. C. T. Price was killed and two other officers were wounded. Thirty-five of the men had fallen.

St Andrew's Day, 1917, was one of great anxiety, but was fairly quiet, apart from the usual shell-fire and sniping. Gen. Hamilton-Moore had received orders to hold Tahta at all costs, and, accordingly, reinforced the 5th H.L.I. with the two companies of the 5th K.O.S.B., that had been left behind when the Yeomanry were relieved. He also raised the number of machine-guns and trench mortars in this section of the line to four of each, and moved two companies of the 5th Argylls, one in close support to the 5th H.L.I., the other into some woods south-east of Tahta.

In the early morning of the 1st December the Turks made two last attempts to break through the northern side of the Nebi Samwil salient: at Tahta, and further to the west, at El Burj. They had also planned a determined attempt to retake Nebi Samwil on the same day.

Just after midnight the Turks commenced a general attack, which however was not pressed with determination. The British artillery opened fire, but the steepness of the sides of the valley prevented the shells from searching it properly. The enemy could creep up comparatively close without machine-guns and rifles being able to reach them.

About 1 a.m. a heavy attack developed against the right of the 5th H.L.I. and it was driven off the ridge. Col. Morrison counter-attacked with his company of 5th Argylls, but in the darkness it missed its direction. Gen. Hamilton-Moore suspected that the enemy on the ridge were a covering party to a larger attacking party behind, who would aim for Tahta, and proceeded at once to collect his reserves in order to drive the Turks back. Meanwhile, the 157th Brigade trench mortars, the weapons best suited for such a situation, were pouring their shells among the rocks and into the hollows where the Turks were lying, undoubtedly demoralizing them and inflicting many casualties. At 4.30 a.m. a company of the 5th Argylls rushed the captured portion of the ridge, and retook it with little loss, the Turks hardly waiting to receive the assault.

Except for constant rifle and machine-gun fire the remainder of the night passed quietly, and the Turks abandoned all further attempts on Tahta.

During this night the 5th H.L.I. lost a further three officers and twenty-two other ranks, including Lieut. G. A. Sillars, killed. In the thirty hours that it had been in the line it had lost nine officers and forty-seven other ranks. Since the 7th November this battalion had suffered twenty-four officer casualties.

During the night of 1-2nd December the 157th Brigade was relieved by the 30th Brigade of the 10th Division, and set out once more on its march to the plains, leaving behind a thoroughly worsted enemy.

Whilst the Turks were attacking at Tahta, they were also attacking further west.

The 3rd Australian Light Horse Brigade were holding the line in front of El Burj, when, at 1.20 a.m. on the 1st December, 500 Turkish storm troops, fresh from Galicia, attacked with bombs and drove them off the crest of a small but important ridge north of that place, taking two trenches. The Australians, being cavalry, had not been issued with grenades, so that they were at a disadvantage, but managed in the darkness to cling to the reverse slope of the ridge just below the crest. Not thirty yards away on the other

BEIT UR EL TAHTA AND EL BURJ

side of the crest were Turks throwing stick bombs at them, and elsewhere the enemy were bringing a heavy fire to bear from machine-guns and automatic rifles.

A company of 4th R.S.F., about 130 strong, was hurried forward, and arrived at the scene of action, just as the Turks were developing another attack, intended to thrust the Australians off the hill altogether. Some Gloucester Yeomanry were also brought forward. 2nd Lieut. J. Boughey, 5th R.S.F., had hurried on ahead, leading forward a small party of grenadiers. Grasping the situation, he at once attacked the horde of Turks, catching them in the flank with a shower of bombs. Many of the enemy fell, a brief, hot encounter ensued, but the sudden attack from an unexpected quarter had dumbfounded them, and in a few seconds the Turks, who a moment before had been advancing to victory, were fleeing for their lives down the slope, pursued by Boughey and his men, who hurled Mills grenades after them as they ran. The Fusiliers were furious at losing their rest,[1] and vented their wrath to the full on the Turks. Boughey had outrun the others, and at the foot of the slope a party of twenty-five Turks surrendered to him.

A few moments later, as he turned round to go for more bombs, he was shot through the head, and died soon afterwards. His gallantry undoubtedly saved a critical situation, and Brig.-Gen. L. C. Wilson, of the 3rd Australian Light Horse Brigade, when thanking Lt.-Col. Stewart-Richardson for his help, called special attention to Boughey's conduct. For his gallant action on this occasion, 2nd Lieut. J. H. Boughey was awarded the Victoria Cross.

Another company of the 4th R.S.F. was brought forward, and their bombers went into the line, which was holding up the enemy attack on the main position. Between 2 a.m. and 6 a.m. these gallant Turks attacked three times, but each time were repulsed with heavy losses, the bombers and Lewis gunners of the 4th R.S.F. doing very deadly work. At

[1] One Fusilier was heard to shout the following, as he threw bomb after bomb at the fleeing Turks: "They mairched us a hunner miles! (Tak' that, ya ——!) An' we've been in five fechts! (Anither yin, ya ——!) and they said we wur relieved! (Tak' that, ya ——!) and we're oot oor beds anither nicht! (Swalla that, ya ——!)"

dawn the Turks tried to retire, but found that they could not, because of enfilade fire from some Australians with machine-guns, in addition to an artillery barrage in their rear, both of which caused them heavy casualties. Two parties, one of Australians and the other of the 4th R.S.F., now moved towards the flanks of the entangled enemy, the survivors of whom surrendered forthwith. In all, six officers and a hundred and six unwounded and sixty wounded Turks were taken prisoners. Over a hundred enemy dead were found close to the British trenches, and there were many more lying at points near by, so that it is believed that not a man of this Turkish battalion escaped. The captured Turks were wearing shrapnel helmets for the first time on this front. Among the prisoners was a German battalion commander. This ended the last Turkish attempt to cut the Roman Road.

In addition to 2nd Lieut. Boughey, the 4th R.S.F. only lost three other ranks killed and six wounded. The total British losses in this affair were nine killed and forty-seven wounded.

The 4th R.S.F. was withdrawn on the evening of the 1st, and rejoined the 155th Brigade at Amwas. The 4th K.O.S.B. also rejoined. On the following day the Brigade marched to Ramleh.

The 156th Brigade was relieved on the night of 1-2nd December by a brigade of the 10th Division, and it, also, set out for Ramleh viâ Kubab.

The losses of the three brigades in warding off these Turkish attacks from the 28th November to the 1st December were as follows :

155TH BRIGADE.

Unit.	Killed and Died of Wounds.		Wounded.		Total.	
	Officers.	O.R.	Officers.	O.R.	Officers.	O.R.
4th R.S.F. - -	1	13	1	23	2	36
5th R.S.F. - -	—	10	4	18	4	28
4th K.O.S.B. -	1	7	1	24	2	31
5th K.O.S.B. -	1	1	—	12	1	13
155th M.G. Coy. -	—	3	—	2	—	5
155th L.T.M. Battery	—	3	—	—	—	3
	3	37	6	79	9	116

BEIT UR EL TAHTA AND EL BURJ

To the names, mentioned in the text, of officers who gave up their lives must be added that of Capt. A. B. M'Creath 5th K.O.S.B.

156TH BRIGADE.

Unit.	Killed and Died of Wounds.		Wounded.		Total.	
	Officers.	O.R.	Officers.	O.R.	Officers.	O.R.
4th Royal Scots	—	—	—	—	—	—
7th Royal Scots	—	—	1	4	1	4
7th Cameronians	2	11	1	34	3	45
8th Cameronians	—	3	1	9	1	12
	2	14	3	47	5	61

157TH BRIGADE.

Unit.	Killed and Died of Wounds.		Wounded.		Total.	
	Officers.	O.R.	Officers.	O.R.	Officers.	O.R.
Brigade H.Q.	—	—	—	2	—	2
5th H.L.I.	3	18	6	36	9	54
6th H.L.I.	—	1	1	2	1	3
7th H.L.I.	—	1	1	2	1	3
5th A. & S.H.	—	2	—	5	—	7
157th M.G. Coy.	—	3	—	1	—	4
	3	25	8	48	11	73

We can only estimate the Turkish casualties in this counter-movement, but everything points to their having been very severe. Moreover, they lost this opportunity, probably the best they ever had in the Jerusalem campaign, of turning a British victory into disaster.

On the day of the last attacks on Tahta and El Burj they made three determined attacks on the Nebi Samwil position, but the British had had time to prepare the defence, and the 60th Division drove them off with a loss of at least 500 killed. The Turks had hoped to break into the base of the Nebi Samwil salient, and to recapture its commanding apex at the same time, but they had failed. After a few more engagements on the northern front, the Turks evacuated Foka, Suffa, and elsewhere, giving up all they had regained.

While the Turks had been fighting for Nebi Samwil, the 53rd Division had advanced from the south, and the 60th Division had closed in from the west. 6-inch howitzers, 60-pounders and many 18-pounders, besides mountain guns, were brought forward from the plains along the hill-roads, of which those from Jimzu to Nebi Samwil and Kuryet el Enab to Biddu had been fashioned and improved under the Lowland Royal Engineers. On 8th December, the 53rd, 60th, and 74th[1] Divisions attacked and took most of the remaining positions covering Jerusalem. The capture of the Nebi Samwil ridge was completed by the 74th before dawn on the 9th, and on the same day Jerusalem fell for the twenty-third time in its history, and for the first time was captured by the British. After 600 years the Christian had returned.

It is interesting to note that the total losses of the whole of the 20th Corps during the last battle for Jerusalem, that is on 8-9th December were 827. Of these, the 60th Division suffered 553, an extremely light figure considering the strength of the defences captured and the difficulties of the ground.[2]

The cost to the Lowland Division in battle casualties for the seizure and defence of the key position of Nebi Samwil was over 1000 officers and men. There can be no more significant comment on the part played by the Lowland Division in the capture of Jerusalem.

It was the lot of one or two of the Lowland units to march through some Australian camps as they made for Ramleh. As the remnants passed along, ragged, hungry, weary, some marching with puttees tied round bleeding feet, others with boot soles minus their uppers tied over their socks, the generous-hearted Colonials, learning that these small parties were all that were left of lusty battalions, came out and cheered as only brave, strong men can cheer when their feelings are deeply stirred.

[1] The 74th was commanded by Major-General E. S. Girdwood, C.B., late of the 156th Brigade.

[2] The total British casualties from 28th November to 10th December —inclusive of the fighting about Tahta, Foka, Nebi Samwil and around Jerusalem—are given by W. T. Massey as 1667.

CHAPTER XXVII

(3RD DECEMBER, 1917 TO 11TH APRIL, 1918)

THE BATTLE OF JAFFA—THE PASSAGE OF THE AUJA

"So fierce was his onset this day that the Turks very soon all turned off from his irresistible attack, and left a free passage to our army. Thus at last, despite their wounds, our men reached the Standard, the ranks were formed again and the host proceeded to Arsuf, outside which town it pitched its tents." (*Itinerarium Regis Ricardi*.)
King Richard I., the Lion-Hearted, at his victory outside Arsuf over the army of Saladin on the 7th September, 1191.

THE 155th Brigade reached the neighbourhood of Ramleh on 2nd December, the 156th and 157th on the following day. There, a few days were spent in reorganization and the absorption of a few drafts which arrived. Some units that were near Surafend managed to get new service dress and boots for their men. There was a spell of bright sunshine, water was available for the washing both of bodies and of clothes, and bivouac areas were gay with lines of blankets, shirts, socks, and so on, drying in the sun. By the time the Division reached the low country again, not a man had seen a cigarette for days, but some were now obtained, and the relief was unspeakable. One Machine-Gun Company, on its way to Ramleh, on encamping for one night, found that the cook's fire could not be lit, because there was not a match in the whole unit. They had to wait for the next company.

On the 5th December the 155th marched out to take over the line north of Jaffa. The last stage of the move was done after nightfall, as otherwise it would have been under Turkish observation. Before the column arrived at its bivouac area, the rain began, and it continued incessantly for five days, producing the most miserable conditions for the troops. The 157th Brigade moved on the 6th to an area near Selmeh, three and a half miles east of Jaffa, but the ground was flooded next day, so that rifles and equipment sank in the quagmire. These were recovered, and on the following day it moved to another area where there had been some attempt at a drainage system. The 156th moved out at about 2 p.m. on the 7th to march the nine miles to Selmeh, but by this time the ground was one vast sea of watery mud and slime. The rate of march was about a mile an hour, and inky darkness soon closed down. The troops, not too fit after their long spell of hardships, were carrying packs and blankets again for the first time since Gaza, and frequently sank to their knees in the morasses which spread everywhere. Equipment and clothes were sodden and heavy with rain. Marching was a weariness and a toil, and, buffeted and lashed by wind and rain, many collapsed and fell out. There was no foothold for the camels, and they staggered and slipped and fell in all directions. Ropes broke and loads collapsed, and, when it was once " barracked " to re-adjust the load, it was almost impossible to coax a beast to its feet again. Their struggles seemed only to embed the animals deeper in the mire, and many wretched beasts fell down for the last time on that night. The worst place was where the track crossed a wadi about twenty feet deep. It was impassable for the camels and for the wheeled transport, which had now rejoined the Division. They had to find another way across, and followed by a detour early the next morning. Advance parties had got fires and tea ready, but by the time the 156th Brigade arrived, about 11.30 p.m. of the 7th, all the fires had been put out by the rain, and officers and men could only sit about, sleepless, and wait in misery for the morning, when the deluge subsided into a drizzle. The plight of the 155th Brigade, which had taken over a line of posts overlooking the southern shores of the River Auja, and of the 157th Brigade, bivouacked in a ploughed field, were very little better. For pure misery, without the excitement of

BATTLE OF JAFFA—PASSAGE OF AUJA

battle, it was one of the worst experiences that the Lowlanders had.

On the evening of the 8th the 156th Brigade took over the line between the 155th and the sea. Its reserves were at Sarona. This was a German-Jewish colony, with good houses, surrounded by orange groves. Needless to say all people who had German connections were at once segregated. The buildings supplied good billets to half of the 156th Brigade, and the groves refreshing fruit to the whole Division. All the troops of the Division were re-clothed and re-equipped, and some more badly needed drafts of men arrived. The Turks shelled the lines intermittently, but caused few casualties, and work on the improvement of the defences was carried on apace.

News came on 9th December of the surrender of Jerusalem. Two days later Sir Edmund Allenby entered the Holy City on foot by the Jaffa Gate, which the Arabs call " The Friend." For centuries there had been current among the Arabs a prophecy that from the West would come a deliverer, bearing a name which signified a Prophet, who would deliver Judaea from the Turk, and at whose advent the waters of the Nile would flow into the Holy Land. The prophecy had been literally fulfilled, for the name Allenby[1] as an Arabic word signifies " The Prophet," while the pipe-line laid across the weary miles of desert carried the waters of the Nile from the Sweet Water Canal in Egypt, for the refreshment of the British troops in Palestine. No other city in the world is so sacred to so many great religions, and the moral effect of this victory cannot be over-estimated. Four of the greatest cities of the Moslem world, Mecca, Jerusalem, Baghdad and Cairo, were now under British influence. It was certain that the Turks and their German allies would attempt to recover Jerusalem as soon as possible; failure to do so would be taken by Orientals as an acknowledgment of British superiority.

Two immediate problems lay before Gen. Allenby. Jerusalem and its port and natural base of supplies, Jaffa,

[1] El-Nebi : Allenby.

had to be made secure. Jerusalem was the problem of the 20th Corps, Jaffa of the 21st.

Just north of Jaffa, the Turks held strong positions on high ground near the sea, at Khurbet Hadrah and Sheikh Muannis. The first is within six miles of the port and the second within four, so that, as soon as they could get heavy guns into position, not only the town but the roadstead would be at their mercy. At this time, as Turkish observers could easily see, Jaffa was being used as a landing place for stores, which otherwise could hardly have been brought forward, as the railway and land transport in general had long been working at their utmost capacity. As it was, all movement on the south bank of the river attracted instant fire from the Turkish field guns, and they were not above sniping at single individuals. The Division had three or four dozen men killed or wounded as a result of these unpleasant attentions. It was essential that without delay the Turks be driven from these positions and forced to take up others further up the coast.

The great problem was how to get at these positions in order to capture them. The village of Sheikh Muannis and the ruin of Khurbet Hadrah are on the southern ends of two low parallel spurs, which run north and south. The country about them is mostly open grass land, with a few gardens, groves and farms, so that they have excellent fields of fire all round them. The former is about a mile and a half from the coast and the latter a similar distance further inland. These spurs terminate abruptly in steep slopes some five hundred yards from the perennial River Auja, which winds about across their front until it reaches the sea, fulfilling the part of a broad, deep moat. Under normal conditions this river has a depth of from ten to twelve feet and a breadth of from forty to fifty yards. The stream has a speed of anything up to three miles an hour, but forty-eight hours of rain will transform it into a rushing torrent, and add another fathom to its depth, a grave consideration for troops who have to force its passage, and, if successful, to maintain themselves on the other side. Within the Divisional sector there were the following crossings : where the river

BATTLE OF JAFFA—PASSAGE OF AUJA 479

spread out a little in crossing the beach, a ford which was liable to shift with the strength of the stream, and in flood time to disappear altogether ; at Jerisheh to the south-east of Muannis, a mill dam partially destroyed ; to the south of Hadrah a mill dam and stone bridge partially demolished. There were some more bridges further east, but they were too far away from the coastal positions and lay behind the Turkish lines, which crossed the Auja about the Hadrah stone bridge, and ran over Bald Hill, a commanding position covering the village and orange groves of Mulebbis on the south side of the river. The ford was the only practicable crossing in existence. Any others would have to be made.

On either bank, and especially on the southern, stretch several thousand yards of level areas of black cotton soil, which, after rain, are transformed into miry swamps. Apart from a few gardens and orange groves, all of which could be searched with fire, it is a level, coverless area, which defenders on the northern banks can sweep from end to end at the easiest ranges. The British were superior in artillery, but, even so, with a very modest force of machine-gunners and riflemen, and with well-concealed artillery, the Turk could have made them pay a terrible price, had they been compelled to force the passage of the Auja by daylight.

Now, on the 24th November, a week after the capture of Jaffa, cavalry of the Australian and New Zealand Mounted Division and infantry of the 54th Division had seized these crossings, but the Turks, with their wonderful powers of recuperation, were recovering from the effects of their disastrous retreat, and counter-attacked in force at 3 a.m. on the following morning. The British had no artillery, the few available river crossings were swept by fire ; and the force which had crossed was only extricated with difficulty, after suffering many casualties. This first attempt did not augur well for the second.

Lt.-Gen. Sir E. S. Bulfin, G.O.C. 21st Corps, held a conference of divisional commanders at Jaffa on 12th December, and disclosed the Corps plan for the driving of the Turks up the coast. Commencing at dawn on the 21st December, there was to be a twenty-four hours bombardment of the whole Turkish position, warships shelling the strong artillery positions of Tel el Rekket and El Jelil near the coast. Covering troops from the 52nd Division were to be thrown across the Auja after nightfall, when bridges were to be built. The three divisions, advancing on a wide front, the 52nd across the Auja, the 54th for Mulebbis, and the 75th on the right for Bireh, were then to commence a forward movement, the successive stages of which would last almost two days, that is from the night of the 21st until the afternoon of the 22nd. These were deliberate methods, and, whilst it was certain that the bombardment would warn the enemy to be ready for the attempt, it was very doubtful whether it would be extensive enough to search out and destroy sufficient of the enemy's artillery and machine-guns to prevent them inflicting extremely heavy casualties, before the bridges were built and the assaulting troops had got across. The fact that it seemed the only feasible method to the tried experts who had considered the problem showed how great were the difficulties to be faced.

There was an alternative, that of a surprise, and Major-Gen. Hill discussed it carefully with his Brigadiers.

On the night of 13-14th December a daring reconnaissance of the Auja was carried out at a point about 2500 yards west of Jerisheh Mill, and south-west of Muannis, by Lieut. G. Stanley Smith, with Lance-Cpl. J. M'Gregor, and Ptes. R. Horsburgh, R. Liddell, and T. Newton, all of the 4th R.S. A boat made by the Divisional Royal Engineers of a wooden framework covered by a tarpaulin, and lined inside with straw, was carried down to the river bank at night. Lewis gun teams of the 8th Cameronians took up covering positions. The voyagers then, at 8 p.m. set out in their craft, navigating her with five paddles. Owing to brilliant starlight the surface of the river looked very white, and it seemed impossible for any sentry within 200 yards not to have seen them. They crossed to the northern bank. They found no sentry for 200 yards up or down from their crossing place. There was long grass, which was not prickly, but gave a good foothold and good cover. Beyond the bank was a bare

BATTLE OF JAFFA—PASSAGE OF AUJA 481

field, in which it would be easy to entrench. After three hours they returned safely without having heard or seen anyone. Smith estimated the breadth of the river at eighty feet and its speed at about two miles an hour. This helped to confirm Gen. Hill in his opinion of the possibility of a surprise attack.

On the next day, the 14th, Gen. Hill submitted to the Corps Commander a scheme, in detail, for a surprise attack by the Division with no preliminary bombardment. Such a surprise could only succeed if the Royal Engineers could bridge the Auja, and if the bulk of the Division could be brought down to its banks, and got across to the other side without the Turks' knowledge. It entailed perfect organization and discipline throughout the Division. Every possibility had to be thought of and provided for. There must be no mistakes. After considering the plan and the difficulties to be overcome, Gen. Bulfin and his staff thought it hardly possible that the feat could be carried through to a successful conclusion. However, Gen. Hill knew his Division and had entire confidence in it. Gen. Bulfin finally sanctioned the scheme to take place on the night of the 20th December, but with the proviso that, if it failed, the Division was to be prepared to take its place in the regular Corps attack, commencing on the next day, for he had decided to go on with his own plan as well. Gen. Hill asked for cavalry, with which to follow up his crossing of the river. Unfortunately, his request was refused.

The Division, then, stood committed to a night attack across a river fordable only at its mouth, and for practical purposes unbridged. Major-Gen. Hill had staked his reputation on its success, and, how thoroughly his Division, from the Brigade Commanders to the latest joined privates, supported him, we shall see. The *esprit de corps* of the Division had always been of the highest order, and on this occasion its value was especially evident. The whole Division was on its mettle.

In addition to their positions at Muannis and Hadrah, aeroplane reconnaissance and other information showed the Turks to have some rifle pits and entrenchments at various places on the northern bank, and especially to cover the ford at the mouth. Further information had to be obtained as to the enemy system of sentries and patrols. Everything had to be done without awakening Turkish suspicions.

The 155th Brigade was to cross by two bridges of boats at a point about 1200 yards east of Jerisheh Mill. This spot was at the southern end of a tongue of land formed by a sharp bend southwards of the river, being chosen because the flanks of the troops who had crossed could be easily covered from the southern banks. Within 200 yards to the east lay an orange grove, suitable for the concealment of bridging material and stores for the attempt. The part nearest the river was rather thin, and had to be camouflaged on the night before the material was assembled. Patrols of the 5th K.O.S.B. cleared the south bank of the river from this area to the eastward for over 500 yards, on one occasion expelling some Turks from a trench near the south end of Hadrah Bridge.

The 156th Brigade was to cross by another pair of bridges at a point south-west of Muannis, and about 2500 yards west of Jerisheh Mill. The latter was probably an aiming point for Turkish artillery, and accordingly was avoided. At this crossing point, also, there was a grove where building material could be concealed. Listening posts were established along the south bank of the river, and these detected no Turkish patrols passing along the north bank within 700 yards of the point of intended crossing. A similar laxity of patrolling was noticed to right and left. The crossing places of the 155th and 156th Brigades had been chosen with the object of avoiding river bank defences and of pushing columns round the flanks and rear of the main positions.

The 157th Brigade was to cross at the ford, which was commanded by a strong system of trenches in the coastal sand-hills, besides rifle pits on the edge of the river. The 7th H.L.I. was to cross with the 156th Brigade, and to capture these entrenchments by surprise attack from their left flank and rear. The existence and exact location of this

BATTLE OF JAFFA—PASSAGE OF AUJA

ford, however, had still to be settled. This was done by a most daring reconnaissance.

In the evening of the 15th December Lt.-Col. Jas. Anderson, officer commanding the 6th H.L.I., Lieut. C. H. Hills, and two other officers of his battalion, made their way to the shore post of the 8th Cameronians, who at the time were holding the coastal position of the line. It was about 300 yards from the mouth of the Auja and the same distance from the edge of the surf. There was no moon, but a very bright planet in the west prevented the night from being absolutely dark. Col. Anderson and Hills then stripped. A covering party was sent out, and, having obtained all the information possible from the officer of the post, Col. Anderson and Hills made for the sea, the former carrying a pole with which to take soundings. They were both strong swimmers, and the water was warmer than the night air. They made their way along, until they had got past the mouth of the river. Before coming out of the sea, they remained lying in the water close to the beach to see if any of the enemy were about. Finding all clear, they hurried across the open to where they guessed the ford to be. They were now within eighty yards of Turkish trenches, which had machine-guns trained on the ford, and at any moment they might have been seen by a Turkish sentry. Getting into the water, they proceeded to grope about for the ford. The river water was very cold, it was flowing fast, and they had to dig their hands and feet into the sand and gravel of its bed in order to prevent the current from sweeping them back towards the surf. A Turk, afterwards taken prisoner, stated that he was on sentry duty at this time, and thought that he saw some heads moving in the water, but was not certain enough to raise an alarm. After a good deal of groping about, Col. Anderson found the bar which formed the ford. He crossed it, finding that it was from two and a half to three feet deep in the middle, and about twenty-four yards wide. He drove in a peg on the south bank to indicate the entrance to the ford. The sides were sloping and sandy, and the floor was of sand and gravel. Above it, the river was from eight to ten feet deep, and the banks were flat and swampy. They then estimated the distance from the ford to the edge of the Mediterranean,[1] re-entered the sea, and made their way back, very cold but completely successful.

For this exploit Lt.-Col. Jas. Anderson received a bar to his D.S.O., and Lieut. C. H. Hills was awarded the Military Cross.

Meanwhile, the C.R.E., Lt.-Col. L. Fortescue-Wells, and his company commanders, Major B. I. Rolling, Major G. W. Streeten and Major K. B. Griffiths-Williams, were solving one of the greatest problems of all—that of crossing the Auja where there were no fords. Failure here meant only one available crossing, and that well defended by the Turks.

The selection of the best material out of the little that was available required much consideration. The sections of the bridges had to be light enough to be carried by man-power over bad ground and in darkness, and at the same time the bridges must be strong and steady enough to bear marching troops. Finally it was decided to use floating piers made by stretching 2300 gallon canvas tanks round specially designed frameworks of timber. The tops of these floating piers, boats, rafts, or coracles, as they have been variously termed, were decked in with boarding. Road-bearers of timber were then made for the purpose of joining the piers, and were boarded over, the whole being designed so that these could be easily connected to the piers when the latter were in position. In order to deaden the sound of men's feet the planking of the bridges was covered with several layers of thick carpets taken from the houses of the German colony in Sarona. The 413th (Lowland) Field Company, with all the carpenters and joiners of the other companies attached, carried out the timber work at Jaffa.[2] These bridges were tested on a pond at Selmeh, near Jaffa, and the Engineers were thoroughly practised in making up the piers into bridges. Rope attachments were also made for pulling

---

[1] The Mediterranean is almost tideless, so that the water's edge was a good point to which to measure.

[2] I am indebted for these details to Major G. W. Streeten, R.E., late of the 410th (Lowland) Field Company.

BATTLE OF JAFFA—PASSAGE OF AUJA 485

some of these craft backwards and forwards across the river as ferry boats. The capacity of each raft was fifteen, exclusive of the two Royal Engineers who navigated it, and life-belts were provided for all when crossing. Many difficult and secret reconnaissances had to be made at night to ascertain the exact width of the river and height of its banks, because steep ascents at the Turkish ends of the bridges might cause disastrous delay and cost many lives.

To mention just one incident : Sapper R. S. Paton, 410th Company, swam across the river on the night of 18th December, and ascertained its width at the crossing place selected for the 155th Brigade.

The transportation of the sections and other Royal Engineers' material across the mud-flats to the places of concealment was a great problem. Heavy rain commenced to fall on the 18th and continued until the morning of the 20th, transforming the river plain into an almost impassable quagmire. By careful organization and accurate timing, one caravan after another, seventy camels at a time, was taken to the orange groves and bushes ; cactus hedges were breached ; the material was stowed away in a lane or a farm courtyard, or below some undergrowth ; and the caravans had safely returned before daylight, so that the Turks saw and suspected nothing. As Gen. Allenby stated in his despatches, " the chief difficulty lay in concealing the collection and preparation of rafts and bridging material."

The Royal Engineers also made control and signal dug-outs in the groves near the crossings, besides improving roads, preparing duck-boards, and so on. For heavier traffic, a barrel-pier bridge was prepared by the 412th Company to be thrown across near Jerisheh Mill as soon as the crossings had been secured.

The Divisional artillery, under Brig.-Gen. E. C. Massy, had to be prepared to shell a number of different positions, and to give support to a series of attacks, which would be flung at different times and at different places along a front of several miles. This had to be done without shelling their own side in the dark, and their time-table had to be flexible enough to admit of sudden readjustment. To avoid uncovering the surprise on the night of the attack by their bombardment, they accustomed the Turks to a regular evening bombardment of these places for the few days preceding 20th December. The machine-gun companies acted similarly. Warships also paid periodic visits, shelling the enemy at Muannis, and about Jelil further up the coast.

Certain of the Divisional guns were allotted definite objectives. The remainder were pooled for the purpose of switching barrages in different directions, not only to clear the way for the attacking columns, but by the blaze of their shell-bursts to direct them to their proper goals.

Using a pond in Sarona village, as many as possible of the infantry were practised daily in embarking and disembarking from the canvas boats. Those detailed for certain objectives were practised nightly in cutting gaps in cactus hedges and finding their way by compass through thick orange groves.

These were a few of the things that had to be thought out. In the end, however, final success would depend on the staff organization, and on the discipline of the troops; but it was the same steady and silent Division that had waited with thinned ranks for the final evacuation of Cape Helles that was now to move as steadily and silently across the Auja. There was to be no rifle shooting. Everything was to be done with the bayonet or bomb; that is, at close quarters. This order was carried out to the letter.

The three brigades were to cross simultaneously on the evening of the 20th, and at 10.30 p.m. the artillery was to open fire and the first assaulting parties were to move forward. Prior to that hour no Turks were to be disturbed.

On the 18th the 54th Division took over the line on the right from the 52nd Division, and the Australian and New Zealand Mounted Division on the left. By the night of the 19-20th great reserves of small arms ammunition, bombs, barbed wire and other Royal Engineers' material had been hidden close to the crossing places.

The whole scheme worked out so closely to the original plans, that it will be convenient now to narrate what happened.

BATTLE OF JAFFA—PASSAGE OF AUJA

At the outset the fates seemed to be against the attempt. But for a few tracks, the river-flats were slimy swamps. The rain had eased off by nightfall, but a watery moon jeopardized success by peeping between the scudding clouds. However, the Divisional Royal Engineers got to work and contrived tracks over the mud by the best means they had to hand. They cut great canvas tanks in two and spread them over the ground. At one place was a field of vegetables of the cabbage tribe. These were uprooted and packed tightly together, so that their stout shaws gave the slush a firmer consistency, before it was covered with tarpaulins. Fascines were laid down and covered with long screens of cloth or sacking material. The 12th Loyal North Lancs. Pioneer Battalion, under Lt.-Col. W. T. C. Beckett, gave great help to the Royal Engineers in this work. The improvization of these roads contributed greatly to the success of the affair.[1]

The downpour had had one advantage: it had flooded the Turkish trenches on the river banks.

In the centre, as the artillery started its usual slow nightly bombardment at 8 p.m., the 156th Brigade, Brig.-Gen. A. H. Leggett, got four rafts afloat, and the covering party, two officers and eighty other ranks of the 7th Cameronians (two companies), commenced to paddle across. They were all over within thirty-five minutes, and, with eight Lewis guns, had formed, in a muddy stretch of open flat, a crescent-shaped bridge-head, about 450 yards wide and 250 yards deep. This unit, under Lt.-Col. J. G. P. Romanes, was to be in reserve. The remainder then commenced to cross similarly: the 7th H.L.I., Lt.-Col. E. S. Gibbons, destined to carry from the flank the trenches covering the ford; the 4th R.S., Lt.-Col. A. M. Mitchell, to take Slag Heap Farm, about a mile from the

---

[1] All of these canvas tanks, etc., had to be accounted for to Ordnance. The two halves of each tank were sewn together, and the result was as efficient as the original. The half of one, however, was missing, and this could only be explained by its having been lost whilst in use as stated. According to a certain authority they had not been put to their proper use, and the result was a file of correspondence which lasted over a period of several months, and grew into a most ponderous bundle.

crossing place and west of Muannis ; the 8th Cameronians, Lt.-Col. J. M. Findlay, to take, from their flank and rear, the trenches south and south-west of Muannis ; and the 7th R.S., Lt.-Col. W. C. Peebles, to push through and occupy Muannis on its low height.

Meanwhile, the first bridge for this crossing was being constructed. Three-quarters of it was completed when grave difficulties arose. Some pontoons were holed and made water, so that they had to be replaced by others. These had to be carried over mud in which men sank up to their knees. The canvas and wood of the bridging material were sodden with rain, and extremely heavy. Gen. Leggett saw that the first bridge would not be ready in time, and that he could not get sufficient men across by the ferrying for an attack commencing at 10.30 p.m. He telephoned Gen. Hill, and, as the Turks were still undisturbed, the latter ordered a postponement of the attack for thirty minutes.

Everything now depended on the signallers of the Division, under Major Angwin, giving timely warning to all concerned. Failure to do so would probably result in a premature attack somewhere, and confusion. However, their organization also stood the test, and word was sent to all units soon after 10 p.m.

This postponement was a relief to the 155th Brigade, whose Royal Engineers and carrying parties of 4th K.O.S.B. had to work in a narrow lane between two sections of the grove, the only place possible. The canvas pontoons were so heavy, as a result of the torrential rains, that the number of men who could get hold of them could only carry them at a very slow pace and for a very short distance at a time.

In addition to the covering party, the following troops intended for this crossing had been ferried over by 11 p.m.: one company, 7th Cameronians ; four companies, 7th H.L.I. ; four companies, 4th R.S. ; and one company, 7th R.S. The remainder had still to cross, the bridge was unfinished, and the ferrying still proceeded, but there could be no further delay. The artillery were moving their fire

BATTLE OF JAFFA—PASSAGE OF AUJA

to Muannis, Slag Heap Farm, and other objectives. A few hundred yards to the east, on the northern side, a large walled orange grove ran down to the river, and within it, on the banks, were Turkish trenches. The company of 7th Cameronians at once set out for this; and by 12.40 a.m. had secured a house at its north-west corner, to which, later on, they carried 500 bombs and 50,000 rounds of small arms ammunition, the brigade reserve. The 7th H.L.I. also set out at once for the ford about two-thirds of a mile to the west. Ten minutes later, the 4th R.S. moved out for Slag Heap Farm, without waiting for the 7th R.S. or 8th Cameronians. The ferry continued working steadily, the bridge was completed, and troops were tramping over its pads of rich carpets by 11.50 p.m., so that by midnight the Brigade was across. Within five minutes after the last battalion had moved from the north bank, the ground near the bridge was subjected to a heavy outburst of enemy shelling. The last two battalions passed the field headquarters of the 4th R.S. at 1.15 a.m., and before 2 a.m. this battalion had rushed and captured Slag Heap Farm, after a short sharp fight, killing a number of Turks, capturing two, and also a machine-gun. The capture of this farm and the building in the orange grove helped to make the bridge-head more secure.

The whole Division was on the move by this time. The routes to be followed by the different battalions were not easy. The ground for almost a mile beyond the bridge crossings was water-logged, so that the pace was greatly retarded by slippery, adhesive mud and pools of slimy water. At different points direction had to be changed. It was pitch dark, and the ground was quite unknown, but for small sectors which could be studied from the south bank or in aeroplane photographs. All movements were made by compass, and every unit throughout the Division reached its objective. So completely surprised were the Turks, that, as a rule, they did not know that there was anything wrong until they saw our men ready to bayonet them if they resisted. For this reason, the attackers' casualties were negligible.

After marching side by side for three-quarters of a mile, the 8th Cameronians turned eastwards, whilst the 7th R.S. went on to attack Muannis. The latter, after rushing two sentry posts and meeting odd parties of Turks, bayoneting twenty of them, rushed the village, and, after a sharp fight, in which many of the enemy were killed, took it at 3 a.m., with two officers and twenty-five other ranks as prisoners. Just north of the village a machine-gun [1] was captured after a brief passage of arms, and the 7th R.S. prepared to defend the village from counter-attack, especially from the north and east.

To the east of Slag Heap Farm was an orange grove, and through this, although its mud was almost impassable, the 8th Cameronians made their way. On the eastern side was a building called Keystone House, lying on the western flank of some Turkish entrenchments, and in the rear of others. Near this house was another, the headquarters of the Turkish battalion holding these defences. This building was bombed, and the commander of the 131st Regiment, two officers, and sixteen other ranks, with a machine-gun, surrendered. Keystone House was next taken, and with it one prisoner. The Cameronians were now right into the rear of the enemy trenches, and by 4 a.m., they had "mopped them up," having taken in the process eighteen more prisoners.

At dawn the 7th Cameronians sent out parties, which cleared the orange groves by the river, and collected twenty-four prisoners.

By 6 a.m. the 156th Brigade had entrenched on its objectives, and was holding a strong line north of Muannis, ready for any counter-attack; but none came. The surprise had been complete, and everywhere quantities of equipment and stores had been captured.

Meanwhile, three companies of the 7th H.L.I. had advanced over the mud-flats to the trenches on the sand-hills, whilst the fourth had headed further to the left,

---

[1] This machine-gun had the Ottoman Arms engraved on it, and is believed to have been one of many sent as a gift to the Turks by the German Emperor.

making for the trenches close to the ford and also a small eminence called Smith's Knob,[1] on which there was an enemy post. As the one party got near, and the trenches could be made out, a machine-gun opened fire, but the position was at once rushed and the gunner bayoneted. Two lines of trenches were taken by the larger party at 11.40 p.m. and 11.50 p.m. respectively. The British artillery barrage was now moving up the sand-hills northward. The Turks never expected an attack from this direction or in such weather, and again the surprise was complete. In the ford trenches two Turkish officers were found asleep, but, on being awakened, showed fight with their revolvers, and so had to be bayoneted. Dugouts and trenches were numerous, but were systematically searched. Occasionally there was resistance, but it was rapidly dealt with, and a considerable number of Turks were bayoneted. The captures of the 7th H.L.I. on this night included four officers, sixty-two other ranks, and three machine-guns. Cpl. M'Bride, 7th H.L.I., went out along the beach single-handed to deal with an enemy sniper, and returned with one Turkish officer and four other ranks as prisoners.

The 7th H.L.I. now gave the signal that they had captured the trenches covering the ford—the steady light of an electric torch. Two companies of the brigade reserve, the 5th H-L.I., Major J. B. Neilson, had been waiting on the south side of the river to help the 7th H.L.I., if need be. 300 yards south of the river were the 6th H.L.I., Lt.-Col. Jas. Anderson, and 5th A. & S. H., Lt.-Col. C. L. Barlow, in the order named, ready to cross. By this time the enemy had realized that the British were attacking, and their artillery commenced to shell the ford and the beach on both sides, whilst their machine-guns also opened a long range fire. At this juncture another crisis arose. The river had risen and widened so much that the ford could not be found. A Royal Engineer officer and his men were stripped and searching about in the water, but the peg marking the

[1] After, I believe, Lt. G. S. Smith, 4th R. S., who made the first reconnaissance across the Auja.

crossing had disappeared, and they could only find water deep enough to drown a man. Lt.-Col. J. Anderson was the only one present who knew the place, his patrol companion being in hospital. He at once went forward, stripped, and went into the river. He swam about until he discovered the ford, now with a swift current of water running over it, four and a half feet deep. He showed the Royal Engineers where it lay, and they drove in their stakes and ran two ropes across, one above and one below the ford, forming safety lines for the troops to catch hold of. Meanwhile, Col. Anderson had commenced pushing his battalion across in fours abreast, the men linking their arms. Every now and then the dark waters were lit up by the bursts of the Turkish shells, but company after company pressed steadily on through the river, their kilts floating round the men as they trod deeper and deeper into the cold stream. Major W. M. Anderson, 6th H.L.I., commanding the advanced companies, observing that the Turkish shell-fire was sweeping a fairly well-defined area on the further shore, directed his men round this, and so saved many casualties. The 6th H.L.I. crossed with a loss of only thirty, and proceeded to form up ready for the sweeping advance northward through the dunes. After them came the 5th Argylls, also with arms linked, and four abreast, the upstream man holding the safety line. The disturbance of the bed of the ford by the men's feet caused the rush of the stream to carry away sand and gravel, so that the water was now considerably deeper, and some of the Highlanders were up to their necks before they were across. The Argylls had only about half a dozen casualties, and began to form up on the right of the 6th H.L.I. There had been some narrow escapes and clever rescues, but not a man in either unit was lost, and everyone arrived fully equipped and ready for action. The smallness of both units' casualties was probably due to the men's bodies being mostly submerged in water, which is a good deflector. Moreover, Cpl. Reid and Pte. Macfarlane, of the 7th H.L.I., found and rushed a signal dug-out in view of the ford, which was probably in touch with the Turkish artillery. The latter incident

BATTLE OF JAFFA—PASSAGE OF AUJA 493

happened shortly after the 6th H.L.I. had commenced to cross, and the enemy shelling of the ford became blind and erratic.

Punctually at the time laid down, 1.50 a.m., the 5th A. & S.H. and 6th H.L.I. again commenced to advance, the latter directing. The Turks had a series of trenches which ran across the dunes at right angles to the coast and covered Tel el Rekket, a height of 132 feet, which was two miles from the ford, and was the final objective of the 6th H.L.I. There was some nervous machine-gun and rifle-fire from the Turks, but, advancing steadily and silently through the sand-hills, the 6th H.L.I. came to and charged its first trench at 2.25 a.m., and the 5th Argylls its first nine minutes later. All was surprise and disorder among the Turks, and they never waited for the kilted men. As soon as they could make them out in the darkness, they picked up their machine-guns and bolted from their trenches and bivouacs, some of the officers in their night-attire. Meanwhile, the Divisional artillery barrage moved with clockwork regularity. The strongest enemy line was about 1000 yards short of Rekket. The Turks kept up a rapid but ill-aimed 'fire. The 6th H.L.I. and Argylls advanced steadily to within twenty yards, and then charged with the bayonet, but again the Turks bolted into the darkness. One complete machine-gun, the tripod of another, and twenty prisoners were taken in this trench. By 3.30 a.m. the 6th H.L.I. had taken Tel el Rekket, and the Argylls were extending their line to the right. The Turks had some artillery behind Rekket. The guns just managed to get away in the darkness, but their ammunition limbers were captured. Besides the items mentioned, two Lewis guns, an enemy camp, and quantities of 'stores were taken.

After dawn Gen. Hamilton-Moore saw that the buildings of El Makhras, about 1000 yards inland from Rekket, were very lightly held, so he pushed the 5th Argylls further out to the right and occupied them. The 157th Brigade then linked up with the 156th Brigade, which sent troops forward and occupied the northern end of the Muannis Ridge. The Turks were still holding the dunes north of

Rekket strongly, but a good defensive line had now been secured. Every officer and man in the 6th H.L.I. and 5th Argylls was soaked to the skin, heavy rain began at 6 a.m. and continued till 9 o'clock of the following morning, there was a bitterly cold wind, and it had been impossible to bring forward a single greatcoat, blanket, or bivouac-sheet, but nothing could damp the cheerfulness of the two battalions. As usual, they made the best of things, and worked hard on their defences.

The task of the 155th Brigade, Brig.-Gen. J. B. Pollok-M'Call, had its own special difficulties and features. After Khurbet Hadrah had been captured, Turkish artillery south of the Auja about Mulebbis and Bald Hill could shell it from its flank and right rear. This would render consolidation difficult, but would have to be endured until the 54th Division on the right took these places as planned by Gen. Bulfin. In addition, the Turks held a bridgehead on the south bank of the river at the partially demolished stone bridge south of Hadrah. This would need a special attack. Further, a small party of about twenty with two Lewis guns were to demonstrate about 1500 yards east of this stone bridge.

Two nights prior to the attack a party of 5th K.O.S.B. drove the Turks out of a house about 600 yards north of the orange grove, in which the bridging material for this crossing was to be concealed on the following night. This house was put in a state of defence so as to keep off enemy parties who might try to approach the orange grove and crossing place from the direction of Hadrah stone bridge. Two machine-guns were mounted on the upper flat, so that they could fire at a range of 600 yards into the enemy's trenches covering the stone bridge. Before the attack pits were also dug at this house, and four Stokes trench mortars were mounted in them. This building was known as "Borderers' Hut."

After nightfall small posts of 5th K.O.S.B. moved to points on the south side of the river at either side of the tongue, where the crossing was planned to take place, in order to keep enemy patrols from entering it. The slow

BATTLE OF JAFFA—PASSAGE OF AUJA 495

and difficult work of dragging the pontoons for the bridge down to the river then commenced. At 11 p.m. the covering party, two companies of the 5th K.O.S.B., Lt.-Col. R. N. Coulson, were ferried across, a position covering the crossing was dug, and a patrol with a Lewis gun was pushed out to two houses, called Mother and Son, which lay to the north of the tongue, and would form an outwork.

Half an hour later the British barrage commenced to light up the ridges, and the platoon of 5th K.O.S.B. stationed well to the east of Borderers' Hut commenced to shoot across the Auja, drawing considerable fire in answer, and distracting the enemy's attention.

About midnight, as the 7th H.L.I. were clearing up the ford trenches, the Turkish artillery opened fire and shelled some points near the 155th Brigade, but ineffectually.

At about 1 a.m. the battalions which were to assault Hadrah, arrived at the crossing place, but it was evident that no bridge would be ready for some time, and accordingly they were ferried across. Meanwhile, heavy firing was heard as the 156th Brigade attacked near Muannis. The 5th R.S.F., Lt.-Col. R. W. Paton, were all across by 2 a.m., and the 4th R.S.F., Lt.-Col. N. G. Stewart-Richardson, by 3.30 a.m. They at once set out. There was the same mud, and the same splendid guidance and organization. Having reached the western slope of Hadrah Ridge, the 5th R.S.F. closed up to the artillery barrage. Parties of the enemy were seen, but there was no firing. When the barrage lifted, the 5th R.S.F. went in with the bayonet in two long single ranks. Again the Turks were completely surprised. The first prisoner on being asked regarding "Mitrailleuse," at once led parties of Fusiliers to two machine-guns ready manned, whose gunners were immediately bayoneted, before they could fire a shot. Prisoners captured were taken along with the advancing Fusiliers, the only way to prevent their escaping when the attackers were so few and the night so dark. In a short while, the 5th R.S.F. had swept over the whole Hadrah position, and had taken two machine-guns, two automatic rifles, three officers, including a battalion commander, and a hundred and nineteen men, including nine wounded. Here, as elsewhere, many were taken asleep in their dug-outs.

The 5th R.S.F. occupied Hadrah, and the 4th R.S.F. came forward, taking up a line on the ridge facing towards the east. The whole position was then consolidated.

In the meantime the 5th K.O.S.B. had disposed of the Turkish post at the stone bridge. One company had to be brought back over the river for this purpose, and, the moment the last Fusilier had stepped ashore, the first man of this company stepped aboard a canvas boat. As the assaulting battalions deployed for the attack, the four Stokes guns in Borderers' Hut opened fire for five minutes on the Turkish bridgehead, and, just as the first light of dawn was showing in the east, Lieut. M'Bryde, 5th K.O.S.B., led his company forward to the attack. He divided his men into two parties. One rushed the trench on the south side of the river, whilst, with the other, he dashed across the remains of the stone bridge to an island in the stream, and thence across a mill weir (a causeway) to the further bank, where he seized a bridge-head position. The Turks defending Hadrah bridge fought hard. Sgt. Seaton rushed an automatic rifle, bayoneted the officer and took four prisoners. However, only fifteen prisoners were taken here, for the enemy resisted stubbornly. About twenty refused to surrender, and were driven back by the bayonets of the Borderers into the river, where, weighted down by loads of bombs and equipment, they sank and were drowned.

Again there was complete success, with losses that were almost negligible. The whole 155th Brigade had only nine casualties in this night attack.

So ended the first and most important stage of this great and complicated exploit. In a single night the Division had crossed what seemed to the Turkish Higher Command an almost impassable natural obstacle. It had thrust the enemy coastal flank back about two and a half miles on a front of three miles, threatening the communications of the Mulebbis and Bald Hill positions south of the Auja. The Turks had not held this part of their line in strength,

PILLAR ERECTED TO COMMEMORATE THE
CROSSING OF THE AUJA BY THE 155TH BRIGADE

The Auja is seen in the background. Similar pillars were erected at the crossings of the 156th and 157th Brigades.

BATTLE OF JAFFA—PASSAGE OF AUJA

probably because they thought a few thousand men sufficient to hold such an inaccessible position, especially when their men were so urgently required elsewhere. Over 100 Turkish dead were buried. Eleven enemy officers and 305 other ranks were captured, along with ten machine-guns, and great quantities of equipment and stores. All of this had been achieved at a cost to the Division of barely 100 casualties.

The following day was spent in preparing for the counter-attacks which the Turks were too disorganized to make. From the Mulebbis district they shelled the captured positions, and especially Hadrah, interfering with the work of consolidation. 2nd Lieut. M'Culloch, of the 261st Brigade, R.F.A., was killed at Hadrah in the early morning of the 21st, whilst on observation duty. The Divisional Royal Engineers worked almost continuously. Water supplies on the north bank were searched out. The pontoon bridge for the 155th Brigade crossing was completed at 6.30 a.m. on the 21st. Approaches and roads were improved. A start was made to repair the Hadrah stone bridge, but this place was not covered by the high ground south of the Auja, as were the others, so that work could not be carried on during daylight, because of shell-fire from the Mulebbis district. The barrel bridge for heavy traffic was completed south of Muannis on the morning of the 22nd. This brought the number of available bridges up to three.

The 4th and 5th K.O.S.B. relieved the 4th and 5th R.S.F. in the line during the afternoon of the 21st.

During the night of 21-22nd December the 54th Division took Bald Hill with forty-four prisoners, killing fifty-two of the enemy. This, following on the crossing of the Auja, caused the Turks to retire from Mulebbis and Fejja at dawn, and later in the day from Rantieh.

The roadstead of Jaffa had been made secure by the capture of the Tel el Rekket, Muannis and Hadrah. It now remained to make these new positions safe by pushing the Turks back still further, so that their artillery could not get at the bridges across the Auja. Before the Turks had recovered from their disorganization, the whole Division was to advance about three and a half miles, spreading out on a front of about seven.

The entire Divisional artillery crossed the Auja during the early morning of the 22nd, with the exception of a howitzer which got badly bogged. The ground was in a terrible condition, and it was 9.45 a.m. before the first battery arrived to support the 155th Brigade. This brigade launched its attack at 10.15 a.m., the battalions "leap-frogging" each other in succession as the various objectives were taken one after another. The artillery and machine-gunners followed, opening fire on the enemy as targets offered, but the Turks were not ready for any proper resistance. They consisted mainly of mounted troops, and only fired from long ranges and bolted before the Scottish troops got anywhere near them. The general direction of the 155th Brigade was to the east-north-east across the new northern front of the 54th Division. In the centre, the 156th Brigade was advancing to the north-east, and on the left, the 157th Brigade to the north-north-east. The whole Divisional infantry was moving forward over the open grassy swells of ground in lines of skirmishers and innumerable small columns of men. Behind, followed the strings of pack-animals with spare ammunition, and the machine-guns, the teams, gunners and limbers of the artillery, the ambulance waggons, and other details. The R.A.M.C. had little to do, the casualties being even less than on the night of the crossing. Overhead, British aeroplanes bombed and machine-gunned the Turks as they withdrew, inflicting many casualties.

Here and there the enemy were entrenched, but in few places was there any opposition. Heavy rifle-fire was opened on the 155th Brigade by some Turks on high ground at Sheikh el Ballutah to its left. Gen. Pollok-M'Call sent the 5th R.S.F. at them, under Lt.-Col. R. W. Paton, excellent covering fire being given by a section of the 155th Company's machine-guns under Lieut. Anderson. The Fusiliers went straight up the slopes under a harassing fire, and dislodged 400 Turkish cavalry, a force as strong as themselves, which made off to some woods a mile away.

BATTLE OF JAFFA—PASSAGE OF AUJA 499

In another place, the 4th K.O.S.B. captured 17,000 rounds of small arms ammunition, which showed that the Turks' poor resistance was not due to lack of ammunition.

Early in his advance Gen. Leggett saw some parties of Turks entrenched in the distance. He kept the guns of the 264th Brigade close up, and when the enemy opened fire, they found themselves under a hail of shrapnel which drove them from their trenches.

On the left of the 157th Brigade, H.M.S. *Grafton*, three monitors, and two destroyers were shelling Jelil, one of its last objectives, and Arsuf, nearly two miles further up the coast. Numbers of Turks were seen by the 157th Brigade, but they offered little resistance, and when Gen. Hamilton-Moore's troops reached Jelil about noon, he saw that he could quite well go on to Haram with its prominent white mosque, and Arsuf, hidden 600 yards further north. Permission was granted to undertake this further advance, and before 2.30 p.m. both places had been occupied, and the enemy were thus prevented from obtaining even a long-range view of Jaffa, now over ten miles distant.

During the last two miles of the advance, the Division, and especially the 156th Brigade, was shelled by the enemy artillery, but the artillery formation was good, and casualties were few, and by 3 p.m. the troops were digging in on the new line. The right of the 155th Brigade now rested on the bridges over the Auja near Ferrekhiyeh, where touch had been gained with the 54th Division. This is about four miles, as the crow flies, from Hadrah, and is north of Mulebbis. From Ferrekhiyeh the line curved to the north-west over some low hills, through Sheikh Ballutah, near which the 155th and 156th Brigades linked up. It then ran across a long elevation, called Argyll Ridge, to 300 yards north of the extensive ruins of the Crusaders' castle of Arsuf on cliffs overlooking the sea. To the north stretched the plain of Sharon.

On this day the Turks were driven back another five miles in the coastal sector, so that, in all, Major-Gen. Hill had now driven them back seven miles from the Auja, and had secured a good defensive line, with its bridge communications in comparative safety. As a rule along the entire front the enemy had been pushed down the slope on to lower ground. The nearest point in the Turkish lines to Jaffa had been at the ford of the Auja, about three and a half miles away; it was now beyond the Ferrekhiyeh area, about twelve miles away, and had no observation. A few rounds of shell fired by an enemy naval gun some months afterwards at a range of nearly twenty miles fell in Jaffa. With this exception the port was quite free from enemy bombardment after this operation.

There is no space to quote the congratulatory messages sent by the Commander-in-Chief, Gen. Sir Edmund H. H. Allenby, the G.O.C. 21st Corps, Lt.-Gen. Sir Edward S. Bulfin, and others, to Major-Gen. John Hill. The forethought, organization, and discipline of the whole Division, the Staff, Engineers, Artillery, Infantry, and everyone, were well-nigh perfect, and it was because of this, and because of Gen. Hill's confidence in his Division and insistence on the scheme, that such a great victory was won at such a small expenditure of human life and of treasure.

Part of Gen. Allenby's reference to the operation in his despatch of 18th September, 1918, runs as follows: "The successful crossing of the Nahr el Auja reflects great credit on the 52nd (Lowland) Division. It involved considerable preparation, the details of which were thought out with care and precision. . . . The fact that the enemy were taken by surprise, and that all resistance was overcome with the bayonet without a shot being fired, bears testimony to the discipline of this Division."

The casualties of the 155th, 156th, and 157th Brigades for the three days' operation were as follows:

155TH BRIGADE.

Unit.	Killed and Died of Wounds.		Wounded.		Total.	
	Officers.	O.R.	Officers.	O.R.	Officers.	O.R.
4th R.S.F.	—	3	1	1	1	4
5th R.S.F.	—	—	3	3	3	3
4th K.O.S.B.	—	1	—	1	—	2
5th K.O.S.B.	—	1	—	5	—	6
155th M.G. Coy.	—	—	—	2	—	2
	—	5	4	12	4	17

BATTLE OF JAFFA—PASSAGE OF AUJA

156TH BRIGADE.

Unit.	Killed and Died of Wounds.		Wounded.		Total.	
	Officers.	O.R.	Officers.	O.R.	Officers.	O.R.
4th Royal Scots	—	5	1	21	1	26
7th Royal Scots	—	—	1	1	1	1
7th Cameronians	—	—	—	2	—	2
8th Cameronians	—	1	1	6	1	7
	—	6	3	30	3	36

157TH BRIGADE.

Unit.	Killed and Died of Wounds.		Wounded.		Total.	
	Officers.	O.R.	Officers.	O.R.	Officers.	O.R.
5th H.L.I.	—	—	—	3	—	3
6th H.L.I.	—	7	1	25	1	32
7th H.L.I.	—	2	—	3	—	5
5th A. & S.H.	—	—	2	8	2	8
157th M.G. Coy.	—	1	—	3	—	4
	—	10	3	42	3	52

We know that the Turks lost over 400 officers and men, and they would probably have had much greater casualties and lost more material if British cavalry had been available.

In a measure, history had repeated itself, for the Crusaders under Richard Cœur de Lion had defeated the soldiers of the Crescent under the great Saladin in a battle fought in this area. Arsuf, hundreds of years before the Crusaders built their castle, had been the site of Apollonia, an ancient Greek settlement. Three marble columns were taken from its ruins by the Divisional Royal Engineers, and placed as memorials at the points on the Auja where the three brigades crossed on that wonderful night. The inscription on the column raised for the 155th Brigade runs as follows : "On the night 20-21st December, 1917, the 155th Brigade, 52nd (Lowland) Division crossed the Auja at this spot by rafts and a light bridge and took the Turkish positions on Kh. Hadrah." Similar statements are carved deeply into the other two columns for the 156th and 157th Brigades.

In addition to its association with the splendid operation, of which it saw the close, the 22nd December has one memory which is a very sad one. On this day there died

Col. Fred. Morrison, C.B., T.D., the Commanding Officer of the 5th H.L.I. He went to hospital very unwillingly, for he wished to stay with his men. An attack of dysentery and pneumonia undermined a constitution worn out by long and hard campaigning, and he passed away. As a man and as a soldier, no one in the Division was more loved and respected, and especially so in his own battalion, which he loved in return. At an age when many would have hesitated to shoulder the burdens and fatigues of campaigning, he remained with his battalion, and refused to accept the home leave to which he was so fully entitled. The memory that he once commanded the 5th H.L.I. will be one of that battalion's greatest treasures.

On the 26th December the Turks anticipated a British advance by determined attacks on the positions covering Jerusalem. As soon as their assaults were spent, Gen. Allenby counter-attacked, and by the evening of the 30th December the 20th Corps had advanced on a front of twelve miles to a depth varying from six to three miles. As a result of this advance his force was in a far better position to cover Jerusalem, and his second problem was solved.

There now followed a period of three months, during which the Division held the coastal sector of the line. The front to be held was a long one, so that two infantry brigades always had to be in the line. However, the British had started to dig first, and had secured many advantages of observation, so that the time was not too onerous. The usual shellings, patrol fights, small attacks, and sniping took place. The enemy were planning their defences, and therefore had to do a good deal of reconnoitring. Accordingly, our snipers went out in pairs before dawn to selected positions, and waited for them, occasionally bagging an unwary Boche or Turk, for several German regiments had been brought into the line opposite the Division. The Germans that the Division met in the east were undoubtedly inferior to the Turk in scouting and night patrol work. On one occasion a patrol of eight Germans approached a small post of the 6th H.L.I. before daybreak on 27th December. Cpl. Manson, who was on duty, promptly

BATTLE OF JAFFA—PASSAGE OF AUJA 503

gave the alarm, and then with one other man rushed them with the bayonet. There was a short scuffle, some firing, one German escaped, but the remaining seven, including their leader, surrendered. All of the enemy patrols, however, were not so rapidly disposed of, and sometimes small actions resulted from these petty encounters. Each unit paid a small toll to the Turkish artillery. On the 7th January Lieut. R. G. Gardner, 5th H.L.I., was killed by enemy shell-fire, and on the 12th March Lieut. Murray, 155th Machine-Gun Company.

When units went into reserve they were billeted in the houses of the German colonists of Sarona. The men of this colony had fled with the Turks, and the women and children had been removed to Jaffa, where it was less easy for them to communicate with the enemy. The weather was often wet, and nearly always bitterly cold, until the end of January, so that these billets were regarded as a great boon, although those who used them, being accustomed to sleeping in the open, usually caught cold. Christmas was heralded by bad rain squalls, which continued throughout the day, blowing down bivouacs, flooding trenches, and washing out the cooks' fires. All the available transport of the army was required to bring forward the regular rations and supplies, so that there was none available for parcel or even letter mails, and very few had any extras for their dinner on that day. A few obtained some tobacco, and this was duly shared round. By New Year's Day the weather was clearer, but as cold as ever. The 6th H.L.I. celebrated the day by holding regimental sports, and the spirits of all were as usual, of the highest. Re-clothing, re-equipping, washing and hard training filled in most of the time of units in reserve.

On the 11th January Brig.-Gen. J. B. Pollok-M'Call, C.M.G., D.S.O., went home on leave from the 155th Brigade, his command being taken over by Lt.-Col. James Anderson, 6th H.L.I. As events turned out, Gen. Pollok-M'Call did not return to the Division, and the 155th Brigade lost a commander who had served with it since the first landing of the Division on Gallipoli. Except his personal friends, few knew that he had suffered continuously from dyspepsia. What this meant in the bitterly cold rain storms of the Judaean Highlands, when bully-beef and biscuits, washed down usually with cold water, was the only fare obtainable, can be imagined. He was one of the keenest and most observant soldiers in the Division, and was ever ready to sacrifice himself.

In January the flowers, for which Syria is famous, began to bloom, and by the end of February the rolling downs in the area held by the Division became a vast garden of lilies, anemones, poppies and an endless variety of other flowers. The wild animal life of the country also added an interest to the daily routine. While lying in the line near Arsuf, some good fox hunting was to be had, and the Fusiliers had their first meet on 6th March, when a silver grey fox made for the Turkish lines, but was headed off. A horseman (R.S.F.) rode right through the posts into No Man's Land, and an article published in *The Palestine News*, the army paper, contained the following : " Fox was raised in Jelil covert, and after skirting Tandy's earths (our dug-outs), led the field through heavy wire on to ground which is at present under dispute between Tandy and his neighbour Abdul." Good fish were obtained from the sea at Arsuf by bombing the water, and gathering them while still floating stunned by the explosion.

On 18th March H.R.H. The Duke of Connaught reviewed the 157th Brigade, which happened to be out of the line, at Sarona, and presented decorations to various officers and men of the Division. He afterwards motored to a hill close to the 156th Brigade Headquarters and viewed the enemy's line.

On the evening of the same day the 5th H.L.I. gave a fancy-dress ball to all officers within reach, whether from the Division or not. It was attended by Gen. Hill and his Staff, and was an unqualified success. According to the invitation the guests arrived in pairs, one of whom was always a "lady," the latter usually a nice looking young subaltern, well shaved. Mention must not be omitted of " The Thistletops," the Divisional troupe of pierrots, which

CONVOY WITH THE DIVISION SAILING FOR FRANCE IN APRIL 1918
Two ships of convoy and escort not shown.

BATTLE OF JAFFA—PASSAGE OF AUJA 505

was the child of Gen. Hill, and played to crowded houses in the Jaffa Theatre. Nor must we forget "The Tangerines" of the 2nd Lowland Field Ambulance. Some of the best soldiers of the Division turned out to be among its best humourists, and these entertainments, with battalion sports, did much to help everyone along.

The flower of the Turkish army had been destroyed, and Turkey was no longer dangerous. Jerusalem was safe, and the trend of Eastern thought forecasted a defeat of the Central Powers. Plans were ready and preparations far advanced for a new advance in Palestine, probably in April, which was intended to break the Turkish power as thoroughly as the October advance ultimately did, but the news from Europe became very ominous. Ludendorff had promised victory to the Central Powers before the summer of 1918 at a cost of 400,000 men. The war would then have been decided before the United States was properly ready, so he calculated. And, accordingly, there followed the German offensives of March, 1918, in the area of the Somme, when the enemy was only held back with the greatest of difficulty, and it became evident that the Allies would need the best troops that they had in order to save Paris and the whole situation in France.

Towards the end of March intimation was received that the Division would be relieved by the 7th Indian Division, and on the last day of the month Lowland advance parties were sent to Kantara. The relief was completed on the 3rd April, the 155th and 157th Brigades being the last in the line. At the same time Brig.-Gen. E. C. Massy, C.B., C.M.G., D.S.O., was transferred to the 7th Indian Division, with the whole of the 52nd Division's artillery, the 261st, 262nd, and 264th Brigades, R.F.A., and the 52nd Divisional Ammunition Column. The Lowlanders had learnt to rely on Gen. Massy and his artillerymen. This was the first real break in the composition of the Division, and everyone regretted it. However, infantry were mostly in demand in France, whilst guns were still needed in Palestine, and a transfer helped to simplify the great problem of overseas transportation. For the same reason, the Divisional Train, Royal Army Service Corps, and all transport animals and waggons were also left behind, and the Division parted with many tried and trusted friends. The collapse of Russia in February, 1918, followed by that of Roumania a few days later, had freed not only the armies of the Central Powers on their Eastern Front, but also over 1,000,000 prisoners of war held by Russia. The help of the splendid young troops of the United States, who were not worn by years of warfare, as were those of Britain and her allies, was badly needed, but the majority of them could only be brought across in British vessels, convoyed by British warships.

The Division concentrated at Surafend, the 156th Brigade being the first to arrive on 28th March. On 3rd April this brigade entrained at Ludd for Kantara, and on the 5th arrived at Alexandria. The 155th reached that port on the 6th, and the 157th on the 8th. Drafts had now brought most of the units up to almost full strength. On the 8th April Brig.-Gen. P. S. Allan, D.S.O., assumed command of the 155th Brigade, Lt.-Col. James Anderson rejoining the 6th H.L.I. On this and succeeding days the Division embarked on the troopships, *Canberra, Caledonia, Indarra, Kaiser-I-Hind, Leasowe Castle, Malwa,* and *Omrah,* and, convoyed by six Japanese destroyers and a British cruiser, sailed from Alexandria, at 2.30 p.m. on the 11th April, for Marseilles.

Almost three years had elapsed since the Lowland Division had sailed eastward along the Mediterranean, and it now had time for a little retrospection. It had fought on Gallipoli to the very last. With Australians and New Zealanders it had played the leading parts in fighting for and making a way across the Sinai Desert. After a long and hard struggle before Gaza it had swept with the cavalry up the coast, at times leading the way, and had hammered the Turks back from the sea, and shattered them. With the 75th Division it had dashed into the Judaean Highlands and seized the key position to Jerusalem. Tired and battle-worn, it had filled the gap at Suffa, and had hurled back Turkish attacks which had been intended to breach the

BATTLE OF JAFFA—PASSAGE OF AUJA

British line. Finally, by sheer efficiency and wonderful stealth, it had seized the passage of the Auja.[1]

The Division had fought in all kinds of country, and in all weathers and temperatures, ranging from the hard frost and blizzards of the moorlands of Gallipoli, and the bitterly cold hail storms of the Judaean Highlands, to the mid-day heat of summer in the desert. It had experienced twelve months of trench warfare, and was now thoroughly trained for open warfare, and hardened to endure long marches and great privations.

Now, it was on its way to take part in the most colossal battle that the world has known.

[1] A Turkish officer, taken prisoner by the 7th H.L.I. at the Auja, expressed surprise that the Lowlanders whom he saw were not men of great stature, as it was current among the Turks that the troops of the 52nd Division were very tall men. It is interesting to note this, in view of the rule that in the legendary lore of all peoples, great soldiers and heroes always develop into giants as the stories are re-told and time goes on.

FRANCE

CHAPTER XXVIII

(12TH APRIL TO 28TH JUNE, 1918)

FRANCE

> The sun rises bright in France,
>   And fair sets he;
> But he has tint the blythe blink he had,
>   In my ain countrie!
> ALLAN CUNNINGHAM.

THE Division had not finished with trench warfare yet, although, like everyone else, they were wearied of it. However, France had one great attraction, its proximity to home. "Home leaves" for both officers and men in the East had been very few, so that some, who had escaped wounds sufficiently severe to send them to the British Isles, had not seen their native country for years. Everyone knew that in France the granting of leave went on almost continually, and the magic word "home" passed about the troopships' decks.

During the voyage the weather was fine and the sea smooth. The transports steamed in two parallel lines abreast, a compact formation, but one which gave a poor target to submarines. The usual routine was followed and the usual precautions were taken. The Division mounted machine-guns on the transports, besides supplying ammunition carriers for the ships' guns, but no U-boats were seen. On the 17th April, beneath grey skies, the transports steamed in line ahead through the entrance gate of the boom defences of Marseilles. The entrainment of the Division commenced at once, and, by the 19th, the last troops, the 157th Brigade, had entrained. The weather was intensely cold, with rain and snow, and the journey took three days, but, as usual, everyone made the best of it. The route was through Orleans, Versailles and Amiens, and the destination Abbeville and the small places in its neighbourhood.

A fortnight previously the Germans had failed in their great attempt to drive a wedge between the British and French armies, in order to hem in the former on the sea coast, while they defeated the latter. They had been finally held up eight miles from the important railway centre of Amiens. If this city had fallen, the only railroad between the Channel Ports and Paris would have been the circuitous one through Abbeville. On the 7th April Ludendorff had commenced another attack, this time to destroy the British left in Flanders, and to capture Calais and Boulogne, after which he hoped to fight through Amiens to Paris and final victory. The worst crisis of this battle actually occurred whilst the Division was entraining and travelling north. When it reached Abbeville and proceeded to billets in the villages about the mouth of the Somme, this was over, the French reserves were arriving, and there was a lull in the battle.

The Division remained in the neighbourhood of Abbeville until the 25th. The time was spent in training and in replacing the animals and equipment, which had been left behind in Palestine. Its next move was to a reserve area about Aire and the Forest of Nieppe, lying opposite the point where the German salient south of Ypres was nearest Calais and Boulogne. The struggle for these ports flared up again on 25th April, but after four days of fighting it subsided into trench warfare with small local actions. Ludendorff had gained ground, but he had failed in his main object and was held at bay.

Whilst near Aire many lectures were given on the conditions of warfare in France, at one of which, on the 3rd May, Sir Douglas Haig was present, and spoke to the officers assembled. Route marching and general training was carried on, especial attention being paid to training in gas warfare. A change which took place soon after the Division's arrival in France was the organization of the machine-gun companies into the 52nd Machine-Gun Battalion. The companies remained with their old brigades so far as was possible in subsequent moves.

On the 6th May the Division commenced to move to the Vimy Ridge area, where it remained until the 19-21st of July, during which days it was relieved by the 8th Division. The different units took turns in the line, and the usual patrolling and trench warfare was carried on. Some small trench raids and reconnaissances were carried out by the different battalions, and there were several encounters between patrols, in which the Lowlanders usually got the better of it. As a rule, however, enemy patrols were rarely met with. Several gas-projector attacks were made from the Division's lines, and both sides shelled with gas, H.E., and shrapnel, the British carrying out some very destructive bombardments of the German lines. Early in the morning of 27th May, a heavy shell, fired by the enemy at long range, fell on one end of a hut near Mont St. Eloi, in which men of the 1/2nd Lowland Field Ambulance were sleeping. Twelve were killed outright, and twenty-five more or less seriously wounded. It was the first enemy shell fired in that area on that morning. A 7th H.L.I. patrol of twelve men, under 2nd Lieut. M'Cormack, ambushed an enemy patrol of twenty during the night of 1st July, killing eight of them, wounding five, and capturing two. On the night of the 3-4th July working parties of the 6th H.L.I. were shelled, and lost Lieut. J. Todd and three other ranks killed, and five other ranks wounded. Lieut. J. M. Molyneux, 7th R.S., was mortally wounded on the 9th July whilst on patrol duty. On the average, the casualties of the Division during this period were not heavy. Sometimes a brigade would lose sixty officers and men in a month, and sometimes as few as ten.

The granting of "home leave" commenced during the second week of May.

The 19th of May saw a change in the command of the 155th Brigade, when Brig.-Gen. J. Forbes-Robertson, V.C., D.S.O., M.C., assumed command, vice Brig.-Gen. P. S. Allan, D.S.O.

The reorganization of infantry brigades from a strength of four battalions each to one of three, necessitated a parting with the junior battalion of each brigade. These were the 5th K.O.S.B., Lt.-Col. R. N. Coulson, in the 155th; the 8th Cameronians, Lt.-Col. J. M. Findlay, in the 156th; and the 5th A. & S.H., Lt.-Col. C. L. Barlow, in the 157th. Much to the regret of everyone, and, with many farewell messages of good-will from Gen. Hill, Brigade Commanders, and the other battalions, these three left the 52nd Division, the first two on 27th June, and the last on the following day, for Bambecque, in Belgian Flanders, to become the 103rd Brigade of the 34th Division. Certainly, no division was more united in itself than was the Lowland, and long campaigning over many battlefields had brought about a very strong feeling of comradeship and respect between the various units. Traditions of common privations and achievement had been established, which nothing could destroy, and the remaining units felt that three old and trusty friends had gone, when these three battalions left the Division.[1]

[1] A brief record of the splendid manner in which the new 103rd Brigade carried on, in the 34th Division, the traditions and spirit of the 52nd, is given in Appendix IV. See also *The Thirty-Fourth Division, 1915-1919*, by Lt.-Col. J. Shakespear, C.M.G., C.I.E., D.S.O.

CHAPTER XXIX

(29TH JUNE TO 31ST AUGUST, 1918)

THE SECOND BATTLE OF THE SOMME: THE BREAKING OF THE HINDENBURG (SIEGFRIED) LINE ABOUT HÉNIN HILL

"The assault of the great breach was confided to Major-General M'Kinnon's brigade, preceded by a storming party of five hundred men, under Major Manners, of the Seventy Fourth . . . the enemy had strongly retrenched it, and maintained a hot fire of musketry upon them from traverses on either side; the top of the breach was also raked with grape, from two guns flanking it at a distance of a few yards. . . . by desperate efforts directed along the parapets on both flanks, the assailants succeeded in turning the retrenchments."

The 74th Regiment (later H.L.I.) at Ciudad Rodrigo, 19th January, 1812. From the *Official Historical Record of the 74th Regiment*, compiled at the Adjutant-General's Office, Horse Guards.

On the 19th, 20th, and 21st July the Division moved to an area west of Bethune, where it was in General Headquarters reserve. The 31st July saw it back again in the line, holding the Oppy Sector before Arras, where it relieved the Canadian 4th Division. During this period every precaution was taken to prevent the enemy from identifying the formations opposite to them before Arras, as the former were obviously becoming nervous and apprehensive of a British attack. British patrolling was firstly of a purely defensive nature, and finally was forbidden altogether. On the night of 6th August a party of the enemy raided a post of the 4th K.O.S.B. They were driven off, but not before they had killed an officer and four men, wounded eight other ranks, and taken two prisoners. Between the

14th and 16th the Division was relieved by the 8th Division, and moved back into reserve about Villers Chatel and Aubigny. There, all arms and equipment were thoroughly overhauled, all surplus baggage was sent to a dump at Aubigny, and the Division was warned to be prepared to move at a few hours' notice. It was evident to all that some very large forward movement was close at hand, and a brief summary of the general situation will help us to understand what this was to be.

For almost four years the Allies and the Central Powers had faced each other on a front stretching from Switzerland to the North Sea. Many attempts had been made by both sides to break through the opposing fronts, but all had failed. During the spring of 1918 the German Higher Command made its mightiest efforts, and had only been held up after both sides had suffered immense losses, and after the Allied front had been bent back in many places. Gen. Ludendorff's main object had been to drive a wedge between the British and French armies, and afterwards to defeat them piecemeal before the United States could place its full force in the field. With this intention, he had continued attacking at certain points after it had become really useless for him to persist in doing so, and was fast using up those vast reserves which gave him the initiative. After his tremendous drive towards Amiens, and his deadly thrust south of Ypres, he had launched his last great offensive, between 26th May and 18th July, aiming principally across the rivers Aisne and Marne, towards Paris, with its irreplaceable munition factories. The plan of Gen. Foch, who had been appointed supreme Commander-in-Chief of the Allied armies on the 26th March, was to inflict the heaviest losses on the enemy, whilst giving ground where necessary, and, when ready, to deliver a series of counter offensives. Each great counter-attack was to cease, as soon as it was evident that a further advance in its area would prove too costly. As one counter-attack of the Allies died down, another was to burst out on a totally different front. He intended to submit the enemy to a constant series of surprises and to keep the battle mobile. Gen. Ludendorff had, however,

SECOND BATTLE OF THE SOMME 517

the great advantage of interior lines of communication, whilst Gen. Foch had to transport his men around the outside of the great salients which ran towards Amiens and Paris. On the other hand, Gen. Ludendorff had used up nearly all his reserves, whilst those of Gen. Foch were increasing daily, largely because of the arrival of troops from the United States. On 18th July, Gen. Foch, with French, British, and American troops, delivered his first great counter-offensive, and by the 4th August the salient, which had stretched along the Marne and Ourcq towards Paris, had ceased to exist,[1] and, more important still, Gen. Ludendorff had used up a large proportion of his best troops, and had been made to realize that he had definitely failed to divide the Allied armies. Most serious of all was the weakening of the German morale, which, after the prolonged strain of the war, could not stand adversity as that of the Allies had done.

On the 8th August Gen. Haig struck with British Imperial and Colonial troops, including Australian veterans of Gallipoli, at the apex of the salient, which stretched towards Amiens, and by nightfall had driven the German line back and removed the menace from that great railway centre. Ludendorff called the 8th August the German Army's "black day." The initiative had finally passed to Foch, who had now been created a Marshal of France. Attack and counter-attack succeeded one another in different parts of the line, preventing Ludendorff from concentrating his reserves, forcing him to throw them in piecemeal, and all working up to that final crescendo of gigantic battles, which was to commence on the 23rd August. Foch fought to free his own communications, and to sever those of Ludendorff into the great salients, which the latter still held. Ludendorff had realised that he had failed, and was fighting for a draw. The German front at this time has been likened in shape to a sickle, the handle lying in Champagne between Verdun and Switzerland, the point resting on the Belgian coast, and the outside curve of the blade being towards

[1] See Appendix IV. for the part played by the 103rd Brigade near Soissons in this counter offensive.

Paris. His armies in the most western portion of this curve, that is to say in the wilderness of the Somme Valley, had penetrated farthest into French territory, and he now sought to withdraw them.

Stretching from the north of Arras, and running generally in a south-easterly direction, before Cambrai and St. Quentin, was a belt of fortified country, varying from 7000 to 10,000 yards in depth. It consisted of numerous fortified villages and other positions, linked up by lines of entrenchments, which assumed the nature of permanent fortifications. The wire entanglements in this area were hundreds of yards in depth. Immense trenches had been fashioned to checkmate a tank attack. In short, after their experience in the Battle of the Somme, 1916, the German Higher Command had not ceased to use every means available to build an impregnable system of fortifications. This was known as the Hindenburg Line, the section between Arras and a point to the south of Cambrai being called the Siegfried system, and those further south, the Hunding and Brunehilde zones. Ludendorff's plan was to hold the line of upland between Arras and the Oise until he could make an orderly retreat to the Siegfried system for winter quarters. He thought that he could hold the Hindenburg Line indefinitely, and that from behind it the Central Powers could bargain for an advantageous peace; but everything depended on his being able to give his men sufficient rest and time to recover their morale behind its fortifications. This, Foch and Haig determined that he should not do.

At first Foch wished Haig to direct his next blow at the central portion of this position, on which Ludendorff was endeavouring to stand, but Haig persuaded him that the better plan was to strike at the Arras corner of the great Somme Valley salient, and so outflank the heights between Arras and the Oise from the north. This meant an attack on the Siegfried System, but, on the other hand, the ground north of the Ancre was less shell-pitted, and more suitable for tanks.

Among the divisions which Sir Douglas Haig had

SECOND BATTLE OF THE SOMME 519

gathered together in Sir Julian Byng's Third Army, which was to deliver the attack, was the 52nd. The veterans of Gallipoli were well represented in that force. Besides the New Zealand Division, there were the 42nd (East Lancs.) and 63rd (Royal Naval) Divisions.

The battle opened on the 21st August and was a complete surprise to the enemy, nine divisions driving in the German front north of the Ancre. Next day, the 22nd, five divisions of Gen. Rawlinson's Fourth Army struck another successful blow further to the south, between Albert and the Somme. The Germans were now in retreat on a wide front, and in order to cripple their withdrawal, it was time for the main attack. Whilst Rawlinson fought his way forward along the Somme, Byng struck again with his chief weight at the northern corner of the great salient.

The 52nd Division, was part of the 6th Army Corps, and on the 22nd of August received orders to attack through the 59th Division at Boiseaux St. Marc in the early morning of the following day. The 156th Brigade, was detailed for this attack. Sixty motor lorries were promised to move it to its assembly area, but the roads were choked with artillery and transport, and by 4 p.m. of the 22nd only thirty-two lorries had reported. Largely through the energy of Major Curtis, G.S., 52nd Division, and of Capt. H. Sayer, Brigade-Major, 156th Brigade, these difficulties were overcome, although some companies of the 4th R.S. had to march from Bretencourt to the jumping-off place south of Mercatel. Their officers had no time for a preliminary reconnaissance, and they had to march practically straight into action, arriving just in time for the commencement of the attack at 4.55 a.m. At that moment the British artillery opened fire, the concentration being very heavy, and averaging one gun to each twelve yards of front.

Twelve minutes later, the 156th Brigade went forward. Nine tanks were to have gone forward with the brigade, three for each battalion, but these, evidently delayed by the congestion of the roads, had not arrived, and, accordingly, the infantry went forward without them. The frontage of the brigade was about 1820 yards. On the right was the

4th R.S., Major J. M. Slater; the 7th R.S., Lt.-Col. W. T. Ewing, was in the centre; and the 7th Cameronians, Lt.-Col. J. G. P. Romanes, was on the left. Each battalion, with a strength of about twenty-two officers and 620 other ranks, attacked on a front of one company, and supplied its own supports and reserves. The formation adopted was one in which each section of men advanced in a separate little clump, forming a tiny but compact unit which could act at once against machine-guns and small strong-points. This brigade, and especially the 7th R.S., had been harassed during the previous night by hostile bombing and mustard gas shelling, and had suffered many casualties thereby.

The country is open and rolling, and they were advancing to the east-north-east, astride a long low swell of ground. To the south-east of this runs the depression of the Cojeul River, a very small stream. In this depression lay a series of villages, which, like all others in this terrible area, were simply heaps of loose bricks, stones, and wreckage, fortified with machine-gun emplacements, concrete dug-outs, and so on. It was a heavy morning following on a close, stuffy night. The surprise was complete, the Germans offered little resistance, and by 6.45 a.m. all objectives had been taken, an advance of about two-thirds of a mile having been made. 200 prisoners were taken at a cost of about 168 casualties, the latter being principally due to the enemy bombardment and machine-gun fire.

At this point the tanks caught up with the infantry and passed through to exploit the ground in front, whilst the brigade consolidated and pushed out patrols on its flanks. Each section of three tanks was guided by a scout and followed by a company from each battalion. They cleared the ground for 500 yards in front of the captured trenches, and then returned. By 7.35 a.m. the position was consolidated, the battalions being disposed in depth. The German artillery retaliated with a heavy shell-fire, but it was not very effective. During the day the flanks were pushed forward another 500 yards, the right being close to the outskirts of the battered ruins, which had been Hénin-sur-Cojeul. The 56th Division had advanced on the right of the 156th

SECOND BATTLE OF THE SOMME

Brigade, but on the left the 2nd Canadian Division had been held up by the fortified ruins of Neuville Vitasse, which the enemy were holding very strongly.

Directly to the east of Hénin-sur-Cojeul lies an extensive rounded elevation known as Hénin Hill. Its highest part runs north and south for about a mile and a half, and has a spur running from its centre eastward for 1000 yards. Its greatest elevation is about 105 feet. South-east of this hill and before the front of the 56th Division, which was on the 52nd's right, lay the remains of Croisilles, a defended village of great strength. During the night orders came for the 56th Division to capture Hénin Hill and Croisilles, and for the 52nd Division, and 2nd Canadian Division, further to the left, to conform. The Siegfried Line ran from north-west to south-east behind Neuville Vitasse, Hénin-sur-Cojeul, and Croisilles, and its front wire and parapets crossed the top of Hénin Hill just behind the highest point, and followed the spur which ran to the east. From the summit of the hill another trench system ran out southward along the crest-line of the main ridge to Croisilles and St. Léger. The wire and entrenchments belonging to positions in use by the enemy in the country eastward of the Siegfried Line and St. Léger can only be described as an endless maze. In addition, the whole of the countryside, south and west of Arras, had been defended and fought over repeatedly, fresh lines being dug and wired and broken up again each time, so that it was literally covered with derelict trenches, entanglements, and all the debris of many overlapping battlefields.

The 157th Brigade, which had also moved forward, was instructed to advance on the 24th on the left of the 56th Division. The final objective given to the 157th Brigade was that portion of the Siegfried Line which ran behind the crest-line of Hénin Hill. This entailed an advance of a mile and a half, with the trench system, which ran southward along the main ridge towards Croisilles, on its flank. It was understood that this trench system would be taken in flank and rear by the 56th Division. The 156th Brigade was to push forward, behind and on the left of the 157th, to a sunken road beyond or to the north-east of Hénin-sur-Cojeul.

After a march of four miles in darkness and latterly in mist, over derelict wire and shell holes, the 157th Brigade, moving forward through the right of the 156th Brigade, attacked promptly at 7 a.m. The 6th H.L.I. was on the right, and the 5th H.L.I. on the left, the 7th H.L.I. being in reserve. As the troops moved off the artillery commenced. It was a misty morning, which prevented enemy observation, and about ten minutes elapsed before the enemy barrage came down on its lines, in time to catch only the headquarters of the leading battalions and the 7th H.L.I. A few minutes later enemy machine-guns and trench mortars also opened fire. These formed the principal German resistance.

Hénin-sur-Cojeul was captured with little difficulty, together with two machine-guns, and the 157th Brigade commenced to move up the western slopes of Hénin Hill towards the Siegfried Line. The 56th Division had come up on the right, but it was found that it had stopped its advance short of Hénin Hill. Lt.-Col. J. Anderson tried to get in touch with the battalion commander on his right, but he could not do so, and the officer in command of the company on the left of the 56th Division stated that he had reached his final objective and saw no option but to stay there. This objective was in line with the first objective of the 157th Brigade. The British artillery barrage also ceased to go forward, and the advancing 157th Brigade began to suffer casualties from our own guns. There must have been some serious omission or mistake in the instructions issued for the artillery on this day. That the 6th Corps, to which formation the 52nd Division belonged at the time, intended Hénin Hill to be captured became very evident in a couple of hours. The 157th Brigade's orders were clear, and it continued to carry them out. By 11.30 a.m., the 5th and 6th H.L.I. had pushed forward and, despite their exposed right flank, had captured their second objective, and, close to the summit, found themselves right up against the Hindenburg Line, and involved in a labyrinth

SECOND BATTLE OF THE SOMME

of wire from 400 to 500 yards wide. Into their right flank came a heavy enfilade fire from German machine-gun nests on the main ridge. British artillery was still pouring heavy shells on the front trench before the H.L.I., and it was manifest that the former did not know that the attack of the 157th Brigade was to be carried so far. These two battalions could advance no further. Frequent messages were sent back for the British barrage to be lifted 500 to 800 yards, so that the H.L.I. could assault the Hindenburg Line, which at this hour was evidently not too strongly held, but, owing to the destruction of artillery communications, it was not until about 1 p.m. that this British shell-fire was stopped. Meanwhile, both assaulting battalions had suffered severely, and the Germans had time to bring up more machine-guns to develop frontal and enfilade fire.

Whilst the 157th Brigade was endeavouring to assault the Hindenburg Line, the 156th Brigade had pushed forward, until by 4 p.m. a company of the 4th R.S. was in touch with the left of the 5th H.L.I. In the centre was the 7th R.S., and on its left the 7th Cameronians in touch with the Canadians, who had taken the sugar factory on the south-eastern outskirts of Neuville Vitasse. This village, however, still held out. The 7th R.S. and 7th Cameronians now sent patrols forward, who found the Hindenburg Line before them held very strongly by the enemy with machine-guns.

At 1.4 p.m. the Headquarters of 6th Corps sent urgent orders for the capture of Hénin Hill. Gen. Hamilton-Moore arranged with the 5th and 6th H.L.I., who by this time had posts of men actually within the wire of the Hindenburg Line, for another assault at about 4 p.m. This was to have been preceded by an artillery bombardment but, again owing to the breaking of communications, the artillery only had time for a thin bombardment lasting three minutes, before it was time to attack. Both 5th and 6th H.L.I. had lost heavily, especially in officers, but they fought their way forward. The entanglement had been very little damaged by artillery fire, and was almost impenetrable, but they pushed through wherever there seemed to be a way. By 5 p.m. some 5th H.L.I. had penetrated this wire and were trying to work across an open stretch lying beyond, which was swept by machine-gun and trench mortar fire from their front and right flank. The enemy kept up a very heavy shell-fire, but by 5.45 p.m. some of these Light Infantrymen had obtained a footing in the first trench. This was all that they could do, however, for a counter-attack developed, and they found themselves quite detached and in the midst of a sea of wire. A few officers who were left now tried to withdraw these men, and some of the party were extricated, bringing with them two prisoners, but a number were captured. Three officers of the 5th H.L.I. were taken, and, of these, two were seriously wounded.

The enemy machine-gun fire was increasing; night was drawing on; the 157th Brigade's right flank was quite " in the air," and no further advance was possible. Accordingly, this Brigade was withdrawn a few hundred yards to a line consisting mainly of odd shell holes and ditches, where it lay during a bombardment which the enemy artillery put down between 8 p.m. and 9.30 p.m. At 4 a.m. on the 25th there followed another heavy bombardment, aimed probably in the hope of catching concentrations of troops preparing for another assault.

" There is no doubt that on this day the Hindenburg Line was very lightly held by the enemy, and had our Heavy Artillery barrage not stopped us, and the troops on our right been able to come on, we should have had little difficulty in capturing it " (Gen. Hamilton-Moore). The delay gave the Germans time to bring up fresh machine-guns and trench mortars, with which they inflicted very severe losses on the 157th Brigade. The 157th Trench Mortars never came into action, because of the system of transport by limber waggons. These vehicles could only take them a certain distance forward over the shell-pitted wire-strewn countryside, after which the guns and ammunition had to be man-handled, and, under conditions of open warfare, the men had not the physical strength to carry them far enough. With the use of pack-animals they might have been made available. The casualties of the 157th Brigade on this day amounted to twenty-six officers and 450 other ranks killed and wounded, besides three officers and eighty-two other ranks missing, many of the latter being also wounded. This was over one-quarter of the Brigade's strength. Both assaulting battalions had lost their commanding officers, Lt.-Col. James Anderson, C.M.G., D.S.O., 6th H.L.I., and Lt.-Col. J. B. Neilson, C.M.G., D.S.O., 5th H.L.I., being among the severely wounded.

Nevertheless, the 157th Brigade had made an advance of about a mile in depth and had taken two of its three objectives.

On the following day the front held by the 52nd and 56th Divisions passed from the 6th to the 17th Corps.

During this day patrols found that the Hindenburg Line was being reinforced. It was evident that it could not be broken now without an adequate artillery preparation, and during the day the guns of both sides heavily shelled the opposing lines, the Germans using large quantities of mustard gas shells.

The 56th Division on the right was still held up at the ruins of Croisilles, and the 2nd Canadian Division on the left was still fighting for the wastes of Neuville Vitasse.

The 26th August, 1918, is famous in the annals of the British forces, Imperial and Colonial, for, on this day, the Canadian Corps, under Gen. Sir Arthur Currie, with the 51st (Highland) Division fighting in its ranks, and the 52nd (Lowland) Division on its right flank, broke into and swung across the Siegfried section of the Hindenburg Line, shattering all the German dreams of its impregnability and Gen. Ludendorff's plans for a stand during the winter behind its fortifications.

On the 24th the 156th Brigade had pushed forward for a depth of over a mile along the low elevation, across part of which it had previously advanced. It still lay over this rising ground, and was now about two-thirds of a mile from the front trenches of the Hindenburg Line, which ran across this spur at the eastern end of its highest part. This portion of the Hindenburg Line was to be the objective on the 26th of the 155th Brigade, Brig.-Gen. J. Forbes-Robertson. There, it was to await the Canadian Corps, which would come up on its left, and then, with the Colonials, it was to fight its way down the Hindenburg Line towards the south-east. The attack was to commence at 3 a.m., while it was still night, and was to be made through the left and centre of the 156th Brigade's line. It will be noticed how the hours for assault were constantly varied, so that the enemy never knew when they were going to be attacked.

Again there was unavoidable congestion of traffic and a dark wet night, but at 3 a.m. the front line of the 155th Brigade moved forward to the attack under a most efficient barrage, which crept forward at the rate of 100 yards in four minutes. Some of the companies were delayed and had to follow, deploying and advancing as they came to the place of assembly. The 5th R.S.F., Lt.-Col. D. M. Murray-Lyon, was on the right, and the 4th R.S.F., Lt.-Col. B. Cruddas, on the left. The 4th K.O.S.B., Lt.-Col. R. Dashwood-Tandy, was in reserve.

The enemy were again taken by surprise, and, although fairly numerous and holding positions of renowned strength, quickly gave way before the determined advance. At one point two trench mortars with some machine-guns held out stubbornly, but they were disposed of by showers of rifle grenades. The "mopping-up" proceeded, and the Royal Engineers (410th Company) gave great assistance in searching for mines and booby-traps. This latter duty was always efficiently carried out by the Royal Engineers after the various assaults of the Division. By 5.30 a.m. the 155th Brigade had broken into the Hindenburg Line, and secured its objectives. Neuville Vitasse still held out and the Canadians were taking it by means of an attack round its northern flank, so that for several hours the 155th Brigade had two exposed flanks to watch, in addition to its front. At 8.20 a.m., however, the Canadians, who had taken Monchy-le-Preux, a very strongly held litter of ruins on a hill further north, gained touch with the left of the 155th Brigade, which swung round until it faced south-

SECOND BATTLE OF THE SOMME 527

east. Meanwhile, on the left of the 155th Brigade the 2nd Canadian Division attacked Wancourt Ridge.

At 10 a.m. the 156th Brigade followed the 155th into the break that it had made in the Hindenburg Line, whilst the 4th R.S. on the right pushed patrols into the section opposite to it. These found the line empty for a distance, but came under heavy fire from a machine-gun nest on the eastern edge of the summit of Hénin Hill.

The 4th K.O.S.B. were brought forward into a sunken road in the captured portion of the Hindenburg Line, and at 3.30 p.m., followed by the 4th R.S.F., and with the 5th R.S.F. near to assist in the " mopping up," moved towards Hénin Hill. As was the rule, the principal enemy resistance was from well hidden machine-guns, which usually continued firing until they were found, and their gunners shot, bombed, or bayoneted. Just before 5 p.m. the 4th K.O.S.B. were seen climbing to the top of the hill in extended order. Some machine-guns of the 155th Company caught an enemy party on the summit, driving them back, and soon afterwards word arrived that Hénin Hill had been captured. A machine-gun on the eastern edge held out for some time, but was finally blown up by the Stokes trench mortars. However, as with all gently-rounded hills, the top of Hénin Hill was very extensive, and its summit seemed always to be receding from the climber. The whole of its higher part had not been captured. Trenches on the summit were still held by the enemy, who pressed close up against the 155th Brigade, whilst their artillery shelled the captured area heavily, as if they intended to try to recover it. The 56th Division on the right was still held up outside Croisilles and south-west of Hénin Hill. To the north, that is on the left of the 155th, the 2nd Canadian Division had captured Wancourt Tower, but fighting went on in this locality all through the succeeding night.

Nothing further could be done on that day, and so the 155th Brigade clung to the north-western side of Hénin Hill, and held the captured section of the Hindenburg Line, with the Canadians on their left flank. On the same evening the 156th Brigade concentrated, to be ready to follow up an attack to be made by the 157th Brigade on the following day, the 27th. This attack was to be made south-eastwards along the Hindenburg Line, in which there was now a rapidly widening breach. It will be noticed how the right flank of this advance, and later its rear, would be exposed so long as Croisilles and its neighbourhood managed to hold out against the 56th Division. The first objective of this attack was to be Fontaine-les-Croisilles, which lay to the south-east directly behind the Hindenburg front line. After this, if possible, the advance was to be continued to Hendecourt-les-Cagnicourt and Riencourt-les-Cagnicourt, further to the south-east, but the latter advance would be impossible so long as Croisilles and its neighbourhood remained in enemy hands.

Major-Gen. Hill ordered the attack as follows. The 157th Brigade was to advance at 9.20 a.m. Having cleared the northern end of Hénin Hill, which was then to be "mopped up" by the 155th Brigade, the 157th was to move, with its front across the front trenches of the Hindenburg Line, down that system and take Fontaine-les-Croisilles. The 56th Division was to attack on its right from the southern end of Hénin Hill, Croisilles and the ground immediately behind it being in its line of advance. At 10.3 a.m. the 156th Brigade was to advance, coming up on the left of the 157th Brigade. Further to the left, the 2nd Canadian Division was to advance.

The 157th Brigade moved off behind its artillery barrage punctually to the minute. The 6th H.L.I., Lt.-Col. W. Menzies Anderson, formed the right assaulting battalion, and the 7th H.L.I., Lt.-Col. E. S. Gibbons, the left. The 5th H.L.I., Lt.-Col. D. E. Brand, followed in reserve. Owing to the condition of the ground, the artillerymen had had difficulty in getting their guns into position in time, and had to bring them into action as they arrived, so that at first the barrage was a little ragged, but it rapidly improved. The wire was a tremendous obstacle, being not only very thick but of great depth. Very heavy fire came from enemy trench mortars and machine-guns at the outset, and this, coupled with the barbed wire, slowed down the speed of

SECOND BATTLE OF THE SOMME

the advance at the start. Casualties were very heavy, but the leadership of the officers was good, the men were determined, and they picked their way through the wire, attacking and taking enemy strong points and machine-gun positions, as they came to them. After the capture of the trenches on the northern part of the summit of Hénin Hill, and on its eastern slopes, the Germans were forced into precipitate retreat. Further lines and expanses of barbed wire had to be passed through, but by noon the 157th Brigade had reached and passed the Sensée River. When it was moving up the eastern slope towards Fontaine-les-Croisilles, it was caught in enfilade by a heavy machine-gun and trench mortar fire directed from some slopes near its right flank.

It was then discovered that the 56th Division had been unable to advance along the eastern slopes of Hénin Hill, and that it was still hung up before Croisilles. Not only was the right flank of the 157th Brigade in the air, but the enemy were in position near its right rear, and it was now found impossible, because of the intensity of the enfilade machine-gun fire, to move the brigade reserve from the left, originally expected to be the exposed flank, to the right.

The 56th Division could not get forward. Accordingly, at 1.16 p.m. Major-Gen. Hill ordered the 155th Brigade, Brig.-Gen. J. Forbes-Robertson, to attack southwards from the Hindenburg Line and clear the trenches which lay in rear of the front line of the Germans who were holding up the 56th Division on the southern portion of Hénin Hill. These trenches lay some 1500 to 2000 yards away, being behind the right rear of the 157th Brigade, and north of Croisilles. The 155th Brigade successfully accomplished this attack during the afternoon, killing and driving off numbers of machine-gunners.

By this time the 156th Brigade had moved forward. The 4th R.S., Major J. M. Slater, was on the right; the 7th R.S., Lt.-Col. W. T. Ewing, was on the left; and the 7th Cameronians, Lt.-Col. J. G. P. Romanes, was in reserve. Their captures included over 500 prisoners with over eighty machine-guns. They had taken Cherisy, so prolonging to the north the line of the 157th, which, having passed through Fontaine-les-Croisilles, now touched the eastern edge of those ruins. From this line no further advance was possible at the time, owing to the fact that the 2nd Canadian Division was held up further north by heavy enfilade fire, as was the 157th Brigade to the south.

The 157th Brigade was now engaged in a desperate battle. The Germans had reinforced their front line and could be seen dribbling their reinforcements forward over the slopes, using communication trenches and sunken roads. A strong force was working its way round the right flank of the 6th H.L.I., and was firing into its right rear. The ground was, of course, quite unknown to our people, and was a vast labyrinth of wire and trenches. The Germans, on the other hand, knew every line of approach, and every " pill-box." There now ensued a series of the fiercest fights between the kilted men and the enemy. A glance at the map will show the reason. A further advance down the front trenches of the Siegfried line would be extemely difficult so long as Croisilles was held by the Germans. On the other hand, if the 157th Brigade could establish itself in the trench systems south of Fontaine-les-Croisilles, the hitherto impregnable area of Croisilles would be threatened with envelopment, and the Germans would be compelled to evacuate.

It is impossible in a history of these dimensions even to mention the numerous deeds of gallantry by all ranks of the 52nd Division, especially during the period that it fought in France, but there are some which were so outstanding that they cannot be passed by. Lieut. D. L. MacIntyre, A. & S.H., Adjutant of the 6th H.L.I., had already distinguished himself by his constant presence in the firing line, where he had, by his coolness under the heaviest shell and machine-gun fire, inspired the confidence of all ranks. On this day he was acting as second-in-command, and, as the 6th H.L.I. had only six officers left when it went into action, he was in charge of the firing line during the attack. He " showed throughout most courageous and skilful leading in face of heavy machine-gun fire. When barbed wire was encountered, he personally reconnoitred it before leading his

SECOND BATTLE OF THE SOMME

men forward. On one occasion when extra strong entanglements were reached, he organized and took forward a party of men, and under heavy machine-gun fire supervised the making of gaps. Later, when the greater part of our line was definitely held up, Lieut. MacIntyre rallied a small party, pushed forward through the enemy barrage in pursuit of an enemy machine-gun detachment, and ran them to earth in a 'pill-box' a short distance ahead, killing three and capturing an officer, ten other ranks, and five machine-guns. In this (Humber) redoubt he and his party (comprising about six men, which included his servant, Pte. Andrew Taylor, and Sgt. James Smith, both of whom distinguished themselves) raided three 'pill-boxes' and disposed of the occupants, thus enabling the battalion to capture the redoubt. When the battalion was ordered to take up a defensive position Lieut. MacIntyre, after he had been relieved of command of the firing line, reconnoitred the right flank which was exposed. When doing this an enemy machine-gun opened fire close to him. Without any hesitation he rushed it single-handed, put the team to flight, and brought in the gun. On returning to the redoubt he continued to show splendid spirit while supervising consolidation.

"The success of the advance was largely due to Lieut. MacIntyre's fine leadership and initiative, and his gallantry and leading was an inspiring example to all." (Quoted from the Official Report.)

For his conspicuous gallantry on this day Lieut. David Lowe MacIntyre was awarded the Victoria Cross.

In order to cut the eastern communications of Croisilles and to encircle it, preparations were now made by the 157th Brigade to continue the attack further southward, but the Division found itself fighting on two fronts, facing east and south-west. Every brigade was engaged, there were no reserves available, and accordingly the 157th was ordered to consolidate its position.

The 6th H.L.I. was in the salient of this area, and, despite rapidly thinning ranks due to a fire which came from front, flank and rear, was stubbornly retaining what it had captured. It reported its position by pigeon and asked for ammunition, which was delivered by aeroplane four hours later. The fighting continued into the night, and at 11.30 p.m. the enemy made a determined counter-attack with machine-guns and bombs on the Humber Redoubt, which was in the right rear of the 6th H.L.I., but this attack was repulsed.

The two assaulting battalions of the 157th Brigade now represented a rifle strength of about 200 each. The 6th H.L.I. had gone into action on the 24th with twenty-three officers and 750 other ranks: it came out three days later with six officers and 223 other ranks. With these reduced numbers this Brigade was holding a front measuring about two miles. It had "mopped up" Fontaine-les-Croisilles, and was holding the eastern and southern edges of that village. From the latter its front ran two-thirds of a mile, approximately, to the south-east, and then bent back at an acute angle, because of the manner in which that flank stretched towards the rear of Croisilles. The apex of this salient on the right was less than a mile from the north-western outskirts of that litter of fortified ruins.

The time had now arrived for the 52nd Division to rest for a few days, and to recruit its sadly depleted ranks. It had lost nearly half of its personnel in battle casualties, the officers, as usual, having suffered most severely, but it had succeeded in making a separate break in the front system of trenches in the Siegfried section of the Hindenburg Line, having torn a gap nearly four miles in width. It had also seized a position that would force the evacuation of Croisilles, which, in spite of persistent attacks had so far held up the division on its right. It will be noted how the direction of the Division's attacks had veered round from the north-east, through the east, to the south.

It was because of such rapid advances on the part of the 52nd and other divisions that the enemy were never given time to make a stand, and were forced to throw their reserves in anywhere. This resulted in great confusion in the enemy lines, and, on many occasions, elements of the same German divisions were identified on widely separated parts of the battle front.

SECOND BATTLE OF THE SOMME

The 155th and 157th Brigades were relieved in the early hours of the 28th August by the 57th Division. The 156th Brigade was relieved at the same time by the 2nd Canadian Division. The Lowland Division then moved to bivouac areas near Mercatel, where they remained until the 31st August, refitting and reorganizing. The Divisional Artillery remained to support the 56th Division.

The break through the Siegfried system of the Hindenburg Line into the northern corner of the great Somme Valley salient had outflanked the whole German line from Arras to Soissons, which was now in a state of flux. One place after another was falling to attacks which never ceased against some part of the enemy front, and Bapaume, the great barrier on the road from Arras to Cambrai, fell to the New Zealanders on the 29th of August.

CHAPTER XXX

(31ST AUGUST TO 7TH SEPTEMBER, 1918)

THE SECOND BATTLE OF ARRAS, OR OF THE SCARPE: THE STORMING OF THE DROCOURT-QUÉANT SWITCH OF THE HINDENBURG LINE

" Now, gentlemen, it is our turn—Montjoie and Saint Denis! France—France and Scotland for ever! Trot—gallop—comrades—les Gardes Eccossais follow me—CHARGE ! "

The Marquis of Huntly at the Battle near Bitche in Alsace against a German army in 1634.

JAMES GRANT.

THE evening of the 31st August found the 52nd Division again under orders for the front line. The enemy had given up Croisilles, and by 5 p.m. on that day the 56th Division had advanced to ground north and south of Bullecourt, but had been unable to clear that village, and lay on its western edge.

The 155th Brigade relieved the 56th Division in the line before Bullecourt, the 156th Brigade being in support, the 157th Brigade remaining in reserve about Hénin Hill.

Of all the dreadful collections of ruins on the Western Front, Bullecourt was one of the most desolate. It was also one of the most strongly fortified, having an extensive system of strong bomb-proof shelters connected by underground tunnels. By means of these the enemy constantly moved their machine-guns and trench mortars to new positions, thus making it very difficult for the attackers to locate them. Bullecourt had been taken by the British, but the Germans had come out of their tunnels and other hiding places in their rear, bombing and machine-gunning them from behind, so that it became untenable. On the morning of the 1st September the 155th Brigade commenced to clear up the situation in Bullecourt. The 4th K.O.S.B., Major P. L. P. Laing, were on the right, and the 4th R.S.F., Lt.-Col. B. Cruddas, on the left, a party of Royal Engineers (410th Company) assisting by searching for mines, booby-traps, and subterranean passages. The 155th Brigade's method of clearing up the place was simple, but thorough and systematic. Patrols searched every nook and cranny, and threw bombs into every cellar, hole and tunnel whenever a movement was heard. Many Germans came out and surrendered, and the process of "mopping up" was so complete that no enemy parties were left to harass the Fusiliers or Borderers from the rear. By mid-day Bullecourt was almost entirely ours, both above and below ground, although during the forthcoming attack the 5th R.S.F. left men in the place to ensure that no enemy snipers or machine-gunners had been overlooked.

In the meantime, the 57th Division had captured Hendecourt-les-Cagnicourt on the left, and the 3rd Division was holding Longatte on the right. It was also reported that the 3rd Division had its troops in Noreuil, which lay south-east of Longatte. Running north and south and to the east of Bullecourt lies a long low ridge, over which, towards the south-east, ran the front trenches of the Hindenburg (Siegfried) Line.

At 5.55 p.m. the 155th Brigade, Brig.-Gen. J. Forbes-Robertson, was to continue the advance down the Hindenburg Line and seize this ridge.

The 57th Division was to advance on its left and the 3rd Division on its right. The final objective was Quéant.

The 4th K.O.S.B., Major P. L. P. Laing, was on the right, and the 4th R.S.F., Lt.-Col. B. Cruddas, on the left, the 5th R.S.F., Lt.-Col. D. M. Murray-Lyon, being in support.

The barrage stood for ten minutes on the enemy trenches, and then moved forward at the rate of 100 yards in five minutes. The Fusiliers and Borderers advanced behind it in the usual artillery formation, with strong "mopping up" parties in rear to dispose of hidden machine-guns. The ground was badly cut up and covered with obstacles, and the enemy machine-gunners were excellent, but their artillery barrage was weak, probably because of the general retreat in progress. The attack of the Fusiliers on the left went forward according to plan, and that of the Borderers on the right did so for the first 600 yards, but later they came under heavy machine-gun fire from the south, which caused heavy casualties. Attempts were made to get into touch with the division on the right, but unsuccessfully, excepting at a point south-east of Bullecourt, and fire from German machine-guns made it evident that Noreuil and the district to the north of it were still in enemy hands.

About 150 Borderers fell by this machine-gun fire, but the advance was continued until finally held up on a line about 1000 yards south-east of Bullecourt, where a position was consolidated for the night, the work being carried out under a bombardment of gas shells. By 8 p.m. the 4th R.S.F. had reached a line south of Riencourt-les-Cagnicourt, which the 57th Division had been seen to enter. These Fusiliers now formed a defensive flank facing south to link up with the Borderers' left.

During the attack, 2nd Lieut. J. B. Frew, 4th R.S.F., saw a party of the enemy in Tank Trench on his right firing on the advancing 4th K.O.S.B. Leaving Pte. M'Callum to engage them with rifle-fire, which the latter did standing on the parados, he sent Sgt. Burnett and two men by a detour to get into Tank Trench below the enemy and to bomb up it. He then proceeded to bomb down the trench. The Germans, finding themselves vigorously bombed from both flanks, and under rifle-fire from the front, surrendered, and fifty-two prisoners with four machine-guns were taken by this handful of men.

At 8.17 p.m. the enemy attempted to work round the right flank of the 4th K.O.S.B. with machine-guns, but this movement was checked by a field artillery barrage. It was finally stopped by a company of 5th R.S.F. coming forward and forming a defensive flank on the Borderers' right.

SECOND BATTLE OF ARRAS

The 155th Brigade was now close up to Quéant, with its left in touch with the 57th Division, but with its right drawn back in order to cover that flank until the 3rd Division should be able to advance.

This was a time when the artillery seemed never to cease, and when one gigantic battle grew out of another, each one increasing in magnitude.

The Second Battle of the Somme, or of Bapaume, as it is also called, which breached the Hindenburg Line and wiped out the great Amiens salient, was finished; but the Second Battle of Arras, or of the Scarpe, was already begun.

" The 1st September marks the close of the second stage in the British offensive. Having in the first stage freed Amiens by our brilliant success east of that town, in the second stage the troops of the Third and Fourth Armies, comprising twenty-three British divisions, by skilful leading, hard fighting, and relentless and unremitting pursuit, in ten days had driven thirty-five German divisions from one side of the old Somme battlefield to the other, thereby turning the line of the River Somme. In so doing they had inflicted upon the enemy the heaviest losses in killed and wounded, and had taken from him over 34,000 prisoners and 270 guns." (Gen. Sir Douglas Haig.)

This thrust into and along the Hindenburg Line had outflanked everything to the south, and the enemy were becoming disorganized and losing heart, but there still remained another possible winter defence line for the Germans. The Hindenburg Line from Quéant to the southeast was still intact, and, with that village as a pivot, there ran northwards another fortified line, known as the Drocourt–Quéant Switch. This had been constructed to link up the Hindenburg (Siegfried) Line proper with the old German front south of Lens, after the First Battle of Arras had destroyed what was originally intended to form the northern Siegfried pivot. In Flanders, the German salient, which stretched towards Boulogne, was being driven in by British Imperial troops, and the capture of Kemmel Hill was imminent. The great road-centre of Peronne on the Somme, north-west of St. Quentin, was captured on the

1st September by Australians. The French north of
Soissons were also pushing forward. Ludendorff was
being pressed back relentlessly across the wilderness of the
Somme area; but he still hoped to shepherd his battered
divisions behind the Drocourt–Quéant Switch and the
Hindenburg Line proper to the south. This Drocourt-
Quéant line had become the key of the whole German front,
and Ludendorff had no less than eleven divisions on the nine
miles between the Sensée and Quéant.

Meanwhile, at the close of the 1st of September, portions
of Gen. Sir H. S. Horne's First Army, and Gen. Sir Julian
Byng's Third Army were already close up to the Drocourt-
Quéant Switch. Once again Sir Douglas Haig was ready
to shatter Gen. Ludendorff's plans. In the early morning
of the 2nd September the right wing of the First Army,
and the left wing of the Third Army, composed of Sir
Charles Fergusson's 17th Corps, and comprising the
52nd, 57th and 63rd Divisions, were all astride the Arras–
Cambrai road, and ready to attack the Drocourt–Quéant
line. The 52nd Division was ordered to attack the pivotal
area of Quéant.

The general plan of this day's operations was that the
Canadian Corps should attack this line south of the River
Scarpe at 5 a.m. As it broke through, the 57th Division
was also to push in on its right, and to manoeuvre into a
position from which to attack Quéant from the north. To
the south of the 52nd Division, the 3rd Division was to
advance against the villages of Noreuil and Lagnicourt.
When these flanking movements had developed sufficiently,
the 52nd Division was to attack and seize the Hindenburg
Line about Quéant. From the map it will be noticed how
the Hindenburg Line skirted the south-eastern edge of
Quéant and then ran almost due east for about four miles
until it reached the Canal du Nord.

The attack of the Canadian Corps and 57th Division, the
artillery of the former being reinforced by the guns of the
52nd Division, commenced at 5 a.m., and by 8 a.m. word
came that they had broken the Drocourt-Quéant line.
Meanwhile, the 4th K.O.S.B. had pushed patrols south

and effected touch with the 3rd Division north of Noreuil. The 3rd Division, owing to strenuous opposition east of Noreuil, was not able to make any substantial progress throughout the day, but, although the advance to the south of Quéant had not yet been made, the attack of the 52nd Division could not longer be postponed.

At 8.45 a.m. the 156th Brigade, Brig.-Gen. A. H. Leggett, commenced to advance through the front of the 155th Brigade, its objective being a stretch of about 700 yards of the Hindenburg Line between Riencourt-les-Cagnicourt and Quéant. The 7th Cameronians, Lt.-Col. J. G. P. Romanes, was on the right, and the 4th R.S., Lt.-Col. A. M. Mitchell, on the left, the northern objective of the latter being the Moulin Sans Souci—a windmill standing out prominently on a small spur. The 7th R.S., Lt.-Col. W. T. Ewing, was in reserve.

The Division did not have the use of its own guns, and the supporting artillery had encountered great difficulties in getting the guns into position. The barrage crept forward at the rate of 100 yards in four minutes, but was weak, and had no perceptible effect on the wire, which was of great depth. The entanglements lay in three very thick belts to a total depth of some 200 yards.

The 7th Cameronians advanced through considerable machine-gun fire from the flanks, and reached this wire, but, despite persistent efforts, could get no further. Sgt. M'Gregor with four or five men succeeded in penetrating the wire, and reached the front trench, where they were attacked by thirteen Germans, all of whom they killed. This individual effort was followed by a heavy counter-attack and the little party had to withdraw to shell holes in front of the trench.

The right of the 4th R.S., also, was held up, but its extreme left managed to get through and capture the Moulin Sans Souci. Vigorous and determined action followed promptly. Lt.-Col. Mitchell immediately pushed his reserve company into the gap with orders to work down the trenches of the Hindenburg Line. Gen. Leggett further strengthened the position with two Stokes trench mortars and a section of machine-guns. These took up a position on the high ground near the mill, and began to bombard and sweep the enemy trenches in enfilade. This combined attack drove the Germans out, and, when the final rushes were made, only isolated machine-gunners were met with. By 3 p.m. the whole of the front line on the 156th Brigade's front had been captured, together with three field guns and ten machine-guns. By 4.30 p.m. 7th Cameronians and 4th R.S. had occupied their final objectives, and gained touch with the 57th Division on the left.

The 7th R.S. now pushed through to clear 800 yards of the Hindenburg support line, which lay about two-thirds of a mile beyond the line just captured. This support line ran to the south-east behind Quéant, until it crossed the Canal du Nord to the north of the Hindenburg front line. These Royal Scots met with no opposition, the enemy having fled, but, owing to the maze of trenches and the masses of wire, they did not complete this operation until nearly midnight.

Both 4th R.S. and 7th Cameronians had sent patrols to reconnoitre Quéant, which the Royal Air Force had reported clear of Germans, but the Lowlanders found it still held by machine-gunners. However, later in the night, the enemy fire ceased, and by 11 p.m. patrols of the 7th Cameronians reported the place evacuated. At 4.30 a.m. on the 3rd September, patrols were sent out with orders to push on, if possible, to Pronville, but these had to return owing to the density and violence of the British barrage.

In the meantime, to exploit the success of the movement, the 63rd Division, supported by the artillery of the 52nd, had moved to the south-eastward through the 57th Division. The enemy, demoralized by the collapse of a system which they had regarded as impregnable, had given way everywhere, and the 63rd Division was now holding the Hindenburg support line to the north-east of Quéant, that is, on the right of the 7th R.S.

The 155th Brigade had swung forward its left, the 4th R.S.F., keeping touch with the right of the 156th Brigade as it advanced, but the 4th K.O.S.B. on the other flank

SECOND BATTLE OF ARRAS

could not get forward as the 3rd Division had been held up further to the south. During the afternoon the 5th R.S.F. had pushed patrols southward, capturing four machine-guns and gaining touch with the 3rd Division at a point some 500 to 600 yards north-east of Noreuil.

Whilst holding high ground covering the right flank, two sections of the 155th Machine-Gunners caught parties of enemy artillery retiring across the open. Men and horses, with guns and limbers, were seen to fall and scatter.

The close of the day thus found the 52nd Division with its left flank thrust forward through the Hindenburg Line north of Quéant, and its right drawn back and facing almost south.

During the night the Guards relieved the 3rd Division. At 5.40 a.m. on the 3rd of September the Guards Division attacked and fought its way forward to the high ground south of Quéant. The 155th Brigade, at the same time, advanced eastward on its left, the 4th R.S.F. leading, being followed by the 4th K.O.S.B. and the 5th R.S.F. It cleared the Hindenburg front line as far as the south of Quéant, meeting with no opposition, and the operation was completed by 9 a.m. One company of the 4th R.S.F. captured five 77 mm. and four 10.5 cm. guns.

The enemy was in full retreat. It was now the turn of the 157th Brigade to advance, and, with the 7th H.L.I. on the right, the 5th H.L.I. on the left, and the 6th H.L.I. in reserve, it moved forward at 11.45 a.m. through Quéant and Pronville to a trench line east of the latter place. No opposition was met with as the advance of the 63rd Division had already forced the thoroughly beaten enemy out of the objectives, but prisoners and machine-guns were captured. The 63rd, covered by the artillery of the 52nd Division, continued to exploit the success, and seized Tadpole Copse, a height less than a mile east of the Canal du Nord from which its guns swept the Bapaume–Cambrai road. This road was Ludendorff's main artery of retreat in the northern area of the great Amiens salient. The 155th Brigade came up, and at 12.5 p.m. relieved the 157th Brigade, which again pushed forward, and cleared the Hindenburg Line as far as Tadpole Copse, making further captures, but meeting with no serious resistance. After the capture of the Drocourt-Quéant Switch the uppermost thought in the minds of the enemy was to find refuge as soon as possible behind the line of the Canal du Nord. The 63rd Division captured Inchy-en-Artois and obtained a footing in Moeuvres, two villages on the western bank of the Canal du Nord, but could not get across that great trench, as its eastern bank was very strongly held. In fact, the advance here had reached the last line of defence on which Ludendorff could hope to make a stand during the winter of 1918-19.

The Division was in Corps Support on the west of Quéant from the 4th to the 6th, and on the 7th moved to bivouacs at St. Léger, where it lay in Corps Reserve. There it refitted and once more filled up its depleted ranks. The Divisional artillery remained in support of the 63rd Division. At 7 p.m. on the 4th the guns of the Division successfully engaged the enemy debouching from Bourlon Wood in an attempt to retake Inchy-en-Artois. This village and Moeuvres, especially the latter, forthwith became the objects of great contention.

The Battle of the Scarpe, which had grown out of the Battle of Bapaume was now over. Sir Douglas Haig refers as follows to this victory :

" On the 2nd September the Drocourt-Quéant line was broken, the maze of trenches at the junction of that line and the Hindenburg system was stormed and the enemy was thrown into precipitate retreat on the whole front south of it." He tells how, in " this gallant feat of arms, the Canadian Corps attacked on the left, whilst on the right the attack of the 17th Corps, launched at the same hour by the 52nd and 57th Divisions, directed its main force on the triangle of fortifications marking the junction of the Hindenburg and Drocourt-Quéant lines north-west of the village of Quéant. Pressed with equal vigour it met with success equally complete. There was stern fighting in the network of trenches both north and south of Quéant, in which neighbourhood the 52nd (Lowland) Division performed

SECOND BATTLE OF ARRAS

distinguished service, and by the progress they made greatly assisted our advance farther north. Early in the afternoon our troops had cleared the triangle, and the 63rd Division had passed through to exploit the success gained. During the day 8000 prisoners had been taken and many guns."

During the whole of the operations, which commenced with the breaking of the Hindenburg Line on the 26th August, and led up to the storming of the Drocourt-Quéant Switch, all forming part of the Second Battle of Arras, or of the Scarpe, the British took over 16,000 prisoners and about 200 guns. In this battle ten British, Imperial and Colonial, divisions attacked and overthrew thirteen German divisions holding a fortified line of immense strength.

"The feat was beyond doubt one of the greatest in the campaign, and it made Ludendorff's plan for an intermediate stand impossible. He had no time for counter-attacks, but hurried his troops in the south behind the Canal du Nord, and, in place of the old Switch, put his trust in the line of water and marsh in the Sensée Valley east of Etaing which protected Douai, and which was continued southward from Marquion by the Agache River and the Canal du Nord." (John Buchan.)

The results of the battles of Amiens, Bapaume, and the Scarpe rapidly declared themselves. By the night of 8th September Gen. Ludendorff had withdrawn to the general line Vermand, less than six miles west of St. Quentin, Epéhy, Havrincourt, and thence along the east bank of the Canal du Nord.

For a week the Allies struck no great blow, but in Flanders the British and Belgians, and to the south the French, were steadily working into the invaders' fronts in many places, and speeding up their retreat.

Marshal Foch was manoeuvring the Allied armies into position for that final battle, for which he had been preparing since July.

The losses of the Division for the period of these operations were as follows. It will be noted that the figures of the 155th Brigade cover the period 26th August to the 7th September, whilst those of the 156th and 157th are given for two separate periods. The figures of captures are shown as covering similar periods. It must be borne in mind that many of the missing were wounded, that some of them were afterwards returned as killed, while some of the wounded died.

155TH BRIGADE—26TH AUGUST TO 7TH SEPTEMBER.

Unit.	Killed. Offrs.	O.R.	Wounded. Offrs.	O.R.	Missing. Offrs.	O.R.	Total. Offrs.	O.R.
Brigade H.Q.	—	—	2	—	—	—	2	—
4th R.S.F.	—	20	8	135	—	4	8	159
5th R.S.F.	3	15	6	167	—	1	9	183
4th K.O.S.B.	3	30	9	150	—	2	12	182
155th L.T.M. Bty.	—	1	—	7	—	—	—	8
	6	66	25	459	—	7	31	532

The officers who gave up their lives were as follows: 5th R.S.F., Capt. G. C. Millar, Lieut. C. E. Gordon, 2nd Lieut. S. B. Hurst; 4th K.O.S.B., Lieut. E. C. R. Hamilton-Johnston, 2nd Lieut. M. Nettleship, 2nd Lieut. J. A. Walker.

156TH BRIGADE—22ND TO 28TH AUGUST.

Unit.	Killed. Offrs.	O.R.	Wounded. Offrs.	O.R.	Wounded (Gassed).[1] Offrs.	O.R.	Missing. Offrs.	O.R.	Total. Offrs.	O.R.
4th R.S.	—	27	3	114	3	98	—	10	6	249
7th R.S.	1	16	5	80	2	251	—	1	8	348
7th Cams.	—	10	3	89	—	42	—	—	3	141
	1	53	11	283	5	391	—	11	17	738

Capt. K. MacKenzie, 7th R.S., was among the killed.

156TH BRIGADE—1ST TO 7TH SEPTEMBER.

Unit.	Killed. Officers.	O.R.	Wounded. Officers.	O.R.	Total. Officers.	O.R.
4th Royal Scots	3	8	—	7	3	15
7th Royal Scots	—	—	—	—	—	—
7th Cameronians	—	11	7	54	7	65
	3	19	7	61	10	80

[1] Separate figures for the gassed are given because they are large. As a rule less than five per cent. of the wounded came under that category.

SECOND BATTLE OF ARRAS

The killed of the 4th R.S. included Lieut. J. G. Mylne, Lieut. S. MacDonald, and 2nd Lieut. T. J. Turner, all of whom fell at the storming of the Drocourt-Quéant Switch.

157TH BRIGADE—22ND TO 31ST AUGUST.

Unit.	Killed. Officers.	O.R.	Wounded. Officers.	O.R.	Missing. Officers.	O.R.	Total. Officers.	O.R.
5th H.L.I.	4	19	8	256	3[1]	59	15	334
6th H.L.I.	5	40	12	298	—	23	17	361
7th H.L.I.	5	58	9	249	—	23	14	330
Other Units	—	—	—	3	—	—	—	3
	14	117	29	806	3	105	46	1028

The officers who are recorded as killed or died of wounds are as follows: 5th H.L.I., Capt. T. A. Fyfe, Lieut. F. Legate, Lieut. A. H. Malcolm, 2nd Lieut. E. D. Turner; 6th H.L.I., Lieut. C. Bruce, Lieut. R. J. A. Cumming, Lieut. W. D. Thompson, 2nd Lieut. K. A. MacIntosh, 2nd Lieut. F. G. Smith; 7th H.L.I., Capt. A. Morton (R.A.M.C.), Capt. S. E. Youden, Lieut. N. D. Galbraith, 2nd Lieut. W. H. M'Callum, 2nd Lieut. J. H. Pullar.

During the first week of September the 157th Brigade lost one officer killed and eight other ranks wounded. The former was Capt. and Quartermaster John Russell, 7th H.L.I., killed on the 5th, a most popular and efficient officer, who had seen considerable service in the war. On the 7th, when moving from the Quéant area to Corps Reserve, the 5th H.L.I. lost forty-seven men gassed near Pronville.

During the whole period from the 22nd August to the 7th September, other units in the 52nd Division, apart from the three infantry brigades, lost sixteen officers and ninety-nine other ranks. This brought the total losses of the Division for these battles to 121 officers and 2494 other ranks.

[1] Two of these were wounded.

The captures made by the Division during this period were as follows:

155TH BRIGADE.

Prisoners:	26th August to 7th September.
Officers	2
Other ranks	334

Artillery, etc.:	
10.5 cm.	4
77 mm.	5
Trench mortars	31
Machine-guns	62
Anti-tank rifles	13

156TH BRIGADE.

Prisoners:	22nd to 28th August.	1st to 7th September.
Officers	10	—
Other ranks	731	11

Artillery, etc.:		
5.9 inch	1	—
77 mm.	2	3
Field guns	4	—
Minenwerfer	7	—
Trench mortars	12	13
Machine-guns	79	23
Anti-tank rifles	6	—

157TH BRIGADE.

Prisoners:	23rd to 28th August.	1st to 7th September.
Officers	5	1
Other ranks	195	52

Artillery, etc.:		
Field guns	6	5
Machine-guns	48	11
Trench mortars	20	1

The total captures by the Division for the whole period amounted to:

Prisoners:	
Officers	18
Other ranks	1323

Artillery, etc.:	
Guns	30
Machine-guns	223
Trench mortars, etc.	84

SECOND BATTLE OF ARRAS

An incident, which showed the equanimity of the Jock in particular, and the British Tommy in general, occurred during the afternoon of the 4th of September, when the 156th Brigade were at work clearing the battlefield west of Quéant. Mr. (now Sir Harry) Lauder gave two concerts to an audience, which collected very rapidly amongst the barbed wire and shell holes, and consisted of a thousand or more men of every arm of the service. Even Germans were there to listen, for our cavalry escorting prisoners to the rear were tempted to stop. Artillery limbers returning empty stopped—everything stopped—except Harry Lauder and the " clumping and bumping " of the big shells that the enemy were planting on the other side of the ridge. " Roamin' in the Gloamin'," and other old favourites were enjoyed, and laughter seemed unrestrained and carefree, although, doubtless, many hearts were full.

CHAPTER XXXI

(8TH TO 26TH SEPTEMBER, 1918)

MOEUVRES

"Like Autumn's dark storms, pouring from two echoing hills, towards each other approached the heroes. Like two deep streams from high rocks meeting, mixing, roaring on the plain; loud, rough and dark in battle meet Lochlin and Innis-fail.
Chief mixes his strokes with chief, and man with man; steel, clanging, sounds on steel."

OSSIAN.

THE Canal du Nord had been under construction at the outbreak of war and portions of it were dry. The result was that, opposite to Cambrai, there was a gap of three or four miles in Ludendorff's water line before it joined up with the Hindenburg (Siegfried) Line. The village of Moeuvres was at the southern end of this gap. The front lines of this great trench system skirted the southern edge of this village, before they ran south-east again and crossed the Canal du Nord about two miles further to the south. The support lines passed through the midst of its ruins, and crossed the dry canal directly behind them, before they ran to the south and then south-east. If the Germans held Moeuvres, the British could not continue the process of rolling up the Hindenburg Line from its north-western flank, and this fortified village also served as an outwork on the southern flank of the defences east of the canal, helping to close the gap. Cambrai, the principal road and railway centre through which Ludendorff fed this section of his front, lay directly behind this gap. For these reasons, it was of immense importance to the Germans that Moeuvres should be held by their troops. The struggle for its possession entailed for the Division eleven days of the bitterest fighting, during which Moeuvres was continually drenched by poison gas and bombarded with H.E. and shrapnel, until at last that tormented litter of trench-seamed and blackened ruins passed finally into British hands.

On 15th September the Division again commenced to move forward, although its battalions were reduced to little more than fifty per cent. of normal strength. The 155th Brigade took over Moeuvres on the night of the 15-16th from the 57th Division. The 4th K.O.S.B., Lt.-Col. E. C. Hill-Whitson, was in the line defending Moeuvres, the 4th R.S.F., Lt.-Col. Cruddas, being in support, and the 5th R.S.F., Lt.-Col. D. M. Murray-Lyon, in reserve.

By this date the village had already changed hands several times, and, although many walls were still standing and one or two buildings could even boast of a roof, it was rapidly becoming as desolate as any in this stricken area. Moeuvres was defended by a chain of about a dozen small posts, which ran from north to south, and touched its eastern edge. Many of them were very shallow and gave very poor shelter, but they were all that were available. One of these posts was about 150 yards from the north side of the village, and lay in a gentle hollow which ran northeast to the Canal du Nord. It was at the angle of a ditch which ran (east-north-east) down to the canal, and from this point an old enemy trench ran to the south-east over a gentle rise to the slopes close to the canal. Thus, it had two lines of approach from the canal, the banks of which were in German hands. From its map indication this post was known as E.14 Central. It was taken and retaken many times.

Beyond heavy shell-fire and sniping, the 4th K.O.S.B. was not attacked during the 16th, but E.14 Central was lost and recovered by the 57th Division. During the following night the Borderers extended their line to the left to include this post, and the 157th Brigade took over the line further to the north. The 5th H.L.I., Lt.-Col. D. E. Brand, was on the right, in touch with the Borderers on the edge of Moeuvres, and the 6th H.L.I., Lt.-Col. W. Menzies Anderson, on the left, holding Inchy-en-Artois. The 7th H.L.I., Lt.-Col. E. S. Gibbons, was in support.

At 10.30 a.m. on the 17th about thirty of the enemy tried to raid E.14 Central, but were driven off by artillery and rifle-fire. The Germans were, however, determined to retake Moeuvres. At 6.25 p.m. they put down an intense barrage on the line of posts and the village, and searched the communications behind. Thirty minutes later troops of the Prussian Guards attacked Moeuvres simultaneously from the north-east, east, and south-east. The Borderers' right, on high ground south of Moeuvres, repulsed the Germans, but the left, on lower ground, was driven back through the village to trenches on its western side. This attack also drove in the extreme right of the 5th H.L.I., and surrounded two of that unit's defensive posts, so that it had to draw its flank back until it faced south-west. Overhead, enemy aeroplanes were directing the Guardsmen's advance by dropping flares. There were now gaps in the Borderers' line, all wires had been cut by shell-fire, and for a while the situation was obscure, but it was soon evident that the greater part of Moeuvres was again in German hands. The S.O.S. signal had been given and the British barrage was falling on the German lines. At 8.15 p.m. a company of the 4th R.S.F. moved up and secured a position on the left of the Borderers' right, that is, on the western edge of the village. As the British line had withdrawn to the western side of Moeuvres, the enemy barrage had followed it. Later, during the evening, two companies of 5th R.S.F. were pushed forward to reinforce the line of the 4th K.O.S.B., and link up with the right of the 5th H.L.I. Bitter fighting continued, but by this time the German attack was held up, and by 10.30 p.m. the line of the 155th was re-established on the western edge of Moeuvres, and in touch with the British Guards on its right, and the 157th on its left.

The artillery bombardments of both sides never ceased. During the 18th the enemy could be seen pushing men into

Moeuvres, and at 5.30 p.m. they attacked the British line west of the village. They obtained a footing in one place, but were bombed back by 2nd Lieut. D. M. Yuille, 4th R.S.F., with three of his men. Elsewhere the attack was held off, and it failed.

During this day the Divisional artillery were busy cutting gaps in the enemy wire east of the canal, and it was evident that another great battle was developing. Major-Gen. Hill made preparations to retake Moeuvres on the next day. The 4th K.O.S.B. was withdrawn into reserve, and the 4th and 5th R.S.F. took over the line, the latter being on the right.

All through the 19th our heavy artillery shelled the eastern part of Moeuvres. The German counter-attacks to push the British away from the village continued. During the early morning of the 19th several bombing attacks on the right of the 5th H.L.I. were repelled. About 5.20 p.m. the enemy bombarded one of the 5th R.S.F. posts south of the village with their trench mortars and then attacked, but this also was repulsed. At 7 p.m. it was the British turn to attack. At that hour a barrage fell on the whole village for five minutes, and then crept forward one hundred yards in every four minutes, until it rested on the great dry trench of the Canal du Nord, barring all enemy reinforcements. Behind it moved the assault: two companies of the 5th R.S.F. on the right, attacking north-east through the village, and then along the Hindenburg Line; three companies of the 4th R.S.F. in the centre, attacking eastward and clearing the village; and two companies of the 7th H.L.I., which unit was temporarily attached to the 155th Brigade, on the left attacking eastward with the object of re-establishing the two 5th H.L.I. posts, which were now within the enemy's lines. The German barrage came down at 7.5 p.m., but by 8.30 p.m. the 4th R.S.F. were well into the village, and fifteen minutes later some of its men had reached its eastern side, but there were held up. Moeuvres was strongly held by the enemy, and confused fighting went on throughout the night, whilst the shell-fire never ceased. The 7th H.L.I. recaptured a post on the northern edge of Moeuvres, and by 8 p.m. the 5th H.L.I. had swung forward to the light railway, finding one of their lost posts, which had been garrisoned by Cpl. David Hunter and six men, still holding out. Early in the morning of the 20th a company of 4th K.O.S.B. was sent to clear a trench south of Moeuvres, and reached the canal but was pushed back to the village. As the 20th drew on, it was evident that the Fusiliers had fought their way through and had retaken Moeuvres, and from 5.30 a.m. to 6.30 a.m. the enemy put down a very heavy artillery barrage on its area, but, as often happened, the good workmanship in the German dug-outs saved many British casualties. Units obtained touch, and by 10.30 a.m. the village was clear of the enemy. One officer and thirty-one other ranks of the 1st Prussian Guards, R.D., were taken prisoner during this operation, and four machine-guns and two trench mortars were captured.

Lt.-Col. E. S. Gibbons, D.S.O., the popular and efficient commanding officer of the 7th H.L.I., was mortally wounded and died on this day.

The 157th Brigade was relieved during the night of the 19-20th by the 5th Canadian Infantry Brigade, and went into reserve, where it was rejoined by the 7th H.L.I.

The 157th Brigade now had an opportunity to realize what Cpl. Hunter's post had done. With only what remained of one day's ration, their iron ration, and a bottle full of water, they had found themselves in a small trench in the open, cut off by the German advance. They had no information, and no orders beyond those given when the post was first occupied by them, but Hunter and his men had held on for ninety-six hours. During the last three days the German barrage and the British barrage each had passed over them twice. Hunter had sent a patrol of two men to report his position. One got through before dawn on the 19th, but the other was killed. Several times parties of the enemy had approached his trench, but he had driven them off. Their fate, if the Germans could have taken time to deal with them, was inevitable, and yet they hung on in stubborn faith that the ground would be retaken.

MOEUVRES

Finally, on the evening of the 19th, they had found British troops around them once more, and were relieved by a platoon of the 5th H.L.I.

Cpl. David F. Hunter, 5th H.L.I., was awarded the Victoria Cross, and his six men received the D.C.M.

At 5 p.m. on the 20th enemy infantry were seen advancing from the Canal du Nord to attack Moeuvres from the north-east, but were dispersed by the British artillery. The enemy retaliated by deluging Moeuvres and its rear with H.E. and gas.

The 156th Brigade relieved the 155th at 8 p.m. on the same day, and the latter moved to the rear of Inchy-en-Artois for a rest.

Moeuvres was in British hands, but the enemy were in close contact everywhere, and still held E.14 Central. The 4th R.S., Lt.-Col. A. M. Mitchell, took over the line on the right, and the 7th R.S., Lt.-Col. W. T. Ewing, on the left. The 7th Cameronians, Lt.-Col. J. G. P. Romanes, was in reserve west of Moeuvres, and the 4th R.S.F., Lt.-Col. B. Cruddas, which was attached to the 156th Brigade, was behind it, ready to counter-attack, if necessary.

At 2.50 p.m. on the 21st the Germans suddenly opened a heavy bombardment on Moeuvres, and at 3.30 p.m. the Prussian Guards again attacked. Their first objective was the spur which ran north-east and south-west on the south-eastern side of Moeuvres, and from which could be obtained a good view of the valley to the south-west. Two of the most northern posts of the 7th R.S. had already suffered heavily from the enemy fire, and were now annihilated. The enemy worked up the saps to the front and flanks of the posts in overwhelming numbers. Their movements were partially obscured by heavy dust raised by the shell-fire, and they bombed as they came. By sheer weight of numbers the posts of the 7th R.S. were driven off the ridge, and by 4 p.m. the enemy were in possession, and looking down on Moeuvres. They at once commenced to push exploiting parties westward. The Prussian Guardsmen, however, were not to be allowed to remain on the ridge for long. A counter-attack was at once launched by the reserve company of the 7th R.S., together with the remnants of the garrisons of the posts, and by 4.45 p.m. the last Guardsman had been hunted from the position. Lieut. A. S. Miller and 2nd Lieut. A. E. Watson won Military Crosses by their gallant leading. These two officers and a few men had a desperate struggle outside one " pill-box," before it was captured with two machine-guns. One enemy officer and twelve other ranks were afterwards counted dead outside this " pill-box." Over forty Prussian Guardsmen were found dead on the ground after this counter-attack.

Further north the enemy attacks were not so vigorous, and were repelled. At 5 p.m. large bodies of the enemy, moving westward along a trench towards the Canal and Moeuvres, were caught by our artillery, and their attack did not materialize.

At 8 p.m. four platoons of the 4th R.S. rushed and captured E.14 Central, and took three machine-guns.

This was the last big attack that the Germans succeeded in launching against Moeuvres, and the night that followed its repulse passed quietly, but for the usual shelling, trench mortar bombing, and sniping. On the 22nd the enemy appeared to be preparing further attacks, and at 6.30 a.m. and 4 p.m. their guns and trench mortars bombarded heavily the defences of the village, but each time our artillery counter preparation was rapid and vigorous, and no attacks followed. At 6.41 p.m., however, there was a burst of intense enemy shelling and an attack was launched against our southern position. Again the British artillery barrage came down quickly, the German attack collapsed before it reached our lines, and by 9.30 p.m. everything was comparatively quiet.

On the 23rd the enemy turned their attention once more to the northern portion of Moeuvres. At 4.30 a.m. they tried to effect a lodgment by bombing up the ditch that led to E.14 Central, but the garrison was alert, and the attack was repelled. Whenever the enemy artillery shelled Moeuvres now, it brought with it such a strenuous retaliation from the British that the German guns rapidly became silent. Every night the defensive posts were improved a little, and the British hold on Moeuvres grew tighter.

On this day Major-Gen. J. Hill, C.B., D.S.O., I.A., A.D.C., handed over the command of the 52nd Division to Major-Gen. F. J. Marshall. Gen. Hill's name will always be associated with the Lowland Division's fighting march from Gaza to Nebi Samwil, with the passage of the Auja, with the breaking of the Hindenburg Line, and with the holding of Moeuvres, the gate of the Canal du Nord. When those of the men of the Lowland Division who were bivouacked in the neighbourhood heard that he was leaving, they came out in force, and lined the roads, cheering him farewell.

During the night of the 23-24th the 155th Brigade relieved the 156th, which passed into Divisional Reserve. Sleep was impossible for those holding the Moeuvres defences, so that periods of duty there were necessarily short. The 156th Brigade had about 220 casualties during these four days, 20-23rd September.

The 4th K.O.S.B. was in the line on the right, and the 4th R.S.F. on the left, the 5th R.S.F. being in reserve. The 24th was confined mostly to bombardments and sniping, but at 4.50 a.m. on the 25th, the enemy, under cover of an artillery and trench mortar barrage, attacked E.14 Central and captured it. The British artillery replied promptly, and the 4th R.S.F. quickly counter-attacked, and recaptured the post. On the following day, the 26th at 5 a.m., it was again attacked and taken by the Germans. On this occasion Stokes guns were turned on the trench and the ditch that ran back from it to the canal. After recapture by the Fusiliers, both were found "full of dead Huns," killed by the Stokes shells. Shortly after this the Canadians on the left formed a joint post with the 4th R.S.F. at this point. At 1 p.m. an attack was made on a post held by the 4th K.O.S.B. in the front trench of the Hindenburg support line, where it left the eastern edge of Moeuvres. The Germans captured it, but they were promptly driven out again, and the position was re-established. These repeated attacks showed how anxious the enemy were to obtain a footing in Moeuvres, with a view to its recapture, but the time was rapidly drawing near when the British were to attack in great strength from the neighbourhood of this village, and finally breach the last enemy defences.

On the 25th of September Brig.-Gen. J. Forbes-Robertson, V.C., D.S.O., M.C., handed over the command of the 155th Brigade to Brig.-Gen. G. H. Harrison.

CHAPTER XXXII

(27TH SEPTEMBER TO 11TH NOVEMBER, 1918)

THE CANAL DU NORD—HERCHIES—MONS

But never had they faced in field so stern a charge before,
And never had they felt the sweep of Scotland's broad claymore.
Not fiercer pours the avalanche adown the steep incline,
That rises o'er the parent springs of rough and rapid Rhine—
Scarce swifter shoots the bolt from Heaven than came the Scottish band,
Right up against the guarded trench, and o'er it sword in hand.
    The Island of the Scots. A Ballad of the Scots Regiment which fought with France against Germany in 1697.

THE lateral communications of Ludendorff's front from the north of Verdun to the west of Lille—that is to say, of two-thirds of the whole—depended almost entirely on the main-line railway, which ran from Thionville in Lorraine, through Longuyon, Mezières, Hirson, and Valenciennes to Lille. Lying behind the centre of this section is the hill and moorland country of the Ardennes—a mass of limestone uplands seamed by countless precipitous ravines and gorges, and with few roads and railways, so that it forms a great natural obstacle. To the south-east of Verdun the German front was well supplied with railway communications, both lateral and forward, from the great supply centres on the Rhine. From Verdun to the Flemish coast, its communications depended mainly on two great routes: the Thionville–Lille railway, which supplied both forward and lateral communications to the greater portion of this front; and the system of railways radiating westward from Liège, which lies on the Meuse in the gap between the Ardennes and the Dutch frontier. If Marshal Foch could thrust forward through Cambrai and Maubeuge to the Ardennes, and thus cut the Thionville–Lille line, the whole German front to the west would have to be fed through the railway which ran through Aix-la-Chapelle to Liège. This would be impossible, and colossal disaster to the German armies would result. The last remaining great barrier, from which Gen. Ludendorff might ward off this thrust, was the defensive line composed of the Douai water zone, the Canal du Nord and the Siegfried system. He reinforced this line accordingly at the expense of his front in Flanders, where extensive mud-flats had always helped the German defence. Other interior lines of defence had been planned, but these had remained little more than plans, because so much of the German effort had been absorbed in fortifying this Siegfried system, and probably, also, because the enemy regarded the latter as impregnable. By the Battle of Havrincourt and Epéhy, which lasted from the 12-18th September, and other advances, Gen. Haig had now brought his armies close up to the line which was Gen. Ludendorff's last hope of defence against this great disaster.

Disaster also threatened from another quarter. The American Army had come into being, and on 12th September had destroyed the great St. Mihiel salient. Gen. Pershing was now within twenty miles of Metz, and was very near Germany's own frontier. This caused Ludendorff to fear an advance into Lorraine, despite the immensely difficult country that lay before Pershing, and he reinforced this front also at the expense of his Flemish positions.

Marshal Foch now prepared to do what Gen. Ludendorff thought impossible—to strike on several sections of the Western Front at once. It was decided that, as soon as possible after Gen. Pershing's great victory, " four convergent and simultaneous offensives should be launched by the Allies as follows :

" By the Americans west of the Meuse in the direction of Mezières ;

" By the French west of the Argonne in close cooperation with the American attack and with the same objective ;

"By the British on the St. Quentin–Cambrai front in the general direction of Maubeuge;

"By Belgian and Allied forces in Flanders in the direction of Ghent." (Sir Douglas Haig.)

The French and Americans were to press the Germans before them into the Ardennes, tearing open their line west of Metz. The British were to cut the enemy in two, and shut the western half of their army in the Belgian bottle-shaped area, of which the country between the Ardennes and the Dutch frontier was the neck. The Allies in Flanders were to free the sea-coast.

Success for the French and American attack, or for the British, would make retreat impossible. "The results to be obtained from these different attacks depended in a peculiarly large degree upon the British attack in the centre. It was here that the enemy's defences were most highly organized. If these were broken, the threat directed at his vital systems of lateral communication would, of necessity, react upon his defence elsewhere." (Sir Douglas Haig.) If they held, Ludendorff would be able to move reinforcements to his left, and, aided by the difficult country which lay before the Americans and French, to ward off their attack.

Gen. Haig's armies had borne the heaviest share of the summer fighting, and their casualties had been very heavy, so that the task which now confronted them could not be lightly undertaken. "Moreover, the political effects of an unsuccessful attack upon a position so well known as the Hindenburg Line would be large, and would go far to revive the declining morale not only of the German Army but of the German people." (Sir Douglas Haig.) Nevertheless, in spite of this, and of the trepidation of the British Government, Sir Douglas Haig decided that he was in a position to make a successful attack, for he knew what his troops could do.

It will be remembered that between Ludendorff's water line, and the northern end of that part of the Siegfried system which he still retained, there was a gap of a few miles. This gap was covered by the great dry ditch of the Canal du Nord, which the enemy regarded as an impassable obstacle for tanks. The canal followed a shallow valley, the eastern or German side of which was a ridge running north and south. This height provided excellent views of the western or British side, where the ground sloped a little more gently. Northward from the Hindenburg support line ran two auxiliary trench and wire systems, the Canal du Nord line close to the canal, and the Marquion line along the crest of the ridge. These, with the Hindenburg system, and the usual indescribable network of fortified villages and trenches which spread everywhere, resulted in the gentle open slopes of the western side being swept by tiers of machine-guns, and being very open to artillery observation. Sir Douglas Haig's plan was to break through this gap and seize Bourlon Wood and other positions which lay behind. This movement would result in turning the flank of the Siegfried system which after a two days' bombardment, he would take by storm. The success of the attempt to break through the gap " depended upon the ability of our troops to debouch from the neighbourhood of Moeuvres " (Sir Douglas Haig). After the canal had been crossed, divisions were to spread out fanwise, turning the enemy defences north and south, and so widening the gap. This task was entrusted to Gen. Horne's First Army, the troops primarily concerned in the attack being the 52nd and 63rd Divisions of the 17th Corps, under Lt.-Gen. Sir Charles Fergusson, and the 4th and 1st Canadian Divisions of the Canadian Corps, under Lt.-Gen. Sir Arthur Currie. After the crossing of the canal had been secured, nine divisions of the First Army, and of the 4th and 6th Corps of Gen. Byng's Third Army were to widen the gap still further and exploit the success.

The 52nd Division was to attack southwards from Moeuvres, down the trench systems on both sides of the Canal du Nord for over a mile, until it obtained touch with the Guards' Division of the Sixth Army, which would then be attacking westwards. The 157th Brigade was to attack southwards from Moeuvres, clearing the Canal du Nord and the Hindenburg front line west of the canal. The 156th Brigade was to attack eastwards across the Canal du Nord, south of the Moeuvres–Graincourt road. It was then to

CANAL DU NORD TO MONS

turn right-handed, clearing the trenches to the south-east, on the further side of the canal, until it also joined hands with the Guards.

On the left of the 156th Brigade, the 63rd Division was to cross the Canal du Nord and fight its way, firstly to the east, and then to the south along the Hindenburg support line. Further to the north the 4th Canadian Division was to assault eastward from Inchy-en-Artois, and on its left the 1st Canadian Division was to attack in an easterly and then in a north-easterly direction.

Three points must be noted, as follows :

(1) Both the 156th and 157th Brigades would have to debouch from a very small area immediately south of Moeuvres, and in different directions ;

(2) Because of the ceaseless fighting for Moeuvres the Prussian Guardsmen in that area were always on the *qui vive* ; and

(3) Because of the enveloping lines of the projected attacks by the 63rd and the Guards' Divisions, the Lowland Division would be certain to find itself blocked out from taking any part in the further advance.

The most careful organization had to be thought out to cope with the difficulties of the debouchment, one of which was that the barrage of the 156th Brigade would tend unavoidably to restrict and congest the left of the 157th Brigade.

The 6th H.L.I., Lt.-Col. W. M. Anderson, was to clear the Hindenburg front line, and the 7th H.L.I., Major C. Gibb, the Canal du Nord and its immediate neighbourhood. The 5th H.L.I., Lt.-Col. D. E. Brand, was in reserve.

The 156th Brigade was to be led by the 4th R.S., Lt.-Col. A. M. Mitchell, that unit being followed by the 7th Cameronians, Lt.-Col. J. G. P. Romanes. The 7th R.S., Lt.-Col. W. T. Ewing, was in reserve.

At 5.20 a.m. on the 27th of September, in the half-light of early dawn, the barrage came down in front of each brigade. Immediately, three parties from the 5th H.L.I. rushed three enemy machine-gun posts which were within a few score yards of the British lines. After fifteen minutes, during which the trench mortars thickened the shrapnel of the artillery, the barrage before the 156th Brigade commenced to move eastwards, while the barrage in front of the 157th Brigade moved in a southerly direction. Behind the latter moved three tanks, zigzagging over the wire, followed by the 6th H.L.I., spreading out as its men emerged from the trenches, its " mopping up " parties systematically clearing the enemy dug-outs and trenches. The German Guardsmen fought hard, their bomb-proofs having protected them from the barrage, but within two hours the 6th H.L.I. had reached its objective about level with the lock south of the Bapaume–Cambrai road, and was in touch with the Welch Guards.

Immediately after the 6th had commenced to advance, the 7th H.L.I. had followed, dropping platoons at intervals into the dry bed of the canal, which had brick sides, ruined in many places, and was about twenty feet deep. The second company of this unit should have been echeloned to the right of the first, but it had missed its way and arrived late. Its commander, taking his direction from the barrage, moved along parallel to it and west of the Hindenburg Line. When he reached a trench (Cow Alley) just north of the Bapaume–Cambrai road, he cut across the front of the 6th H.L.I. over the Hindenburg Line, and arrived in his proper place just to time. This company suffered a good deal from machine-gun nests hidden in a spoil-heap on the eastern bank. With the cooperation of some parties of 7th H.L.I. these machine-gun nests were rapidly destroyed. The tanks safely negotiated the canal by a crossing made by German engineers to one side of the ruins of the Bapaume–Cambrai road bridge. After the canal had been cleared, the 156th Brigade could be seen still fighting its way forward on the eastern bank, and large parties of the enemy were observed retreating across country before the Royal Scots. The 6th and 7th H.L.I. aided the movement with supporting fire.

Meanwhile, at 5.30, the 4th R.S. had commenced to fight their way forward. One minute after the British barrage opened, the Germans were bombarding the Royal Scots with trench mortar bombs and gas shells. When the barrage moved forward the Royal Scots kept close up to it,

CANAL DU NORD TO MONS

Behind them moved a company of 7th Cameronians, who were to follow across the canal, clear a long trench, and secure touch with the Guards to the south. As soon as the leading waves got over the crest of the ridge south-west of Moeuvres, they came under heavy machine-gun fire from both flanks and from the eastern slopes. At the same time they found themselves enmeshed in wire entanglements concealed by the undergrowth. This caused them heavy losses, and they had to bomb their way to the canal, the barrage creeping well ahead of them. About the left of the 4th R.S., and on either side of the Moeuvres–Graincourt road, the canal banks are raised about twenty feet above the surrounding country. The Royal Scots had to work without the help of tanks, because of the obstacle presented by the canal. " Having attained the trench immediately west of the canal, the men were reorganized and an attempt made to gain the bank by a frontal attack. It was at once evident that this would be very costly if successful, and bombing parties were organized to work round the left flank. These fought back the enemy traverse until held up by the last short stretch of trench, at the end of which was a small ' pill-box ' and two machine-guns. Quickly a heavy covering fire was arranged, and Cpl. Foggo, dashing forward, threw two bombs into the post and, joined by others, cleared the post and gained the top of the canal bank immediately south of the road crossing." (*History 4th Royal Scots.*) The company of 7th Cameronians had helped the 4th R.S. in this attack, and now followed the latter as its men scrambled down into and across the canal, and began to clear the trenches on the western side. The Canal du Nord had been crossed.

Stubborn resistance was met with at many points, but by 9.55 a.m. the Royal Scots had reached their objective, a trench junction (Leopard and Lion trenches) just north of the Bapaume–Cambrai road.

The company of 7th Cameronians referred to had lost heavily in crossing the canal, and only one of its officers was left. It was reinforced by another company from its own unit, which by this time had also crossed the canal. The whole of the 7th Cameronians now pressed southward, continuing the clearing process. Lance-Cpl. J. Clark rushed one German machine-gun post single-handed, killing or capturing all within it. This is one incident of many. After a while their advance was delayed, because of heavy machine-gun fire, which came from the ridge to the west, where the men of the 63rd Division were held up in their work of clearing the Hindenburg support line. However, the Cameronians got into the trenches and bombed their way along, so that by 2.30 p.m. they had reached a point about 1000 yards south of the Bapaume–Cambrai road, and were in touch with the Guards. *En route* they had taken about 200 prisoners, who surrendered practically without a fight. By 2.30 p.m. the 63rd Division was again advancing along the Hindenburg support line, and the 7th Cameronians cleared the ground south of the Bapaume–Cambrai road as far east as the wire of that system.

The Division had blotted out of existence a stretch of the German position with a frontage of about a mile and a quarter, and a depth of a mile. The 157th Brigade had captured forty-four machine-guns, two trench mortars, and two anti-tank rifles, besides one officer and 234 other ranks prisoners. The 156th Brigade had taken between 450 and 500 prisoners from twelve different Prussian cavalry regiments, besides numerous machine-guns and trench mortars.

Through the gap torn by these four divisions the other nine were now pouring on the demoralized enemy, and by the evening of the 29th the rent was thirteen miles wide and nearly five miles deep. Bourlon Wood had been captured, and, about three and a half miles to the east, could be seen the spires of Cambrai. Over 10,000 prisoners and 200 guns had been captured. Tanks were across the Canal du Nord, but, most important of all, the advance had turned the flank of the Douai water line to the north and of the Hindenburg (Siegfried) system to the south, and was still proceeding. By the following evening Cambrai was menaced from the north and west.

On the 28th September the King of the Belgians commenced his thrust for Ghent, and the guns of Sir Douglas

CANAL DU NORD TO MONS

Haig continued their deluge on the Siegfried system, which had commenced on the previous day On the morning of Sunday the 29th, Sir Douglas Haig struck again, this time assaulting on a twelve mile front the Siegfried system south of the break already made. Shaken by the outflanking movement to the north, and bombarded for two days by an overwhelming artillery, the main Siegfried system of the Hindenburg Line was stormed and crumbled into ruins, and with it disappeared Ludendorff's last hope of wintering behind that mighty line of field fortifications.

On the 30th September the 155th Brigade moved forward to the neighbourhood of Anneux on the south-west of Cambrai, which the enemy were making great efforts to save. On the following day it crossed the Canal de l'Escaut, and, from a front held by the 63rd Division, attacked the small suburb, the Faubourg de Paris. The 4th R.S.F., Major J. Bruce, was on the right, and the 5th R.S.F., Lt.-Col. D. M. Murray-Lyon, on the left, the 4th K.O.S.B., Lt.-Col. E. C. Hill-Whitson, being in reserve. The average strength of these battalions was about 350. Low-flying enemy aircraft spotted the assembly of the troops. The advance was over open fields without cover. The British barrage fell beyond one machine-gun post, and did not touch many others on the flanks, and especially in the outskirts of Cambrai. The result was that, after heavy casualties had been suffered, the advance was held up.

Among those killed on this day was Captain W. F. Templeton, 4th R.S.F., a splendid character, who might well be styled the poet of the Division, because of the charming verses he wrote whilst serving with it. He was hit three times before he finally collapsed.

The 4th R.S.F. lost six officers and 106 other ranks in this attack, and the 5th R.S.F. eleven officers and 164 other ranks. Capt. P. Lavell of the 155th Trench Mortars was amongst the killed.

Early in the morning of the 2nd October an attempt was made by a company of the 4th K.O.S.B. to take the machine-gun redoubt west of the Faubourg de Paris, which had done much to hold up the previous attack, but again the enemy barrage was too heavy. On the evening of the same day, however, it was captured by a strong fighting patrol.

During the whole of the 3rd of October the artillery kept up an intermittent local bombardment of the Faubourg de Paris, which, while it warned the enemy to expect an attack, did not touch their machine-gun positions in the outskirts of Cambrai. In fact, only an overwhelming bombardment lasting for days could have thoroughly searched all of these suburbs. At 11 p.m. two companies of the 4th K.O.S.B. attacked it from the south-west, and again a withering fire swept the area. All of the officers and many other ranks fell, and although some Borderers actually reached the buildings, the remnants were driven back and the attack failed.

The 155th Brigade had now hardly the rifle strength of a battalion, and on the night of the 4-5th October it was relieved by the 157th Brigade, which had been lying in support in the Marcoing line about Cantingneul Mill. The enemy artillery and aeroplanes did their best to get rid of their great stores of ammunition lying in Cambrai, and the shell-fire and bombing during this period was heavy and persistent. Box respirators had to be worn almost continuously.

On the 1st of October the 6th H.L.I. lost by this shell-fire Major G. P. Speirs, Croix de Guerre, died of wounds, one other rank killed, and nine wounded. Major Speirs was a thorough sportsman, and had been present at every battle in Gallipoli, Sinai, Palestine, and France, in which the 6th H.L.I. had fought. " No officer ever gave more devoted service to his country, and it is typical of his care for the comfort of the battalion that it was while supervising the cooking of a meal for the men that he received his first wound on this day " (Lieut.-Col. James Anderson). He received his second and fatal wound when being carried to the dressing station.

The 157th Brigade was relieved by units of the 57th Division during the night of 5-6th October, and the Division, with sadly thinned ranks, moved back for a rest to the eastward of Arras.

CANAL DU NORD TO MONS

The losses of the Division during the months of September and October can be estimated from the following figures:

155TH BRIGADE—15TH TO 22ND SEPTEMBER.
(Moeuvres.)

Unit.	Killed.		Wounded, including Wounded and Missing.		Missing, etc.		Total.	
	Officers.	O.R.	Officers.	O.R.	Officers.	O.R.	Officers.	O.R.
4th R.S.F. -	1	11	6	83	1	28	8	122
5th R.S.F. -	1	9	3	50	—	21	4	80
4th K.O.S.B. -	—	13	4	61	—	20	4	94
155th L.T.M.Bty. —	—	—	—	1	—	—	—	1
	2	33	13	195	1	69	16	297

Capt. A. D. H. Clark-Kennedy, 5th R.S.F., was among the killed.

155TH BRIGADE—1ST TO 31ST OCTOBER.
(Principally Faubourg de Paris.)

Unit.	Killed and Died of Wounds.		Wounded.		Missing.		Total.	
	Officers.	O.R.	Officers.	O.R.	Officers.	O.R.	Officers.	O.R.
4th R.S.F. -	2	9	4	116	—	2	6	127
5th R.S.F. -	2	15	9	146	—	3	11	164
4th K.O.S.B. -	2	?	1	?	3[1]	?	6	?[2]

In addition to Capt. W. F. Templeton, the dead included 2nd Lieut. F. S. Burleigh, 4th R.S.F., Lieuts. R. Montgomerie and R. F. W. Henderson, 6th Royal Scots, attached 5th R.S.F., and Lieut. G. Fair, and Lieut. Kirkwood, 4th K.O.S.B.

156TH BRIGADE—8TH TO 30TH SEPTEMBER.
(Moeuvres and Canal du Nord.)

Unit.	Killed and Died of Wounds.		Wounded.		Missing.		Total.	
	Officers.	O.R.	Officers.	O.R.	Officers.	O.R.	Officers.	O.R.
Brigade H.Q. -	—	—	1	—	—	—	1	—
4th Royal Scots	4	37	13	133	—	7	17	177
7th Royal Scots	3	14	2	41	1	46	6	101
7th Cameronians	4	17	1	77	—	12	5	106
156th T.M. Bty.	—	—	—	1	—	—	—	1
Brigade Signal Section -	—	—	—	2	—	—	—	2
	11	68	17	254	1	65	29	387

[1] All of these were wounded.

[2] The writer has been unable to get accurate figures of casualties in other ranks of the 4th K.O.S.B. They are believed to be between 130 and 150, of whom some were missing, but the majority killed or wounded.

The 4th R.S. lost six officers and eighty-one other ranks in the defence of Moeuvres, including Lieuts. Hudson and Thomson, killed. Eleven officers and ninety-six other ranks were the casualties of the same battalion in forcing the Canal du Nord, and included Lieut. A. W. W. Hawkes and 2nd Lieut. G. W. Sinclair, killed. The 7th R.S. suffered most of their casualties in repelling the attack of the Prussian Guards on the 21st September. Of their missing, the officer and most of the men were wounded. Their killed included Lieuts. T. A. Herdman, and L. Muirhead, and 2nd Lieut. R. P. Innes.

157TH BRIGADE—7TH TO 30TH SEPTEMBER.
(Defence of Moeuvres and Canal du Nord.)

Unit.	Killed and Died of Wounds.		Wounded.		Missing.		Total.	
	Officers.	O.R.	Officers.	O.R.	Officers.	O.R.	Officers.	O.R.
5th H.L.I.	3	14	4	95	—	4	7	113
6th H.L.I.	3	19	6	102	—	12	9	133
7th H.L.I.	5	13	1	99	—	8	6	120
Other Units	—	—	—	13	—	—	—	13
	11	46	11	309	—	24	22	379

Apart from the men gassed on the 7th, the 5th H.L.I. sustained most of its casualties while defending Moeuvres on the 19th. Capt. W. F. Donald, M.C., and Lieut. A. Bryson were killed on this day. Capt. K. Ross, R.A.M.C., fell two days previously. The 6th H.L.I. lost most of its men on the 27th. In addition to Lieut. M'Craken, Lieuts. E. A. Hitchcock and W. H. Aikman were numbered among its dead. The 7th H.L.I. lost three officers and sixty-five other ranks at the Canal du Nord, and most of the remainder in the defence of Moeuvres. In addition to Col. Gibbons, its dead included Lieuts. W. P. Mackie, J. R. G. Muir, and J. M. Smith, and 2nd Lieut. H. L. Vallance, the last two on the 27th.

157TH BRIGADE—1ST TO 31ST OCTOBER.
(West of Cambrai.)

Unit.	Killed and Died of Wounds.		Wounded.		Missing.		Total.	
	Officers.	O.R.	Officers.	O.R.	Officers.	O.R.	Officers.	O.R.
5th H.L.I.	—	1	4	—	—	—	4	1
6th H.L.I.	1	1	—	9	—	—	1	10
7th H.L.I.	—	1	—	8	—	—	—	9
	1[1]	3	4	17	—	—	5	20

[1] The death of Major Speirs has already been referred to.

The total strength of the 4th R.S.F. on the 1st October was fourteen officers and 315 other ranks. By the following morning its companies had only two officers and ninety riflemen left. The 5th R.S.F. had twenty-seven officers and 502 other ranks with the unit on the 1st of October, but in a few days had been reduced by battle casualties alone to sixteen officers and 338 other ranks. The position with the 4th K.O.S.B. was similar. The 156th Brigade was rather better, its average effective strength per battalion on the 28th September being thirty-six officers and 709 other ranks, but it must be remembered that every unit in the Division during these operations was from time to time receiving drafts of officers and men, and especially of the former. Despite this, the strength of the 6th H.L.I. at the end of September was only twenty-three officers and 394 other ranks, and the 5th and 7th H.L.I. had about the same numbers. The Division had been fighting and marching since the 22nd of August, and the need for rest and replenishment of its depleted ranks was obvious.

The Turkish army in Palestine had collapsed before Allenby on the 19th September. Bulgaria had asked for an armistice on the 26th. In France the greatest battle in history was raging on a 250 mile front, and had already been decided against the enemy. The British in the centre were already through the last German defences in one place, and before them lay unspoiled open country, where the enemy would have to fight without the bomb-proof shelters to which they had grown used. In the action which began on 26th September, thirty British and two American infantry divisions and one British cavalry division had engaged and defeated thirty-nine German divisions, and taken over 36,000 prisoners and 380 guns. From this time onwards Ludendorff was only fighting to postpone final defeat, which was certain to come.

On the 4th October Pershing commenced his advance between the Meuse and the Aire. On the 8th Haig assaulted the remainder of the Siegfried zone, and it in turn disappeared in one vast cataclysm. Cambrai fell on the following night as a result of an encircling movement from the north by the Canadian Corps. The immense difficulties of the country before them delayed Gouraud and Pershing, so that the retreating German centre was not pinned in the trap which had been prepared. Nevertheless, by 8th October Germany was finally beaten, and her great armies had begun to disintegrate.

Disaster succeeded disaster for the Central Powers. Italy began her final attack on Austria on the 24th October, and ten days later the latter collapsed. Turkey surrendered on the 30th October. Germany was left alone, and was retreating all along the line from Lorraine to the sea.

On the 19th October the Division once more set out to march to the front line. During this advance the Divisional Royal Engineers distinguished themselves in their searches for enemy mines and booby-traps. Many bridges were also constructed, one of ninety feet span at Douai, built by the 410th Company, being ready for traffic within fifty hours, despite great difficulties. The 156th Brigade led, and the route lay through Lens, Auby, north of Douai, to Hergnies on the Jard Canal, north of Valenciennes, where it took over the outpost line from the 8th Division on the 28th October. A few days later it was joined by the 157th Brigade. It was a low-lying and flooded country, with excellent fields of fire for machine-guns, and with numerous canals and rivers, which the enemy had tried to make impassable. The British plan in this area was to hold the enemy on this line while working round his flanks. It was known that the Germans were nearing a general collapse.

Haig took Valenciennes on the 2nd of November, cutting Ludendorff's lateral communications, so that his army was broken into two pieces. For the greater portion of the western of these two pieces the bottle-neck of Liège was the only line of retreat, and gigantic disaster was inevitable. Pershing, fighting in a veritable wilderness, had broken through the Kriemhilde system of the Hindenburg Line on the 15th of October, and by the 4th of November was in a position to shell the railway between Montmedy and Longuyon, threatening the retreat of all the Germans between the Meuse and the British. In Flanders the sea

CANAL DU NORD TO MONS

coast had been recaptured, and Ghent was about to fall. The German retreat was becoming a rout.

On the night of the 7-8th November, 7th Cameronian and 7th H.L.I. patrols got across the enemy water defences by means of canvas rafts, such as had been used on the Auja, and by broken bridges. On the following day the Division learnt that the Germans had asked for and been given the terms of an armistice, and it also became known that they had abandoned the water defences before the 156th and 157th Brigades. The code word, "Hunt," reached the 52nd on the morning of the 8th; both brigades crossed the canal, and a hot pursuit followed, no attention being paid to exposed flanks. The Belgian frontier was crossed at Bonsecours on the 9th, and the troops received a great ovation everywhere.

The principal rearguard resistance came from machine and field guns. The 10th of November found the 156th Brigade attacking, from the west, Herchies, a village six miles north-west of Mons. The Germans were holding the place with machine-guns, together with some field guns about 3000 yards behind. The 7th Cameronians, Major W. Mather, led the attack. On the right, advancing from the south, was the 157th Brigade, with the 6th H.L.I., Lt.-Col. W. M. Anderson, leading. The 7th Cameronians passed through Herchies at 4.20 p.m., taking two machine-guns and seventeen prisoners, and by 1 a.m. were on high ground between Erbaut and Jurbise. The 6th H.L.I. took their last two prisoners of war on the 10th. By 7 a.m. on the 11th patrols of the 7th Cameronians had entered Jurbise, and the 155th Brigade was continuing the pursuit, with the 4th R.S.F., Major Barfoot, in the van. The 5th H.L.I. Lt.-Col. D. E. Brand, was pushing on for the Mons–Jurbise road. There was no opposition and it was reached by 9 a.m. "We quite expected orders to continue the pursuit. But of a sudden there arose a clatter of hoofs and an obviously excited transport officer dashed up to the Commanding Officer, brandishing one of the pink forms we had learned to hate. But never before had an Army Form borne such a message as this: ' Hostilities will cease at 11.00; until further orders units will not move beyond the position occupied at that time.' At last there had dawned the day for which we had lived—and so many had died. Strange to relate there was no tremendous excitement. Perhaps the philosopher spoke truly when he said that one always has a feeling of regret on doing a thing for the last time. Perhaps we had been fed on rumours so often that we took this for one. Perhaps we were too weary in mind and body to grasp the significance of the stupendous news. Or was it that our thoughts turned at this time to those grand men who had given their lives for this great end ? Whatever the reason, the fact remains that there was no enthusiasm in keeping with the event." (*History 5th H.L.I.*) The bands played, and everyone felt relieved, but there were many sad hearts.

The Division had a few casualties on the 10th November, as follows :

Unit.	Killed and Died of Wounds.	Other Ranks Wounded.	Killed and Missing.
4th Royal Scots	—	5	—
7th Royal Scots	1	3	—
7th Cameronians	4	7	1
6th H.L.I.	1	2	—
	6	17	1

The good people of Herchies have erected a memorial to these men, who fell when all was so nearly over.

The 4th R.S.F. had passed through Jurbise, north of Mons, and it is believed that, at 11 a.m. on the 11th, some of their men stood on the very ground where Royal Scots Fusiliers of the old Expeditionary Force had fought at the outbreak of the war.

On the 15th November took place the official entry of Gen. Horne's Army into Mons, every brigade of the 52nd Division being well represented. Special comment must be made about Major D. Yuille, who led the party which represented the 155th Brigade in the procession. At an age when most men might reasonably have been expected to watch the war from a comfortable fireside, he had left his schoolmastering and gone to Gallipoli with the 4th R.S.F., serving as its quartermaster. He was never away from his battalion during the war for sickness or any other reason, with the exception of four weeks' leave in Palestine, and one in France, and he never once failed his battalion or brigade.[1]

We will now bid farewell to the Division. Its units passed through the various stages of demobilization, until finally the cadres returned to their headquarters, where later they grew into renewed life as part of the revived Territorial Force of Scotland. Some of the units have changed; some have amalgamated; but the spirit of the 52nd (Lowland) Division will always remain the same.

In a work of this size there is no space to tell of the honours and distinctions which the Division received. Let it suffice to say that it won five Victoria Crosses,[2] and that, latterly, it ranked fourth on the list of divisions which the Germans held most in dread.

Perhaps no division had been more fortunate in its Commanders and Brigadiers. Throughout these pages we have followed them as they played their parts and passed across the stage, and it remains, briefly, to take leave of those who held the different commands in the final scene.

Major-Gen. F. J. Marshall, C.M.G., D.S.O., was the last war-time commander of the Division. His command had been a short one, only lasting for some seven weeks, but in that time his skill and determination had made him respected as a worthy successor to those who had gone before.

Brig.-Gen. G. H. Harrison, D.S.O., similarly had commanded the 155th Brigade for a comparatively short period, but he will be remembered with gratitude by his Brigade for his fine soldierly qualities and for his cheerful personality.

Brig.-Gen. A. H. Leggett, C.M.G., D.S.O., had served continuously with the Division since Gallipoli days, and had held command of the 156th Brigade from the early months

[1] The case of Captain and Quartermaster J. Phillips, 7th Cameronians, is very similar as to age and good service. He was only away from his battalion for twelve days in hospital in Egypt during the entire war.

[2] A sixth Victoria Cross was won by the late Sergt. L. M'Guffie, 5th K.O.S.B., on 28th September, 1918, when serving in Flanders, near Wytschaete, in the 103rd Brigade.

of 1917. To a deep knowledge of warfare and a natural aptitude for arms he added an abounding common sense. It is safe to say that no commander in the army held a warmer place in the hearts of those under him than this B.G.C. 156th Brigade.

Brig.-Gen. C. D. Hamilton-Moore, C.M.G., D.S.O., commanding the 157th Brigade, had served with the Division for upwards of two years. He had led his Brigade with the utmost success throughout the stirring days of the advance in Palestine as well as in the constant fighting in France, and by his real kindliness and consideration had won the affectionate regard of officers and men.

It only remains now, as we close this story of the 52nd Division, to salute those comrades who have gone on before and who remain as silent witnesses in many lands. Some were killed in battle, some died of their wounds, and some of disease, but all gave up their lives in defence of their country's and the Empire's honour. Some lie on the bleak moorlands of Gallipoli, and some in the sands of the Sinai Desert; some sleep on the plains and highlands of Judaea, and some in the sea; some were laid to rest in the fields of France and Belgium, and some in their own beloved island home; but all will live for ever in the grateful hearts of their fellow-countrymen, whom they died to save.

> Blow out, you bugles, over the rich Dead!
> There's none of these so lonely and poor of old,
> But, dying, has made us rarer gifts than gold.
> These laid the world away; poured out the red
> Sweet wine of youth; gave up the years to be
> Of work and joy, and that unhoped serene,
> That men call age; and those who would have been,
> Their sons, they gave, their immortality.
>
> RUPERT BROOKE.

APPENDIX I

THE TRANSPORT COMPANIES OF THE LOWLAND DIVISIONAL TRAIN AND THE 10TH (IRISH) DIVISION

The Transport Companies of the Lowland Divisional Train embarked at Port Said for Salonica on the 13-14th October, 1915, reaching the latter port on the 19th. They were at once attached to the 10th (Irish) Division, which was just arriving from Suvla Bay. With the 10th Division they entrained for Doiran, and marched to a position in the hills overlooking Strumnitza. This Division was attacked by ten enemy divisions during the middle of December, but was saved from envelopment by fog and retreated. After about five days' marching, the 10th Division concentrated outside Salonica, and was soon afterwards moved to the Struma Valley. In September, 1917, it was moved to Palestine, where Lt.-Col. P. C. de la Prynne, D.S.O., took over the command, exchanging with Lt.-Col. J. S. Matthew, C.M.G., D.S.O., T.D., who returned to the 52nd Division. The Lowland Divisional Train was now known as the 10th Divisional Train.

In the first week of November, 1917, the 10th Division took part in the attack on the Turkish centre and left. It relieved the 52nd Division in the first week of December, and after the capture of Jerusalem, took part in repelling the Turkish attempts to retake that city. Until September, 1918, it was in the centre of the British line, lying to the north of Jerusalem.

After Gen. Allenby had broken through the Turkish right on the coast, the whole line advanced, and with it the 10th Division, helping to capture Nablus (Shechem), and reaching a point about seven miles north-east of that place. This ended the fighting so far as the 10th Division was concerned. The 10th Divisional Train remained with this Division until the end of the war, and was demobilized in Egypt.

APPENDIX II

THE 7TH H.L.I. AND 8TH CAMERONIAN TRENCH MORTAR TEAMS IN MESOPOTAMIA

WHILST at Kantara in 1916 a trench mortar team, recruited from the 7th H.L.I., was sent to Mesopotamia, where it was attached to the 7th (Indian) Division. This team took part in the advance on Baghdad, serving in the battle of Sanna-i-yat. It proceeded to Palestine with the 7th (Indian) Division, and took part in the fighting from March, 1918, until the armistice with the Turks. Throughout its travels this small unit retained its identity.

A similar trench mortar team was recruited from the 8th Cameronians and sent to Mesopotamia in 1916. Under Lieuts. Sharp and Begg it rendered most efficient service throughout the campaign and retained its identity until the end of the war.

APPENDIX III

THE LOWLAND ROYAL FIELD ARTILLERY AND THE 7TH (INDIAN) DIVISION

WHEN the 52nd (Lowland) Division left Palestine for France, its artillery was transferred to the 7th (Indian) Division. After its attachment to the 7th (Indian) Division, the Lowland Artillery took part in all of the principal fighting in the coastal sector immediately north of Jaffa.

On 28-29th May, 1918, it supported the infantry in an advance of the line for a mile and a half on a seven mile front. On 8-10th June, the " Sisters," an elevation of great importance to the enemy for observation purposes, was captured by the 7th Division, the Lowland gunners carrying out the artillery work.

During July and August the batteries were often in action replying to the Turks.

On the 19th July the Lowland gunners supported a large trench raid on the Tabsor system, a village and some heights fortified so that they formed the key of the Turkish defences in the coastal sector.

By means of a variety of feints and artifices, Gen. Allenby had persuaded the Turks that his next attack would be on their left, and all the while he was secretly concentrating his forces for a break-through on the coast. At 4.30 a.m. on the 19th September, 1918, the guns of 21st Corps opened fire on the Turkish positions, those of the 261st, 262nd, and 264th Brigades being turned on the Tabsor system. By 9 a.m. the enemy's reserve lines had everywhere been seized by the infantry, and the

APPENDIX III

way was open for the cavalry, who at once commenced that whirlwind advance which took them eventually into Damascus on the 1st October. The Lowland gunners followed up the infantry, assisting them in clearing up the enemy positions, but there was little more fighting for them to do, as the Turkish army had collapsed completely. The 7th (Indian) Division continued its advance up the coast, reaching Haifa on the 29th September. On the 3rd October it set out in three columns for Beirut. A composite brigade was formed from the R.F.A. and led the way with Column 'C.' It camped on successive nights at the following places: Acre, Ras Nakura, Ras el Ain, N. el Kasmiye, Sidon, El Damur, Beirut. During eight days this column marched ninety-six miles. On all sides was found a country famine-stricken and impoverished by Turkish misrule. Mortality among the horses and sickness among the officers and men were heavy. After a few days' rest it continued its advance, and the artillery reached Tripolis on the 26th October, having marched about 270 miles in thirty-eight days. The Lowland gunners remained there until the 22nd November, when they commenced to trek back to Egypt. A sad feature of the stay at Tripolis was the number of men who died from disease after the Armistice. The Lowland Artillery reached Cairo on the 20th December. During the Egyptian trouble in March, 1919, mobile columns were formed from the Lowland gunners, which did excellent patrol work under the most trying conditions. They remained at Abbassiah, outside Cairo, until August, 1919, when their demobilization was completed.

The Higher Command can change the organization of an army, but it cannot change the feelings of the men. Soon after the Armistice, a senior officer asked a Lowland gunner to what he belonged. The man's reply was, " 52nd, the Lowland Division."

APPENDIX III

The losses of the Lowland Artillery during various periods of its service with the 52nd and 7th (Indian) Division are as follows:

PERIOD.	Killed, Died of Wounds and Disease.		Wounded.	
	Officers.	O.R.	Officers.	O.R.
1915. 6th to 21st July (Cape Helles and Anzac)	—	3	1	13
,, 2nd to 30th August (Suvla and Anzac)	—	4	2	17
,, 9th Sept. to 19th Decr. (Up to Evacuation of Suvla and Anzac)	1	10	—	16
1916. (Sinai)	3	16	—	4
1917. 1st January to 13th October (Palestine)	1	7	4	38
,, 27th October to 7th December (Advance in Palestine)	2	5	6	32
1917-18. 8th December, 1917, to 20th September, 1918 (Auja and Tabsor Operations)	1	10	3	22
1918-19. 10th Oct., 1918, to 5th June, 1919 (Tripoli and Egypt)	1	45	—	1
	9	100	16	143

APPENDIX IV

A BRIEF ACCOUNT OF THE 103RD INFANTRY BRIGADE,
JUNE TO NOVEMBER, 1918

OWING to the lack of men it had been decided to reduce infantry divisions in France to three brigades of three battalions each instead of four battalions. In the case of the 52nd Division, the G.O.C. decided to shed the junior battalion in the army list in each brigade, and so the following battalions had to leave the old Division: 5th K.O.S.B. (Lt.-Col. R. N. Coulson, D.S.O.), 8th Cameronians (Lt.-Col. J. M. Findlay, D.S.O.), and 5th A. & S.H. (Lt.-Col. C. L. Barlow, D.S.O.).

These battalions embussed at St. Eloi at 10.30 a.m. on 28th June, 1918, and after a tedious journey arrived some twelve hours later at Bambecque, near Ypres. Here they found they were to form a Scottish Brigade of the 34th Division, and were fortunate in having to command them, Brig.-Gen. J. G. Chaplin, D.S.O., from the Cameronians. The Divisional Commander was Major-Gen. C. L. Nicholson, K.C.B., C.M.G.

After a fortnight the Division entrained at Wayenberg on 16th July for the south. On the 18th the Division arrived at Senlis, near Paris. After some very heavy marching through woods and by night so as to prevent observation by the Germans, it arrived on 23rd July in front of Coutremin and Tigny, near Soissons.

The Germans at the beginning of July had made a determined attempt to break through the French lines on either side of Rheims. On the west of this town they were so far successful, and crossed the Marne on a front Chateau Thierry–Epernay. They were eventually hung up

APPENDIX IV

and caught in a salient, and Mangin counter-attacked on a front Fontenoy–Bellieu. The Germans realized their danger and threw in reinforcements, forty enemy divisions being engaged in this single sector. Gen. Foch had applied to the British, and as a result four divisions were sent to help in this counter-attack—the 51st and 62nd to Gouraud east of Rheims, and the 15th and 34th to Mangin on the west of the salient.

On 23rd July the other two brigades of the Division took part in the attack on Coutremin and Tigny, but the 103rd Brigade was kept in reserve.

After a night march through woods under shell-fire, the Brigade constituted the right of the Division in the attack on Beugneux Ridge, advancing through the French front line at zero hour, 4.10 a.m. on 29th July. All three battalions lost very severely, the casualties amounting in each case to more than one-third of the effective strength. Owing to the stubbornness of the defence and the inevitable lack of reconnaissance, due to the advance taking place over ground which the officers had never seen, the attack was beaten off.

Three days later, the front being narrowed down, and with a greater weight of artillery, the 34th Division again attacked the heights. The 103rd Brigade was opposite Beugneux village, which was on the slope of a hill. Immediately in front of the village was a wooded knoll, point 158, which held a nest of machine-guns. The 5th K.O.S.B. were to turn this wood from the south-east and the 5th A. & S.H. from the north-west, while the 8th Cameronians were in close reserve.

At 4.49 a.m. on 1st August, behind a heavy barrage and in a dense morning mist, the battalions advanced to the assault through high growing corn. The Germans at once put down a counter-barrage with their artillery and machine-guns and men fell fast. The troops were not, however, this time to be denied, and in spite of casualties the wooded knoll was ours. Just as the headquarters of the 5th K.O.S.B. reached the far edge of Hill 158, about a hundred Argylls, all of whose officers had fallen, emerged from its wooded

APPENDIX IV

cover. Two K.O.S.B. officers were sent to them, and with a cheer they went up the hill to the next objective. This was taken after stiff fighting, and to the credit of the Division fell the capture of the key to the position which had been holding up the whole French advance.

The French passed through our lines and swept the enemy back without a pause to the River Vesle.

An index to the severity of the fighting is the fact that the 5th A. & S.H. came out of action with only one of their officers—the C.O., Lt.-Col. Barlow, having been killed at the head of his men during the capture of Hill 158. The other units also suffered severely.

Warm letters of congratulation on the work done by the Division were received from Gens. Mangin and Penet, the former's special order of the day reading as follows :

" You came into the battle at its fiercest moment. The enemy, defeated the first time, brought up against us his best divisions, in numbers superior to our own. You continued to advance, foot after foot, in spite of his bitter resistance, and you held on to the conquered ground notwithstanding the violence of his counter-attack. Then, on 1st August side by side with your French comrades, you carried the height dominating the country between the Aisne and the Ourcq, which the defenders had been ordered to hold at all costs. Having failed in his attempts to retake the height with his last reserve, the enemy was compelled to retreat, pursued and harassed for a distance of seven miles. All you English and Scottish troops, both young soldiers and victors of Flanders and Palestine, have shown the magnificent qualities of your race, namely, indomitable courage and tenacity. You have won the admiration of your brothers in arms. Your country will be proud of you, for to you and your commanders is due in a large measure the victory which we have just gained against the barbarous enemies of all free peoples. I am happy to have you under my command and I thank you."

On 7th August, after a succession of moves by march, bus, and rail, the 34th Division found itself once again in the British area, near Ypres.

APPENDIX IV

After some time in the Ypres sector the Brigade, now under the command of Brig.-Gen. R. I. Rawson, D.S.O., took part in the advance over Kemmel Hill, which the Germans were forced to evacuate.

The next part of the line held by the Brigade was just short of Wytschaete, and on 28th September this famous ridge was taken by the Division after a successful attack.

During the fighting on this day Sgt. M'Guffie, of the 5th K.O.S.B., performed prodigies of valour, and richly deserved the Victoria Cross which was subsequently awarded. At the storming of Piccadilly Farm, when his platoon commander was killed, he took command and, rushing some dug-outs, captured two officers and twelve other prisoners. Later, on the St. Eloi road he saw a party of British prisoners being led off by some Germans. Without a thought he dashed out and, single-handed, disarmed the escort and released twelve prisoners, whom the Germans had taken from a neighbouring battalion. His next exploit was to rush up to a German " pill-box," which was holding up the advance with machine-guns, and fire rifle-grenades through the loopholes. He thus captured the " pill-box " and its garrison. Altogether he was credited with two officers and twenty other ranks whom he brought in alive. Sad to relate this gallant soldier was killed by a shell a few days later near Kruseik, and never knew of the honour he had won.

The next serious engagement was the capture on 14th October of Ghelewe and the line of the Lys on the outskirts of Menin. The first objective was Ghelewe, and this, under a heavy barrage, was encircled by three companies of the 8th Cameronians on the right and three of the 5th K.O.S.B. on the left, their respective fourth companies mopping up the village when the enveloping troops had passed on. Ghelewe itself was meantime masked by the smoke of thermite and H.E. shells. The advance to the second objective was then made by the same two battalions, this entailing the capture of a number of " pill-boxes " and farms. The 5th A. & S.H., who had been in reserve, then carried on the advance and captured the third objective on the line of the River Lys. Altogether the engagement was a most successful one, and though casualties were severe they were not out of proportion to the results gained.

After some days' rest the Division again pushed forward, and on 31st October, in conjunction with tanks supplied by the French, fought a most successful action at Anseghem being again congratulated by the French.

Shortly after this came the signing of the Armistice, and thereafter the Brigade advanced into Germany and formed part of the British Army of the Rhine.

INDEX

ABBASSIAH (Cairo), 246, 579.
Abbeville, 512.
Abraham, 248.
Abukir, 13 ; historical associations of, 13 *n*., 14.
Abu Shusheh, 426.
Achi Baba, 26-38, 153, 156, 162, 178, 206, 213, 221, 222, 240.
Achi Baba Nullah, 26-28, 82-85, 103, 140, 150, 163-166, 187, 218, 235.
Acre, 579.
Agnew, Capt. J., 118 ; afterwards Major, 206.
Agnew, Lt. J. S., 438.
Aikman, Lt. W. H., 569.
Ainslie, 2nd Lt. A., 332.
Aire, 512, 569.
Aisne [river], 516, 583.
Aitchison, 2nd Lt. I. D., 68.
Aitken, Lt., 197, 198.
Aix-la-Chapelle, 558.
Akaba, Gulf of, 249.
Akir [Ekron], 414, 423, 424, 426, 429.
Aku, 416.
Albert, 519.
Aleppo, 359.
Alexander, Lt. I. M., 127.
Alexander, Major J., 230.
Alexander the Great, 247, 264, 308.
Alexandria, 13, 14, 31, 65, 506.
Ali el Muntar, 309-323, 327, 328, 330, 334, 337, 353.
Allan, Brig.-Gen. P. S., 506, 513.
Allan, Capt. J. S., quoted, 415, 420-421.
Allan, Lt. C. F., 68.
Allan, Lt. D. B., 181.
Allenby, Gen. E. H. H., 346, 355-357 ; quoted, 358 ; 359, 369 ; quoted, 372 ; 373 ; quoted, 409-410, 412 ; 413 ; quoted, 424, 426, 427 ; 429 ; quoted, 445 ; 477 ; quoted, 485, 500 ; 575, 578.
Ambulance (1st L.F.), 4 ; embarked at Devonport on *Karoa*, 11 ; at Port Said, 11, 14 ; at Mudros, 14 ; landed on Gallipoli, 27-28th June 1915, 14 ; in operations at Cape Helles, 65, 76, 81, 188, 219 ; commanded by Col. G. H. Edington, 65 ; by Lt.-Col. J. W. Leitch, 295 ; at final evacuation of Cape Helles, 237, 239 ; in operations in Sinai, 278, 279, 295-296, 299 ; in operations in Palestine, 322, 339, 371.
Ambulance (2nd L.F.), 4 ; embarked at Plymouth on *Manitou*, 11 ; at Port Said, 11, 15 ; landed on Gallipoli, 30th Aug. 1915, 148 ; commanded by Lt.-Col. Moffat, 148 ; in operations at Cape Helles, 188 ; in operations in Sinai, 278-279 ; in operations in Palestine, 322, 371, 376 ; in operations in France, 513.
Ambulance (3rd L.F.), 4 ; embarked at Devonport on *Karoa*, 11 ; at Port Said, 11, 14 ; at Mudros, 14 ; landed on Gallipoli, 3rd July 1915, 14, 76 ; commanded by Lt.-Col. Young, 81 ; in operations at Cape Helles, 81, 188, 219 ; in final evacuation of Cape Helles, 235-237, 239 ; in operations in Sinai, 258-259, 278-279 ; in operations in Palestine, 322, 339, 371, 376, 417.

Amiens, 512, 516, 517, 542.
Amman, 427.
Amru, 248.
Amwas, 466, 472.
Ancre [river], 518, 519.
Andania, H.M.S., 11, 13.
Anderson, Capt. J. K., 443-445, 456.
Anderson, Lt., 498.
Anderson, 2nd Lt., 210.
Anderson, Lt.-Col. J., 102; quoted, 108, 110; 111; quoted, 113, 117, 123; 143; quoted, 177, 188-189, 200; 218, 230; quoted, 230, 252-253, 300, 301-302; 315, 349, 351, 352, 373, 385, 394, 435; quoted, 438; 441, 453, 468, 483-484, 491-492, 503, 506, 522, 525; quoted, 566.
Anderson, Lt.-Col. W. Menzies, 526, 550.
Anderson, Lt. R. B., 326, 329, 332.
Anderson, Major W. M., 492; afterwards Lt.-Col., 561, 571.
Angwin, Major, 488.
Anneux, 565.
Anseghem, 585.
Antiochus IV., 264.
Anzac, 14, 24, 26, 43, 70, 77, 88, 163-166, 169-172, 190, 192, 213, 215, 221, 222, 226.
Anzac Point, 273, 280.
Arber, Lt., 161.
Archangel, 20.
Argonne, 558.
Argyll Ridge, 499.
Argyll and Sutherland Highlanders (5th Bn.), joined H.L.I. Bde., 7; recruiting area, 10; embarked at Devonport on *Andania*, 11; at Alexandria, 11, 13, 14; at Mudros, 13; landed on Gallipoli, 3rd July 1915, 14; at Ghurka Bluff, 78-80; commanded by Lt.-Col. D. Darroch, 103; in battle of 12-13th July 1915, 102-110, 123-124; losses of, 127-128; in fighting in Krithia Nullah, 21st Nov.-7th Dec. 1915, 185-192; in attack on G.11a and G.12, 201; losses of, 202; in final garrison at Cape Helles, 230; at Hill 70, 263; at Canterbury Hill, 267; in reserve at Gaza, 315; in action, 327-330; losses of, 332-333; at Tank Redoubt, 349-350; losses of, 350; in attack at Wadi Hesi, 375; attack Sausage Ridge, 385-387; losses of, 389; attack Kummam, 394-398; losses of, 398; at Mansurah, 426; in reserve at Tahta, 468; in support of 5th H.L.I., 469; losses of, 473; in night attack at Auja, 491-494; losses of, 501; leave 157th Bde., 514; join 5th K.O.S.B. and 8th Cameronians as 103rd Bde., 514; to Bambecque, 28th June 1918, 514; achievements of 103rd Bde., 581-585.
Armstrong, Major E., 119.
Arras, 515, 518, 521, 533, 566.
Arsuf, 499, 501, 504.
Artillery (Divisional), 5, 8; recruiting area, 10; embark at Devonport, 11; at Port Said, 11, 14; at Mudros, 14; Glasgow Howitzers (4th) landed on Gallipoli, 21-24th June 1915, 14; at Gully Ravine, 45; 4th Battery attached 29th Div.; 5th to Anzacs, 46; in battle of 28th June 1915, 51; at Anzac, 163-166; commanded by Gen. Birdwood, 166; at Suvla Bay, 166-167; strength of, 3rd Sept. 1915, 167; at Lala Baba, 172; concentrate at Kantara, 171; 2nd Lowland Bde. at El Kubri, 251; 2nd and 4th rejoin Div. at Kantara, 252; joined by 3rd and 5th Bdes., 265; renumbered, 265; 260th, 262nd, 263rd at Romani, 267, 275, 277; losses of, 293; renumbered, 298; reorganized, 305; 261st in action at El Sire, 316; 261st, 262nd in 2nd Battle of Gaza, 318-319, 323, 327; losses of, 336; Turkish losses, 337; 261st, 262nd, 264th at 3rd Battle of Gaza, 360, 363; 264th at mouth of Wadi Hesi, 374, 381, 383; 261st to Esdud with 157th Bde., 393; 264th at Burkah and Brown Hill, 404; 261st at Katrah, 415, 416; 261st, 262nd, 264th at Mansurah, 426; 264th at Beit

INDEX

Likia, 437; at Biddu, 447; 261st at Hadrah, 497; artillery transferred to 7th (Indian) Division, 505; in fighting in coastal sector, 578-579; losses of, 580.
Ascalon, 377, 380, 391, 402.
Ashurbanipal, 247.
Atawineh Ridge, 311.
Aubigny, 516.
Augustus Caesar, 248.
Auja [river], 425, 427, 429, 459, 475-507, 580.
Austin, 2nd Lt., 209.
Australian and New Zealand Army Corps, 28, 77, 163-166, 248, 266, 267, 270, 276, 289-294, 300, 306, 310, 351, 392, 413, 479; Australian L. H., 171, 256, 261-262, 279-280, 286, 393, 399, 413; New Zealand Rifle Brigade, 279, 287.

Backhouse Post, 81.
Baghdad, 354, 477, 577.
Baikie, Brig.-Gen. Sir H. S., 42; quoted, 42-44; 48; quoted, 73, 113-114.
Bald Hill, 479, 494, 496, 497.
Balfour, Lt.-Col. J. R., 88, 139.
Balin, 412.
Balkan War 1912-13, 12.
Ballah, 246, 249.
Ballarat, H.M.S., 8, 11, 13.
Ballybunion, 250, 279.
Bambecque, 514, 581.
Bapaume, 533, 537, 542, 543.
Barfoot, Major, 571.
Barlow, Lt.-Col. C. L., 375, 385, 394, 453, 468, 491, 514, 581, 583.
Barnett, Lt. I., 127.
Baxter, Lt. J., 398.
Beach Post, 344.
Beckett, Lt.-Col. W. T. C., 487.
Beersheba, 306, 310-313, 351, 356-361, 373, 399, 427.
Begg, Lieut., 577.
Beirut, 579.
Beit Anan, 434-436, 439, 446, 455, 456, 460, 465.
Beit Dukka, 434-436, 438, 446, 459, 465, 468.
Beit Duras, 395.
Beit Iksa, 445,

Beit Izza, 441, 447, 448, 454, 455, 460.
Beit Jibrin, 396, 403, 412.
Beit Likia, 432-434, 437, 441, 444, 462-466.
Beit Sira, 460, 463, 467.
Beit Surik, 441, 454.
Beitunia, 440, 453.
Beit Ur el Tahta [Lower Bethhoron], 429, 458-474.
Beit Ur el Foka [Upper Bethhoron], 440, 459, 463, 467, 473.
Belgians, King of the, 564.
Bell, Capt. G. C., 146.
Bellieu, 582.
Berfilya, 432-433, 439, 461.
Berkusie, 412.
Beshshit, 409, 411, 414, 415, 417, 419.
Bethune, 515.
Beugneux, 582.
Biddu, 439-441, 446, 447, 448, 453, 474.
Bikanir Camel Corps, at Dueidar, 255-263; losses of, 262.
Bir Abu Dujak, 287.
Bir Abu Hamra, 271, 272, 280, 281, 282, 283, 287, 288, 289, 291.
Bir Bayud [oasis], 255, 263, 269.
Bir el Abd, 254, 263, 269, 274, 292, 303.
Bir el Arais, 254.
Bir el Dueidar, 250, 254, 327.
Bir el Gilban, 250.
Bir el Hamisah, 275.
Bir el Mageibra [oasis], 255, 270. 274.
Bir Jemameh, 390.
Bir Nebala, 442.
Bir Salmana, 267, 269, 292.
Bireh, 480.
Bird, Major W. T., 62, 63, 75, 98, 127.
Birdwood, Gen. Sir Wm., 166, 169, 170, 172, 212, 213, 239.
Black, Lt. C. S. P., 108.
Black, Major C. S., quoted, 109-110, 132, 174, 240.
Black, Sgt., 438.
Blair, Capt. R., quoted, 77; 99, 120; afterwards Major, 406.
Blazed Hill, 321, 331.
Bolton, Capt., 408.
Boomerang Redoubt, 47, 49, 51.
" Borderers' Hut," 494-496.

INDEX

Border Regiment, 1st Bn., 47, 51, 63, 64.
Boswell, Lt.-Col. J. D., 159, 219.
Boughey, 2nd Lt. F. H. S. H. P., 471, 472.
Boulogne, 512, 537.
Bourlon Wood, 560-564.
Bowen, Lt. and Q.M. H., 337.
Boyd, Capt. E. R., quoted, 347, 363; quoted, 370, 400, 415, 430, 431, 438.
Boyd, Lt. R. M. S., 128.
Braidwood, Pte., 183.
Braithwaite, Major-Gen. W. P., 69.
Brand, Major D. E., 387; afterwards Lt.-Col., 528, 549, 561, 571.
Bramwell, Capt. and Adjt. C. J., 58, 68.
Bretencourt, 519.
Bridge, Lt.-Col. B. G., 179.
Brigades—
86th Brigade, at Gully Ravine, 47; 71.
87th Brigade, at Gully Ravine, 47; in battle of 28th June, 1915, 49, 54, 71; sent to Cape Helles, 168; attached to 52nd Div., 205; in fighting in Krithia Nullah, 20th Dec. 1915, 205.
88th Brigade, 34, 39; relieved by 156th Bde., 48; attempt on H.12, 61, 71, 74.
103rd Brigade, formed of 5th K.O.S.B., 8th Cameronians and 5th A. & S.H., 581; commanded by Brig.-Gen. J. G. Chaplin, 581; entrain at Wayenberg, 581; arrive at Senlis, 581; in reserve at attack on Coutremin and Tigny, 582; in attack on Beugneux Ridge, 582-583; congratulated by Gens. Mangin and Penet, 583; near Ypres, 583; commanded by Brig.-Gen. R. I. Rawson, 584; in attack on Kemmel Hill, 584; at Wytschaete, 584; at Ghelewe and River Lys, 584-585; formed part of Army of the Rhine, 585.
127th Brigade, 279, 288.
155th Brigade, commanded by Brig.-Gen. F. Erskine, 4; composition of, 4; embarkation of, at Liverpool, 11; at Mudros, 11, 14; at Alexandria, 11, 14; landed on Gallipoli, 6th, 7th, 14th June 1915, 14; ambulance embarked at Devonport, 11; at Port Said, 11, 14; at Mudros, 14; landed on Gallipoli, 6th-14th June 1915, 14, 32; attached 42nd Div., 39; in reserve at battle of 28th June 1915, 51; in forward trenches, 78; in battle of 12th-13th July 1915, 83-101, 113; losses of, 126-127; relieve 157th Bde. 3rd Oct. 1915, 142; in support at Krithia Nullah, 15th-30th Nov. 1915, 179; in attacks of G.11a and G.12, 194-195; losses of, 202; relieve 157th Bde., 205; attack in Krithia Nullah 29th Dec. 1915, 208; relieved by 88th Bde., 210; losses of, 210; in final garrison at Cape Helles, 217-241; at Port Said, 246; at Kantara, 250; temporarily commanded by Lt.-Col. A. H. Leggett, 255; at Romani, 267, 276, 292; losses of, 293; in training at Mahemdia, 299; advance to El Arish, 299-303; at El Burj, 308; at Sheikh Zowaid, 308; into Palestine, 309; at Khan Yunus, 309; at In Seirat, 309; at 2nd Battle of Gaza, 315-329; losses of, 331-332; actions in sand-hills, 353; at 3rd Battle of Gaza, 362, 364; losses of, 371; to mouth of Wadi Hesi, 374, 377; attack Sausage Ridge, 378; losses of, 384; at Herbieh, 399; towards Beshshit, 411; attack Mughar and Katrah, 414-424; losses of, 425; at Ramleh, 430; at Berfilya, 433; at Beit Likia, 437; attack El Jib, 447-451; losses of, 456; at Beit Sira and Suffa, 460; near El Burj, 464; at Beit Sira, 467; losses of, 472; at Ramleh, 475; take over line

north of Jaffa, 475; in night attack at Auja, 482-497; memorial to, 501; relieved on 3rd April 1918, 505; at Alexandria, 506; commanded by Brig.-Gen. P. S. Allan, 506; sail for Marseilles 11th April 1918, 506; commanded by Brig.-Gen. J. Forbes-Robertson, 513; lose 5th K.O.S.B., 514; in 2nd Battle of Somme, 26th-28th Aug. 1918, 526-533; relieved by 57th Div., 533; at Bullecourt, 534; in 2nd Battle of Arras, 31st Aug.-7th Sept. 1918, 534-542; losses of, 544; captures of, 546; at Moeuvres 15th-20th Sept. 1918, 549-553; again, 24th-26th Sept. 1918, 30th Sept.-4th Oct. 1918, 555; S.W. of Cambrai, 30th Sept. 1918, 564; attack Faubourg de Paris, 564-566; losses of, Sept. and Oct. 1918, 567; effective strength, 1st Oct. 1918, 569; towards Mons, 10th Nov. 1918, 571; represented at entry into Mons, 15th Nov. 1918, 572.

156th Brigade, commanded by Brig-Gen. Stuart Hare, 4; composition of, 4; 5th and 6th Bns. Cameronians taken out of, 6; 4th and 7th Bns. R.S. join Bde., 7; commanded by Brig.-Gen. W. Scott-Moncrieff, 7; embarkation of at Devonport, 8, 11; at Liverpool, 11; at Mudros, 11, 14; at Alexandria, 11; Ambulance embarked at Devonport, 11; at Port Said, 11; Bde. re-embarked at Alexandria, 8th June 1915, 13; at Mudros, 13; landed on Gallipoli, June 1915, 14; attached 29th Div., 39, 40, 41; at Gully Ravine, 47; relieve 88th Bde., 48; in battle of 28th June 1915, 49, 52, 57; to take H.12, 59; message from Brig.-Gen Scott-Moncrieff, 60; H.Q. Staff hold bombing saps, 64; relieved by 29th Div., 65; losses of, in battle of 28th June 1915, 66-68; commended by Sir Ian Hamilton, 71, by Gen. de Lisle, 72; remarks on share in battle, 73-74; commanded by Lt.-Col. P. C. Palin, 78; at Ghurka Bluff, 78; relieved by 88th Bde., 81; sent to Backhouse Post, 81; in Divisional reserve, 85; in battle of 12th-13th July 1915, 97-99; losses of, 126-127; at Krithia Nullah, 15th-30th Nov. 1915, 179-190; plan of attack, 179; losses of, 183, 210; in final garrison at Cape Helles, 217, 218-241; at Ballah, 246; at Kantara, 250; at Mahemdia, 266; commanded by Brig.-Gen. E. S. Girdwood, 268; at Romani, 276, 277; losses of, 293; in training at Mahemdia, 299; advance to El Arish, 299-303; commanded by Brig. Gen. A. H. Leggett, 308; at Sheikh Zowaid, 308; into Palestine, 309; at Khan Yunus, 311; rejoin Div. at In Seirat, 314; behind Mansurah, 317; at 2nd Battle of Gaza, 318, 322, 328; losses of 331, 332; at Sana Redoubt, 351; attached to 54th Div. at 3rd Battle of Gaza, 361-370; losses of, 370-371; towards Wadi Hesi, 377, 384; Headquarters' patrol take Ascalon, 391; at Mejdel, 399; at Esdud and Kummam, 402; joined by Yeomanry, 403; attack Burkah and Brown Hill, 403; losses of, 408; at Beshshit, 414; at Ludd, 430; at Beit Likia, 433; attack El Jib, 447-453; losses of, 456; at Beit Anan, 460; at Beit Likia, 462; at Beit Sira, 463; losses of, 473; at Ramleh, 475; near Selmeh, 476; in night attack at Auja, 482-497; memorial to, 501; relieved 31st March 1918, 505; at Alexandria, 506; sail for Marseilles, 11th April 1918, 506; lose 8th Cameronians, 514; in 2nd Battle of the

INDEX 591

Somme, 22nd-28th Aug. 1918, 519-533; relieved by 2nd Canadian Div., 533; supports 155th Bde. at Bullecourt, 534; in 2nd Battle of Arras, 2nd-7th Sept. 1918, 539-542; losses of, 544-545; captures of, 546; at Moeuvres, 20th-23rd Sept. 1918, 553-555; attack across Canal du Nord, 27th-28th Sept. 1918, 561-564; captures of, 564; losses of, Sept. 1918, 567-568; effective strength, 28th Sept. 1918, 569; in outpost line on Jard Canal, 28th Oct. 1918, 570-571; attack Herchies, 10th Nov. 1918, 571; losses of, 572; represented at entry into Mons, 15th Nov. 1918, 572.
157th Brigade, commanded by Brig.-Gen. P. W. Hendry, 4; composition of, 4; 9th H.L.I. taken out of, 6; 5th A. & S.H. joined Bde., 7; embarkation of, at Devonport, 11; at Alexandria, 11, 14; Ambulance embarked at Plymouth, 11, at Port Said, 11; Bde. arrived at Mudros, 14; landed on Gallipoli, 3rd July 1915, 14, 76; in forward trenches, 78; commanded by Col. W. H. Millar, 79; in battle of 12-13th July 1915, 83-89, 102-119, 125; commanded by Brig.-Gen. H. G. Casson, 132; in action, 135; relieved by 155th Bde., 3rd Oct. 1915, 142; total effective strength of, 30th Sept. 1915, 149, Oct. 1915, 160; in fighting in Krithia Nullah, 21st Nov.-5th Dec. 1915, 184-192; losses of 202; at G.11a, 204; in final garrison at Cape Helles, 218-241; at Ballah, 246; at Ballybunion, 250; at Kantara, 250; at Romani, 267, 276-277, 292; in training at Katib Gannit, 299; commanded by Brig.-Gen. C. D. Hamilton-Moore, 299; advance to El Arish, 299-303; at Sheikh Zowaid, 308; into Palestine, 309; at In Seirat, 309; at Wadi Ghuzze, 311; at El Burjaliye, 315; losses of, 316; in reserve at second Battle of Gaza, 320; in action, 327-330; losses of, 332-333; in reserve near Wadi Nukhabir, 353; march to the mouth of Wadi Hesi, 373; attack Sausage Ridge, 384; losses of, 389; towards Esdud, 392; attack Kummam, 394-398; losses of, 398; at Yebnah, 414; at Ludd, 430; at Beit Likia, 433; losses of, 439; attack Er Ram, 447; at Beit Izza, 454-455, 460; losses of, 457; defend Tahta, 468-470; losses of, 473; at Ramleh, 475; near Selmeh, 476; in night attack at Auja, 482-497; memorial to, 501; reviewed by Duke of Connaught, 504; relieved on 3rd April 1918, 505; at Alexandria, 506; sail for Marseilles, 11th April 1918, 506; lose 5th A. & S.H., 514; at second Battle of the Somme, 24-28th August 1918, 521-533; relieved by 57th Div., 533; at Hénin Hill, 534; in second Battle of Arras, 3-7th Sept. 1918, 541-542; losses of, 545; captures of, 546; at Moeuvres, 16-20th Sept. 1918, 549-553; attack southward from Moeuvres, 27-28th Sept. 1918, 561-562; captures of, 564; relieve 155th Bde. near Cambrai, 4-5th Oct. 1918, 566; losses of Sept. and Oct. 1918, 568; effective strength, 30th Sept. 1918, 569; on outpost line on Jard Canal, 570-571; towards Mons, 10th Nov. 1918, 571; losses of, 572; represented at entry into Mons, 15th Nov. 1918, 572.
158th Brigade at Romani, 270, 274, 276, 277.
161st Brigade, 277.
Brindlay, Lt. C. S., 260.

INDEX

British Navy, 153, 157, 181, 283, 305, 318.
Broadfoot, 2nd Lt. W. A., 117, 128.
Brooke, Rupert, quoted, 574.
Brotherstone, Capt., 283.
Brown, Capt. J. R., 331, 333.
Brown, Capt. R., 349, 396.
Brown Hill, 400-411.
Brown House, 100.
Brown, Lt.-Col. A., 278.
Brown, 2nd Lt. D., 145.
Brown, Lt. Sorley, quoted, 92, 100, 216-217, 224.
Brown, Lt. W., 68.
Brown, Major R., 206.
Bruce, Capt. A. C. A., 261.
Bruce, Lt. C., 545.
Bruce, Major J., 415, 565.
Brunton, 2nd Lt. J. M., 348.
Bryson, Lt. A., 568.
Buchan, John, quoted, 543.
Buchan, Pipe-Major A., 53.
Buchanan, Pte. T., 145.
Buchanan, Capt. W. L., 439.
Bulair, 21, 23, 164.
Bulfin, Lt.-Gen. Sir E. S., 359, 479, 481, 500.
Bulldog, T.B.D., 238.
Bullecourt, 534-536.
Bulman, Lt. A., 127.
Burberah, 382, 385, 389, 401.
Burkah, 400-411.
Burleigh, 2nd Lt. F. S., 567.
Burnett, Sgt., 536.
Burrows, Capt. A., quoted, 159.
Burt, Lt. H., 344.
Butani, 405, 406.
Byng, Sir Julian, 519, 538, 560.
Byzantium—*See* Constantinople.

CAIRNS, Lt., 210.
Cairo, 477, 579.
Calais, 512.
Caledonia, H.M.S., 506.
Caley, Lt.-Col., 61.
Caliph Omar, 248.
Cambrai, 533, 548, 558, 559, 564, 569.
Cambyses, 247, 264.
Camel Corps—
  Bikanir, 255-263, 276.
  Imperial, 273.
  Transport, 297.
Camel Hill, 328.

Camels, 246, 259, 262, 269, 271, 297-298.
Campbell, Capt., 469.
Campbell, Capt. L. R., 197.
Campbell, 2nd Lt. J., 323, 332.
Campbell, Major, 467.
Cameronians (5th Bn.), 4; sent to France, Nov. 1914, 6.
Cameronians (6th Bn.), 4; sent to France, March 1915, 6.
Cameronians (7th Bn.), 4; recruiting area, 10; embarked at Liverpool on *Empress of Britain*, 11; at Alexandria, 11, 14; at Mudros, 14; landed on Gallipoli, 13-14th June 1915, 14; in reserve at battle of 28th June 1915, 50; commanded by Lt.-Col. J. B. Wilson, 50; trench relief, 52, 55; attack H.12, 59-63, 64; losses of, 67-68; combined with 8th Bn., 74-75; commanded by Major W. T. Bird, 75; in battle of 12-13th July 1915, 98-99; temporarily commanded by Capt. R. Blair, 99; losses of, 126; in fighting in Krithia Nullah, 15-30th Nov. 1915, 179-190; in last garrison at Cape Helles, 218-241; reformed into separate unit under Lt.-Col. J. G. P. Romanes, 249-250; at Hill 70, 263: at Romani, 270, 289-290; at 2nd Battle of Gaza, 318-320, 328-330; losses of, 331, 333; action by patrols, 339; ambush laid by, 348-349; attack of, on Umbrella Hill, 361-369; losses of, 370-371; hold Ascalon, 402; attack Burkah, 404-410; losses of, 408; attack Nebi Samwil, 441-444; in reserve at Beit Sira, 463; at Tahta, 464; losses of, 473; in night attack at Auja, 488-489; losses of, 501; at 2nd Battle of the Somme, 520; in reserve, 529; in 2nd battle of Arras, 2nd Sept. 1918, 539-540; losses of, 544; in reserve at Moeuvres, 553; at Canal du Nord, 563-564; lead attack on Herchies, 10th Nov. 1918, 571; last prisoners taken, 10th Nov. 1918, 571; enter

INDEX

Jurbise, 11th Nov. 1918, 571; losses of, 572.
Cameronians (8th Bn.), 4; recruiting area, 10; embarked at Devonport on *Ballarat*, 8, 11; at Mudros, 11, 14; landed on Gallipoli, 13-14th June 1915, 14; in Rest Camp, 39; in Eski Lines, 40; commanded by Lt.-Col. H. M. Hannan, 40; losses of, 48; in battle of 28th June 1915, 49; commanded by Major J. M. Findlay, 50; attacks by, 51, 57, 61, 64; losses of, 67, 68; commended by Gen. de Lisle, 72; combined with 7th Bn., 74-75; commanded by Major W. T. Bird, 75; in battle of 12-13th July 1915, 98-99; temporarily commanded by Capt. R. Blair, 99; losses of, 126, 127; in fighting in Krithia Nullah, 15-30th Nov. 1915, 179-190; in last garrison at Cape Helles, 218-241; reformed into separate unit under Lt.-Col. R. N. Coulson, 249-250; at Pelusium, 263; commanded by Lt.-Col. J. M. Findlay, 289; at Romani, 289-290; losses of, 293; in reserve at 2nd battle of Gaza, 320, 327-330; losses of, 331, 333; at Suffolk Ridge, 347; at Umbrella Hill, 362; at El Arish Redoubt, 362-369; losses of, 370-371; attack Burkah and Brown Hill, 404-410; losses of, 408, 409; attack Nebi Samwil, 441-444, 451; at Beit Sira, 463; losses of, 473; gun teams at Auja, 480; in night attack at Auja, 488, 490; losses of, 501; leave 156th Bde., 514; join 5th K.O.S.B. and 5th A. & S.H. as 103rd Bde., 514; to Bambecque, 27th June 1918, 514; achievements of 103rd Bde., 581-585; Trench Mortar Team in Mesopotamia, 577.
Canadian Army Corps, 2nd Div., 521, 525-528, 538, 542; 1st and 4th Divs., 560.
Canal de l'Escaut, 565.
Canal du Nord, 538, 548, 556, 557.
Canberra, H.M.S., 506.

Canterbury Hill, 267, 272, 279, 280, 286, 288.
Cantingneul Mill, 566.
Care, 2nd Lt. G. B., 333.
Carlyle, 2nd Lt. R., 127.
Carmel, Mount, 356.
Carmichael, Lt. R. H., 128.
Casson, Brig.-Gen. H. G., 132, 184, 205, 291, 299.
Casson's Landing.—*See* "S" Beach.
Cavalry (British), 266, 279, 298, 300, 359, 369, 372, 376, 389-392, 399, 423, 426, 464.
Chabrias, 248.
Champagne, 517.
Chanak [town], 21, 22, 24, 26.
Chaplin, Brig.-Gen. J. G., 581.
Chateau Thierry, 581.
Chauvel, Lt.-Gen. Sir H. G., 359.
Cherisy, 529.
Chetwode, Lt.-Gen. Sir P. W., 303, 359.
Chocolate Hill, 172.
Chunuk Bair, 164, 165.
Church, Capt. W. Campbell, 68.
Clark, Capt. and Adj. R. Vere, 68.
Clark, Capt. D., 68.
Clark, Capt. G. M., 409.
Clark, Lance-Cpl. J., 564.
Clark, Major, 119.
Clark, Pte, 455.
Clark, Sgt. J., 183.
Clarke, Lt. J. S. D., 398.
Clark-Kennedy, Capt. A. D. H., 567.
Clark-Kennedy, Capt. A. R., 332.
Cleugh, Pte., 112.
Clifford, Signalling-Cpl., 261.
Cochrane, Capt. W. F., 324, 325, 332.
Cochrane, Major W. E. A., 93.
Code names for Bdes., Gaza, 340.
Coeur de Lion, Richard, 440, 501.
Cojeul [river], 520.
Clapperton-Stewart, Major R. A., 110, 119; quoted, 124; 206.
Coltart, Lt., 348-349.
Colville, Lance-Cpl., 342.
Conder, Lt. C. R., 374.
Connal, Lt.-Col. K. H. M., 159.
Connaught, Duke of, 504.
Considine, Lt. P. F., 68.
Constantinople, 20, 23.

INDEX

Cook, Major J. B., 319; afterwards Lt.-Col., 336, 343, 380, 382, 383, 415, 422, 449, 450, 456.
Cornwallis, H.M.S., 172.
Corps Expéditionnaire Française d'Orient, 28, 81, 83, 88-101, 105, 113, 122, 136, 213, 220.
Coulson, Major R. N., 218, 230; afterwards Lt.-Col., 250, 495, 514, 581.
Coutremin, 581, 582.
Cowan, 2nd Lt. R., 109, 128.
Coyle, Pte., 107.
Craig, 2nd Lt. J. M., 341, 342.
Crawford, Lt. and Adj., 261.
Cree, Lt. R. S., 409.
Crombie, Lt. S. P., 332.
Crombie, Major, 326.
Cruddas, Lt.-Col. B., 526, 535, 549, 553.
Cumming, 2nd Lt. A., 330, 333.
Cumming, Lt. R. J. A., 545.
Cunningham, Capt. S. A., 127.
Curran, Col. W., 283.
Currie, Lt.-Gen. Sir Arthur, 525, 560.
Curtis, Major, 519.
Cyclist Company (Divisional), 133, 276, 282-283, 291, 293, 321, 323.

DALGLEISH, 2nd Lt. W., 366, 409.
Daly, Capt. C. G., 108.
Daly, Capt. J. F., 108.
Damascus, 357.
Dardanelles, 7, 19, 82, 218.
" Dardanelles Cup," 156, 246.
Dardanus, 22.
Darius, 247.
Darius Ochus, 248.
Darroch, Lt.-Col. Duncan, 103, 110, 206.
Dashwood-Tandy, Lt.-Col. R., 379, 415, 449, 462, 526.
Davidson, Lt., 108.
Davidson, 2nd Lt. F. B., 143.
Davie, Lt. F., 196, 331, 333.
Davies, Lt.-Gen. Sir F. J., 134, 156; quoted, 202-203; 213, 239.
Dawes, Lt. E., 371.
Dawson, Capt. J. D., 55, 68.
Deas, Lt. A. O., 201.
Deir el Belah, 314, 338-339, 361, 369-370.
Deir Sineid, 377, 384, 389.

de la Prynne, Lt.-Col. P. C., 265, 575.
de Lisle, Major-Gen., 46, 52, 63, 72.
de Robeck, Vice-Admiral Sir J., 239.
De Tott's Battery, 25.
Delilah's Neck, 328.
Denbigh, Lord, 265.
Desert fighting, features of, 252-253, 256-257, 268, 278-279.
Desert Mounted Corps, 361, 369, 372, 376.
Devonport, 8, 11.
Dewar, C.Q.M.S., 41.
Dickson, Lt. G., 128.
Divisions (Army)—
  2nd Lowland Division, *see* 52nd (Lowland) Division.
  3rd, 535, 539.
  7th (Indian), 505, 577-579.
  10th (Irish), 168, 359, 575-576.
  13th, 213.
  29th, 28, 34, 51, 59, 63, 65, 69, 71, 77, 88, 133, 138, 213.
  34th, 583.
  42nd Division, at Achi Baba, 28; in battle of 12th-13th July 1915, 76, 103; attack by, 133; in fighting near Romani, 266, 270, 279, 286; in fighting at Katia, 299; advance to El Arish, 300-303; ordered to France, 305; at 2nd Battle of the Somme, 519.
  51st (Highland), 525.
  52nd (Lowland) Division, formation of, 3; mobilization of, 3; disposition of, 4; commanded by Major-Gen. G. G. A. Egerton, 4; equipment of, 5; billeting of, 5; volunteer for overseas, 5; changes in composition of, 6-7; in Gretna disaster, 8; recruiting area, 10; embarkation of, 11; movements before landing on Gallipoli, 14; landed on Gallipoli, 18; total losses to 13th July 1915, 128; whole Div. in front line, 17th Aug. 1915, 138, 141; sick and wounded on strength of, during Sept. and Oct. 1915, 146; commanded by Major-Gen. the

INDEX

Hon. H. A. Lawrence, 17th Sept. 1915, 148; Band of, 154, 155; reinforced by Lowland Mounted Bde., Oct. 1915, 159-160; sick and wounded on strength of, during Nov. and Dec. 1915, 176; strength of, 7th Jan. 1916, 228; 9th Jan. 1916, 230; evacuate Gallipoli, 172, 212-241; to Egypt, 246; at Suez Canal, 246; at Kantara, 250-251; to El Arish, 266; commanded by Major-Gen. W. G. B. Smith, C.M.G., 11th July 1916, 267; at Romani, 266; Mobile Column organized, 270; disposition of, 276-277; losses of, 294; advance to El Arish, 299-303; in reserve near Gaza 308, 313; at 2nd Battle of Gaza, 314-334; constructed redoubts, 336; to attack Sausage Ridge, 378; attack Mughar and Katrah, 413; disposition of, 429-430; near Jerusalem, 458; part played in capture of Jerusalem, 458, 474; night attack at Auja, 480-497; congratulatory messages to, 500; hold coastal sector, Dec. 1917 to Mar. 1919, 502; at Surafend, 506; entrain for Kantara, 506; sailed from Alexandria for Marseilles, 11th April 1918, 506; achievements of, 506-507; reached Marseilles, 17th April 1918, 511; entrained for Abbeville, 511; at Aire and Forest of Nieppe, 512; at Vimy Ridge, 6th May-21st July 1918, 513; G.H.Q. Reserve, 515; to Villers Chatel and Aubigny, 516; part of 6th A.C., 519; at 2nd Battle of the Somme, 23rd-28th Aug. 1918, 519-533; at Hindenburg Line, 26th Aug. 1918, 525; at 2nd Battle of Arras, 31st Aug.-7th Sept. 1918, 534-542; losses of, 544-545; captures of, 546; attack Canal du Nord, 560-564; losses of, Sept. and Oct. 1918, 567-569; total strength of, 1st Oct. 1918, 569; represented in official entry into Mons, 572; farewell to Div., 573-574.
53rd (Welsh), 305, 308, 310, 327, 359.
54th (East-Anglian), 305, 308, 314, 359, 361-370, 373, 429, 459, 463-464, 497.
56th, 520-529.
57th, 535, 536, 538, 543, 548.
60th, 359, 429, 454-455, 462, 473.
63rd (R.N.), 28, 121-125, 519, 542-3, 560, 561, 565.
74th, 315, 359, 465-468.
75th, 359, 369, 373, 407, 413, 425-426, 431, 439, 441, 445, 446, 448, 454.
Divisional Band, 154-155, 179, 187.
Dobell, Gen., 311, 333.
Doiran, 575.
Donald, Capt. W. F., 568.
Douai, 564, 570.
Douglas, Lt. R., 96, 127.
Douglas, Major-Gen. Sir W., 134, 135.
Dow, Lt., 199.
Downie, Major A. M., 111, 128.
Drage, Major, 276.
Drocourt-Quéant Switch, 537-538.
Dueidar, operations at, 245-263, 266-269, 272, 279, 287.
Duff, 2nd Lt. A., 68.
Duff, Lt. W., 68.
Dumbell Hill, 335.
Dun, Capt. J., 323, 332.
Dunfermline, 5.
Dunglass, Lt.-Col., Lord, 159.
Dunn, Capt., 91.
Dunn, Lt.-Col. S. R., 16, 50, 53, 68.
Dunning, Lt.-Col. M., 371.
Dykes, Capt. J. J., 127.

EASSON, CAPT. D. E. C., 128.
Eastern Mule Track, 78.
Edgar, H.M. cruiser, 179.
Edington, Col., quoted, 14, 65; quoted, 65, 66, 100, 175, 188, 228, 237.
Edmond, 2nd Lt. J., 352.
Edwards, 2nd Lt. N. R., 333.
Egerton, Major-Gen. G. G. A., 4, 9, 40, 72; quoted, 74; 103, 148.

INDEX

Egyptian Expeditionary Force, 252.
Egyptian Labour Corps, 268, 296.
El Afein, 299.
El Arish, 247, 249, 266-269, 295-308, 339, 361, 365-371.
El Burj, 308, 458-474.
El Burjaliye, 308, 309, 314-316.
El Damur, 579.
El Dhaheriye, 429.
El Jelil, 480, 486, 499, 504.
El Jib [Gibeon], 429-457.
El Kubeibeh, 403, 412, 415, 424.
El Maadan, 295, 303.
El Makhras, 493.
El Mesmiye [El Mesmuyeh], 413.
El Rabah, 269, 275, 292, 299.
El Salt, 357.
El Sire [or El Sier], 309, 314-319, 323, 327, 336, 339.
El Tine, 426.
Elliot, Lt. A. S., 57, 68.
Elliot, Lt.-Col. H. H., 360.
Elliot, 2nd Lt. J. B., 444, 456.
Empress of Britain, H.M.S., 11, 13, 14.
Enver Bey, 77, 355.
Epéhy, 543, 548.
Epernay, 581.
Er Ram, 445, 447.
Erskine, Brig.-Gen. F., 4, 39, 96, 97, 121, 139.
Erzerum, 253.
Esani, 307.
Esarhaddon, 247.
Esdraelon, Plain of, 356.
Esdud [Ashdod], 392, 394, 395, 399, 401, 402, 403, 404, 405.
Eski Lines, 40, 87, 154, 228.
Ewing, Dr., quoted, 66, 75, 131, 149-150, 154, 189, 238.
Ewing, Major W. T., 404 ; afterwards Lt.-Col., 520, 529, 539, 553, 561.
" Eye-witness," quoted, 52, 53.

Fair, Lt. G., 567.
Farquhar, Lt.-Col. J., 315, 360.
Fejja, 497.
Ferguson, 2nd Lt. F., 127.
Ferguson, Pte., 344.
Fergusson, Sir Charles, 538, 560.
Ferrekhiyeh, 499.
Fevzi Pasha, 358.
Findlay, Rev. A. Fyfe, quoted, 353.

Findlay, Major J. A., 195, 386-387, 389.
Findlay, Lt. J. T., 68.
Findlay, Major J. M., 40, 50, 57 ; afterwards Lt.-Col., 289, 347, 362, 404, 441, 443, 451, 463, 488, 514, 581.
Findlay, Lt. S., 291, 293.
Fleming, Lt. M. J. H., 117-118, 128.
Flett, Lt. J. G., 181.
Foch, Gen., afterwards Marshal, 516-518, 543, 558, 582.
Foggo, Cpl., 563.
Fontenoy, 582.
Fontaine-les-Croisilles, 521, 525, 527, 528-534.
Forbes-Robertson, Brig-Gen. J., 513, 526, 529, 535, 556.
Forrest, Major W. T., quoted, 94, 114-115, 117 ; 324, 332.
Fortescue-Wells, Lt.-Col. L., 362, 484.
Foster, 2nd Lt. J. R., 330.
Fox, Pte., 421.
Franklin, Capt. and Bde.-Major, 456.
Frankau, 2nd Lt. P. E., 371.
Frew, 2nd Lt. J. B., 536.
Frost, Capt., 199.
Fyfe, Lt. J., 183.
Fyfe, Capt. T. A., 545.

Gairdner, Capt. E. D., 341, 342.
Galbraith, Lt.-Col. J. H., 103, 119 ; quoted, 123 ; 161, 184, 218, 230, 315, 329.
Galbraith, Lt. N. D., 545.
Galbraith, Lt. W. B., 128.
Gallipoli, operations at, 15-241 ; evacuation decided on, 169 ; opposition of Sir Ian Hamilton to, 169 ; visit of Lord Kitchener, 169 ; reasons for failure of operations, 170 ; blizzard on, 187-190 ; total losses in campaign of, 239-240.
Galloway, Lt. R. N., 68.
Gandy, Capt. W. H., 105, 128.
Gardner, Lt. R. G., 503.
Gas masks, issue of, 138.
Gaskell, Lt.-Col. J. G., 360.
Gaza, operations at, 306-311, 312-334, 335-354, 355-371.
Gaza–Beersheba road, 348.

INDEX 597

Gebel Maghara, 300, 304.
Gemmell, Capt. S. A., 128.
Gemmell, Sgt., 396.
George, H.M. King, 9.
Ghelewe, 584.
Ghent, 559, 564.
Ghurka Bluff, 25, 29, 46, 78, 80, 130.
Ghurkas (3rd Bn.), 407-408.
Gibb, 2nd Lt., 326, 332.
Gibb, Major C., 561.
Gibbons, Lt.-Col. E. S., 375, 394, 397, 435, 468, 487, 528, 550, 552, 568.
Gibraltar, 10.
Gibson, 2nd Lt. R. J., 68.
Girdwood, Capt. E. S., 59-61; afterwards Brig.-Gen., 268, 286, 289; afterwards Major-Gen., 308, 474.
Glasgow Highlanders (9th Bn. H.L.I.), 4; sent to France, Nov. 1914, 6.
Glendinning, Capt. T. H., 282, 321, 332.
Godfrey de Bouillon, 432.
Goldthorpe, Lt.-Col. F. H., 320.
Goliath, H.M.S., 31.
Gordon, Lt. C. E., 544.
Gouraud, Gen., 46, 47, 69, 582.
Gowan, Cpl. G., 54.
Grafton, H.M.S., 499.
Graham, Lt., 420.
Graham, Sgt., 341.
Graincourt, 563.
Grant, 2nd Lt. A., 331, 333.
Grant, 2nd Lt. W. G., 316, 333.
Gray, Capt. J., 406.
Gray, Major J., 53, 68.
Green Hill, 317, 318, 320, 322.
Greenshields, Lt. T. B., 182.
Greer, Major W. W., 232, 322.
Greig, Pte. J., 200.
Gretna, railway disaster near, 8.
Griffith-Williams, Major K.B., 484.
Guards Div., 541, 550, 560-563.
Guest, Lt. R., 281.
" Gully " Beach, *see* " Y2 " Beach.
Gully Ravine, 25, 28, 45-49, 54, 56, 62, 78, 79, 130, 218.
Gunn, Sgt. J., 63.

HAIFA, 356, 579.
Haig, Sir Douglas, 512, 517, 518; quoted, 537; 538; quoted, 542-543, 558; quoted, 558-559; 559; quoted, 560; 565, 569, 570.
Haldane, Lord, formed Territorial Force, 3.
Hamilton, Sir Ian, 7, 17, 24, 30, 31, 39, 42; quoted, 69, 70, 71, 72, 77; 80; quoted, 94; 97; quoted 99-100; 120; quoted, 122-123; 138, 141, 153, 157, 164, 166, 168; handed over command, 169; quoted, 169.
Hamilton, Capt. J., 267.
Hamilton, Major J. D. L., 8, 9.
Hamilton-Grierson, 2nd Lt. J. G., 127.
Hamilton-Johnston, Lt. E. C. R., 544.
Hamilton-Moore, Brig.-Gen. C. D., 299, 315, 327, 329, 373, 384, 389, 392, 393, 396, 402, 414, 426, 434, 436, 437, 453, 454, 469, 493, 499, 523; quoted, 524; 574.
Hampshire Regiment, 63, 64.
Hannan, Capt. D., 347.
Hannan, Lt.-Col. H. M., 40.
Happy Valley, 317, 327.
Haram, 499.
Hardie, Lt., 200.
Hare, Brig.-Gen. Stuart, 4, 361.
Haricot Redoubt, 29, 30, 40, 46.
Harper, Sgt. G., 110.
Harrison, Brig.-Gen. G. H., 573.
Harrison, Lt. R., 398.
Hart, Capt. J. G., 353.
Hassan, Col., quoted, 70.
Havrincourt, 543, 548.
Hawkes, Lt. A. W. W., 568.
Haws, Lt., 55.
Hebron, 358.
Heliopolis, 246.
Hellabi, 462.
Helles, Cape, operations at, 14-212; evacuation of, 212-241.
Hellespont, *see* Dardanelles.
Hendecourt-les-Cagnicourt, 535.
Henderson, Lt. A., 293.
Henderson, 2nd Lt. A. H. M., 92, 127.
Henderson, Major J. N., 52, 68.
Henderson, Lt. R. F. W., 567.
Hendry, Brig.-Gen. P. W., 4, 76, 78, 132.
Henery, 2nd Lt., 332.
Hénin Hill, 521, 522, 527, 528, 529.
Hénin-sur-Cojeul, 520, 521, 522.

Herbertson, Major J., 127.
Herbieh, 374, 377, 384, 385, 399, 401.
Herchies, 557-571.
Herdman, Lt. T. A., 568.
Hereira, 315, 360.
Hewison, Capt., 119.
Hewison, Lt. A., 454.
Highland Light Infantry (5th Bn.), 4; recruiting area, 10; embarked at Devonport on *Transylvania*, 11; at Alexandria, 11, 14; at Mudros, 14; landed on Gallipoli, 3rd July 1915, 14; attached to 1st Dublin Fusiliers and 1st Munsters, 78; at Achi Baba Nullah, 78, 80; History of, quoted, 79-80; in battle of 12th-13th July 1915, 111-112, 120; History of, quoted, 104, 108, 111, 112; relieve 6th H.L.I., 125; losses of, 127, 128; in attack of 13th Aug. 1915, 135-137; find by, 138; dig saps, 143; sniping by, 144; advance bombing station, 160; in fighting in Krithia Nullah, 21st Nov.-7th Dec. 1915, 184-192; in attack on G.11a and G.12, 192-201; losses of, 202; in final garrison at Cape Helles, 230; at Hill 70, 263; at Mahemdia, 277; History of, quoted, 298; at El Burjaliye, 314-15; on Lees Hill, 327, 330; losses of, 332; at Outpost Hill, 343; at Tank Redoubt, 349-350; losses of, 350; at Sheikh Abbas, 351-352; in attack at Wadi Hesi, 374; at Ras Abu Ameirah, 374-375; attack Sausage Ridge, 385-387; losses of, 389; at Esdud, 394; occupied Beit Anan, 435-436, 437-438; losses of, 439; at Tahta, 468; losses of, 473; in night attack at Auja, 491; losses of, 501; death of Col. F. Morrison, 502; at 2nd Battle of the Somme, 522-525; in reserve, 528; at 2nd Battle of Arras, 3rd-4th Sept. 1918, 541; losses of, 545; at Moeuvres, 550-553; in reserve at Canal du Nord, 561-562; towards Mons, 11th Nov. 1918, 571; History of, quoted, 571-572.

Highland Light Infantry (6th Bn.), 4; recruiting area, 10; embarked at Devonport on *Transylvania*, 11; at Alexandria, 11, 14; at Mudros, 14; landed on Gallipoli, 3rd July 1915, 14; at Achi Baba Nullah, 78, 80; commanded by Major Jas. Anderson, 102; in battle of 12-13th July 1915, 83, 102-112, 115-119; commended by Sir Ian Hamilton, 123; at Parsons Road and Trotman Road, 125; losses of, 127-128; find by, 142; dig saps, 143; in fighting in Krithia Nullah, 21st Nov.-7th Dec. 1915, 185-192; in attack on G.11a and G.12, 200; losses of, 202; in final garrison at Cape Helles, 218-241; at Hill 70, 263; at Mahemdia, 277; at El Burjaliye, 315-316; on Lees Hill, 327, 330; losses of, 332; at Wadi Endless, 349; losses of, 350-351; at Sheikh Abbas, 351-352; in attack at Wadi Hesi, 374; at Herbieh, 374; attack Sausage Ridge, 385-389; losses of, 389; in reserve at Esdud, 394; losses of, 398; occupied Dukka, 436-438; losses of, 439; at Beit Izza, 441; at Tahta, 468-470; losses of, 473; reconnaissance of Auja by officers of, 483; in night attack at Auja, 491-494; losses of, 501; at Vimy Ridge, 513; at 2nd Battle of Somme, 522-533; in reserve at 2nd Battle of Arras, 3-4th Sept 1918, 541; losses of, 545; at Inchy-en-Artois, 550; in Hindenburg front line, 561-562; attack Herchies, 10th Nov. 1918, 571; last prisoners taken, 10th Nov. 1918, 571; losses of, 572.

Highland Light Infantry (7th Bn.), 4; recruiting area, 10; embarked at Devonport on *Transylvania*, 11; at Alexandria, 11, 14; at Mudros, 14; landed on Gallipoli, 3rd July 1915, 14; at Achi Baba Nullah, 78, 80;

INDEX

commanded by Lt.-Col. J. H. Galbraith, 103; in battle of 12-13th July 1915, 102-106, 114, 118-120, 123, 125; losses of, 127-128; capture part of H.11a, 20th Oct. 1915, 161; in fighting in Krithia Nullah, 21st Nov.-7th Dec. 1915, 185-192; in attack on G.11a and G.12, 196, 201; losses of, 202; in last garrison at Cape Helles, 218-241; at El Burjaliye, 314; on Lees Hill, 327-330; losses of, 332-333; in attack at Wadi Hesi, 375; losses of, 389; attack Kummam, 394-398; losses of, 398; at Mansurah, 426; occupy Beit Anan, 435-436; at Tahta, 468; losses of, 473; in night attack at Auja, 487, 490-495; losses of, 501; ambush enemy patrol at Vimy Ridge, 513; in reserve at 2nd Battle of the Somme, 522; in action, 528; at 2nd Battle of Arras, 3-4th Sept 1918, 541; losses of, 545; in support at Moeuvres, 550-552; attack Canal du Nord, 561-562; cross Jard Canal, 8th Nov. 1918, 571; Trench Mortar Team in Mesopotamia, 577.
Highland Light Infantry Brigade, see 157th.
Hill 70, 260, 263.
Hill 158, 582, 583.
Hill, Cpl. J., 258, 260.
Hill, Major-Gen. John, 353, 371, 373, 379, 384, 394, 413, 414, 419, 447, 460, 465, 480, 481, 488, 499-500, 504, 514, 529, 551, 555.
Hills, Lt. C. H., 483-484.
Hill-Whitson, Lt.-Col. E. C., 549, 565.
Hind, Pte. A., 56.
Hindenburg Line, 518-574.
Hirson, 557.
Hissarlik Point, 25, 130.
Hitchcock, Lt. E. A., 568.
Hod el Enna, 279.
Hod Salmana, 266.
Hodge, Capt. H. F., 276, 282.
Holy Family, The, 248.
Hong Kong and Singapore Mountain Battery, 448.

Horne, Gen. Sir H. S., 249 n., 538, 560, 572.
Horsburgh, Pte. R., 480.
Howat, Capt. J., 68.
Hudson, Lt., 568.
Huj, 360, 390, 392.
Hunter, C.S.M. Donald, 143.
Hunter, Cpl. David F., 553. VC
Hunter-Weston, Gen., 39, 47, 69, 72, 103, 123, 134.
Hunter-Weston Hill, 213, 225.
Hurst, 2nd Lt. S. B., 544.
Hutchison, 2nd Lt. J. W., 456.
Hythe, H.M.S., 158.

IDA, Mt., 21, 130.
Imbros, 12, 144, 156, 189.
Immingham, S.S., 16-17.
Implacable Landing, see " X " Beach.
In Seirat, 309-311, 314.
Inchy-en-Artois, 542.
Indarra, H.M.S., 506.
Innes, Lt. J. B., 92, 127.
Innes, 2nd Lt. R. P., 568.
Innes, Lt. W. K., 92.
Invergordon, 5.
Ismail Oglu Tepe, 166.
Ismalia, 273.

JACK, Pte., 397.
Jackson, 2nd Lt. T., 127.
Jacob, 248.
Jaffa, 267, 357, 393, 427, 430, 446, 475-507.
Japanese Prince, H.M.S., 15.
Jedireh, 447.
Jemal Pasha, 355.
Jericho, 357.
Jerusalem, 356-359, 373, 425-432, 440, 454, 457, 462, 474, 477, 478, 502, 505, 575.
Jerisheh, 479, 480, 482, 485.
Johnston, Capt. J. Howard, 135.
Johnstone, 2nd Lt. W. J., 68.
Joseph, 246, 248.
Joshua, 442.
Jowitt, Major T. L., 119, 120, 128.
Julius Caesar, 247.
Junction Station, 357, 360, 373, 402-403, 410, 412, 425-426, 429.

KAIAJAK AGHALA, 166.
Kaiser-i-Hind, H.M.S., 506.
Kanli Dere, 26.

INDEX

Kantara, 247-251, 254-256, 262-269, 279, 505, 506, 577.
Kara Dagh, 21.
Karm, 360, 399.
Karoa, H.M.S., 11, 14.
Katia, 247-249, 253-257, 262-266, 272, 292, 295.
Katib Abu Asab, 250, 260-262.
Katib Gannit, 271, 272, 277, 279, 280, 281, 283, 285, 291.
Katrah, 403, 411-428, 429.
Kauwakah, 372.
Kavak Tepe, 166, 172.
Kearsey, Lt.-Col. A. H. C., 342, 379, 415, 449, 450.
Kelly, Cpl., 180.
Kelly, Cpl. A. R., 112.
Kelly, C.Q.M.S., 438.
Kemmel Hill, 537, 584.
Kennedy, Pte. H., 207.
Kennedy, Capt. W. D., 324, 332.
Kennedy, Major J. C., 323.
Kenneth, Capt. A., 127.
Kereves Dere, 25, 28, 29, 46, 82, 85, 91, 94, 106.
Kerr, 2nd Lt. J., 425.
Keystone House, 490.
Khamsin, 252.
Khan Surafend, 429, 475, 506.
Khan Yunus, 306, 308-309, 369.
Khirbet el Bir, 319.
Khirbet Sihan, 319.
Khurbet Hadrah, 478, 479, 481, 482, 494, 495, 496, 497, 499, 501.
Khurbet Hebra, 418.
Kilid Bahr [village], 21, 22, 26.
Kilid Bahr Plateau, 164.
King, Capt. A. C., 387.
King's Own Scottish Borderers (4th Bn.), 4; recruiting area, 10; embarked at Liverpool on *Empress of Britain*, 11; at Alexandria, 11, 14; at Mudros, 14; landed on Gallipoli, 14th June 1915, 14; in front lines, 39; commanded by Lt.-Col. J. M'Neile, 88; in battle of 12-13th July 1915, 88, 92-96, 114-115, 124; losses of, 126-127; strength of, 13th Sept. 1915, 141; advance bomb-sap, 160; support 5th R.S.F., 208; losses of, 210; evacuate Cape Helles, 219; represented in final garrison, 230; in reserve at 2nd Battle of Gaza, 320; in action, 324, 326, 329; losses of, 331-332; attack Sausage Ridge, 378-383; losses of, 384; attack Mughar, 415-423; losses of, 425; support attack on El Jib, 449-450; attack Suffa, 462; attached to 156th Bde, 463; rejoin 155th Bde. at Amwas, 472; losses of, 472; in night attack at Auja, 482; losses of, 500; in reserve at 2nd Battle of the Somme, 526; in action, 527; at Bullecourt, 535; at 2nd Battle of Arras, 31st Aug.-7th Sept. 1918, 535-536, 540-541; losses of, 544; defend Moeuvres, 549-553, 555; in reserve at Faubourg de Paris, 565; in action, 565.
King's Own Scottish Borderers (5th Bn.), 4; recruiting area, 10; embarked at Liverpool on *Mauretania*, 11; at Mudros, 11, 14; landed on Gallipoli, 6-7th June 1915, 14; at Cape Helles, 34; attached R.N.D., 39; commanded by Lt.-Col. W. J. Millar, 88; in battle of 12-13th July 1915, 88, 95; commended by Sir Ian Hamilton, 123; losses of, 126-127; advance bomb-sap, 160; support 5th R.S.F., 29th Dec. 1915, 208; losses of, 210; evacuate Cape Helles, 219; represented in final garrison, 230; at Pelusium, 263, 281; at 2nd Battle of Gaza, 319-330; losses of, 331-332; raid on Sea Post, 342-346; attack Sausage Ridge, 378-383; losses of, 384; at Katrah and Mughar, 415-423; losses of, 425; attack El Jib, 449-450; attack Suffa, 462; near El Burj, 464; at Two Tree Post, 465; reinforced by Australians, 465; hold Two Tree Post, 469; losses of, 472; in night attack at Auja, 494-497; losses of, 500; leave 155th Bde., 514; join with 8th Cameronians and 5th A. & S.H. to form 103rd Bde., 514; to Bambecque, 27th June 1915,

INDEX

514; trench mortar team in Mesopotamia, 577; achievements of 103rd Bde., 581-585.
Kirbe, Lt., 199.
Kiretch Tepe Sirt, 166.
Kirkwood, Lt., 567.
Kirte Dere, 26.
Kitchener, Lord, 42, 71, 169, 374.
Koe, Brig.-Gen. L. C., 132, 179, 218, 267-268.
Koe's Landing, see " Y " Beach.
Koja Chemen Tepe, 165, 166.
Krithia Nullah, 26-28, 35, 46, 78, 82, 141, 144, 150, 154, 160-162, 173-190, 191-203, 204-211, 213, 218.
Kubeibeh [Emmaus], 436-439, 441, 444, 446, 447, 454.
Kulundia, 447.
Kum Kale [village], 21, 22, 31, 38.
Kummam, 393, 394, 395, 399, 402, 403, 404, 405.
Kurd Hill, 314-318, 335, 337.
Kuryet el Enab, 439, 474.
Kut el Amara, 265.
Kyle, Lt. H., 127.

LABYRINTH (trenches), 318, 323.
Lagnicourt, 538.
Laing, Capt. P. L. P., 285, 421; afterwards Major, 535.
Laird, Lt., 110.
Lamb, 2nd Lt., 329.
Lancashire Landing, see " W " Beach.
Lancers, Hyderabad, 438.
Lang, Capt. and Adj. J. C., 92, 127.
Lang, Capt. W. B., 128.
Larbert, 5, 8.
Latron, 463.
Lauder, Pte. D. Ross, 135.
Lauder, Sir Harry, 547.
Lavell, Capt. P., 565.
Law, Lt., 332.
Lawrence, Major-Gen. the Hon. H. A., 148, 218, 239, 266-267, 271-272, 287, 294.
Lawson, Lt. G., 293.
Leasowe Castle, H.M.S., 506.
Lees, Hill, 317, 320, 321, 327, 329, 330, 331, 335, 336.
Lees, Lt. J., 285; afterwards Capt. 332.
Legate, Lt. F., 545.
Leggat, 2nd Lt. W., 68.

Legge Valley, 164.
Leggett, Lt.-Col. A. H., 161, 194, 208, 255, 259, 261, 262, 266; quoted, 274; 274, 276; afterwards Brig.-Gen., 308, 315, 328, 361, 367, 377; quoted, 378-379; 391, 402-404, 414, 441; quoted, 441-442; 450, 452, 462, 464, 487, 488, 499, 539, 573.
Leitch, Major J. W., 65; afterwards Lt.-Col., quoted, 295, 296; 339, 371.
Leith, Lt. E. M., 193, 198, 200.
Lemnos, 12, 156, 245.
Lens, 537.
Liddell, Pte. R., 480.
Liège, 557.
Lille, 557.
Linton, Capt. G. P., 119.
Lipsett, Lance-Cpl. J., 443, 445.
Liverpool, 8, 9, 10, 11.
Lockhart, 2nd Lt. D. B., 455.
Logan, Capt., 38.
Logan, Lt., 326.
Lone Pine Ridge, 164-166.
Longatte, 535.
Longuyon, 557, 570.
Lowe, Coy. Sgt.-Maj., 41, 54, 63.
Lownie, Pte. W., 54.
Ludd [Lydda], 427, 430-434, 446, 459, 506.
Ludendorff, Gen., 505, 512, 516, 517, 518, 525, 541, 542, 543, 548, 557, 558, 559, 565, 570.
Lumgair, Capt. R. R. M., 324, 325, 332.
Lunn, Pte. A., 54.
Lusitania, H.M.S., 8.
Lyell, 2nd Lt. D., 55, 98, 127.
Lyle, Lt.-Col. F., 206.
Lys [river], 584, 585.

M'ASLAN, Pte. J., 259.
M'Bride, Cpl., 491.
M'Bryde, Lt., 496.
M'Callum, 2nd Lt. W. H., 545.
M'Callum, Pte., 536.
M'Clelland, 2nd Lt., 55; afterwards Capt., 391.
M'Coll, 2nd Lt. M. B., 127.
M'Cowan, Lt. H., 68.
Macrae, Capt. W. D., 388.
M'Craken, Lt., 568.
M'Creath, Capt. R. B., 473.
M'Culloch, 2nd Lt., 497.

M'Culloch, Lt. W., 196.
M'Diarmid, 2nd Lt., 257.
MacDonald, Capt. J., 120, 128.
Macdonald, Lt. S., 545.
M'Donald, Pte., R.A.M.C., 258, 259.
M'Ewan, Lt. G. L., 128.
Macfarlane, 2nd Lt. W. B., 127.
Macfarlane, Pte., 492.
M'Glashan, Lt. J. E., 128.
M'George, Lt., 345.
M'Gillivray, 2nd Lt. A. R., 466.
M'Gregor, Lance-Cpl. J., 480.
M'Guffie, Capt. A. J., 465.
M'Guffie, Sergt. L., 573, 584.
MacKay, Pte. J., 369.
M'Kean, Sgt.-Major M., 199.
M'Keever, Capt. L. L., 384.
MacKenzie, Capt. K., 544.
MacKenzie, Lt. F. B., 55, 56, 63.
M'Kenzie, Lt. R. P., 332.
M'Kersie, Lt. A. J., 128.
Mackie, Capt. R. E., 68.
Mackie, Lt. W. P., 568.
Mackie, Sgt. A., 398.
M'Kie, R.Q.M.S., 207.
M'Kinnon, Lt. G., 345, 381.
M'Kirdy, Capt. R. F., 128.
Macindoe, Capt. C. A. D., 68.
Macindoe, Lt. R. C. B., 68.
MacInnes, Capt. N., 65.
MacIntosh, Cpl. R., 201.
MacIntosh, 2nd Lt. K. A., 545.
M'Intosh, Lt., 195, 209.
MacIntyre, 2nd Lt. D. L., 455 ; afterwards Lt., 530-531.
M'Intyre, Pte. J., 56.
MacLachlan, Sgt. A., 105.
MacLaine, Lt.-Col. R. G., 380, 381.
M'Lardie, Lt. P., 201, 207.
Maclay, 2nd Lt. J. W., 68.
Maclay, 2nd Lt. W. S., 68.
Maclean, Brig.-Gen. C. A. H., 441.
M'Lean, Cpl., 350.
MacLean, Lt. H., 60 ; afterwards Capt., 348-349.
M'Lellan, Capt. L., 468.
M'Lellan, Piper K., 105.
M'Leod, Lt., 336.
M'Mahon, Sir H., 169.
M'Neil, Capt. A. H., 119.
M'Neile, Lt.-Col. J., 88, 92-94, 127.
M'Naughton, Lt., 209, 210.
Macquaker, Capt., 388.
M'Quaker, Lt. G. W., 422, 425.
M'Queen, Pte. E., 108.

M'Rorie, Capt. R. D., 367, 371.
Machine Gun Companies: 155th, 120, 184, 277, 283, 319, 323, 325, 406, 451, 512-513, 527, 541.
156th, 289, 370, 404-408, 463.
157th, 376, 396, 398, 435, 441.
Magdhaba, 304, 369.
Mahemdia, 248, 266, 268, 269, 271, 275, 277, 291.
Maher, Surg.-Gen., 296.
Mahon, Lt.-Gen. Sir B., 170.
Majestic, H.M.S., 12, 31.
Malcolm, Lt. A. H., 545.
Malcolm, 2nd Lt. J. W., 112, 128.
Malta, 10, 12, 31, 65.
Malwa, H.M.S., 506.
Mangin, Gen., 582, quoted, 583.
Manitou, H.M.S., 11.
Manson, Cpl., 502.
Mansura, 309, 313-319, 330, 331, 335, 336, 339, 346, 426, 430.
Marne [river], 516, 517, 581.
Marquette, H.M.S., 11.
Marseilles, 506, 511.
Marshall, Major-Gen. F. J., 555, 573.
Martin, Col., 296.
Martin, 2nd Lt., 128.
Masaid, 303.
Masnou, Gen., 123.
Massy, Brig.-Gen. E. C., 360, 403, 447, 485, 505.
Mather, Major W., 571.
Matthew, Lt.-Col. J. S., 400, 575.
Mathew-Lannowe, Lt.-Col. B. H. H., 206, 315, 349.
Maubeuge, 559.
Mauretania, H.M.S., 8, 11, 13, 15.
Mavor, Lt., 110.
Maxwell, Gen. Sir J., 169, 249.
Maxwell, 2nd Lt. J., 127.
Maxwell, Lt. W. F. J., 134.
May, 2nd Lt. R. E., 116, 128.
Mazar, 269, 299.
Melrose, Pte. T., 112.
Mecca, 477.
Mediterranean Expeditionary Force, 17, 148, 170, 252.
Meiklejohn, Lt., 180.
Mejdel, 391, 392, 393, 399, 401, 402, 411.
Memorial Columns on Auja, 501.
Mendur, 335, 336.
Menin, 584.

INDEX 603

Mercantile Marine, 157.
Mercatel, 519.
Mercer, Lt. W. M., 463.
Mercian, H.M.S., 11.
Meredith, Mount, 272, 279.
Mesopotamia, 577.
Messudiyeh, 427.
Metz, 558.
Meuse [river], 557, 569.
Mezières, 557, 558.
Middlesex Hill, 317, 321, 322, 328, 330, 370.
Mill, 2nd Lt. W. H., 127.
Millar, Capt. G. C., 544.
Millar, Col. W. H., 79, 102, 135, 139.
Millar, Lt. W., 107, 108, 121.
Millar, Lt.-Col. W. J., 88, 96, 123, 160.
Miller, Lt. A. S., 554.
Miller, Lt., 258, 261.
Milligan, Major J., 282.
Milne, Lt. J. S., 350.
Mitchell, Capt. A. M., 181; afterwards Major, 234; afterwards Lt.-Col., 349, 362, 404, 406, 407, 451, 463, 464, 487, 539, 553, 561.
Mitchell, Capt. J. M., 8, 9.
Mitchell, Lt., 210.
Mitylene, 164.
Moeuvres, 542, 548-556, 560, 561, 563.
Moffat, Lt.-Col., 148.
Monchy-le-Preux, 527.
Monteith, R.S.M., 387.
Monro, Sir C., quoted, 157, 158; 169-170; quoted, 170, 171; 172; quoted, 212; 218; quoted, 226.
Mons, 557-572.
Montgomerie, Lt. R., 567.
Montmedy, 570.
Mount St. Eloi, 513, 581, 584.
Moore, Lt. G. A. C., 68.
Moore, 2nd Lt. J. C., 332.
Morham, Lt. J., 64.
Morrison, Capt. R., 200.
Morrison, Col. F. L., 104, 143, 160, 192, 200, 276, 315, 343, 349, 374, 385, 394, 435, 468, 470, 502.
Morto Bay, 25, 26, 27, 130, 140, 156, 225, 240.
Morton, Capt. A., 545.
Morton, Capt. G., 112, 128.
Moulin Sans Souci, 539.
Moulourja, 17.

Mowat, Capt. C. J. C., 68.
Moya Harab, 247, 250.
Mudros, 11-17, 65, 76, 160, 219, 233, 234, 235.
Mughar, 403, 411-428.
Muir, Lt. A., 182.
Muir, Lt. J. R. G., 568.
Muirhead, Lt. L., 568.
Mulebbis, 479, 480, 494, 496, 497, 499.
Munitions, shortage of, 42-44, 69, 170, 323.
Munro, Lt. R., 350.
Murphy, Sgt. T., 91.
Murray, Lt., 503.
Murray, Lt.-Gen. Sir A., 218, 249, 250, 252-253; quoted, 254; 266, 269; quoted, 271; 272, 275; quoted, 286; 287; quoted, 287; 294, 310-312, 331, 333, 346.
Murray, R.S.M., 421.
Murray-Lyon, Lt.-Col. D. M., 526, 535, 549, 565.
Mylne, Lt. J. G., 545.
Mysore, 449.

NAANE, 426.
Nahr el Kasmiye, 579.
Nahr Sukereir, 396, 410.
Napoleon, 248.
Narrows, The, 21, 22, 23, 24, 26, 138, 164, 237.
Nazareth, 248.
Nebi Samwil [Mizpeh or Mountjoye], 429-457.
Nebi Yesir's Tomb, 303.
Nebala, 442, 451.
Negiliat, 275.
Neilson, 2nd Lt. J. T., 371.
Neilson, Lt. J. A., 182.
Neilson, Major J. B., 193, 195, 230, 469, 491; afterwards Lt.-Col., 525.
Nelson Bn., R.N.D., 121, 122, 137.
Nesmith, Capt. J., 128.
Nettleship, 2nd Lt. M., 544.
Neuville Vitasse, 521, 523, 525, 526.
Newton, Pte. T., 480.
Nicholas, Grand Duke, 253.
Nicholl, John, 431.
Nicholson, Lt., 323, 332.
Nicholson, Major-Gen. C. L., 581.
Nicol, 2nd Lt. A., 107, 128.

Nieppe, Forest of, 512.
Nimmo, Capt. A. P., 420, 425.
Nineveh, 307.
Nish, Fall of, 174.
Noble, 2nd Lt. D., 407.
Noreuil, 535, 536, 538.
Northampton Mound, 347.

OGHRATINA, 254, 255, 256, 263, 270, 274, 275.
Oise [river], 518.
Old British Trenches, 347, 351, 352.
Oliphant, Lt., 195.
Omrah, H.M.S., 506.
On, 246.
Orkney, Lt. R., 159.
Orleans, 512.
Osborne, Lt. J. S., 299.
Ourcq, 517.
Ourcq [river], 583.
Outpost Hill, 317-331, 343, 365, 370.
Ovens, Lt. W. R., 325.

PALESTINE, 267.
Palestine, physical features of, 338, 353, 356-358 ; fulfilment of prophecies, 354, 477.
Palin, Lt.-Col. P. C., 78, 81.
Paris, 516.
Parker, Brig.-Gen., 281.
Partridge, S.S., 237.
Pasha Dâgh, 22, 26, 27.
Paterson, Lt. C., 68.
Paton, Capt. R. W., 282 ; afterwards Major, 382-383, 416-417, 450, 462 ; afterwards Lt.-Col., 495, 498.
Paton, Sapper R. S., 485.
Paton, Sgt. A. Y., 117-118.
Patrick, 2nd Lt. J. B., 127.
Pattison, 2nd Lt. R. M., 68.
Peebles, Capt. J. R., 68.
Peebles, Lt.-Col. W. C., 8, 50 ; quoted, 56; 80, 97, 123, 160, 174, 179, 218, 230, 276, 320, 328, 362, 404, 405, 451 ; quoted, 452 ; 463, 488.
Pelusium, 248, 254, 264, 267, 272-275, 279-280, 283, 285-288.
Pender, Lt. G., 333.
Penet, Gen., 583.
Penman, Capt., 344, 345.
Periscope rifles, issue of, 144.

Peronne, 537.
Pershing, Gen., 558, 569, 570.
Philip, Lt. A. W., 329, 333.
Phillips, Capt. and Q.M. J., 573.
Piccadilly Farm, 584.
Pink Farm, 65.
Pirie, Capt., 325, 332.
Pitchford, Lt. D. M., 198.
Plymouth, 10, 11.
Plymouth Bn., R.N.D., 115.
Pollard, Lt. A. H., 293.
Pollock, Capt. J. Dunbar, 52, 68.
Pollock, Lance-Cpl. D., 364.
Pollok, Lt. J. M., quoted, 324-325.
Pollok-M'Call, Lt.-Col. J. B., 88, 96 ; quoted, 119, 123 ; afterwards Brig.-Gen., 139, 179, 194, 208, 284, 291, 315, 327, 329, 342, 362, 378, 379, 382, 383, 384, 411, 414, 419-420, 448, 450, 460, 462 ; quoted, 464 ; 494, 498, 503.
Porteous, 2nd Lt. G., 456.
Port Said, 11, 246, 248, 266, 575.
Portsmouth Bn., R.N.D., 122.
Preston, Col., quoted, 359, 390, 410, 423, 430.
Price, 2nd Lt. C. T., 469.
Prince George, H.M.B., 234.
Prince of Wales, H.R.H. The, 252.
Pronville, 545.
Ptolemy Philadelphus, 247.
Pullar, 2nd Lt. J. H., 545.

QUÉANT, 535, 537.
Queen's Hill, 317, 321.
Quentin's Hill Junction, 8.

RAFA, 249, 304, 306, 308-310, 339, 354, 369.
Raffin, Cpl., 259, 261.
" Rakaten," 138.
Ram Allah, 445.
Rameses the Great, 247.
Ramleh, 427-432, 446, 472-475.
Ramsay, Capt. A. K., 411.
Ramsay, Lance-Cpl., 421.
Rankine, Cpl. J., 54.
Rantieh, 497.
Ras Abu Ameirah, 374-379, 383-385.
Ras el Ain, 579.
Ras Nakura, 579.
Rawlinson, Gen., 519.
Rawson, Brig.-Gen., 584.
Redford barracks, 5.

INDEX 605

Reid, Cpl., 492.
Reindeer, H.M.S., 16-17.
Requin, 318.
Rest Camp (Cape Helles), 32-41.
Rheims, 581.
Rhododendron Ridge, 164-166.
Richardson, Cpl. T., quoted, 94.
Riencourt-les-Cagnicourt, 536.
Rifaat, Col., quoted, 69-70.
Ritchie, Private, R.A.M.C., 258-259.
River Clyde, H.M.S., 25, 232, 236.
River Clyde Landing, see "V" Beach.
Roberts, Capt. F., 255, 257-259, 263.
Roberts, 2nd Lt. D. F., 371.
Robertson, Capt. J., 68.
Robertson, 2nd Lt. B. H., 68.
Robertson, Lt.-Col. C. C., 285.
Robertson, 2nd Lt. L. D., 425.
Robertson, Lt. W. R., 409.
Robertson, Pte. R., 54.
Rodger, Lt. W., 80.
Rodgers, Capt., 209.
Rogers, Capt. A. N., 452, 456.
Rolling, Lt.-Col. B. I., 425-426, 484.
Romanes, Lt.-Col. J. G. P., 289, 320, 361, 404, 442, 451, 463, 487, 520, 529, 539, 553, 561.
Romani, 264-294.
Rosie, Sgt., 56.
Ross, Capt. G. A. S., 68.
Ross, Capt. K., 568.
Ross, Lt., 420.
Ross, Lance-Cpl. A., 62.
Rowan, Lt. J. L., 105.
Rowland, 2nd Lt. S. J., 371.
Royal Engineers, 51, 94, 132, 158, 179, 255, 259, 268, 335, 362, 368, 374, 376, 393, 425-426, 491, 526.
Royal Engineers (Divisional), 4; recruiting area, 10; in operations at Cape Helles, 88, 102, 188, 193, 208-210; in operations in Sinai, 251, 254, 256, 278, 297, 304; in operations in Palestine, 313, 399, 439, 474, 480; in operations in France, 570.
Royal Flying Corps, 144, 263, 266, 267, 269, 274, 275, 292, 300, 305, 327, 336-337, 374, 377, 481, 540.
Royal Naval Division, 28, 121-125; renamed 63rd (R.N.), 519, 542, 560, 561, 565.

Royal Scots (4th Bn.), joined S.R. Bde., 7; recruiting area, 10; embarked at Liverpool on *Empress of Britain*, 11; at Alexandria, 11, 14; at Mudros, 14; landed on Gallipoli, 12-14th June 1915, 14; commended by Sir Ian Hamilton, 16-17; in action, 40, 41; losses of, 48; in battle of 28th June 1915, 50; commanded by Lt.-Col. S. R. Dunn, 50; attacks by, 51, 53-55; commended by Gen. de Lisle, 63; repulse attack, 63-64; relieved by Hampshire Rgt., 64; return, 64; losses of, 67-68; commended by Sir Ian Hamilton, 72-73; combined with 7th R.S., 75; commanded by Lt.-Col. W. C. Peebles, 75; memorial service by Dr. Ewing, 75; at Ghurka Bluff, 80; in battle of 12-13th July 1915, 97-99; losses of, 126; reformed into separate unit under Col. A. Young, 134; rifle strength, Aug. 1915, 141; combined with 7th R.S., 174; in fighting in Krithia Nullah, 15-30th Nov. 1915, 179-190; strength of, 7th Jan. 1916, 228; in last garrison at Cape Helles, 218-241; reformed into separate unit under Col. A. Young, 246; sent to Pelusium, 263; at Romani, 286; at 2nd Battle of Gaza, 318, 320; losses of, 331, 333; at Suffolk Ridge, 348; patrol fighting, 349; attack El Arish Redoubt, 362-369; losses of, 370-371; attack Brown Hill, 404-410; losses of, 408-409; relieve 75th Div. at Beit Surik, 441; at Nebi Samwil, 451; attached to 155th Bde. at El Burj, 463; rejoin 156th Bde., 467; reconnaissance of Auja by members of, 480; in night attack at Auja, 487, 489; losses of, 501; at 2nd Battle of the Somme, 520, 523, 529; in 2nd Battle of Arras, 2nd Sept. 1918, 539, 540; losses of, 544-545; at Moeuvres, 553-555; at Canal du Nord, 562-563; History of, quoted, 563;

at Herchies, 10th Nov. 1918, 571; losses of, 572.
Royal Scots (5th Bn.), 36, 38.
Royal Scots (7th Bn.), joined S.R. Bde., 7; in Gretna railway disaster, 8-9; recruiting area, 10; embarked at Liverpool on *Empress of Britain*, 11; at Alexandria, 11, 14; at Mudros, 14; landed on Gallipoli, 12-14th June 1915, 14; in battle of 28th June 1915, 50, 55; commanded by Lt.-Col. W. C. Peebles, 50; repulse attack, 63; losses of, 67, 68; commended by Sir Ian Hamilton, 72-73; combined with 4th R.S., 75; at Gurkha Bluff, 80; in battle of 12-13th July 1915, 97-98; commended by Sir Ian Hamilton, 123; losses of, 126, 127; reformed into separate unit, 134; receive draft of survivors of Gretna disaster, 3rd Oct. 1915, 145; scheme to capture trench at Krithia Nullah, 160; combined with 4th R.S., 174; in fighting in Krithia Nullah, 15-30th Nov. 1915, 179-190; strength of, 7th Jan. 1916, 228; in last garrison at Cape Helles, 218-241; reformed into separate unit, 246; at Hill 70, 263; at Romani, 270, 286; History of, quoted, 309; at 2nd Battle of Gaza, 318-320, 328; losses of, 331, 333; company of, at Umbrella Hill, 362-369; losses of, 370; attack Burkah, 404-410; losses of, 408; relieve 75th Div. at Biddu, 441; at Nebi Samwil, 451; at Beit Sira, 463; losses of, 473; in night attack at Auja, 489, 490; losses of, 501; at 2nd Battle of the Somme, 520-523, 529; in reserve at 2nd Battle of Arras, 2nd Sept. 1918, 539; in action, 540; losses of, 544; at Moeuvres, 553-555; in reserve at Canal du Nord, 561; at Herchies, 10th Nov. 1918, 571; losses of, 572.
Royal Scots Fusiliers (4th Bn.), 4; recruiting area, 10; embarked at Liverpool on *Mauretania*, 11;
at Mudros, 11, 14; landed on Gallipoli, 6th-7th June 1915, 14; at Cape Helles, 34, 38, 40; commanded by Lt.-Col. J. R. Balfour, 88; in battle of 12th-13th July, 1915, 88-91, 95-97, 113, 125; losses of, 126-127; support 5th R.S.F., 29th Dec., 1915, 208; losses of, 210; in final garrison at Cape Helles, 219-241; at Dueidar, 260-263; losses of, 262; at Romani, 267, 276-277; at Khan Yunus, 308; in 2nd Battle of Gaza, 319-330; losses of, 331-332; on outpost duty near Wadi Hesi, 377; attack Sausage Ridge, 380-383; losses of, 384; at Beshshit, 415; losses of, 425; in reserve at attack on El Jib, 449-450; near Tahta, 460; attack Suffa, 462; near El Burj, 464; assist Australian L.H. Bde., 471; rejoin 155th Bde. at Amwas, 472; losses of, 472; in night attack at Auja, 496; losses of, 500; in 2nd Battle of the Somme, 526-527; at Bullecourt, 535; at 2nd Battle of Arras, 31st Aug. 1918, 535, 536, 540-541; losses of, 544; in support of 4th K.O.S.B. at Moeuvres, 549; in action, 550-551; attached to 156th Bde. at Moeuvres, 553; rejoin 155th at Moeuvres, 555; attack Faubourg de Paris, 565; losses of, 565; towards Mons, 10th Nov. 1918, 571, 572.
Royal Scots Fusiliers (5th Bn.), 4; recruiting area, 10; embarked at Liverpool on *Mauretania*, 11; at Mudros, 11, 14; landed on Gallipoli, 6th-7th June, 1915, 14; at Cape Helles, 34, 36, 38, 40; relieved, 78; commanded by Lt.-Col. J. B. Pollok-M'Call, 88; in reserve at battle of 12th-13th July, 1915, 88; in action, 95-97; losses of two companies while digging trenches, 99; commended by Sir Ian Hamilton 123; losses of, 126-127; temporarily commanded by Major Russell, 139; incident at bomb station, 145; in attack on G.11a

INDEX 607

and G.12, 194-197; losses of, 196; attack trenches, 29th Dec. 1915, 208-210; losses of, 210; represented in final garrison at Cape Helles, 219-241; at Dueidar, 255-263; losses of, 262; at Romani, 285; in 2nd Battle of Gaza, 319-330; losses of, 331-332; at Umbrella Hill, 340-343; on Outpost Duty near Wadi Hesi, 377; attack Sausage Ridge, 380-383; losses of, 384; occupy Beshshit, 414; attack Katrah, 415-423; losses of, 425; attack El Jib, 449-450; attack Suffa, 462; near El Burj, 464; at Beit Sira, 467; assist Australian L.H. Bde., 471; losses of, 472; in night attack at Auja, 495-496; losses of, 500; in 2nd Battle of the Somme, 526-527; at Bullecourt, 535; in support, east of Bullecourt, 535-536; at 2nd Battle of Arras, 2nd Sept., 1918, 541; losses of, 544; in reserve at Moeuvres, 549; in action, 550-551; in reserve, 555; attack Faubourg de Paris, 565; losses of, 565.
Royal Welch Fusiliers (5th Bn.), 277, 285, 290.
Royston, Mount, 272, 280, 286, 287, 288, 289.
Russell, Capt. and Q.-M. John, 545.
Russell, 2nd Lt. H. G., 106, 127.
Russell, 2nd Lt. J., 333.
Russell, Major, 139.
Rutherford, Capt. R. W. G., 68.

SABKET EL BARDAWIL, 248, 271, 300, 301.
Saghir Dere, see Gully Ravine.
Saladin, 248.
Salonica, 15, 575.
Salvesen, Lt. C. R., 9.
Samothrace, 12, 189.
Samson's Ridge, 315, 327, 335, 336, 363.
Sana Redoubt, 351.
Sanders, Lt.-Col. J. M. B., 320.
Sanderson, Capt. H., 127.
Sanderson, Major A. W., 55, 68.
Sanna-i-yat, 577.
Sarona, 477, 484, 503, 504.
Sarpi, 245.

Sausage Ridge, 374-385.
Sayer, Capt. H., 519.
"S" Beach, 25.
Scarpe [river], 538, 542, 543.
Scimitar Hill, 166.
Scorpion, H.M. destroyer, 47.
Scott, Lt., 196.
Scott, Lt. J., 180.
Scott, 2nd Lt. J. W., 68.
Scott-Elliot, Lt., 281.
Scott-Moncrieff, Brig.-Gen. W., 7, 18, 39, 48, 52, 59, 60-61, 68, 72, 74.
Scottish Rifle Brigade, see 156th.
Scottish Rifles, see Cameronians.
Scutari, 23.
Sea Post, 342, 343, 344, 345.
Seaton, Sgt., 496.
Sedd el Bahr [village], 21, 22, 24, 25, 27, 28, 82, 140, 169, 213, 232, 234.
Selmeh, 476, 484.
Senlis, 581.
Sennacherib, 247, 296.
Sensée River, 529.
Sharia, 358, 369, 372, 373, 390.
Sharp, Lieut., 577.
Sharon, Plain of, 426, 446, 499.
Shechem (Nablus), 357, 427, 575.
Sheikh Abbas Ridge, 309, 313, 314, 327, 335-338, 346, 347, 351, 353.
Sheikh Ajlin, 315, 327, 335, 336.
Sheikh el Ballutah, 498, 499.
Sheikh Hassan, 369, 373.
Sheikh Muannis, 478, 480, 481, 482, 486, 488, 489, 490, 493, 495, 497.
Sheikh Zowaid, 308.
Shellal, 307, 314, 315, 335.
Sheppard, Lt.-Col., 167, 171.
Shilta, 459, 460-464, 467.
Shropshire, H.M.S., 11, 13.
Sidi Bishr, 268, 270.
Sidon, 579.
Sillars, Lt. G. A., 470.
Simpson, Lt.-Col. G. S., 252, 281, 316, 323, 336.
Simson, Lt.-Col., 319, 326, 332.
Sinai, description of, 246-249.
Sinclair, Lt. G. W., 568.
Slag Heap Farm, 487, 489, 490.
Slater, Major J. M., 520, 529.
Small Nullah, 187.
Smith, Capt. M., 452.
Smith, Lt. E., 127.

INDEX

Smith, 2nd Lt. F. G., 545.
Smith, Lt. G. S., 480, 491 n.
Smith, Lt. J. M., 568.
Smith, Lt. J. O., 371.
Smith, Major-Gen. W. E. B., 267, 315, 342, 353.
Smith, Sgt. James, 531.
Smith's Knob, 491.
Smyrna, 24.
Sollum, 252.
Somme [river], 512; 2nd Battle of, 515-533, 537.
South Scottish Brigade, see 155th.
Speirs, Capt. G. C. F., 284.
Speirs, Major G. P., 566.
Spence, Chaplain J., 444.
Stavely, Capt. C. M., 239.
Stewart, C.Q.M.S., 199.
Stewart, Lt., 64, 325.
Stewart, 2nd Lt. J. S., 128.
Stewart, Maj. R. R., 163.
Stewart, Major W., 127.
Stewart, Pte. J., 143.
Stewart-Richardson, Lt.-Col. A. G. 449, 460, 462, 471, 495.
Stirling, 4.
Stirling Ordnance Depot, 7.
St. Léger, 521.
St. Mihiel, 558.
Stockdale, Col., 74.
Stokes, Bugler, 140.
Stopford, Lt.-Gen. Sir F., 134.
Stout, Lt. T., 68.
St. Quentin, 543, 559.
Strachan, Lt., 196.
Street, Gen. H. E., quoted, 103.
Streeten, Capt. G. W., 251; afterwards Major, 484.
Strong Point, 273, 280.
Strumnitza, 575.
Sturrock, Lt. G. R., 127.
Suffa, 460, 462-464, 468, 473, 506.
Suffolk Regiment (5th Bn.), 362, 366.
Suffolk Ridge, 347, 348, 351, 352, 353.
Surrender of Jerusalem, 477.
Sutherland, Lt. H. E., 262; afterwards Capt., 421-422.
Suez Canal, 20, 246-263.
Suvla, 23, 82, 133-138, 164-166, 169-172, 190, 192, 213, 215, 221, 222, 225, 575, 580.
Switzerland, 517.

TABSOR, 587, 580.
Tadpole Copse, 541-542.
Talbot, H.M. cruiser, 47.
Tank Redoubt, 337, 349, 351.
Tanks, 365, 519-520, 564.
Taylor, Pte. Andrew, 531.
Taylor, Lt. D. M., 68.
Taylor, Major, 33.
Taylor, Surg.-Major D. R., 100, 127.
Taylor, Capt. R. S., 295, 296.
Tekke, Cape, 24, 139, 225, 227.
Tekke Tepe, 166.
Tel el Ahmar, 336.
Tel el Murre, 410.
Tel el Rekket, 480, 493, 494, 497.
Tel el Sharia, 311.
Tel el Turmus, 396, 403.
Tel Nejile, 390.
Temple, Lance-Cpl. J., 178.
Templeton, Capt. W. F., quoted, 245, 264, 333, 565, 567.
Templeton, Lt. A. D., 68.
Tenedos, 12.
Ternuka, 412, 424.
Thionville, 557.
Thom, Lt. L. W., 333.
Thompson, Major H., 230, 260-263; afterwards Lt.-Col., 276, 319, 320, 322, 332, 333.
Thompson, Lt. W. D., 545.
Thomson, Lt., 568.
Thomson, Lt. E. J., 55, 68.
Thomson, 2nd Lt. F. W., 68.
Thomson, Major P. M'L., 205, 206.
Thothmes III., 247.
Tidd, Capt. E. G., 128.
Tigny, 581, 582.
Tillicoutry, 5.
Tina, Plain of, 248, 250, 273, 286.
Townsend, Captain, 387.
Townsend, Coy. Segt.-Major, 323.
Transylvania, H.M.S., 11, 13.
Trench names, Gallipoli, 150.
Trench names, Gaza, 347.
Trench system, Cape Helles, 34-36.
Tripolis, 579, 580.
Triumph, H.M.S., 12, 31.
Turk Top, 255.
Turner, Lt., 199, 320, 345.
Turner, 2nd Lt. E. D., 545.
Turner, 2nd Lt. T. J., 545.
Tweedie, 2nd Lt. A., 332.
Tweedie, Col., A. D. M. S., 371.

INDEX

Twelve Tree Copse, 78.
Two Tree Post, 465, 468.

UM AGBA, 266.
Umbrella Hill, 336, 340, 341, 342, 343, 346 n, 361, 362, 364, 365, 368, 370, 371.
Ushant, 10.
Uzun Keupru, 23.

" V " BEACH, 24, 25, 31, 32, 225, 226, 231-236.
Valenciennes, 557, 570.
Vallance, 2nd Lt. H. L., 568.
Verdun, 517, 557.
Vermand, 543.
Versailles, 512.
Vesle [river], 582.
Victoria Cross, awards of, 135, 342, 471, 531, 553, 584.
Villers Chatel, 516.
Vimy Ridge, 513.
von Falkenhayn, Gen., 355, 359, 410.
von Kressenstein, Gen. Kress, 270-271, 274-276, 280, 282, 284, 288-292, 294, 358, 359, 424.

WADDLE, Sgt. J., 199.
Wadi Abbeideh, 442.
Wadi el Arish, 304.
Wadi el Ghor, 419.
Wadi el Nukhabir, 316, 353.
Wadi Endless, 347, 349.
Wadi Ghuzze, 307-314, 337, 339, 353.
Wadi Hannina, 442.
Wadi Hesi, 358, 372-390, 391, 394, 401.
Wadi Janus [Brook Kedron], 414, 415, 418.
Wadi Mejma, 404, 405.
Wadi Selman [Ajalon], 435, 460.
Wadi Shellal el Ghor, 418.
Walker, 2nd Lt. J. A., 544.
Walker, Major, 265.
Wallace, Capt. A., 92, 127.
Wallace, 2nd Lt. J., 348.
Wancourt Ridge, 527.
Wancourt Tower, 527.
Wardle, Major, 224.
Warren [trenches], 318, 323.
Watson, Lt., 180.
Watson, Lt. A. E., 554.
Watson, Capt. E., 161.

Watson, 2nd Lt. E., 63.
Watson, Capt. and Adj. J. M., 425.
Watson, Capt. W. G. D., 332.
Watson, Capt. W., quoted, 167; 171; afterwards Major, 282.
Watson, Lt. W. J., 154, 187.
Waugh, Sgt., 325.
Wayenberg, 581.
" W " Beach, 24, 27, 31, 65, 77, 130, 206, 224-226, 234-238.
Weber Pasha, 80.
Webster, Lt. J., 396.
Weli Sheikh Nuran, 304, 306.
Weller, Lt. G. H., 128.
Wellington Ridge, 272, 274, 277, 280, 285, 286, 287, 289, 290.
Wells, Lt.-Col. L. Fortescue, 362, 484.
Welsh, Capt. T., 127.
Wemyss, Vice-Admiral, 239.
Whitton, Capt. P., 68.
Wightman, Capt. A. J., 56, 57.
Wilkie, Capt., 209.
Williams, Capt. A. E., 315.
Williams, Crawsley, 302.
Wilson, 2nd Lt. A. N., 456.
Wilson, Lt.-Col. G. T. B., 160, 276.
Wilson, 2nd Lt. J., 107, 159.
Wilson, Lt.-Col. J. Boyd, 50, 60, 68.
Wilson, Brig.-Gen. L. C., 471.
Winchester, Lt. H. W., 367.
Wolverine, H.M. destroyer, 47.
Wood, 259.
Wood, Lt. J., 420, 425.
Woodhead, 2nd Lt. P., 127.
Wright, 259.
Wyllie, Lt. M., 108.
Wytschaete, 573 n, 584.

" X " BEACH, 24, 41, 130, 175, 188, 206.

" Y " BEACH, 25, 41.
" Y2 " Beach, 24, 225, 237.
Yebnah (Jamnia or Ibelin), 411, 414, 426, 429, 430.
Yeomanry, 4, 10, 159, 179, 182, 219, 250, 254-257, 259, 260, 262, 266, 286, 294, 380, 382, 392, 403, 413-416, 420-421, 425, 440, 459-463.
Yilderim (Lightning Army Group), 356.
Youden, Capt. S. E., 545.

Young, Col. A., 134, 174.
Young, Lt. A., 68.
Young, Capt. E. T., 68.
Young, Capt. H. R., 91, 97; afterwards Major, 332, 333.
Young, Lt.-Col. J., quoted, 81, 90, 100-101, 117, 147, 148, 214-215, 232, 235-237, 258-259, 286-287; 371; quoted, 392, 417-418, 432, 446.
Young, Pte., 62.
Young, Lt. W. S., 371.
Ypres, 512, 516, 583, 584.
Yuille, 2nd Lt. D. M., 551.
Yuille, Major D., quoted, 89, 90, 461; 572-573.

DIVISIONAL SIGN

155TH

156TH

157TH

BRIGADE SIGNS

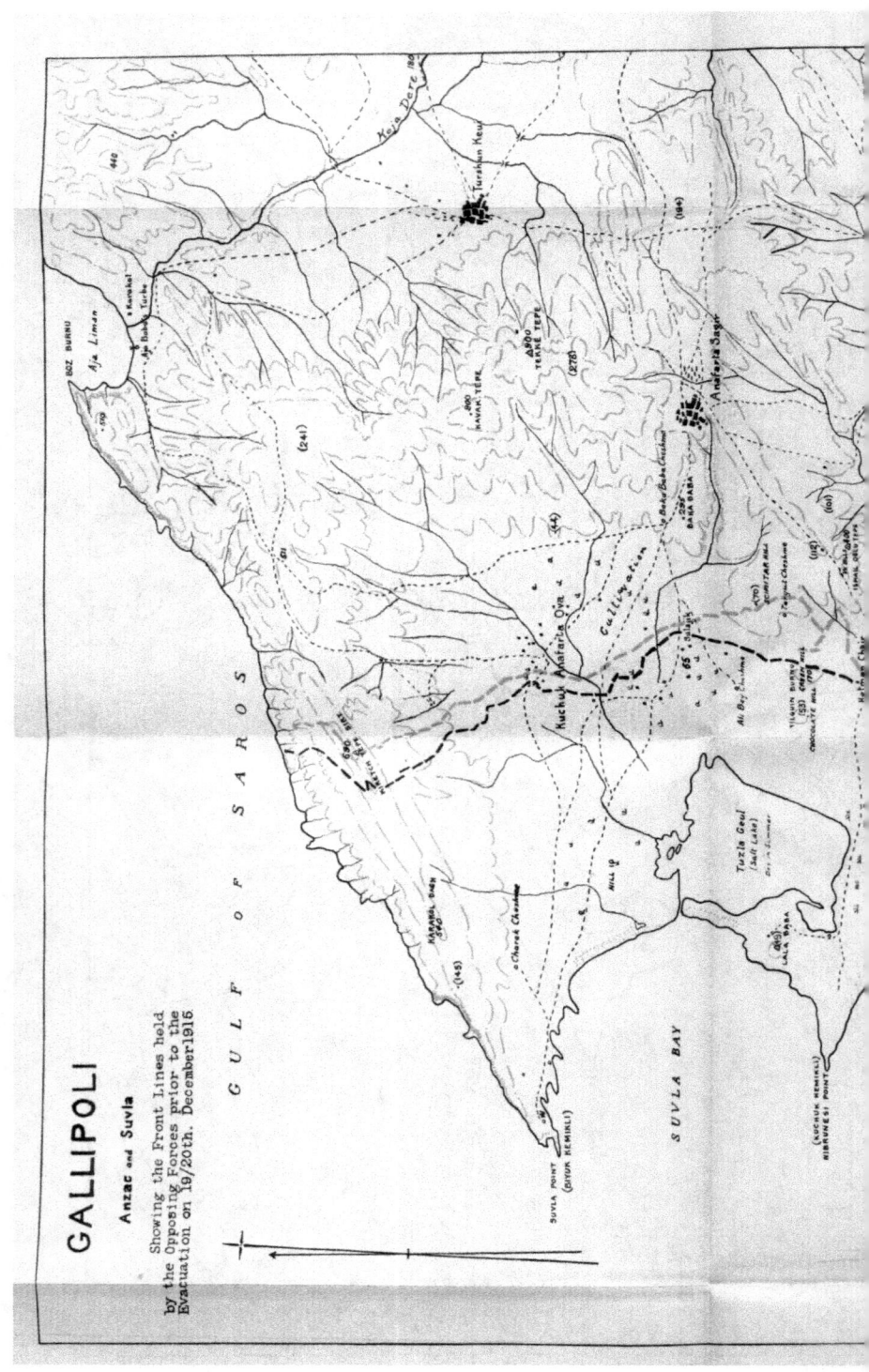

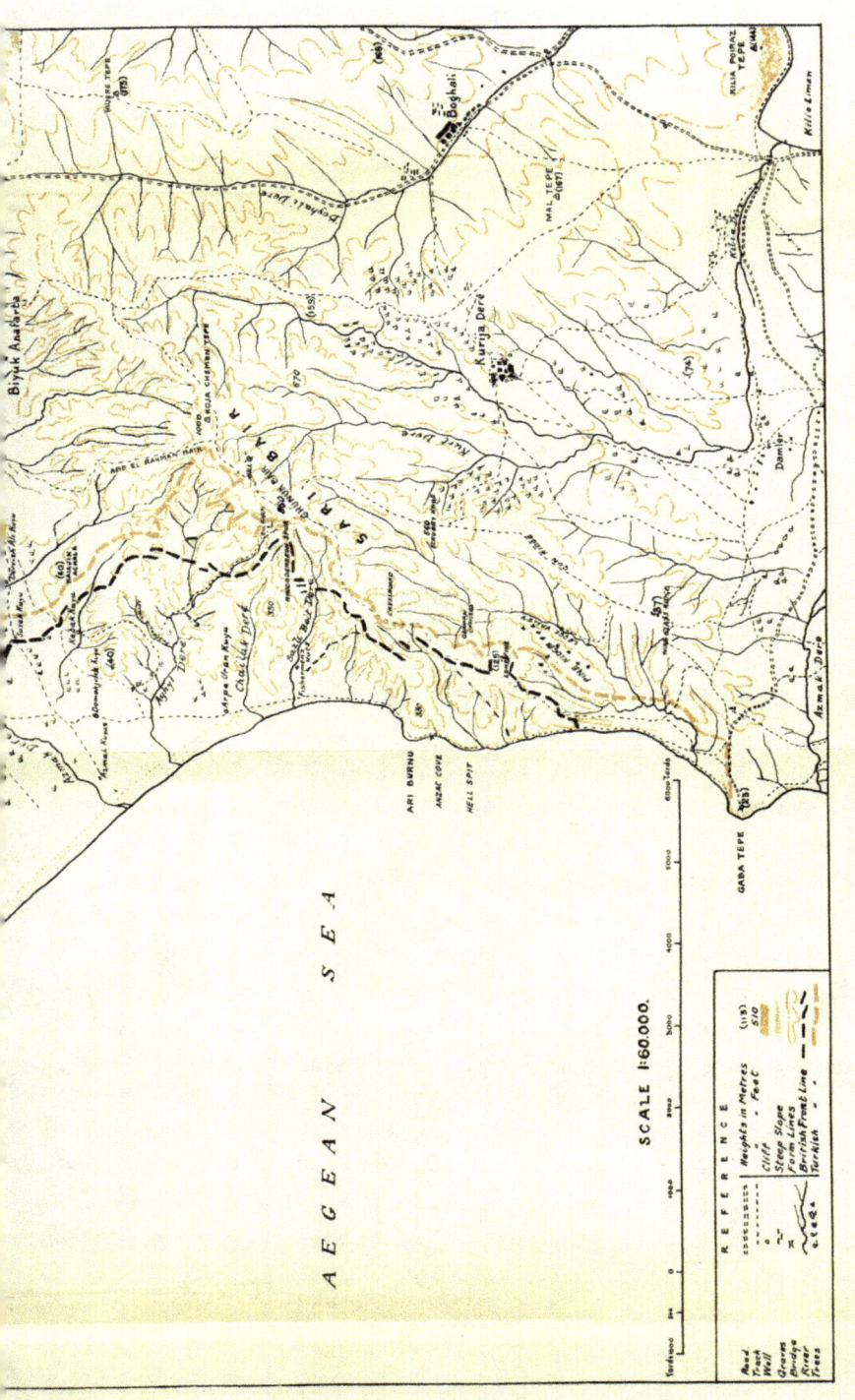

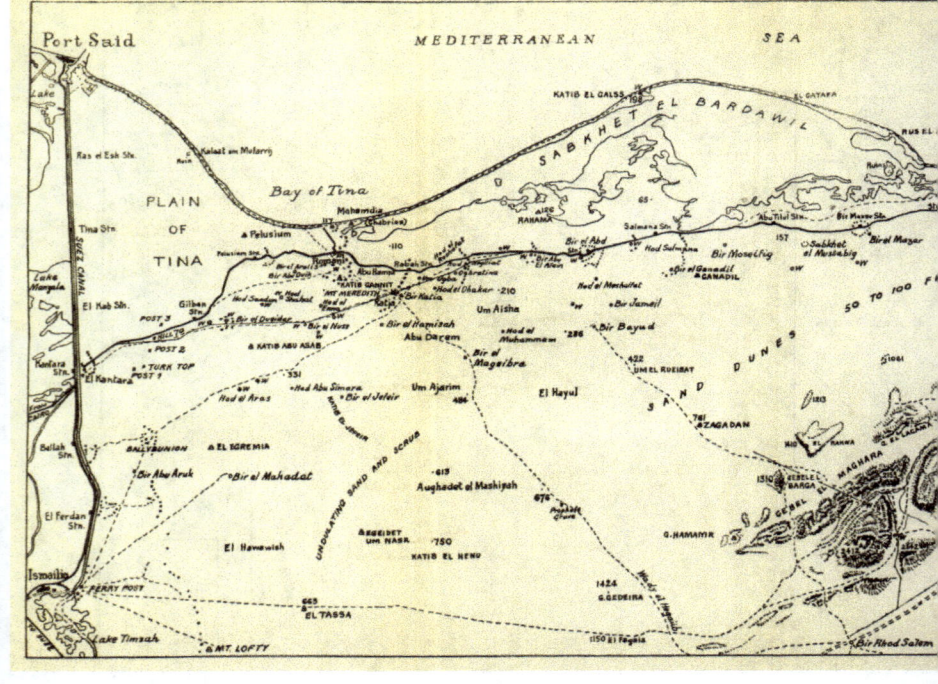

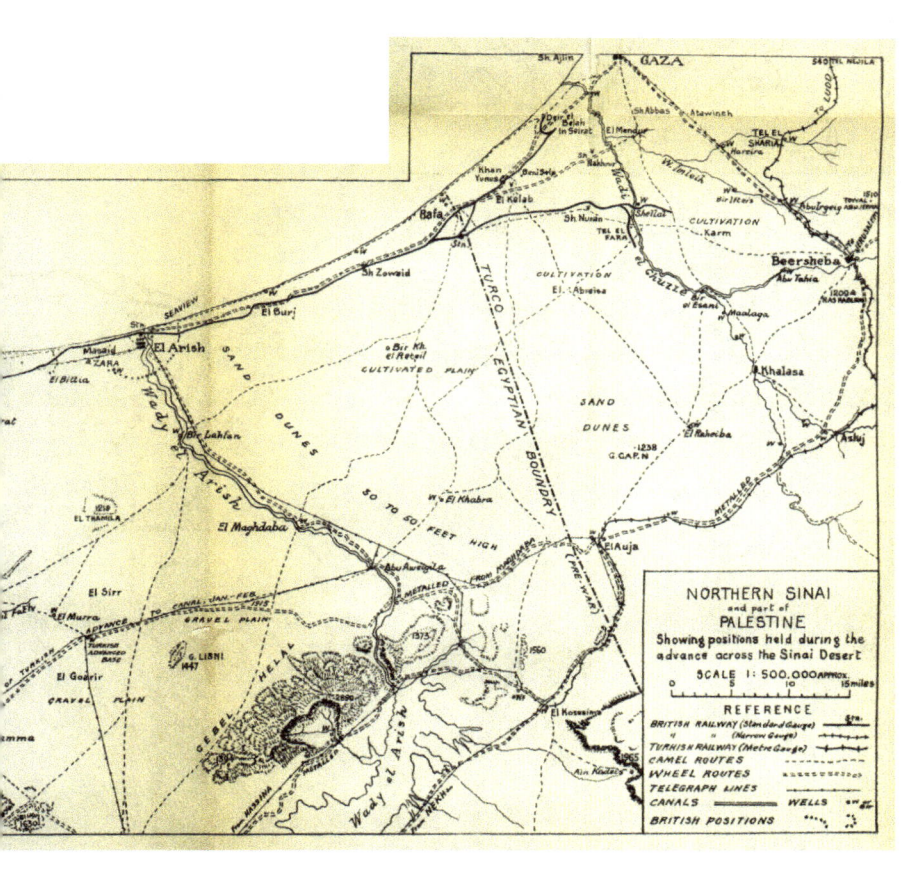

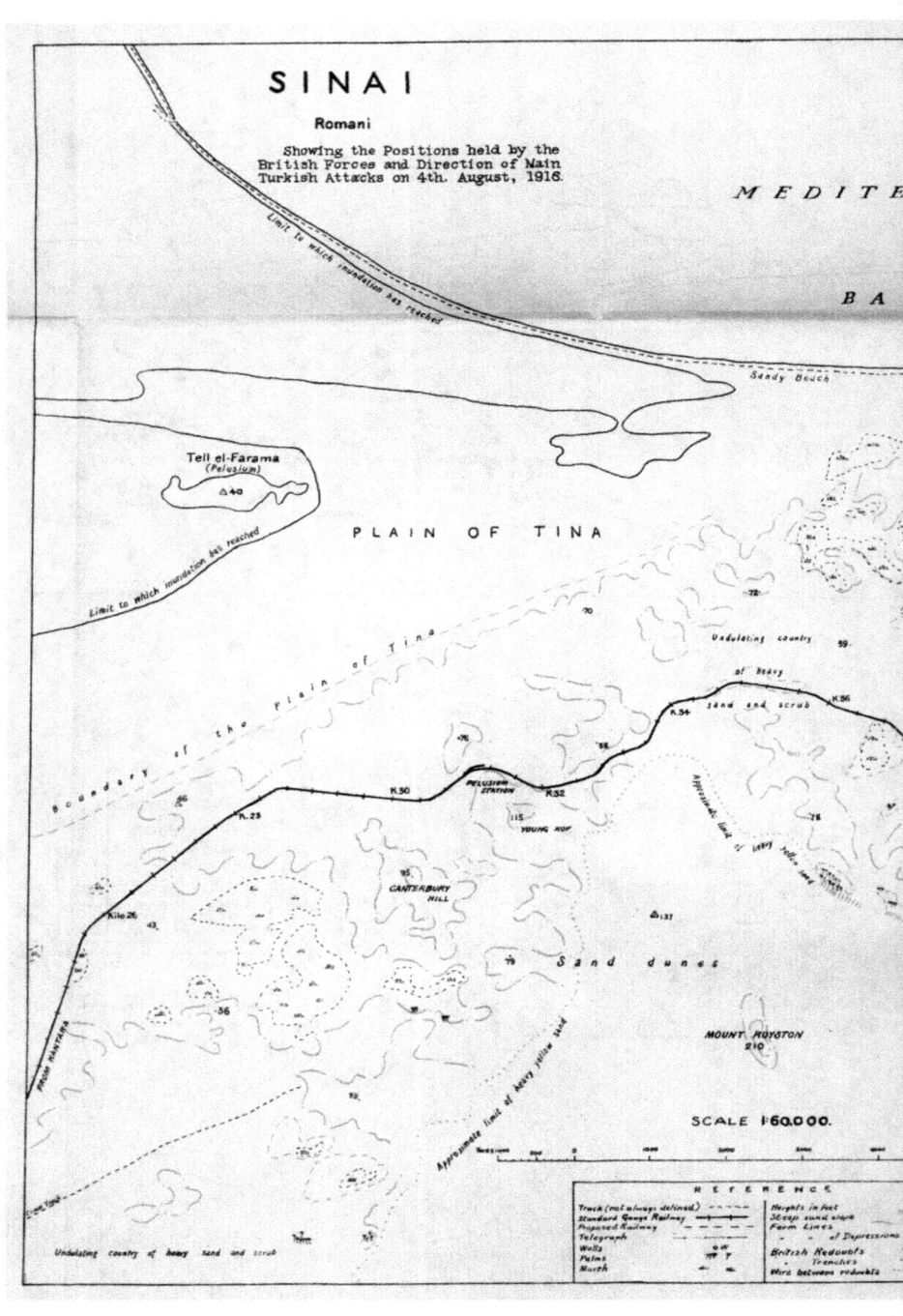

ANEAN SEA
TINA
PORT SAID – GAZA CARAVAN ROUTE
Mahamdiya
DRY BED OF LAKE BARDAWIL
Covered with dry salt and small patches of brine
BLAIRE POST
No 9
No 8
No 10a
Sabkhet el-Romani
K 42
K 40
ROMANI STATION
No 7
No 7a
No 6
Hod el Sofiyia
K 44
Bir el-Romani
Ghozlan
K 46
K 45
No 23
Etmaler
No 5
No 4
Bir Abu Hamra
No 22
No 22a
No 3
Katib Gannit
No 21a
No 21
No 1
No 2
WELLINGTON RIDGE
MOUNT MEREDITH
KATIA
KANTARA – EL ARISH CARAVAN ROUTE
Telegraph (Disused)
Bir el Maraia

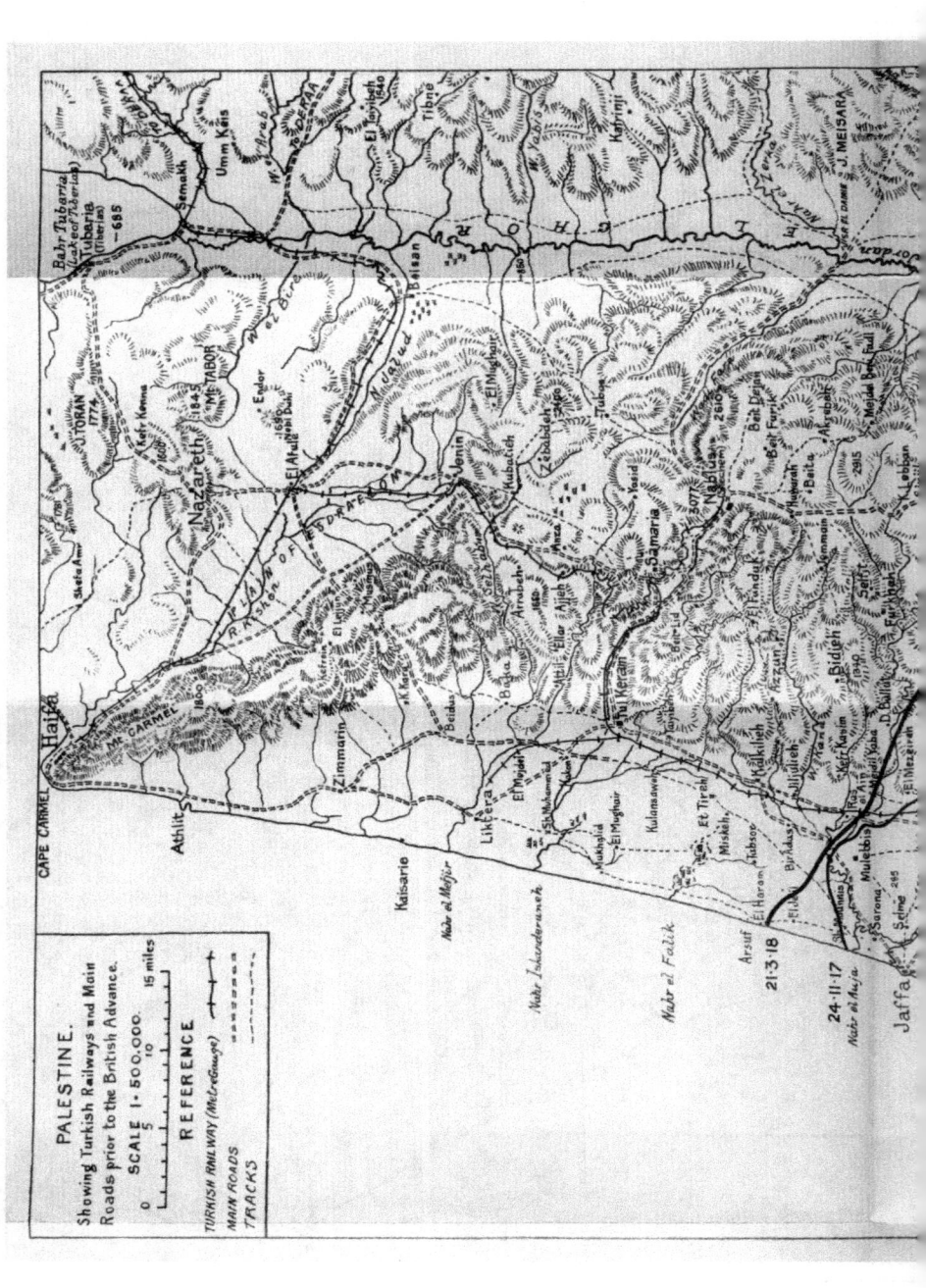

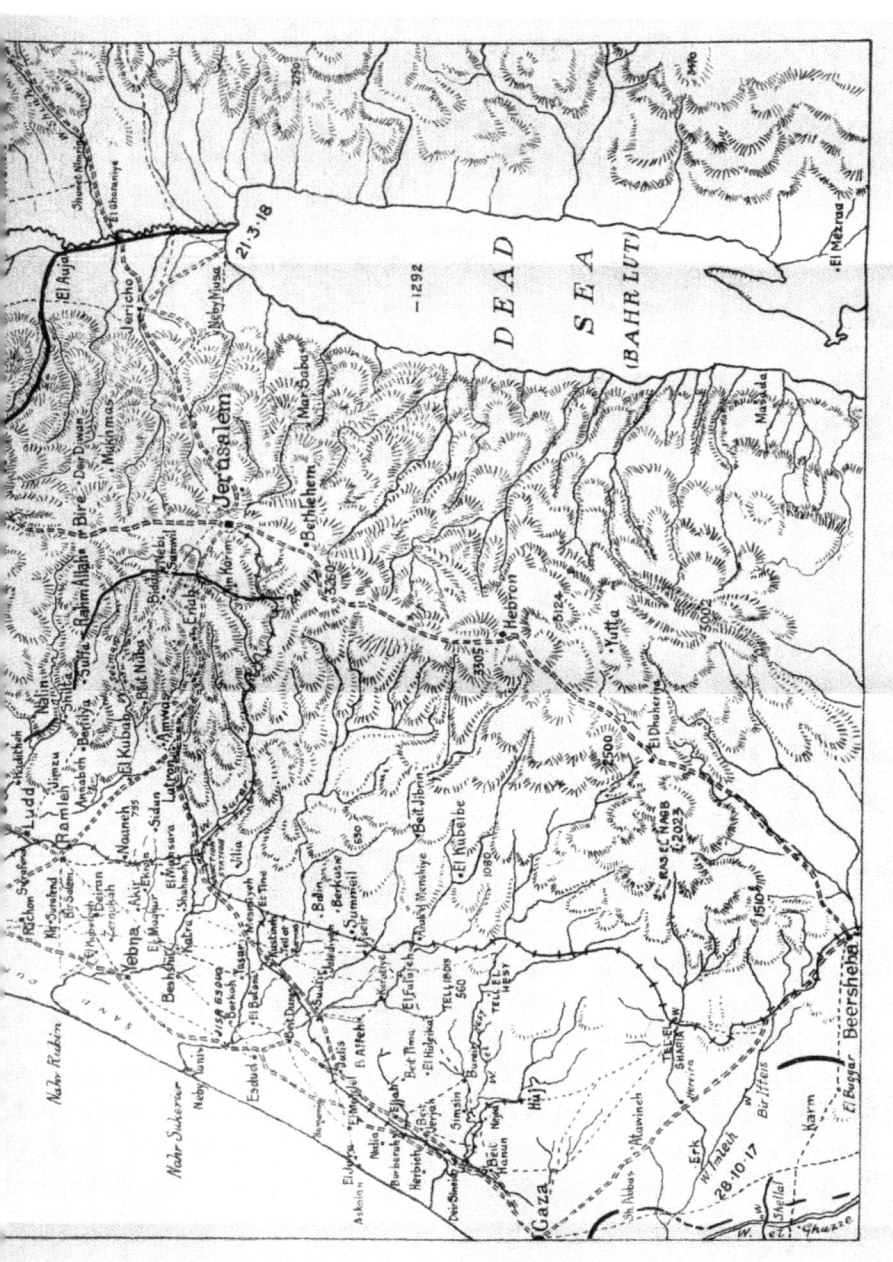

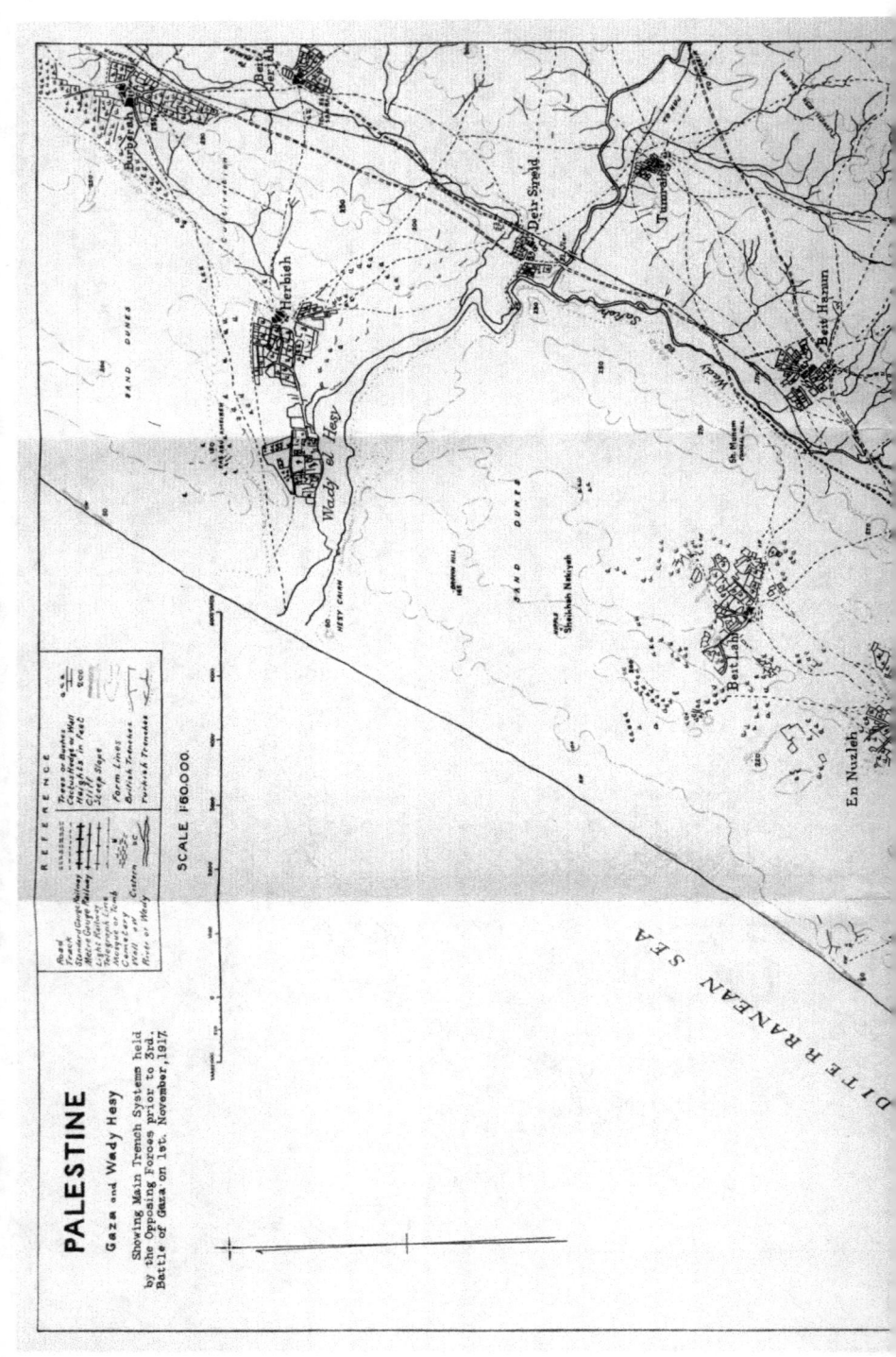

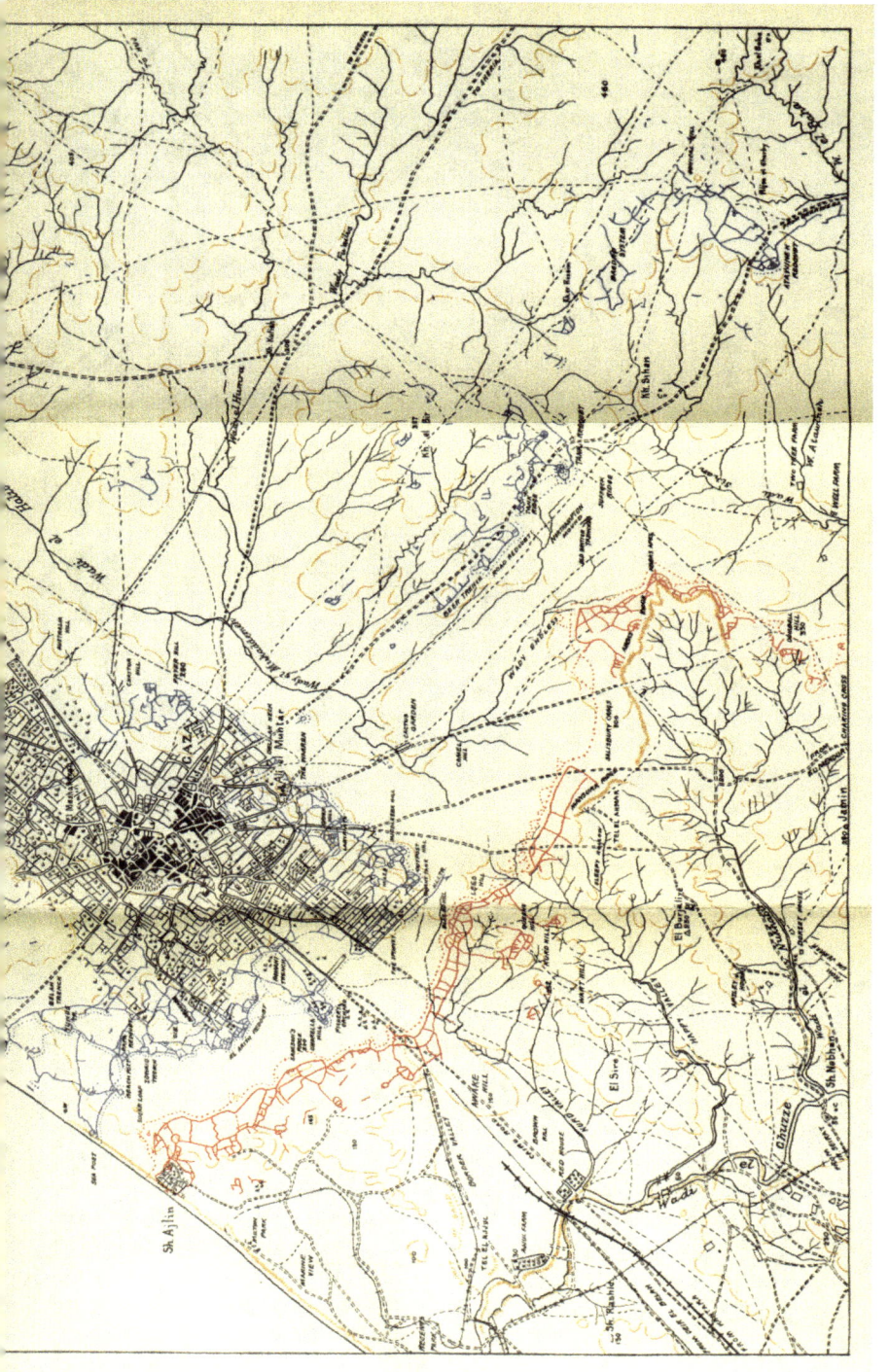

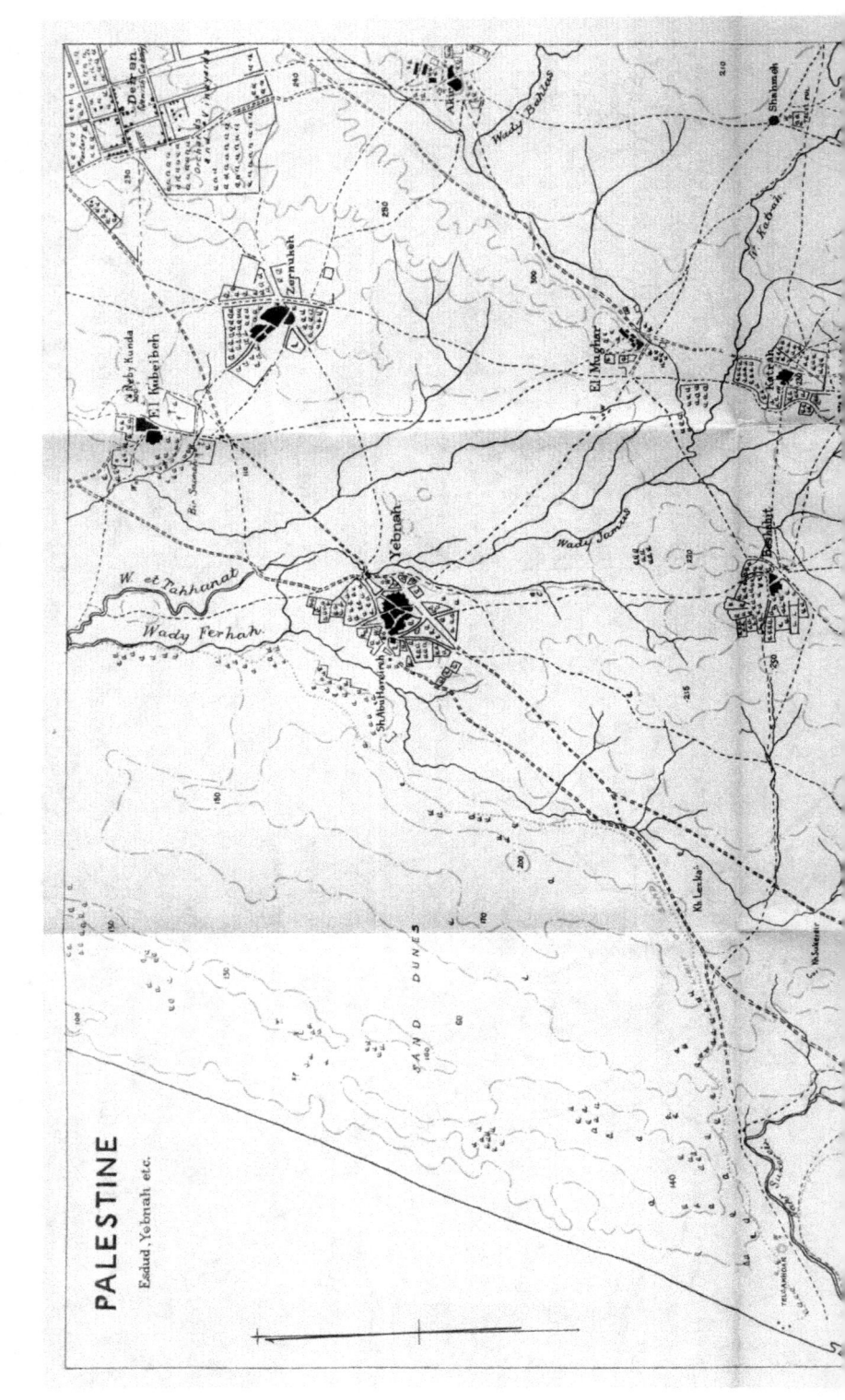

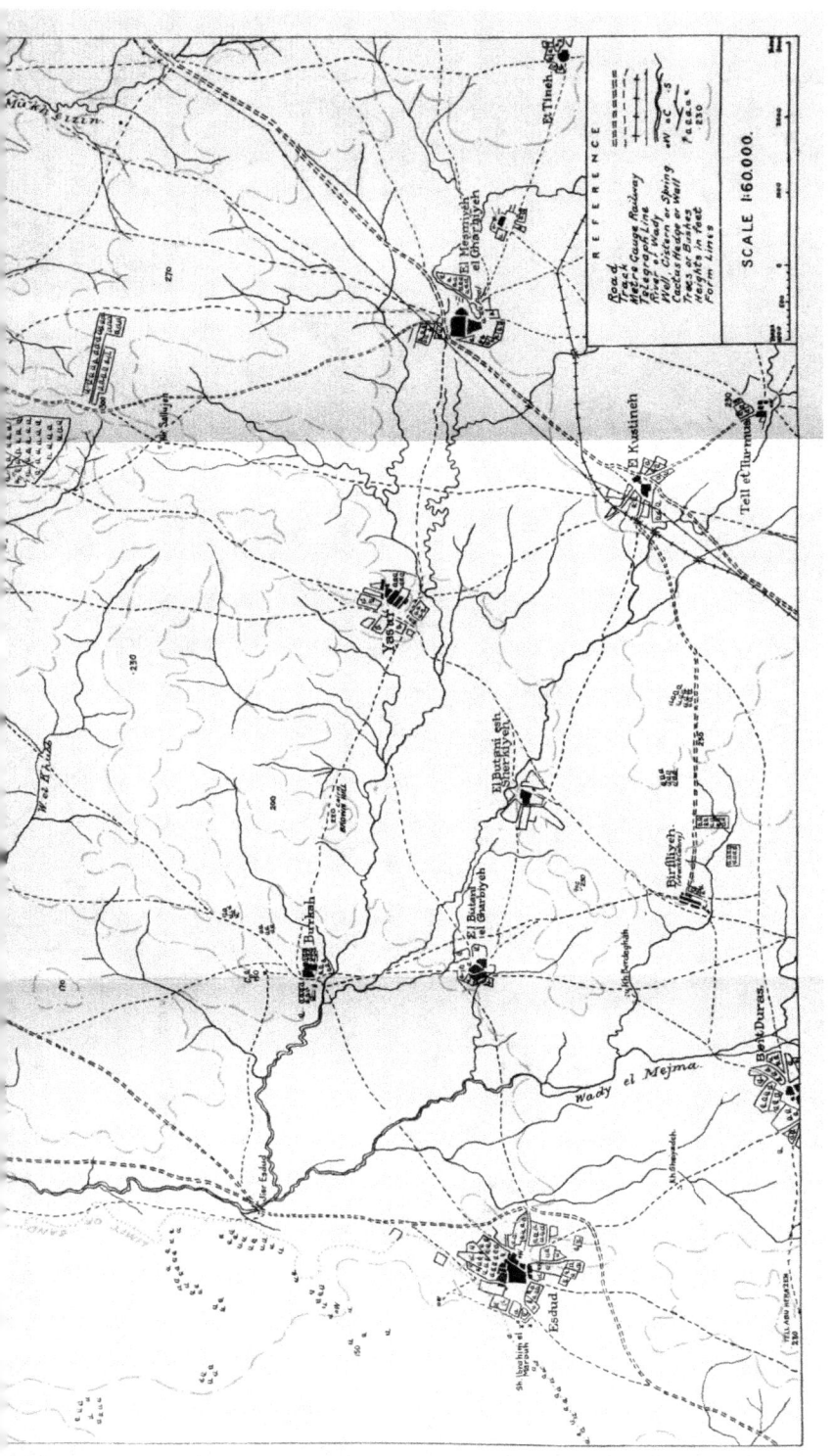

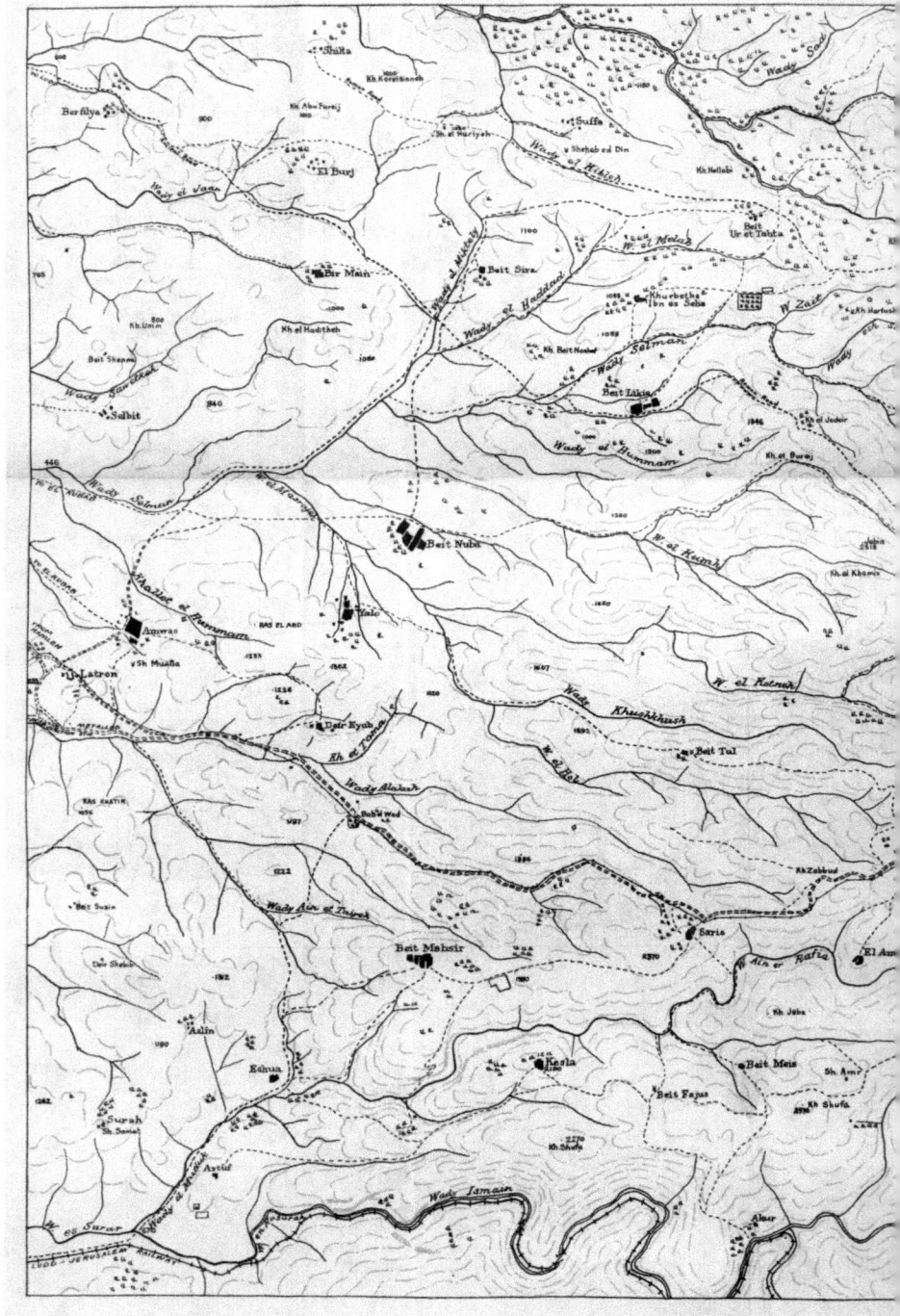

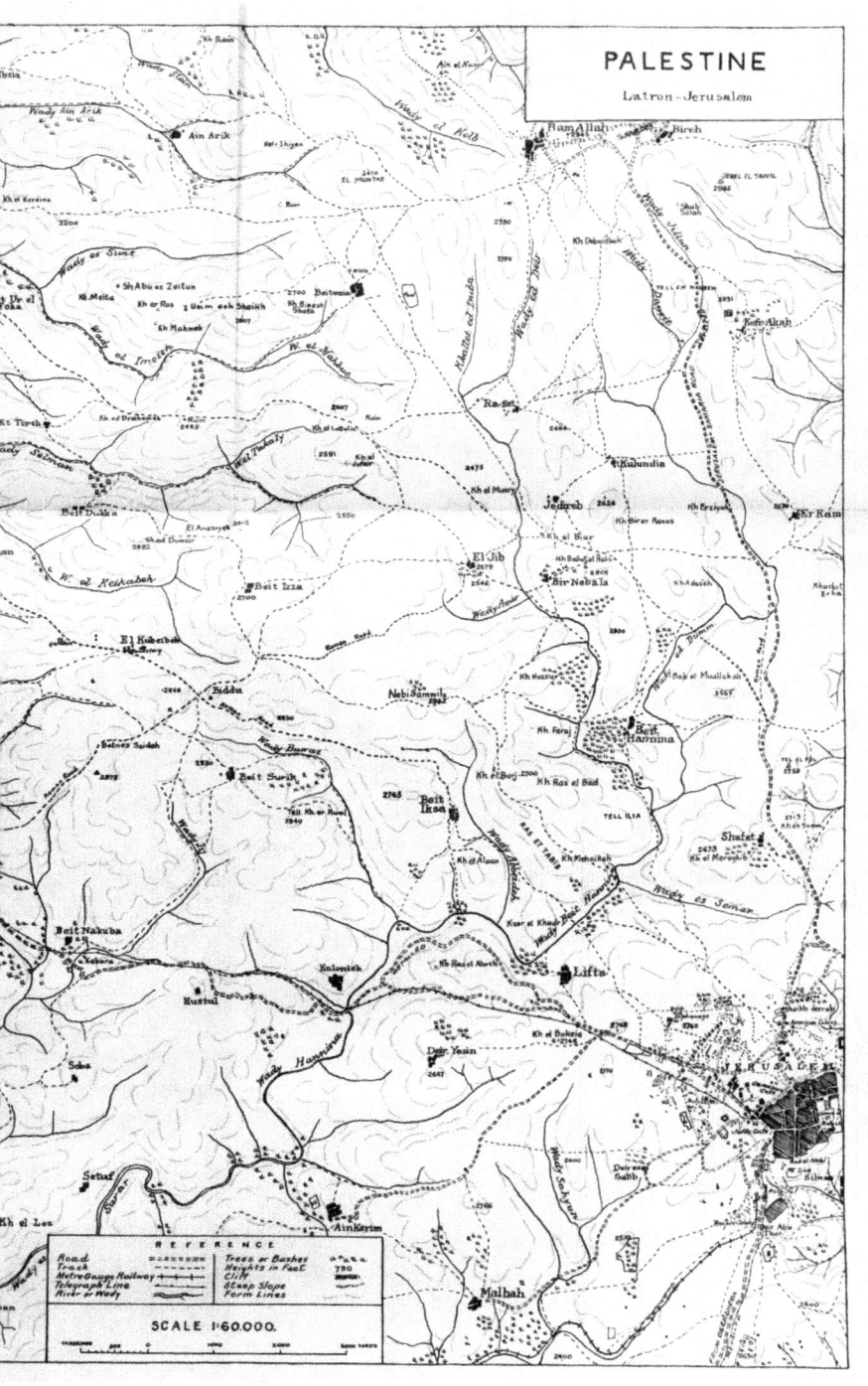

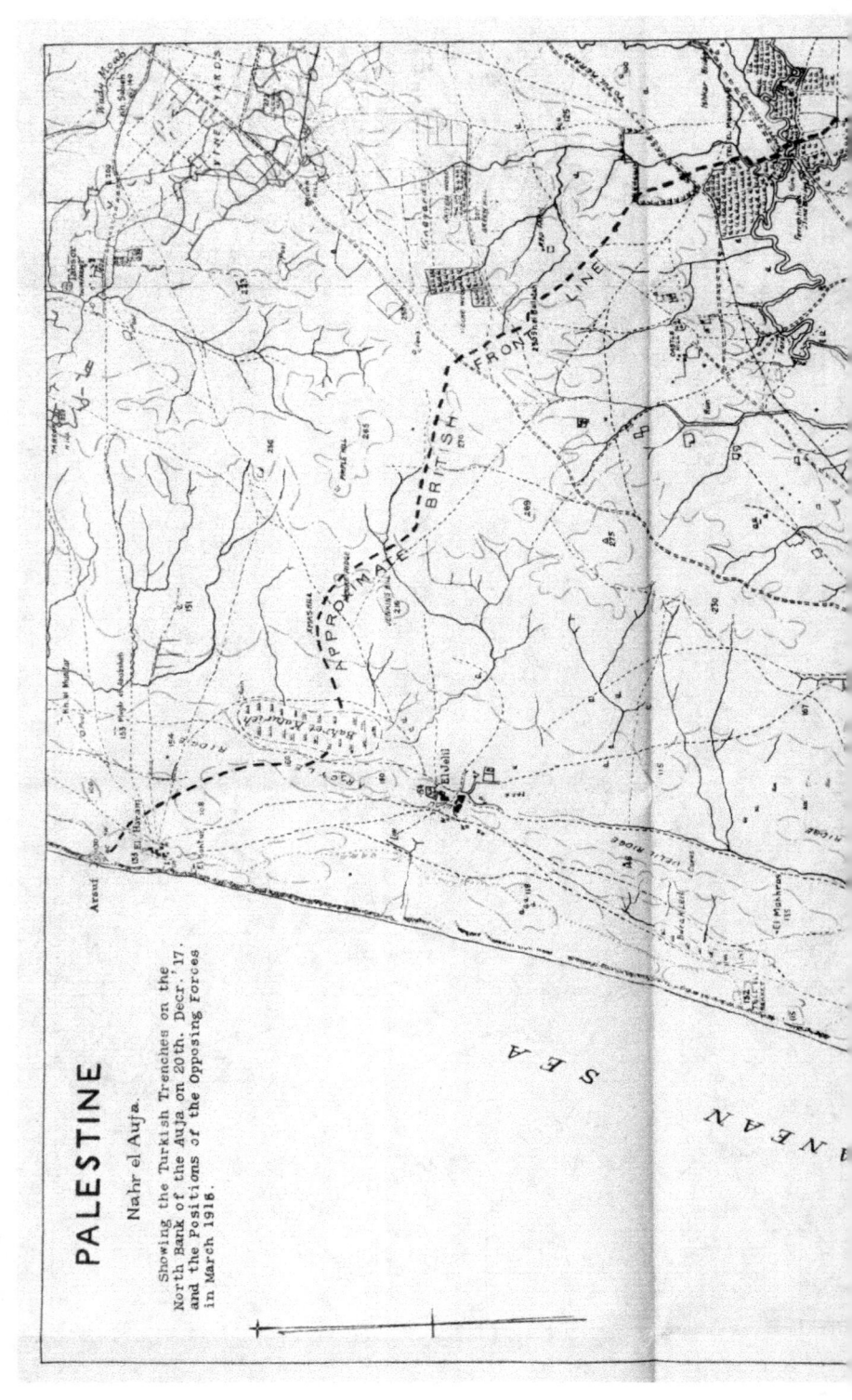

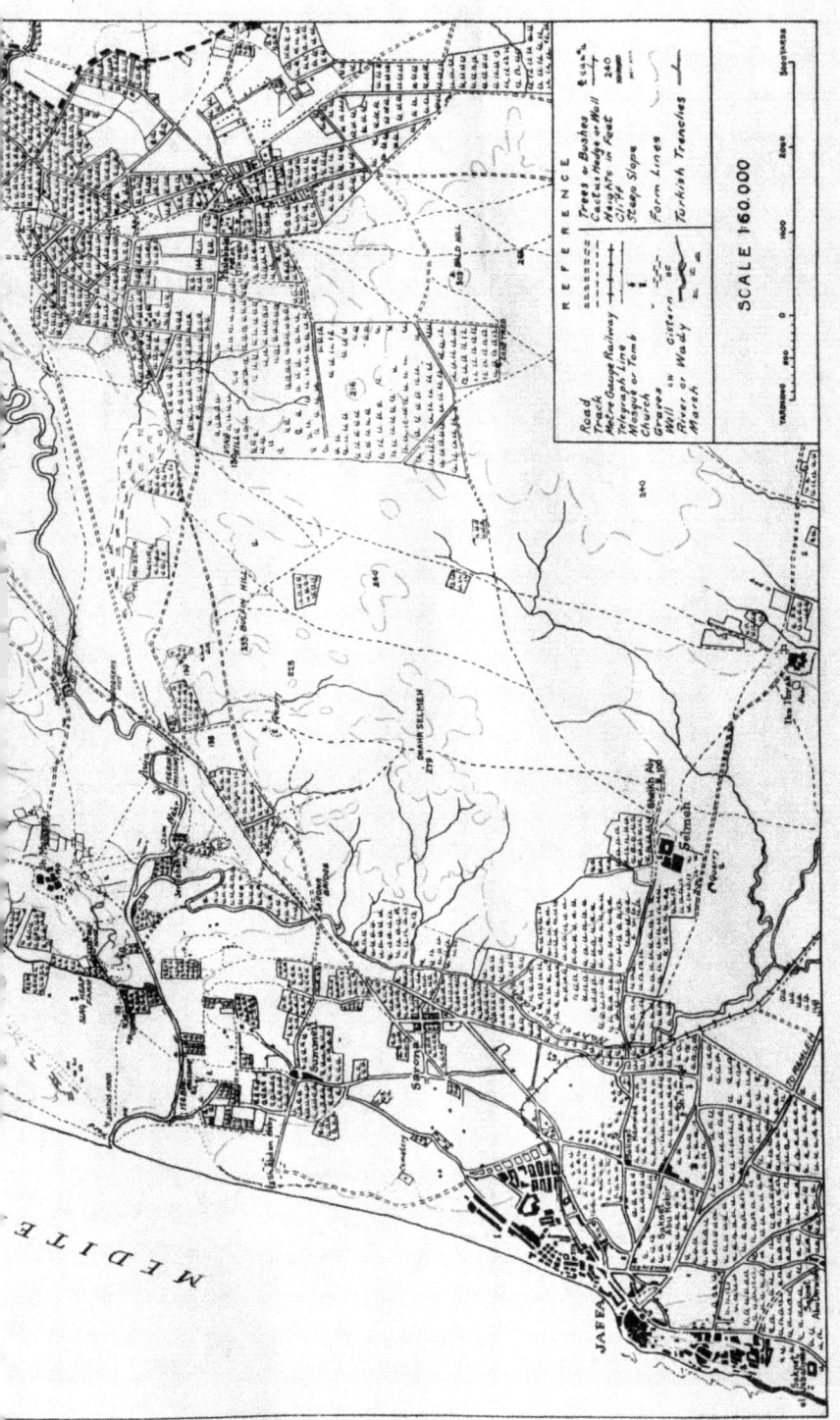

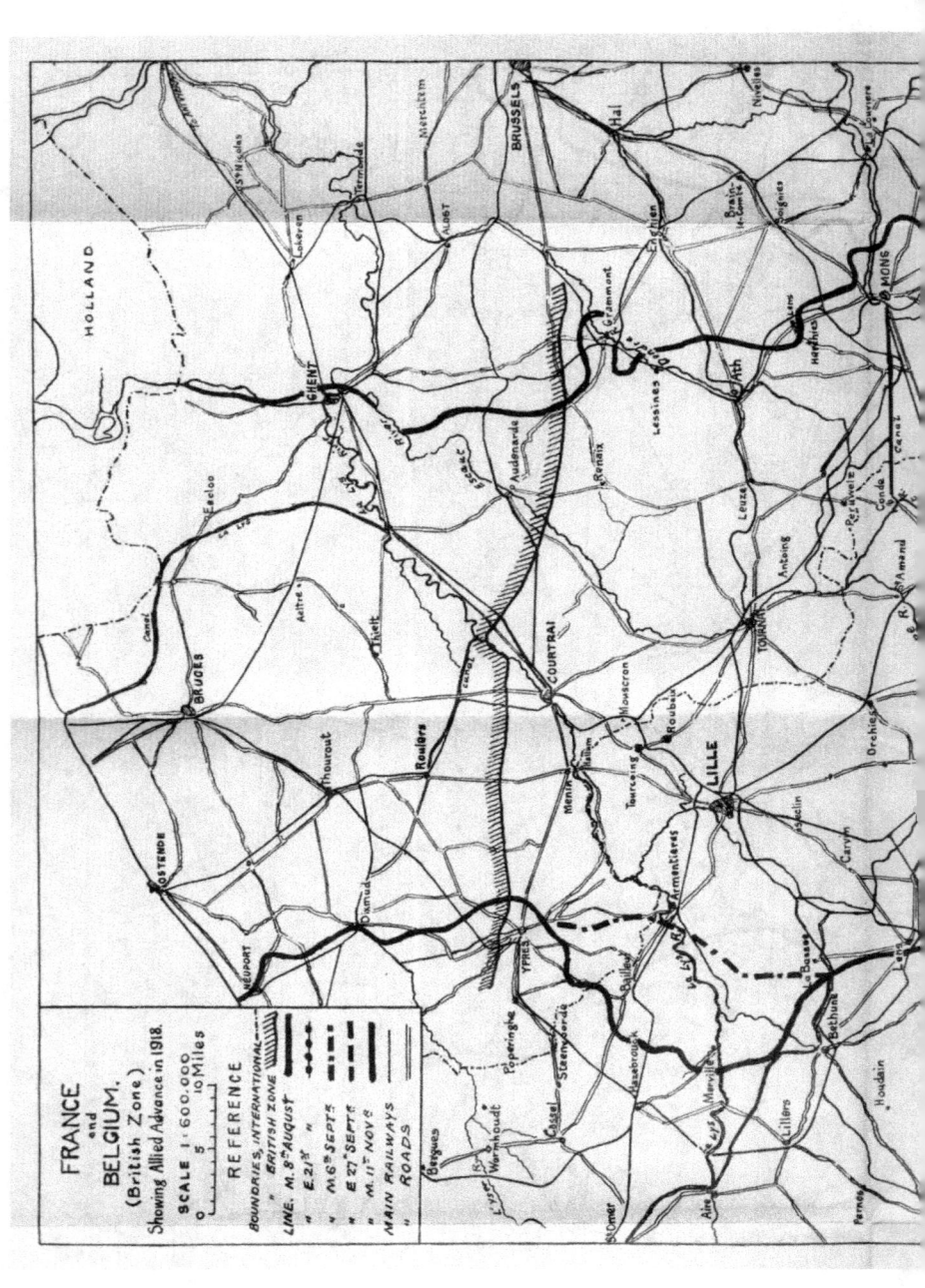

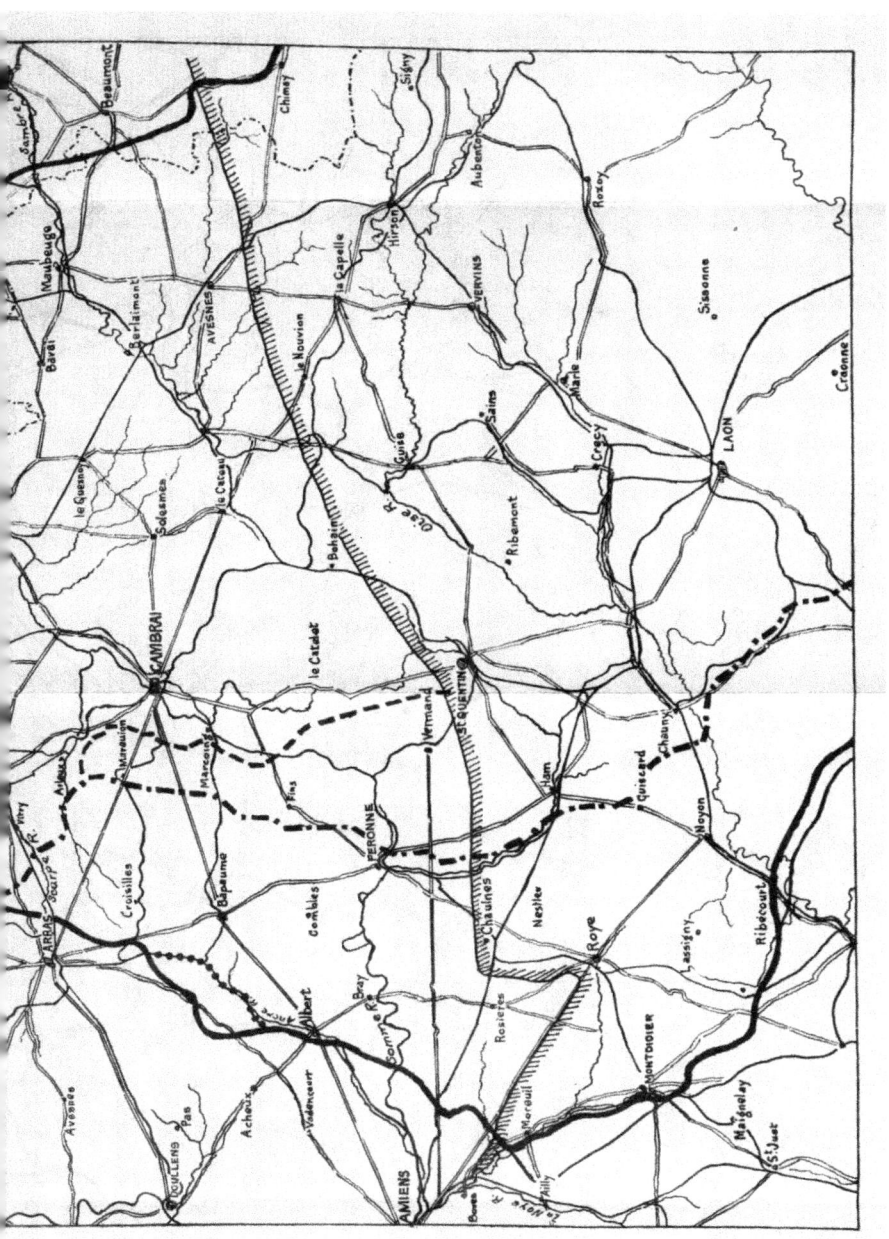

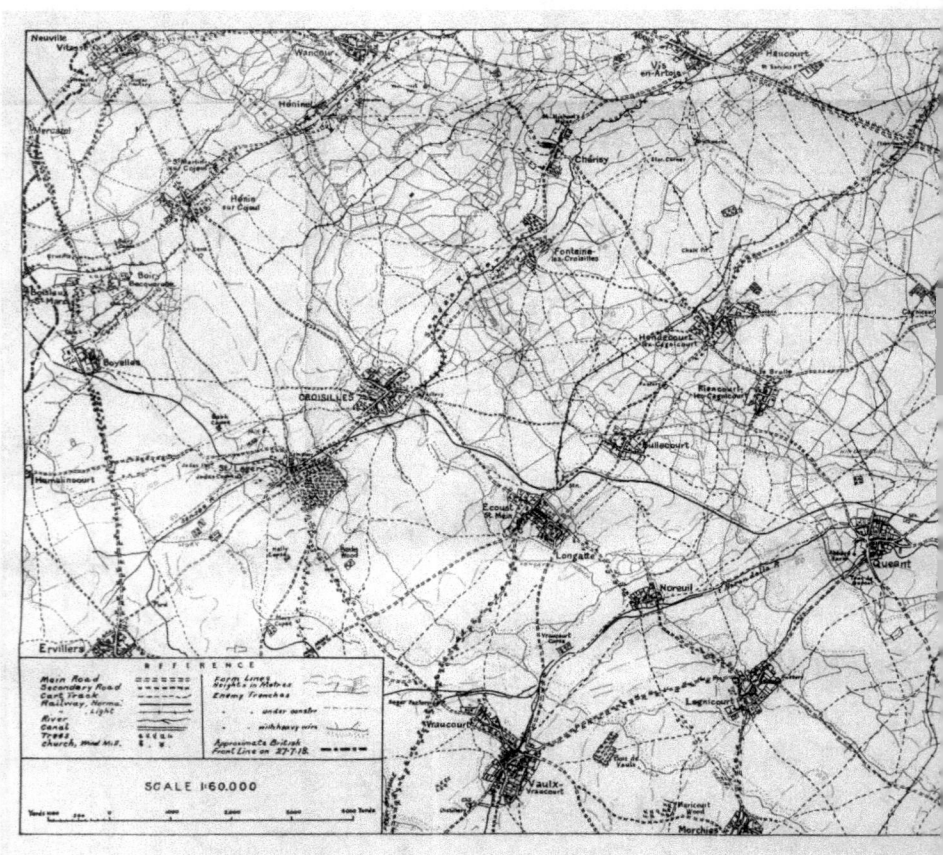

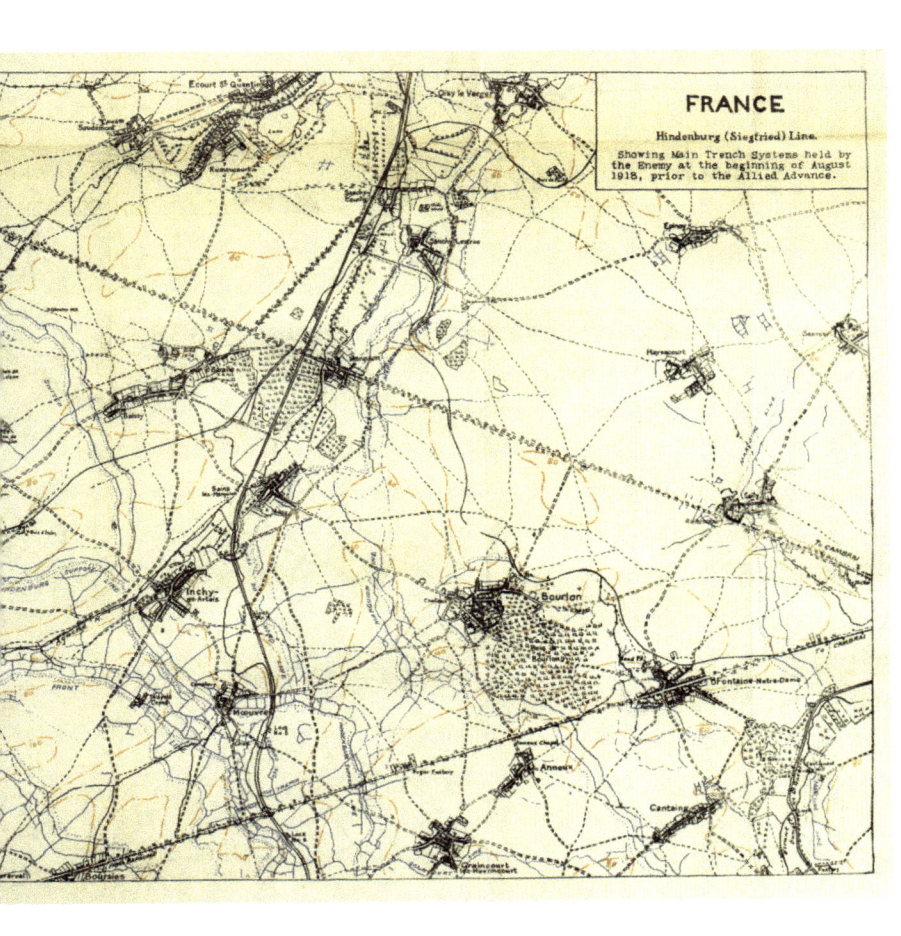

www.ingramcontent.com/pod-product-compliance
Lightning Source LLC
Chambersburg PA
CBHW070753300426
44111CB00014B/2386